SPENSER STUDIES

XXIV

SPENSER STUDIES

A Renaissance Poetry Annual

XXIV

Special Issue
Spenser and Platonism

GUEST EDITORS
Kenneth Borris
Jon Quitslund
Carol Kaske

SPENSER STUDIES GENERAL EDITORS
William A. Oram
Anne Lake Prescott
Thomas P. Roche, Jr.

AMS PRESS, INC.
New York

SPENSER STUDIES
A RENAISSANCE POETRY ANNUAL
Volume XXIV

Guest Editors: Kenneth Borris, Jon Quitslund, and Carol Kaske
General Editors: Anne Lake Prescott, William A. Oram,
and Thomas P. Roche, Jr.

Spenser Studies is published annually by AMS Press, Inc. as a forum for Spenser scholarship and criticism and related Renaissance subjects. Manuscripts must be double-spaced, including notes, which should be grouped at the end and should be prepared according to *The Chicago Manual of Style.* Authors of essay-length manuscripts should include an abstract of 100–150 words and provide a disk version of the article, preferably in a Windows-compatible format. One copy of each manuscript should be sent to Thomas P. Roche, Jr., Program of Liberal Studies, 215 O'Shaugnessy Hall, University of Notre Dame, Notre Dame, IN 46556; one copy to Anne Lake Prescott, Department of English, Barnard College, Columbia University, 3009 Broadway, New York, NY 10027–6598; and one copy to William A. Oram, Department of English, Smith College, Northampton, MA 01063.

Please send inquiries concerning subscriptions or the availability of earlier volumes to AMS Press, Inc., Brooklyn Navy Yard, 63 Flushing Ave. – Unit #221, Brooklyn, NY 11205–1073, USA.

ISSN 0195–9468

International Standard Book Numbers

Set ISBN-10: 0–404–19200–9
Set ISBN-13: 978–0–404–19200–6

Vol. XXIV ISBN-10: 0–404–19224–6
Vol. XXIV ISBN-13: 978–0–404–19224–2

AMS PRESS, INC.
Brooklyn Navy Yard, 63 Flushing Avenue – Unit #221
Brooklyn, NY 11205–1073, USA
www.amspressinc.com

MANUFACTURED IN THE UNITED STATES OF AMERICA

Contents

Spenser and Platonism

Forum: The Relation of the *Fowre Hymnes* to *The Faerie Queene*

Illustrations

Index

KENNETH BORRIS, JON QUITSLUND,
AND CAROL KASKE

Introduction: Spenser and Platonism

THE SEEDS FOR this project were planted in 2000, at the conference of the Renaissance Society of America in Florence, where the three coeditors had organized a session on Spenser and Florentine Platonism. A year later, Andrew Hadfield stimulated us further by anecdotally reporting an apparent decline of interest in the poet's Platonic affinities in his *Cambridge Companion to Spenser*.[1] As our volume seeks to show, this dimension of Spenser's mind and art continues to offer opportunities for inquiries that are as significant and revealing as any other. Surveying a wide range of Spenser's engagements with Platonic thought, the collection presents diverse interpretive positions. Our subject's current vitality and openness to new research will, we think, be apparent to readers. In early modernity (absent latter-day efforts to distinguish sharply between Plato's authentic doctrines and later Neoplatonic adaptations), Platonic philosophy appeared as a "broad stream," and we use "Platonism" inclusively here in that sense.[2] While the kinds of Platonism pertinent to Spenser at various points in his life are disputable, as well as the extent to which he accepted, modified, or countered Plato's legacy, that philosophy's fundamental relevance to assessment and appreciation of his poetry is beyond dispute.

From the late 1950s through the 1980s, study of the Platonic aspects of Spenser's texts yielded two specialized books[3] and countless notes, journal articles, and chapters in books, besides informing more general Spenser monographs such as those of William Nelson, Alastair Fowler, Thomas P. Roche, Jr., John Erskine Hankins, A. Kent Hieatt, Humphrey Tonkin, and James Nohrnberg. During this period, most leading Spenserians significantly addressed aspects of the poet's relations with Platonism in one or more publications. A substantial range of related articles appeared in *The Spenser Encyclopedia* of 1990, reflecting interests that had emerged in previous decades.[4] Scholarly engagement with this topic was declining by that time, however, and relatively few pertinent studies were published from 1991 to 2008.[5] The major exception, Jon Quitslund's *Spenser's Supreme Fiction* of 2001, was the late harvest of researches that had begun in the 1960s, complicated by the author's keen interest in the reformation of early modern studies during the 1980s and 1990s.

Relaunching study of Spenser and Platonism may now be timely. The decline of interest in this historicizing topic coincided with the ascendancy of new historicism and cultural materialism, which transformed Anglo-American study of early modern English literature by emphasizing its implication in social practices, political institutions, colonial circumstances, and material culture, and by privileging much that prior literary historicism had underprivileged. As culture in general became conceptualized as text, so the potential interpretive scope of literary scholars burgeoned, and the centrality of "major works of art" was to be "jostled now by an array of other texts and images."[6] That was not an altogether new development, for the scholars associated with the Warburg Institute in London, who strongly influenced Spenser studies in the 1960s and 1970s,[7] had long anticipated new historicist multidisciplinarities and "thick descriptions" of "cultural performances," though in a different way that stressed intellectual and iconographical contexts rather than sociopolitical ones. In the subsequent poststructuralist historicisms, intellectual history remained topical mainly where it was relevant to their new emphases, and to studies of the body, gender, and sexuality. Insofar as early modern philosophies received notice, skepticism rose in appeal, in accord with ideological trends within the literary academy,[8] while other philosophical schools of at least equal sixteenth-century importance depreciated. The new hermeneutics of suspicion, whereby cultural artifacts, their creators, and their milieus are to be warily demystified, gained currency in both Spenser and Shakespeare studies. Yet, unlike Shakespeareans, Spenserians apparently continued to assume that their poet had little interest in former modes of skepticism.[9]

What were once innovative approaches became in their turn formulaic; various "afterwords" seeking new means and topics of inquiry, such as David Kastan's *Shakespeare After Theory*, have been circulating for over a decade.[10] One recent account of Spenser studies discerns "a resurgence of specifically historical work, untrammeled by explicit theoretical webbing"; and another finds a newly "inclusive perspective," whereby Spenserians tacitly meld different aspects of varied approaches without subscribing narrowly to any.[11] Whatever the status and longevity of these perceived trends, the history of ideas has been aptly chastened and refreshed by the reconceptualizations of critical practice in recent decades, and remains indispensable to historical inquiry. Even former experiences of physical reality and its representation in texts were informed by prevalent ideologies. As one of the two premier exemplars of allegorism in Western fiction, together with Dante's *Divina commedia*, Spenser's *Faerie Queene* has its own distinctive relation to ideas, which he seeks to materialize textually. The interaction of his language and imagery with intellectual contexts has unique interpretive importance, and the poem's conceptual dimensions can be illuminated in many ways.

While the Anglo-American literary academy was reducing its investment in the early modern domains of philosophical learning, serious study of the period's intellectual movements and their participation in broad cultural changes continued in departments of history and philosophy. Nothing could more strikingly instance this paradox of historiographical fashion than the explosion of interest in Marsilio Ficino (1433–99), the leading Renaissance exponent of the Platonic inheritance, and a key figure for European thought and culture of the time. Besides receiving much new interpretive attention, Ficino has sparked an international enterprise, now far advanced, to translate his extensive corpus of writings into English. Never before have the resources for investigation in this field been so ample and so accessible. Changes in concepts of literary historicism and texts as well as shifts in topics of interest now call for reassessments of Spenser's Platonism; and recent transformations that other disciplines have wrought in current knowledge of early modern philosophy provide new contexts for interpretation of his poetry.

Meanwhile, as Spenser's philosophical affinities and Platonism were becoming unfashionable for scholarly inquiry, his engagement with Protestant and Catholic doctrines and practices were attracting fresh scrutiny, probably because their obvious sociopolitical resonances suited the new historiographical trends. From 1991 to date, Kenneth Borris, John King, Harold L. Weatherby, Darryl Gless, Richard Mallette, and Carol Kaske all published monographs on the relations of Spenser's poetry to religious contexts. Within their spatial constraints the recent Cambridge and Palgrave Spenser *Companions* both allocate a chapter to religion, yet not to philosophy; the forthcoming *Oxford Handbook of Edmund Spenser* will include chapters on both. In regard to Platonism, if Spenser's religious concerns invite inquiry, so should his relations with Platonic doctrines, for they interact with Christianity extensively in his writings. Surveying the schools of ancient philosophy, Augustine had remarked, "there are none who come nearer to us [i.e., Christians] than the Platonists,"[12] and such assumptions were part of Platonism's appeal in Spenser's time. Further, since conjunctions of Platonism and Christian thought (whether Protestant or Catholic) produced contradictions as well as complementarities, inquiry into Spenser's engagement with Platonism should appeal to contemporary interest in heterodoxies, fideist and other skepticisms, and the problems of religious belief. When a writer embraces both Christian and non-Christian traditions, as Spenser does to some extent, any frictions and rivalries between them in his texts illuminate his distinctive aspirations, doctrinal compromises, and fault lines of credence. Insofar as Spenser turned to Plato, ancient Platonists, and their Renaissance elaborators such as Ficino and Pico della Mirandola (1463–94), he would have been interested in considering the insights of human reason from the pagans onward, and the possibilities of supplementing the resources of magisterial Protestant thought such as Calvin's.

In any case, philosophical contexts in general have much to contribute to Spenser studies, for poetry was commonly defined as humankind's "first philosophy," and otherwise as an instrument or part of philosophy that mediated between that discipline and history.[13] As many of the poet's contemporaries attest, he was admirably learned; several specifically praise his philosophical expertise;[14] and heroic poetry was supposed to survey human knowledge.[15] His expressions of interest in Platonism extend from *The Shepheardes Calender* (1579) to the *Fowre Hymnes* (1596). While Spenser drew on diverse philosophical schools[16] and, unlike Milton, cultivated a magnanimous intellectual eclecticism rather than seeking to refine any specific system,[17] engagement with Platonism was certainly a major factor in his intellectual formation and poesis. In different ways at different times, his relationship with elements of that philosophy was, as the word "engagement" indicates, intrigued, enthusiastic, and critical. Its resources seem to have "both deeply challenged and energized his creativity."[18]

Platonism was particularly significant for Spenser's era because European culture had been transformed through a distinctive metamorphosis of Platonic knowledge. An amalgam of doctrines with a range of common themes, Platonism had already evolved in several phases across two millennia, and had become intricately involved with Christianity. Yet the singular character of the Renaissance owes much to the recovery and new dissemination, beginning in the mid-fifteenth century, of the full series of Plato's dialogues. That process further involved parallel treatment of his ancient successors, and of texts attributed to his legendary predecessors, Orpheus and Hermes Trismegistus. New developments of Platonism thus proceeded in both popular and learned texts, while diverse contemporary responses developed across the verbal and visual arts, the learned disciplines, and the circumstances of everyday life in educated circles. Spenser himself embraced this cultural phenomenon in his poetry, and did so most obviously in his representations of love, beauty, gender, sexuality, and poetic inspiration. As Plato's newly available *Phaedrus* and *Symposium* had sparked a vogue for Platonizing reconceptualizations of love and beauty in European thought and culture, so Spenser represents himself primarily as a poet of love and beauty. Whether we find that he adapts, modifies, or criticizes those doctrines, Platonic theory thus has central importance for much of his poetry, and both the Cambridge and Palgrave Spenser *Companions* refer more to Platonic than Aristotelian contexts.[19]

Theories of love and beauty are the aspect of Spenser's Platonism most likely to elicit general interest now, as in the past. Although the cultural effects of the early modern fashion for Platonizing accounts of love are sometimes criticized, mainly for encouraging abstracted perceptions of the beloved,[20] the effects of that idealizing impulse were complex and not wholly unfavorable. Along with Spenser, many verbal and visual artists were drawn to amorous and aesthetic idealization.[21] In general, Platonic love theory argued that external physical beauties, though significant, are inferior to internal beauties of mind and character; it opposed exploitative fixations upon superficialities of appearance. The advocates of such idealization partly sought to help lovers discern and live up to ideals attributed to the beloved. By exalting the inner qualities of women, Renaissance Platonic love theory also encouraged critical reconsideration of the Aristotelian definition of woman as a natural deficiency, so to speak, or an imperfect man.[22] By advocating that apart from activities requiring physical strength, women are equal to men in all respects, including their aptitude for learning, Plato's *Republic* and *Laws* helped to authorize early modern efforts to enhance the status of women.[23] Pursuit of virtue is central to *The Faerie Queene*, and masculine and feminine capacities for virtue could readily appear unequal from an Aristotelian standpoint, yet identical to Platonists.[24] Spenser introduces each book of that poem by extrapolating its formative archetype of virtue from a feminine source. The views of Platonic writers might diverge in the domains of love, gender, and sexuality, depending on what they chose to emphasize or revise, but they tended to promote attitudes that were progressive for the time.[25] The protofeminist impulses that Spenser evinces in some contexts, and his relatively relaxed depictions of male same-sex desire, reflect an awareness of Platonic precedents and their influence.[26]

The most clearly Platonic and Ficinian notion in Spenser's canon is that a beneficial kind of frenzy or madness magnifies creative achievement in love, in literature, and in the highest human endeavors.[27] As *The Shepheardes Calender*'s commentator E. K. recognized in the *October* eclogue (1579), the poet refers to and enacts amorous and poetic frenzies, and he continued to do so throughout his poetic career. Insofar as early modern women were involved in eros and erotic emotions, in which they may have been more interested than men, the notion of this benign frenzy tended to elevate them to the philosophic realm as both subjects and readers. The Renaissance recovery of Plato's dialogues on love and the cultural transmutations of their ideas, which Spenser's poetry exemplifies,[28] are among the fundamental motives of the early modern history of the emotions. Those dialogues reshaped the possibilities of understanding eros and the esthetic domain.

These comments only begin to illustrate how the poet's interactions with early modern Platonism can be of current interest; we could further pursue ramifications into the realms of poetics, metaphysics, epistemology, natural philosophy, and politics. Plato's writings pertained to the active as well as the contemplative and studious paths in life, for the *Republic* and *Laws* were foundational texts for sixteenth-century civic humanism. Scholars interested in applying ideological analyses and the hermeneutics of suspicion to early modern contexts may find the *Republic* helpful for exploring how writers of that time could themselves formulate critiques of socially prevalent misperceptions and illusions: a major theme of Spenser's *Faerie Queene* from the outset. Yet for study of this allegorical fabulist, it is perhaps most relevant that, as Sir Philip Sidney says in his *Defence of Poetry*, "whosoever well considereth" the "body" of Plato's work "shall find that . . . though the inside and strength were philosophy, the skin, as it were, and beauty depended most of poetry" (75). Just as that philosopher, like his major followers such as Ficino, "very often" borrows "the masking raiment of poesy" through usage of figurative discourse, illustrative fables, and dialogic interactions of characters (75, 93), no other philosophical school offered resources of expression that more nearly approached Spenser's own poetic practice of romancing ideas, and possibly Ideas, in *The Faerie Queene*.

Among the diverse studies gathered in this volume, those by Carol Kaske and Valery Rees appear first because they supply a foundation, either terminological or bibliographical, for future work. Kaske surveys the "hallmarks" or distinctively Platonic terms and concepts, of which at least one should normally be present in a literary work or passage before it can be properly called Platonic. After surveying corresponding themes and concerns of Spenser and Marsilio Ficino, Plato's Renaissance apostle, Rees provides a substantial appendix that argues for Spenser's early acquisition of Platonic learning by examining the availability and use of related works in the Oxbridge and London milieus, especially at Cambridge University where Spenser studied. At Oxford in 1583, a member of an audience noticed that the lecturer, Giordano Bruno, was plagiarizing from Ficino.

In addition, these two essays as well as those of Eugene Hill and Anne Lake Prescott highlight a single Platonist in Spenser's intellectual milieu who is relatively underused by or unknown to Spenserians: respectively, Flaminio Nobili, Ficino, Everard Digby, and Guy le Fèvre de la Boderie. Prescott thus elucidates *Faerie Queene* Book I.x, with its literal and allusively implied mountains of contemplation, while Kaske considers *Faerie Queene* IV.ii–iii with its patterns of unfolding and infolding. Hill discovers syncretism between Aristotle and Plato in Everard Digby, one of Spenser's Cambridge contemporaries; and Prescott finds it between Christian contemplation and Plato in both Spenser and Guy le Fèvre de la Boderie. Prescott's examples clarify the sixteenth-century cultural significances of "syncretism." The oddness of her intertexts (such as reasoning by anagram) sets a baseline against which Spenser's more reasonable—yet still sometimes odd or weird—poesis can be measured.

Assessing Digby's obscure and still-unedited Latin treatise, Hill further discerns compelling circumstantial evidence for his influence on the poet. These two writers, Hill argues, evince thematic and modal similarities in that Spenser's Platonic romance involves Neo-Aristotelian organizational categories, and evinces an "epistemology of identification" (whereby in knowing something you come to resemble it). By a curious twist of bibliographical fate, the so-called *Theology of Aristotle*—really a Neoplatonic work, a translation of an Arabic paraphrase of Proclus's *Elements of Theology*—became for Digby and some other scholars a proof that Aristotle's works contain a latent Platonic meaning if read allegorically. The Platonizing aspects of Aristotle's sixteenth-century reception warrant investigation of *The Faerie Queene* along those lines. Certainly Digby's case demonstrates the difficulties of assuming any clear-cut distinctions or incompatibilities between Aristotelian and Platonic modes of thought in the poet's time.

Andrew Escobedo and Kenneth Borris then proceed to consider how Spenser's poetic relates to Platonic theories of beauty and love. Surveying a range of enamorments in *The Faerie Queene*, Escobedo assesses the role of erotic rapture, such as Plato had celebrated in the

Symposium and *Phaedrus*, in Spenser's representations of his protagonists' agency and moral development in their varied quests. Their
enraptured experience typically ensures the authenticity of their ensuing ventures. Insofar as Scudamour exercises choice at the Temple
of Venus, he appears a more ambiguous figure outside that normative
paradigm. Platonic rapture, Escobedo shows, is fundamental for assessment of Spenserian heroism and poetic endeavor, just as this poet
aims to fashion readers according to his characterological models.

Platonism was also a major force in sixteenth-century literary theories and practice, and Borris, like Richard McCabe later in this volume, seeks to clarify how Spenser's poetic relates to that cultural
context. In literary applications, Platonism had two contrary modes:
censure of poetry, following Plato's *Republic*; and advocacy of the art,
following some contexts in that dialogue and others. To forestall
such censure, Spenser shaped his own poetic in accord with Platonic
doctrines of beauty, love, ecstatic furor, mimetic idealism, icastic
imitation, and the philosopher's mission of bringing enlightenment.
In Books III to V of *The Faerie Queene*, the stories of Merlin's mirror
and of the true and false Florimells thus engage and refute antipoetic
critiques such as Plato's and Stephen Gosson's. Yet through his depiction of Florimell's impostor, Spenser mocks mimetic artists, especially
poets, who violate his literary principles. He sought the status of a
philosopher-poet, and Florimell herself instantiates his quest for poetic truth through the manifestation of beauty, which induces heroism through its evocation of eros according to Socrates (IV. pr.3).

Several subsequent essays in this collection concern themselves
with the extent to which *The Faerie Queene* represents a coherent
fictive world, a *kosmos* that provides a meaningful and dynamic environment within which characters and their actions take shape. The
sources for world-making poetry can be found in pre-Socratic
thought, which was organized and elaborated in Plato's *Timaeus*; a
broad and continuous tradition in poetry and philosophy developed
out of that seminal text. Catherine Gimelli Martin traces Spenser's
appeals to the tetrad of four elements back to Plato, placing *The
Faerie Queene* (Book II in particular) in literary, philosophical, and
mythographic contexts, and mapping the narrative's movement across
a continuum that is geographical as well as ethical and psychological.
Jon Quitslund's essay also deals primarily with Book II and with
Spenser's representation of human consciousness within a dynamic
cosmos. Focusing on Guyon's descent into Mammon's cave, Quitslund reads that episode, and several others thematically related to it
in the 1590 *Faerie Queene*, in the light of Marsilio Ficino's description,
in his *Three Books on Life*, of melancholia and various medical and

magical techniques for overcoming its ill effects. Quitslund argues that a Platonic program, explicable in terms of Ficino's astrological medicine and therapeutic magic, links the episodes in Mammon's cave, Alma's castle, Acrasia's bower, and the garden of Venus and Adonis in a coherent sequence.

Starting from a recognition that Spenser's account of Adonis's garden "is most obviously a cosmological fiction," Kenneth Gross's essay moves from the cosmic frame of reference to speculation on the introspective, metafictional aspect of the garden's meaning, as "an image of the mind making itself up even as it seems to make up nature." For analogues to Spenser's imaginative activity, Gross refers to Nicholas of Cusa as well as to Plato and Plotinus. In his conclusion, he entertains the idea that other places in *The Faerie Queene*—Mammon's cave, for example—could also be regarded as allegories of the mind's activity. Support for this idea can be found in Quitslund's essay.

While primarily devoted to the *Fowre Hymnes*, Ayesha Ramachandran's essay includes a wide-ranging discussion of the cosmological (and indeed, cosmogonic) aspect of Spenser's poetry. She finds a "synthesis of radically different philosophical traditions" in the *Hymnes*, and touches on themes that other contributors address with a focus primarily on *The Faerie Queene*. Bringing both Lucretius and Spenser's near-contemporary Michael Marullus into a discussion that has been dominated by authors more obviously in the Platonic line of succession, she reminds us of Ficino's enduring interest in Lucretius and of the seminal influence of *De rerum natura* on a host of sixteenth-century writers (such as Marullus, Pierre de Ronsard, Du Bartas, Pontus de Tyard, and Bruno) who dealt imaginatively with the themes of an emergent early modern natural philosophy.

Paul Suttie's essay poses a challenge to such critics as Martin and Quitslund, and to others who see Spenser as either a syncretist or a synthesizer of ideas drawn from different philosophical traditions. While granting that the broad Platonic tradition greatly influenced Spenser's thinking, he finds Spenser's loyalties—to Queen Elizabeth and her policies, and to the waywardness of "earthly or naturall" Eros—often at odds with a Platonic worldview and the kind of "luminous truth" that one expects from a thoroughgoing Platonist.

This volume closes with a four-part Forum on the relationship of Spenser's relatively neglected *Fowre Hymnes* to his *Faerie Queene*, by the "four hims": Richard McCabe, Kenneth Borris, Gordon Teskey, and Jon Quitslund. The *Hymnes* have particular importance for consideration of Spenser and Platonism. They are the poet's most philosophically and theologically discursive texts, as their genre mandates,

and so they express his Platonic learning most explicitly. What may
they have to tell us about the tropes, contents, and contexts of his
other works, especially of his most elaborately covert poem, *The
Faerie Queene*?

McCabe and Borris find that Spenser's hymnic and heroic poems
are intimately related. McCabe considers how all Spenser's publications of 1596 jointly relate to the course of his poetic career in the
1590s, within its particular English and colonial circumstances. Like
Borris in his previous essay on poetics in this volume, McCabe newly
demonstrates the importance of Plato's *Republic* for Spenser's poetic,
and on account of his different emphases he supplements as well as
complements Borris's study.[29] McCabe further shows, for example,
that the *Hymnes* involve a defense of poetry extending that argument
of the 1596 *Faerie Queene*. These contributors concur that Spenser's
poetic advocacy proceeds both "*via* and *versus* Plato," in McCabe's
phrase, to claim true philosophical status. After challenging Robert
Ellrodt's claim that all four hymns and their Platonic learning postdate
The Faerie Queene, Borris's essay for the Forum concludes that the
origins, composition, tropes, and contents of these texts overlap in
various ways. A selection of textual examples show that the *Hymnes*
have much heuristic value for exploring the Platonic capacities of
Spenser's allegory of Faery.

Focusing on the *Hymnes* themselves, Teskey illuminates Spenser's
poetic by reading them backwards, so that their praises of love and
beauty culminate in the first hymn's honoring of eros. Insofar as
Spenser's hymnic tetralogy is dialectical, the interactive articulation
of its components qualifies its own sequential order, and the poet's
publication of the first two shows that they remained important to
him. He was deeply drawn both to eros in the world and to what
Teskey considers, in some hymnic contexts, the "chilly" abstractions
of Neoplatonism. The *Hymnes* explore the interinvolvements of those
Spenserian impulses apparent too in *The Faerie Queene*'s allegorical
realm of materialized ideals and idealized materialities.[30] In this essay
as elsewhere, Teskey recognizes the centrality of textual play to
Spenserian writing and reading; early modern humanists enjoyed in-
versions, deliberate paradoxes, and symbolic enigmas, as the Socratic
dictum of *serio ludere* adopted by Ficino, Pico, and others enjoins.[31]

Quitslund assesses the *Hymnes* in relation to Spenser's other poems
both early and late, so as to identify structural, thematic, and cognitive homologies across the poet's canon. The *Hymnes* reveal philosophical and theological expertise such as Spenser encoded in his
heroic poem. Partly derived from Ficino, Spenser's accounts of love
and beauty in the first two hymns, for example, accord with passages

in both installments of *The Faerie Queene,* and with an early Platoniz-ing sonnet incorporated in the *Amoretti.* While encouraging the sifting of truths from illusions, this poet envisions an interplay of coexistent flux and cosmic order, "competing as figure and ground for the poet's and his readers' attention."

The assembling of this volume has been an exciting intellectual adventure. Most of all we thank the regular editors of *Spenser Studies,* William B. Oram, Anne Lake Prescott, and Thomas P. Roche, Jr. for supporting our initial proposal for a special issue on Spenser's Platonism; and also, at AMS Press, our editors Jack Hopper, who advised us in the initial stages, and David Ramm, who presided genially over our collection's publication. All admirers of Elizabethan literature are deeply indebted to AMS Press for publishing *Spenser Studies* and thus advancing knowledge of this great poet. We further thank Michael J. B. Allen, Michael Bristol, Meredith Donaldson, Andrew Escobedo, and Faith Wallis for further assistance, and the contributors for their commitment to this project, their fine work, and their patience. During this volume's gestation, we the editors have ourselves learned much from them and from each other, and the collaboration has been for us a splendid experience.

Kenneth Borris, McGill University
Jon Quitslund, The George Washington University
Carol Kaske, Cornell University

NOTES

1. Hadfield, "Introduction: The Relevance of Edmund Spenser," in *The Cambridge Companion to Spenser,* ed. Andrew Hadfield (Cambridge: Cambridge University Press, 2001), 12n33.

2. See Jon A. Quitslund, "Platonism," in A. C. Hamilton et al., eds., *The Spenser Encyclopedia* (Toronto: University of Toronto Press, 1990), 546–48; hereafter designated *SE.*

3. Elizabeth Bieman, *Plato Baptized: Towards the Interpretation of Spenser's Mimetic Fictions* (Toronto: University of Toronto Press, 1988); Robert Ellrodt, *Neoplatonism in the Poetry of Spenser* (Geneva: Droz, 1960).

4. In addition to "Platonism" in *SE,* see Quitslund's "beauty," 81–82; Michael J. B. Allen, "Ficino, Marsilio," 305–07; Elizabeth Bieman, "*Fowre Hymnes,*" 315–17; Douglas Brooks-Davies, "mysteries," 485–87; Robert L. Reid, "psychology, Platonic," 568–70; and György Szónyi, "hermeticism," 358–59.

5. Whereas searching the *MLA Bibliography* with the terms "Spenser" plus "Plat★" and "Neoplat★" yields 36 items for the years 1960 to 1990, it yields only 10 for

1991–2008. The ratio per year drops more than 50%. That figure likely underestimates the actual extent of decline because it does not take into account the unannounced treatment of Platonism within monographs addressing Spenser, which was relatively extensive between 1960 and 1990.

6.   Quoting Catherine Gallagher and Stephen Greenblatt, *Practicing New Historicism* (Chicago: University of Chicago Press, 2000), 9.

7.   Two exemplars of that influence are Alastair Fowler, *Spenser and the Numbers of Time* (London: Routledge, 1964); James Nohrnberg, *The Analogy of "The Faerie Queene"* (Princeton: Princeton University Press, 1976). See Carol Kaske, "Hallmarks of Platonism and the Sons of Agape (*Faerie Queene* IV.ii–iv)," this volume.

8.   In *Practicing the New Historicism*, Gallagher and Greenblatt explain that "new historicist readings are more often skeptical, wary, demystifying, critical, and even adversarial" (9).

9.   Many Spenserians seem to have assumed that early modern skepticism has little relevance to this poet and his writings, and yet that is unlikely because he was highly engaged in the intellectual life of his time. His long-term Platonic interests probably indicate an antiskeptical tendency. Compare Colin McGinn, *Shakespeare's Philosophy: Discovering the Meaning Behind the Plays* (New York: Harper Collins, 2006), 3–8.

10.   Kastan, *Shakespeare After Theory* (New York: Routledge, 1999). Also, e.g., Valentine Cunningham, *Reading After Theory* (Oxford: Blackwell, 2002); Terry Eagleton, *After Theory* (London: Allen Lane, 2003). See Brook Thomas, *The New Historicism and Other Old-Fashioned Topics* (Princeton: Princeton University Press, 1991); Douglas Bruster, "The New Materialism in Renaissance Studies," in *Material Culture and Cultural Materialisms in the Middle Ages and Renaissance*, ed. Curtis Perry (Turnhout: Brepols, 2001), 225–38.

11.   Quoting J. B. Lethbridge, "Introduction: Recuperating the Return to History," in *Edmund Spenser: New and Renewed Directions*, ed. Lethbridge (Madison: Fairleigh Dickinson University Press, 2006), 16; Bart van Es, "Introduction," in *A Critical Companion to Spenser Studies*, ed. van Es (Houndmills: Palgrave Macmillan, 2006), 6.

12.   Augustine, *City of God*, ed. David Knowles, trans. Henry Bettenson (Harmondsworth: Penguin, 1972), 8.5.

13.   See Bernard Weinberg, *A History of Literary Criticism in the Italian Renaissance*, 2 vols. (Chicago: University of Chicago Press, 1961), ch. 1; Sir Philip Sidney, *A Defence of Poetry*, in *Miscellaneous Prose*, ed. Katherine Duncan-Jones and Jan van Dorsten (Oxford: Clarendon Press, 1973), 82–94. Cited parenthetically in our text hereafter.

14.   See R. M. Cummings, ed., *Edmund Spenser: The Critical Heritage* (London: Routledge, 1971), 35–194. Lodowick Bryskett and Sir Kenelm Digby specifically praise the poet's philosophical expertise.

15.   See Kenneth Borris, *Allegory and Epic in English Renaissance Literature: Heroic Form in Sidney, Spenser, Milton* (Cambridge: Cambridge University Press, 2000), chs. 1 and 3.

16.   See Andrew Escobedo, "Spenser and Classical Philosophy," forthcoming in *The Oxford Handbook to Edmund Spenser*, ed. Richard McCabe; also, in *SE*, Quitslund, "Platonism," 546–48; and Ronald A. Horton, "Aristotle and His Commentators," 57–60.

17. In this volume, see Carol Kaske's "Hallmarks," on Spenser's pluralism; on his syncretism, see Eugene Hill, "Everard Digby: A Syncretic Philosopher at Spenser's Cambridge," and Ayesha Ramachandran, "Edmund Spenser, Lucretian Neoplatonist: Cosmology in the *Fowre Hymnes*."

18. Kenneth Borris, "Platonism and Spenser's Poetic: Idealized Imitation, Merlin's Mirror, and the Florimells," in this volume.

19. The Palgrave *Companion* indexes eleven pages for "Plato" and "Neoplatonism," none for "Aristotle." The Cambridge *Companion's* ratio is 9:4.

20. Cf. Patrick Cheney, " 'And Doubted Her to Deeme an Earthly Wight': Male Neoplatonic 'Magic' and the Problem of Female Identity in Spenser's Allegory of the Two Florimells," *Studies in Philology* 86 (1989): 310–40.

21. See Borris, "Platonism and Spenser's Poetic," section one, in this volume.

22. See Ian Maclean, *The Renaissance Notion of Woman: A Study in the Fortunes of Scholasticism and Medical Science in European Intellectual Life* (Cambridge: Cambridge University Press, 1980), 8, 24–25, 30–31.

23. *Republic*, 5.451d–57c; 7.540c. *Laws*, 7.804e–805b.

24. Maclean, *Renaissance Notion of Woman*, 54–55.

25. For example, the proto-feminist argument of Book III of Baldassare Castiglione's famous *Libro del cortegiano* adduces Plato's *Republic* as a precedent. However, Plato's dialogues are exploratory rather than mutually consistent, and some comments deprecating femininity in the *Timaeus*, e.g., could be exploited by antifeminists (42ab, 90e–91a). Also, whereas some versions of Platonism favor sex and marriage (as did Spenser), Giordano Bruno's Platonizing *De gli heroici furori* advocates misogynistic asceticism. Yet in the *Timaeus* Plato argues that reproaches of sexual incontinence are unjust because some have greater sexual desire by nature (86be). Plato and Socrates could also be used to counter early modern religious and legal condemnation of same-sexual love (between males most obviously, but also between females). One important context was the *Symposium's* myth of humanity's creation from primal double beings of three types: male/female, male/male, and female/female (189d–92e). See Kenneth Borris, ed., *Same-Sex Desire in the English Renaissance: A Sourcebook of Texts, 1470–1650* (New York: Routledge, 2004), 17.

26. In Book III, Spenser insists on feminine excellence in arms, arts (i.e., the diverse disciplines), and civic policy; Platonic intertexts, cited often in early modernity, include the *Republic* and *Laws* (see note 23 above), and *Critias*, 110be, 112de. In the *January* and *April* eclogues, Spenser's nonjudgmental representation of male same-sex desire, even in connection with his own persona Colin Clout, occasioned criticism. In E. K.'s comment on *January*, the immediate invocation of Plato shows how central Platonic discourse was, in various possible ways, for this issue (compare, e.g., *Charmides*, 153d–54e). On the fuss that nonetheless ensued, see William Webbe, *Of English Poetry*, in *Elizabethan Critical Essays*, ed. G. Gregory Smith, 2 vols. (London: Oxford University Press, 1904), 1:264–65. Yet Spenser continued to represent love between males, including couples presumed to have had sex, with relative equanimity in *The Faerie Queene* (I.vi.17, III.vi.45, IV.x.27–28, VI.v.23–24). Drawing partly on Matteo Boiardo and Lodovico Ariosto's Bradamante/Fiordespina stories in their romantic epics, Spenser has Britomart exploit her masculine disguise to flirt with Amoret, IV.i.5–8.

27.   See Kaske, "Hallmarks" essay, in this volume.

28.   The many relevant studies include Lauren Silberman, *Transforming Desire: Erotic Knowledge in Books III and IV of "The Faerie Queene"* (Berkeley: University of California Press, 1995).

29.   The joint appearance of these two complementary essays in this volume is a happy coincidence, because Borris and McCabe conceived, researched, and wrote them independently.

30.   Their synthesis would presumably depend upon Spenser's characteristic assumption that physicality reflects and hence discloses a transcendental source, as his representations of genuine beauty, e.g., show. (This is not one of Teskey's points in his context, but one that we the editors add here for clarification of our introductory context, with Teskey's approval.)

31.   See Teskey, "allegory," *SE*, 16–22. On *serio ludere*, see Edgar Wind, *Pagan Mysteries in the Renaissance*, rev. ed. (London: Faber, 1958), 236–37.

CAROL KASKE

Hallmarks of Platonism and the Sons of Agape (*Faerie Queene* IV.ii–iv)[1]

The present essay first lays down a foundation of terms and concepts which are distinctively Platonic as they appear in Spenser: Ideas, the four beneficent frenzies, the concomitance of beauty and goodness, ladders, preexistence, and the Platonic cycle of the individual soul from emanation to remeatio. With regard to several of these hallmarks, it introduces a new Platonist, Flaminio Nobili, in a mutually illuminating comparison to Spenser, discovering that Plato means less to his *trattato d'amore* than to Spenser's works. It demonstrates that Spenser throughout his poetry both endorses and enacts the Platonic and Ficinian notion that a certain kind of madness or frenzy fosters vision and creativity. It argues that just as Spenser affirms preexistence in *Heavenly Beautie*, so he implies it in certain other works, including *The Faerie Queene*. It argues that whereas the word "Idea" seems adventitious to the *Hymne of Heavenlie Love,* it plays an important part in *Hymne of Beautie* and in *Amoretti* 45 and 88, manifesting Spenser's tendency to translate Platonic metaphysical concepts into terms of individuals and of the human mind. Then in the second part, proof-texts from the *Fowre Hymnes* serve to reveal some other Platonic concepts such as emanation in an explication both of a story and of its analogous echoes, thus illustrating that tango of retrenchment and discovery that an investigation of a poet's worldview enacts as tastes change. The unity of the sons of Agape with each other and with their community of siblings, in-laws, lovers, and friends exemplifies the unity and equality of a modern social group in the face of diversity.

INTRODUCTION

*T*HIS ESSAY SERVES a dual purpose. First, after situating my approach among certain trends in the last eighty years of Spenser scholarship,

Spenser Studies: A Renaissance Poetry Annual, Volume XXIV, Copyright © 2009 AMS Press, Inc. All rights reserved.

it surveys hallmarks of Platonism, as opposed to those images or doctrines which could by some stretch of the imagination be considered Platonic. The hallmarks of Platonism are as follows: (1) the Ideas or forms, (2) the four divine frenzies, (3) the concomitance of beauty with goodness, (4) the ladder of love, (5) the preexistence of the soul, and (6) emanation. Other hallmarks might be discovered in Spenser by other critics and also by philosophers. In outlining the final hallmark, I apply this approach to an in-depth explication of a specific episode, the Sons of Agape in IV.ii.41–iv.45—my second project, with which the essay ends. This paper has evolved. In "Neoplatonism in Spenser Once More" (2000),[2] I published a list of notions somewhat similar to the one which follows, but it was flawed. From this earlier article, I will incorporate for the sake of completeness some themes and some entire sentences here and there, especially my treatment of Spenser's doctrine of preexistence. On the other hand, I will illustrate some of the hallmarks differently than before, especially the sixth and final one, emanation, by means of an interpretation different from and more Platonic than that which I published in "Neoplatonism," so that the present article constitutes an updating of the earlier one.

There are (at least) two different approaches whereby critics of the early to middle periods of the twentieth century addressed or alluded to Spenser's relation to Plato—approaches that are contrasting yet still visible in the present essay. Spenserians have greeted Platonic interpretations of Spenser with different degrees of credulity and empathy in different periods. In the 1930s and 1940s, a wave of Platonic interpretations washed over Spenser.[3] Also born in the 1930s but fundamentally European in languages, origin, and interests was the movement associated with the Warburg Institute. Starting in the 1930s and continuing until the present day, Aby Warburg and the scholars of the Warburg Institute which he assembled around his library and which he brought with him to London when he fled Nazi Germany, began to influence not only art history and cultural history but literary criticism. Warburg was from the outset interested in the ongoing influence of Greco-Roman antiquity, particularly of its gods but also of its philosophy; he and his followers, however, found it in strange places and in a variety of what Jon Quitslund calls "the Mediterranean cultures."

Warburg was dedicated to interdisciplinarity, and Warburgians study topics such as emblems, astrology, and numerology which cross the boundaries of nations and disciplines, and hence usually escape notice; their documentation also draws on many disciplines. They are dedicated to iconography and "iconology," a discipline Warburg

invented, seeking to decipher the social and cultural meaning of a
visual image with the aid of written texts, as in the study of emblems.
On the other hand, "Warburg was not interested," says Michael Ann
Holly, "in the spiritual world of the Middle Ages." Scholars most
intimately associated with the Institute and its methods include Warburg's original associates Fritz Saxl and Gertrud Bing, Ernst Cassirer,
Frances Yates, Erwin Panofsky, Raymond Klibansky, Jean Seznec,
Sir Ernst Gombrich, D. P. Walker, Charles Schmitt, Joseph Trapp,
and, in the younger generation, Anna Baldwin, Sarah Hutton, Malcolm Smith, Penelope Gouk, and Jill Kraye, and by career and/
or intellectual kinship Edgar Wind and Alastair Fowler, which pair
achieves importance later in this essay. Because of their penchant for
the interdisciplinary and their avoidance of the Christian, Warburg
scholars came up with esoteric sources and analogs, though continuing like the aforementioned Spenser group to cite Plato and his
followers as well, especially the abstruse and neglected followers.[4]
Frances Yates wrote extensively and intriguingly about Spenser in her
book *Astraea: The Imperial Theme* (1975), thus setting for Spenserians a
Neo-historicist agenda. A present-day Spenserian whom I would class
as a disciple of and counterpart to these scholars is James Nohrnberg;
besides generally fitting my characterization of them, he frequently
cites Wind, Panofsky, Yates, and D. P. Walker. Though it was not
their avowed intent, the Warburg scholars were inclined to estrange,
to defamiliarize their chosen subjects. Yates said, and Quitslund
quotes her with approval, " 'I do not think that it is sufficiently
realized how very peculiar the Elizabethan Renaissance was, both
socially and intellectually.' "[5] In his scholarship and in his lectures,
D. P. Walker's favorite word of praise for a Renaissance author
was "odd."

In the middle decades of the twentieth century, particularly in
England, Canada, and the United States, the straightforwardly Platonic critics participating in the "wave" were rejected as anachronis-
tically far-fetched in order to accommodate not only a new
perception that the Renaissance, and Spenser with it, had remained
Christian, but also a new desire—fueled by T. S. Eliot and C. S.
Lewis—to see in Renaissance culture in general and its artists and
writers in particular that unity of the self and of thought and feeling
which a commonsensical, latitudinarian, syncretic, and diffusely Platonic Christianity could supply. This high-minded and widespread
movement exemplifies the now-maligned approach called Christian
humanism; the Warburg scholars, while taking no particular stand
about Christian humanism and while never so widely known and
admired as were the Christian humanists, have in the long run fared

better in critical esteem. The most eloquent and outspoken summary of Christian humanism for our purposes is by Kathleen Williams in her article significantly entitled " 'Eterne in Mutabilitie': The Unified World of *The Faerie Queene*."[6] In 1960, following these critics though writing in France, Robert Ellrodt exulted with only a touch of irony that "with C. S. Lewis, honest Spenser, divested of foreign apparel and antique garb, trod the stage in Elizabethan dress" (7n5).[7] This exemplifies the commonsensical tendencies of the Christian humanists, in contrast to the Warburg scholars, who flaunted their esotericism and did not care whether anyone could possibly live by the worldviews they reported. Ellrodt cites Lewis frequently (among other places, 76n106) and quotes the Williams essay with approval (8n11). Ellrodt primarily set out to prune the excesses of his immediate predecessors, their far-fetched Platonic interpretations and the "outlandishness," as he flippantly termed it, of Greenlaw's titles like "Spenser and Lucretius" (1920) and "Some Ancient Religious Cults in Spenser" (1923) (*Neoplatonism*, 7–8); and he would probably have tarred the Warburg scholars, if he had known them, with the same brush.

Since Ellrodt, for all his idiosyncrasies, is a representative of an entire school of thought about Spenser—Christian humanism—and devotes a clear and deeply researched book to our topic, I will focus the second part of my survey on him. The central thesis in Ellrodt's groundbreaking study is that Spenser, during most of his career until just before its fertile end in 1596, was medieval in his art and thought, including his initial version of Platonic thought, which Ellrodt defined as Timaeic, syncretic, popular, and commonsensical. In 1596, Ellrodt admits, in the *Fowre Hymnes* (Dedication dated 1 September) Spenser began using technical, doctrinaire, Florentine Neoplatonism. This represents the first of two controversial features. If Ellrodt is right on this topic, then my explication of the Sons of Agape, below—a story written for the 1596 installment of *The Faerie Queene* (entered in the Stationer's Register on 20 January, published on 1 November)—is probably wrong, since my Platonism there is quite technical and that passage which alone treats in detail the titular heroes of Book IV (ii–iv) must have taken longer than one year for its gestation. I will discuss this problem of the chronology of Spenser's journey into Platonism further under Hallmark Two, the four frenzies. Ellrodt sought to naturalize Spenser's Platonism, promoting the more commonsensical (or, as Ellrodt calls them, "popular" and "medieval") Platonists like Boethius, Macrobius, Augustine, Bembo, Leo Ebreo, Equicola, Castiglione, Louis le Roy, and Flaminio Nobili. Some Spenserians think of this intellectual community as restricted and constricting, yet it already endorsed many notions which are considered to be Platonic, such as the supposedly Neoplatonic doctrine of the three worlds. I have traced these Warburgian and Ellrodtian currents not to judge them, for this essay participates at times in each, but only to categorize and contextualize the above critics that I use and to illustrate in an admittedly sketchy account how a critic can be allured or repelled by circumambient trends. Ellrodt concluded that Spenser is a Neoplatonizing Christian, not a Christianizing Neoplatonist like Ficino (*Neoplatonism,* 213). This represents Ellrodt's second questionable feature—his approach, which assumes that by assembling verbal parallels, one can assemble a picture of a poet's beliefs and hence of his unchanging self. While Ellrodt's exhaustive scholarship is indispensable for all future research on Spenser's relation to Plato, and while his proposed proportion of Platonism to other worldviews such as Christianity may be generally right, Spenserians no longer attempt to sum up Spenser's ruling ideology in this essentialist way because, whatever the attractions of unity might be, Spenser's thought, *pace* Williams, is not as monolithic as is that of, say, Dante, Herbert, or Milton; he sounds at times narrowly Christian, at times broadly Platonic and syncretic like Ficino, and Spenserians should not homogenize these passages in order to categorize the poet neatly.

Recounting various objections to Ellrodt will balance my frequent reliance on him; and the flavor of some later Spenser critics can be sampled according to the touchstone of their opinions about him. In the present volume, both Valery Rees and Kenneth Borris, particularly in his Forum essay, object to Ellrodt's picture of Spenser's tardy assimilation of Platonism. Borris warns that if Ellrodt were right on this, most of the essays in the present volume would fall to the ground. Before our volume, some critics who take exception to Ellrodt on various grounds, not always his dating, are Elizabeth Bieman and Jon Quitslund, while John Erskine Hankins, Rosemond Tuve, and C. S. Lewis offer a balanced synthesis on the subject. In her book significantly entitled *Plato Baptized*, Elizabeth Bieman criticizes Ellrodt for assuming that one can "separate out the Christian from the Neoplatonic elements in Spenser."[8] Granted, this criticism cuts deep, but most of the critics in our volume seem to believe the two strands can be distinguished at least intellectually, otherwise one cannot analyze an author's syncretism or trace the gradual Christianization or secularization of a poet-speaker's thought as some of us attempt to do. Quitslund criticizes Ellrodt for sympathizing too much with "an older tradition inherited from the Middle Ages" (120–21). In this judgment, one hears echoes of the literary and historical debate that raged in the 1950s as to whether there was a Renaissance, and if so, whether it had to wait until the seventeenth century, at least in England. He warns Ellrodt that Elizabethan thought is complex. As an example, he cites Bateman's intercalation of passages from Agrippa von Nettesheim (a Renaissance humanist and a student of the "occult" sciences under the heady influence of Ficino), into his edition of the medieval encyclopedia *De proprietatibus rerum* by Bartholomaeus Anglicus. True, but the very fact that Bateman chose to translate Bartholomaeus shows sympathy with the Middle Ages; so this fact, however revealing, supports only a mild objection.[9] Hankins in his *Source and Meaning in Spenser's Allegory* gives a valuable survey of scholarship as to what works may be included in the "Platonic" portion of Spenser's oeuvre. Hankins finds that Ellrodt reacted too violently to Bennett's excessive claims for Plato. In general, he objects to Ellrodt's exclusionism, thus proleptically authorizing the present volume: "There is nothing inherently improbable about a Platonic influence upon Spenser and no reason to exclude it in favor of a Christian influence" (239). In regard to a specific passage, however, Hankins applauds Ellrodt's preference for "Christian writers, particularly St. Augustine" over Plato as an analogue, source, or target of allusion for the Garden of Adonis (referring to Ellrodt, 70–92), thus tempering his own global criticism by a local agreement.[10] This is typical of the discriminating way in which most of us use Ellrodt today.

Another compromiser is Rosemond Tuve. She supports Ellrodt in insisting on the medievalism not only of Spenser's outlook but also of that of the two British universities in the sixteenth century. She "does not try to substitute other sources for the Platonic and Neoplatonic sources . . . but [only] to stress the commonness of certain ideas" (53). She nevertheless subscribes conjecturally to Ellrodt's controversial thesis about "Spenser's not using more 'technical' Platonism in pieces of earlier date."[11] Then there is Lewis himself. In my essay, Lewis will be cited piecemeal and ad hoc. To sum up the views of this giant, whose general opinions are already well known, would be to carry coals to Newcastle and would occupy more space and time than it is worth. Suffice it to say that in his nuanced review of *Neoplatonism,* Lewis stands between the Platonists of the "wave" on the one hand and Ellrodt on the other with regard to recognition of distinctive, Florentine, Platonic sources in Spenser. (As for the Warburg scholars, Lewis recommends Wind's flexible and inclusive interpretations of the Italian Renaissance mythological painters as a model for interpreters of Spenser's allegories, saying that one meaning does not preclude other and possibly quite different meanings which

may come to the fore later in the work [160]). While he praises
Neoplatonism, saying "it strengthens my hand," and "in most of this
[treatment of the *Fowre Hymnes*], Dr. Ellrodt seems to me clearly
right," he distances himself slightly from Ellrodt's opinions about the
dating of the *Hymnes*.[12]

Finally, Ellrodt criticizes himself in his recent essay "Fundamental
Modes of Thought" (2005), though on his overall approach, not on
the matter of dating, which looms larger in some people's minds
than in those of others.[13] I had criticized Ellrodt in "Spenser and
Neoplatonism Once More" for being essentialist and too biographical. He is now in approximate agreement with me about Spenser's
contradictions: he says that foregrounding them is one of Spenser's
distinctive habits of mind. This would spring from a Spenser who
was sharply self-contestatory, though in other contexts, Ellrodt gives
a picture (implicitly Empsonian) of the poet's mind as contradictory
because vague and dreamy. This new position was adumbrated in his
original position that Spenser accepts contradictions because medieval
poets did so and Spenser is largely a medieval poet.[14] I agree. The
Middle Ages accepted contradictions regarding both the morality of
bloodshed and the relative value of and right time for the Active and
the Contemplative Lives and their respective concomitants, earthly
and heavenly love; for example, Stephen Hawes did so in the contradictory endings of *The Passetime of Pleasure,* modeled on the endings
of Petrarch's *Trionfi.* For the most striking of medieval contradictions,
one thinks of the contradictory values voiced by the two speakers in
The Owl and the Nightingale, of the third and recantatory part of
Andreas Capellanus's prose treatise *The Art of Courtly Love,* and of
Chaucer's Retractation of the *Canterbury Tales* and his two conclusions to *Troilus and Criseyde.* Nevertheless, Ellrodt rightly concedes,
Spenser foregrounds contradiction more than do his medieval predecessors. Another trait that makes Spenser's philosophy hard to pin
down, Ellrodt acknowledges, is that he is a professional poet, by
which Ellrodt now means that Spenser often says what is rhetorically
appropriate to the genre in which he is writing and not necessarily
what he "really believed," contrary to his previous ideal of the poet
expressing his unitary self. Ellrodt almost admits that Spenser's technical, doctrinaire, Florentine Neoplatonism in the *Hymnes* does not
necessarily mark a conversion but represents obedience to the genre
of the classical hymn, as in those of Marullus (on which see Ramachandran's essay, *infra*). Being a professional poet limited Spenser's
self-expression but freed him as an artist to adapt his personal ideology
to his chosen genre. That Spenser did so has been argued by Patrick
Cheney with regard to Spenser's Retractation in the *Fowre Hymnes*.[15]

These concessions, with which I agree—that Spenser foregrounds contradictions and that he accepts them both because he is in many respects a medieval poet and because he is a professional poet with a concomitant concern for genre—go far towards reconciling Ellrodt's monologic view of Spenser with my polyglossic one and towards liberating the critic to take each passage, at least initially, at face value. Thus we have seen excessive Platonism (that of the initial wave, e.g., Bennett's) corrected by Lewis, Tuve, Williams, Hankins, and Ellrodt; Ellrodt's essentialism corrected by me; Ellrodt's skepticism corrected by Lewis and Hankins; and Lewis's and Ellrodt's common sense and Christianity contrasted with the wider Warburgian horizon of expectation.

Having accounted for contradictions by pluralism in "Spenser's Pluralistic Universe" (1975), *Spenser and Biblical Poetics* (1999), and "Spenser and Neoplatonism Once More," (2000),[16] I now adopt as a working hypothesis that Spenser was often a pluralist and that he does not necessarily conform to Williams's ideal of thematic unity. This working assumption liberates us in looking for elements of Platonism. If we abandon, at least for purposes of this argument, the quest for and assumption of thematic unity on a grand scale espoused by Williams and the New Critics—unity between and among works (such as that which some critics assume to exist between the *Epithalamion* and the *Amoretti* or between major subdivisions such as two or more single *Hymnes* or two or more books of *The Faerie Queene*), we can afford to acknowledge the obvious Platonism manifested by certain subdivisions like the *Hymne of Beautie* (hereafter *HB* in documentation), by the last part of *Colin Clouts Come Home Againe,* by certain sonnets of the *Amoretti* such as 8, 45, and 89, and even by certain passages in the romance-epic such as the Garden of Adonis (III.vi). We should not refuse to test the relevance of a Platonic doctrine just because, as it seems to us, the Spenser we already know could not possibly have believed it. Only after identifying what these Platonic moments are in themselves is it then permissible and necessary to determine their relation to Christianity and to Spenser's other works and values. The relation may be one of pluralism. The poet's stance may change in the course of the poem, and this may be part of the drama. To avoid the "anything-goes" approach that pluralism might entail, I require the change in viewpoint to be signaled by some overt sign, some structural break or change in mood. For example, in the *Cantos of Mutabilitie*, the poet-speaker's partial rejection of Nature's answer to Mutabilitie and his espousal of *contemptus mundi*—"Me seemes that though she all unworthy were/Of th'heavens rule, yet very sooth to say,/In all things else she bears the greatest sway" (VII.viii.1)—is cordoned off as "The Eighth Canto, unperfite."[17] The greatest contradiction in Spenser's thought about love, one confessed by Spenser himself and hence recognized to some extent (if only as a pose) by almost every critic, is the high-minded "Retractation" which the poet-speaker applies to the *Fowre Hymnes*, expressed both in the "Dedication" to the hymns and in the beginning of the *Hymne of Heavenly Love*: "Many lewd layes (ah woe is me the more) . . . " (lines 7–21).[18] The Retractation has been thoroughly discussed many times, from various viewpoints, for example by Cheney and by McCabe in his edition.[19]

A pluralistic approach is familiar in Shakespeare criticism. What Shakespeare says in one play or poem does not necessarily carry over to another nor is it always integrated within its own sonnet or play. For example, Shakespeare does not merit the label Platonist,[20] yet in *Midsummer Night's Dream*, Shakespeare refers to the Platonic doctrine of the madness of the lover and the *furor poeticus* or poetic madness: "The poet's eye in a fine frenzy rolling" (V.1.12), and "the lunatic, the lover, and the poet/Are of imagination all compact" (V.1.7). Spenser agrees. This doctrine of the divine frenzies is uniquely Platonic and thus constitutes what I call a hallmark of Platonism. In another work Shakespeare refers to an even more technical and distinctively Platonic doctrine, the World-soul: "the prophetic soul/ Of the wide world dreaming on things to come" (Sonnet 107, 1–2). In contrast, Spenser, for all his Platonism, never employs this precise term or its Latin equivalent, "Anima Mundi"; therefore, while I allude to this doctrine, I do not dwell on it as a hallmark in Spenser. In another sonnet (53), Shakespeare seems, at least to Stephen Medcalf, to allude to the doctrine of the Idea and its several embodiments: "What is your substance, whereof are you made?" But he inverts it.[21] Hamlet the character exhibits some traits of Ficino's paradigm of the melancholically demented genius. Clearly Shakespeare, without constructing a whole Platonic frame of reference, nevertheless embeds individual Platonic hallmarks, and so, I believe, does Spenser (he does more than that, of course, in the *Fowre Hymnes*). Shakespeare also contradicts himself in one and the same play. *Hamlet* the play acquires its profundity, according to Norman Rabkin, from its insistence on contradictory attitudes toward life, such as the value of rationality as opposed to impulsiveness and the value of life itself.[22] Like Shakespeare in Keats's famous letter, Spenser has negative capability, not in style, to be sure, but in philosophy. One could label Spenser and Shakespeare Platonic, but neither is as thoroughgoing a Platonist as Henry More.

To avoid quibbles, in this essay, I will not always distinguish Plato from the tradition he started; I will sometimes call a Neoplatonic or a Middle Platonic doctrine "Platonic." In this I am following not only the practice of Michael J. B. Allen and my fellow editor Kenneth Borris but also the practice of the Middle Ages and Renaissance, which periods did not have the term "Neoplatonism" (see *OED*). This anachronistic term will be reserved, as it often is, for the Florentine revival of Plato. Neoplatonism sometimes refers to the Middle Platonists such as Plotinus, Porphyry, Iamblichus, and Proclus, but I will consider them not as a separate stage—though they carried intellectual weight, usually unacknowledged, with some individual medieval and Renaissance thinkers and with the continuing, vaguely defined Platonic tradition—but only insofar as they contributed to medieval Platonism and to Florentine Neoplatonism. I realize that I am sidestepping much intellectual history here, but one cannot in the space of an essay consider every subdivision in depth.

The section on hallmarks which follows seeks to highlight for purposes of definition those doctrines that are distinctively Platonic or Neoplatonic. There are two definitions (at least) of Platonism—the strong and the weak, the exclusive and the inclusive. The strong is that proposed by Ellrodt—technical, doctrinaire, Florentine Platonism, in which I would include the fourth book of Castiglione's *Courtier*, despite its popular mode, because Castiglione portrays a hallmark—a complete ladder of contemplation from the lady to God, whereas most Renaissance Platonists do not. The weak definition, considered historically, may contain a hallmark or two but it gathers under a capacious umbrella that diffuse medieval Platonism based ultimately upon the *Timaeus* (as represented in Chalcidius's truncated translation), the *Meno*, the *Phaedo*, and echoes and outlooks of Plato in the philosophers Proclus, the pseudo-Areopagite, Macrobius, Martianus Capella, Aquinas, and Augustine. This weak Platonism was voiced by influential medieval and proto-medieval literary men like Augustine (in his more literary works like the *Confessions* and the *Dialogues*; I cited him before as a philosopher), Boethius, the School of Chartres, Bonaventura, Jean de Meun, Alanus de Insulis, and the poets of the *dolce stil nuovo*. Its favorite doctrines included the creation of the universe by God, a scale of being (albeit not of a strictly Platonic kind) containing certain levels and correspondences, "the one informing spirit, and the essential goodness of all created things" (Ellrodt, *Neoplatonism,* 8–9). These doctrines are indeed Platonic but also characteristic of other philosophies. The differences can be illustrated by my own mistakes. I used to list the concept of transmigration as distinctive, but I no longer do because it is prominent not only in Pythagoras but also in a widely read yet unplatonic writer like Ovid (*Metamorphoses, Book* 15). The Platonism of a hallmark must be obvious. I used to think of the three-storey universe in his *Hymne of Heavenly Beautie* (hereafter *HHB* in documentation; lines 65–70) as distinctively Platonic; but two recent editors now call the notion "medieval" and "traditional."[23] They do so either explicitly or implicitly because a three-storey universe is implied in Dante's *Paradiso* and because Lewis adumbrates it in his repeated contention (though his examples are confusing and incomplete) that things above the moon, while still material, are more durable than things below the moon.[24]

In his 2005 article and its previous Gallic incarnation,[25] Ellrodt "discovered" a virtually unknown Platonist—Flaminio Nobili in his *Trattato dell' amore humano*, published in Italian in 1567 and again in 1580 and translated into French in 1588 by Lavardin. A copy of the first edition of the work was demonstrably owned and marked up (though in a noncommittal way) by Tasso, who was at least distantly acquainted with Nobili[26] and who, of course, served as both a source and a model for Spenser (see for example *A Letter of the Authors*). The work instantiates the always somewhat Platonic genre of the *trattato d'amore*, of which genre the *Fowre Hymnes* is usually described as an embodiment in verse. I will append to my discussion of several hallmarks the conformity or nonconformity to them not only of Spenser but of Nobili. Besides Plato, among several authorities, Nobili cites two other *trattatisti*, Cardinal Bembo in his work *Gli Asolani* and Leone Ebreo in his *Dialoghi d'Amore*. "Spenser could have read it [*Trattato dell' amore humano*] in Italian or in a French translation published in 1588," says Ellrodt; but he concedes with characteristic rigor, "I make no claim for a direct influence in the absence of verbal echoes." Nobili is worth comparing with Spenser as an alleged Platonist. Ellrodt recommends *Trattato dell'amore humano* as a protypical example of one sort of *trattato d'amore*, one that is both Christian and relatively down-to-earth, for example, in its endorsement of marriage, an endorsement exemplified in his *Neoplatonism* in terms of Louis le Roy (99–105 et passim). Ellrodt himself instantiates the commonsensical proclivities shown also by Lewis. Marriage is a touchstone of commonsensical Platonism. Nobili and Spenser (and also Tasso in his epic) all say that if possible, a man should marry the woman he loves; but Nobili observes that marriage makes the love less Platonic.[27] Other loves to which Nobili grants mild approval (as compared to love of God who is one's final end) are love of one's children, one's beneficiaries, and one's students (55v, not quoted or translated by Ellrodt). If we view Spenser's thought as one unified system, his enthusiastic endorsement of marriage and procreation in the *Epithalamion,* the *Amoretti,* and the *Faerie Queene* represents a similarity with Nobili. Spenser does not, however, endorse marriage in the *Fowre Hymnes,* even though the last two of them are Christian, thus rendering the similarity between the two men slightly less striking. If we view Spenser's oeuvre pluralistically, we can say that Spenser conspicuously omitted marriage in the *Hymnes* in order to keep them, or at least the first pair, strictly Platonic and to emphasize the contrasting perspective of the *Amoretti and Epithalamion* (1595), and thus perhaps to exalt Christian love at the expense of Platonic love.

Either way may be right; I mention pluralism in this essay as an enabling assumption not as a thesis to be argued, and not to exclude but to include. Also when dealing with such widespread notions, the source-critic must yield to the cultural historian or historian of ideas, seeking for his chosen author not just sources and targets of allusion but texts that perhaps are only analogues and intertexts. As an intertext, then, Nobili's treatise needs to be studied in depth by an accomplished Italianist. I will treat some hallmarks briefly and some fully. The presence of hallmarks does not necessarily categorize an entire work, let alone the entire oeuvre, as Platonic because the author in question may be pluralistic, like Shakespeare; but hallmarks do provide criteria for assessing the Platonism of individual passages and thus for infusing more rigor into those future studies of Spenser's Platonism which all of us in the present volume hope to inspire in the future. Ellrodt warns, "not because it includes elements also found in the Neoplatonic treatises of the age should a poem be styled Platonic, when those very elements happen to be alien to Platonism or Neoplatonism in spirit or ancestry. To warrant such a labeling, the notions involved should be integral with the Neoplatonic philosophy . . . in its original spirit" (*Neoplatonism,* 29). Such selectivity resembles my present search for hallmarks or distinctively Platonic doctrines. Yet rigor is not the only virtue. As happens with other scholarly topics and trends, that of Platonism has gone through a tango of discovery and retrenchment. My hallmarks represent retrenchment; my explication of the story of the sons of Agape represents—I hope—discovery.

PART ONE: HALLMARKS

1. Ideas

The most obvious indication that a text is Platonic is of course a verbatim reference to Plato's doctrine of the Ideas or Forms. Spenser refers verbatim to Plato's Ideas four times. He goes out of his way to insert a reference to them in each of the last two Hymns. In "Hymne of Heavenly Beautie," the poet-speaker travels mentally to a heaven "Where those *Idees* on high/Enraunged be, which *Plato* so admyrd" (lines 82–83). Christian Platonists like Spenser incorporate the intelligible world as a kind of mezzanine into their heaven which already contains God, the angels, and the souls of the blessed dead. He does not say the Ideas are in the mind of God. As critics mention, Plato in the *Phaedrus* pictures virtuous souls in heaven looking out and up at the Ideas from the apex of the outer shell of the universe; therefore putting souls next to Ideas is not so incongruous as it may seem at first (*Phaedrus* 245c–251b). Previously, in the otherwise intensely biblical *Hymne of Heavenly Love*, he refers to God the Son as an Idea— "Th'Idee of his pure glory" (hereafter *HHL* in documentation, line 284). The "Idee" of Christ's glory would correspond roughly to his glorified self, which consists of the pre-incarnate Word, perpetually existing "in the bosom of the Father" (for this phrase, see John 1:1–5, 18; and *HHL,* lines 30–37), now clothed in glorified flesh. Thirdly, in *Amoretti* 45.7, Spenser claims to contemplate the lady's "Idea." Since this Idea is in the mind, not of God but of the lover, it is an example of Platonic abstraction of the beloved. In the *Hymne of Heavenly Love*, in a parallel of agape to eros, the believer raising his contemplation from the historical Christ to his "Idea" is roughly analogous, as Enid Welsford, McCabe, and the editors of the *YSP* believe, to the lover raising his eyes from the mistress's body to contemplation of her own heavenly Idea in *Amoretti* 45.7.[28] Spenser thus marks these particular hymns as Platonic; and, since the Platonism of the preceding two hymns of love and of beauty is already obvious without this hallmark, the term and concept of "Idees" very likely serves to mark as Platonic the *Fowre Hymnes* as a whole. Judging by the conspicuously adventitious way in which he drags the term into the *Hymne of Heavenly Love*, this status of Platonic Ideas as a hallmark of Platonism seems to have been a motive in Spenser's craft as well. Fourthly, in *Amoretti* 88, the Idea of the beloved is contemplated by the lover as a somewhat inadequate comfort in her absence. In both sonnets, the Ideas, while still admired, have migrated from the Intelligible World not just into a cosmological sphere or the mind of God but into the human mind. The "Idea" of her represents the highest degree that Spenser envisions to which the lover can abstract the beloved; and Spenser egoistically equates it with the lady's ideal self which would normally be pictured as dwelling in the mind of God or at least somewhere in heaven. In the *Amoretti*, the two sonnets shed a Platonic glow of transcendence onto at least their own sonnets and the surrounding and the otherwise related ones and the love they express. Marginal though they are, the references to the Idea in *Amoretti* seem functional within their respective sonnets, whereas those in the two religious Hymns might seem more or less perfunctory. (In the proems of The *Faerie Queene*, according to Borris's essay in the present volume, Spenser engages in an analogous project of idealization in framing his archetypes of the virtues.) Nobili does not mention the Ideas or Forms at all; he uses the word "form" frequently but in a different sense.

The Ideas are involved in a standard Platonic scheme to which Spenser never refers, at least on the literal level, the three Neoplatonic hypostases: the One and/or God, the Angelic Mind which contains the Ideas, and the World-soul. This trinity would constitute another hallmark. But I find no clear literal reference to the World-soul in Spenser—at most, possible symbolic overtones. For his part, Nobili does not explicitly mention the World-soul either. In content, Nobili is really more Aristotelian than Platonic, and the same could be said about the Spenser, not of the hymns, to be sure, but of *The Faerie Queene*.

2. Frenzies

An authentically Platonic doctrine and one that is particularly characteristic of Ficino's Platonism is the doctrine of the four divine *furores* or frenzies. Plato affirmed paradoxically that there is a certain divine kind of madness or frenzy that can conduce to achievement in poetry, prophecy, the priesthood, and most important, in love. Thus the four divine frenzies could be better described as one kind of frenzy, the divine or beneficial, as manifested in these four human occupations. Frenzy is more than just inspiration, it is, as Ficino insists, an alienation of one's mind and a cause of eccentric behavior, particularly of melancholy. In Plato, the notion is voiced in the *Symposium*, the *Ion,* and the *Phaedrus*.[29] The concept had also been expressed in the Middle Ages in Pseudo-Aristotle, Problem 30.1.[30] In diluted form, this hallmark was expressed occasionally even elsewhere in the Middle Ages; but "the creative Eros of the Italian Renaissance reawakened the spirit in the letter," says E. R. Curtius.[31] This notion was restored to the West almost singlehandedly by Ficino. He was fascinated by it, perhaps because, as Klibansky, Panofsky, and Saxl conjecture, though they do not use this modern medical term, he himself was not only melancholy but bipolar, that is, his melancholy brought him "highs," his moments of ecstatic creativity, as well as "lows."[32] Flaminio Nobili extols the blessed lover "stimulated by celestial and divine frenzy/celeste e divino furor sospinto" to selfless interpersonal love on the very last folio of his treatise (fol. 57, not translated or discussed by Ellrodt). The notion that it sometimes helps to be a little crazy stretched the leash upon which reason was supposed to restrain the passions in general and the creative temperament in particular.

Spenser endorsed the notion of the four frenzies too, many times, as Michael J. B. Allen twice remarks in his article "Ficino" in the *Spenser Encyclopedia* (see also Ellrodt, *Neoplatonism,* 31). This is Spenser's most Ficinian theme. Perhaps the clearest occurrence, encompassing both the amatory and the poetic frenzy, is the poet-speaker's lament at the beginning of the *Hymne of Beautie*:

O whither love wilt thou now carry me
What wontlesse fury dost thou now inspire
In my poor heart, too full of thee?[33]

The most Platonic as well as the most Ficinian motif in *Colin* is the notion of the divine frenzies of the lover and the poet. We know Colin is alienated from himself as in a frenzy because an interlocutor warns: "thou hast forgot/Thyself" (lines 616–17). Colin agrees, protesting

Her [Queen Elizabeth's] great excellence,
Lifts me above the measure of my might:
That being filled with furious insolence
I feele myselfe like one yrapt in spright.(lines 620–23)

"Insolence" bears its Latin sense of "unaccustomedness" so that it is the equivalent of "wontlesse furie" in the "Hymne of Beautie." Colin's "celestiall rage," as Cuddie puts it, "that powreth forth those oracles so sage/Of that high power, wherewith thou art possest" (823–26), is correctly and fully glossed by McCabe as Ficinian.

Equally Platonic (I am talking in this essay not about motives but about motifs) is Colin's high-minded love for his queen in the end of *Colin.* It derives from the hallmark "ladders," but it is inextricably bound up with Colin's poetic frenzy here. The poem's last few hundred lines are energized by this among other Platonic motifs. By this point in the poem, Colin has transferred his love from the fickle Rosalind to the distant queen—perhaps because no ordinary woman, only an ideal queen like Elizabeth, deserves Platonic adulation. The poet-speaker portrays the queen as herself a Platonist ascending "in Neoplatonic fashion" to contemplating the heaven of the angels and "the cradle of her own creation," which is, according to McCabe's plausible gloss, "her own heavenly 'Idea' " (*Colin,* lines 612–15). (The motif also encountered here of Love's pacification of warring elements in order to make the world may be originally Platonic, but it is not a hallmark because it seems by Spenser's time to have become part of the common stock of poets.) Thus *Colin Clouts Come Home Againe* has among its many modes a strikingly Ficinian one. In other poems besides *Colin Clouts* and *Fowre Hymnes,* McCabe reports quite a few Ficinian motifs both in his edition of the *Shorter Poems* and also in his book *Pillars of Eternity.*[34] (The single words "rage" and "fury" are, of course, also used by Spenser in their normal, unfavorable senses.) So much for Platonism in Spenser's latest works.

The furor *poeticus* is referred to in Spenser's earliest independently authored work, 1579; in *Shepheardes Calender* "October," Cuddie predicts:

Thou kenst not *Percie* howe the ryme should rage.
O if my temples were distaind with wine,

....

How I could reare the Muse on stately stage,
And teache her tread aloft in buskin fine,
With queinte *Bellona* in her equipage.
But ah my corage cooles ere it be warme.

("October," lines 109–15)

"Rhymes should rage" is Platonic, even though the fact that wine fosters ecstasies of all kinds could have been recognized without Plato's endorsement. E. K.'s Argument and glosses on the poem and on the "Embleme" are even more explicitly Platonic, and chiefly because they glorify poetic madness, especially the gloss on line 110: "O if my) He seemeth here to be rauished with a Poetical furie. For (if one rightly mark) the numbers rise so ful, and the verse groweth so big, that it seemeth he hath forgot the meanenesse of shepheards state and stile" (see also E. K. on lines 21 and 27). Both Cuddie's statement and this apparatus to it represent technical doctrinaire Florentine Neoplatonism. Since E. K. was closely supervised by Spenser, as Spenser's "Postscripte" to his letter to Harvey about his work "Dreames" indicates that he was,[35] this example refutes Ellrodt's thesis that Spenser discovered such Platonism only later in life when he was writing *Colin* (pub. 1595) and *Fowre Hymnes* (pub. 1596).

To bolster his thesis about dating, Ellrodt of course questions, as Spenserians often do, how accurately E. K. represents Spenser's thoughts (*Neoplatonism,* 31–33). Here Ellrodt resorts to a strained argument. He makes light of this early reference both by questioning whether Spenser had by then actually read Plato's and Ficino's treatments of the four frenzies firsthand, which is of course very difficult either to argue or to disprove, and by affirming that E. K. and Spenser could have read about them instead in Minturno's *De Poeta* and that they could have borrowed "the Greek word *Enthousiasmos* used by E. K. . . . from a letter of Cicero" (*Neoplatonism,* 31–32). This question is easy to ask but of little relevance to my present study, which focuses on intellectual indebtedness rather than sources per se, because regardless of where the two friends got them, the character and flavor of the statement remains Neoplatonic, even though it is very early.

I propose as a viable compromise that, in any case, no one, not even Ellrodt, claims that Spenser's adoption of technical doctrinaire Florentine Neoplatonism, whenever that was, burst upon him in one blinding flash. Spenser would be likely to adopt this one hallmark of Platonism before he adopted the others because it is both appealing to poets and comprehensible to amateurs. That one of the alleged exemplars and proponents of Plato's exalted theory is a poet confessedly inferior to Colin, a poet who gets his inspiration from wine and who fails to maintain it for long, makes the theory of the *furor poeticus* no less Platonic; it just distances it by dramatic irony. (For the long and complex debate as to Cuddie's poetic theory and practice, its relation to Piers's more Platonic theory, and Spenser's endorsement of either or both, see the detailed survey of scholarship by Patrick Cheney.)[36]

3. Beauty and Goodness

Another doctrine so obviously Neoplatonic as to require little elaboration is the close though not absolute correlation of beauty and goodness. Spenser affirms: "All that faire is, is by nature good" (*HB* line139) and "All that's good, is beautiful and faire" (*HHB* lines 133). Nobili says, "Nature intends that we infer that within that beautiful body dwells a soul well disposed to be formed in excellent qualities."[37] This stress on the education of the beloved (which is also in Plato) accords with Nobili's stress here and elsewhere on the love of a teacher for his students, and we can also picture what he says as applying to the love of an older man and a younger woman. While mentioning that beauty bespeaks "a soul ready to be trained up in excellent qualities" ("ben disposta formarsi di eccelenti qualità"), however, Nobili does not stress the already-existing spiritual beauty of the beloved nor the lover's mental abstraction of the beloved's divine essence, as much as does Spenser. Spenser comes across as the more Platonic of the two.

4. Ladders

Spenser and many lovers and love-theorists see something divine about the beauty of other human beings and ascribe it to God's especially felicitous creation of them. This much is already expressed by medieval thinkers without benefit of Plato. But in Platonic theory there is a distinctively Platonic variant of this doctrine, and thus another hallmark—the ladder of love, a scale of contemplation based on what is loved and how it is loved. Much has been written about such ladders; I will assemble the primary sources as a foundation for future work and add a few of my own insights. It has little or nothing, beyond a certain progression to a goal and thus a possible parodic force, to do with the Ladder of Lechery allegorized in *Faerie Queene* III.i.45.[38] The Platonic ladder's summit is either God or the Ideas, principally the Idea of beauty. The ladder consists of increasing abstraction in the lover's thinking and less and less materiality in his objects of love. The archetypal unbroken ascent is found, of course, in Plato's *Symposium* itself (209e–12a). It leads the lover from the beauty of an individual body through the beauty of all bodies to the beauty of all souls and up to the Platonic Idea of beauty itself. Then there is, of course, Ficino's Commentary on the *Symposium*, titled "In Convivium Platonis," which naturally alludes to it passim. The account of the ascent in this commentary by Ficino is not as clear as that in Plato and in other commentaries and expansions on him. An unbroken Platonic ascent is found in some other *trattatisti*, for example, the ladder of love as described in the speech attributed to the character Bembo in Castiglione's *The Courtier*.[39]

The erotic ladders of Spenser and Nobili, however, are not complete but terminate far short of the goal—God and / or the Idea of Beauty. *An Hymne of Heauenlie Love* (hereafter *HHL* in documentation) contains no ladder at all until the very last stanza, the ascent to the "Idee of his [Christ's] pure glory":

Then shall thy rauisht soule inspired bee
With heavenly thoughts, farre above humane skil,
And thy bright radiant eyes shall plainely see
Th'Idee of his pure glorie present stil,
Before thy face, that all thy spirits shall fill
With sweete enragement of celestial love,
Kindled through sights of those faire things above.[40]

Note incidentally the locally Platonic descriptions not only of the glorified Christ as an Idea (see Hallmark 1, above) but also of the Beatific Vision as "enragement" (see Hallmark 2, above). The rest of the hymn's architecture is not an ascent but a series of "compositions of place" (on which see Louis Martz, *The Poetry of Meditation*) designed to elicit love for the historical Jesus, the most concrete and least Platonic kind of contemplation imaginable. The poem ends with ascesis and abjection (lines 246–80), which is common to both Christianity and Platonism.

From an outlook similar to that of the *Hymne of Heavenly Love*, Nobili explicitly denies that one can ascend a ladder from love of the lady to love of God. After expounding the standard theory of Platonic love, Nobili objects that he and some other authors he has read feel forced to abandon the love of a beautiful woman in order to contemplate God:

To rise to this Divine Love, I do not know for certain how far womanly beauty is a necessary ladder, for the consideration of the miraculous yet orderly effects of nature, of the regular movements of the celestial spheres, the vital force of light, [and] the perfection of the universe seem to me a safer way to lead us to the knowledge of the supreme beauty rather than losing oneself in the constant contemplation of a face in which one descries on the second day the same art of the Creator as on the first day. And it appears that Bembo [i.e., not Castiglione's character but the historical person, author of *Gli Asolani*] was of this opinion, since, upon introducing that man of great merit, Romito, he makes no mention of a lady at any time but instead calls attention to the eternal Beauties of Heaven, and chiefly to the First [and Final] Cause of all things, that Ocean of beauty and felicity [which, upon borrowing it from the greatest philosophers,] the marvelous Dante explained clearly enough in the last cantos of his *Paradiso*.[41]

(Nobili conveniently forgets that Dante Pilgrim ascended as far as contemplation of the heavenly court by means of a beloved, though by now deceased, woman—Beatrice.) Nobili's skepticism is based both on personal observation of himself and on accounts by other writers such as Petrarch as to the impossibility of heterosexual love's leading the lover to the love of God.

Regarding spiritual beauty, which forms the highest rung of his short ladder of love, Nobili complains, in the first place, that the love of a woman's spiritual beauty is impossible, at least after the initial enthusiasm:

> It certainly never happened to me to know any Lavinello [in Bembo's *Gli Asolani*] fully satisfied with enjoying beauty in the proper way . . . with the eye, the ear, the intellect; but I usually see (with a possible exception at the beginning of enamoration, before the growth and full manifestation of love) that all lovers would have all; . . . if spiritual beauty is meant [by Leone Ebreo, whose *Dialoghi* he is criticizing here], that is, the beauty of the mind of the woman loved, we cannot in this world be united to this beauty, nor see it in its purity for it can only be reached through material and gross bodies; besides, when we shall be able to see it purely [i.e., in heaven], we shall not find our enjoyment in it, but in the Fount of Divine Beauty, our true and complete felicity. [42]

Lavinellos do not exist and spiritual beauty is inaccessible in this life because of the mediation of bodies; in the next life it can be nothing but an afterthought because there everyone is preoccupied with enjoying the Fount of Divine Beauty. Nobili's diagnosis is psychological as well as moral. By referring straightforwardly to his own disillusioning experience ("it never happened to me to know . . . ") and that of other writers on love such as Petrarch, he explicitly questions whether human sexual love, even spiritual love if it were possible, can serve as a way to God. In this quotation, one can see that Nobili is trying to construct an ideology of love that is reasoned, comprehensive, and viable for everyone. Nobili is aiming to elucidate the truth by means of examples both personal and public, rather like his approximate contemporary Montaigne, and this is why he critiques the theory of the Platonic smooth ascent.

While Spenser likewise does not portray the final steps from the lady to God, he climbs a bit farther in that direction. Spenser for his part does affirm, in harmony with Plato and in contrast to Nobili, that one can and should love the spiritual beauty of the beloved, even on this earth, because, according to a powerful Platonic myth, the lovers have already seen each other in the "heavenly bowres" and recognized that they were made out of one mold and hence would love each other after they descended to earth (*HB,* lines 201–10). Moreover, he affirms that the lover can and should abstract from the physical beauty of the beloved an essence which is more perfect than what his eyes can see because he conforms her present image to her appearance in heaven before they both descended into bodies (*HB,* lines 211–38; see "Preexistence.") Spenser's inclusion and Nobili's exclusion of the lover's mental abstraction of the beloved's divine essence stems from the different purposes of each—Nobili to recommend a course of action that is possible and likely, Spenser to enunciate the theory drawn from the precepts of Plato, whether attainable by the many or only by the few: "For lovers eyes more sharply sighted be / Then other mens" (*HB,* lines 232–33). So far, Spenser acts like a professional poet and affirms what his genre demands regardless of its viability.

Although Spenser's lover ascends beyond physical beauty to the spiritual, however, his persona's imagination is no more capable than is that of Nobili's persona of ascending beyond the beauties of the individual beloved to the beauty of all bodies. Their method of argument is different, as we have seen, and not just because the one is in prose and the other in verse.

In Spenser's ladder of love, as is well known, the gap consists most obviously of the twofold Retractation.

> Many lewd layes (ah woe is me the more)
> In praise of that mad fit, which fooles call love,
> I have in th'heat of youth made heretofore,
>
> ....
> And ye that wont with greedy vaine desire
> To read my fault,.....................................
>
> ....
> Sith now that heat is quenched, quench my blame,
> And in her ashes shrowd my dying shame. (*HHL,* lines 8–21)

And at the hymn's climax, he advocates renunciation of any future erotic love:

> All other loves, with which the world doth blind
> Weak fancies, and stirre up affections base,
> Thou must renounce, and utterly displace. (*HHL,* lines 262–64)

Thus Spenser like Nobili ultimately, if not so quickly, abandons love of woman in favor of love of God (as well as of Christ and of God's beloved Sapience), but the lines of reasoning are different. In *Fowre Hymnes,* though not in *Amoretti and Epithalamion,* Spenser totally ignores the Christian solution of marriage in order to sound Platonic, and maintain his pluralism, whereas Nobili accords marriage a Christian if lowly place because he is assembling, from various traditions, practical advice on a love that will make people reasonably happy and benefit the species.

Besides omitting marriage, Spenser the poet-speaker enacts the breakdown of Platonic love even while writing within its framework, similar to Cuddie's enactment of the evanescence of poetic frenzy in "October." Through most of the *Hymn of Beautie,* Spenser or his persona is a performer of the role of Platonic *vates* enacting the theory of the smooth Platonic ascent. The lover seems to be headed towards God or the Idea of Beauty up to line 238 as he abstracts the essence of the individual beloved's spiritual beauty. But at the end, the poet-speaker speaks in his own person (*HB,* lines 273b–87) and stoops to a personal plea for mercy addressed first to Venus (267–80), then to his own mistress (281–87). Already in line 239, just at the point where, according to Plato, he should ascend beyond the individual beloved, that is, from the abstraction of the individual lady's essence (*HB,* lines 232–33) to the beauty of bodies in general, the lover descends to Petrarchan allegories such as Cupid's darts of love, a thousand Graces on the lady's forehead, and a Triumph of Love, motifs which are not philosophical but merely rhetorical and fanciful. A generalized beauty is not represented either in Spenser (until it is implied in the ladder of the beauties of nature in *HHB*) or in Nobili. Instead, Spenser has dramatized his persona's inability to abstract any further, and the next hymn, the *Hymne of Heavenly Love,* makes a new start with the Retractation and proceeds by concrete stories.

Though their means and motives differ, Spenser's and Nobili's recommendation turns out to be the same, and we shall spend less time on it: contemplation of the beauties of nature, especially the visible heavens, and in due course of the beauty of God—chiefly personified in Spenser's case by God's beloved Sapience:

> Beginning then below with th'easie vew
> Of this base world, subject to fleshly eye
> From thence to mount aloft by order dew
> ....
> Of the soare faulcon so I learne to fly. (*HHB,* lines 22–26)

Both men recommend love of our fellow men for God's sake. As mentioned above, Nobili praises selfless interpersonal love (for example, of one's students), as one of the divine frenzies (fol. 57). Besides my analysis of his non-Platonic method of reasoning in *Hymne of Heauenlie Love*, I should mention here that Spenser, when he does reason, constructs a non-Platonic rationale for love of one's fellow man, namely, because 1) God loves them, and therefore all were bought with the same price—Christ's blood; 2) because Christ commanded us to love them in order to multiply the effect of his own love; and, 3) in a (for Spenser) rare moment of commonsensical egalitarianism, because all men must die:

> they shall have like heritage of land,
> However here on higher steps we stand. (*HHL*, lines 200–201)

There are two unremarkable similarities: the repudiation of lust or purely physical desire[43] and the praise of procreation as Godlike and participating in eternity.[44] There is a cryptic passage that seems to be about adulterous courtly love; and if so, it might, as Ellrodt claims, underlie Spenser's House of Busyrane, though the details are not very similar. In this kind of love, the lover will "break the rules [i.e., about marriage] but do it prudently, with great regard for his own honor and for the lady's." Nobili continues: "This love is that of a man not exactly entirely virtuous and rather incontinent than intemperate, as the Philosophers say, whence it has in it more of the human"[45] I report it for what some other scholar can make of it. Neither Ellrodt nor I have located in Nobili any mentions of the metaphysical subtleties of Platonism such as my next two hall-marks—preexistence and emanation. Ellrodt reports that, in content, Nobili depends heavily on Aristotle and on Christian doctrine ("Fundamental Modes," 10–11, 13). Even if one's ladder is broken, it is still Platonic, only a bit less so, because only Plato considers eros to be important enough to merit a philosophical treatise.

5. Preexistence

Two further hallmarks, two distinctively Platonic myths and doctrines which Spenser echoes and dramatizes—preexistence and creation by emanation—concern the origins and final destinations of human souls, their existence before and after their incarnations. Some instances may be either mythical or allegorical, but I will report them here without disputing their literalness or elucidating their symbolism. Their presence shows that at the very least Spenser is trying to sound Platonic.

But first, some preliminary explanations. Transmigration or reincarnation is the migration of the soul at death into another body, be it human or animal. A subset of this—palingenesis—is transmigration into another human being either at birth or in preexistence, as in Plato's Myth of Er (*Republic,* Book 10). I once considered transmigration to be a hallmark of Platonism, but it occurs not only in Vergil in his account of the afterlife in *Aeneid* VI, but also in the unplatonic Ovid's speech of Pythagoras (*Metamorphoses,* XV, 454ff.; both themselves drawing on Plato's Myth of Er). So in this case Plato is just part of the full-voiced choir of Spenser's sources, analogs, and intertexts. Incidentally, if I am right, and so far as I know no one agrees with me, Spenser's transmigrations include one shared with Plato's Myth of Er, and that is transmigration between species. True, Vergil seems a more Platonic source in that he exhibits as does Spenser the distinctively Platonic thousand-year waiting period (VI, 748). But Vergil does not mention transmigration between species, and Plato does; and Ovid, too, dwells on it in the speech of Pythagoras. When Spenser states that some creatures on leaving the Garden of Adonis were "clad with other hew" (III.vi.33), the plain literal meaning of this, given the Renaissance meaning of "hew" as "species," is "changed to another species." Even if one were to agree with that reading of mine here, even this motif would not constitute a hallmark, a unique link between Spenser and Plato, because it is also Ovidian.

Transmigration within humankind happens with surprising frequency in Spenser. He claims that the soul of Chaucer has transmigrated into him (IV.ii.34), but this motif, charming as it is, is not uniquely Platonic.[46] Transmigration occurs in the Garden of Adonis episode, one which is pretty well agreed to be Platonic in some respects—a topic too complex and controversial to explore in detail here—but no motifs in it, including this one, are unique enough to be called hallmarks. What interests us here is that two of the sons of Agape transmigrate at death, and Spenser himself calls it "traduction" (IV.iii.13), which A. C. Hamilton glosses as "transmigration."

Preexistence, however, constitutes a fifth and genuine hallmark of Platonism. It is part of Plato's notion of learning and loving as remembering or anamnesis (*Phaedo,* 72e to 83b; see also *Meno* 81a–c ff.). The *Phaedo* and the *Meno* were known and translated into Latin in the Middle Ages, but their doctrine of preexistence retains a Platonic flavor. Queen Elizabeth is known to have read the *Phaedo*, or some of it, in the original Greek. It is also in the *Phaedrus*, however, and in an erotic context—a dialogue unknown in the Middle Ages and discovered by Florentines (Leonardo Bruni translated the first part of it already in 1424 and then of course Ficino, building on him, translated the entire dialogue in his *Opera Platonis*, 1484), so that its doctrines constitute not only a hallmark, but a Florentine one.

Though few critics acknowledge the fact, it is obvious that preexistence is important to the topic of love in the *Hymne of Beautie*. Women, while advised to love someone eventually, are urged to discriminate and to resist the importunities of lustful lovers by remembering "their first countries sight" (*HB*, line 165). Preexistence justifies the lover who idealizes the beloved on the grounds that they discern the true spiritual beauty that adorned the beloved in "her first perfection," presumably before birth:

> Drawing out of the object of their eyes,
> A more refined forme, which they present
> Unto their mind, voide of all blemishment;
> Which it reducing to her first perfection,
> Beholdeth free from fleshes frayle infection,

Paradoxically, he is thus

> Counting it fairer than it is indeede,
> And yet indeede her fairenesse doth exceede,

because he is envisioning her as she was in preexistence (*HB*, lines 211–39, esp. 213–17, 230–31). Preexistence thus justifies the way in which Britomart "fashiond" Artegall "in her mind, And in" her feigning fancie did pourtray/Him such, as fittest she for love could find,/Wise, warlike, personable, courteous, and kind" (III.iv.5).

Preexistence in Spenser determines that there is only one beloved for every person. Hence, for every enamored couple, in his view, love is a "sympathie,"

> Which they have harbored since their first descent
> Out of their heavenly bowres, where they did see
> And know ech other here belovd to be.
> Then wrong it were that any other twaine
> Should in loves gentle band combined bee,

But those whom heaven did at first ordaine,
And make out of one mould the more t'agree.

(HB, lines 197–207).

Spenser here selects and modifies his sources significantly. Because Plato's *Symposium* and its commentator Ficino do not mention preexistence, critics feel justified in not seeing it in Spenser. Plato's doctrinal arguments for preexistence occur in the *Phaedo* (73a–83b) and the *Meno* (81a–c) and are about learning, not about love. The *Phaedrus* myth, however, employs preexistence to authorize love. This is the true Platonic source for Spenser's view of the prenatal experience:

> when he (the soul) sees the beauty of earth he is transported with the recollection of the true beauty. . . . Few only retain an adequate remembrance of them [i.e., the Ideas in the intelligible world, the world of preexistence]; and they, when they behold here any image of that other world, are rapt in amazement. . . . There was a time when with the rest of the happy band they saw beauty shining in brightness . . . pure ourselves and not yet enshrined in that living tomb . . . the body. . . . we saw her there shining in company with the celestial forms; and coming to earth we find her here too.[47]

What Plato says of beauty Spenser says about one's individual beloved, thus making the link between prenatal and earthly existence not abstract and philosophical but personal and mythical. Spenser frequently does this to Platonic entities.

Among the editors, Welsford totally skips the Spenserian lines in question (she skips from 182 to 211). Ficino, commenting through his translation, keeps the personal but discards the preexistence in Plato: he avoids the topic of preexistence by translating it into astrological destiny. McCabe and Bjorvand–Schell follow suit; they rely on Ficino's *Commentary on the Symposium* 6.6 as an adequate gloss to lines 197–203. But "sympathy . . . composed of starres concent,/ Which they have harbored since their first descent/Out of those heavenly bowers, where they did see/And know each other here beloved to be," is more Platonic than the astrologer Ficino's doctrine, for whom the intellectual kinship becomes purely astrological:

> Those who . . . are born under the same star, are so constituted, that the image of the more beautiful of the two flowing though

the eyes into the soul of the other, corresponds to and agrees completely with a like image formed from its very generation both in the celestial body and in the inner part of the soul.

(I quote the translation followed by Bjorvand-Schell in *Yale Shorter Poems*.) Critics have been unduly influenced by Ficino to downplay preexistence in favor of astrology. They should stick closer to the words of Plato and of *Hymne of Beautie,* lines 197–207.

This preincarnate matchmaking—providential but not biblical—explains Spenser's general endorsement of monogamy throughout his works. It justifies the quixotic searches of many lovers, male or female, for seemingly unattainable beloveds. Of course romancers had always portrayed such quixotic searches without benefit of Neoplatonism, but Spenser must have valued the philosophical justification.

Preexistence can also be discerned in the *Hymne of Love.* It makes a lover (usually the man, but also Britomart in III.ii.24–46) discriminating, not in his mind but in his instincts; it makes him desire not just to quench his lust but to procreate with a beloved who is truly beautiful:

having yet in his deducted spright,
Some sparks remaining of that heavenly fyre,
He is enlumind with that goodly light,
Unto like goodly semblant to aspyre:
Therefore in choice of love, he doth desire
That seemes on earth most heavenly, to embrace.
That same is Beautie, borne of heavenly race.

(*HL,* lines 106–12)

Even if critics have not appreciated Spenser's belief in preexistence, Henry More did. He modestly affirmed preexistence—namely that all human souls preexisted in the World-Soul and thence sinfully or at least frivolously descended to bodies—and on one occasion he voiced this belief in Spenserian stanzas and with an invocation to Spenser ("*Aristo's* [Ariosto's] son").[48]

6. Emanation, Constituting Part Two: The Sons of Agape

The sixth hallmark is the theory of creation by emanation, quite different from both sexual reproduction and the artisanal labors of the

Platonic Demiurge or the God of Genesis, Chapters 1–3. Emanation denotes both a process and its product. According to the *OED*, the product is "an efflux; spec., a beam, flash, ray of light 1646" and also "a person or thing produced by emanation from the Divine Essence 1650. . . . Hence Emanational, adjective, pertaining to the theory of emanation as distinct from creation." These late dates and the absence of the abstract noun from another important dictionary, the *Oxford Latin Dictionary,* need not deter us because, as Lewis and Short's *Dictionary* tells us, the Latin noun had long existed in the Apocrypha, not only in the English translation published at Douai (1582) but also in the Latin Vulgate, still read even by Protestants in Spenser's day, in the book of Sapientia or Wisdom 7:25–26. The Douai version reads:

> For she (Wisdom) is a vapor of the power of God, and a certain, pure emanation of the glory of the almighty God: and therefore no defiled thing cometh into her. 26 For she is the brightness of the eternal light: and the unspotted mirror of God's majesty, and the image of his goodness.

The action of emanation is like that of a fountain (the source) with one or more concentric pools (the product). It also resembles cell division in that it is a means of reproduction that requires neither an artificer nor a second parent, except that the product, the new individual, is somehow remote from and inferior to its parent—perhaps in its greater concreteness and particularity or in its heightened vulnerability to the vicissitudes of mortal life. Emanation is useful to philosophers trying to explain the origin of evil because it enables them to avoid moral dualism by saying that evil gradually increases with corporeality.

But enough of abstractions; they are too reductive. What interests us is their function in a literary context. Let us see how the doctrines both of Ideas and emanation play out not only in the *Fowre Hymnes* but also in the texture of a single episode in the somewhat more concrete world of Spenser's epic-romance, *The Faerie Queene.* I will now explicate a passage about explication, that is, about unfoldings and exfoliations.

In addition to a Christian interpretation of the deaths of Agape's first two sons and her cup of nepenthe, which I have published in *Spenser and Biblical Poetics* and in "Spenser and Neoplatonism,"[49] I want to give a different though compatible interpretation, revealing a syncretic equivocation. I will argue that their entire story contains a myth of origins and of another, a Neoplatonic afterlife: in particular, that the birth of the three sons symbolizes the emanation of the Many from the One; that their careers in adulthood symbolize the further unfolding or differentiation of the Many as their beings dilate; and that the transmigrations of the first two sons into the third symbolize a step in *remeatio* (or *regressio*, *conversio*, or *raptio*)—the return to the One. Oneness-emanation-return or emanation-conversion-return constitutes the standard Platonic cycle of the soul. As Wind admits in his general treatment of emanation,[50] Spenser's sources Ficino and Pico have trouble distinguishing the cycle of the soul into three neat steps like the above, and Spenser doesn't try to; but I shall try to at least hew to the chronological order of the events in the *fabula*. If I am right, the episode tells not only a personal and moral but an ontological and eschatological story. I admit that the brothers do not have a preexistence in some other world as do the lovers in the *Hymne of Beautie*, but they preexisted genetically and obstetrically in Agape as her "branches" (IV.ii.43.3–8). Emanation is one of those technical, Neoplatonic doctrines that Ellrodt denies in Spenser prior to the *Fowre Hymnes* (*Neoplatonism*, 38, 77), as Fowler triumphally points out when defending its presence.[51] Ellrodt does not deal with the Agape episode.

6.1. Birth

The episode of the sons of Agape constitutes, first, in themselves and with their mother, an allegory of kinship, then, in conjunction with Cambell, Canacee, and Cambina, of friendship. That they are brothers is not just a metaphor for Christian brotherly love, though it is that; it is a sign, some of us believe, that they illustrate Neoplatonic emanation, which must be from one common source. Stanzas 41 and 43 of Canto ii have been labeled "vacuous"—and rightly so with respect to Stanza 41, lines 2, 5, and 6, about their boldness and Agape's happiness at their birth:

> Amongst those knights there were three brethren bold,
> Three bolder brethren never were yborn,
> Born of one mother in one happy mold,
> Born at one burden in one happy morn;
> Thrice happy mother, and thrice happy morn,

> That bore three such, three such not to be found;
> Her name was *Agape* whose children werne
> All three as one, the first hight *Priamond,*
> The second *Diamond,* the youngest *Triamond.* (41)

In this stanza, on the literal level, Spenser seems to be just jogging in place. Some of his points could be predicated of any triplets—the triple oneness of the brothers by virtue of their one mother and their simultaneous birth. Stanza 43, however, on their subsequent development, extends the oneness of their birth to their psychology.

> These three did love each other dearely well,
> And with so firm affection were allyde,
> As if but one soule in them all did dwell,
> Which did her power into three parts divide:
> Like three faire branches budding farre and wide,
> That from one roote deriv'd their vitall sap
> And like that roote that doth her life divide,
> Their mother was. . . .   (IV.ii.43)

As adults too, we are told, they are morally one, as if having "one soule." Their natal oneness is again recounted (lines 5–8). In the course of a simile-within-a simile, the "one soule" which makes them loving brothers in adulthood is portrayed as feminine, and originary, and finally as their "roote": that is, their mother Agape herself; for Agape is the "soul" of their relationship. They grow out of a threefold division in Agape's soul, a division which Wind aptly compares to Ficino's characteristic splitting of his gods into three aspects, on which see below. Spenser's insistence that Agape is "one" (41.3; 43.3–6) is supererogatory unless she represents, within her little family, the One or some lower version of it. The birth of triplets from a "single mother" sounds like emanation from the One and the allegory sounds ontological. It suggests that Agape is not only a moral means towards love but Oneness itself. Recall the cachet that Una's name bears—though in her case it refers to moral transparency, not oneness with anyone else.

In Neoplatonic cosmogonies, the One overflows hierarchically first into the Angelic Mind and then into the World-soul, comprising the three hypostases. This represents one standard example of emanation. Spenser never describes this process, but he describes the corresponding Christian trinity in such Neoplatonic terms. In Spenser's *Hymne of Heavenly Love,* in a matrix of Platonized Christianity (yes, we can use such generalizations when we are talking about concepts and small passages), the One or God, moved by love, parthenogenetically "of itself begot" first God the Son (*HHL,* lines 29–35) and then "his second brood" the angels (*HHL,* lines 50–56). In between these two births, God "derived" the Holy Spirit from a combination of Himself and God the Son (lines 36–49; especially 38); in the words of the Apostle's Creed, the Spirit "proceeded" from them, which unique process theologians agree is a Neoplatonic element within Christianity. This process reenacts Spenser's earlier and more Neoplatonic account of the origin of the individual human soul: it "derived was/ At first, out of that great immortall Spright [i.e., suggesting emanation, not creation]/By whom all live to love" (*HB,* lines 106–08). This fecund "immortall Spright" sounds like not only the Holy Spirit but Spenser's Agape, mother of three individual souls. (I do not need to identify this Spright exactly, but given the context it probably designates either the World-soul, Venus Urania, or a Platonized view of God himself.) Similarly and still earlier, in the *Hymne of Love,* the poet-speaker says that the individual lover's "sprite" is "deducted," that is, emanated, not created individually by God's own hand, as orthodox Christianity anthropomorphically believes. That is why it has "some sparks remaining of that heavenly fyre" (*HL,* lines 106–07). This description of the emanation of the individual makes it resemble the emanation of the Holy Spirit, which is admitted by all theologians to be Neoplatonic. To sum up Agape's functions, she fosters unity/ friendship both biologically, in a way which suggests emanation, and morally. No one else, so far as I am aware, draws parallels to Agape and the three brothers from the *Fowre Hymnes.* Similarly, in *Amoretti* 79.11, the lover proclaims that his beloved is "derived" from "that fayre Spirit." As if to cover all the bases, he adds not only that she was "made" by this spirit as orthodoxy demands but also that she was "borne of heavenly seed" like Jesus at his incarnation (to quote the Apostle's Creed again, he was "conceived by the Holy Ghost, born of the Virgin Mary"). Spenser departs from strict Christian orthodoxy so that he can describe the origins both of his gods and of his individuals in terms that are Platonic. The relation of the sons to the mother is the relation of individuals to their Platonic Idea. As such, they parallel the relation of Guyon to the personification Shamefastness in the House of Alma: "You shamefast are, but Shamefastness itself is she." By analogy, the same applies to his companion Arthur's relation to his assigned "date," the personification Prayse-Desire (*Faerie Queene* II.ix.39, 43).

6.2. "Difference Discreet": Further Unfoldings

That Agape divides and branches out to produce these triplets indicates that her genetic legacy is diversified, as emanations sometimes
are. When the triplets grow up, they have different talents for fighting. These are expressed in an unusual stanza and its prelude:

> the first hight *Priamond,*
> The second *Diamond*, the youngest *Triamond.*

> Stout *Priamond*, but not so strong to strike,
> Strong *Diamond*, but not so stout a knight,
> But *Triamond* was stout and strong alike;
> On horsebacke used *Triamond* to fight,
> And *Priamond* on foot had more delight,
> But horse and foot knew *Diamond* to wield:
> With curtax used *Diamond* to smite,
> And *Triamond* to handle spear and shield,
> But spear and curtax both us'd *Priamond* in field.   (IV.ii.42)

That their talents make some difference (though not so much as the
interpreter might wish) in the course of their lives is acknowledged
when their mother returning home "in warlike fresh array/Them
found all three according to their kind" (IV.ii.53.3–4). A. C. Hamilton glosses these lines as follows: "3–4 Each is arrayed according to
his ability." Diamond has a curtaxe because it is his specialty and
presumably Priamond the cross-trainer has one too; Triamond has a
horse because horsemanship is his specialty, and presumably Diamond
the cross-trainer has one too. The story does not tell us what array
Priamond wears for exercising his talent of endurance, though it
would certainly include a shield, nor does it specify the accoutrement
for Triamond who combines endurance with aggressiveness. To render the pattern algebraically, let the letters "a" through "f" signify
the talents:

> Pri. has a, Di. has b, Tri. has a + b.
> Tri. has c, Pri. has d, Di. has c + d.
> Di. has e, Tri. has f, Pri. has e + f.

Each brother excels in combining two athletic talents that appear singly in each of his two brothers. I read this positively: the implication is that friendship need not be based on identity, it can be based on the interdependence of different skills.

Building on Wind and Fowler,[52] I will argue that stanzas 42 and 43 are allegories of Ficinian emanation (both Wind [210] and Fowler already say that) and that they constitute a celebration of unity and equality in diversity. Stanza 42 consists, Wind reveals, of a Neoplatonic "unfolding" of the sort affected by Ficino (210). Unfolding is a kind of emanation—the kind that produces more than one individual. Wind has found and summarized a very similar example of such an unfolding, permutation,[53] or differentiation, one found in Ficino's commentary on Plotinus:

Ficino started with a triad of gods—Mercury, Venus, and Apollo—and expanded it into an ennead, that is, a ninefold series, because each of the three gods asserts his power for himself and also in combination with one of the others. The nine possible variations are listed by Ficino in this sequence: (1) Mercury, (2) Mercury-Venus, (3) Mercury-Apollo, (4) Venus, (5)Venus-Mercury, (6)Venus-Apollo, (7) Apollo, (8) Apollo-Mercury, (9) Apollo-Venus.[54]

This thought-pattern is very close to Spenser's in Stanza 42–closer than any other analogues which have been proposed, as I will show. Even so, Spenser's nine variations are more complex than Ficino's, involving not only three persons but six qualities—strong versus stout, sword versus axe, and mounted versus on foot.

Fowler agrees with Wind about Spenser and adds his own Ficinian example of unfolding—apportionment of the three theological virtues to the persons of the Trinity and the worshipper of each. Fowler quotes Ficino: "The soul approaches God through faith, hope, and charity—faith chiefly to the Son, love to the Spirit, hope to the Father. In return, God gives the soul three graces: light from the Son, joy from the Spirit, strength from the Father. He gives light principally as a reward for faith, joy as a reward for hope, and strength as a reward for love." [55] This pattern is complex but loose; one does not feel as one does with Ficino's gods and Spenser's martial skills that we have before us all the possible variations. Nevertheless this, too, is an analogue.

An internal analogue to the differentiated brothers is the twin sisters Amoret and Belphoebe, who "twixt them two did share/

The heritage of all celestial grace" (III.vi.4). This implies they are complementary. They are extremely diverse. In fact, one wonders why Spenser makes them twins at all. Building on "twixt them both did share," Kathleen Williams explains correctly that they represent two legitimate types of woman; other critics explain that they represent the two usual, church-approved sexual lifestyles, the virgin and the wife (see, for example, Hamilton's notes on III.vi.3.9 and III.vi.4.6–9). Their differences are emphasized in order to show that they exhaust the possibilities, as the truest permutations do. So it is with Agape's triplets.

While we are considering thematic analogues to emanation or unfolding, we should consider formal ones. Stanzas 41.8–9 to 42.9 are an extreme example of Spenser's "unpacking stanza," as I call it, or in standard rhetorical terms, *epanados*, or *divisio* plus *inclusio*. At the House of Busyrane, Cupid is followed by

> *Reproch, Repentaunce, Shame*;
> *Reproch* the first, *Shame* next, *Repent* behinde:
> *Repentaunce* feeble, sorowfull, and lame;
> *Reproch* despightful, careless, and unkinde;
> *Shame* most ill favourd, bestiall, and blinde:
> *Shame* lowrd, *Repentaunce* sigh'd, *Reproch* did scold;
> *Reproch* sharpe stings, *Repentaunce* whips entwined,
> *Shame* burning brond-yrons in her hand did hold:
> All three to each unlike, yet all made in one mould[56]

Upton and Todd in the *Variorum* were the first to cite these as an analogue to the brothers. These clearly constitute a unity in diversity. Nothing is said about their parentage unless one gives a genetic meaning, possibly a womb, to "all made in one mould," which could imply they are siblings. A. C. Hamilton's notes on the way the three names are permuted in III.xii.24 constitute a masterly explication which is too complicated to quote or summarize here. The parallel of this threesome with that of the brothers includes both the assignment of particular traits (albeit wholly distinct ones), to each person, the affirmation of their oneness, and some relationship between them, in this case, according to the effects of an illicit love affair, especially on the woman.

Another example of *epanados*, in which the relationship of six elements is even closer since it is one of musical harmony, is the stanza and its prelude describing the music in the Bower of Bliss:

Birdes, voices, instruments, winds, waters all agree.
The joyous birdes shrouded in cheerful shade,
Their notes unto the voice attempred sweet;
Th'angelicall soft trembling voices made
To th'instruments divine respondence meet:
The silver sounding instruments did meet
With the base murmure of the waters fall:
The waters fall with difference discreet,
Now soft, now loud, unto the wind did call:
The gentle warbling wind low answered to all.   (II.xii.70–71)[57]

Of course, the intents, tones, and types of discourse here are very different, since both the brothers' stanza and the stanza itemizing Amoret's tormentors serve for descriptive classification while the music-stanza elicits aesthetic pleasure. Nevertheless this analogue, while not Neoplatonic in content, enacts the workings of Neoplatonic unfolding. All three unpackings are heralded by what E. R. Curtius in his monumental survey of topoi calls a summation-schema;[58] beginning and/or ending with a summation, what I more colloquially call "bookends": at the beginning of IV.ii.41 is a bookend: "there were three brethren bold, /Three bolder brethren never were yborne," and then some rhetorically irrelevant material, and finally another bookend at the end of the stanza ("whose children werne/All three as one, the first hight Priamond . . . " etc. Then comes a further description of each brother without bookends (42). In the House of Busyrane, at the beginning is the bookend "Behind him was Reproch, Repentaunce, Shame" and at the end is another: "All three to each unlike, yet all made in one mould." In the music-stanza, the initial bookend is "Birds, voices, instruments, winds, waters all agree" and the final bookend is simply "all." The summative "all" appears in the last lines of every *epanados* or unpacking that I have quoted. The music-stanza and the brothers-stanza employ the bookends to Neoplatonic effect by displaying the distribution of traits and their ultimate unity. The summation or "bookend" corresponds to the One. The brothers-stanza and the music-stanza include a pair of opposites: just as "stout" is a defensive skill and "strong to strike" an offensive, so high and low notes are juxtaposed when "silver sounding instruments did meet/With the base murmure of the waters fall." And the water makes sounds "now soft, now loud."

These similarities could indicate that IV.ii.42 is not distinctively Neoplatonic but only rhetorical. But it could still be philosophical as well as rhetorical: Spenser may have noticed at some point in his education that the triads typical of Neoplatonic emanation resembled his own well-worn figures—summation, *epanados*, division, and inclusion—and thus could be enacted by them.

The doctrine of emanation is extensively dramatized, including one stanza that unpacks civility, in the spectacle of the dancing graces on Mount Acidale. Much has been written on this beautiful episode, some of it relevant to this essay. I will merely summarize what pertains to emanation. As is well known, the Three Graces as Venus's handmaidens represent an unfolding of Venus, and the ring of one hundred naked and dancing ladies in turn represent an unfolding of the Graces. Unfoldings, though by no means unique to Platonism, dramatize with especial aptness the theme of the Many produced by emanation from the One, constituting, as Kenneth Borris has phrased it in a private communication, a mental *habitus* of Spenser's, what Ellrodt would have classed as a "fundamental mode of thought." Unfoldings can be pictured either as circles or as disks—disks like the fountain in the center of concentric pools which serves as the archetypal symbol of Platonic emanation. As Louis Martz argued in a lecture in Chapel Hill, N. C., at the summer Medieval and Renaissance Institute in 1979, the several circles in the Graces episode and elsewhere in Book VI occur on various Platonic levels, one of them evil, some of them social, one of them cosmic—namely the stellification of Ariadne's crown. The "Three Disgraces" as Borris calls them, Decetto, Defetto, and Despetto, unpack the Blatant Beast and thus neatly parody not only the Graces, as Fowler, Ronald Bond, and others have discovered[59] but the sons of Agape.

6.3. Egalitarianism and Matter

The brothers are like the persons of the Christian Trinity but unlike the three Neoplatonic hypostases in that they are not ranked, despite their necessarily successive emergence from the womb, in which sequence Priamond is the "eldest." This equality can be seen in stanzas 41 and 43. The three Neoplatonic hypostases are usually ranked, as when Ficino frequently refers to the Angelic Mind as higher than the World-soul (e.g., *De Vita* III.i). But in the passage cited by Fowler, Ficino pictures the persons of the Christian trinity as all on the same ontological level, as Trinitarian orthodoxy demands. For all his Platonism, Spenser too, describing the trinity in the *Hymn of Heavenly Love*, describes the last two members of the Trinity, though born or emanating successively in time, as being on the same ontological level; he subordinates only the angels (and not very clearly at that) and all of them of course to God. Unlike most schemata in the Middle Ages and the Renaissance, those of the brothers and the Trinity are egalitarian.[60] I do not push the parallel so far as to interpret the brothers as the Trinity, as some critics have done. The brothers are not that exalted, and it would render ludicrous the notion of one of them marrying Canacee. Spenser seems here to associate diversity not with hierarchy but with interdependency. Social formations too are examples of the interplay of the One and the Many. Other analogues to this association in this period are rare. One is voiced in St. Paul's famous metaphor of the Body of Christ and in its secular version, the fable of Menenius Agrippa, about the body and the members. Spenser's praise of a group as a mosaic of diverse but equal members strikes a rare responsive chord because it is an ideal of great social resonance today.

Wind finds in Spenser a similarly egalitarian (or almost egalitarian) relation between two contrasting half brothers controlled and infolded by the personification Concord:

> On either side of her, two young men stood,
> Both strongly arm'd, as fearing one another;
> Yet were they brethren both of halfe the blood,
> Begotten by two fathers of one mother,
> Though of contrarie natures each to other:
> The one of them hight *Love*, the other *Hate*,
> *Hate* was the elder, *Love* the younger brother;
> Yet was the younger stronger in his state
> Then th'elder, and him maystred still in all debate.
>
> Natheless that Dame so well them tempred both,
> That she them forced hand to joyne in hand,
> Albe that *Hatred* was thereto full loth,
> And turn'd his face away, as he did stand,
> Unwilling to behold that lovely band.   (*FQ* IV.x.32–33)

In forcing them to combine, Concord is an example of infolding, as Wind points out (211), and she forces them to experience unity and thus make a step towards the One—a step similar to Priamond's

and Diamond's absorption into Triamond. Because Love and Hate
are not only diverse like the sons of Agape but contrary, Concord
creates a *concordia discors* or even a *coincidentia oppositorum*. Concord is
in a sense the One, or a lower emanation of it, like Agape, though
a One with a split personality. Although derived originally from
Empedocles, the cosmological level of Concord's conciliatory actions
is also Platonic, as Spenser shows by attributing these actions to Love
and incorporating them in a Platonic context both in *Hymn of Love*
(lines 56–91) and in *Colin* (lines 841–58).[61] Wind says that Concord,
having as it were digested Love and Hate, then illustrates an unfolding
like Agape's by bringing forth Peace and Friendship, her harmonious
and explicitly biological children.[62] It is not clear who the fathers of
Love and Hate are. Whereas IV.ii.42, the stanza describing the threefold union of Agape's sons, being specifically about friendship, could
be merely psychological and ontological (IV,ii.42), Concord's symbolism of community cries out for a political application as well.
Concord and her staff could symbolize the government of a nation
subsuming tension and producing "Peace." Thoughts about the One
and the Many are inherent in theories of the State. In addition, after
Triamond receives the souls of his brothers, we see another and
looser amalgamation which begins the process of state-formation—a
multifaceted foursome that results from the final uniting of Cambell
and Canacee, Triamond and Cambina as siblings; Cambell and Triamond, Cambina and Canacee as friends; and Cambell and Cambina,
Triamond and Canacee as lovers, who may also be called friends.[63]
The nation has replaced Agape as another representative of the One.

6.4. Fighting and the Father

That emanations of Agape should excel in warfare is an incongruity
which seems due to the inevitable romance-epic ingredients of "wars
and knights" (VII.vi.37). Also, as Jon Quitslund reminds me, Spenser
subscribes to the widespread belief that love often begins in enmity,
as in the *innamoramento* of Britomart and Artegall, as Jessica Wolfe
has recently argued.[64] Again, martial skills have the advantage of being
susceptible of that fine differentiation which Spenser needs here. It
is their father's talent which has determined that the sons shall be
military men:

showing forth signes of their fathers blood,
They loved armes, and knighthood did ensue,
Seeking adventures, where they any knew. (IV.ii.46)

The father would seem incompatible with my interpretation since emanation is sexless, like cell division. I counter that the father disappears after sowing his seed, plays no further part in the story, and is mentioned as little as possible, whereas the mother and her role are praised at tedious length. If Spenser in his notion of genetic inheritance is following Galen, then the mother has input; if Spenser is following Aristotle, the traditional authority, the father supplies all the form, that is, the traits, and the mother supplies the passive matter; I go with this interpretation as being the historically more probable one. But in so doing, she distributes the various traits among the sons. Ficino says—and he is quoted in relation to Spenser by Hankins—that matter is the principle of individuation or differentiation.[65] In accordance with her presumed role as matter, Agape accepts passively the father's seed bearing its military form, its knightliness, but it is she who distributes its various components into diverse individuals.

6.5. Survey of Scholarship

Consideration of the alternative interpretations of IV.ii.41–43 that have been offered will show the rich suggestiveness of the story and why the Wind-Fowler interpretation is necessary, though perhaps not sufficient. In the eighteenth century, Todd and Upton find the stanzas beautiful and discover analogues not only within the works of Spenser but also in Ovid (whose parallels with Spenser here are rather diffuse and weak), whereas Wind and to an extent Fowler represent modern taste and call the stanzas vacuous and pedantic to the untutored mind if it is not equipped with Neoplatonism. Neoplatonism makes the episode beautiful partly by supplying a oneness which transcends physical death—eschatologically, the return to the One and morally, a unified society.

On a general and realistic level, Hankins adduces a statement from Aristotle: "Best of all," says Hankins, "is the friendship of brothers, when nature, fortune, and virtue happily conspire to join them by blood and by a common outlook on things." Hankins does not cite the place in Aristotle (perhaps he got it by way of Heffner and De-Moss in the *Variorum*, on IV.ix.1, the Amyas-Placidas story—critics who are cited by him above, 143). Hankins continues: "Spenser has illustrated this passage in the three sons of Agape" (143–44). If the *Faerie Queene* were a realistic novel, this would be all the explanation we would need, but certain elements of Spenser's story are symbolic and seem to apply to those not blessed with siblings. Clearly the quest of Agape represents love of kin of the special, maternal variety. As Nelson says, the brothers too represent among other things love of kin.[66] That siblings can also be friends without implying incest, as in Hankins's quotation from Aristotle, is implied in Spenser's curious noun for Cambell, Canacee's brother, "her dearest friend" (IV.iii.35.5). In most interpretations of Spenser, though not in all of the analogues, the episode's main theme has always seemed to be friendship.

Following Roche, Nohrnberg cites the emblem of the three-bodied Geryon *in bono* either for friendship or for love of siblings; he cites other entities which possess three bodies, three souls, or both, all interpreted as friendship or concord; but this resemblance only takes us so far because the union is congenital.[67] Spenser portrays souls that are differentiated, souls that transmigrate into a living brother one by one as they die, and Geryon's subdivisions by and large do not. Nohrnberg cites one apt analogue in Silius Italicus's *Punica* (I, 278–82) in which with the help of the Fates, two souls enter their fighting brother sequentially "duraeque sorores/tertia bis rupto torquerent stamina filo" ["for whom the stern Sisters spun a third lease of life when the thread had twice been snapped"]: and they do so in fulfillment of a parent's prayer as a consolation for the brothers' future bodily death. Vergil's Evander tells a similar story about a man named Erulus (or Herilus) who had two extra souls (*Aeneid,* VIII, 564–67).[68] All these extra souls, however, are not called brothers; they are anonymous and without affection; any affection resides in the parent who gave them; they are life-extenders and no more. Only in Wind's analogue (the gods) and that of Fowler (the Trinity) do the characters have differing yet not hierarchical traits. This seemingly significant permutation of the brothers' talents does not occur in most of the many narrative and emblematic sources that scholars cite for triplicity; in them, oneness is stressed without differentiation, which indicates where Spenser's originality came into play. Only Nelson explains differentiation.

A salient fact about the brothers is that in Book IV's title heading, occupying half a page, Triamond has a different name, "Telamond," one always interpreted, by those who consider it, as "perfect world." The prefix *Tela*—does indeed derive from Greek *teleios,* "finished,

complete, perfect.''[69] Although this etymology remains a faint over-
tone because Spenser did not incorporate the name into the story
itself, nevertheless it must be considered.

Nelson constructs an apt interpretation of the differentiation, the
battle, the deaths, and the name Telamond: "Spenser is careful to
show that each of the three sons of Agape has a particular knightly
excellence but not all of the excellences which a knight might have
(IV.ii.42).'' Each is somehow incomplete. One of them needs to
somehow absorb the different talents of the other brothers in order
for him to defeat Cambell and win Canacee. Servius interprets Erulus,
the man with the three souls in *Aeneid* VIII lines 564–67, by saying
"the three souls stand for a great and complete man.''[70] Servius's Latin
has "perfectum,'' one meaning of which is "complete,'' just as one
meaning of *teleios* is "complete.'' Both words imply the end of a
process and Erulus's extra souls manifest themselves sequentially. This
implies that *Tela-* was to have become Triamond's name only after he
absorbed his two brothers. Nelson cites moralists that posit equality as
one basis for friendship (243–44). Then and only then, says Nelson
about Spenser's characters, is Triamond equal to Cambell, his present
competitor, potential kinsman, and future friend. Triamond's final
"parity'' with Cambell, he continues, is shown by his endurance and
by his acquisition of a sorceress as an ally (Cambina) to match that
of Cambell (Canacee).

Jefferson B. Fletcher propounded this interpretation to Nelson but
admitted that the extra souls all die before Triamond fights Cambell
to a draw and becomes his friend. Finessing this objection makes
Nelson's account ambivalent and confusing (Nelson, 244). I would
finesse it by citing Hamilton's observation on "trebly wext''
(IV.ii.52) that a residue of the killed brothers stays on in Triamond
inasmuch as Spenser closes the tale by saying that Triamond subsequently lived "a long . . . life'' (IV.iii.52.5). This residue of longevity
is a significant alteration of fate in that initially all three of the threads
signifying their lives were said to be "short'' (ii.50). Presumably,
then, the full complement of manliness lingers on as well, as is shown
by Triamond subsequently fighting Cambell to a draw with no end
in sight. Nelson's sources Vergil and Servius are incomplete only in
that they do not account for the great affection of the brothers—illustrating love of kin as in the three kinds of love enumerated in IV.ix.1.
Vergil's narrator Evander mentions no affection between Erulus's
three souls; transmigration is for Nelson just a mythical device for
rolling all three brothers into one (244), whereas I will argue it is
also a reunion and a *remeatio* for each of them. Properly understood,

Nelson's interpretation illuminates the purpose of the battle (to demonstrate parity) and, by implication, that of the timed transmigrations
(not only to preserve the first two brothers but also to measure the
damage [mitigated by the magic ring] that each of them has managed
to inflict on Cambell in order to soften him up for Triamond).

Many critics vaguely allegorize the brothers as the medieval or
Neoplatonic three worlds (terrestrial, celestial, and invisible or supercelestial, the realm of God and of souls) or as some other traditional
or made-up triad of worlds. Thus Priamond is said by these critics to
symbolize the sensible, terrestrial world; Diamond the visible celestial
heavens; and Triamond (or Telamond?) the supercelestial heavens,
the third and highest storey of the universe, "unmoving, incorrupt,
and spotless bright" (*HHB,* line 68). This interpretation is tenable
only until one is discovered that not only makes sense of the alternative name on the title page but also remains true to the literal details
of the story.

The interpretation of the suffix (-mond or—mund) as "world" is
questionable. This second element was common in literature and in
life, for example in Spenser's Christian name "Edmund." Perhaps
one could say, reductively, that Spenser liked names that reminded
him of his own. "Mund" or "mond" as a noun or element of a
compound does not really derive from Latin mundus, world, because
the man's name "Edmund" (and also "Sigmund") go back to the
Anglo-Saxon, where the word "mond" or "mund" means not
"world" but, in its first and basic meaning, "hand," and by extension,
protection.[71] Because of its commonness and its other meaning, I do
not see the necessity of etymologizing the suffix at all.

Although the three worlds play an important role in the *Fowre
Hymnes* and the *Mutabilitie Cantos,* nothing else in the episode relates
to cosmology, except perhaps for the journey of Diamond's soul to
"her native home" (IV.iii.30.9). Cosmology does not appear in the
analogues either. Nor do the three Neoplatonic worlds find much
of a counterpart in the brothers The picture of one of them marrying
Canacee is ludicrous, whereas a three-souled man would be acceptable. The Neoplatonic three worlds are hierarchically ordered, both
in size and in purity from matter, whereas the brothers are equal.
Whatever superiority one may credit to Triamond when he becomes
Telamond, the twice-killed Diamond is certainly not superior to
Priamond as the celestial world is to the terrestrial one. Moreover,
the brothers emanated not from each other as the worlds did in Plato
and his commentators but from a fourth person, Agape. Agape, not
Triamond, is the character who could be envisaged on a higher, less
material plane of existence like the supercelestial world, being an

abstraction of their shared virtue, but the story requires three people, not four. We shall see that the perfected Triamond has one of her characteristics, but that is all.

Pace David Burchmore and most of the critics, the concept contributes nothing to the interpretation of this episode; in fact, this extra meaning blurs in the reader's mind the other and relevant meanings.[72] We need to clear the decks. But it is in the names, you may say. The prefixes or first elements of the names—one, two, and three—are indeed relevant; but they do not necessarily involve the three worlds. They fit the chronological sequence in which the brothers transmigrated into Triamond, which also happens to be the sequence in which they were born (IV.ii.41). Their firstness, secondness, and thirdness allude to their birth-order, their death-order, and the maximum number of souls that each brother managed to possess at any one time.

Both glosses, Nelson's "complete man" and the medieval and Neoplatonic three worlds, could coexist; but Nelson's man saves more of the phenomena and is more parsimonious. In fact, many of the preceding analogues may have been present in Spenser's mind and in those of his readers. Most of them could be attached, not to the worlds, it is true, but to the Neoplatonic emanations proposed by Wind and Fowler and to Nelson's interpretation of the extra souls as forming Triamond into "a complete man" and thus a worthy husband and brother-in-law.

6.6. Death, Transmigration, and *Remeatio / Regressio*

The Three Fates granted Agape her wish that the souls of Priamond and Diamond should become parts of Triamond:

> Graunt this, that when ye shred with fatall knife
> His line, which is the eldest of the three,
> Which is of them the shortest, as I see
> Eftsoones his life may pass into the next;
> And when the next shall likewise ended bee,
> Unto the third, that his may so be trebly wext

They graunted it.   (IV.ii.52–53)

She does not tell her sons anything about the transaction. Spenser records the fulfillment when first Priamond and then Diamond transmigrate into a surviving brother. Priamond's final destiny is described with eschatological specificity:

> His wearie ghost assoyld from fleshly band,
> Did not as other wont, directly fly
> Unto her rest in Plutoes griesly land,
> Ne into ayre did vanish presently,
> Ne changed was into a starre in sky:
> But through *traduction* was eftsoones derived,
> Like as his mother prayd the Destinie,
> Into his other brethren, that survived,
> In whom he liv'd a new, of former life deprived.
>
> (IV.iii.13, my emphasis)

A. C. Hamilton glosses the word "traduction" as "transmigration."
    When two people contribute their souls to a third person so that he becomes "trebly wext," or three in one, the act can aptly symbolize a step in the process called *remeatio, regressio,* or returning to the One. With no explicit connection to this particular episode, Fowler aptly defines *remeatio* as simply "the returning phase of the cosmic rhythm" and illustrates it in the titular knights and Arthur: "the missions [from the Faerie court] correspond to the Neoplatonic *emanatio,* the quests themselves to the *raptio* or *conversio,* and the [implied future] ingathering of the virtues in the complete person of Arthur to the return or *remeatio*" ("Neoplatonic Order," 75). In this phase, the three souls of the brothers become one in the sense of inhabiting a single body. This gives the incident at the very least a Platonic patina. Priamond first transmigrates into Diamond; next, having been killed again there, as the plural "brethren" implies, he further transmigrates into Triamond. Diamond also transmigrates at death into Triamond, and undergoes after this another step of *remeatio*: his departing soul, having been killed a second and final time within the body of Triamond, ascends to "her native home" which is a literal Platonic allusion to the world of preexistence, sometimes identified with a particular planet in the celestial world (IV.iii.30.9; see Hamilton's notes ad loc.; also "unto her native planet shall retire," *HB,* lines 99–105). Though not compatible with Christianity,[73] traduction is compatible with preexistence in that the stay on one's "native planet" could be just a temporary phase in a soul's preexistence, perhaps the counterpart of the Garden's thousand-year waiting period, before the next incarnation.

On the moral level, "traduction" symbolizes empathy and brotherly love, dramatized in many other places in the episode including the very next stanza. Although Agape says nothing to her sons about the peculiar fate she has arranged for them, "she warned them to tend their safeties well,/And love each other deare (IV.ii.53)." This does not occur in the cited analogs. I have already argued in two previous studies (*Spenser* and "Neoplatonism") that traduction in particular symbolizes the Eucharistic commonality of the living and the dead as a remedy for death—an interpretation developing out of Cambina's Christian-acting cup of nepenthe wherewith she magically calms and reconciles the combatants Triamond and Cambell and thus in effect unites Triamond also with Canacee, the woman he fights to win. I would like to add here to my statements and to Nohrnberg's adumbration thereof[74] that when the deceased brothers unite with their siblings, their unity resembles that brotherly love attributed to the church, both the militant and the triumphant, as the Body of Christ. Both Agape's stanza quoted above, requesting the transmigration of the two doomed brothers, and its fulfillment in the narrative of Canto iii (IV.ii.53, iii.9–50), represent, on the moral level, steps through larger and larger groups towards not only the body of Christ but the commonwealth.

But this transmigration means more than friendship; in the metaphysical allegory, it means *remeatio*, a step in returning to the One. *The Hymne of Beautie* describes this *remeatio* literally:

> But that faire lampe [the beautiful soul]
> ....
> Shall never be extinguisht nor decay,
> But when the vitall spirits do expyre,
> Unto her native planet shall retyre,
> For it is heavenly borne and can not die,
> Being a parcell of the purest skie.   (*HB*, lines 99–105)

An emanation could literally be called a "parcel" of what it emanated from, such as the One.[75] But an orthodox Christian could not call his soul a "parcel" of anything, except of the body of Christ, the Church. For a Platonist, that individual piece of beauty which constitutes the individual soul will join other "parcels" in its native planet and all of them together will ascend to make up one thing, the purest sky (that is, the supercelestial heavens from which it initially emanated), and in that sense will be reabsorbed into the One. This account of the *remeatio* gives us a third term from the *Fowre Hymnes* identifying the soul as an emanation: there was "deducted," and "derived," and now there is "parcel."

We can accept both Christian and pagan meanings in this episode because its alleged subject, friendliness, is a virtue in both classical and Christian thought. Here the *Faerie Queene* echoes not Christian eschatology but the Platonic eschatology of the *Fowre Hymnes*, thus indicating their mutual philosophical relation at this point.. When the soul returns to its "native planet" and thence to "the purest sky," this sounds, within the discourse of the *Hymnes*, like sober doctrine. Through the lens of a work which is agreed to be conspicuously Platonic—namely the *Fowre Hymnes*—I bring out the Platonic coloring of phrases regarding the sons of Agape in *The Faerie Queene*. A continuation of the theme of friends merging identities occurs in the tournament for Florimell's girdle, as Judith Anderson has pointed out: Cambell and Triamond "literally fight for one another."[76] First Cambell, then Triamond, each don their friend's armor, symbolizing the exchange of identities between Plato's friends and lovers; they both win the prize but cannot agree because each wants his friend to have it all. Since it is Florimell's girdle, they cannot usefully divide it. Wearing another person's armor also represents a material parallel to Spenser's myth of transmigration.

But when the two brothers die, the transmigration of Priamond's soul into Diamond, and of both their souls into Triamond (not treated by Wind or Fowler but affirmed by Roche, 16–17) is not just about friendship; it is philosophical Neoplatonism because it illustrates the entire cycle of the soul, as Nohrnberg implies, ending with infolding or *remeatio*, the return to the One, or a step in that direction (Nohrnberg, 617; his connection of all this to Telamond/Triamond is remote). Fowler finds other examples of the cycle of the soul in the *Faerie Queene* but not this one ("Emanations," 61). Their deaths are almost the reverse of their birth in which Agape "did her life divide" into three. On the literal level, the added souls contribute to Triamond's endurance in the battle for Canacee (e.g., IV.iii.30–31, 35). As we have seen, Triamond will have "a long and happy life" (IV.iii.52), as if the extra lives of his brothers deposited in Triamond a residue of longevity.

The Faerie Queene aptly mimes the emanation and *remeatio/regressus/reversio* of the three souls in terms of water: Spenser says about the Thames and the Medway whose marriage provides the climax of Book IV what he might have said of the souls of the brothers:

All which long sundred, doe at last accord
To joyne in one, ere to the sea they come,
So flowing all from one, all one at last become.   (IV.xi.43)

Another internal analogue, as Kenneth Borris has reminded me, is the efflux of courtesy from Queen Elizabeth and its return to her when her courtiers themselves behave courteously and thus adorn her court (VI Proem 7). As I have said, the relation of the brothers to Agape is like that of examples to an abstraction or a Platonic Idea. Their death, our present concern, brings an abstraction down to earth. They do not return to Agape, let alone anything higher, though Priamond's soul, when killed a second time in Triamond's body, returns to its "native home," which implies preexistence. Morally, though, Triamond continues to dramatize *agape* in his generosity to Cambell in the ensuing tournament for Florimell's girdle discussed above.

Instead of Triamond's being killed and returning to the One, to Agape, or to his "native home," the outcome of the battle as engineered by Cambina's seemingly Christian magic is a group of four, literally pictured as such at IV.ii.30. A. Kent Hieatt (*SE*, "Tetrad") and A. C. Hamilton (note to IV.iii.52) picture it as a tetrad, an "x" in a rectangle.[77] Each of the four corners or members of the group relates to the others by three kinds of love, to wit: love of kin, in that not only the brothers but Cambell and Canacee, Cambina and Triamond are siblings; sexual love; and "zeale of friends combynd with vertues meet"—kinds listed by Spenser a few cantos later in the Amidas-Placidas-Paeana episode (IV.ix.1). By contributing to a tetrad, Triamond joins the other three friends, lovers, and kinfolk in symbolizing the building of a "nation" (mentioned by Hieatt, "Tetrad")—an earthly version of the One. Critics and cultural theorists have noticed, perhaps too stridently, how politics tends to replace metaphysics as the major theme both in the later books of *The Faerie Queene* and in Early Modern culture at large.[78]

This tetrad fulfills the same function as the original triad of the brothers—to exhibit unity in diversity. In this case there is diversity of sex and possibly as a result a degree of hierarchy of the husbands over the wives. Nevertheless, the future wives—Cambina and Canacee—gain some dominance by their magic, especially Cambina with her masterful behavior on the battlefield, and in this Cambina like her half brothers carries on the work and thus represents an emanation of her mother Agape. Even her name sounds like "combine." As for Cambell and Canacee, initially, they exemplify love of kin just as the three brothers do. But because their parents are not allegorical and are not in fact even mentioned, they do not represent emanations of anything. They do, however, represent familial unity.

There are (at least) two kinds of social unity in the story of the sons of Agape; not only the brothers' allegorical and Platonic origin and transmigration but also the (somewhat) realistic growth of male bonding between the surviving brother and his prospective brother-in-law Cambell based on their now-equal prowess. "As soon as he gives up his sister," says Dorothy Stephens of Cambell, "he finds a friend."[79] This is as far as the incest theme found in the source, for instance in Chaucer and Gower, carries over to Spenser (see A. C. Hamilton's gloss on IV.ii.35). A mild version of incestuous desire is dramatized by Cambell's ambivalence expressed in his plan not only to choose a bridegroom for his sister but also to fight him. Cambell manifests an unhealthy reluctance to graduate from love of kin, the lowest form of love in Spenser's survey of kinds in IV.ix.1–2, to exogamy, to the highest form of love, friendship. In Spenser, Cambell shrinks from exogamy not primarily because of any physical eros between him and his sister but because of the common sentiment that "nobody is good enough to become a part of our family"—a reluctance found also in parents of couples.

CONCLUSION

In Part One, "Hallmarks," I have surveyed in greater or less detail six distinctively Platonic doctrines: first, on the metaphysical level, the Ideas or Forms, and then on the human level the four divine frenzies, the concomitance of physical with spiritual beauty, ladders of contemplation (whether broken or continuous), preexistence, and emanation.

New notions in my survey of hallmarks are as follows: I have given a sketchy and derivative description of a Neoplatonist newly rediscovered by Ellrodt—Flaminio Nobili—and determined that on the whole (and he is more amenable to categorization than is Spenser because he is writing a single unified treatise on the subject) he is less Platonic than is Spenser. The Platonic doctrine of the Four Frenzies dawned on Spenser as early as the "October" Eclogue and E. K's gloss on it in 1579 and remained with him throughout his poetic career. In another example of such doctrinaire Platonism, Spenser affirms preexistence pervasively and seriously in the first two hymns (in *HL*, for example, line 106) and he seems to imply it elsewhere in Books III and IV. Critics have avoided admitting this, sticking to a Ficinian personal but astrological interpretation of the major passage (*HB*, lines 197–203) because they lack the authorization that a pluralistic approach would supply. Spenser's picture in the *Hymne of Heavenly Beautie* of souls meeting each other as future lovers during their preexistence seems to have been original with him. Plato said in the *Phaedrus* (250–56) that each soul first sees in preexistence not the beloved, as in Spenser, but the Idea of beauty and then when on earth he or she recognizes it and loves it. Spenser has personalized Plato's original statement.

In Part Two, "The Sons of Agape," which interpretively applies my exposition of the sixth hallmark, emanation, to an episode of *The Faerie Queene,* I have argued that Agape symbolizes the One or some lower emanation and analogue of it such as Venus and that she dramatizes how the Many issues from the One genetically. Along the same lines, I have elaborated on Wind's and Fowler's notion that her sons are emanations from her who are equal yet conspicuously differentiated. Her bargain with the Fates arranges for their final unity. In an analogous group in the Temple of Venus, Wind rightly claims that Love, Hate, Peace, and Friendship are emanations of the personification Concord whether or not they are also her biological children, and that by forcing two of them to join hands and thus infold back into her "lovely band," she forces them to enact *remeatio*—the final stage in the Platonic cycle of a soul and the Platonic meaning, as Fowler adds, of the ingathering of Spenser's titular knights to Arthur and to Gloriana's court. Bizarre analogues to the story such as people with extra souls and three-bodied monsters symbolizing friends dramatize social unity in the building of a commonwealth as a remedy for death. I have advanced a partly political defense for the beauty and relevance of the curious "unpacking" stanza about the brothers (IV.ii.42) as well as other "unpacking" stanzas in *The Faerie Queene.* Throughout, openmindedness is encouraged by tracing the ebb and flow of literary taste and how it felt or must have felt to belong to this or that movement.

Cornell University

NOTES

1. Joseph B. Dallett, Alice Colby-Hall, Michael Twomey, Thomas D. Hill, William J. Kennedy, and my fellow editors Ken Borris and Jon Quitslund contributed in various ways to this essay. In Spenser quotations, I have normalized *u* and *v*.

2. "Neoplatonism in Spenser Once More," *Religion and Literature* 32.2 (2000), 157–69. I am grateful to the editors of *Religion and Literature* for permission to paraphrase and quote from parts of the article.

3. See J. S. Harrison in Spenser, Variorum *Works,* ed. Edwin A. Greenlaw, et al. 11 vols. (Baltimore: Johns Hopkins University Press (1932–58), 1:501–05. See also Josephine Waters Bennett in "Spenser's Garden of Adonis," *PMLA* 47 (1932): 46–80, and two subsequent articles by her in *Studies in Philology* defending Spenser's Platonism against Brents Stirling. This selective survey complements that of Valery Rees in the present volume; it focuses on Spenser and Plato not on Spenser and Ficino, emphasizes the work of the Warburg Institute, and cites a few more recent critics. Since at least some Platonism is obvious in the *Fowre Hymnes,* I have not listed the many investigators of that.

4. Holly, "Aby Warburg," in "Interpretations of the Renaissance," in *Encyclopedia of the Renaissance,* ed. Paul Grendler et al. (New York: Charles Scribner's Sons, 1999), vol. 5. Besides this quotation, many of the above points were inspired by or based loosely on her article. For detailed evidence of the interests and approaches of the Warburg school, see the *Journal of the Warburg and Courtauld Institutes.*

5. Jon Quitslund, *Spenser's Supreme Fiction: Platonic Natural Philosophy and "The Faerie Queene"* (Toronto: University of Toronto Press, 2001), 121.

6. *ELH* 19 (1952): 115–30; reprinted in *Critical Essays on Spenser from ELH,* no editor (Baltimore: Johns Hopkins University Press, 1970), 59–74, and also in *That Soueraine Light: Essays in Honor of Edmund Spenser 1552–1952* (Baltimore: Johns Hopkins University Press, 1952), 35–50.

7. *Neoplatonism in the Poetry of Spenser* (Genève: Librairie Droz, 1960 [reprint Folcroft, PA: Folcroft Press, 1969]), "Introduction," 7–8. Hereafter cited by *Neoplatonism* and page in text.

8. *Plato Baptized: Towards the Interpretation of Spenser's Mimetic Fictions,* (Toronto: University of Toronto Press, 1988), 248, n 9.

9. Quitslund, 120–22.

10. John Erskine Hankins, *Source and Meaning in Spenser's Allegory: A Study of The Faerie Queene* (Oxford: Clarendon Press, 1971), 234–39, esp. 235–37.

11. "Spenserus," in *Essays by Rosemond Tuve,* ed. Thomas P. Roche, Jr. (Princeton: Princeton University Press, 1970), 162n27. Ellrodt quotes earlier works of Tuve extensively in *Neoplatonism,* 91.

12. Lewis says in his review of *Neoplatonism* in *Ètudes Anglaises* reprinted in *Studies in Medieval and Renaissance Literature,* ed. Walter Hooper (Cambridge: Cambridge University Press, 1966), 160, 151, 150, first, that "the dating [Ellrodt] accepts is not really necessary to his main position" (150)—which is that the technical, esoteric Platonism which Bennett and others attributed to Spenser is unjustified. Lewis expresses his agreement that the Platonism even of the *Fowre Hymnes* is attenuated both by Christianity and by earthly love by saying,"In most of this Dr. Ellrodt seems to me clearly right" (151). Lewis hypothesizes that Spenser might have begun with that short-lived enthusiasm in his youth to which he lays claim in the Retractation, writing his first two hymns "with the accuracy of a neophyte." If so, "the lack of demonstrably Neoplatonic echoes in the rest of Spenser's work [aside from the *Fowre Hymnes* and certain sonnets in the *Amoretti*] would then represent, not (as in Dr.

Ellrodt's picture) a period when he was still ignorant of their system, but a period in which he learned to sit to it more and more loosely" (150).

13.   Robert Ellrodt, "Fundamental Modes of Thought, Imagination, and Sensibility in the Poetry of Spenser," *Spenser Studies* 20 (2005): 1, hereafter "Fundamental Modes." When Ellrodt said Spenser was a "professional poet" in *Neoplatonism* (32) he was simply naturalizing Spenser's early adoption of the technical doctrinaire notion of poetic madness, not advocating pluralism; but in "Fundamental Modes," 2, he does invoke professionalism along with rhetoric to explain Spenser's contradictions, i.e., his pluralism.

14.   "Fundamental Modes," 5 and 9.

15.   Patrick Cheney, *Spenser's Famous Flight: A Renaissance Idea of a Literary Career* (Toronto: University of Toronto Press, 1993), 196–211, summarizes past interpretations of Spenser's Retractation of the first two Hymns. For his part, similarly to Ellrodt's recent position, Cheney interprets the Retractation in terms of professionalism, not in any crass patron-pleasing sense but in imitation of the career pattern of DuBartas, who advised the old poet to turn at the last to divine poetry (197–99 ff.).

16.   "Spenser's Pluralistic Universe: The View from the Mount of Contemplation (F. Q. I.x)," in *Contemporary Thought on Edmund Spenser,* Richard C. Frushell and Bernard J. Vondersmith, eds., (Carbondale, IL: University of Southern Illinois Press: 1975), 121–49, 230–33 ; *Spenser and Biblical Poetics* (Ithaca, NY: Cornell University Press, 1999), hereafter cited by short title "*Spenser*" and page in text, see Index s.v. "contradictions"; and "Neoplatonism," in which, for criticism of Ellrodt on this point, see 157.

17.   A. C. Hamilton, et al., eds., *The Faerie Queene* (London: Longmans, 2001). All references to *The Faerie Queene* will be to this edition.

18.   Dedication to *Fowre Hymnes*, 452, and *HHL*, lines 8–21.

19.   *Edmund Spenser: The Shorter Poems,* ed. Richard A. McCabe (London: Penguin, 1999) in his general Introduction, xv–xviii; 705–07. Unless otherwise noted, all references to Spenser's poetry aside from *The Faerie Queene* are to this edition. On this point, see again Cheney, 197–99.

20.   See, e.g., J. B. Leishman in his chapter "Shakespeare's Un-Platonic Hyperbole" in his *Themes and Variations in Shakespeare's Sonnets* (London: Hutchinson University Library, 1963): "what in Shakespeare . . . seems to be Platonism is really inverted Platonism," 149.

21.   For an example of the kind of inversion of Plato that Leishman is talking about, see Stephen Medcalf, " Shakespeare on Beauty, Truth, and Transcendence," in Anna Baldwin and Sarah Hutton, eds., *Platonism and the English Imagination* (Cambridge: Cambridge University Press, 1994), 117–25, especially on Sonnet 53, e.g., the antiplatonic "acknowledgement of a single actual person as the standard and guarantee of value" (122).

22.   See Norman Rabkin on Shakespeare's pluralism, which he sums up in his broader term "complementarity," in *Shakespeare and the Common Understanding*, NY: Free Press, 1967), ch. 1, passim, esp. 6–9 on *Hamlet.* See also his *Shakespeare and the Problem of Meaning* (Chicago: University. of Chicago Press, 1981), 67 on *Antony and Cleopatra* and 34 on *Henry V* which reads in part: "In *Henry V*, Shakespeare created a work whose ultimate power is precisely the fact that it points in two

opposite directions . . . " like the familiar drawing of a rabbit that is also a duck. Jon Quitslund anticipated me in seeing something like pluralism in Spenser in that he too invokes Rabkin on Shakespeare as a model (320n23). Quitslund called the structure not pluralism, my word, but "complementarity," a term he borrows from Rabkin, though complementarity includes emotional ambivalence towards one and the same image—a valuable esthetic response, but one whose existence is not only less remarkable but also harder to prove than are my propositional contradictions such as that between I.x.1.9 and II.i.33.4.

23.   William A. Oram, et al., eds., *The Yale Edition of the Shorter Poems of Edmund Spenser* (hereafter *YSP*) (New Haven: Yale University Press, 1989); Richard A. McCabe, ed., *Edmund Spenser: The Shorter Poems*, both glossing *HHB* approximately lines 64–77.

24.   *The Discarded Image: An Introduction to Medieval and Renaissance Literature* (Cambridge: Cambridge University Press, 1967), 108–09; see also 121.

25.   "Les structures fondamentales de la pensée et de la sensibilité dans l'oeuvre poétique de Spenser," *Annales de la Facultè des Lettres de Nice 18, Ètudes Anglo-Americaines* (1972): 5–16.

26.   *Il Trattato dell'Amore Humano di Flaminio Nobili*, ed., with Tasso's marginalia, Pier Desiderio Pasolini (Rome, Ermanno Loescher, 1895). As Pasolini complains, Tasso's notes are noncommittal, but Tasso probably was sympathetic because he was using the book in preparing himself for a self-organized debate, in connection with a wedding, on a list of questions on love (Introduction, Sections IV and V). I have consulted this edition, but in my text I will cite the first edition, *Trattato dell'Amore Humano, Composto, & donato ha già molti anni da M. Flaminio Nobili* (Lucca: Busdraghi, 1567). Since Nobili's book is available, if at all, in a rare edition and in collections of rare books in universities, I will give also the page and note number of Ellrodt's 2005 article, which is readily available, wherever I cite Nobili, so that readers can check the Italian. In the two passages I cite and Ellrodt does not, I will append the Italian as well. There is also a French translation which I have been unable to access (*Traité de l'amour humain*, trans. J. de Lavardin [Paris: Lucas Breyel, 1588]). For their acquaintance, see C. P. Brand, *Torquato Tasso: A Study Of The Poet And Of His Contribution to English Literature* (Cambridge: Cambridge University Press, 1965), 73.

27.   Though Nobili recommends marrying the woman one loves (22r–v); but late in the book he admits that marriage makes the love less Platonic because "the constant contemplation of a face on which one descries on the second day the same art of the Creator as on the first day" is not as uplifting as is contemplating the beauties of the universe (25r–v).

28.   Enid Welsford, ed., *Fowre Hymnes, Epithalamion: A Study of Edmund Spenser's Doctrine of Love* (Oxford: Blackwell, 1967). All three are annotating *HHL* line 284. Compare Teskey's resistant reading of the phrase, "Th'Idee of his pure glory" in the present volume.

29.   In the *Symposium*, see Stephanus numbers 205d–07c, 210–12a, cited in note 91 of Sears Jayne's translation of Ficino's *Commentary on Plato's Symposium on Love* (Dallas TX: Spring Publications, 1985), 178. See Hugh Maclean on the *Fowre Hymnes* in his first and second editions of *Edmund Spenser's Poetry* (New York: Norton, 1968, 1982); Maclean's edition of the hymns is the most useful for our purposes

since Welsford's (1967) inasmuch as it quotes extensively in English in the notes from Ficino's commentary on the *Symposium*; these notes were excised along with the *Fowre Hymnes* themselves in subsequent Norton editions. In the *Ion*, see 534–42; in the *Phaedrus*, 244a–45b, especially 245a.

30.   Becker number 953a. This Pseudo-Aristotelian work entitled *Problemata* was available with an explanation by Pietro d'Abano (Mantua: 1475), to whom Ficino refers; see Ficino's *De vita—Three Books on Life,* ed. Kaske and Clark (Binghamton, NY: Medieval and Renaissance Texts and Studies, 1989) I.v, notes 7, 8, 12, and 13, citing Ps.-Aristotle, Becker number 954a–b. Problem 30.1 stresses the beneficent side of melancholy and thus its bipolarity as much as does Ficino.

31.   *European Literature and the Latin Middle Ages,* trans. Willard Trask (London: Routledge, 1953), Excursus 8, "The Poet's Divine Frenzy," 474–75. For faint survivals of the four frenzies from Plato and Aristotle in medieval poetics, see Kaske and Clark, eds., Introduction, n24.

32.   His description of his symptoms occurs in many places over his entire career; for the "highs" distinctive to bipolar disorder and produced by certain states of the melancholic humor black bile, see for example in *Three Books on Life,* Introduction, 23, 30, and 77 and *De vita* I.iv–vi, esp. v, lines 52–66, esp. 55–66 and our notes 7 and 8; on I.v–vi, note 2. Raymond Klibansky, Irwin Panofsky and Fritz Saxl, *Saturn and Melancholy: Studies in the History of Natural Philosophy, Religion, and Art* (London: Nelson, 1964), 255–56 and esp. 261, discuss "the dangerous bipolarity of Saturn," though they do not of course anticipate that "bipolarity" will become a twentieth-century medical term of art. The four frenzies arise from a special and beneficial form of the fourth humor, black bile, a humor which, until Ficino, had almost always been viewed as the cause only of melancholy in the narrow psychological sense—what we call the "lows." This beneficial form implies that oscillation which characterizes bipolarism. Ficino mentioned the four beneficial frenzies in general as early as 1457 in his Letter 7 to Peregrino Agli (*Letters,* trans. various, vol. 1 [London: Shepheard-Walwyn, 1975], 42–48). For original Latin, see Ficino's *Opera omnia,* 4 vols., ed. M. Sancipriano and P. O. Kristeller, Basle, 1576, facs. rpt. Turin, Bottega d'Erasmo, 1959), 287, 612, and Ficino's entire dialog *In Platonis Iovem [sic,* for *Ionem] . . . epitome,* ★1281, ff.. See also Ficino's commentary on the *Symposium,* 7.13–15; for English see Jayne, *Commentary.* See also Ficino on *Phaedrus* 243e–45a on which see *Marsilio Ficino and the Phaedran Charioteer, Introductions, Texts, Translations,* by Michael J. B. Allen (Berkeley: University of California Press, 1981) Summae Chs. 13–14, 140–44. See *Platonic Theology,* 13.2, ed. James Hankins and William Bowen, trans. Michael J. B. Allen (Cambridge MA: Harvard University Press, 2004), 126–31. Michael J. B. Allen gave full attention to Spenser's adoption of this notion in his paper "Ficino's Concept of the Poet" at the Neo-Latin Seminar of the Modern Language association New York, 1974. In print, Allen has published much on this notion, most notably for Spenser in his entry "Ficino" in the *Spenser Encyclopedia,* ed. A. C. Hamilton et al. (Toronto: University of Toronto Press, 1990), hereafter designated *SE.*

33.   *HB,* lines 1–3. See notes thereon by McCabe in *Shorter Poems* and by Richard Schell and Einar Bjorvand in *YSP.*

34.   *The Pillars of Eternity: Time and Providence in "The Faerie Queene"* (Dublin: Irish Academic Press, 1989).

35. In *Three Proper and Wittie Familiar Letters,* "Postscripte," Spenser happily announces that E. K. has glossed his recently completed *Dreams,* a lost work. See *Variorum, Prose,* 9:18.

36. Cheney, *Famous Flight,* 27–38. In "October," what I am calling a Platonic poetics Cheney calls an Orphic poetics. William J. Kennedy, in "The Virgilian Legacies of Petrarch's *Bucolicum Carmen* and Spenser's *Shepheardes Calender,*" *The Early Renaissance, Acta,* vol. 9 (1982): 97–100, laments that Renaissance commentators tend to ignore irony and merge different speakers.

37. "Natura . . . vuole, che facciamo ragione, che dentro a quel bel corpo dimori anima a formarsi di eccelenti qualità, ben disposta" (16v). Note that the lady's beauty bespeaks not her present but only her potential spiritual beauty to be nurtured by her husband. I will quote Nobili in English as translated by Ellrodt, with occasional emendations and additions by Kennedy and me. I give the page of Ellrodt 's "Fundamental Modes" article on Nobili for those who want to consult the Italian; when the Italian is not quoted in Ellrodt's article, as in this case, I append it from the first edition (1567).

38. Alastair Fowler, "Six Knights at Castle Joyous," *Studies in Philology* 56 (1959): 583–99; James Hutton, "Spenser and the 'Cinq Points en Amours,' " *Modern Language Notes* 57.8 (1942): 657–60. So much for literary history. In the synchronic context of Spenser's total oeuvre, this Ladder of Lechery in III.i.45 could be seen as a bawdy parody of the Ladder of Love in the *HB.*

39. The facts of publication for the smooth ascenders are as follows: Ficino, *Commentary,* Speech VI, Chapters 6, 8, 10 ad fin., 18 ad fin., and 19. This discrepancy could be because, according to Jayne, 6, in Speech VI, Ficino is really commenting on Plotinus, *Enneads* l.6.4–9. *The Book of the Courtier,* trans. Charles Singleton (Garden City, NY: Doubleday, 1959), sections (66)–(68), 351–54. Three other prophets of the smooth ascent are as follows: Nobili cites as such both Pietro Bembo, *Gli Asolani,* insofar as his character Lavinello is his raisonneur; and Leone Ebreo, *Dialoghi d'Amore* by way of his character Philo, fol. 17r–v, quoted and translated by Ellrodt, "Fundamental," 11n57. Another smooth ascent, occasionally mentioned by Ellrodt, is portrayed in Girolamo Benivieni's *Canzone d'amore,* especially as commented upon by Pico della Mirandola; see the latter's *Commentary on a Canzone of Benivieni,* ed. and trans. Sears Jayne (New York: Peter Lang, 1984). Ellrodt, *Neoplatonism,* 29–31 offers a convenient summary of the typical smooth and complete ascent based on Bembo's speech in *The Courtier.*

40. *Hymne of Heavenly Love,* hereafter in documentation *HHL,* lines 281–87. On line 284, see editors' notes in *YSP;* Welsford; and McCabe in *Shorter Poems.*

41. Fol. 25r–v trans. Ellrodt 13n63. The above is basically Ellrodt's translation of the Italian in "Fundamental," 13n63, with my revisions and those of Kennedy. Phrases in square brackets are those that Ellrodt skips and we supply.

42. Nobili, fol. 17r–v quoted and trans. by Ellrodt, "Fundamental," 11n57.

43. *HB,* lines 69–73; Nobili, fols. 20v and 21r quoted and translated by Ellrodt, "Fundamental" 12 and n58 .

44. *HL,* lines 99–105; Nobili, fol. 15v–16r quoted and translated by Ellrodt, "Fundamental," 11n55).

45. Nobili, fol. 21v quoted and translated by Ellrodt "Fundamental," 12 and n59.

46.   For a list of other poetic transmigrations, see Elizabeth D. Harvey, "Nomadic Souls: Pythagoras, Spenser, Donne," *Spenser Studies* 22 (2007): 258.

47.   *Phaedrus* 249–50; for other references to lovers in heaven before or after incarnation, see 245b–c, 248d–e, 250–51b, 252c–d, 257a.

48.   See his "The Praeexistency of the Soul," ed. William B. Hunter, in *The English Spenserians: The Poetry of Giles Fletcher, George Wither, Michael Drayton, Phineas Fletcher and Henry More* (Salt Lake City, UT: University of Utah Press, 1977), 403–40; esp. stanzas 1 and 4, 404–05 and notes. See also Sarah Hutton, 73, and Dominic Scott, 145–47 and nn. 11 and 12, in Baldwin and Hutton, eds.

49.   In "Neoplatonism," 161, I allegorize Triamond's incorporation of his two dead brothers as mourning and the church's communion between the dead and the living. In my book, I both say this and allegorize the socially unifying effect of Cambina's cup of nepenthe on Cambell and Triamond as the socially unifying function of the Eucharist (*Spenser,* 49–50).

50.   See *Pagan Mysteries in the Renaissance,* rev. ed. (London: Faber and Faber, 1968). For Wind's admission that the various versions of the three stages in the cycle of the soul are not really coextensive, see 38n9.

51.   "Emanations of Glory: Neoplatonic Order in Spenser's Faerie Queen [sic]," hereafter "Emanations," in *A Theatre for Spenserians* ed. Judith Kennedy and James Reither (Toronto: University of Toronto Press, 1973), 56, taunting Ellrodt with this discovery of technical Platonism in *The Faerie Queene.*

52.   See Wind, 37–41 on emanations in general; 128–29, for Ficino's unfolding or permutation of three gods into triplets including solos and combinations; and 210–11 on the sons of Agape as representatives of "unfolding" or explicatio (or, by implication, emanation), balanced by the sons or employees of Concord as "infolding" of opposites into one. See Fowler, "Emanations," 56–57.

53.   See *OED* online, "Permutation . . . 3 *Math.*" Senses b and c. I take it this describes a list in which a person can be stout but not strong, or strong but not stout, or both together, and that exhausts the possibilities. One permutation familiar to every schoolboy in the Middle Ages and the Renaissance, and hence not distinctively Platonic, is the derivation of the four humors and temperaments, the four seasons, and many another tetrad from combinations of the four qualities—hot, cold, moist, and dry. Water is cold and wet, air hot and wet, etc.

54.   Wind, 128, paraphrasing Ficino's commentary on a chapter of Plotinus which he titles, "On the Threefold Return of the Soul to the Divine (*De triplici reditu animae ad divinum),"* *Opera* (Basle, 1567), 1559.

55.   Fowler 57 and his n12, citing and quoting *Opera* 1.443.

56.   III.xii.24. Dorothy Stephens in her edition *The Faerie Queene Books Three and Four* (Indianapolis: Hackett, 2006) also notes this internal parallel at IV.ii.42.7.

57.   Another use of the figure "unpacking," *epanados*, division, or *inclusio* is Belphoebe's question about Timias's depression and Timias's point for point reply, too lengthy to analyze here (IV.viii.14–17).

58.   Curtius, 289–91.

59.   Bond, "Despetto, Decetto, and Defetto" in *SE*; cf. also Fowler "Neoplatonic Order," 64–66.

60.   Nohrnberg quotes W. H. Auden's interpretation of the brothers as equals, 608.

61.   As parallels to *HL,* lines 78–91, McCabe cites Plato, *Symposium,* 188a, and Ficino, *In Convivium Platonis Commentarium,* 3.2.

62.   IV.x.34.2; Wind, 128.

63.   These combinations occur in IV.iii.43–52; they represent, among other things "the nation," as Hieatt notes in his article "Tetrads" in *SE.*

64.   "Spenser, Homer, and the Mythology of Strife," *Renaissance Quarterly* 58.4 (2005): 1220–88.

65.   "Through many seeds is distributed the vigour of a single Idea, and the weakness of their virtue [that of the seeds] is compensated by number. By the same reasoning, matter is led into many forms under only one seed. Dimension, always subject to division, adds to the innumerable multitude of this world," Ficino, *Commentarius in Plotinum,* iii, "De Providentia," xvii in *Opera,* Basle: 1576), 1697, translated by Hankins, 261. Hankins is using the 1561 ed.; the page number, however, is the same in the 1576 ed. which I use.

66.   William Nelson, *The Poetry of Edmund Spenser, A Study* (New York: Columbia University Press, 1963), hereafter cited by page number in text, 238.

67.   Thomas P. Roche, Jr., *The Kindly Flame: A Study of the Third and Fourth Books of Spenser's "Faerie Queene"* (Princeton: Princeton University Press, 1964), 18; James Nohrnberg, *The Analogy of "The Faerie Queene,"* (Princeton: Princeton University Press, 1976), 610–11, both hereafter cited by name and page number in text.

68.   Cited by Hamilton, by Nohrnberg, and by Patrick Cheney, "Triamond," in the *SE.*

69.   See Liddell and Scott's *Greek-English Lexicon.* See Roche, 15–17.

70.   Servius on *Aen.* 8.560–67: "tres animas magnum, & perfectum indicat virum," in *P. Virgilii Maronis . . . universum poema. Cum absoluta Servii . . . interpretatione* (Venice: Heirs of . . . Bonelli, 1574).

71.   See *An Anglo-Saxon Dictionary* by Joseph Bosworth, ed. T. Northcote Toller (Oxford: Oxford University Press, 1898), s.v. "Eadmund . . . [Ead *happy,* mund *protection*]." Spenser may or may not have known Anglo-Saxon; it was a new and fashionable subject dear to the heart of his friend Camden; but he must have known that his Christian name was not of Latin derivation because he knew of his famous Anglo-Saxon namesake: he recounts and laments the iconoclastic destruction of St. Edmund's shrine at Bury in *Ruins of Time,* line 418. Of course Spenser if he wished could have arrived at the meaning "first, second, and third worlds" for the brothers' names by drawing a fanciful or punning etymology, a frequent practice in the Middle Ages and the Renaissance.

72.   David Burchmore, "Triamond, Agape, and the Fates: Neoplatonic Cosmology in Spenser's Legend of Friendship," *Spenser Studies* 5 (1984): 45–64. Burchmore's history of the various concepts of the three "worlds" seemingly invoked by the brothers' names is valuable in itself, but his equations of all the various triads is loose, relying on the ancient principle (handy for poets but risky for exegetes, although endorsed by famous critics including Wind and Roche) that any triad is equatable with any other triad.

73.   Dante identifies the notion of an afterlife on one's native planet with Platonic (i.e., Timaeic) rather than Christian eschatology, see *Paradiso,* 4.22–24 and Sinclair's note 6 on 4.49–54 in *Dante's Paradiso: Italian Text with English Translation and Comment by John D. Sinclair* (Oxford: Galaxy, 1961). Shortly after Spenser, Sir John

Davies in his "Nosce Teipsum," cited by Ellrodt in regard to the recycling babes in the Garden of Adonis (79–80 and n125 on III.vi.33, 35), regards the notion of traduction as heretical, though Davies mainly objects to seeing it as the origin of souls, whereas Spenser here uses the notion for the preservation of dead souls. Ellrodt uses the heretical status of a doctrine as an argument that Spenser could not possibly have intended to express it.

74.   Nohrnberg says of Agape's general call to unity, "the ecclesiastical community is a fellowship," 615. Regarding Spenser's implied formation of a commonwealth from his four-groups, in "Tetrads" in *SE*, Kent Hieatt says that tetrads harmonize, among other groups, "the nation."

75.   *OED* "parcel . . . A, sb. 1. *gen*. A part *of* anything . . . b. A component part (*of* something), something included in a whole."

76.   "Cambell, Canacee, Cambina," in *SE* and IV.iv, 26–27, 33–36.

77.   Hieatt, "Tetrad," *SE,* and Hamilton, ed., note to IV.iii.52.

78.   See e.g., David Lee Miller: Tudor apologists were trying to conflate "English imperium with Biblical millennium," *The Poem's Two Bodies: The Poetics of the 1590 "Faerie Queene"* (Princeton: Princeton University Press, 1988), 115. See also Regina Schwartz, *Sacramental Poetics at the Dawn of Secularism: When God Left the World* (Stanford: Stanford University Press, 2008), 18–35.

79.   Stephens, ed., on IV.iii.49.5 The following interpretation is based partly on Stephens and the analogue she cites, namely Sheila Cavanaugh's parallels between the tournament for Canacee and Levi-Strauss's famous statements on the incest-taboo as a means to exogamy; see *Wanton Eyes and Chaste Desires* (Bloomington: Indiana University Press, 1994), 78–79.

VALERY REES

Ficinian Ideas in the Poetry of Edmund Spenser

Tracing specific influences in Spenser is no straightforward task, but this essay revisits the question of Spenser's Platonism through interests he can be shown to have shared with Marsilio Ficino. These include the interplay of stability and change, which fascinated them both, and which both took as a reflection of the relationship between ultimate reality and the passing illusory show in which they felt most of our earthly life is spent. Both writers concern themselves with ascent to the supercelestial world of reality, and with the role that beauty and love may play in this ascent. They likewise share a commitment to the importance and potential of the immortal human soul. Spenser also draws on Platonic theories of poetry expounded by Ficino. An appendix is provided which traces in detail the extent to which the works of Ficino and Plato were available to Spenser and his contemporaries in England, and particularly in Cambridge during his residence there.

*A*LMOST A CENTURY separates the death of the Florentine philosopher Marsilio Ficino in 1499 and the publication of *The Faerie Queene* in 1590 and 1596. This was time enough to allow Ficino's ideas to spread widely, eliciting both positive response and challenge in most of the princely courts, universities, and theological schools of Europe. Any examination of Spenser's response to Ficinian ideas must therefore allow for this more general diffusion. It must also accommodate the fact that Spenser rarely cites specific authors. Yet, he certainly had the opportunity during his time at Cambridge to read certain works of Ficino and also to engage with the dialogues of Plato through Ficino's commentaries and introductions (see Fig. 1).[1] Even if Spenser had failed to make much use of this opportunity, it would

Spenser Studies: A Renaissance Poetry Annual, Volume XXIV, Copyright © 2009 AMS Press, Inc. All rights reserved.

Fig. 1. Ficino's *Argumentum* introducing his translation of Plato's *Statesman*, in *Platonis opera omnia* (Basel: Froben, 1532), by kind permission of the Master and Fellows of St. John's College, Cambridge. Ficino's summaries and commentaries served as an important introduction to the works of Plato even for readers who were able to approach the text in Greek. For others, his translations remained the main path towards acquaintance with Plato and provided the basis for other translations well into the nineteenth century.

be hard to imagine that he was unacquainted with the broad outlines of Ficino's thought, given their currency. Among Spenser's closest friends, Gabriel Harvey appears to have read Ficino's letters, and Sir Walter Ralegh to have owned Ficino's *Opera omnia*.[2] That Ficino was well known in English academic circles is illustrated by events in Oxford in 1583, when Giordano Bruno's plagiarism of Ficino was recognized by a member of his lecture audience.[3] Nevertheless, in the richly layered modes of expression that make up Spenser's own work it is difficult to distinguish the extent to which he relied upon any particular philosophical approach. So it is not surprising that debate over his alleged Platonic tendencies, mediated by Ficino or otherwise, has run a long course.[4]

The principal issues in a controversy already well established were delineated in 1932 by Josephine Waters Bennett in an article which emphasized the Platonic features of Spenser's Garden of Adonis in Book III of *The Faerie Queene*, locating it on the border between the immaterial world of pure forms and the manifest creation.[5] Her interpretation was swiftly challenged by Brents Stirling, who insisted upon a more earthly interpretation of the Garden, without need of Platonic theory.[6] Their controversy sparked across the pages of learned journals for some years and brought to light many important facets of classical mythology, but they continued to disagree over the interpretation of key terms in the poem.[7] In 1952, Sears Jayne picked up some problems already signalled by Stirling relating to the term "Platonism" in the Renaissance, arising from the complexity of traditions woven together under that label. He distinguished three phases of Platonic influence on English Renaissance writers, but added little light to the debate by denying the availability or influence of Ficino's work.[8] Reasserting that influence, in a study published in 1960, Robert Ellrodt concluded that Spenser's first two hymns published in his *Fowre Hymnes* of 1596 evince "unmistakable indebtedness to Ficino," and even his "dominant influence," among Renaissance Platonists, in these particular texts.[9] Spenser's dedication for the *Hymnes* states that he wrote the first pair in his youth. However, Ellrodt claims they were actually written around 1596 in their present form, and that before 1596 the influence on Spenser of Plato, his ancient followers, and learned Renaissance Platonists such as Ficino was indirect, absorbed through popular intermediaries such as Pietro Bembo and Castglione.[10] Until Spenser had completed *The Faerie Queene*, in Ellrodt's view, his Platonism was largely a mix of medieval Platonism (that of St. Augustine, Petrarch, and Dante) and of popularized Renaissance Platonic aesthetics, even if it revealed a gradually deepening interest through the passing years.

Nevertheless, the controversy was by no means exhausted, for in subsequent studies too numerous to list here, by scholars including C. S. Lewis, William Nelson, Maurice Evans, Kathleen Williams, Thomas P. Roche, Jr., John Erskine Hankins, Alastair Fowler, Lila Geller, James Nohrnberg, Humphrey Tonkin, Michael J. B. Allen, David W. Burchmore, Elizabeth Bieman, and Elizabeth Jane Bellamy, the extent of Spenser's ancient and Renaissance Platonic learning before the mid 1590s was deemed much broader than Ellrodt had assumed.[11] Most recently, Jon A. Quitslund's *Spenser's Supreme Fiction* has brought Ficino and Cristoforo Landino into much greater prominence. Quitslund stresses how these two scholars revitalized learning and helped its spread into courtly circles.[12] While it is true that Ficino's approach to philosophical inquiry was often still underpinned with scholastic arguments drawn from Aquinas and from his own Aristotelian education, he brought immensely important new sources into circulation through his unceasing work of translation and exposition. Quitslund's account allows this contribution to be appreciated.[13] Meanwhile other Spenserians have pursued different interpretative approaches. Among recent works, Syrithe Pugh has revived interest in Spenser's use of Ovid.[14] Harold Weatherby focuses on the influence of the Greek patristic texts (e.g., John of Damascus, John Chrysostom, Tertullian, and Dionysius), highlighting the importance of the transfiguration in a theology where sin and mortality are attributed to a change in our nature at the fall. For him, Una is clothed in the light of Mount Tabor, and the Garden of Adonis is an Eden allegory, more specifically an allegory of the sexual aspects of Eden: its contrast to the Bower of Bliss represents for him the allegorical core of the work. But perhaps he gives too little attention to the fact that Greek patristic texts were also part of Ficino's blend of Christian Platonism.[15] James Broaddus concentrates on the physiological aspects of sexuality in the Garden, and its implications for society.[16] Others interpret passages in the context of religious discourses of the Reformation[17] or find the setting of Elizabethan politics, wars, and Ireland to be a revealing approach to the understanding of Spenser's work.[18]

It is not my aim to reopen the Platonic debate, nor to insist upon any simplistic reading of Spenser. However, coming to Spenser from Ficino, I find it likely that a reader of the *Fowre Hymnes* and certain passages of *The Faerie Queene* can be helped by some understanding of the material that Ficino had laid before Renaissance writers and readers. These ideas were widely current within the circles for whom the poet wrote, and many of them appear to resonate within his verse. This article will therefore attempt to illustrate in a simple way a few of the more important strands, in the hope that this may serve as an introduction to Ficino's relevance to Spenser. The philosopher's works are now more accessible than ever to the student of English literature.[19]

Stability and Change

To begin with a theme that is often taken last because it makes its formal appearance only at the end of the *Faerie Queene*,[20] the concept of mutability plays an important part in Spenser's thinking. For Ficino, likewise, the whole drift of philosophy is described as "the ascent from the things which flow and rise and fall to those which truly are, and always remain the same." [21]

Ficino seems to hold a view of life as a drama conducted somewhat in the dark. Writing in consolation to a friend whose son, Michele, had died at the very outset of a promising career, he says,

> It is the opinion of the ancient sages . . . that men, that is souls, come down into this life from God Himself as though into a comedy or tragedy, where all things commonly considered favourable or adverse are merely fables: imagined riches and poverty, imagined kings and slaves, and likewise imagined birth and death. Perhaps the Platonic saying, "The human race is God's play on earth," points to this.
>
> The author of this play and fable is God Himself, who is also the Father of souls. He therefore sends them down from on high into this play as the actors; but it is the nature of the world which gives them their parts.[22]

The world in which we move is a shadow world. It is not reality. We merely come here for a time, to perform the actions allotted to us. Of Michele, Ficino says, "He was sent by God to play for a short while, and you merely dressed him for a particular part. Once he was dressed for the play, you spared no effort to instruct him. He has gone back, not from life, but from a particular play in life, into the very substance of life."[23]

Sometimes Ficino presents the notion of the world from which we have come and to which we may return in a more recognizably Christian-Platonist form, referring to it frequently as "our true home." In a long and important letter to King Ferrante of Naples, written as if by his deceased father, King Alfonso,[24] Ficino describes how the soul of Alfonso now resides in the celestial world, in a realm of immeasurable light. Because the minds of men are "everlasting rays of the eternal Sun," they are able to spring back to that realm whenever they are free from the dark cloud of the body. This happens "when they value mortal things as nothing, especially when weighed against the eternal." The body is the shadow of the transparent mind, bonded to it by spirit; but through devotion or love, and righteous action, the individual may fly back to the celestial homeland. Here he may feast upon the food of the gods. But this realm of the gods is itself only the shadow of another world, the supercelestial: "Here, my son, here alone, I say, one lives the truest, clearest, best, and most joyful life, where all life is nothing but truth, clarity, goodness and joy in its fullness. Here in that immeasurable light of lights we see all the lights of the ideal forms, and in those lights we clearly behold everything as it really is, just like someone seeing in the sun all the rays emanating from it and in those rays all the individual colours which are created from them."[25]

This supercelestial realm is our true home, and Alfonso duly sings its praises, encouraging his son to follow a path in life that will enable him to fly there too and stressing the unbroken connection between the sublime realm and earth: "But look, Ferdinand, look up and see a miracle! Borne on the wings of a seraph, I fly back to the sublime realm of the Thrones in a single moment; and yet, rather like a ray of light, I do not leave your home."[26]

In his letters, Ficino can present the elements of Platonic philosophy in a freely adapted fashion, suited to the particular needs of his reader and sometimes employing, as in this case, imaginative devices to ease or sweeten the path of comprehension. For this reason the letters were very popular at the time as an introduction to Platonic thought, and of course they retain this character to the present day.[27] But for more detail on how he locates this supercelestial homeland in terms of change and mutability, we may turn to a more formal treatise.

At the beginning of his eighteen books of *Platonic Theology*, Ficino sets out clearly the different levels of being and the position of the soul within them.[28] Bodies are at the lowest of these levels. Quality, or "active power," is the name he gives to the next level, then soul. All these three are subject to change, but soul differs from the levels below it by being not subject additionally to division. Above soul is angelic mind: this too is indivisible but it is also unchanging. Angelic mind, or "Angel," seems to have a universal compass.[29] This presents no contradiction if we remember that it is the Neoplatonic principle of emanation that creates the level, not the principle of division. The level of angelic mind corresponds to the realm of those universal powers which pagan theology had named as gods: intelligence (Mercury), love (Venus), discipline (Saturn), and the rest, though Ficino does not dwell on these correspondences in a work dedicated to showing the Christian face of Platonic philosophy.[30] It is worth underlining the fact that this realm is indivisible, thus the individual gods (and likewise angels) would be mere aspects of a single greater power.

Beyond angelic mind is God. God is presented as the light of truth which angelic mind seeks. God cannot be described or defined, but is the still point round which all turns, and towards which the soul may ascend. Thus from the outset of the *Platonic Theology*, this major work which inquires into the immortality of souls, Ficino sets out a framework of existence in levels. Yet, although the soul's place in the hierarchy of being seems to be at the midpoint between the realm of God and the realm of Body, Ficino also postulates its freedom of movement in either direction. Constant involvement in and attachment to bodily desires can cause its imprisonment in matter, but he is in no doubt as to the possibility, and desirability, of the alternative, despite the many difficulties that may be experienced on the way:

Our human minds "immured in darkness and a sightless dungeon"[31] may look in vain for that light, and we are often driven to doubt our own provenance. But I pray that as heavenly souls longing with desire for our heavenly home we may cast off the bonds of our terrestrial chains; cast them off as swiftly as possible, so that, uplifted on Platonic wings and with God as our guide, we may fly unhindered to our ethereal abode, where we will straightway look with joy on the excellence of our own human nature.[32]

If "casting off the terrestrial chains" means casting off the body itself, this passage would imply that the fortunate soul who can make this journey does so only after death, a view that would be unexceptionable even to the strictest theologian. However, in later writing, and in the relative freedom of his letters, it is clear that Ficino holds the view that the ascent can be made within our lifetime. Even in this more formal tract, he uses a phrase which confirms the latter interpretation, when he seeks to demonstrate "that the soul is completely indissoluble, because it holds together the different levels of

nature; next, that it is preeminent, because it presides over the framework of the world; and finally that it is most blessed when it steals
into the bosom of the divine."[33] Stealing into the bosom of the divine
(*dum se divinis insinuat*) suggests that the place of the soul is with God,
even while it is still connected to life on earth in the body. Ficino
is thus encouraging the reader to seek and find a union with the
divine that will then transform the life.

There will be more to say about this under the heading of love,
but it is worth noting here that this encouragement is also at the
heart of Ficino's *Argumentum* (Introduction) to the *Platonic Theology*,
a short separate outline which he sent to Lorenzo de' Medici in
advance of the full text and later incorporated in the second book of
his letters.[34] There he clarifies that there are three steps of contemplation according to the Platonic tradition. The first "ascends from the
body through the soul to God." The second involves dwelling in
contemplation of the divine. But a third step again "descends to the
soul and the body."[35] Any attempt to separate some incorporeal part
of the being (e.g., the "intellect") from the full person is thus denied,
and Ficino holds that "The divine light is not demonstrated by the
skill of the reason but understood in the clear serenity of a devout
life."[36] In this way we see that the stability and unchanging quality
of the light of the supreme is not dissociated from the changing world
of action and matter, but illuminates that world, and gives it its life
and motion. On the other hand, he upholds the need for separation
of the mind from earthly concerns during the exercise of contemplation, but the integrity of the creation is not diminished by this, nor
is that of the human being. [37]

When Spenser's Mutabilitie appears at the end of *The Faerie
Queene*, she is presented as the governing principle of the entire
preceding narrative, but she can represent only part of a whole that
now calls out for completion. Her claim to rule the world of gods
as well as men is a false one:

> Proud *Change* (not pleasd, in mortall things,
>   beneath the Moone, to raigne)
> Pretends, as well of Gods, as Men,
>   to be the Soueraine.[38]

While everything that moves and changes is subject to the laws of
mutability, it is to be seen against that which does not move or
change, as the poet tells us in the last lines of the third *Canto of Mutabilitie*:

For, all that moueth doth in *Change* delight:
But thence-forth all shall rest eternally
With Him that is the God of Sabbaoth hight. (VII.viii.2)

And he closes that final canto with a plea for the experience of that
Sabbath of eternal rest, which can be granted only by and in the
presence of the Lord of Hosts: "O! that great Sabbaoth God, grant
me that Sabaoths sight."[39]

Spenser thus directs our gaze to a realm beyond the sway of mutability. Glimpses of this destination have already appeared in Book I
through Una, and in Book III, where the Garden of Adonis opens a
window into the divine realm. There in nature's seminary, a thousand
"naked babes" are daily clothed in mortal form to go out into the
world, and to the garden they return to be renewed, replanted for a
thousand years, an echo of Plato's myth of Er.[40] There time and
change still operate, but being and form are not the same:

All things from thence [Chaos] doe their first being fetch,
   And borrow matter, whereof they are made,
   Which when as forme and feature it does ketch,
   Becomes a bodie, and doth then inuade
   The state of life, out of the griesly shade.
   That substance is eterne, and bideth so,
   Ne when the life decayes, and forme does fade,
   Doth it consume, and into nothing go,
But chaunged is, and often altred to and fro.

The substance is not chaunged, nor altered,
   But th'only forme and outward fashion;
   For euery substance is conditioned
   To change her hew, and sundry formes to don,
   Meet for her temper and complexion:
   For formes are variable and decay,
   By course of kind, and by occasion;
   And that faire flower of beautie fades away,
As doth the lilly fresh before the sunny ray.

Great enimy to it, and to all the rest,
   That in the *Gardin* of Adonis springs,
   Is wicked *Time*, who with his scyth addrest,
   Does mow the flowring herbes and goodly things,

And all their glory to the ground downe flings,
Where they doe wither, and are fowly mard:
He flyes about, and with his flaggy wings
Beates downe both leaues and buds without regard,
Ne euer pittie may relent his malice hard.   (III.vi.37–39)[41]

From a Platonic standpoint, in the last two stanzas of the *Cantos of Mutabilitie* Spenser would seem to indicate that the whole of his "darke conceite" or allegorical tale has been a tale of shadows as compared with the light of that world into which he now craves entry, beyond the transient shadow-world of life on earth.[42] Dwelling on the things that change has been the task of the narrative account, an epic tale by any standards; but the significance of that change and decay is now defined by its contrast with what does not change and decay. The "unperfite" eighth canto of the seventh book can thus be seen as the culmination of *The Faerie Queene*, and as one of the keys to the allegory. That world beyond change is also presented in the *Hymne of Heavenly Love* and that of *Heavenly Beauty* as the most desirable, the true destination of the soul. It may therefore indicate how Spenser's writing relates to that of his outwardly very different forebear Ficino.

Ascent to the Supercelestial World

Ficino returned time and again to the theme of how the ascent might be made from the world of change to the world of unity. Spenser's deployment of Duessa and Una would seem to position him on similar ground. Una reflects the idea of unity as the binding of the world's parts in mutual love, while Duessa, quite apart from any intended allegorization of the Church of Rome, stands for two-faced duality, pretense, and counterfeit: for everything, in a word, that is opposed to the One, and that is unreal. But Una plays a part in dispelling ignorance and leading towards another state.

For Ficino, this is ascent, and he describes it in various ways: as steps, as stages, as a ladder, and as rapture.[43] But in an introductory essay to the commentary on Plato's *Philebus* already quoted above he says:

the minds of those practising philosophy, having recovered their wings through wisdom and justice, as soon as they have left the body, fly back to the heavenly kingdom. In heaven they perform the same duties as on earth. United with God in truth, they rejoice. United with each other in freedom, they give thanks. They watch over men dutifully, and as interpreters of God and as prophets, what they have set in motion here they complete there. They turn the minds of men towards God. They interpret the secret mysteries of God to human minds.[44]

The location of this heaven is the supercelestial world. In spite of the fact that he speaks here of the minds leaving their bodies, we can safely assume, from what he discusses both later in this essay and elsewhere, that this is a temporary separation from the body, achieved by an effort of intellect: they will by and by return to the body.[45] The training of the mind towards reason and metaphysical thought leads it towards the good. There are elements in the human condition that make it difficult to achieve the ascent, in particular a propensity for distraction and agitation. There are also the more legitimate constant requirements of the physical world.

In an early letter to Giovanni Cavalcanti, Ficino had explored the difficulties of making this ascent:

The soul in this body has two principal impediments. First, it is drawn into many activities and much agitation, and its different activities weaken and obstruct each other, for it is very hard to apply the mind to different things at the same time. Secondly, the soul is engaged in inferior activities much earlier, more attentively and more often than in higher ones, not only because of the condition of its abysmal dwelling but also because of the corporeal service assigned to men for a time by God. And so it is that when we wish to consider the incorporeal, we function for the most part feebly, and perceive it dimly as though through a cloud. But whenever the actions of eating, accumulating, feeling or imagining either entirely cease or are greatly reduced, then the vision of the mind will be correspondingly sharpened, so that whatever is observed by the mind is observed more clearly under the power of this light. Then indeed the soul will observe through itself, and it will see that light of the intellect more clearly than it now sees the light of the senses through the glass windows of this bodily prison. Entirely at peace, it will perceive through its own perfect transparency the highest impressions in the light of the divine sun. . . . Nor will the mind then gaze as if at painted images, but rather at real objects, of which all other things are images.[46]

Moreover we cannot reach the good unless there is some reciprocal drawing from the good itself: "no one ascends unless God has in some measure first descended into him."[47] Or as he expresses it later, in the Preface to his St. Paul Commentary,

> We should, under Paul's guidance, use all our powers to lift ourselves up to mind which contemplates the divine. . . . But since that contemplation of the mind cannot reach the divine with the powers of its own intelligence, there seem again to be three stages for us, . . . [through] faith, hope and love, the gifts of the Holy Spirit, but chiefly love, towering over all knowledge and uniting us with the order of the seraphs. . . . In seraphic love that ineffable warmth of the Holy Spirit will be kindled in us. In this life-giving warmth, the light and wisdom of the divine word will at once shine out. Endowed by grace with these divine gifts, we shall attain the incomparable gift, from the Father, of ability, by which we shall be strong enough to perceive the mysteries divinely unveiled to Paul.[48]

But even when it reaches that happy state of union, the soul has not arrived at a static destination. In an earlier letter Ficino explains that "Philosophy, to express it in a few words, is the ascent of the mind from the lower regions to the highest, and from darkness to light. Its origin is an impulse of the divine mind; its middle steps are the faculties and the disciplines which we have described and its end is the possession of the highest good. Finally, its fruit is the right government of men."[49] The soul which has ascended may also descend. In fact, it does so with freedom and with love.

This is an area in which Spenser seems to have some difficulty with the application of Ficino's Platonic ideas to a Christian hermeneutic. When he speaks

> Of that same time when no more *Change* shall be,
> But stedfast rest of all things firmely stayd
> Vpon the pillours of Eternity,

there is little to indicate that he is thinking of an ascent and a return (VII.viii.2). It seems to be more a reference to the world to come, when the soul will have cast off its mortal form, rather than to the ability of mankind to move between the two realms. Yet for Ficino, mankind can achieve union with the divine in this life. In doing so a person's life will be lit up with divine light, as it was at the outset. In the fourth section of the commentary on Plato's *Symposium*, which was extremely popular during Spenser's lifetime,[50] Ficino relates how the soul is born from God and is illumined by His rays, giving an innate light by which it can recognize all things below. But soon, coming closer to God by virtue of this spark, it receives another brighter, infused light: "With these [lights] joined together, as though with two wings, it is able to fly through the heavenly region. And if it always used that divine light, it would always cleave to the divine things; the earth would be empty of rational animals."[51] Being free, but also subject to the promptings of nature, the soul neglects to use its divine light, and descends into the body. However, it can recover this light through the process of contemplation of the divine, and thus regains its freedom of movement between the worlds.

For Spenser the answer seems less clear. While the invocations of the *Fowre Hymnes* appear to envisage some contemplative union of the poet with the divine in this life, achieved by means of inspiration, the narrative of *The Faerie Queene* would often seem to deny that, involving as it does a constant engagement in the emotional realm and the vagaries of life. Perfect peace, as we have seen, appears to belong to the world to come. But there are perhaps some moments during the narrative that offer a glimpse of the possibility, and Spenser insists in the *Letter to Ralegh* that *The Faerie Queene* is a continued allegory.[52] Moreover, the "unperfite" eighth canto may perhaps not be "unperfite" after all. For that which does not move or change because it is utterly single may be fitly dealt with in few words. The very simplicity and unity of the unmoving One does not require the extended lyrical display or narrative exploits that occupy the previous books. Perhaps, like the hidden cantilever of a bridge or stair, the small bulk of this eighth canto can sustain a massive counterweight of words. In the *Fowre Hymnes* there is a definite move towards ascent. Whatever their dating (i.e., whether they were conceived together or apart),[53] there seems to be a progression intended, an ascent to the supercelestial world, that fits very well with Ficino's understanding of ascent. But to consider ascent in the hymns we must look more closely at ideas of beauty and love.

BEAUTY

For Ficino, the function of beauty is to lift the soul to higher things.
Taking Diotima's account of love and beauty in Plato's *Symposium*
as his foundation, he says: "The ray of beauty . . . has the power to
be reflected back to what it came from, and it draws the lover with
it. But it descends first from God, and passes through the Angel and
the Soul as if they were made of glass; and from the Soul it easily
emanates into the body prepared to receive it. Then from that body . . . it shines out, especially through the eyes, the transparent windows of the soul."[54] From there it "flies onward, through the air,"
and penetrating the eyes of the beholder "pierces his soul, kindles
his appetite and then leads the wounded soul and the kindled appetite
to their healing place." Ascending by the same route as it had descended, it returns through Soul, through Angel and finally back
to God.[55]
    Beauty is delicate, perfect and blessed, and may itself perfect its
beholders: "Delicate in that, by a certain sweetness of its own it
allures to itself the appetite of all things. Perfect in that, when the
things which it has attracted approach, it illuminates them with its
own rays and perfects them. Blessed in that it fills the illuminated
objects with eternal good [thing]s."[56] Again, in a letter based on the
Phaedrus, he expresses the role of beauty thus:

> we do indeed perceive the reflection of divine beauty with our
> eyes and mark the resonance of divine harmony with our
> ears. . . . Thus when the soul has received through the physical
> senses those images which are within material objects, we re-
> member what we knew before when we existed outside the
> prison of the body. The soul is fired by this memory, and
> shaking its wings, by degrees purges itself from contact with
> the body and its filth and becomes wholly possessed by divine
> frenzy. . . . Regaining the memory of the true and divine beauty
> by the appearance of beauty that the eyes perceive, we desire
> the former with a secret and unutterable ardour of the mind.
> This Plato calls "divine love" which he defines as the desire to
> return again to the contemplation of divine beauty.[57]

In the Plato summaries, he says that through physical beauty we
can "use our judgement to hunt out the beauty of the soul, the beauty

of the angelic mind, and the beauty of God."[58] For beauty is "nothing other than the splendour of the highest good, shining in those things which are perceived by eyes, ears and mind, and by means of them turning sight, hearing and mind towards the Good itself. From this it comes about that beauty is a circle of divine light, emanating from the Good, abiding in the Good, and forever turned back towards the Good by means of the Good."[59]

This is a high calling indeed for beauty, and Spenser also appears to treat love as the desire for beauty, both in *The Faerie Queene* and the *Fowre Hymnes*. It is especially significant that he places the *Hymne of Heavenly Beauty* after the *Hymne of Heavenly Love*. To those who deny the Platonism of Spenser, this must create some difficulty, since the hymns do seem to proceed by progression, and heavenly beauty does seem to carry the author beyond the realm reached in the *Hymne of Heavenly Love*.[60] There, through adoration of Christ, he is taken—by ravishment—to the realm of the one Idea:

> Thenceforth all worlds desire will in thee dye,
> And all earthes glorie on which men do gaze,
> Seeme durt and drosse in thy pure sighted eye,
> Compar'd to that celestiall beauties blaze,
> Whose glorious beames all fleshly sense doth daze
> With admiration of their passing light,
> Blinding the eyes and lumining the spright.
>
> Then shall thy rauisht soule inspired bee
> With heauenly thoughts, farre aboue humane skil,
> And thy bright radiant eyes shall plainely see
> Th'Idee of his pure glorie present still,
> Before thy face, that all thy spirits shall fill
> With sweete enragement of celestiall loue,
> Kindled through sight of those faire things aboue.
>
> (*HHL*, lines 274–87)

But in the *Hymne of Heavenly Beauty* that completes the cycle, he reaches a realm of bliss and reality which seems to surpass the "Idee" of pure glory and reach the source of glory itself. Beauty carries him "aloft through heavenly contemplation" to the sun of which Ficino spoke, to the footstool of God, the mercy seat, the immortal light. There in God's bosom sits Sapience, "the soueraine dearling of the Deity"—a high place indeed for philosophy—and the description of ecstasy with which the hymn concludes seems to eclipse all else:

But who so may, thrise happie man him hold,
Of all on earth, whom God so much doth grace,
And lets his owne Beloued to behold:
For in the view of her celestiall face,
All ioy, all blisse, all happinesse haue place

....

In which they see such admirable things,
As carries them into an extasy,
And heare such heauenly notes, and carolings
Of Gods high praise, that filles the brasen sky,
And feele such ioy and pleasure inwardly,
That maketh them all worldly cares forget,
And onely thinke on that before them set.

                                        (*HHB*, lines 239–66)

Having reached this place in the presence of God, a place which
is reminiscent of the union described by Ficino, though Spenser stops
short of calling it such, the soul is now sure that "All other sights
but fayned shadowes bee," and it feeds with "fastened mynd," finding fullness of joy and contentment (lines 273–87). In his final lines,
he apparently expresses the hope that he may look to that light while
still in this life, because he expresses the wish that, possessed of the
pleasures such contemplation brings, his "straying thoughts" may
"henceforth forever rest" (line 301). The highest valuation is placed
once again on the stillness and stability that is beyond the realm of
movement and change, and he would seem to regard it as an anchor
for the mind that has once attained it.

                                    LOVE

In Ficino, it is love rather than beauty that holds primacy, though
admittedly as described in the commentary on the *Symposium*, it is
beauty that first generates love, and sets in motion that wonderful
continuous circle of attraction that begins with God, flows to the
world, and returns again to God.[61] Thus occasionally Ficino anticipates the near merging of love and beauty found in Spenser's fourth
hymn. The light of beauty is described there as

> that soueraine light,
> From whose pure beams al perfect beauty springs,
> That kindleth loue in euery godly spright,
> Euen the loue of God. . . .   (lines 295–98)

We have already noted in the quotations above how closely love and beauty are linked in Ficino. Love to Ficino is a mighty power. It "runs to meet us even before we start looking."[62] It is the main topic, through many twists and turns, of the entire commentary on the *Symposium*, whose more familiar name (and the name he gave to his own vernacular translation) is "On Love."[63] While he spends much time in that work exploring Plato's concept that love is a god, in his letters he turns rather to its complement, that God is love, or as more fully expressed in the first Epistle of John, "God is love. He that dwelleth in love dwelleth in God, and God in him."[64]

This was the text he chose for an address to the people of Florence, on the occasion of his inauguration as a canon of the cathedral in 1487, that he included in his published letters. He has no doubt that love is of the utmost cosmic significance: "The whole creation has been brought into being and is sustained because God Himself, the Creator, willed this from the beginning and wills it now."[65] The divine creation is thus an act of love. This is a far cry from the homoerotic love often associated with Plato's *Symposium* and *Phaedrus*.[66] But it is the love of the final section of the *Fowre Hymnes*, and may also be the love that is glimpsed behind the allegory in *The Faerie Queene*.

Divine love, Ficino says, "loves and cares for the common good of all." Human love likewise only finds its fulfillment in the common good of all. From this he moves to the idea that the soul becomes divine "not because God shines a glimmer of his light upon our understanding but because our will blazes with the flames of divine love." Having established that "he who dwells in love dwells in God," he must then proceed to the slightly trickier proposition that "God dwells in him": "But how dwelleth God in him? How, I ask, dwelleth the infinite God in the finite soul? Being embraced, our soul indeed dwells in God, but God, being all-embracing, dwells in the soul. Almighty God certainly dwells even where love is absent, but as the all-seeing judge, the avenger and dispenser of punishment. On the other hand, where love abounds, most merciful God dwells as the redeeming Eucharist and the inexhaustible bestower of all graces."

The sermon reaches its climax as he considers again the role of love in the context of human life:

O omnipotent love, which is God and which makes all
things, sustains all things and perfects all things!

O love most wise, which fires the soul through divine inspiration and miraculously transforms it into God!

O love, beyond all doubt most bounteous, which joins the
infinite grace of the Creator with something created and
finite. . . .

Through the Eucharist, celebrated there on that occasion, man and
God are joined through love:

At His entry our hearts will immediately rejoice, and no one
will take our joy from us. For out of His extraordinary love He
will make us lie down in a green pasture; He will give us to
drink of the stream of His joy; He will restore us at this Paschal
meal with manna from heaven and He will nourish us with the
bread of angels.

Therefore, through love alone we shall see and taste today
how sweet the Lord is; we shall realise immediately how great
is the bounty of His sweetness, which He has preserved for
those alone who love Him. For we shall be drunk with the
abundance of His house; our hearts' desire will be satisfied
when His glory shall appear.[67]

This remarkable oration, replete with biblical allusions, is only one
of many occasions on which Ficino expounds the importance of
joining in the cosmic flow of love, by which God brings forth the
creation, and through which he draws the creation back to himself.
The specific role of the human being is to participate in this flow.
In Spenser, we see a cosmic flow of love bringing forth the material
universe in *Colin Clouts Come Home Againe* (lines 841–86), and Colin,
Spenser's own fictive persona, is presented there as the priest of love.

Ficino meanwhile develops the same text on love (I John 4:16)
further in another letter from the same period, to support the essential
identity of love and knowledge:

"God is Love; and he that dwelleth in Love dwelleth in God,
and God in him." But if that Love is the yearning, spur and
need in our love, and yet God is in need of nothing, being all

good, in what way, then, is God Himself that Love? He is the fire, He is the light and He is the joy in that Love. Thus God is Love. But the fire of that Love has been kindled in the soul. The light lives in God, and joy in both God and the soul, just as the same ray of sunlight in a concave mirror remains light in itself, but appears as fire in wood, and from the fire light arises there too. Therefore he who dwells in the fire of that Love at once dwells in the very light of God, and at once divine joy dwells in him.

Indeed, a heavenly body instantly communicates light before heat to transparent bodies, as they are very like itself, but to earthly bodies, which are quite unlike itself, it imparts heat before light. Thus when these bodies are cleansed by fire and made most like Heaven, they immediately give back the light. So the soul, hedged about by the earthly body, should begin with love for God, that, cleansed by love, it may then partake of the divine light and of the joy within that light.[68]

Ficino carefully distinguishes between the two aspects of love represented in Latin by *charitas* and *amor*. *Charitas* means love with no personal desire or yearning, as in brotherly love, the love of God for man, or lovingkindness. *Amor* generally contains an element of desire, even in man's love for God. Spenser too is skilled in deploying the differences between them, and this perhaps distinguishes the first two of his *Hymnes* from the second pair.

Ficino's letter to Matteo of Forlì, a papal Commissioner, written sometime between 1481 and 1484, spells out the transformative power of love on four different levels, human, natural, celestial, and divine, describing them as four "reasons":

The first is human, I say, because love indeed is the true foundation of friendship. But such is the power of friendship that by this alone the human race can live in peace and bliss even without any laws; but once friendship is taken away, neither laws nor any other human endeavours could bring about that bliss. I need hardly add that it is love that makes men so quick to invention, so forceful in speech, so amenable, congenial, courteous and faithful to common custom.

The natural reason is of this kind: some likeness is always the cause of love. This, indeed, is clearly seen in the stars and elements, and in plants and animals. Therefore whoever is most

inclined to love human beings is considered closest of all to that
ideal pattern of the human race according to which the divine
artificer has created men. On the other hand, those who are
least inclined to love are furthest from the divine pattern and
most distant from human kind.

The third reason . . . , the celestial reason, we learn from the
astronomers: those people are usually more inclined towards
love at whose birth Venus and Mercury are so placed that . . .
they uphold the guiding powers of the indwelling spirit through
their concordant will.[69]

At this point he reminds the reader that "lust, which longs for touch,
is one thing, but quite another is love, which rests content in beholding, hearing, and contemplating."

He then gives the fourth reason, which is particularly relevant to
the burden of Spenser's fourth hymn, and is related explicitly to
Plato's *Phaedrus* (249–56) and *Symposium* (210–12):

Since the forms of all things are causal in the divine mind and
some of their shadows appear in our world, nothing reminds
us of the beauty of the Creator Himself more quickly than the
beauty of created things. Nor does Plato think that it is as easy
for us to investigate divine wisdom through human wisdom,
or as easy to investigate the other powers of God through any
other human powers, as it is to find divine beauty through
human beauty and, having found it, to love it. This is because
the reflection of the other powers that are in God accords with
minds alone and is perceived by them alone, while the image
of divine beauty expresses itself throughout creation and is perceived clearly not only by the mind but by the eyes as well, the
most perceptive of all the senses. Hence Plato considers that
love of the divine arises from human love.

He therefore defines love as nothing but the yearning for
beauty. Beauty, however, he defines as nothing but grace: I
mean grace from the three Graces, that is, grace implanted in
three activities especially, and coming likewise from three divine beings. For through the grace of harmony in music Apollo
entices those listening; through the grace of colour and form
Venus captivates those watching; and through the wonderful

grace of intelligence and eloquence Mercury turns men to himself, especially those who practise contemplation, and fires them with love of divine contemplation and beauty.[70]

The significance of all this is that beauty plays a key role in transforming human love into divine love, transforming the lover at the same time, and making him or her divine, as the title of the letter declares.[71] "Indeed, understanding does not usually transform us into what we understand," Ficino concludes, "but love does transform us into what we love. For this reason our Plato considers that it is by this very yearning for divine beauty rather than by the pursuit of knowledge or by any other power that the mind, regaining its wings, flies back to its true home."[72]

I have quoted this letter at length because it is an important formulation, and one in which, as in Spenser, the roles of love and beauty are inextricably entwined. In its mock-scholastic disputational style it is pushing against the borders of letter-writing, but in so doing it also illustrates the earnestness with which Ficino used his letters to convey philosophical thought. The transformative power of love becomes for him a theme of ever-growing importance as his years advance. In Spenser, the transformative power of love, or its failure to transform, weaves through the many sections of *The Faerie Queene* as he explores a great variety of amorous encounters.[73]

THE SOUL

There is much more that could be said about Ficino's philosophy that has a bearing on Spenser's poetry. For example, Ficino had plenty of advice for participants in courtly life,[74] for the role of philosopher or poet, and for the ruler.[75] Promoting Plato's ideal of the philosopher-king, he may have helped to form at least some part of the composite image of Spenser's Gloriana as indeed it contributed to the public persona of the real Queen whom Spenser celebrated. But among such further topics, perhaps the most significant are Ficino's views of the soul, as they represent a new formulation of the place of man in the creation—a formulation that gained wide currency. Ficino stresses the centrality of soul: "Since [the soul] is the true bond of everything in the universe, when it passes into some things, it does not abandon others, but it moves into individuals while forever preserving all things. It can with justice, accordingly, be called nature's centre, the mean of everything in the universe, the succession or chain of the world, the countenance of all things, and the knot and bond of the world."[76]

The "knot and bond of the world" is also described as love, stressing again how closely bound together are those central ideas of Ficino's philosophy—beauty, unity, love, and the soul:

> The desire for propagating one's own perfection, which is innate in everything, explains the latent enfolded fecundity of everything; it makes seeds develop into an embryo, it draws out the powers of each thing from its heart, and conceives offspring; and by "opening" these offspring, as though with a set of keys, brings them into the light. Thus since they are the works of one artificer and members of the same machine, and are mutually alike in their being and living, all the world's parts are bound together with a mutual love. We are justly entitled to call love, therefore, the perpetual knot and bond of the world, the motionless prop and stay of its parts, and the firm foundation of the whole machine.[77]

Similarly, if we consider Ficino's early *Theological Dialogue between God and the Soul*[78] or his *Theological Prayer to God*,[79] these may also have had some bearing on Spenser's *Hymns*. The *Dialogue* is an outpouring of yearning for union, together with a poetic description of the nature of the divine, and it culminates in the rapture of the soul into union with the divine. The *Prayer* hymns the divine light and pours out loving thanks for God's innumerable acts of beneficence.

LITERARY STRATEGIES

Spenser also seems to have been influenced by the importance that Ficino ascribes to poetic frenzy and "the mysteries," including the communication of philosophical truths in poetic veils. An early letter on the four frenzies—and in particular on divine love and poetry—circulated widely long before its publication in print. True inspiration, he argues, depends upon ecstasy, and in the ecstatic state the soul has access to the world it enjoyed before it was imprisoned in the body:

It uses the ears as messengers as though they were chinks in this darkness. By the ears . . . the soul receives the echoes of that incomparable music, by which it is led back to the deep and silent memory of the harmony which it previously enjoyed. The whole soul then kindles with desire to fly back to its rightful home, so that it may enjoy that true music again. It realizes that as long as it is enclosed in the dark abode of the body it can in no way reach that music. It therefore strives wholeheartedly to imitate it. [80]

The "deep and silent memory" may then be expressed through music. This is not conventional song and instrumental music, which he calls a "superficial and vulgar" imitation that merely soothes:

Some, who imitate the divine and heavenly harmony with deeper and sounder judgment, render a sense of its inner reason and knowledge into verse, feet and numbers. It is these who, inspired by the divine spirit, give forth with full voice the most solemn and glorious song. Plato calls this solemn music and poetry the most effective imitation of the celestial harmony. . . . It expresses with fire the most profound and, as a poet would say, prophetic meanings, in the numbers of voice and movement. . . . [It] delight(s) the ear . . . and brings to the mind the finest nourishment, most like the food of the gods and so seems to come very close to God.[81]

Ficino expands these early ideas of poetic *furor*, based on Plato's *Ion* and *Phaedrus*, in his *Platonic Theology* XIII.2.5, and he also himself experimented with some forms of poetry, writing hymns to be sung to the lyre. Although most of Ficino's writing is in prose, in a letter to his young friend Martin Prenninger of Konstanz, written on 9 June 1492, he admitted that in his youth he had, for his own private use, translated the Orphic *Argonautica*, Orphic and Homeric hymns, and hymns of Proclus, as well as Hesiod's *Theogony*, that treasury of poets' myths.[82] It may have been just such songs that he used when he took up his own lyre to sing, an Orphic custom revived by Ficino and his circle, described both by him and other participants on many occasions.[83] In fact, he was still singing Orphic hymns to the lyre five years after his ordination as a Catholic priest, as he describes in a letter to Sebastiano Foresi, fellow poet, musician, and priest, dated 8 September 1479.[84] But not wishing to appear to be encouraging the worship of the ancient gods and the *daemons*, he never published these hymns.

Ficino's wariness of poetry extended further: in a letter to Braccio Martelli on *daemons*, he says that that "The craft of poetry has vigorously aroused . . . misapprehensions . . . because it makes use of an eloquence perfectly suited to produce entrancement and seemingly magical attraction; it is also easily able to charm and entice minds, and therefore it produces in us a belief in utterly impossible things."[85] Ficino was deeply conscious of Plato's ambivalence towards the poets, yet on the whole his own views are more positive.[86] He delights in Platonic allegories such as the Cave, the Phaedran charioteer, and the Wings, expounding them frequently both in his letters and commentaries.[87] The wings are usually interpreted as love and reason. In the letter to Matteo of Forli already quoted, he notes the importance of the three Graces—that is, of harmony in sound, beauty of color and form, and eloquence—and observes that whereas understanding "does not usually transform us into what we understand . . . love does transform us into what we love," and so it is the desire for beauty that gives the mind power to return home.[88]

Ficino also wrote a number of allegorical fables of his own devising, some to elucidate his commentary on Plato's *Philebus*,[89] and a series of moral allegories inspired by the fables of Bartolomeo Scala.[90] Sharing the general Renaissance veneration for Virgil as a proto-Christian allegorist, Ficino borrows the allegory of the golden bough from Virgil's *Aeneid* (VI, 140–48), and interprets it in relation to scriptural passages from St. John.[91] One feels he would have been sympathetic to the idea of a Christian epic on which Spenser embarked. He also frequently reminds his readers that the ancients used the veil of poetry to express great truths that the mind can hardly grasp. In addition, he notices and admires in Plato a subtle blend of prose and poetry, to which he also aspired himself. Prose, he said, is "free of restrictions" and "reaches its point more swiftly," but poetry "should delight, soothe and enrapture through the blending of harmonies and imagery."[92] It was perhaps partly because of his own skill in the use of language and his appreciation of its special powers that Ficino had so much influence on poets within his own circle, quite apart from opening for them the treasure house of Platonic ideas.[93]

ASSESSING THE DEBT

Spenser's poetry, as we have seen, relates in many ways to the ideas Marsilio Ficino was expounding in Florence before the Reformation. Yet Ficino was only one among many humanist sources available to Spenser. Many writers contributed to that renewal of confidence in the classical traditions of philosophy and poetry as being worthy of playing a part in authentic Christian expression. Yet Ficino's voice was certainly an important one. Spenser wrote for an audience among whom many were familiar with the broad outlines of Ficino's Platonism, and with the work of French and Italian writers of the intervening century who were themselves steeped in his influence.[94] There was also considerable familiarity with some of Ficino's sources, often through his translations, as well as his work on magic and medicine, the ever-popular *Three Books on Life*.[95]

As a poet, Spenser creates and describes, responds, and evokes through imagery, through narrative and through atmospherics. Only rarely and in prose does he discuss the origin or development of his ideas.[96] Yet, while he does not pay particular court to the figure of Marsilio Ficino by name, Spenser's writings nonetheless evince significant Ficinian affinities and influence, most clearly in the *Fowre Hymnes*.[97] I have tried in this paper to present a short introduction to the writings of Ficino that are of especial relevance to the study of Spenser and the Platonic aspects of his intellectual context. The passages chosen for illustration have been drawn from the wide range of Ficino's writings and selected for their ability to indicate how the broad tenor of his concerns complements some of Spenser's. For further illumination, however, the lover of Spenser can do no better than turn to Ficino's works themselves, to gain a deeper understanding of one important part of the rich treasury of ideas current in the poet's day. The main aim here has been to draw attention to questions of the nature and purpose of human life that seem to underlie Spenser's allegory, and which resonate also in Ficino's thought. Though the philosopher and the poet diverge in their forms of expression, producing works that differ widely in their style and coloring, the two writers share a passionate interest in the potential of mankind and a belief in the stability and permanence of a more perfect world of which this world is but the shadow.

School of Economic Science, London

Appendix
Availability of the Works of Ficino and Plato and Their Place in the Cambridge Curriculum

The aim of this appendix is to clear up some of the doubts that have been expressed concerning the currency of the works of Ficino and of Plato during Spenser's lifetime. The two are closely related because it was often through the Latin translations of Ficino that English readers read Plato. His translations were equipped with introductory summaries (*argumenta*) and helpful commentaries informed by his own studies of Plotinus and the later Neoplatonic commentary tradition. These additions favored the development of a Christian Platonism and rendered Plato's texts more accessible and more acceptable to the Christian reader (see Fig. 1).

The important questions to be answered are:

1. Were Ficino's Plato translations and commentaries available to Spenser in Cambridge?
2. Was Plato being read and studied as part of the university curriculum?
3. Were the works of Plato available in versions other than Ficino's?
4. Were the works of Plato available more widely to English readers beyond Cambridge?
5. Which other works of Ficino were available to English readers?

But first, some words on the background to my inquiry, its methods, and the works in question.

Background and Method

Sears Reynolds Jayne, in his final work, *Plato in Renaissance England* (Dordrecht and London: Kluwer Academic Publishers, 1995), expressed the view that, contrary to earlier beliefs, Plato was little known and little studied in Renaissance England. While allowing that Henry VIII had taken some steps to encourage the study of Plato at Cambridge, and that the glosses for Spenser's *Shepheardes Calendar* include references to Plato, he based his negative findings on a survey of book publishing, of book ownership, and of specific allusions to Plato.

Against this background of negativity, and in view of the debates around Spenser's own Platonism, it seemed worth looking again for fresh data, especially since Jayne's approach seemed to overlook three important points:

(i) Focusing so closely on English book publishing undervalues the importance of continental publishing in the English book trade during the Tudor period, especially for academic works written in Latin.

(ii) Reliance on records of book ownership in the period is fraught with difficulties due to the extremely patchy nature of the evidence. These difficulties also affect my own findings and will be further discussed below.

(iii) Jayne's assumption that writers will refer specifically to Plato or Ficino when using ideas derived from their reading is not always applicable. It applies to Ascham, who was at pains in his *Scholemaster* to commend specific authors to his readers; but it does not apply to a poet like Spenser, who follows the pattern, praised by the ancients, of bees taking nectar from many flowers and distilling it into honey whose sweetness cannot be ascribed to any particular flower from which the nectar came. (Seneca, *Epistle* 84, "On Gathering Ideas," and St. Basil, *Homilia ad Adolescentes*, 7–8, both specifically apply this metaphor to reading, and their texts were popular with humanist educators.)

Given these concerns about the underlying premises of Jayne's methodology, I decided to visit a number of college libraries in Cambridge to see what I could piece together of their holdings of Ficino and Plato at the time Spenser was there. Having found some interesting results in Cambridge, I extended the search to Oxford, and in a small and partial way to London. I shall present a summary of what I found and why I consider these findings significant. My own survey is more limited in scope than that of Jayne, but it has a precise relevance to Spenser, and offers grounds for a more positive view.

In Cambridge I visited individual colleges, consulting their early records and the books themselves. Important supplementary evidence came from E. S. Leedham-Green's *Books in Cambridge Inventories* (2 vols., Cambridge: Cambridge University Press, 1986), which will be referred to hereafter as Leedham-Green, *Inventories*. In Oxford, nearly all the early holdings of the college libraries have been very well recorded on OLIS, the library catalogue of Oxford University, with full details of provenance where available; but I still visited the individual libraries. For the Bodleian's own books there seems to be less provenance information, but this library (the original University library) was less accessible to readers before its overhaul by Thomas Bodley at the very end of the sixteenth century, and college libraries are therefore more important. Other useful catalogues for Oxford were Dennis Rhodes, *Catalogue of Incunabula in All the Libraries of Oxford University Outside the Bodleian* (1982), and Paul Morgan, *The Inter-collegiate Catalogue of pre-1640 Foreign Books in Oxford* (provisional printout, 1979). Library and college histories were also consulted for both Oxford and Cambridge.

GENERAL AVAILABILITY OF FICINO'S PLATO TRANSLATIONS AND COMMENTARIES

Ficino, the first Renaissance scholar to have access to the full range of Plato's dialogues, started to translate them from Greek as early as 1463, and to write commentaries on them. These circulated at first in manuscript, but were eventually committed to print as the *Platonis Opera*, together with Ficino's *argumenta* (summaries) and commentaries (Florence: Lorenzo Veneto, 1484). A second revised edition followed (Venice: Bernardino de Choris, 1491), which included a work of his own, the *Platonic Theology*, which had first been published separately in 1482. A further revision of the commentaries, *Commentaria in Platonem*, appeared a few years later (Florence: Lorenzo Francisco, 1496). Subsequent editions of the *Platonis Opera* after Ficino's lifetime appeared in 1517 and 1556 (Venice); 1518, 1522, and 1533 (Paris); 1532, 1539, 1546, 1551, 1561 (Basel); and 1548, 1550, 1556, 1557, 1567 (Lyons). There were eight more editions still within Spenser's lifetime, and numerous individual works from the set were published separately. See Paul Oskar Kristeller, *Supplementum Ficinianum*, 2 vols. (Florence: Olschki, 1937), vol. I, lx–lxiv; corrected and updated in Kristeller, *Marsilio Ficino and His Work after Five Hundred Years* (Florence: Olschki, 1987), 114–16. The 1561 Basel edition of Plato's works uses the later translation of Janus Cornarius, but still introduces each item with Ficino's *argumentum* and includes his commentaries.

Some of Ficino's commentaries also circulated individually, such as the *De amore*, a work of his own based loosely upon interpretation of the *Symposium*, which enjoyed wide readership in manuscript and in the printed version of the collected works. It also came out in two separate editions in 1544 (Florence and Rome), both in Italian translation. Ficino's three books on life, *De vita libri tres*, collectively often considered a medical work, should also be counted among the commentaries since the third and largest book originated as a section of his Plotinus commentary. (I have discussed possible reasons for its removal in "Marsilio Ficino and the Rise of Philosophic Interests in Buda," *Italy and Hungary: Humanism and Art in the Early Renaissance*, ed. Péter Farbaky, Louis Waldman and Fiorella Gioffredi Superbi [Florence: Leo S. Olschki, forthcoming 2009]).

De vita libri tres first appeared in print in 1489 (the printed edition predates the dedicatory manuscript copies) with further editions of 1494, 1498, 1501, 1506 and sixteen more prior to 1580. The main Plotinus commentary, without this section, was published with the Plotinus translation in Florence by Antonio Miscomini in 1492, and in Basel in 1540, 1559, 1562, and 1580.

A further volume of Neoplatonic texts in Ficino's translations appeared in 1497 from the Aldine press in Venice, consisting of Iamblichus's *De mysteriis Aegyptiorum, Chaldaeorum, Assyriorum*, two Proclus extracts, Porphyry on gods and demons, Synesius's *On dreams*, Psellus's *On daemons*, Priscian of Lydia's version of Theophrastus's commentary on Aristotle's *De anima* and a few other shorter items. The second edition of this collection (Venice: Aldus, 1516), and subsequent editions, included Ficino's own *De vita* and his famous version of the *Corpus Hermeticum* (usually known then as the *Pimander* of Hermes Trismegistus), first published on its own in 1471 and frequently thereafter. Five Tornaesius editions of the Iamblichus collection followed from Lyons in 1549, 1552, 1577, 1578, and 1607. These various editions of the collection will all be referred to simply as Iamblichus or *De Mysteriis*, together with the date of the edition.

Ficino's own Letters (*Epistolae*) carried his ideas to correspondents across Europe and he published them as a collection (Venice: Matteo Capcasa, 1495; reprinted Nuremberg: Anton Koberger, 1497); they were later included in the Basel *Opera omnia* of Ficino. As letters, they are often more specific and spontaneous than a formal commentary, thus offering the same Platonizing commentary and exposition but in a more readily accessible form.

Through the international book trade, there were thus ample opportunities for book buyers in England to obtain copies of Ficino's translations of the works of Plato and his later followers, as well as the commentaries he wrote on them. In addition, many of the commentaries were gathered together with Ficino's own works in his *Opera omnia* published in Basel by Henricus Petri in 1561 and again in 1576. For a full list of all Ficino's works, see Kristeller as cited above, *Supplementum*, I, lvii–lxxiii; and *Marsilio Ficino and His Work*, 114–16.

1. Were Ficino's Plato translations and commentaries available to Spenser in Cambridge?

At Spenser's own college, Pembroke, famous for educating churchmen, the initial results were disappointing: there are five sets of sixteenth-century editions of Plato's *Opera omnia* among the card index of early holdings of the library, one of the *Timaeus* separately, and an edition of Ficino's Plotinus translation. However, on inspection most of these turn out to be seventeenth—or eighteenth-century gifts, except the *Timaeus* which is in Greek, and the Plotinus (Basel: Perna, 1580, Greek and Latin text), for which there is no provenance information (a difficulty frequently encountered in work with early library collections). Ficino's own two-volume *Opera omnia* (Basel: Henricus Petri, 1561) is in the library, but given with many other works by John Gaskarth in the eighteenth century; and there is an additional copy of the first volume, but without provenance details. However, the second edition of Ficino's translation of Iamblichus and other texts (Venice, 1516) is present, and two further editions of this work from 1570 and 1587 (Lyons: Johan. Tornaesium). The two later editions are in small format, 16° and 32°, suggesting that they were for pocket reading, but there is no indication of provenance. The 1516 edition was the gift of Lancelot Andrews (1555–1626), a student at Pembroke in the 1570s and later a leading bishop and chief of the authorized translators of the Bible under King James. Although it most probably came to Pembroke's library only on the bishop's death, he was a contemporary of Spenser's at Pembroke, joining the college just two years after him, and they had both previously been pupils of Richard Mulcaster at Merchant Taylors' School. A shared interest in such Platonic works is therefore quite likely. Also on the positive side, evidence of the presence in Spenser's time of two important other works, Ficino's *Platonis Opera* of 1484 and his *Letters*, came to light subsequently by another route, as will be discussed below. But it is worth reflecting for a moment on some of the difficulties, over and above lack of provenance data, which attend the interpretation of information gathered through college library searches.

Ownership of books was generally a personal matter. Books might therefore move on from one college to another with their owners, or be passed down within families, unless they were left in bequests. College libraries tended to contain large works, for reference and consultation, mainly by the fellows, and even then these works were generally chained to the desks. Many of the former chained books are still in pristine condition, leading one to wonder how often they were in fact consulted. Smaller books were more likely to circulate from hand to hand, and if popular would end up in a very ragged condition, eventually being discarded. Smaller books might also be borrowed from college libraries by the fellows, and were sometimes not returned.

Masters often sold books to their pupils, who then sold them back for reissue. This particularly applied to texts for study. Similar arrangements existed with the booksellers. Occasionally wealthy men kept their student books into old age. Only rarely do we have inventories of the books of individuals or booksellers, and then they were conducted as part of the probate process. No register survives before 1501, and surviving inventories begin only from 1535. Those we have are naturally skewed in favor of larger books as these would be listed by name and accorded a known cash value by the probate officials, while smaller books would often be lumped together, being worth only a few pence each and thus scarcely worth the officials' time to list separately. The appraisers worked in pairs, "with one appraiser calling out titles, sometimes not very clearly, while another, not very tidily, wrote them down" (Leedham-Green, *Inventories*, I, xii). Where two or more titles were bound together, only the first title would be entered, and often bindings represent a large part of the value. A poorly bound book might therefore not get listed.

Controversial or suspect books would be quietly spirited away prior to the arrival of the assessor. It is also a limitation that the inventories of individual libraries that survive relate to scholars who died in Cambridge. We do not have any list of the books in Spenser's own possession that burned when his house was attacked in Ireland. Nor do we know what Gabriel Harvey possibly lent him.

Even libraries kept few detailed records, or few that have survived, of their original collections and early donations. This might not matter so much were it not the case that many books were removed from their original places by Henry VIII at the dissolution of the monasteries, and again by the Marian commissioners in 1557, and those of Elizabeth sent to hunt out popish works. However some of these inspection inventories survive. Information about books in the lists was generally kept as brief as possible, no doubt to minimize untoward consequences and seizures. Nevertheless in Cambridge in 1557, two cartloads of books inspected were found heretical and burned. (See Peter D. Clarke, *Corpus of British Medieval Library Catalogues*, vol. 10, *The University and College Libraries of Cambridge* [London: British Library and British Academy, 2002], 399.) From the list drawn up for the Marian commissioners visiting Pembroke in

1557 we can safely say that although the College does not now hold any early copies of Ficino's works, at the time of their visit it did possess the *editio princeps* of his Plato translations (Florence, 1484). It is listed as a gift of John Camberton, a fellow of the college and vice chancellor of the university in 1488. There is no further information about it, and it is no longer there, but at least we know that Ficino's Plato had been present in Pembroke earlier in the Tudor period.

Furthermore, a Pembroke scholar by the name of William Robinson, who achieved his BA in 1541/2 and was elected fellow in 1543, proceeding to MA that year, died possessed of eighty-four books, including a copy of Ficino's *Epistolae* (*Letters*), which are so rich in philosophical content (see Fig. 2). His will, to which probate was granted in January 1548, gave his books to the college library (Leedham Green, *Inventories*, I, 95–98), but this one is no longer there. In 1551, Anthony Hall of Pembroke died possessed of a Latin Plato, worth 6s 8d, and left some money to Robinson's father "for certain books I had of his sonnes unpaid for" (Leedham-Green, *Inventories*, 117–18). In 1559 one Edyll willed his *Opera Platonis* to Pembroke (though we do not know which edition). Edyll came from Cumberland to matriculate as a pensioner of Christ's College in 1544. He proceeded to the BA in 1546/7, and in 1547 migrated to Pembroke to take up a fellowship. There he received his MA in 1549, and took the tonsure in London in 1554, proceeding to a Bachelor of Divinity in 1556 followed by a fellowship at Jesus College in 1558/9. The Plato appears to be a Latin translation and was "to go from chamber to chamber yerely as they have St Austyn." Edyll lived in reasonable comfort: he died possessed of the trappings for a horse, a pair of virginals, a pair of clavichords and a lute. He also owned Rhetoric texts in Latin and Greek and a number of Hebrew books (Leedham-Green, *Inventories*, I, 232–34). Another volume, a Greek and Latin Plotinus (therefore probably Pietro Perna's edition of 1580), was given to the college by a John Wistfield in 1598 (who also gave a Greek-Latin edition of Iamblichus [Heidelberg, 1598], but the Latin is that of Arcerius, not Ficino).

The other principal Cambridge colleges in which humanist studies were likely to be embraced by Spenser's time were Christ's, founded by Lady Margaret Beaufort; Queens', which had been home to Erasmus from 1511; St. John's, also Lady Margaret's foundation; and Trinity. The latter two became the leading centers for the study of Greek. There was also the Library of the University, reestablished by Andrew Perne, although its holdings would not at that time have been generally available to students or even their teachers. (See Patrick Collinson, David McKitterick, and Elisabeth S. Leedham-Green, *Andrew Perne: Quatercentenary Studies*, Cambridge: Cambridge Bibliographical Society, 1991.)

Fig. 2.   Ficino, *Epistolae*, first edition (Venice: Matteo Capcasa, 1495), John Colet's copy, by kind permission of the Warden and Fellows of All Souls' College, Oxford. Ficino's letters cover a wide range of moral and philosophic questions; written to over 200 individuals over a time span of almost forty years, they provide an accessible introduction to Platonic philosophy.

2. Was Plato being read and studied as part of the university curriculum?

The content of the Cambridge University Arts course and its increasingly humanistic character during the sixteenth century were discussed by Lisa Jardine in her article, "Humanism and the Sixteenth Century Cambridge Arts Course," *History of Education* 4.1 (1975): 16–31. Jardine uses evidence drawn from the inventories of members of the university who died in residence between 1535 and 1590, and also relates it to that presented from similar lists for Oxford described in Mark H. Curtis, "Library Catalogues and Tudor Oxford and Cambridge," *Studies in the Renaissance* 5 (1958): 111–20. These lists have since been superseded by the relevant volumes of the *Corpus of British Medieval Library Catalogues* (London: British Library, 1995–), and by Leedham-Green, *Inventories* (cited above). Neither Jardine's data nor the later lists reflect an especially strong presence of Plato, though some interesting findings from the later lists will be presented below. Jardine's general conclusions relate more to the development of rhetoric as a technique than to the content of the works used, Platonic or otherwise.

Attempts to interpret changes in the university statutes in favor of Platonic philosophy have also faltered. Even if possession of one work of Plato was formally required at Trinity in 1552, there is no evidence that this was honored or enforced in practice (see Jayne, *Plato in Renaissance England*, 93, citing Trinity College Statutes). Likewise the assertion that a work of Plato was a required text in the university statutes of 1549 and 1570, and in those of Trinity College, has not so far been confirmed by definite evidence of teaching practice (Philip Gaskell, *Trinity College Library*, Cambridge: Cambridge University Press, 1980).

Yet, we can detect a keen interest in Plato from the reign of Henry VIII, as Jayne himself charts. The first Regius Professor of Greek was John Cheke (1514–57) of St. John's College, who taught Plato at least in tutorials until 1544 when he became tutor to the future king Edward VI. His successor in the chair was Nicholas Carr, originally at Pembroke but transferred by the king to Trinity College on its foundation in 1546. Public lectures on Plato were instituted there and were said to have been very popular. (See Jayne, *Plato in Renaissance England*, 90; and Thomas Wilson, *De vita et obitu duorum fratrum Suffolciensium* [London, 1551] cited there.) Carr also translated sections of Plato's *Laws*, *Symposium*, and *Timaeus* and wrote commentaries on them. Meanwhile, in 1545, at St. John's College, Plato had been included in the philosophy course as well as the Greek course.

Fig. 3.   Ficino's Plato translations (Paris: Badius, 1522), the copy of James Pylkington, Master of St. John's 1559–61, reproduced by kind permission of the Master and Fellows of St. John's College, Cambridge.

Turning to the presence of books in college libraries, we find that at Christ's College, both the Plotinus in Ficino's translation (Basel: Perna, 1580) and the Greek works of Plato (Basel: Froben 1551) carry no positive identification that they entered the library early, though it is possible. They may conceivably have been in the original gift of the founder Margaret Beaufort (1443–1509), but are not recorded as such, and when re-bound in the eighteenth century they were also trimmed, thus losing any information on their origin and donation. The only certain gift of a Ficino work from Lady Margaret is a copy of his translation of the two short works of Dionysius, *Mystic Theology* and *Divine Names*, bound into a large volume of other works by Dionysius (Strasbourg, 1502/3). After her death, much of Lady Margaret's estate was directed rather to the newer college she was founding, St. John's.

At St. John's, under Bishop John Fisher, there were at least two Plato volumes definitely in the old library during Spenser's time at Cambridge, one in Greek and one in Ficino's Latin. The Latin edition was Ficino's translation, republished by Jodocus Badius Ascensius in Paris in 1522. This was donated by James Pylkington, who was Master of the college in 1559–1561 (see Fig. 3). The Greek volume (probably Basel: Ioan. Valderum, 1534), valued at 10 shillings at probate, was donated by another fellow of the college, Miles Buckley, in 1559. Some of his books were left to his nephew Edward, but the Greek Plato was reserved specifically in his will for the college: "I give to the poore Scholers of our house all the little bokes that stand on the nether shelfe in the corner of the studdye/ at the discrecion of mr Lakyn & sir Cobbe. . . . I gyve plato in greke to our librarie" (see Leedham-Green, *Inventories*, I, 245).

There is one curious entry in the list prepared by the bursars of St. John's College for the Marian commissioners in 1557: the book is simply designated "*de re medica*" with the author given as Mercellius Ficinus. This book appears to have been acquired since the previous inventory of 1544. It is no longer present, but it could have been either Ficino's short plague treatise or his *De vita*. Peter Clarke suggests it was the latter work (Clarke, *Corpus of British Medieval Library Catalogues*, vol. 10, 632); yet *De vita* is generally a much longer book, and certainly one which might invoke the disapproval of the commissioners if they examined it. Of course, deliberate concealment is one possible explanation, and the haste with which this particular list was prepared another (Clark: *Corpus*, 625). However there is a sixty-four leaf 8vo edition of books I and II of *De vita* (i.e., the more "medical" parts of the work, and small in format) in an Italian translation by Lucio Fauno (Venice: Tramezzino, 1548); one is in the possession of the University Library (shelfmark Bute.533). Ficino's plague treatise is also a small work of some 52 quarto leaves in its first edition (Florence: San Jacopo di Ripoli, 1481), reprinted in 1522 (Siena and Florence: Giunti), and again in Florence in 1523. Further editions followed from the same house (Venice: Giunti, 1556 and Florence: Giunti, 1576), these latter two in 8vo format. In addition, his plague treatise was the subject of discussion in a sixty-four page 8vo book by Giovanni Francesco Boccalino, *De causis pestilentiae urbem Venetam opprimentis anno MDLVI* (Venice: Gabriele Iolitum, 1556), which names Ficino on its title page. The Boccalino volume is still extant at St. John's, though it is recorded as bequeathed by John Collins (1571–1634; shelfmark Ll.13.14 [3]).

St. John's most famous Ficino volume is the *Opera Platonis* that belonged to John Dee (Basel: Froben, 1532; see Fig. 1). This is a work much used by Dee during Spenser's lifetime. It is heavily annotated and he took it with him on his travels. However, on his death it passed into the hands of Patrick Saunders and came to the library only in 1684, donated by Peter Gunning (1614–84), who became Master of the college in 1661, Regius Professor of Divinity, and later Bishop of Ely.

For the books of Trinity College left to it by its various Masters in its early years, no information is available despite the college's fame for Greek studies and the proud presence of a much later bust of Plato in the library (from the 1750s). The fact that there were only a few copies of Plato in the earliest surviving catalogues suggests that members of the college most likely had their own. William Liffe (or Lyffe), for example, was at Trinity from 1560 and was elected a fellow in 1563. When he died at the age of 26, in 1569, he left 122 books, including Plato and Aristotle in Greek—but these went to his pupils and not to the college (Leedham-Green, *Inventories*, I, 302–05). Nicholas Sharpe, who died in 1576, owned two copies of Plato, one in Latin, one in Greek. As already noted with Edyll, readers of Plato were often men of substance. Sharpe was at Trinity from 1566 and lived in style: besides 112 volumes (representing 92 titles), his inventory for probate includes copious and elegant apparel and linens, a rapier, a dagger, and a lute (Leedham-Green, *Inventories*, I, 316–19). It is not clear what became of his books, but the estate was administered by his brother in London.

One college copy of Plato at Trinity (shelfmark OL 86) was probably the 1578 edition of Plato edited and published by Stephanus (Henri Etienne) and translated by Serranus (Jean de Serres), but it is no longer extant. On this important edition see S. K. Heninger, Jr., "Sidney and Serranus' Plato," *English Literary Renaissance* 13 (1983): 146–61; and his *Sidney and Spenser: The Poet as Maker* (University Park, PA: Pennsylvania State University Press, 1989), 317, 396, and 533, n186. Trinity's copy of Ficino's *Commentaries* on Plato (Florence: de Alpa, 1496, 2vo) that was at one time in the library is there no longer, probably alienated before 1667. (For the early years of Trinity's library see Gaskell, *Trinity College Library*; and David McKitterick, *The Making of the Wren Library*, Cambridge: Cambridge University Press, 1995).

At Queens' College there is no record of copies of Ficino's own works, but of his translations there is a Plotinus, in the 1580 edition, as well as the Serranus translation of Plato (Greek and Latin parallel text, 3 vols., 1578). Proclus's commentary *In Timaeum* (Basel, 1534) is present in Greek, and Proclus's *Platonic Theology* came into the library later in a 1618 edition. Given the interest in Greek studies at Queens' under Erasmus, this is a very slender showing, and one that presumably much underestimates the former extent of interest in Platonic learning there. The books of that earlier period seem to have disappeared, though a list records that Sir Thomas Smith (1513–77) had left a Latin Plato, which is thus earlier than the Serranus edition of 1578, as well as French translations of the *Symposium* and *Timaeus*, and a copy of Castiglione's *Il Cortegiano*—all relevant to our questions, but rarely found in the Oxford and Cambridge libraries.

At Corpus Christi, Matthew Parker, the future Archbishop of Canterbury, was an important collector and benefactor between 1533 and 1553. Among extant works that belonged to him are copies of Ficino's translation of Plato (Paris: Joanne Parvo and Jodocus Badius, 1518) and of Plotinus (Florence: Antonio Miscomini, 1492), and a copy of Ficino's own *De vita libri tres* (Basel: Cratandrum and Bebel, 1532). The latter work, like many other continental books, was imported as loose folds of pages and was bound in England, in this case in London.

In 1569, Gonville and Caius College also had Greek and Latin works of Plato, some of which had belonged to Henry VIII's physician Thomas Wendy (d.1560). He left an Aldine edition of Plato (Venice: 1513) to Gonville Hall (see Elisabeth Leedham-Green, "A Catalogue of Caius College Library, 1569," in *Proceedings of the Cambridge Bibliographical Society*, 8 [1981–84]: 29–41; and P. Grierson, "John Caius' Library," Biographical History of Gonville and Caius College 7 [1978]: 508–25).

At the University Library we know that Francis Bacon (1561–1626) gave a Latin Plato "in the early 1570s" (i.e., soon after he entered Trinity College at the age of twelve) and also a Greek one. The Latin is the Cornarius edition (1561) with Ficino's interpretative additions. (Elisabeth Leedham-Green and David McKitterick, "A Catalogue of Cambridge University Library in 1583," in *Books and Collectors, 1200–1700: Essays Presented to Andrew Watson*, ed. J. P. Carley and C. G. C. Tite [London: British Library, 1996], 153–235, at 180.) Bacon's interest in Plato is noteworthy: he gave another copy of the latter's works "well bound and claspt" in Serranus's edition, to St. Alban's Grammar School. His enthusiasm for Plato probably predated his arrival in Cambridge, as his mother and her father, Sir Anthony Cooke, were keen humanist scholars.

We might wonder what happened to the libraries of the early humanist reformers from Cambridge—Andrew Perne, Thomas Cranmer, John Whitgift, and the like—all enthusiastic students of Greek. Cranmer's books, acquired by the Earl of Arundel, went to the Lumley Library and thence to the royal collection. They have thus ended up in the British Library and are hard to distinguish, although one copy of Ficino's *Letters* (shelfmark IA.7529) is thought to have been his (see David Selwyn, *The Library of Thomas Cranmer* [Oxford: Oxford Bibliographical Society], 1996; N. R. Ker, *Medieval Libraries of Great Britain*, 2nd ed. [London: Royal Historical Society], 1964). Perne, Master of Peterhouse for 35 years, worked hard to build up the University Library. He had 3,000 titles of his own when he died in 1589, a quarter more than the great library of John Dee, including a Plotinus that went to Peterhouse and a Plato valued at 6s. 7d. (This may have been the five-volume edition with Ficino's translation in 16° format, published at Lyons by Tornaesius in 1550). He also had a Hermes *Pimander* (which Ficino translated), one of twelve small books valued together at twelve pence. Archbishop Whitgift (1530–1604), who had been Perne's protégé, left his books at Lambeth Palace for future archbishops.

Several other Cambridge scholars included in Elizabeth Leedham-Green's *Inventories* had unspecified works of Ficino worth only a few pennies: one was owned by Perman in 1545, valued at eightpence; another, owned by Nevell in 1548, was worth just a penny. Townley in 1549, Benyngworth in 1551, and Pember (tutor to Roger Ascham) in 1560 each had one worth six to eight pence (*Inventories*, II, 343–44). They were thus relatively small works, and quite affordable even to scholars who had few possessions. Ficino's *De vita* appears by name, valued at a maximum of tenpence: one was owned by Townley in 1549, by Gylpin in 1551, and by Roberts in 1579/80. After that, values of fourpence (Lorkin, 1591) and threepence (Mote, 1592) are recorded, perhaps indicating the same copy changing hands in ever-declining condition (*Inventories*, II, 343–44). Lorkin is almost certainly Thomas Lorkin, Regius Professor of Physic (medicine), 1564–91. The one and only reference to a contemporary copy of Ficino's *Letters* was the one mentioned above belonging to Robinson, a fellow of Pembroke. When he died in 1547/8 it was valued at sixpence. Of the two complete editions of the letters, the first (Venice: Capcasa, 1495) is folio, but the second (Nuremberg: Koberger, 1497) is quarto. From the price, it would be reasonable to surmise that Robinson's copy was of the second smaller edition. Although a small selection of six letters was published in 1519, this would have been so slender as to be unlikely to fetch sixpence when it was almost thirty years old, and so Robinson's copy was most likely to have been a well-worn copy of the full 1497 edition. While other books were left to the college library, Robinson's will specifies, "I geve to the yonge scholers of Pembroke hall all my bookes of philosophy beinge under the price of xij d a booke to be geven at the desposicion of mr. Askew, Mr. grendall and Mr. Weste" (Leedham-Green, *Inventories*, I, 95). The absence of the *Letters* now is therefore not surprising. Perhaps it was even one of those books that were passed around and avidly read until they literally fell apart.

Ficino's translation of the later Neoplatonic writers, the "Iamblichus" volume already mentioned, occurs in the inventories four times. The first owner, Nevell, who died in 1548, was already mentioned above as possessing another untitled Ficino work; the next

Iamblichus owner is anonymous (c. 1558); then Welles died possessed of one in 1569–70, and another anonymous owner in 1588–89. Of course, whether this could have been the same book passing down the generations, it is not possible to know. A few works of Proclus and Synesius on their own crop up in these lists, probably indicating individual Greek texts. Such is the entry for a small stock of seven unbound texts of Proclus's *De sphaera* at the bookseller Pilgrim. Their value in this state is only fourpence a piece, but they were clearly required for use in the teaching of mathematics.

Plotinus does not appear in private hands, or at the bookseller, but Plato does, though sometimes in unidentifiable form. Of twenty-five folio copies of his *Opera* appearing up to and including the entries for Perne and Tillman, in 1589, eleven are identified as Greek, eight as Latin, one as dual-language text and the rest are unspecified. One Latin copy is identified as a Ficino translation, belonging to A. Hatcher in 1587. He has been identified with John Hatcher, a fellow of St. John's in 1533, Regius Professor of Physic around 1554 and Vice-Chancellor of the University in 1579–80. He accumulated great wealth, and built himself a grand house on the remains of the Augustinian Friary in the city, but died childless, leaving 576 books (Leedham-Green, *Inventories*, I, 367–82; see also W. M. Palmer, *Cambridgeshire Doctors in the Olden Time, 1466–1827* [Cambridge, 1911]). The dual-language Greek/Latin copy belonged to Ambrose Barker of Essex, in 1583. He entered Christ's College, became a deacon there, then a priest in 1573. He was moderately prosperous: two of his doublets had lace, he possessed a bow and arrows, a grey gelding with two saddles and a silver pot of some value. His library consisted mainly of Calvinist books but also contained Latin literature and some Hebrew and French. His Plato was a valuable one, worth thirty shillings (Leedham-Green, *Inventories*, I, 351–54). This was almost certainly the Serranus edition, since most other copies of the Plato *Opera* ranged from five to nine shillings.

Individual works of Plato recorded in the inventories included nine *Laws*, two *Gorgias*, two *Menexenus*, three *Timaeus* (but these are not Ficino's) and two *Divini Platonis Gemmae*, a tiny book of sayings put together by Liburnius in Venice (1530). One of the latter is ascribed, wrongly, to Ficino.

To sum up for Cambridge as a whole, although few of the early holdings of college libraries are documented on the union catalogue of the University, the individual libraries are repositories of much information, as are the books themselves when available. Inspection inventories drawn up by royal commissioners add to the picture, and probate valuation records for the goods of those scholars who died while still resident in the city offer fascinating, if highly select, glimpses. Among what was certainly a rapid increase of books in circulation during the Tudor period, we can find from all these records just a few copies of Ficino's translations and commentaries that survive in their original locations in Cambridge. We find traces of a few more, no longer extant, including the copy of his *Letters* at Pembroke. The original owners of these works, where they can be identified, were often men of considerable substance in the academic, ecclesiastic, or medical worlds.

3. Were the works of Plato available in versions other than Ficino's?

Reference has already been made to two copies of the Serranus (Jean de Serres, 1540–98) translations of Plato into Latin, published in three handsome folio volumes by Henri Estienne (Stephanus), whose numbering system is still standard for modern editions of Plato. These became prized editions in several libraries at the end of the sixteenth century and the first half of the seventeenth. The editors' intention was to correct Ficino's Neoplatonizing commentaries with a translation more rooted in Reformation thinking: Serranus and Stephanus were both Huguenots.

Serranus dedicated the first volume of this work to Queen Elizabeth, in gratitude for her help to the Huguenot exile community after the St. Bartholomew's Day Massacre of 1572. A copy was also sent to Sir Philip Sidney, who was living with his uncle, the Earl of Leicester, to whom Spenser was at that time secretary. Spenser would thus have been among the first to be familiar with this alternative version of Plato, not long after leaving the university.

In addition to the Serranus volumes, there were still medieval and early humanist copies of individual dialogues of Plato in circulation. For the *Timaeus*, Calcidius's partial rendering, dating back to the fourth century and popular throughout the Middle Ages, remained accessible. To it were now added the many works listed by Jayne (*Plato in Renaissance England*, Appendix 1a, 143–47) and discussed in detail by James Hankins in *Plato in the Italian Renaissance* (2 vols., Leiden: Brill, 1991). Among these are translations by Pier Candido Decembrio (*The Republic*), Leonardo Bruni (*Phaedo, Apology, Crito, Letters* and part of the *Phaedrus*) and Rinuccio Aretino (*Euthyphro* and the pseudo-Platonic *Axiochus*). Jayne shows that they were in Oxford, Cambridge, London, and some of the larger abbeys before the dissolution. Many ended up after the dissolution in the royal collections, and thus eventually in the British Library. They are sometimes over-looked because they circulated in manuscript rather than print, but given the small numbers of surviving and traceable printed works of Plato noted above, manuscript copies should by no means be dismissed from a role in spreading knowledge of Plato, especially in the fifteenth century. However, by the sixteenth century, it still seems likely that it was primarily Ficino's much-published versions in print that formed and shaped opinion, with or without their derivatives in French and Italian (see below); from 1578 onwards, those were supplemented by the alternative Serranus translation. A minority of scholars were also reading Plato in Greek, but quite possibly with the help of Ficino's introductory material.

4. Were the works of Plato available more widely to readers beyond Cambridge?

While Cambridge had particular importance for Spenser's formal education, London and Oxford were also significant centers of culture and learning, so that it was clearly desirable to extend the search for available texts. Since London had no university, the relevant holdings would be among royal libraries or the libraries of individual courtiers. Here James P. Carley's volumes in the *Corpus of British Medieval Library Catalogues* presented itself as a guide: specifically vol. 7, *The Libraries of King Henry VIII* (London: British Library, 2000). But in fact it yielded little. Ficino's Plotinus (Florence: 1492) was in the Upper Library at Westminster in 1542 (now in the British Library, IB 27193), together with an unspecified work of Plato, probably Ficino's *Opera Platonis* of 1484 (present whereabouts not given). The king's personal library, his "privy books," were not listed, and may account for some more titles—perhaps for some of the further British Library holdings, where early provenance information is often unavailable. Carley's later volume, *The Books of King Henry VIII and His Wives* (London: British Library, 2004), makes no mention of Ficino or Plato, but it is more of a popular overview than a detailed examination. Meanwhile London was a thriving commercial metropolis, with a resident Italian community and an established trade in the importation of books. Moreover, the presence of English scholars in Italy renders it quite likely that copies of important books found their way into royal and private collections, just as they did in other royal and ducal courts. It is frustrating that we have only isolated evidence of the presence of Plato in court circles, such as that in the library of John Dee at Mortlake. Dee, as we have seen, annotated his *Platonis opera* heavily; it also accompanied him on his travels. It is the working copies of such books that are of greatest interest, those owned by or accessible to scholars and writers.

Of the private libraries covered in Robert Fehrenbach and Elisabeth Leedham-Green's *Private Libraries in Renaissance England: A Collection and Catalogue of Tudor and Early-Stuart Book Lists* (Binghamton, NY: Medieval and Renaissance Texts and Studies, 1992), volumes 4 and 5, there are a few interesting entries. In Oxford, John Mitchel, servant to the Regius Professor of medicine, had an unspecified work of Marsilio Ficino and ten other books in 1572; Philip Johnson, taberdar of the Queen's College, Oxford, and later a fellow, had 300 books including a copy of *De vita* valued at three pence in 1576. The following year John Tatham, Dean of Merton and later Proctor of the University, in charge of Lincoln College, had another copy of it—or possibly it was the same one, for there is no way of knowing among these inventories how often the same books may reappear under new ownership. A copy of *De vita* was probably also owned by John Simpson, fellow of Exeter College, though it is listed as "Vicinius." He also owned a tiny book in 24ᵗᵒ called *Gemma Platonis*, attributed to Ficino but the same as Luburnio's *Divini Platonis Gemmae* listed above, here in a later edition (Paris: B. Prevost, 1554).

Ficino's *De vita* took on an apparently English garb when reissued by Timothy Bright (1550–1615) in a combined edition with his own *Hygieina: de sanitate tuenda* of 1581 and *Therapeutica* of 1583 (Frankfurt: Wechel, 1598). This threefold work, incorporating Ficino's *De vita*, and hence purveying a thoroughly Plotinian and Proclan world view, was intended to be of use to practicing physicians. Different versions of this collection exist, with or without the third book; but a copy in Cambridge University Library has all three (Frankfurt, 1598; shelfmark Keynes A.4.33). Bright's own medical interests included melancholy, on which Ficino was the leading authority. A Cambridge scholar, Bright had also studied abroad before moving to London, to St. Bartholomew the Less, where from 1573 and for just over twenty years he practiced medicine. It appears that he was not properly licensed to do so, as in court records of November 1587 he was sentenced in absentia: "Dr Bright, having often been summoned, and not appearing, was sent to prison, viz. to the Fleet." From 1594 he was a clergyman, and was later honored by Queen Elizabeth for his reinvention of shorthand (*Characterie*).

For the college libraries at Oxford, some publications are of particular use, especially J. R. Liddell, "The Library of Corpus Christi

College, Oxford in the Sixteenth Century," *The Library*, 4th ser., 18 (1938): 385–416. The Oxford volume of the *Corpus of British Medieval Library Catalogues* has not yet been published; but existing library catalogues were helpful and, as at Cambridge, college visits were valuable.

Some library holdings are on the borderline of relevance to our period: for example, Queen's College, whose library was entirely renewed in a later period, nevertheless has a 1580 Plotinus in sixteenth-century Oxford bindings (BB.y.320). We can thus narrow its arrival in Oxford down to around twenty years from 1580, but no closer. They also have a copy of the 1496 Florence edition of Ficino's Plato commentaries, but it came by bequest of Robert Mason, who died in 1841. There is no way of telling where it spent the intervening three hundred and fifty years. All Souls' has a copy of Ficino's Plotinus translation in the bilingual text edition of Pietro Perna (Basel, 1580) that carries on the title page the inscription "emit aere suo Anno 1582 mens. Decembr." However, the name is crossed out, and since the comment is in Latin, we cannot know the nationality of the original purchaser. The same book bears an additional manuscript quotation in Greek at the foot of the title page. Another copy of this work belonging to Merton is in sixteenth-century Oxford binding, but its only known provenance is later, from the library of the Idealist philosopher Francis Herbert Bradley (1846–1924). Keble College has a fine copy of the Plato commentaries (HJ 85; Florence: Lorenzo de Alopa, 1496); but it belonged originally to Nicholas Báthory, bishop of Vác in Hungary, friend of the author, and somehow made its way to Oxford between the end of the Turkish occupation of Buda in 1686 and the nineteenth century. (See Dennis E. Rhodes, "Battista Guarini and a Book at Oxford," *Journal of the Warburg and Courtauld Institutes*, 37 [1974]: 349–53.) Ruling out as many as possible of such volumes, the following tally of translations definitely in Oxford during Spenser's lifetime can be deduced.

Among books given to the library of St. John's College, which was founded in 1555 mainly for the education of clergy, is a small cluster of relevant items: Gabriel Dunne, who died in 1558, was the last abbot of Buckfast before its dissolution and later a canon of St. Paul's. He gave the college a fine copy of Ficino's translations of Plato in the 1551 edition of Froben from Basel (shelfmark Xx.3.19; see Fig. 4). The library itself was not built until 1596–98 but then attracted further gifts from scholars of Spenser's own generation who had valued their studies of Plato. Thus from the bequest of Henry Price, college librarian (died 1600), came a translation of Dionysius with commentaries (a volume which contains a small but important

Fig. 4.   Ficino's Plato translations (Basel: Froben, 1551) donated to
St. John's College, Oxford, in 1558 by Gabriel Dunne, last Abbot of
Buckfast, canon of St. Paul's Cathedral, London. By permission of the
President and Scholars of St. John Baptist College in the University of
Oxford.

contribution from Ficino) and a copy of Ficino's *Opera omnia* (Basel,
1576) which bears numerous annotations on his *De Christiana religione*
and *De vita*, as well as the short work on plague treatment (Price
seems to have been a physician). The two volumes of Ficino's *Opera*
(shelfmarks Gamma 1.13 and 14) bear marks that suggest they were
chained, and intended as a reference work. The fact that Price did
not annotate the second volume, although it contains Ficino's Plato
commentaries and *argumenta*, is less significant in view of the fact that
he had another copy of those: we know that he left Greek and Latin
copies of Plato and Aristotle to a Dr. Matthew Gwinne, physician
and literary luminary, who also took part in the debates with Giordano Bruno in 1583. It would naturally be of great interest were we
able to trace that volume of Ficino's Plato too, and to follow the
reading patterns of Price and Gwinne through any further annotations.

Another physician, Sir William Paddy (1554–1634), graduate of
St. John's College and physician to King James I, gave many hundreds
of his books to the library, including a copy of Ficino's Plotinus
translations (shelfmark Gamma 2.14; Basel: Thomas Guarin,
1559–this is the same edition as Pietro Perna). The date of these gifts
appears to be 1602. A copy of Antonio Telesio's *Libellus de Coloribus*
has part of Ficino's *Timaeus* translation bound in with it (also from
Price), and a further copy of Ficino's *De vita* is bound with Hippocra-
tes but in a copy whose provenance is unknown (HB4/4.a.5.20).
The library also has a Greek Plato with Proclus's commentaries on

Timaeus and *Republic* (Shelfmark Lambda 1.16; Basel: Valderum, 1534), the gift of Dr. Cole; and what at first sight looks like a 1569 copy of Ficino's *Platonic Theology* but which turns out to be a commentary on the first book of his *De vita* by the German schoolmaster and professor of medicine, Georg Pictorius (Basel: Henricpetri, 1569).

At Christ Church, the Cornarius Plato (shelfmark AB.1.14; Basel: Froben, 1561) was donated to the college by a D. (Dominus?) Willoughby, the year after its printing, in 1562. This is among the earliest gifts given to Christ Church whose library opened in that year. We know little of the donor, apart from the fact that he is said to have been Thomas Willoughby, an alumnus of Westminster School who became a student of Christ Church in 1569, some years after the gift. The book itself has been rebound.

Ficino's commentaries in his two-volume *Opera omnia* are also in Christ Church library, although one volume was catalogued long ago under the wrong date, and the other under the wrong title as *Sententiae Pulcherrimae* (Basel: 1576 edition; see Fig. 5). Both volumes bear the signature of Samuel Purchas, who matriculated from St. John's College in 1594 and graduated BA in 1597, MA in 1600. He entered the church and wrote accounts of travels all over the world without ever leaving England. He served as chaplain to the Archbishop of Canterbury from 1613 or 1614, that same George Abbot who had challenged Bruno in Oxford in 1583. Purchas's volumes bear his name; it is not known where or when he acquired them. Another Christ Church holding is an unusual Latin Plotinus (Basel: Ioannes Soter, 1540) which belonged to Arthur Bedell (fl. 1553–83) and is also signed Joannes Revin (shelfmark Hyp.L.59; see Fig. 6).

At Corpus Christi, Richard Fox (1448–1528), Bishop of Winchester and Henry VII's trusted advisor, gave two volumes of the first Aldine edition of Plato in Greek (shelfmark delta.5.13 and 14; Venice: 1513) to the college, and Ficino's *Opera Platonis* (Florence: Lorenzo Francisco de Alopa: 1484), although this bears an additional autograph note with the name Richard Porson.

Balliol has or had a number of the early fifteenth-century manuscript translations of individual Plato dialogues by Leonardo Bruni, Pietro Candido Decembrio, and Rinuccio Aretino. Two of these are now lost. Of printed books, a late gift of Iamblichus also bears a much earlier signature of Samuel Flemyng (shelfmark 0635e05; see Fig. 7). I have not yet been able to identify him. One member of a Flemming family, Robert (1416–83), who studied at Oxford, embraced humanist studies in Italy, leaving his books to Lincoln College; but he died before the Iamblichus was printed. Jayne mentions a Samuel Flemyng

Fig. 5. Ficino's *Opera omnia* (Basel: Henricpetri, 1576), title page of vol. 1, belonging to Samuel Purchas, by kind permission of the Governing Body of Christ Church, Oxford.

as a tutor using Plato at King's College in Cambridge (*Plato in Renaissance England*, 111).

New College has a copy, without provenance information, of Ficino's Plato translations (Venice, 1491). This is the edition that also contains Ficino's own *Platonic Theology*, not generally found in England outside the *Opera omnia*. There is also an Aldine Greek edition of Plato (Venice, 1513) in sixteenth-century bindings, as well as the Greek edition by Simon Grynaeus and Joannes Oporinus of Proclus's commentaries (Basel: Ioan. Valderum, 1534); but again, their provenance is unknown. The two volumes of Ficino's *Opera omnia* (Basel, 1576) both belonged to John Sharrock of Cornwall, who matriculated in 1582. A copy of Ficino's Plotinus (Florence: 1492) in Magdalen College (shelfmark Arch.B III.5.4) is without provenance information.

Jesus College's holdings, though of great interest in themselves (they include Edward Herbert's copy of Ficino's Iamblichus translation), were all donated to the college around or after 1640, with no

Fig. 6. Ficino's Plotinus translation (Basel: Ioannes Soter, 1540), belonging to Arthur Bedell (fl. 1553–1583), reproduced by kind permission of the Governing Body of Christ Church, Oxford.

certain English provenance prior to their immediate past owners. Queen's College has Grynaeus's edition of Ficino's Plato translations (Basel: Froben, 1546), provenance unknown; and a set of the Serranus Plato that had belonged to William Hutchenson, whom I have tentatively identified as the Rector of All Saints, Castle Camps, who was born in 1563 and died in 1604. He was a Doctor of Divinity and was under the patronage of the Earl of Oxford. Nine complete sets of the three-volume Serranus Plato arrived in Oxford college libraries at the end of the sixteenth century or beginning of the seventeenth.

5. Which other works of Ficino were available to English readers?

Among Ficino's own writings, his letters (*Epistolae*) deserve a special mention because of their accessibility to beginners in Platonic philosophy. Their presence was noted in Pembroke earlier (Robinson's

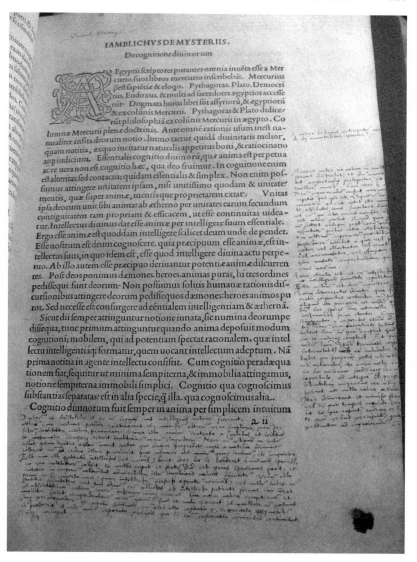

Fig. 7.   Ficino's Iamblichus (Venice: Aldus Manutius, 1497) first page, with marginal annotations later trimmed, and ownership signature of Samuel Flemyng, reproduced by kind permission of the Master and Fellows of Balliol College, Oxford.

copy). In Oxford, two copies of Ficino's *Letters* are of particular interest. These are both of the *editio princeps* (Venice: Capcasa, 1495). One, at All Souls' College, belonged to John Colet (1469–1519), who taught in Oxford, visited Italy, became Dean of St. Paul's and ultimately founder of St. Paul's School, famous for its program of classical education. This copy bears marginal notes throughout the volume as well as his own transcription of two letters to him from Ficino, written in 1499, and a draft of his own reply to the first (shelfmark L.R.4.d.19; see Figs. 2 and 8). The other copy of this work belongs to Corpus Christi (shelfmark Φ.A.3.4). In 1597 Richard Cobb, a graduate of the college and licensed preacher, bequeathed his copy of the *Letters* to his college; but it had been in England for a long time as it is inscribed by Johannis Godfridus, stating that he is a monk of Boxley Abbey in Kent, a Cistercian monastery that was dissolved in 1538. Godfridus also states that he paid 19 shillings and 7 pence for the book, suggesting that it was perhaps quite new when he bought it. Another hand bears the date 8 February 1530, but it is hard to know whether this is necessarily related to Godfridus's inscription.

A copy of the Ficino *Letters* in the smaller 4to size (Nuremberg: Anton Koberger, 1497, shelfmark Φ.C.1.13) was given to Corpus Christi by its founder Bishop Fox, who had also given the two volumes of Plato in Greek and Ficino's *Opera Platonis* mentioned above.

Ficino's *Opera omnia* already mentioned includes, besides the Plato and Plotinus commentaries and his versions of the later Platonists, several of his own works that had already been published separately (see note 2 in the accompanying essay). *De Christiana religione* was available in Latin (1476, 1500, 1507, 1510, 1518, 1559, and 1578) and Tuscan (1474, 1484, and 1568). His eighteen-book *Platonic Theology* had appeared in 1482, 1524, and 1559 and his *Letters* in 1495 and 1497. *De vita*, as already mentioned, enjoyed twenty-one editions. His short treatise in Tuscan on the treatment of plague had five editions, as well as being translated into Latin for the *Opera omnia*. Apart from *De vita*, the few copies of the *Letters*, and possibly the plague treatise, none of these individual works seem to have been acquired in England—or if they were, they either have not survived or cannot now be traced. But copies of the *Opera omnia* made all these works available.

The fact that Ficino's works were mostly in Latin would not have deterred an educated university reader, since Latin fluency was expected. For example, in 1573, a rule at Corpus required that Latin must be spoken at all times during full term, and a scholar would be

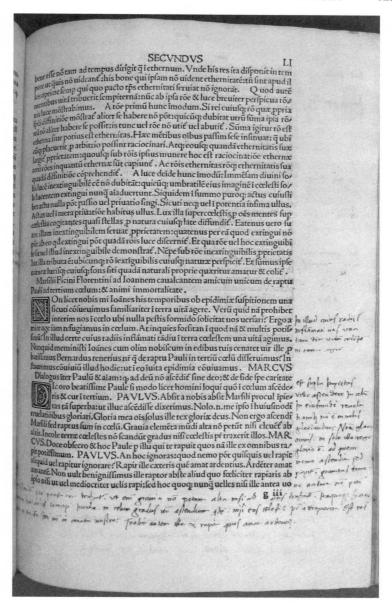

Fig. 8. Ficino's *Letters* (see fig. 2), John Colet's copy with his annotations on the *Rapture of St. Paul*, reproduced by kind permission of the Warden and Fellows of All Souls' College, Oxford.

"subject to the heaviest penalties for speaking English," which included being "beaten at the buttery hatch" (Corpus Christi College
archives). The French translations of Ficino's *Symposium* commentary
(*De amore*) are often said to have become as popular as the Latin
original or its Tuscan printed edition of 1544. Jean de la Haye
brought out a French translation in 1546 in 8vo format, and Guy
Lefèvre de la Boderie issued another French version of it in 1578
and 1589, following the success of his translations of two other works
by Ficino, *De la religion chrestienne* (1578) and *Les trois livres de la vie*
in 1582. Yet these books were almost totally absent from college
libraries, perhaps because of the currency of Latin there. If they were
read, they must have passed privately from hand to hand, as with
many other compact books.

CONCLUSION

Some copies of Ficino's work have certainly been lost, and others
perhaps destroyed or removed to quite unexpected locations, so that
any census of surviving traceable Tudor copies is bound to underesti-
mate Ficino's former currency in England. The purging of libraries
during the Henrician Reformation and the removal of potentially
incriminating books before visits of the Edwardian or Marian commissioners' visits may have added to the natural losses of the passing
years. Nevertheless, enough copies of Ficino's work remain to show
that his work was known in England during Spenser's youth, and the
speed with which Bruno's plagiarism was recognized is a powerful
confirmation. Some of these copies were in libraries, others in private
ownership. Many of the men who were reading Ficino were in positions of influence in the church and in the universities, some of them
also at court. They were men whose views would go on to influence
pupils and pupils' pupils over a considerable period of time. In addition, used copies of Ficino's works could change hands for relatively
small sums of money, making them affordable even to scholars of
modest means. The accessibility of Ficinian Platonism can therefore
now be accepted, and it scarcely needed to be part of an official
curriculum for its influence to be felt. Sixteenth-century desires to
read Plato, ways of approaching Plato, and practices of incorporating
Socratic wisdom into practical Christianity are at bottom unmeasur-
able, but it was certainly possible for Spenser to read Plato and to
have conversations about Ficinian Platonism from his student years
onwards.

Acknowledgements

In compiling this appendix I have been helped by many scholars to whom I acknowl-edge sincere gratitude. Dr. Elisabeth Leedham-Green, Fellow of Darwin College and Archivist of Corpus Christi, doyenne of studies on the university and its libraries in general, offered freely of her wisdom, insight, and practical assistance. I would also like to thank individually the librarians who fetched many tomes for inspection and who answered my endless questions with great patience and generosity: at Cambridge, Mrs. Patricia Aske, Librarian of Pembroke College; Miss Candace Guite and Mrs. Anne Keith, Librarians of Christ's College; Mrs. Karen Begg, Librarian, and Dr. Andrew Zurcher, Fellow, of Queens' College; Dr. Jonathan Harrison, Special Collections Librarian of St. John's College; Prof. David McKitterick, Librar-ian, and Miss Joanna Ball, Sub-Librarian, of Trinity College; in Oxford, Dr. Norma Aubertin-Potter, Librarian in Charge at All Souls'; Dr. Penelope Bulloch, Librarian of Balliol; Dr. Sara Wheale at the Bodleian Library; Dr. Cristina Neagu, Librarian at Christ Church; Dr. Anne Taylor, Acting Librarian at Corpus Christi, and Mr. Julian Reid, Archivist; Miss Sarah Cobbold, Librarian of Jesus College; Mrs. Marga-ret Sarosi, Librarian of Keble College; Dr. Christine Ferdinand, Librarian of Magda-lene College; Dr. Julia Walworth, Fellow Librarian of Merton College; Mrs. Amanda Saville, Librarian, Mr. Paul Ivanovic, Cataloguer of Rare Books, and Mrs. Veronika Vernier, Historic Collections Assistant, at the Queen's College; Dr. Naomi Van Loo, Librarian of New College; Dr. Malcolm Vale, Fellow Librarian, Mrs. Catherine Hilliard, Librarian, and Mrs. Ruth Ogden, Library Administrator at St. Johns Col-lege. Finally I would like to thank the editors of this volume of *Spenser Studies* for their unfailing interest and encouragement, without which this task would not have been undertaken.

Notes

1.   When Spenser entered Pembroke Hall in 1569, texts of Plato were available and Ficino's translations and commentaries were in use. In fact, to read Plato in the sixteenth century often meant to read Ficino. For discussion of the Cambridge curriculum and availability of specific works in England during the Tudor period, see the Appendix to this article.

2.   See *Gabriel Harvey's Marginalia*, ed. G. C. M. Smith (Stratford: Shakespeare Head, 1913), for a comment in his commonplace book that indicates reading of the *Letters* (105); for Ralegh's ownership of what is almost certainly Ficino's *Opera omnia*, see Walter Oakeshott, "Sir Walter Ralegh's Library," *The Library*, 5th ser., 23 (1968): 285–327, at 318. I am grateful to Kenneth Borris and Jon Quitslund for drawing these cases to my attention. The *Opera omnia*, published in Basel in 1561 and again in 1576, is a two-volume folio work gathering all of Ficino's own writings: *On the Christian Religion*; the *Platonic Theology*; his unfinished commentary on St. Paul's Epistles and some sermons; his *Letters*; an early treatise on *Pleasure*; the *argumenta*

and commentaries that had accompanied his translations of Plato and Plotinus; his *Three Books on Life*; and the translations of other Neoplatonic works: in other words, almost everything except the actual translations of Plato and Plotinus. Ficino's Plato translation, in some editions entitled *Omnia divini Platonis opera*, was a one-volume work; so was his Plotinus translation, sometimes entitled *Opera omnia Plotini*. Ralegh's list specifies a two-volume folio work.

3. George Abbot (1562–1633) was, at the time of Bruno's visit, a student at Balliol College. He later became a leading figure in the university (and from 1611 Archbishop of Canterbury). He described Bruno's visit some twenty years after the event in a book directed against Thomas Hill's *Quartron of Reasons of Catholike Religion* that had been secretly printed and was circulating widely. From the vividness of his account (a digression in his general argument against Hill) it would appear that Bruno's presence had made a strong impression on him: he eloquently derides Bruno's bombast, his ambition, appearance and Italian accent, and then relates how "a grave man, & both then and now of good place in that University, seemed to himselfe, some where to have read those things which the Doctor propounded; but silencing his conceit till he heard him the second time, remembered himselfe then, and repayring to his study, found both the former and the later Lecture, taken almost verbatim out of the works of Marsilius Ficinus." Abbot, *The Reasons Which Doctour Hill Hath Brought, for the Upholding of Papistry, . . . Unmasked and Shewed to Be Very Weake* (Oxford: Joseph Barnes, 1604) fol. 4v—5. Quoted in Robert McNulty, "Bruno at Oxford," *Renaissance News* 13.4 (Winter 1960): 300–305; see also Cristina Neagu, "Reading Copernicus: Giordano Bruno's Lectures at Oxford," *Christ Church Library Newsletter* 5.1 (Michaelmas 2008): 8–13. McNulty tentatively identifies the "grave man" in question as Martin Culpepper, who was Warden of New College at the time in question. Stressing the polemical nature of the description, Neagu presents a more positive view of Bruno's visit, but the basic fact that he was discovered appropriating Ficinian material is not in dispute.

4. Excellent introductory surveys can be found in *The Spenser Encyclopedia*, ed. A. C. Hamilton et al. (Toronto: University of Toronto Press, 1988). See especially Michael J. B. Allen, "Ficino"; Jon Quitslund, "Beauty" and "Platonism"; and Elizabeth Bieman, "*Fowre Hymnes*."

5. Josephine Waters Bennett, "Spenser's Garden of Adonis," *PMLA* 47 (1932): 46–80.

6. Brents Stirling, "The Philosophy of Spenser's Garden of Adonis," *PMLA* 49 (1934): 501–38.

7. Bennett's reply to Stirling is "Spenser's Garden of Adonis Revisited" in *JEGP* 41 (1942): 53–78. This was followed by Stirling's response, "Spenser's 'Platonic' Garden," ibid., 482–86, and a further rejoinder by Bennett, ibid., 486–89. The stanza at the heart of their contention was III.vi.36.

8. Sears Jayne, "Ficino and the Platonism of the English Renaissance," *Comparative Literature* 4.3 (1952): 214–38. Given the numerous editions of Ficino's work listed in the Appendix to this paper, Jayne's insistence on their unavailability seems exaggerated. Besides those noted in the Appendix, at least eight different works by Ficino appear in *John Dee's Library Catalogue* of 1583, ed. Julian Roberts and Andrew G. Watson (London: Bibliographical Society, 1990), and Dee made his collection

available to other readers. Despite Jayne's significant contribution to Ficino scholar-ship in rendering the *De amore* into English (see note 11), he has maintained a curiously prejudiced view of Ficino, right down to his most recent monograph, *Plato in Renaissance England* (Dordrecht: Kluwer, 1995). See also note 2.

9.   Robert Ellrodt, *Neoplatonism in the Poetry of Spenser* (Geneva: Droz, 1960), 118, 137–39.

10.   Castiglione's *Book of the Courtier*, first published by the Aldine press in Venice in 1528, was translated into English by Thomas Hoby in 1561 and was particularly important in England. See especially Bembo's last speech at the end of Book IV which presents several strands of Plato's philosophy of love and beauty as interpreted by Ficino. Thomas Elyot's *Boke Named the Governour* (London: T. Berthelet, 1531) had already paved the way for the reception of this, not least through his high valuation of Plato: "But aboue all other, the warkes of Plato wolde be most studiously radde whan the iugement of a man is come to perfection, and by the other studies is instructed in the fourme of speakynge that philosophers used. Lorde god, what incomparable swetnesse of wordes and mater shall he finde in the saide warkes of Plato and Cicero; wherin is ioyned grauitie with dilectation, excellent wysedome with diuine eloquence, absolute vertue with pleasure incredible, and euery place is so infarced with profitable counsaile, ioyned with honestie . . . " (I, 11).

11.   Ellrodt's work nonetheless remains a valuable resource, especially for informa-tion on some of the vernacular texts in which ideas of the Florentine Platonists were adapted and distributed in courtly circles across Europe during the sixteenth century: e.g., the writings of Castiglione, Leone Ebreo, Louis Le Roy, Mario Equicola, Pontus de Tyard, Guy Lefèvre de la Boderie, etc.

12.   Jon Quitslund, *Spenser's Supreme Fiction: Platonic Natural Philosophy and the Faerie Queene* (Toronto: University of Toronto Press, 2001). Landino's commentary on Virgil, published in 1481, was celebrated by Ficino in a song of praise (*Letters*, **5**:49) which was also published with Landino's work. The two men were closely related in thought and in friendship. Ficino is also a major character in Landino's *Disputationes Camaldulenses*. I cite the former's letters from *The Letters of Marsilio Ficino* (London: Shepheard Walwyn, 1975–), 8 vols., 9–12 forthcoming. Hereafter cited as *Letters*, with the volume number in bold Arabic (to distinguish from the Roman numerals of Ficino's own book-divisions, which are sometimes different), and the number of the letter within that volume. Page numbers are added parenthetically where neces-sary, in the case of long letters.

13.   Ficino used many new sources, ranging from the Greek Church Fathers to Neoplatonic texts of late antiquity. On his scholastic roots, see Paul Oscar Kristeller, "The Scholastic Background of Marsilio Ficino," *Traditio* 2 (1944): 257–318, re-printed in *Studies in Renaissance Thought and Letters* (Rome: Edizioni di Storia e Letteratura, 1969); idem, *Renaissance Thought and its Sources* (New York: Columbia University Press, 1979); Ardis Collins, *The Secular is Sacred* (The Hague: Martinus Nijhoff, 1974); Brian Copenhaver, "Scholastic Philosophy and Renaissance Magic in the *De Vita* of Marsilio Ficino," *Renaissance Quarterly* 37 (1984): 523–24. Some of Ficino's works (e.g., the *Platonic Theology*) are more scholastic in style than others (e.g., *De amore*, *De vita*, *Letters*).

14.   Syrithe Pugh, *Spenser and Ovid* (Aldershot: Ashgate, 2005).

15.   Harold L. Weatherby, *Mirrors of Celestial Grace: Patristic Theology in Spenser's Allegory* (Toronto: University of Toronto Press, 1994).

16.   James W. Broaddus, *Spenser's Allegory of Love: Social Vision in Books III, IV and V of "The Faerie Queene"* (Madison: Fairleigh Dickinson University Press, 1995).

17.   Richard Mallette, *Spenser and the Discourses of Reformation England* (Lincoln: University of Nebraska Press, 1997); Darryl J. Gless, *Interpretation and Theology in Spenser* (Cambridge: Cambridge University Press, 1994).

18.   Kenneth Borris, *Spenser's Poetics of Prophecy in "The Faerie Queene" V* (Victoria: University of Victoria Press, 1991); Patricia Coughlan, ed., *Spenser and Ireland: An Interdisciplinary Perspective* (Cork: Cork University Press, 1989).

19.   Besides the extensive scholarly literature on Ficino, many of his works can now be read in English translation. The first to appear—a reflection of its importance for English writers of the Renaissance—was Sears Reynold Jayne's translation of *De amore* (Columbia, MO: University of Missouri Press, 1944); he revised this extensively as *Marsilio Ficino: Commentary on Plato's Symposium on Love* (Dallas: Spring Publications, 1985). Next came an early treatise from Book II of Ficino's Letters, "Five Questions Concerning the Mind," translated by J. L. Burroughs in *The Renaissance Philosophy of Man*, ed. E. Cassirer, P. O. Kristeller and J. H. Randall (Chicago: University of Chicago Press 1948; reprinted 1956, 1971), 185–212, and reissued in *A Cultural Introduction to Philosophy from Antiquity to Descartes*, ed. J. J. McDermott (New York: Alfred Knopf, 1985), 637–46.

Translation of the complete series of letters (twelve volumes) was undertaken by members of the Language Department of the School of Economic Science, as *The Letters of Marsilio Ficino*. See note 12 above, which explains my citation system for this text.

Ficino's *Three Books on Life* should be read in the masterly edition of Carol V. Kaske and John R. Clark (Binghamton: Medieval and Renaissance Texts and Studies, 1989).

Michael J. B. Allen's many translations include several of Ficino's commentaries on Plato, *Marsilio Ficino: The Philebus Commentary* (Berkeley: University of California Press, 1975, revised 1979; rpt. Tempe, AZ: Medieval and Renaissance Texts and Studies, 2000); *Marsilio Ficino and the Phaedran Charioteer* (Berkeley: University of California Press, 1981); *Icastes: Marsilio Ficino's Interpretation of Plato's Sophist* (Berkeley: University of California Press, 1989); with James Hankins, the important *Platonic Theology*, 6 vols., (Cambridge MA: Harvard University Press, I Tatti Renaissance Library, 2001–06). Most recently, a new version of the *Phaedrus* and *Ion* commentaries has been published as the first in a series of Ficino's Plato Commentaries in the I Tatti Renaissance Library (2008).

Arthur Farndell has translated twenty-five of the shorter Plato commentaries and *argumenta* for Plato's letters as *Gardens of Philosophy* (London: Shepheard-Walwyn, 2006); four of the longer ones are presented in the same series: *Parmenides* as *Evermore Shall Be So* (2008), *Republic* and *Laws* as *When Philosophers Rule* (2009), and *Timaeus* as *All Things Natural* (forthcoming). The *Parmenides* commentary is also in preparation for the I Tatti series by Maude Vanhaelen, and my translation of his sermons and his commentary on the Epistles of St. Paul will appear in that series in due course.

Ficino's Plotinus commentaries, and his paraphrases of Iamblichus still await a translator, as do his extracts from Proclus, Dionysius, and Porphyry, though one extract from Porphyry, on Daemons, can be found in *Letters* **7**, 29. See also Brian Copenhaver, "Hermes Trismegistus, Proclus and the Question of a Philosophy of Magic in the Renaissance," in *Hermeticism and the Renaissance*, ed. I. Merkel and A. G. Debus (Washington: Folger Shakespeare Library, 1988), for Ficino's translation of Proclus on magic. For Hermes Trismegistus, three translations are useful. Though Ficino's own translation is not their starting point, they are from scholars deeply versed in Ficino: Brian Copenhaver, *Hermetica* (Cambridge: Cambridge University Press, 1992); *The Way of Hermes*, trans. Clement Salaman, Dorine van Oyen, William Wharton and Jean-Pierre Mahé (London: Duckworth, 1999); *Asclepius*, trans. Clement Salaman (London: Duckworth, 2007).

20.   The *Cantos of Mutabilitie* were added late to the published text, in 1609, ten years after Spenser's death.

21.   Ficino, *Letters*, **3**:18 (28). This letter, written before 1474 (possibly as early as 1469), accompanies his *Life of Plato*, and was intended as introductory material for the study of Plato. It originally formed part of his public lectures on Plato's *Philebus* but in 1477 Ficino added both this and the *Life of Plato* to his collection of letters. See Allen, *Philebus Commentary*, 8.

22.   Ficino, *Letters*, **7**:49, written to the lawyer and poet Ugolino Verino. Ficino is citing Plotinus's treatise on Providence, *Enneads*, III, 2 and 3. Plato speaks of man as the puppet of the gods in *Laws*, I:644–45.

23.   *Letters*, **7**:49.

24.   Ficino claims to have heard Alfonso's prophecy uttered in heaven, and is now translating it from the angelic tongue into the language of men. Alfonso's discourse is reminiscent of the significant father-to-son speeches in Virgil, *Aeneid*, VI:679–892; and the *Corpus Hermeticum*, books 4, 5, 8, 10, 12 and 13.

25.   *Letters*, **5**:13 (27).

26.   Ibid.

27.   Ficino collected the letters into twelve books for publication. They circulated in manuscript at first, but were printed in 1495 in Florence, and again soon after in Nuremberg in1497. Thereafter the letters were included in editions of the *Opera omnia*, which during Spenser's lifetime were published twice in Basel for the international book trade, in 1561 and 1576. For the availability of the *Letters* and the *Opera omnia* in the core collections of English libraries, suggesting that the letters were readily available during the sixteenth century, see note 8 above and Appendix.

28.   Ficino devoted much attention to the soul, writing his eighteen-book *Platonic Theology* to defend the immortality of individual souls. He also endorses the concept of a universal soul of the world. For him, the individual soul is "an everlasting ray of the eternal Sun"; it is incorporeal and divine in nature; it is linked to the body by *spiritus*. Because man is thus both corporeal and incorporeal, he stands on the horizon between the incorporeal and the physical worlds. The soul has powers, including pure intellect, will, and the five senses. See my section on Soul, and any of Ficino's writings, but perhaps especially *Letters*, **1**:110 and 115; **5**:13; *De amore* IV.3–4; and *Platonic Theology* passim.

29.   By "Angel" Ficino means that ontological level of first emanation from the One. It can be understood as the realm of Platonic ideas, and it allows a link between the unmoving One and the moving plural world of soul (which would otherwise

be irreconcilable opposites). Sometimes this world of "Angelic mind" is seen as the realm of ancient gods and stellar influences, filled with daemons doing their bidding; it is also the traditional realm of Christian angels conveying messages between God and man (see his sermon "On the Star of the Magi," *Letters*, **6**: Appendix).

30.   Some revealing passages in the *Platonic Theology* are IV.1.14 and XVIII.5; but see rather *De vita*, III, *passim*, where he pursues the correspondences between the heavenly aspects of these powers and human use of them. See also *Letters*, **5**:47.

31.   Virgil, *Aeneid*, VI.734.

32.   *Platonic Theology*, I.1.1.

33.   *Platonic Theology*, I.1.3.

34.   Although the Introduction was drafted in 1476 and is incorporated by Ficino into the second book of the Letters (*Opera omnia*, 706–16), the covering letter conveying it to Lorenzo appears in the third book (*Letters*, **2**:37). The text can now be read in an Appendix to the translation of *Platonic Theology* by Allen and Hankins, 6:220–75. It is called there (273) a "retrospective overview, a *praegustatio*," of the *Platonic Theology* that finally appeared in 1482. This *Argumentum* is not to be confused with the dedicatory Preface to Lorenzo that also accompanied the *Platonic Theology* proper in its final version.

35.   *Argumentum*, 221.

36.   Ibid., 241.

37.   In his last work, the *Commentary on the Epistles of St. Paul*, Ficino lays great stress on the separation of the mind from earthly concerns, in response to the text of St. Paul's experience of rapture. But throughout his life he maintains the essential integrity of the human person, mind, body and spirit, seeking to reassure people of the divine aspects of human nature and to increase its strength and power—even though the *Platonic Theology* begins from the premise that mankind can never be happy in life because the mind is never at rest, and the body is frail.

38.   These lines are inscribed below the title of the first *Canto of Mutabilitie* in the 1609 edition as "argument." The precise status of these cantos (this one is billed as part of Book VII) cannot be ascertained since it remains unknown whether they are in fact surviving fragments of a lost book. I am indebted to Andrew Zurcher for pointing out the unreliability of Spenser's agent after his death. Though seven is an unusual number of books for an epic, Giovanni Pico's *Heptaplus* affords an interesting model. Throughout, I cite Spenser's texts from his Variorum *Works*, ed. Edwin Greenlaw et al., 10 vols. (Baltimore: Johns Hopkins University Press, 1932–57), and abbreviate the *Hymnes'* titles *HL, HB, HHL, HHB*.

39.   *Faerie Queene*, VII.viii.2. The play on words between "Sabbaoth" and "Sabaoth" in line 9 may easily escape the modern reader familiar with a different system of Hebrew transliteration, but they refer respectively to the "Lord of Hosts" (*Tsevaot*) and the "Sabbath" (*Shabbat*).

40.   Plato, *Republic*, X.614–18, cf. Virgil, *Aeneid* VI.730–51. For the period of a thousand years spent journeying under the earth, see Plato, *Republic*, 615a; Virgil interprets the thousand years as a purification period for all souls.

41.   Jon Quitslund relates this passage to a distinction between the innate parts of the soul and the rational part of the soul which is infused from its supercelestial source; Spenser's verses therefore cannot be read as a simple recycling of beings. See

Supreme Fiction, 201–02. In *De Amore* IV.4, Ficino speaks of the twin lights of the soul, one innate and one infused from above, but elsewhere the distinction is less obvious, certainly not amounting to two "souls" (see note 28 above); the bodily aspect of soul is attributed rather to *spiritus*, which is neither wholly corporeal nor wholly incorporeal (described as "a body not a body, as it were" in his *De Vita*, III.3). On the innate and infused souls, see further Quitslund, *Supreme Fiction*, 252–55.

42.   Spenser calls the *Faerie Queene* a "darke conceit" in his dedicatory letter to Sir Walter Ralegh, dated 23 January 1589.

43.   For the steps or stages, see *Letters*, **1**, 123; *Platonic Theology*, 12.1.1; and the St. Paul Commentary, Preface.

44.   *Letters*, **3**:18 (31); see also my note 21. This passage has its basis in Plato's *Phaedrus*. See Allen, *Phaedran Charioteer*, esp. 100–102.

45.   For the separation of mind from body, see Ficino, *Letters*, **1**:110, 115 and 123; his Commentary on the Epistles of St. Paul, IV and IX, and *Platonic Theology*, XIII.2. Cf. the return from the light back to the darkened world in Plato's cave allegory to which Ficino often refers, *Republic*, VII.519d, and the return of the enlightened soul in *Corpus Hermeticum*, I.32. Ficino's views on cyclical return or palingenesis are harder to interpret, but see Carol Kaske, "Ficino's Pre-Incarnational Scenarios," in *Neoplatonism and the Arts*, ed. Liana Cheney and John Hendrix (Lewiston: Edwin Mellen Press, 2002), 53–64, at 54–55. See also Michael J. B. Allen, "Life as a Dead Platonist," in *Marsilio Ficino: His Theology, His Philosophy, His Legacy*, ed. Michael J. B. Allen and Valery Rees with Martin Davies (Leiden: Brill, 2002), 159–78.

46.   *Letters*, **1**:39.

47.   Cf. *Letters*, **2**:25.

48.   *Opera omnia*, 425.

49.   *Letters*, **3**:18 (31).

50.   See Appendix.

51.   *De amore*, IV.4, trans. Jayne (1985), 76. More extensive discussion of the descent of the soul occurs in many places, e.g., *Platonic Theology*, XVIII.4; Letters, X (*Opera*, 917); and in the commentary on *Enneads*, IV, 8, *Plotini opera* (Basel: Pietro Perna, 1580; facsim. rpt., Paris: Phénix, 2005) 468–76. For a detailed exposition related to Ficino's *Phaedrus* commentary, see Michael J. B. Allen, *The Platonism of Marsilio Ficino* (Berkeley: University of California Press, 1984), 165–84.

52.   My prior section points out that Una and the Garden of Adonis open windows into the divine realm. Several other such moments of glimpsed potential have been suggested to me by Kenneth Borris, such as the vision of New Jerusalem that Contemplation affords to Redcross (I.x.46ff), the manifestation of the Graces to Colin Clout on Mount Acidale (VI.x.4–30), and the allegorical apotheosis of Pastorella at Belgard (VI.xii.3–22). On the latter, see Borris, "Sub Rosa: Pastorella's Allegorical Homecoming, and Closure in the 1596 *Faerie Queene*," *Spenser Studies* 21 (2006): 133–80.

53.   Spenser's own dedicatory letter suggests that the first two hymns are from his youth, and the latter two more recent and a retraction. There are however grounds for treating them as a unit. Cf. Spenser's Variorum *Works*, 7:657–62.

54.   *De amore*, VI.10, trans. Jayne (1985), 126.

55.   Ficino, following Plato, is talking mainly here of the love between an older and a younger man. But the same process *mutatis mutandis* applies to the love between a man and a woman with which Spenser is concerned.

56. *De amore*, VI.10, trans. Jayne (1985), 129–30.

57. *Letters*, **1**:7 (44).

58. Summary of *Protagoras*, trans. Farndell, *Gardens of Philosophy*, 66.

59. Summary of *Hippias*, or "On the Beautiful and Noble," trans. Farndell, *Gardens of Philosophy*, 28. Diotima's teaching to Socrates is again specifically cited.

60. Like Ficino, Spenser often treats love as the desire for beauty. Cf. *Letters*, **1**:42: "The soul, consumed by the divine brilliance which shines in the beauteous man as though in a mirror, is seized unknowingly by that brilliance and is drawn upward as by a hook, so that the soul becomes God."

61. Ficino, *De amore*, II.2.

62. *De amore*, VII.17.

63. The translation, entitled *Sopra lo amore o ver Convito di Platone*, was made by Ficino for Bernardo Nero and Antonio Manetti, but was not published in print until 1544.

64. 1 John 4:16.

65. *Letters*, **7**:41 (48). The following few quotations are all from this "letter" (which was in fact a sermon).

66. For a recent discussion, see John Dillon, "The Platonic Sage in Love," *Studia Humaniora Tartuensia* 4.B.3 (2003): 1–8 (available online at http://www.ut.ee/klassik/sht/2003/dillon1.pdf).

67. *Letters*, **7**:41 (49–50).

68. *Letters*, **7**:56, entitled "To know God we should begin with love for God."

69. *Letters*, **6**:42 (55).

70. Ibid.

71. It is entitled "He who transforms human love into divine is transformed from man into God."

72. *Letters*, **6**:42 (56).

73. See, e.g., Broaddus, *Spenser's Allegory of Love*.

74. See my article "Ficino's Advice to Princes" in *Marsilio Ficino: His Theology, His Philosophy, His Legacy*, 339–57.

75. Ficino expands on the Platonic figure of the philosopher-king (*Republic*, V, 473d) in several letters, and in his introduction to Plato's *Statesman*; but a particularly interesting discussion of where "philosopher" and "ruler" overlap is found in his summary of a work now no longer ascribed to Plato, which Ficino calls the "Book on Philosophy or the Lover." There he says, "The philosopher's function is to know the divine and govern the human: the first aspect includes contemplative philosophy, while the second embraces practical philosophy. The philosopher first contemplates, through wisdom, the divine or absolute nature of the Good. Then he governs human affairs by directing men's activities towards their end in this Good. But there are two prerequisites for this. The first is a recognition of what human nature is and of how it is delivered from evil and led to the Good: this condition the Philosopher meets through insight. The second is putting in order people's attitudes and actions, moderating and restraining them in such a way that they easily incline towards the Good. . . . The government of human affairs rests on these two conditions." Trans. Farndell, *Gardens of Philosophy*, 10.

76. *Platonic Theology*, III.2.3.

77. Ficino, *De amore* III.3, trans. Jayne (1985), 67; but adapted following Michael J. B. Allen, "Marsilio Ficino's Interpretation of Plato's *Timaeus*," in his *Plato's Third Eye* (Aldershot: Ashgate, 1995), XI, 400.

78. *Letters*, **1**:4.

79. *Letters*, **1**:116.

80. *Letters*, **1**:7. This letter was written in 1457 to Peregrino Agli, in response to receiving some verses from him. Ficino was twenty-four years old, and Agli several years younger. In a forthcoming paper, I plan to discuss their relationship, and a lengthy hymn of praise written in Sapphic stanzas by Ficino.

81. *Letters*, **1**:7 (46).

82. Ficino, *Epistolae* XI.24, *Opera omnia*, 933–35.

83. For example, *Letters*, **1**, 1; **4**, 11. Ficino's skill with the lyre was described by Bishop Campano: "If curly-haired Apollo should play upon Marsilio's cithara, Apollo would fall defeated in both dexterity of hand and singing. There is frenzy; when he sings, as a lover to the singing of his beloved, he plucks his lyre in harmony with the melody and rhythm of the song. Then his eyes burn, he leaps to his feet, and he discovers music which he never learnt by rote." (Marsilii citharam crispus si tentet Apollo | Et dextra et cantu victus Apollo cadet | Et furor est, cum cantat amans cantante puella | Ad flexum, ad nutum percutit ille lyram | Tunc ardenti oculi, tunc planta exsurgit utraque | Et quos non didicit, comperit ille modos.) Kristeller, *Supplementum Ficinianum*, II:230. See also D. P. Walker, "Le Chant Orphique de Marsile Ficin," in *Musique et poésie au XVe siècle* (Paris: Colloques internationaux de CNRS, 1954), 17–28; and "Ficino's *Spiritus* and Music," *Annales Musicologiques* 1 (1953): 131–50; both reprinted in his *Music, Spirit and Language in the Renaissance*, ed. Penelope Gouk (London: Ashgate, 1985); see also Angela Voss, "*Orpheus redivivus*: The Musical Magic of Marsilio Ficino," in *Marsilio Ficino: His Theology, His Philosophy, His Legacy*, 227–41.

84. *Letters*, **4**:11.

85. *Letters*, **7**:29 (36). This letter mainly consists of a translation of Porphyry's work *On daemons* which Ficino produced some time between 1486 and 1488.

86. For an excellent discussion of this apparent disparity, see Michael J. B. Allen, *Synoptic Art* (Florence: Leo Olschki, 1998), 93–123.

87. For example, *Letters*, **3**:26, **4**:48, and his commentaries on *Phaedrus* and the *Republic*. The wings motif also occurs in many other places, e.g., at the opening of his *De Christiana religione* of 1474, representing the necessary combination of love and reason.

88. *Letters*, **6**:42 (56).

89. For the fables on pleasure, see Allen, *Ficino: The Philebus Commentary*, 454–79. Ficino later replaced them with other material but added them to the tenth book of his Letters.

90. *Letters*, **6**:11–16 and 22–24.

91. See *Letters*, **7**:19.

92. *Letters*, **2**:3 (9).

93. Ficino is also an important transmitter of much traditional material of a more Aristotelian or Patristic hue. His use of scholastic arguments from Thomas Aquinas has been mentioned above. For Patristic elements in Spenser, see note 15. However

the emphasis here has necessarily been on Ficino's relevance to Spenser's engagement with Platonism.

94.   Besides Castiglione, Leone Ebreo, and Guy Lefèvre de la Boderie, this would include Ronsard, Du Bellay, and perhaps even Giordano Bruno.

95.   His translations included Hermes Trismegistus, Plotinus, Iamblichus, Porphyry, some Proclus and Dionysius as well as the ubiquitous Plato. Ellrodt has listed the French editions of Plato available to Spenser and his readers in *Neoplatonism*, 224–27. By 1592, there were twenty-three editions of Ficino's full Latin translations of Plato in print: six published in Italy, five in Basel and one in Geneva, besides eleven in France (from Paris and Lyons). For these and a complete list of his other works see Kristeller, *Supplementum Ficinianum*, lvii—lxxv; updated in *Marsilio Ficino and His Work after Five Hundred Years*, 112–21. The key collection of Iamblichus and other Platonists was published by the Aldine press in 1497 and again in 1516, and was followed by four further printings in Lyons during the sixteenth century. Hermes was printed sixteen times (in addition to inclusion in the *Opera omnia*), including editions in Paris, Cracow and Hamburg as well as Italy. The *Three Books on Life* had no less than twenty-seven editions by the end of the 1590s. For the availability of these works in England, see Appendix.

96.   See the *Letter to Ralegh* of 1589 accompanying the *Faerie Queene*, which expounds to some extent the purpose of his allegory or "dark conceit."

97.   These affinities can be followed in several annotated editions of the *Hymnes*, such as *Edmund Spenser's Poetry*, ed. Hugh Maclean, 2nd ed. (New York: Norton, 1982); *Spenser: Fowre Hymnes, Epithalamion*, ed. Enid Welsford (Oxford: Blackwell, 1967); *The Shorter Poems of Edmund Spenser*, ed. William Oram et al. (Yale: Yale University Press, 1989); and *Edmund Spenser: The Shorter Poems*, ed. Richard A. McCabe (London: Penguin, 1999). See also the *Spenser Encylopedia* articles cited in note 4 above. Even Ellrodt, though minimizing Spenser's Platonism, acknowledged that evidence of close study of learned Florentine Platonic views on love and beauty appears in the *Hymnes* and some of the *Amoretti* (*Neoplatonism*, 118, 121, 211–13).

EUGENE D. HILL

Everard Digby: A Syncretic Philosopher at Spenser's Cambridge

This essay affords a look at intellectual activity in the Cambridge of Spenser's day by way of an introduction to a large Neo-Latin volume of metaphysics entitled the *Theoria Analytica*, published by Everard Digby in 1579. Digby's defense of metaphysics against the Ramist assault thereupon is explored, along with his remarkable efforts to read Neoplatonic mysteries (including alchemy and Kabbalah) into the *Posterior Analytics* of Aristotle. The structure of Digby's tome exhibits similarities to patterns detected by Spenserians of a numerological bent. In its overall linkage of Platonic and Aristotelian themes and in its epistemology of identification—by which the reader is formed into the likeness of what he reads—the *Theoria* exhibits striking affinities with Spenser's *Faerie Queene*. Everard Digby, Spenser's Cambridge contemporary, has furnished us with a virtual charter for the poet's allegorical invention.

*I*N 1579 A PAIR OF SCHOLARS, each with degrees from Cambridge earlier in the decade, published a first book. For Edmund Spenser, that book was *The Shepheardes Calender*, and it opened a career honored now by bookcases of scholarly investigations and two professional journals. For the other young man, Everard Digby (not to be confused with the unrelated namesake a generation later, a Gunpowder conspirator), the book was the *Theoria Analytica*, and this extensive Latin treatise on logic and metaphysics would be largely forgotten, commemorated at length only in a pair of unpublished doctoral dissertations defended, with odd simultaneity, in 1980.[1] Spenser and Digby are not known to have been acquainted, though Digby was something of a character, notorious in later years for his in-college pranks and already in the 1570s a well regarded young

teacher of philosophy, who might well have attracted Spenser's atten-
tions. More importantly, though, the *Theoria* bears important witness
to the ways one Elizabethan Platonist practiced a vigorous syncretic
approach to ancient philosophy, uniting Aristotelian and Platonic
terms and themes in a way familiar to readers of *The Faerie
Queene*—that insistently Neoplatonizing romance built on a foundation of Neo-Aristotelian ethical categories. The *Theoria* affords us a
look at what ideas came to mind, and what books came to hand, in
Platonizing circles at Cambridge in the 1570s. If one wished to invent
a figure who could show us something of Plato-spinning during
Spenser's university days, one would invent somebody like Everard
Digby.

The neglect of the *Theoria* can be readily understood, of course.
Even the full title makes the point: *Theoria Analytica, Viam ad Mon-
archiam Scientiarum demonstrans, totius Philosophiae & reliquarum Scientiarum, necnon primorum postremorumque Philosophorum mysteria arcanaque
dogmata enucleans. In tres libros digesta.*[2] Few readers today will tackle
a book offering well over four hundred pages of scholastic Latin.
Who now has the taste—or the genius—of the young Leibniz, who
read scholastic metaphysics (as he later recalled) with a pleasure akin
to that of reading a novel?[3]

Digby was controversial in the 1580s for his attack on the fashionable Ramist philosophy, of which attack more below. But Digby was
forgotten by the seventeenth century, not to be seriously explored
until Charles de Rémusat came upon the *Theoria* in preparing his
Histoire de la philosophie en Angleterre depuis Bacon jusqu'à Locke (2nd
ed., 1878). As an historian of philosophy, Rémusat looks for anticipa-
tions of ideas with a future; thus he links Digby on the mind with
Leibniz. But he rightly views as Digby's "pensée fondamentale . . .
celle d'une ressemblance, d'une correspondence, d'une certaine iden-
tité entre la nature et l'esprit, entre le monde et l'intelligence, entre
les objets et les idées." And he aptly admires the web of analogy
that dominates the *Theoria*: "Le symbole, la métaphore, en un mot
l'imagination figurative, envahit sa cosmologie, sa théologie, sa psy-
chologie."[4]

The case for Digby was challenged some dozen years later by
another erudite historian of philosophy, Jakob Freudenthal of Breslau,
who demonstrated something Rémusat had missed: much of Digby's
learning, many of his impressive citations in the *Theoria* that had
impressed the Frenchman, came from intermediate sources—in particular from the kabbalistic dialogues of Johannes Reuchlin. For the
German there is nothing original, and nothing of interest, in Digby,

just dead medieval ideas in rebarbative late Scholastic language. Freudenthal heaps particular scorn on Digby's substantial neglect of "clear-thinking humanists" in favor of *Schwärmgeister*—superstitious enthusiasts, among whom the professor at Breslau numbers Ficino.[5] Freudenthal extinguished the briefly renewed interest in Digby—perhaps appropriately for philosophers, but most regrettably for *seizièmistes*, in particular those who want to know about Platonism in Elizabethan Cambridge, for whom Ficino is a master and not a superannuated denizen of medieval thought.

More recent work has not done much for Digby, who goes unmentioned in Copenhaver and Schmitt's *Renaissance Philosophy* (1992) and is only glancingly treated in Schmitt and Skinner's *Cambridge History of Renaissance Philosophy* (1988). Schmitt, though, was quite generous to Digby in his book *John Case and Aristotelianism in Renaissance England* (1983), where he remarks: "Digby's treatise has some claim to be considered the first British philosophical work since the Middle Ages to be addressed to a learned international audience"; "it is the first serious, published philosophical work in Britain after the coming of the Reformation."[6] Schmitt's half-dozen pages on the *Theoria* only begin to suggest the work's interest and do not broach its significance for students of Elizabethan poetry in general, and Edmund Spenser in particular.

So there is good reason to attempt here to sketch the key motifs and leading themes of Digby's neglected 1579 tome. Let us begin at the beginning, with my own translation (literal, all too painfully literal) of the initiating movement of the *Theoria*. Digby's preface to the book begins with this assertion about the *Posterior Analytics*:

> Reading through Aristotle's exceptional work about demonstration, after long contemplation, I seemed to comprehend . . . the very beginnings of knowledge [*scientiae primordia*]. When these were properly understood and stored deep in my mind, I found that what I frequently accepted as a borrowing from the wisest men was true: in Aristotle something lies hid [*aliquid latere*] which does not appear at first glance, and which—drunk deep rather than tasted—gives delight.
>
> (*Theoria*, sig. A1r.)

Digby believed that Aristotle was the author of the *Liber de causis*, though that work is in fact, as Thomas Aquinas recognized, an Arabic paraphrase of the *Elements of Theology* of Proclus. Digby was, accordingly, prepared to find the emanationist metaphysics of the *De causis* hidden in the seemingly naturalistic Aristotelian corpus. This notion of latency ("*aliquid latere*") is the crucial one for Digby. The "wisest men" who held such a view are not specified at this point, but from his book as a whole there can be little doubt that Digby had in mind Reuchlin and Lefèvre d'Etaples. The latter could not be more explicit on the matter. Lefèvre wrote: "It should not be hidden from you [*te latere non debet*] that through all the philosophy of Aristotle there is a certain hidden and latent secret analogy [*abditam latentemque esse quandam secretam analogiam*]." Even when Aristotle seems to be talking about transitory things, he is laboring at something weightier: he is in fact talking "also of divine things [*pariter divina tractare*]." I have been quoting from Lefèvre's Preface to the Paraphrase on the *Physics* (1492), but similar language can be found in the Frenchman's edition of the *Metaphysics* (1515): "in this work the highest divine things are adumbrated under the covers of natural things, like fire in flint." In his metaphysics, Lefèvre asserts, Aristotle transmitted the *divina mysteria* of the Egyptian priests and the Chaldean magi; and, in the Preface to his edition of the Organon (1501), Lefèvre makes the same claim for logic.[7]

So the "wisest men" Digby praises in beginning his book are Reuchlin and Lefèvre—masters of early sixteenth-century high syncretic Platonism. But who are the proponents of "today's method of learning and teaching arts," for whom this view of Aristotle as latently Neoplatonic smacks of irrelevant near-mysticism—*Schwärmerei* of the first water? Here a bit of intellectual history must be reviewed.

As Cesare Vasoli has shown in *La dialettica e la retorica dell'Umanesimo* (1968), the sixteenth century produced a school of thinkers whose object it was to free logic from the metaphysical implications it held for mystical Neoplatonists like Lefèvre. For these thinkers logic was not a key to the hidden structure of a multileveled world, but a tool for the construction of human discourse. In place of a logic of demonstration, they developed a logic of a distinctly rhetorical character. Authors of this school had either to reject the *Posterior Analytics* or to reinterpret the work to meet their needs.

The first alternative was chosen by Marius Nizolius in his *De veris principiis et vera ratione philosophandi contra pseudophilosophos* (1553). In this volume Nizolius calls for "the demolition of Dialectics and Metaphysics by their very roots . . . so that they will never be able to revive."[8] The *oracula* and the *arcana* of traditional metaphysics are at once useless and false. In their place Nizolius would establish rhetoric as a new logic of the concrete. As for the *Posterior Analytics*, Nizolius needs only a brief chapter to demolish "a book not only composed by Aristotle in vain, but also to the great detriment of students of philosophy, who are constrained to spend good hours on nonsense of no moment." Nizolius writes:

> I do not know how so many interpreters, who have interpreted these trifles, and so many men, who read them to this day, have been so stupid and so blind as not to see nor to understand, that in this entire book of Aristotle, nothing else is involved but what does not exist and cannot be related or taught, and that the whole human race has been deceived and deluded by this veritable fable.[9]

The second alternative, that of reinterpreting the *Posterior Analytics*, was adopted quite explicitly by Philipp Melanchthon. In a text of 1518, Melanchthon recalls having advised his teacher and friend Franciscus Stadianus, who was setting out to read the *Posterior Analytics*, that "therein Aristotle was teaching rhetoric [*illic ab Aristotele Rhetorica doceri*]."[10]

Peter Ramus may be said to have combined these two positions: he both denigrated the *Posterior Analytics* and reinterpreted the work to suit his own purposes. In the *Aristotelicae Animadversiones*, Ramus attacks the Aristotelian theory of demonstration:

> O false and sophistic glory of demonstration: for so many years demonstration has been engaged in lust with the adulterous sophists of all good disciplines, but has not yet given birth to any knowledge [*ullam scientiam*], but has contaminated all realms of knowledge [*omnes*] with its miscarriages. Let it be called therefore harlot, not mother; for there is hardly a discipline in which the insane lust for demonstrating, i.e. for obscuring (thus the Aristotelians speak, ironically) has not brought on heavy shadows.[11]

Rejecting the primacy of demonstration, Ramus nonetheless insists upon the importance of analysis, which he calls "the life and soul of the logical art." "For analysis," he writes, "is the touchstone by which we may test logical gold." But Ramus holds a quite restricted notion of analysis. Here is the definition he offers: "Logical analysis is the examination and the exploration of a disputation already invented and arranged." Analysis is not limited to one art,

though stringent Aristotelians wrongly accord pride of place to geometrical analysis. Rather, analysis is the *"pars exercitationis* in every
art, both first and last."[12]

Ramus insists that it is *he* who is the real Aristotelian, since (as he
says) "I refer the entire logical art to analysis." He believes that
the self-professed Artistotelians actually spurn their master's teaching,
since they refuse to present analysis as a practical exercise, one best
carried out (Ramus insists) on passages from good poets and orators.
Indeed, by analysis, the Frenchman seems often to mean little more
than *explication de texte.* By means of analysis, he writes, "we examine
and unweave a disputation."[13]

Ramus remarks that commentators believe that the "obscurity [of
the *Analytics*] pleased Aristotle"; but they are wrong. "All of logic,
which is contained in the *Analytics*" (Ramus rejects the division between Prior and Posterior), "is *per se facillima . . . et clarissima,* though
it is now rendered difficult and obscure by various clouds." These
"interposed clouds" will melt away if one bears in mind the definition
of logic as the *ars bene disserendi.* The art has two parts, invention and
disposition; and disposition is the same as judgment, or analysis. The
Analytics may be a disordered work, but from it one simple principle
may be derived. If one arranges one's arguments in descending order
of natural priority, one will construct a suitably perspicuous discourse.
And that is the function of logic, the "art of arguing well."[14]

This attempt on Ramus's part to separate analysis from invention
was bitterly contested by Jacques Charpentier, a professor at the Sor-
bonne whom Digby held in the highest esteem. Carpentarius (to
follow Digby for once in giving the Latin version of the name) insists
that "the analytical art" of Aristotle "pertains not less, but perhaps
even more, to investigation, than to explaining what has already
been found." Charpentier holds that there is for "intelligent" readers
"nothing more admirable" in the Organon than the *Analytics.* Against
Ramus, Charpentier reasserts that the *Analytics* provides the techniques for exact demonstration, not merely for ordering what one
knows.[15]

The same view of the *Posterior Analytics* was taken in what was
Digby's preferred commentary on the Organon, that of the Academy
of Louvain. In the introduction to its treatment of the *Posterior Analytics,* the Louvain volume asserts that "since knowledge [*scientia*] is
acquired only through demonstration, this discipline—expressing
demonstration and natural reason—is certainly to be used by anyone
who is thinking about finding any new knowledge and bringing it
to light."[16]

This sketch of the sixteenth-century debate about the *Posterior Analytics* allows us to return to the opening sentence of Digby's Preface with heightened understanding. An informed contemporary reader would have recognized what Digby was up to: he was combining Lefèvre's theory of the mystical latency of the Aristotelian text with Charpentier's defense against the Ramists of the *Posterior Analytics* as a tool for discovery. In sum, the *Theoria* represents an effort to read metaphysics as the latent meaning of logic. Such a venture goes counter to Ramus's persistent efforts to downgrade metaphysics at the expense of dialectic. Indeed, one of the best students of sixteenth-century thought, Peter Petersen, could say that Ramism lacked a metaphysics: "dem Ramismus . . . fehlte die Metaphysik."[17] Walter Ong makes the same point when he notes that "there is no room for metaphysics as such in the Ramist canon."[18]

In his *Scholae metaphysicae* Ramus acknowledges that Aristotle wished to establish "a certain art, the greatest of all, different from logic." But he was, Ramus asserts, wrong to do so, and his books of metaphysics are mere "heaps of logical tautologies." Aristotle's *Metaphysics* is "nothing but logic obscured by many logical and some theological sophistries." The general science that Aristotle sought in his *Metaphysics* is in fact, the Frenchman holds, dialectic. But "theology"—here as often a synonym for metaphysics—"is not the most general art but, on the contrary, the most specific of all arts." In his commentary on the *Metaphysics*, Ramus repeatedly finds that the attempt at linking logic with theology results in confusion and needless difficulty.[19] Digby insists upon maintaining the link and working through the difficulty, with frequent gibes at the perverters and deniers of transmitted wisdom. Have we not, the Cantabrigian asks, neglected mature fruit ripened by the sun of wisdom and "as unclean pigs are wont to do," devoured "the acrid, unripe, putrid, corrupt fruit" of torn boughs?[20] Few Elizabethan university folk would have missed the target here: "boughs" is of course, in the Latin, *ramos*.

It is Ramus who is "the perverter [*inversorem*] of our youth," "the distorter [*contortorem*] of every *scientia*." Understanding nothing himself, he wishes to ensure that his followers also understand nothing. And he has fascinated the minds of youth, easily diverted by a pleasing surface, and drawn them away from the mistress [*domina*] they should be pursuing: she is no less than "the art of arts, the science of sciences [*scientiarum scientiam*], the investigator of things occult, the doctrine of perfect things, the messenger of divine things."[21]

The hyperbolic language here provides a taste of the Digbeian rhetoric. Suffice it to say that the author of the *Theoria* proposes to follow Aristotle in resolving (the analysis of the title) phenomena into a few overarching principles. In the Preface these principles remain unspecified. But Digby does note that Aristotle "insinuates that he has kept silent many things" about which he had speculated, though "many vestiges of such speculation exist in his writings." Indeed, Digby remarks, when teaching the *Posterior Analytics*—"a book to whose explication I was so much given over"—at Cambridge, he has looked beyond the Philosopher's words to his intended meaning:

> I divined a certain higher and simpler notion of the principle than I was able to observe formed or expressed in the words of the Philosophers, containing every complex of notions, surpassing dignity, transcending universality, and finally through its splendor sending forth noble lights under the pale shade of Erebus and dispelling deep night.

This truth will be like the unique ray of Titan, illuminating the entire globe. Only traces of it are to be found in Aristotle, diffused here and there. With this talk of "an uncovering of the divine ray" and of a science even beyond Aristotle,[22] Digby is hinting at the kabbalistic theory he will expound at the core of the *Theoria*.

For readers of Spenser three aspects of Digby's book merit presentation: the treatise's overall structure; its account of epistemology; and its treatment of esoteric sciences, in particular of alchemy and of Kabbalah.

Digby's Preface offers, in his inimitable prose, an account of the book's structure:

> It has three parts. The first is the ascent from the proposed question, or conclusion knowable through discursive demonstration, through complex and incomplex principles, ascending by way of apprehension to the first notion *simpliciter*, which is the first scientific *lumen simpliciter*. The second is the demonstration by the *radii* emitted from the first *lumen*, showing in what manner the *lumen* is absolutely in itself, and how it goes out from the principle into the universal intelligence, diffusing itself successively. By what grades, and with what measure Angels, Spirits, Daemons, and Men are illuminated by the first, which is the first notion and perception of our intelligence, by which we understand that we know and know that we understand. The third teaches the effect of the two preceding, which is

scientia and the species thereof, of which this like a general instrument is the demonstrative and artificial fashioner of all conclusions in all matters.[23]

Resisting the temptation to respond "You can say that again, Randy," I wish to put the trajectory Digby specifies here into more accessible language. The *Theoria* begins with continual ascent; in its central book a commanding perspective is attained; the conclusion of the work combines descent with knowledge and self-knowledge. The book, that is to say, enacts a journey out and back—a circular journey. Indeed, the *Theoria* exhibits precisely that form—variously called circular, recessed or ring form—whose significant presence in Elizabethan poetry has been demonstrated by major scholarship of the past half century.

In a recent book the late Mary Douglas explains that the construction of a full-scale "ring is a triumph of chiastic ordering."[24] The basic structure represents an expansion of the ABCBA pattern familiar in musical composition; Fowler speaks of "a return to things previously mentioned (or things resembling them) in reverse order" and adduces Cedric Whitman's analysis of the ring composition of the *Iliad* as a structure of what Fowler calls "recessed symmetries."[25] In her chapter "How to Construct and Recognize a Ring," Douglas provides seven identifying criteria, including parallel sections and what she calls "central loading"—this last being the equivalent of Fowler's numerological center, often the triumphator at the middle of the triumph.[26]

In his monograph of 1960, A. Kent Hieatt showed that a template of this sort gave meaningful shape to Spenser's "Epithalamion." A persistent balancing of elements equally distant from the center (Books I and VI, II and V, III and IV) was found in *The Faerie Queene* by James Nohrnberg in a major book of 1976. Fowler finds numerical and spatial patterns of this kind "almost universal [among poets] in the period 1580–1680."[27] So we are dealing with a principle of structuring widely instantiated in the period, perhaps most brilliantly in Spenser. Digby's *Theoria* represents the surest example of symmetrically recessed structure to be found in Elizabethan literature. This point has not been made in the scholarship on Digby, but I believe it can be established to any reader's satisfaction. The structure is there to be observed; and the author in effect tells us as much.

Digby clearly exhibits the key markers of ring composition as formulated by Douglas in her Terry Lectures, *Thinking in Circles* (2007): emphasis on the balance of beginning and ending, and the presence of a semantically privileged middle. Digby lays particular stress on the connection between opening and conclusion. In the final sentence of the first chapter of the *Theoria* he writes that "it is characteristic of analysis to intimate the end in the beginning." The initial sentence of that chapter is: "For the beginner the end is to be recalled in memory, and for the one concluding, the opening." In the final words of the terminal chapter of the *Theoria*, Digby returns to this principle: "the end shines forth for the beginner, and the beginning for the one concluding."[28]

The treatise also exhibits what Fowler would call a triumphal center. The book has a total of fifty-nine chapters, the central chapter being the ninth of the second book, entitled "Mundus suprasupremus," the longest chapter in the *Theoria* and the one in which the highest of Digby's high secrets are unveiled. The book as a whole clearly exhibits a definite literary shape. Digby even hints at this in one passage, where he compares the procedures of correct analysis (his, as opposed to Ramus's) with "the scansion of poems, which in the most perfect and most august meter begin and end with the same (metrical) foot."[29]

Mary Douglas, an anthropologist, believes that the skill of writing in ring form—of thinking in circles—exhibits the craftsmanship of high style, of self-authenticating expertise. The form of symmetrical composition indicates the author's control of arcane knowledge: "however simple the form of community, the members normally need to distinguish a high style from the low-style speech that serves for work or domestic life. Ring composition is used for ceremonial speeches, victory odes, funeral orations, and joyful celebrations. It is also the common form for solemnly reciting myths of origin."[30] Certainly the *Theoria* makes such a structure-based claim for triumphal prestige. But Digby's treatise has in addition both philosophical and polemical points to make by its recursive formation.

Digby gives the *Theoria* this up-and-down pyramidal shape because he believes that the one-way deductive movement of Ramus is precluded by the limits of the human inquirer. For human intellect, Digby writes, "resembles a twilight vision [*tanquam vespertilionis visus*]." If one starts from the top, one is lost in confusion and without any guide. In this connection, Digby several times quotes a passage from Aristotle's *Metaphysics* (993b): "For as the eyes of bats are to the blaze of day, so is the reason of our soul to the things which are by nature most evident of all."[31]

This distinction between the *notiora natura* and the *notiora nobis* represents the crucial one for Digby. As a modern commentator writes, Aristotle "consistently maintains that the proper course in conducting an investigation is to start from what is more intelligible to us, but less intelligible absolutely, and proceed to what is more intelligible absolutely but (before we start the investigation) less intelligible to us."[32]

Digby calls this distinction into play in one of his clearest remarks on the structure of his philosophical project:

> In devising an analysis, I judge that to be the beginning, by which we know something as an acquired *habitus*, in *scientia*, in the better known to us, in the end [the better known] according to nature. In transmitting and teaching sciences, [I judge] that to be the end, which in the beginning (as it were through a cloud) we have guessed at. In resolving which, indeed, after we have been engaged with it for a long while, we acquiesce, in contemplation, in vigilance, in the better known according to [its] nature. Descending from such a *lumen*, delineating and describing the way back, by benefit of the *lumen* of its rays, until at length the conclusion we seek, brought into the presence of light, has become known to us thus not only to be, but (since we see the cause *praesenti lumine*) to be necessary. Awakened therefore by its rays (whether of the good, the true, *lumen*, light, or whatever that is, which is by far most perfect and first according to nature): in its light I hope that I shall see light [*in lumine suo me spero lumen visurum*].[33]

From the Aristotelian *habitus* of science to the awakening of Christian and Neoplatonic illumination—that is the path of the *Theoria*.

To put the matter in other terms, Digby's project in the *Theoria* is to "vectorize" Aristotle, to enlist him in a voyage of ascent. In the *Posterior Analytics*, Aristotle studies the systematics of scientific inference through a careful discussion of demonstration and definition; the book is not organized as a movement up to ever higher ground. Digby pays only passing attention to the systematics of inference. Though he borrows phrases, images, and ideas from the *Posterior Analytics*, he uses them in a spirit altogether different from that of the Aristotelian text. Consider this passage, from the end of the first book of the *Theoria*, as Digby pauses to consider the ground covered:

> In this ascent three discourses are found, and one resting place in each of these, which is so designated in reference to the

things that come before it [*prioribus*], but in reference to the
things that follow [is] the beginning of motion. First is the
confused intention; the apprehension of a middle notion; the
habitus of conclusion; here first it halts. Second: the confused
notion of a principle: the notion of a mediating discourse; and
the *habitus* of the principle; here for the second time it stops.
Third: the confused appetite of light; the anagogical outgoing;
the vision of divine pulchritude making itself seen; and here it
stops for the third time, as in the highest altitude of contemplation of human wit.[34]

The three-part movement is evidently from Aristotelian language of
middles and conclusions to the language of pseudo-Dionysian
Licht-metaphysik.

As exhibited by and formulated in the *Theoria*, this pyramid of
knowing richly recalls the account of Spenserian recessed symmetry
as provided a generation ago by Hieatt, Fowler, and other scholars.
The distinction between the *notiora natura* and the *notiora nobis* underlies at once Aristotelian dialectic, Digbeian metaphysical logic
and—dare one say it?—the theory of allegory accompanying *The
Faerie Queene* in Spenser's *Letter to Ralegh*. For ring composition is
not merely, as Mary Douglas (following many others) takes it to be,
a matter of either poetic craft as a claim to social authority or of
esoteric neoteric patterning as a claim to occult power. Such structur-
ation rests, at least in Elizabethan Cambridge, upon a firm philosophical basis of Aristotelianism as a way toward Platonic insight.

Turning now from structure to argument, we shall look briefly at
features of Digby's epistemology that will be of particular interest to
students of Spenser.

Digby's account of knowledge relies upon an exegetical assumption that permits him to evade the naturalistic thrust of Aristotle's
psychology. Of course, Digby insists, Aristotle never contradicts himself, never differs with himself. Instances of apparent conflict are to
be referred to the subject matter of the works in question. Sometimes
Aristotle wants to remain closer to nature, as in the *De anima*, in
which he discusses the soul as it is linked to the body. Sometimes
he rises higher, as in Digby's favorite text, the *Posterior Analytics*. So
Digby in his epistemology will draw upon the *De anima* when it
suits him to do so, but always as part of his upward spiraling.

Digby treats knowledge as a basic identification of knower and
known, mind and object. Versions of this theme he would have

known from two of his favorite authors, Reuchlin in the *De arte cabalistica*, and Ficino in his commentary on Plotinus. Here let me document the latter.

Ficino exhorted his reader to see in "the divine Plotinus" the reborn spirit of Plato. Varying the metaphor, Ficino instructs his reader to imagine "Plato himself exclaiming toward Plotinus, 'This is my beloved son, in whom I am thoroughly pleased.' "[35] And in Plotinus, Digby would have found what Jean Pépin in a classic article formulates in these words: "Plotin prononce avec la plus grande clarté pour l'identification de l'esprit et de son objet."[36] Here is what Digby would have read in Ficino's Plotinus—the Latin is perhaps accessible, surely more so than Digby's, and for once I shall give it in the original:

Praeterea memento potentiam cognoscendi in ipso cognitionis actu unum quodammodo fieri cum objecto. Et quo magis fit unum, eo perfectiorem esse cognitionem, atque vicissim: & ubi perfectissima est, imo ubicunque vera, ibi unum idemque esse re ipsa cognoscentem potentiam atque cognitum. Intellectus igitur & intellectualis omnis essentia sicut est omnia semper actu, ita & actu cuncta semper intelligit. Rationalis vero natura animae omnia quidem est, sed non semper in actu omnia. Et quatenus actu se confert in aliquam intra se latentium rationem, eatenus sit ipsa ratio, perque hanc intelligit, quae in huius virtute comprehendentur, & intelligendo fit illa. Summatim re vera cognoscere aliquid non est aliud, quam hoc ipsum esse vel fieri.[37]

Digby likewise asserts that the intellect deals in different and opposite ways with divine and material objects: it is related to divine objects as material to form, to material objects as form to material; it illuminates the material objects, and it is illuminated by the divine objects. Understanding divine objects, it is turned into them, so that knower and known are the same; it raises material objects toward its own perfection and likeness.[38]

The notion that the human mind becomes what it knows is so central to Digby's epistemology that he can use it to explain other matters. Thus, at one point, he takes up the issue of how angels can be both in the higher world and on earth. The answer is that, like the mind, they are not bound to the laws of matter; the angels are *"tanquam mens humana, quae una cum sit, omnia fit, & tamen, una est actu, & cum primo intelligibili idem, etiamsi longe illud positione sit semotum* [the angels are like the human mind, which though it is one, becomes all things, and yet is one in act, and the same as the 'prime intelligible,' even though far removed from that in position]."[39]

Along with Ficino's Plotinus commentary, Digby's favorite source on this topic is Aristotle's *De Anima*. According to *De Anima* III, Digby writes, "*intellectus & primum intelligibile idem.*" On the same page, Digby cites Themistius's paraphrase of Book III: "*Nihil aliud est intellectus quam ipsa plane intelligibilia* [the intellect is nothing other certainly than the *intelligibilia* themselves]."[40] And later in the *Theoria*, Digby offers Aristotle's argument that the intellect both makes and becomes all things.[41]

The Aristotle passages in question here have long been *loci vexati*. Aristotle says, "The thinking part of the soul . . . must be potentially identical in character with its object without being the object." Indeed, "in the case of objects which involve no matter, what thinks and what is thought are identical; for speculative knowledge and its object are identical." These passages are from chapter 4. In chapter 5, Aristotle writes that "mind as we have described it is what it is by virtue of becoming all things"; this is the celebrated distinction between the *nous poiētikos* and the *nous pathētikos*, the active or agent intellect and the passive or receptive intellect. In chapter 7, Aristotle asserts that "Actual knowledge is identical with its object"; in the same chapter, we read that "In every case the mind which is actively thinking is the object which it thinks." And in chapter 8, Aristotle specifies that the mind cannot be an object like a stone: "it is not the stone which is present in the soul but its form."[42]

From Aristotle, then—as from the Greek commentators on the Philosopher, from Plotinus and Ficino, as well as the Christian Kabbalists—Digby would have learned that it takes one to know one. In a splendid paper on this notion, which he calls the *Similia similibus* idea, Artur Schneider shows that it was originally meant to explain physical perception. In several branches of pre-Socratic thought, it was believed that there must be a physical correspondence between sense and object: light is known by light, so the eye must be fiery. "Wir denken jedes Element durch ein entsprechendes Element in uns."[43] The soul whose construction is described in Plato's *Timaeus* can know the world because it is composed of the same stuff. But, in Plato and Aristotle, the *similia* theme is expanded: the mind can know the divine only because it is, in a sense, divine itself, like unto God (in the Platonic sense).[44]

For Digby—as for Plotinus, Ficino, and Reuchlin—the *similia* theme was definitive of knowledge in its fullest sense. The best summary I can offer of Digby's epistemology is by way of citation from another English author, Lodowick Bryskett, a close intellectual friend of the poet Spenser. Explaining the Aristotelian account of knowledge in *A Discourse of Civill Life* (published in 1606), Bryskett writes:

> . . . some have said this possible understanding (as we may terme it) to be such a thing, as out of it all things should be made, as if it were in stead of matter; and the other agent understanding to be the worker of all things, and as it were the forme, because this part which before was but in power to things intelligible, becometh through the operation of the agent understanding to be now in act. And for this cause also is it said, that the understanding, and things understood, become more properly and truly one selfe same thing, then of matter and forme it may be said. For it is credible, that both the formes of things and the understanding being immateriall, they do the more perfectly unite themselves, and that the understanding doth so make it selfe equall with the thing understood, that they both become one. To which purpose *Aristotle* said very well, that the reasonable soule, whiles it understandeth things intelligible, becometh one selfe same thing with them. And this is that very act of truth, to wit, the certain science or knowledge of any thing: which knowledge or science is in effect nought else then the things so knowne.[45]

Bryskett's clarity in formulating this notion, familiar in its time, is welcome after Digby's obnubilated profundity. But I think it is Digby who allows us to see the historical and intellectual contexts of the identification thesis in the sixteenth century. However rebarbative the Scholastic prose of Digby's *Theoria Analytica*, it may furnish the intellectual charter for the "pleasing Analysis of all"—the teasingly polyvalent allegory—of Spenser's *Faerie Queene*. (Might the gentle poet here intend a backhand allusion to the somewhat less charming *Theoria Analytica*?) Up and down, in and out, mind and object: these are all inter-involved in ways that surpass the metaphoric and approach the identificational. It may take one to know the other, in all sorts of ways. The Aristotelian "agent intellect": precisely that philosophic-cum-poetic notion may be what is at work in fashioning a Spenserian gentleman.

Students of Renaissance literature are of course familiar with the identity thesis through its amatory version, like this remark in Sidney's *Arcadia*: "indeed the true love hath that excellent nature in it,

that it doth transform the very essence of the lover into the thing
loved, uniting and, as it were, incorporating it with a secret and
inward working."[46] And they are familiar as well with the philosophical version of human malleability, Pico's *Oration on the Dignity of Man*
being abundantly cited in this connection. But the deep rooting of
this idea of the transformation of knower into known—its basis in
Renaissance Aristotelianism—has largely escaped attention.

This essay has dealt with the recessed symmetrical structure of
Digby's treatise and with the identificationist epistemology that underlies that structure. Much of the *Theoria* offers detailed esoteric
material—from Renaissance alchemical texts and Reuchlin's kabbalistic book—that exhibit up-and-down movement through the cosmos
via meditation and experiment. For my last excerpt from Digby I
want to provide a lengthy statement of the Cantabrigian's main alchemical theme. The passage occurs, fittingly, in the chapter "De
Homine" (II.19). The passage is rich; I shall have to provide an
extensive translation. After citing the Virgilian tag, *hic labor hoc opus
est*, to point up the difficulty of describing the dual status of man,
Digby writes:

> This medium is the most marvelous, the greatest consent in
> discord, as of the divine with things human, things human with
> things divine; things animal with things human, things human
> with things animal: in fine, things natural with things animal,
> human and divine. To which nothing is more similar than the
> Philosopher's stone, the marvel of the whole world [*miraculum
> totius mundi*]. For as Hermes says, this is the *apotelesma* [translite-
> rating the Greek] of the entire world, and gives perfection to
> things imperfect, as Roger Bacon teaches in his *Mirror of Al-
> chemy*; and it transforms, penetrates, cleans, clarifies, fixes all
> things, until they are reduced *ad solem*, as Geber teaches in his
> *Sum of Perfection*. By absolutely the same power the human
> mind, the Elixir of all lower forms, on account of the divinity
> which is naturally in it from the first radical grafting of nature,
> even if it becomes more obscure in us and more languid because
> of the surrounding dregs of matter, nevertheless it adapts all
> other things so far as it can and is permitted to the likeness of
> the one, which is a stone and not a stone, of which there is
> not logical predication—if you ask what it is, it is the miracle
> of the whole world and the miracle of miracles. If human wit

in its condition were able to understand this, or even to gaze at its naked likeness or the light of its vestment, at length no miracle would remain in the sensible or the intelligible world. But indeed there are many; nor is anything more similar to the miracle than the *chemia* [Greek transliterated] of light and shadows in one form. Since this is spiritual, and founded above reason, learn from the material Elixir, a miracle almost spiritual. For just as there is one stone, which is not a stone; also just as clarity fixed in density and density in clarity is most volatile over a flame of the fixed, as Bacon attests; and these are like the clear in the fixed, and the fixed in the clear, but with the clear above and the fixed below; nor are these distinguished, nor confounded except miraculously, since they are the same (as Hermes teaches) as the working of the miracles of one thing. Thus Hortulanus explains it: Since (he says) the inferior part is the earth, which is called nurse and ferment; and the higher part is the soul, which vivifies and resuscitates the whole stone, therefore—with separation effected and conjunction celebrated—many miracles are performed in the secret work of nature. In entirely the same way in this scientific alchemy (for just like the alchemist with the lowest materials, so the demonstrator is engaged in resolving the most subtle forms) what is divine in us is, as it were, purely human, and what is human or animal is, as it were, divine. For the divine mind makes the entire man rational. . . . There what is above, is like what is below. Here what is below, is like what is above, by bending, possessing, dominating, and nevertheless the divine is made fast [*figitur*] in the human, and the human in the divine light, sees light—not by dividing superior from inferior, but by confounding both, according to the words of Hortulanus: with separation effected, and also conjunction celebrated.[47]

It would take another essay to unpack everything in the preceding citation.[48] Digby's main point, however, is clear: the mind is like the Stone: it transforms base things into radiant knowledge. The mind is itself, most itself, when it is elsewhere. What Digby offers in his alchemical humanism, then, is nothing less than a Charter for Allegory.

Another celebrated Elizabethan poet from Cambridge, Christopher Marlowe, might very well have had Everard Digby in mind when he placed the following words in the mouth of his character Faustus: "Sweet Analytics, 'tis thou has ravish'd me!" The present essay, though, seeks to make the case for linking the *Theoria* with another capital author of the day. My contention is that Digby's gnarled treatise exhibits pertinent affinities with the elegant spirals of Edmund Spenser. Digby's "veils" of soul-making may, in some measure, be Spenser's as well.

Notes

1. Shaan Akester, "The Life and Works of Everard Digby (c. 1551–1605)," Diss. Oxford 1980; Eugene David Hill, "Image and Argument in an Elizabethan Syncretist: A Study of Everard Digby's *Theoria Analytica*," Diss. Princeton 1980. A word of thanks to Oxford for lending a microfilm of the Akester; mine is available from UMI in Ann Arbor.

2. Here as throughout I regularize spelling in familiar ways (as by replacing the long s) and expand abbreviations. Throughout, I cite from and translate the *Theoria* in a UMI reprint of STC 6843; this reproduces a copy in the McAlpin Collection of the Union Theological Seminary Library which I also had the privilege of consulting. Readers will now find the book on EEBO. No translation exists, nor should one hold one's breath in anticipation.

3. "Selbstschilderung" in Leibniz, *Gesammelte Werke*, ed. G. H. Pertz, series I, vol. 4 (Hannover: Hahn, 1847), 168.

4. Charles de Rémusat, *Histoire de la philosophie en Angleterre depuis Bacon jusqu'à Locke*, 2nd ed. (Paris: Didier, 1878), I: 111, 115.

5. Jakob Freudenthal, "Beiträge zur Geschichte der englischen Philosophie," *Archiv für Geschichte der Philosophie*, 4 (1891): 450–77, and 5 (1892): 1–41. Here I draw from 466–67.

6. Charles B. Schmitt, *John Case and Aristotelianism in Renaissance England* (Kingston: McGill-Queen's University Press, 1983), 47–52; quotations are from 47–48.

7. *The Prefatory Epistles of Jacques Lefèvre d'Etaples and Related Texts*, ed. Eugene F. Rice, Jr. (New York: Columbia University Press, 1972), 6, 5, 356, 20, 87.

8. My translation of the Latin as quoted by Paolo Rossi in his article, "La celebrazione della rettorica e la polemica antimetafisica nel *De Principiis* di Mario Nizolio," in *La Crisi dell'uso dogmatico della ragione*, ed. Antonio Banfi (Rome: Bocca, 1953), 107n; inclusive pagination is 105–21.

9. My translations from a chapter whose title may be rendered "On the false demonstration and false science and false wisdom of the pseudophilosophers, and also of the useless and false book of the *Posterior Analytics*," in Mario Nizolio, *De veris Principiis et Vera Ratione Philosophandi contra Pseudophilosophos*, ed. Quirinus Breen (Rome: Bocca, 1956), II: 147 and 148.

10. Philipp Melanchthon, *De corrigendis adolescentiae studiis*, in *Corpus Reformatorum*, ed. Carl Bretschneider (Halle: Schwetschke, 1843), vol. 11, col. 20.

11.   Quoted in Cesare Vasoli, *La dialettica e la retorica dell'Umanesimo: "Invenzione" e "Methodo" nella cultura del XV e XVI secolo* (Milan: Feltrinelli, 1968), 362.

12.   Ramus, *Scholae dialecticae*, in *Scholae in liberales artes* (Basel, 1569), facsim. rpt., ed. Walter J. Ong (Hildesheim: Olms, 1970), cols. 263, 262, 191.

13.   *Scholae dialecticae*, cols. 194, 300.

14.   *Scholae dialecticae*, cols. 194–96.

15.   Jacobus Carpentarius, *Platonis cum Aristotele in universa philosophia comparatio . . .* (Paris: DuPuys, 1573), 122 and 58; cf. also 55–58, 69, 75.

16.   *Commentaria, in Isagogen Porphyrii et in omnes libros Aristotelis de dialectica . . .* (Louvain: Servatij, 1568), 241.

17.   Peter Petersen, *Geschichte der aristotelischen Philosophie im protestantischen Deutschland* (Leipzig: Meiner, 1921), 140.

18.   See the Preface to Ong's edition of the *Scholae in liberales artes* (cited above, n. 12), xv.

19.   Ramus, *Scholae Metaphysicae*, in *Scholae in liberales artes*, sigs. Nn1v, Nn2r, and p. 834.

20.   *Theoria*, sigs. A2v–A3r.

21.   *Theoria*, sig. A3r–v.

22.   *Theoria*, A4r–B1r–v.

23.   *Theoria*, sigs. B1v–B2r.

24.   Mary Douglas, *Thinking in Circles: An Essay on Ring Composition* (New Haven: Yale University Press, 2007), 31.

25.   Alastair Fowler, *Triumphal Forms: Structural Patterns in Elizabethan Poetry* (Cambridge: Cambridge University Press, 1970), 91–92.

26.   Douglas, *Thinking in Circles*, 31–42; Fowler, *Triumphal Forms*, chapter 4 in particular.

27.   A. Kent Hieatt, *Short Time's Endless Monument: The Symbolism of the Numbers in Edmund Spenser's 'Epithalamion'* (New York: Columbia University Press, 1960); James Nohrnberg, *The Analogy of* The Faerie Queene (Princeton: Princeton University Press, 1976), x–xi; Fowler, ix.

28.   *Theoria*, 1, [424], the latter misnumbered 404.

29.   *Theoria*, 15.

30.   *Thinking in Circles*, 27.

31.   *Theoria*, 37, 6.

32.   J. D. G. Evans, *Aristotle's Concept of Dialectic* (Cambridge: Cambridge University Press, 1977), 68–69.

33.   *Theoria*, 6–7. Cf. Psalm 36.9.

34.   *Theoria*, 86.

35.   Marsilio Ficino, *Opera omnia* (Basel, 1576), facsim. rpt., ed. P. O. Kristeller (Torino : Bottega d'Erasmo, 1962), II: 1548.

36.   Jean Pépin, "Éléments pour une histoire de la relation entre l'intelligence et l'intelligible chez Plotin et dans le néoplatonisme," *Revue philosophique*, 146 (1956): 64.

37.   Ficino, *Opera omnia*, II: 1725.

38.   *Theoria*, 344; cf. 249.

39.   *Theoria*, 218.

40. *Theoria*, 40; *De Anima*, 430a; *Themistii peripatetici lucidissimi Paraphrasis in Aristotelis Posteriora, & Physica*; *In libros item De anima*, trans. Hermolao Barbaro (Venice: Scotum, 1542), 289–99.

41. *Theoria*, 339.

42. *The Basic Works of Aristotle*, ed. Richard McKeon (New York: Random House, 1941), 589, 591, 592, 593, 595.

43. Artur Schneider, "Der Gedanke der Erkenntnis des Gleichen durch Gleiches in antiker und patristischer Zeit," in *Festgabe Cl. Baeumker* (Münster: Aschendorff, 1923), 65–76; the citation is from 67. Schneider's article is that rare thing, a piece of scholarship that one wishes were longer. I have found no comparable work for the later periods.

44. Schneider, 69–70.

45. Lodowick Bryskett, *A Discourse of Civill Life* (London, 1606; facsim. rpt. Amsterdam: Theatrum Orbis Terrarum, 1971), 124–25.

46. Sir Philip Sidney, *The Countess of Pembroke's Arcadia*, ed. Maurice Evans (Harmondsworth: Penguin, 1977), 133–34.

47. *Theoria*, 235–37.

48. For Digby's use of Reuchlinian Kabbalah, see chapter 5, "Digby and the Esoteric Sciences," in Hill (1980).

ANNE LAKE PRESCOTT

Hills of Contemplation and Signifying Circles: Spenser and Guy Le Fèvre de la Boderie

Among the many French poets whom Spenser read, or might well have read, Guy Le Fèvre de la Boderie was the one most determined to versify the cosmos in terms merging Neoplatonism, Christian syncretism, kabbalism, word magic, numerology, and a resolute insistence on Gallic glory and accomplishment. His long poem, *La Galliade* (1578), includes a prefatory sonnet sequence celebrating his employer, the duc d'Anjou, who was at this time courting Queen Elizabeth, as well as lines on the "mount of contemplation" from which the ecstatic and music-filled soul can see the New Jerusalem. The hill is worth comparing to the one in *Faerie Queene* I.x.46–58 up which the hermit Contemplation guides Redcrosse and from which the knight, too, sees the reborn city of David. Both passages are a reminder of how possible it was, if not always logical, for Catholic poets such as Le Fèvre and a Protestant one such as Spenser to combine the Christian with the Platonic. Further to set the two mounts of contemplation in context, this essay offers a small collection of other mountains and ascents with a Christian but also often Platonic atmosphere.

SOME DECADES AGO, in a study that over the years has provoked both admiration and objection, Robert Ellrodt argued that Spenser probably read Ficino's *Sopra l'Amore* in the 1588 edition of a translation by the French Neoplatonic poet Guy Le Fèvre de la Boderie, first published in 1578 as *Discours de l'honneste amour sur le Banquet de Platon*.[1] For Ellrodt, one of the benefits to be had from sorting out which

Renaissance Platonists (I would add semi-Platonists or quasi-Platonists) lie behind Spenser's poetry is the help that such work might provide in determining the degree to which Spenser felt a tension between Christianity and Platonism and to what extent they merged in his mind, logically or not. Certainly Le Fèvre, one of the most syncretic poets of the Renaissance, if one of the most obsessed and self-repetitive, felt no such tension. In the 1578 edition of *Discours*, for example, his dedicatory letter to Marguerite de Valois (sister of Henri III) reports that Ficino thought Plato had prophesied the coming of Christ, bringer of Sapience and Love.[2] After all, MARIE is an anagram of AIMER, and there are clear parallels between Plato's love and the kisses in Solomon's Song of Songs—no wonder that "Marguerite de Valois" is an anagram of "Gise le Verité d'Amour" (lies [dwells?] the truth of Love). The flattery is overdone, Spenser might have thought, but flattering queens is what poets do, even if part of this French poet's name, anagrammatized at the end of the epistle, is "L'Un Guide Orfee." Orpheus did not flatter queens, after all, although that omission might seem a mistake if we remember his death at the hands of angry women.

In this essay I will suggest that there were political as well as literary reasons for English poets to have known Le Fèvre, at least by name, and that his poetry, particularly his long cosmological poem *La Galliade* (1578), is worth remembering, even worth reading, by those who study Spenser. After describing the poem I will take as an example of Spenserian moments that gain further resonance when set next to this French poem the scene (I.x) in which St. George is guided by the hermit Contemplation up a hill, one that the narrator compares to Sinai, Olivet, and Parnassus and from which, with a further ascent, the knight can see the New Jerusalem.[3] James E. Phillips cites this passage from *The Faerie Queene* at the start of his helpful essay on Spenser's religious syncretism.[4] To give this hill and a not dissimilar one in *La Galliade* a fuller context, I will also offer a small mountain range of ones that Spenser and his contemporaries might have known.

Le Fèvre was himself as syncretic a poet as Spenser was likely to find, a devout and meticulously orthodox Catholic with a liking for divine circles, ecstatic ascents, anagrams, and number symbolism whose mind for all its theological orthodoxy hovered somewhere between Platonism and Renaissance occultism. His range of languages was impressive. In Paris he published translations of Jeronimo Muñoz on the supernova of 1572 (1574), of Francesco Giorgio on *L'Harmonie du monde* (1579), of Ficino's *Trois livres de la vie* (*Three Books on Life*, 1582), and, in Antwerp, of a tract on baptism by Severus, "patriarch of Alexandria" (in fact of Antioch). Near Eastern languages fascinated him, as did Italian Neoplatonism and the cosmic circles that were for him even more alive with the sound of music than they were for his French contemporaries.

My focus here is on *La Galliade*, but Le Fèvre wrote other books worth remembering. *L'Encyclie des Secrets de l'Eternité* (1571) merges biblical poetry and divine kisses with macro- and micro-cosmography, celebrations of David with Orphic odes. The picture of Le Fèvre that prefaces it, giving his age as thirty, is encircled by Greek words praying—in an anagram of his full name—"May Holy David bud forth as One Orphically," while below the image a Hebrew poem claims that, like a merged soul, spirit, and body, this poet merges three in one: Virgil, Orpheus, the upstanding Greek (with a pun on "Or-Pe" in Hebrew, "light of the mouth"), and David, the leader and singer (Fig. 1).[5] The author of *Amoretti*, with its allusions to the liturgical calendar, might have also enjoyed the first part of Le Fèvre's *Hymnes Ecclesiastiques* (1579, with a preface dated the previous September), a collection of lyrics—many of them translations—that follow the church year around its circuit.[6] True, Spenser would not have shared the hope that these "ecclesiastical" songs might be a "contrepoison" to psalm translations by those of the "Religion pretendue reformée" (a2–a3v). The volume is very much an elite production, with fancy metrical experiments, dedications to the great and famous, and a title page noting the author's service to the French king's brother, once duc d'Alençon and now duc d'Anjou. A hymn on "divine David, royal prophet and poet," that Israelite "swan," for example, addresses the same duke (V4v–V5). Not a very good poem, it summons all the clichés, including the conventional musical theory whereby we vibrate to David's harp. Some lines may seem awkwardly literal: harping goes through "les trous de mes oreilles" [the holes of my ears] into his "poictrine," his breast, for the ear has *holes*, whereas the eye is mere jelly. A similar theory had led Ficino to say that hearing is nobler than sight because music, for example, finds less impeded access to the brain than images find as they go through the eye.[7]

That same year, Le Fèvre published his *Diverses Meslanges Poétiques*, with poems ranging from an epitaph for a hermaphrodite to a poem on Anjou (the poet's Caesar and Hercules) after the author's return from Flanders, from a translated poem on Copernicus's theory (more witty than worried) to praise of Jodelle's play *Cléopâtre*. Again, Christian belief is at ease with semi-occult theories and an obsession with circles: Anjou is a ramping lion while the sun is in the sign Leo, and he is likewise powerful in August, the month named for the Caesar

ÆTATIS SVÆ AN. XXX.

דְּמוּת הַזֹּאת אֲשֶׁר אַחַת שָׁלוֹשׁ שֵׁמוֹת חוֹפָאת יַחַד
כְּמוֹ נֶפֶשׁ וְעֹם רוּחַ נְשָׁמָה הִיא בְּגוּף אֶחָד
וְהֵ רִאשׁוֹן שְׁמוֹ דָּוִד בְּעִבְרִיִּם הַשָּׂר וָשָׁר
וְהֵ שֵׁנִי שְׁמוֹ אוֹר־פֶּה בְּיַוְנִים יָחִיד יָשָׁר
שְׁלִישִׁי הוּא שְׁמוֹ וִרְגִיל בְּרוֹמִיִּם שָׁלִישׁ זוֹמֵר
וְהוּא וִרְגִיל רֵאשִׁית עוֹשָׂה וְתוֹךְ אוֹר־פֶּה דָּוִד גּוֹמֵר

Fig. 1. Verso title page to Guy Le Fèvre de la Boderie's *L'Encyclie des
Secrets de l'Eternité (1571)*. Image reproduced courtesy of BnF–Gallica.

who brought peace while the great Sun filled the womb of a virgin—a Virgo (next sign after Leo). The little sonnet sequence that Le Fèvre dedicates to Anjou and that this sonnet concludes is, as Rosanna Gorris says in her invaluable edition, a "bizarre" mixture of magical-medical advice, much derived from Ficino's *Three Books on Life*, to his then very sick prince and protector, one he still hoped would be king.[8] And not just of France: Sonnet X tells Anjou that when the duke recovers Le Fèvre is ready to take his harp and calm the waves as the prince, his sword once more at his side, crosses the Channel to win an English crown (by marrying Elizabeth, he means, not by force of arms). If Spenser and Sidney read that, did they laugh or weep?

Le Fèvre's *Galliade* is a versified compendium of French Renaissance Neoplatonic and occultist theories.[9] There are five books or "circles," the total representing the marriage of Heaven and Earth, for 5 is the chief marriage number. One might think that the title, with its "iade" suffix, makes a Virgilian claim, but Le Fèvre is clear that this is no parallel to pagan epic. Rather, his poem—despite the sincere or affected credulity with which it asserts the greatness of everything Gallic—is generically a contribution to Renaissance "scientific" poetry. The title puns on "galliarde" (the universe dances, and in ways that shame the frivolity of mere human bouncing and hoofing), "Gallia" (Gaul, cradle and now again leader of the arts, its earlier Gaulish tongue closely related to Hebrew and Syriac), and the Hebrew "galal" (revolve, rotate, like space and time). I apologize for the length of the following summary, but even if—or because—Le Fèvre had a mind "darkened by Neoplatonic clouds," as one skeptic has said, he probably needs an introduction to Spenserians.[10]

Circle I tracks the twelve peoples descending from the three sons of Noah, the patriarch who himself travels to Italy, bringing with him the Kabbalah and founding a college for its dissemination, as they populate the twelve geographical areas influenced by the twelve signs of the zodiac and the dominating planets. Tracing such migrations allows Le Fèvre to versify a great deal of astrological information and to explain the presiding signs and the history of the places in question, the margins all the while citing ancient authorities and giving information on the Hebraic sources and the significance of the names. Noah gives power over Gaul (a large geographical area including Britain) to Samothes, whom the pseudo-history largely invented by Annius of Viterbo, the "Pseudo-Berosus," identified with Meschech, fourth son of Japhet. But Samothes is also, said this tradition, and *La Galliade* agrees, the same as Dis/Pluto, for as so often in Renaissance mythography the classical gods correspond to biblical figures or their relatives.[11] This was, says Le Fèvre, done under the first sign, Aries, with Mars dominating. In Gallia Samothes teaches astronomy and astrology; his relatives people *Angle*terre, in the northern "angle" of the world, under his brother Gomer, whose name means "perfect, consummation." Gomer's name lives on in "Montgomery," surname of the unfortunate nobleman who inadvertently killed Henri II while jousting but also in the name of a town in Le Fèvre's native Normandy. And now the translation of empire has rotated preeminence back to France. After lines praising mathematics for helping us to explain eclipses and to reform the calendar (Pope Gregory XIII had recently begun to do just that), Le Fèvre closes the circle with a compliment to François Ier for restoring Gallic arts to their ancient glory and with a celebratory list of French writers: Lefèvre d'Etaples, Finé, Erasmus (who called himself Gallic because Holland is part of a greater Gaul), Budé, Pelletier, Belleforest, Amyot, Lazare de Baïf, Ramus, and others.

The second Circle is on architecture, exciting for its relation to mathematics and hence to music and cosmic mysteries but leading also to a discussion of fire, metallurgy, varieties of lumber, and the beauty of Gallic landscapes. Since architecture varies according to climate, it is here that Le Fèvre discusses the various races, adopting from Vitruvius, says the modern editor's note, an explanation based on the belief that solar effects on the bodily humors vary with latitude. From here Le Fèvre modulates to a discussion of humanity's different vocal timbres and registers, the effect of climate on the understanding, and the temperance of the Gallic (i.e., northwestern European) clime that explains the Celtic people's superiority—their prudence, strength, dexterity, and intelligence. This leads to a number of other topics: the construction of the organ, the Golden Age, the Virtue and Reason that differentiate us from animals, and the foundations of Paris and Troy. Le Fèvre associates such foundations with the angels who preside over various geographical areas; Gaul itself has an archangel, Zarfatiel. After tracing the *translatio studii*, the Circle ends with a list of great architects.

Third, appropriately, comes a Circle on the trivium (the triad of grammar, rhetoric, logic) and on Celtic mysteries. Like others who wanted to believe in a Gaulish version of the *prisca theologia*, and with a similar need to explain those unfortunate stories of human sacrifice, Le Fèvre cherished the memory of the druids, convinced of their occult learning. Here, with evidence drawn from ancient sources, are druidical mistletoe ceremonies, herbal wisdom, belief in reincarnation (something Le Fèvre himself rejects), and the significant role of women in Gaulish culture. We get a long summary of Gaulish religion; not all in that religion is praiseworthy, to be sure, but Le Fèvre nevertheless affirms its superiority to others, even to that of Greece. There follow many pages, with marginal citations of Greek Platonists and of the Egyptian mysteries that Renaissance syncretists equated with classical and Hebraic wisdom, on the steps or degrees and varieties of religious ecstasy, the "ravishment of the spirit," and its connection to the bodily humors. Le Fèvre associates the sixth degree with the muses and with revels around Cybele on Ida, but the seventh and last ravishment is, as one would expect from a translator of Ficino's commentary on the *Symposium*, the ecstasy of Love. Here is the Temple of the Graces, described with sensuous lines paraphrasing the Song of Songs and some ecstatic number symbolism. Here are the New Jerusalem and the "haut mont de Sion," the high hill of Sion. Here are Noah's Ark, the hill of Moses, and the vision of the Temple. Here is the place to which David was ravished in heart and thought when anointed king, here the flight of Solomon when singing of the Bridegroom and Spouse, the visions of the Prophets, the Ascension, and St. Paul swept up to the third Heaven to see still unrevealed secrets. Here, finally, is Patmos, from which St. John saw the Lover, the elect, and "the order of all ages." By this time the reader, in Spenser's day or our own, will have anticipated that Le Fèvre now moves to the circling history that has restored Gallic primitive greatness in arts and sciences, its cities, its learning in law, medicine, and other arts ever since Charlemagne, so we end as usual with a list of names.

The author of the *Fowre Hymnes* would have read all this with interest, if sometimes with amusement or irritation at the shameless Gallic self-promotion, but I suspect that for Spenser the most compelling Circle would have been the fourth, on music, bards, and poetry, with debts to such theorists as Boethius or Gaforio and including a compendium of stories recounting music's effects on minds and bodies of people and animals.[12] Such anecdotes, together with claims for music's medicinal, political, moral, and spiritual power, are found in a large number of texts from classical times forward that celebrate music, many of them Italian or French but some English. Spenser himself, or rather E. K. in a gloss on the "October Eclogue," cites the effects of Timotheus's musical modes on Alexander's moods (compare *Galliade* IV. 1032).[13] Le Fèvre's Fourth Circle is among the most energetic of such compendia.

First to understand and practice music, says Le Fèvre, was Bardus, whose name derives from the Chaldean "Bar-d'us," or "son of resonance." Gaulish bards had power over feelings and morals, of course,

but they also had their equivalent of Parnassus: Mount Barri, a Bur-
gundian hill with a name that is a corrupt form of "bardi." There
follows a long section on the music of the spheres, the *anima mundi*
and its numbers (odd are male and even are female, as in the Pythagorean system), harmonics, and intervals. Because the planetary
spheres make music, there is also a section on the distances between
the planets and the corresponding musical intervals. David and Orpheus tuned their instruments to such intervals, one with ten strings
and the other with seven. We read of Orpheus's musical power to
tame animals and savages, as well as of Pythagoras's discovery of the
scale after hearing a blacksmith striking with different sized hammers
(a famous story that Spenser exploits through reversal in *FQ* IV.v.41),
but the Gaulish bards have priority. No wonder music has power,
moreover, for the tetrachord relates to the four seasons, the four
humors, and the four elements, to say nothing of the sense, imagination, intellect, and reason in the tuned human lute, the amorous
harmony sung by the "grand Harpeur du Ciel"—David (IV.568).
But what if such harmony were to cease? Then all is out of tune
("Tout est desaccordé," IV.583) and the golden chain broken ("la
cheine d'or est rompue," IV.603). The monitory lines on such a
terrible possibility were written, the author need not say, during
France's religious civil wars when indeed, as he puts it later when
lamenting confusion and disobedience in the political hierarchy, "le
grand luth du Regne a perdu ses accords" (IV.1174). Take but accord, that is to say the ratio of high and low, of degree, away from
the "great lute of the Kingdom" and hark what discord follows. The
Ulysses of Shakespeare's *Troilus and Cressida* would say the same, and
the speaker of Donne's *First Anniversary* would point out that such a
confusion had long since occurred in a fallen world.[14]

Next comes an extended section often mentioning David and the
musical universe of which his own music is an analogue, a passage
to which I will return shortly. Le Fèvre then sings the universal
harmony as seen among birds, bees, cicadas, mammals such as deer
and the musically tamable elephants, waters, isles, a music-loving
monster from Finland, mermaids, and (lumped together) workers and
children. The poet lists music's many and well-known therapeutic
effects, most notably David's harping away of Saul's madness but also
the famous musical cure of tarantula bites, as well as the role of music
in war. In sum, harmony is everywhere and so, oh court musicians,
use your power wisely to promote due obedience, order, piety, and
harmony. (Le Fèvre is writing several years before Catherine de'
Medici tried to provide just such harmonious effects by the production of *Le Ballet Comique de la Royne*, 1581, a splendid masque with

verses by the likes of Ronsard that is clearly aimed at vibrating Huguenot and Catholic into mutual love; earlier efforts had not worked, one reason for the queen's resort to political murder that rapidly turned into the St. Bartholomew Massacre.) Then follow an address to Anjou and more anagram magic: O ALCIDE L'HEUREUX ("Oh Hercules the Fortunate"). Few can have truly thought of Elizabeth's unimpressive "frog" as Herculean, at least in appearance, but he could plausibly be an "Alcide" because one of his baptismal names was in fact "Hercule." The right music, Le Fèvre continues, can promote female virtue, but ladies and courtiers should avoid the soft song that effeminizes the souls of even the wellborn. Plug your ears with wax, Prince—presumably like Ulysses' sailors sailing by the Sirens. Some thoughts on modes follow, including the claim that Sappho invented the Mixolydian, and the Circle concludes with an exhortation to write religious poetry and with Le Fèvre's own hymns of praise, many incorporating lines from the psalms. Le Fèvre's theories are strongly Platonic, if with many, many allusions to David, but the religious poetry in Circle IV is also intensely biblical. Such syncretism allows him such Christian/Platonic paradoxes as the instruction to praise "L'Un et le Tout" ("the One and All," IV.1664). And again he offers the advice to royal musicians: sing God, sing harmony, sing virtue even at the table of your kings, just as had the Gaulish bards.

Spenser would also have read Circle V, on poets and poetry, with interest. We begin with those Gaulish bards and Bardus's invention of the rules for poetry, an art united to music. Poetry moves to Egypt and thence to the Israelites, as witness, for example, Moses, his sister Miriam, Deborah, David, and Solomon. Then comes Orpheus, who had studied in Egypt, and then an overview of the most famous ancient Greek writers, the ancient classical genres from lyric to "scientific" poetry, and a brief history of the Latin writers. When the barbarians arrive poetry and music must hide, but eventually they are reintroduced by writers in Italy—although there they become lascivious (a stereotype that would have been more than familiar to Spenser). And now at last the circle bends its line back home! Thanks to time and *translatio*, under François I music and poetry returned to the land loved by the bards, as witness such poets as Marot and such composers as Jannequin. But Time does not rest, for now, under Henri II, we have many more such modern bards, among them Jean Dorat (teacher of the Pléiade), Ronsard, du Bellay, Robert Garnier, Tyard, Marguerite de Valois, and Desportes. We end with some more musicians, the most famous nowadays being Orlando Lassus, and with a wish for the immortality of such artists.

If Spenser did indeed look at *La Galliade* as well as at Le Fèvre's translation of Ficino, and particularly if he saw the first of these shortly after its publication in 1578 just as he was working on his *Calender*, he would have read, perhaps with mixed irritation and amusement, the French poet's dedicatory sonnet sequence to his employer, Anjou. Le Fèvre, who worked Anjou's name into nearly every title page over which he had influence, announces himself in the 1578 edition of *La Galliade* as "Secretaire de Monseigneur, & son Interpret aux langues peregrines."[15] The second, and apparently far rarer, edition of 1582 lacks this self-identification but adds a long and abjectly admiring poem to Henri III, who had no liking for his brother, although Le Fèvre retains the equally abject poems to the duke. In 1578 an entire wreath of seventeen sonnets to Elizabeth's young suitor, "Monsieur," would have attracted the attention of anyone—Sidney? Leicester?—glancing at this book.

Whatever his merits as a poet and Platonist, then, Le Fèvre was politically positioned to be noticed. Sidney, moreover, could have heard about him from Christofle Plantin, the French-born printer who settled in Antwerp and made his press famous for his beautifully produced editions of humanists, church fathers, the great multivolumed Polyglot Bible, and Le Fèvre's long *L'Encyclie des Secrets de l'Eternité* (1571) as well as his *Dictionarium Syro-chaldaicum* (1572; 1573), his contribution to the Polyglot. *L'Encyclie*, dedicated to Alençon (as the duke still was) and aflame with Neoplatonic rapture and circles, also sports a large collection of poems with anagrams: CHRISTOFLE PLANTIN, his head full of art/craft/ability is "L'ART PLEINT SON CHEF" (187).[16] Plantin, who had occult tendencies of his own, shared Le Fèvre's love of circles: his impresa, which of course often appears on the title page, was the compass, its top in the sky and its legs describing and presumably about to complete what will be a circle on the earth (not for Plantin Ben Jonson's more discouraged image/impresa of the broken compass with its motto "deest quod ducere orbem"—"that is missing which might complete the circle"). In other words, Le Fèvre not only served a princely duke, heir to his childless brother and of keen interest to English politicians and poets, but he also was connected to the world of northern Renaissance humanist printing and the effort to make ancient Middle Eastern languages available to modern scholars and readers. In his own view, after all, French derived from such tongues.

The first edition, then, appeared just before, and the second just after, the height of Spenser's fear that the queen might make a match with the son of that Catholic Italian/French Jezebel, Catherine de' Medici, a son whose death in the summer of 1584 many ascribed, sometimes with punitive glee, to syphilis. Spenser was not alone, of course, for his antipathy was shared by Sidney, who wrote a widely copied letter to the queen urging her not to go ahead, and by John Stubbs—who lost his right hand, it will be remembered, for denouncing the proposed match in print. Spenser scholars are well aware of such protests against any projected marriage with "Monsieur," but it is also wise to remember that the situation was politically complicated by shifts in allegiances and loyalties that made the French prince a less dreadful prospect to Elizabeth and some of her advisers than one might suppose. Anjou was not only, in 1578, the likely future king of France but also an enemy of the Catholic extremists of the Holy League and an ally, more or less and up to a point, of those "politiques" who were more tolerant of Protestants than was his beleaguered brother. In the three-sided French civil wars he might seem, if not as attractive as the Huguenot Henri de Navarre, then preferable to Henri de Guise, leader of the ultra-papist League, and even to his brother Henri III. As one of Le Fèvre's modern editors has pointed out, moreover, the range of his friendships with and poems to many in his native Normandy and in the Low Countries shows him to be no bigot no matter how steady a Catholic.[17] It is easy to believe that those in Leicester's sphere of patronage and alliance would have heard of Anjou's poet-secretary.

The dedicatory sonnet sequence has received no critical commentary of which I am aware, yet it would repay attention, if not from those interested in French Platonism then from those tracing Anglo-French relations just as the *Shepheardes Calender* was being prepared and printed. The overwrought verses are generically interesting as forming a non-amatory and non-Petrarchan sonnet sequence, one interesting to put with the briefer sequence to Elizabeth by another of Anjou's admirers, the Norman Huguenot printer living in London, Jacques Bellot, who published it during those same years of marital possibility.[18] Sidney and Spenser would have noted, with whatever mixture of reactions, Le Fèvre's association of Anjou with the highest Platonic aspirations and harmonies. One sonnet corrals into a single cosmic and temporal circle the Mosaic, the Hermetic, and the Orphic:

Comme de l'infiny de la Coronne ronde
Decoule la Sagesse au sourgeon eternel,
Tout ainsi par rondeurs son ruisseau perennel
Es siecles retom[b]ez se retorne en ce Monde.
En Luz Israël beut de sa source feconde,

Moyse en arrousa le terroir solennel
Qui est baigné du Nil, le grand Mercure isnel
L'y puisa, et depuis Orfee encor l'y sonde:
   Puis le divin Platon d'Egipte la derive
En la ville où Pallas feist naistre son Olive,
Et d'Athenes Denis sur Seine la borna:
   Si que Paris sans pair de la ville à Minerve,
De Thrace Egipte, et Luz fut faite la reserve,
Où le Rond accomply des Sciences torna.[19]

The mystic circle of *translatio* has returned prominence to where it belongs: France.

There is one mystery concerning this sonnet sequence. Le Fèvre was alert to the occult meaning of numbers and their mysteries, so one may wonder why there are seventeen poems (just as there are, runs the conventional wisdom, seventeen "procreation" ones in Shakespeare's 1609 *Sonnets*). It is highly unlikely, one would assume, that Le Fèvre wrote these sonnets without considering the significance of 17, but 17 is not always a number to welcome: "infaustus," says Petrus Bungus of it in a brief essay that offers nothing but evidence as to why we should fear or dislike it.[20] Bungus might have told Anjou to prefer the sequence of fifteen sonnets in the *Meslanges* (fifteen is a resonant number: there are fifteen steps to the Temple, after all, and Augustine had said when explaining why the Ark floated fifteen cubits above the land that it combines the seven of time and the eight of eternity, thus figuring baptism and resurrection).[21]

There are, I think, two answers. The first involves Le Fèvre's persistent identification of himself with a combined Orpheus and David. David, says *La Galliade*, invented the ten-stringed psaltery that parallels the ten heavens—that is, the ten spheres or angelic "Sephiroth" that are, in the kabbalistic thinking to which Le Fèvre was drawn, ten emanations of God. For his part, Orpheus, so as to parallel the seven planets, invented the seven-stringed heptachord (IV.343–50). It is possible that in his own mind, if not in anything said explicitly to Anjou, Le Fèvre was again letting his inner David bud forth Orphically, as in the anagram of his name. But such is the limited supply of the smaller mystic numbers and the plenitude of ordinary coincidence that it is possible to find another reason, one more down to earth and probably of more immediate interest to those connected with Leicester's foreign policy. By the time *La Galliade* saw print, Anjou had been negotiating for a larger role in the Low Countries, an area that famously comprised, as Spenser was to note allegorically when describing the lost sons ("springals") of the widow Belge in Book V of *The Faerie Queene*, seventeen provinces. That there are seventeen sonnets, then, may be a gesture, although not an explicit one—in such matters a little tact is advantageous in case things go wrong—at Anjou's growing role in European geopolitics. Since 1576 the prince had been negotiating with the Netherlandish States, and in early 1578, perhaps after Le Fèvre had finished writing but before Spenser published the *Calender*, he had begun trying to raise an army for the Netherlands. In July he arrived at the Netherlands, and by late that summer, after some misadventures and evasions, a small army did arrive. By the end of summer that same year it was agreed that Anjou would provide men and horse to the States and be given the title "Defender of the liberty of the Netherlands" against Spanish tyranny, although his powers were limited. And, asked the States-General, would he please persuade Elizabeth to help.[22] She did, eventually, and Spenser allegorizes that help in Book V, but by that time the prince's life and Flemish adventure were over.

If, drawn by his interests and political curiosity, Spenser looked at *La Galliade* before he wrote Book I of *The Faerie Queene* he would have seen the long passage in Circle IV praising David as the archetypal poet-musician whose songs reflect and participate in the nesting analogies of cosmic harmony. In that section, dense with harmonic ratios, angelic hierarchies, and numerology, Le Fèvre tells how the holy verses of David's harp mount up so that the drunken soul leaves Jerusalem for Sion, where on the peak of the Mount of Contemplation she hears those songs whose music surpasses those of Helicon and Parnassus as much as the day surpasses the night's shadow, the Heavens surpass the Earth, stable Eternity surpasses fleeting time, and the sweet voices of the heavenly Sirens [who guide the spheres and make their music] surpass those of the Sisters [the Muses] who dance in a circle atop the double hill [Parnassus]: the soul

> . . . suyvant par les Cieux l'harmonie eslevee
> Vient de Jerusalem jusques dedans Sion
> Sur la croupe du mont de Contemplation,
> Où elle oyt des chansons dont la Musique passe
> Les chansons d'Helicon, ou celles de Parnasse
> Autaunt comme le jour passe l'ombre et la nuit,
> Le Ciel passe la Terre, et que le Temps qui fuit
> Loing loing est devancé de l'Eternité stable,
> Et autant qu'est la voix plus douce et delectable

Des Syrenes des Cieux, que des Seurs qui en rond
Menent la nuit leur bal dessus le double Mont.

(IV.649–58)

As would Spenser, although more explicit in his stress on harmony
and less impressed by the secular muses, Le Fèvre here associates the
upward ascent of the contemplative soul with both biblical and pagan
hills, with religious rapture and poetic inspiration. That it is Sion, hill
and citadel, from which the soul soars to contemplation, is entirely
appropriate, moreover, for Augustine, Jerome, and others (including
Erasmus) had identified the name "Sion" with "specula," or watchtower, and hence with contemplation. Augustine's commentary on
Ps 2 says, "as for Zion, if it means 'Lookout Post,' as some translate
it, we should understand it as nothing other than the Church, whose
gaze is duly lifted with longing toward the contemplation of God's
glory. . . ." The Church, he adds, is a mount "because of its lofty
dignity and stability."[23] An orthodox Catholic as well as Platonist,
Le Fèvre would agree that the Church is a solid rock from which to
take off into the skies of heavenly vision.

Some lines later we read that Davidic song accompanied by the
ten-stringed psaltery (that is, explains the author, the ten-fold order
of the holy angels) leads from "Jerusalem," meaning "vision of
peace," to Sion—the double-peaked hill on which the ecstatic soul
is aflame with holy fire (IV.711–24). The double-peaked hill may
seem to suggest that Le Fèvre is again remembering Parnassus, but
the editor's note argues plausibly that it is rather the twin-peaked
mount seen from Patmos by St. John and that elsewhere the poet
aligns this mount with Christ's double nature and Moses's Sinai (although not everyone agreed on the number of that mountain's peaks).
Filled with such music, says Le Fèvre some lines later, the harmonized
spirit can hear the nuptial song in the Holy City where the morning
stars sing together (IV.865–74). Nor is this surprising, Le Fèvre adds
before letting his sentence come to a close, if Plato is right about
numbers.

After some recuperative time in the House of Holiness, it will be
remembered, a refreshed and well-instructed Redcrosse is led by
Mercie (perhaps cousin to Le Fèvre's "Esprit d'Amour" in IV.565)
"Forth to an hill, that was both steepe and hy," on the top of which
is the hermitage of "an aged holy man" named "heavenly Contemplation" (I.x.46). The hermit calls him what his name, George, shows
him to be—a "man of earth," although by the end of the scene the
knight will have heard that he will one day be called "Saint *George*

of mery England, the signe of victoree" (I.x.61). First, though, with Contemplation as a guide, George climbs "the highest Mount." From there he can see "a goodly Citie" whose "wals and towres were builded high and strong/Of perle and precious stone," a sight that the narrator calls "Too high a ditty for my simple song"—a literary tact familiar to us, if perhaps not to Spenser, from the end of the *Paradiso*.[24] The city, the angel- and saint-filled place of "eternall peace and happinesse," to which Redcrosse longs to go at once, is that of "the great king." And who is the great king? The city is "The new Hierusalem," the one that, as St. George remarks, transcends Gloriana's Cleopolis, and so doubtless the king is God, either in one or three persons. And yet Jerusalem, city of peace, is also the city of David, so it would be nearly impossible to read these stanzas without remembering not only the description of the bridal city in the Bible's book of Revelation but also the psalmist who reigned in the earthly Jerusalem, and perhaps how that same psalmist asked "Who shal ascende into the mountaine of the Lord? and who shal stand in his holie place? Even he that hathe innocent hands, and a pure heart" (Ps. 24, Geneva version).[25] Because the height from which Redcrosse sees this city is the familiar territory of the hermit Contemplation, one might call it, without much distortion, the "mount of contemplation."

As St. George starts his final ascent, it is Sinai, Olivet, and (with delightfully proto-Miltonic arrogance) Parnassus to which Spenser at some length and with almost vatic vigor compares the hill. Needless to say, though, soon the main intertext in these stanzas (53–56) is the Bible's Book of Revelation. Shortly after St. John's apocalyptic vision of "a new heaven, & a new earth" with "the holie citie newe Jerusalem" coming down like "a bride trimmed for her housband" (Revelation 21.1–2, Geneva version), an angel summons the prophet "in the spirit to a great & an hie mountaine." There "he shewed me the great citie, holie Jerusalem, descending out of the heaven from God" (21.9–10). There are other hills in the Bible, of course, and other sights, but none so immediately important for Contemplation as this.[26] It seems right, again, that granted the etymology of "Sion"—the place of "sight" and (says Augustine) of the triumphant church from which to see the New Jerusalem, city of the new David, Christ—that Una, the one true church, should have helped ready Redcrosse for his vision by taking him to the House of Holinesse from which Mercie can then lead him upward. It may also be right, particularly in a Protestant poem, that even Mercie does not, so far as we know, accompany him and the hermit on his climb to what in this world must be the ultimate if still anticipatory vision.

Whatever Spenser's other sources or intertexts, and they must be many, Le Fèvre's passage is worth remembering in terms of the syncretism that some like Phillips find in *The Faerie Queene* but that Ellrodt denies is present in this particular scene.[27] True, for a "man of earth" to trudge up a hill, even an allegorical one, feels different than for an ecstatic soul to move up a staircase or scale of Love or to soar through the cosmos's crystal spheres, and true too that St. George must descend to rejoin Una, kill a dragon, and serve Gloriana in this world, but Christian and biblical hills had long had a Platonic and syncretic shimmer. After all, in his heterosexualized version of the lover's ascent in the *Symposium*, Castiglione's Bembo had compared Love's highest rapture to Hercules's fiery death on the "mountaigne Oeta" as well as the "fyrie bushe of Moses" on Sinai.[28] Even the secular poems that Spenser certainly read include such hills. In *Gerusalemme Liberata* (XVIII.11–16), after a hermit has pointed out his errors, Tasso's Rinaldo climbs Mount Olivet and learns about his future, although despite his clothes blazing white he has no vision, let alone an apocalyptic one. In *Rinaldo* (Book XI) the knight emerges from the Vale of Grief to the Hill of Hope, presided over by a female figure.

Spenser hardly needed literary, biblical, or indeed Platonic tradition, of course, to know that religious or philosophical exaltation can be facilitated by and represented as literal or mental ascent. So long as we think of divinity as somehow "up," flight and hill metaphors will persist, whatever our recent discovery that there is no such thing as "up" in space-time as we now understand it (*out*, maybe, but not *up*). In the years before Spenser published the first half of *The Faerie Queene*, or so a search of Early English Books Online suggests, the word "contemplation" was often, although not always, linked to wings and hills, to raised sight or upward surge. Even our bipedalism, as Ovid had long ago observed, means that we can look to the stars and, says one of Ovid's readers, be "lifted up by governaunce, to the contemplation of God his maker."[29] These images need not be thought of as sources or even as intertexts, but cumulatively, so to speak, they add up to some sort of context—a Pelion on Ossa of spiritual aspiration—for Spenser's own hill. Sometimes, it is true, contemplation involves no spatial movement, or perhaps such movement is already in the past, which is why Robert Southwell can contrast the invisible "sweet fruites of prayer and contemplation" to the "onions, garlicke, and the fleshe pottes of Egipt."[30] Sometimes to contemplate is to fly: "Give me the wings of contemplation, I beseech thee, that endued therewithal I may flie aloft to thee" and "soare upward unto the joies of peace, and unto the delectable, and pleasant state of light."[31] John Dee, commenting on the value of studying Euclidian geometry, urges us to move from the "conjecture, weenyng and opinion" up to the divinely creative world of Number where, he says, "the zelous Philosopher, may win nere this Riverish Ida, this Mountayne of Contemplation: and more then Contemplation."[32]

Another image of ascent, from Thomas à Kempis, makes a moving anticipatory gloss on Contemplation's reminder to St. George that he has work to do before he can actually enter the divine city. Whatever the insistence in Aristotelian ethical thought that virtue must be expressed in action, Thomas's passionate reminder has a felt pain that brings such theory to psychological life. In his *Of the Imitation of Christ*, translated in 1580 by Thomas Rogers, "Lord" tells "Servant" that "we are to exercise our selves with baser works, when we cannot doo the best": "My sonne, thou canst not alwaies abide in the most earnest, and ardent studie of virtue, nor continue in the highest degree of heavenlie contemplation, but of force through original corruption thou art made sometime to come downe unto inferior things, & to beare the burden of this mortal life though unwillinglie and with griefe. For as long as thou carriest about a mortal bodie, thou shalt feele the waight and heavines of the same" (N3v–N4). Generically, Spenser's hermit puts this in terms closer to the Romance stress on service to a lord or lady, but the deeper point is the same: the New Jerusalem is not for us in this world, or not yet. Nor, Socrates might have thought as he finished tucking in his drunken companions after their symposium and left for the day's ordinary occupation, is flesh ready to act upon Diotima's high vision.[33]

Imagining the lines of vision, however, is not as easy as one might suppose. Spatially, John has gone up in spirit to see a city coming down. Whether St. George's gaze is directed yet further up, or aimed down to see a descended city, or cast horizontally is not clear, and indeed illustrations of such visions can be ambiguous.[34] What is so striking in some of the images of heavenly contemplation that Spenser might have seen or certainly saw is just this spatial or perspectival complexity. A picture he certainly knew well is the illustration of John's vision accompanying one of the sonnets in the *Theatre for Worldlings* (1569; Fig. 2) that Van der Noot substituted for the four he dropped from Joachim du Bellay's *Songe* (but that, in 1591, Spenser restored for his *Visions of Bellay*). The image shows St. John on a hill or outcropping high above what must be, if here inaccurately imagined, square walls and buildings of the New Jerusalem. Here the new city is *below* the prophet, just as it is in a little illustration found in the 1575 *Bishops Bible* (R8), while on a smaller hill across the way

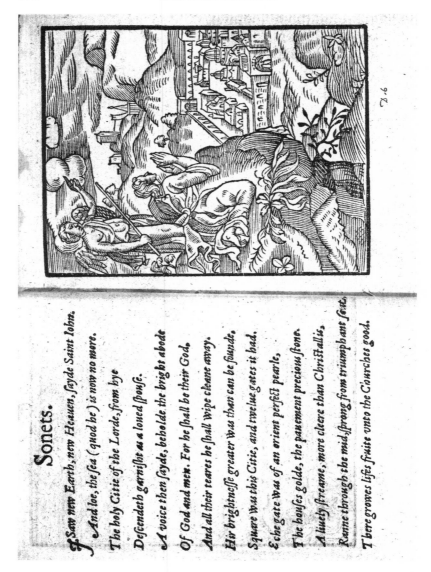

Sonets.

I Saw new Earth, new Heauen, sayde Saint Iohn.
And loe, the sea (quod he) is now no more.
The holy Citie of the Lorde, from hye
Descendeth garnisht as a loued spouse.
A voice then sayde, beholde the bright abode
Of God and men. For he shall be their God,
And all their teares he shall wipe cleane away.
Hir brightnesse greater was then can be founde,
Square was this Citie, and twelue gates it had.
Eche gate was of an orient perfect pearle,
The houses golde, the pauement precious stone.
A liuely streame, more cleere than Chrystallis,
Ranne through the mid,strong from triumphant seat.
There growes lifes fruite vnto the Churches good.

Fig. 2. Illustration of John's vision in Jan Van der Noot's *Theatre for Worldlings* (1569). This item is reproduced by permission of The Huntington Library, San Marino, California.

are some ruins, presumably representing the ruined earthly Jerusalem, the city of Man, or maybe the ruins of Rome, which are *above* the restored city. An angel points up and John's gaze follows the direction of his guide's finger, ignoring the city below. The scene would make more visual sense if the square city were the earthly Jerusalem, but the poem precludes that possibility. The picture's point is clear enough—raise your thoughts to angelic matters—but the physical vectors do not quite parallel the spiritual. Perhaps we are meant to contemplate beyond what even prophets can see.

That same year, 1569, Stephen Batman published *A Christall Glasse of Christian Reformation*. I cannot prove but strongly suspect that Spenser read this work, for Batman had connections with the Sidney family and the many illustrations are attractive. One picture (M4; Fig. 3) illustrates Faith, imagined as a knight with a cross of St. George on his Pauline "shielde of lively faith," making him English but with a Templar look, and carrying the "spere of continuance." Satan lies crushed under his feet and he gazes toward a hill. He is not on a hill himself, but rather looks across a strait of water at a hill on the other side. What he sees on the hill is not, however, the New Jerusalem, for the unimpressive little buildings, like Van der Noot's, fit the English woodcut convention indicating ruins. Again, the knight's eyes go skyward as he contemplates the divine Tetragrammaton. He is not on a hill, the hill that he ignores is worldly, and what he sees is not a city but a name. The atmosphere is biblical, if more Pauline than Apocalyptic, and the knight is without a guide. Nevertheless, one can imagine young Spenser enjoying it.[35]

In that the hermit Contemplation's second hill offers an apocalyptic vision of the New Jerusalem it is, of course, biblical and Christian. Is it also Platonic? Professor Ellrodt once wrote that "To both human and cosmic love, [Spenser] ascribes a heavenly origin, but in the *Faerie Queene* he has no place for 'heavenly love' as conceived by the Platonists, love 'ad divinam pulchritudinem cogitandam' (*In Conv[ivium]* VI.vii). For, when he ascends the mount of Contemplation, he no longer speaks the language of Plato, nor even of a Christian Platonist: he speaks the language of Christian devotion unalloyed and holds forth the vision, not of the Intelligible World, but of the Heavenly Jerusalem (*FQ* X.46–47)" (35). Perhaps. And yet Spenser's was a subculture willing to live with intellectually unguarded borders and pleased by parallels and analogies. The language of Christian devotion, as Ellrodt would doubtless concede, had long been inflected by Platonic language about or conceptions of the intelligible world, perhaps as early as Paul's epistles. Texts read or readable by Spenser during the years in which he was thinking about or writing *The*

Of Faith.

❡Of fayth and the wonderfull working of the same: and
stedfast beliefe of the fathers in olde tyme.

The signification.

❡'He man in armour signifieth all stedfast beleuers of the veritie, being armed with constant zeale of Christianitie, and
weaponed with the shielde of liuely faith, the spere of continu-
aunce, and the sworde of the word of God: The Diuil vnder him
is temptation, being ouercome by faith in Christ Iesus.

M.iiij.   **Faith**

Fig. 3. "Faith," from Stephen Batman's *A Christall Glasse of Christian Reformation* (1569), sig. Miii. Image © The British Libary Board. Shelfmark C.17.d.2.

Faerie Queene can comfortably combine biblical and loosely Platonic language or refer to Platonic images as they imagine an upward look or vertical motion. Let me cite several that even more clearly than those I have already quoted (although not more clearly than does Le Fèvre) perform this syncretic merger.

One example is useful in showing how mingled Platonic and Christian images of contemplation can appear in surprising places. Richard Eden's translation of *The Arte of Navigation* by Martin Cortés (London, 1561) mentions a number of Greek philosophers on the divisions of the world, the elements, the quintessence, man's position as a microcosm in whom we may "contemplate thynges of no lesse admiration, then in the greate worlde." And it was God who created this *mundus* that we may thus contemplate, says the next chapter (the illustrated initial T in the 1589 edition shows a knight on a handsome rearing horse). The text cites Moses and John, and then turns to "the divine Philosopher *Plato*," who "affirmed that eyes were geven to men to beholde the bewtie therof, and to take pleasure in the contemplation of the heavenly bodies" (Av–A5; see Plato's *Timaeus*, section 47). There is, to be sure, no hill here, but both the Bible and Plato justify, even require, our upward contemplative gaze.

Less unexpectedly Platonic is Sheltco à Geveren's *Of the Ende of This World, the Seconde Commyng of Christ*, translated by Thomas Rogers (London, 1577), almost as taken by numbers as is Le Fèvre. The calculations include estimates of the world's age and the conclusion that something very important will happen in 1595. Needless to say, Plato and Pythagoras both figure, and so does the familiar claim that "numbering is given of God himselfe to man, as a necessarie instrument of reasoning and discoursing, without which, the mynde should appeare without a mynde, and all artes and knowledge would vanish." Citing both Plato and scripture, and impressed by the circles, the "order and tyme," of the cosmos, seasons, months, days, and hours, Sheltco says we should through contemplation "ascend into heaven to beholde things celestiall and of continuance," for "God is not a God of confusion" (H2–H3). Le Fèvre would have put that thought in verse (as indeed Spenser did, in *FQ* VII.vii), but no more succinctly.

Last in my small mound of syncretic hills is a text that Spenser would certainly have found engaging, for it has many connections with his own—and includes some of the same pseudo-Berosian history that not only lies behind Le Fèvre's claims on behalf of Gaul's cultural centrality but also haunts *The Faerie Queene* with its memory of giants and eclectic Egypto-classical-biblical mythology. This is *The Voyage of the Wandering Knight* by Jean de Cartigny, based in part on the same parable by Bernard of Clairvaux that structures Stephen Batman's 1569 *Travayled Pilgrime* (quite likely known to Spenser), and translated in 1581 by William Goodyear. As in Spenser's Book I, education by Charity "maketh men consider of things present and visible, as if they were not. *Love* maketh a pure and cleane heart, which may contemplate and beholde heavenly thinges." With "rav-ishings" it "leapeth up to heaven, having by contemplation exceeding great joyfulnesse" and finds "familiaritie with God," longing for him as, in Ps. 41, the hart pants after the living water (P2v–P3).

Texts such as this are hardly major, although those who love Spenser would at least like Cartigny, but like *La Galliade* they show the *ease* of syncretic thinking by solidly Christian writers and the degree to which a path up Parnassus (perhaps with a stop for an Athenian drinking party) can not merely cross but actually merge with those offering a way up Sinai and Olivet.

It is *La Galliade*'s own Sion and Davidic exaltations that I believe we might most appropriately add to the mountain range of contem-plative opportunities, whether as a possible source or as an opportu-nity for comparative contemplation. The hill is of particular relevance to Spenser, I think, precisely because it so comfortably combines biblical and Platonic images of ascent and vision. For all its wild eccentricities, its beyond-patriotic insistence on the impor-tance of a greater Gaul, its lunatic etymologies, and its obsessions with circles and numbers, *La Galliade* is another instance of Renais-sance writers' willingness to merge the biblical and the Platonic, the pseudohistorical and the cosmological, in ways that might make a professional philosopher tear his beard but that can generate aesthetic and psychological excitement. Redcrosse's ascent acquires an acceler-ating energy from remembering such syncretism.

Spenser would also, perhaps, have enjoyed other French Platonic circles (if with a little more skepticism than Le Fèvre), for French Renaissance poets sang circles almost as often as others sang their mistresses. "Je te salue, ô Globe," writes Edouard du Monin, for example, and goes on to say that Christ is both head and tail "of this great roundness." Smiling at the image of Jesus as the worm Ouro-boros is perhaps permissible, although in his defense Monin could point to Christ's nature as both alpha and omega. More impressive may be Monin's claim that that Eternity is born from a point, al-though Jacques Pelletier du Mans praises, rather, "O un! ô deux! dont tout l'œuvre commence" ("Oh one, oh two, from which all creation begins").[36] But St. George himself is urged downhill, back into the world of time's forward linear motion. Some years later Spenser himself would imagine that motion as also circular—in the

Mutabilitie Cantos the seasons and months process forward but also calendrically—and would then long to escape such cycles even if, as Nature says, through them we "dilate" our being. For Spenserian circles, if not Fèvrian ones, are in truth ambiguous. Especially thanks to the earlier Renaissance's at first reluctant acceptance of zero (or to give the usual term in those days, a "cipher"), a circle, an "O" can be a sign for nothing but also the shape of an all, to say nothing of a woman's nether "nothing." The religious implications are intriguing, and all the more so since Greek philosophy, particularly the Aristotelian, had resisted the concept of nothing, zero, naught. Any biblical religion, as has often been said, has linearity: Israelite history is not a set of circles, and individually we age. But Christians such as Spenser and Le Fèvre also move liturgically around a year, which is why *Amoretti* (like Petrarch's *Rime* and du Bellay's *Olive* wreath) lives in such compelling tension between allusions to cyclical seasons and rituals and those to the length of time spent in courting. The Catholic Le Fèvre could not have believed in the myth of eternal return—the cosmos strains toward an Eternity when seasons end and stars fall. Nor, as I have said, was Spenser content with temporal consolations, as witness his longing for the end of mutability. I suspect, though, that Le Fèvre thought he could have his "galliade," and his eternity too, precisely because of the paradoxes inherent in the circle—a nothing, an all, and a motion that bends to meet itself. Temporal circles in all their splendor participate in and will be eventually enclosed by the eternal roundness. Spenser has firm pillars and Le Fèvre wanted ecstasy-inducing circles, but in the New Jerusalem visible from the hill of Contemplation they may be the same thing.

Yet the two poets' circles are not quite the same. Spenser's poetry may be inflected by Platonism, but it also explores circular failure, so to speak, the defects in what should be, but are not, circles. The number of them in Spenser's verse is impressive. In Book VI there are the circles of graces and naked dancing ladies on Mt. Acidale, "perfect" triadic rhythm further indicated by the beloved/dot in the middle, but they vanish when intruded upon, whatever the innate courtesy of the intruder.[37] There is the great circle of the sun, but in *Epithalamion* the imperfections of the solar circle appear in the number symbolism itself.[38] There is the zodiac, but Book V's proem notes the precession of the equinox that Spenser figures as a set of unjust usurpations. Book VII has circles, some of them resembling those of Le Fèvre, but the signs of the Zodiac carry agricultural emblems that recall the curse of Adam. The canto's other processions that represent the mutable world of time are eventually contrasted, interestingly, not with perfected circles of eternity but with eternity's *pillars*—round, presumably, but also forming rectilinear verticals. We end the poem not with a circle but with the Temple, the number symbolism itself indicating escape from the rotations of Time in Cantos vi and vii as Spenser moves to Canto viii, beyond the numbers of the six-day creation or heptad week to the eighth day after the Sabbath, the day of Resurrection. For that matter, if only because the poem is unfinished we never even see the circle of a Round Table presided over by a fully matured Arthur now co-reigning in Cleopolis. One can speculate, though, that the Prince and the virtue he represents will somehow become even more upstanding when free from circling time, a pillar of Magnificence in the City of David.

Barnard College, Columbia University

NOTES

1.   Robert Ellrodt, *Neoplatonism in the Poetry of Spenser* (Travaux d'Humanisme et Renaissance 35; Geneva: Droz, 1960), distinguishes among Renaissance Platonisms and argues that Spenser was not as beguiled by them as some have said; he does not mention *La Galliade*. On Spenser's Platonism see Jon A. Quitslund: "Spenser's Image of Sapience," *Studies in the Renaissance* 16 (1969): 181–213 and his *Spenser's Supreme Fiction: Platonic Natural Philosophy and "The Faerie Queene"* (Toronto: University of Toronto Press, 2001). Whatever the degree of his Platonism, I would add, Spenser can also insist that grace comes *down*—into the flesh, the muck, the world of sin and time—because "Entire affection hateth nicer [i.e., more squeamish] hands" (*FQ* I.viii.40). Spenser unquestionably read some French writers with a Platonic tinge (Ronsard, du Bartas) as well as others more committed to Platonism (Pontus de Tyard, Louis Le Roy). On Tyard, see Carol V. Kaske, "The Bacchus who Wouldn't Wash: *Faerie Queene* II.i–ii," *Renaissance Quarterly* 29.2 (1976): 195–210; her "Spenser and Neoplatonism Once More," *Religion and Literature* 32 (2000), a special issue ed. Daniel Gates, 157–67, traces the fate of the "wave of strictly Platonic interpretations" that "washed over Spenser" early in the last century. Ayesha Ramachandran's wisely balanced essay, "Edmund Spenser, Lucretian Neoplatonist: Cosmology in the *Fowre Hymnes*," in this volume, provides further updating.

2.   Ellrodt's index confuses this Marguerite with her aunt, author of the *Heptaméron*.

3.   The Variorum Spenser cites personifications of Contemplation in a morality play (in which he thinks "ful hevenly" thoughts) and in the *Old Arcadia*, where he holds his "only seat" in the solitary woods and thence can climb on the wings of hope "even unto the stars." See Edmund Spenser, *Works*, ed. Edwin Greenlaw et al. (Baltimore: Johns Hopkins University Press, 1932) I, 289.

4.   James E. Phillips, "Spenser's Syncretistic Religious Imagery," *ELH* 36.1 (1969): 110–30. Spenser's comparison of the hill to Sinai, Olivet, and Parnassus, says

Phillips, exemplifies a syncretism found also in Sidney's friend Philippe de Mornay and others. Phillips, who mentions Le Fèvre but not *La Galliade*, notes that French Platonism was more culturally conservative than the Italian. On French Orphism, including its patriotic association of Gallic bards with ancient mysteries and music, see D. P. Walker: "The Prisca Theologia in France," *Journal of the Warburg and Courtauld Institutes* 17.3/4 (1954): 204–59. Walker, who stresses the impact of Italian Neoplatonism and Orphic or Hermetic thinking on French writers, says that Le Fèvre, "not a great poet" but "odd and interesting," merged patriotic "history" and ancient theology "in an extreme and reckless form" (205). See also Walker's *The Ancient Theology: Studies in Christian Platonism from the Fifteenth to the Eighteenth Century* (Ithaca, NY: Cornell University Press, 1972). Robert Merrill, *Platonism in French Renaissance Poetry* (New York: New York University Press, 1957) is useful on Platonic topics. On poetry with a sometimes Neoplatonic gaze and shifting cosmologies, see Isabelle Pantin, *La Poésie du ciel en France dans la seconde moitié du seizième siècle* (Geneva: Droz, 1995); pp. 94–98 are on Le Fèvre. Perhaps Spenser knew also of the humanist and jurist Louis Le Caron, whose *Dialogues* (1556) engage profoundly with Plato (Ronsard is a speaker in the dialogue on poetry) and who, like Le Fèvre, played a political role during the French civil wars; see the introduction to the modern edition eds. Joan A. Buhlmann and Donald Gilman (Geneva: Droz, 1986).

5.   I thank my colleague Lisa Gordis for translating the Hebrew and my sister Lydia Kirsopp Lake for help with Greek and classical matters. On the anagram, which has been variously translated, see Le Fèvre's *Diverses Meslanges Poétiques*, ed. Rosanna Gorris (Geneva: Droz, 1993, based on the 1582 edition), 69. D. P. Walker, "Orpheus the Theologian and Renaissance Platonists," *Journal of the Warburg and Courtauld Institutes* 16.1/2 (1953): 110–20, notes the anagram and its implications. Le Fèvre goes further than most Renaissance poets in perceiving language as weighty with essential meanings; hence his compulsive anagram-making. Had Spenser claimed that Guyon is Young or Book IV's Lust a Slut (with a gender change), or even that an errant Calidore might as well be Road-Lice, Le Fèvre would have perceived in him a fellow believer in names as packed hieroglyphs of identity. It must have been pleasurable for him to find lurking in his very name two great musicians famed for quasi-magical effects.

6.   On this text see Franco Giacone, "Bible et esthétique: *Les Hymnes Ecclesiastiques* de Guy Le Fèvre de La Boderie," in *Cité des Hommes, Cité de Dieu: Travaux sur la littérature de la Renaissance en l'honneur de Daniel Ménager* (Geneva: Droz, 2003), 393–406, who notes the relative absence of direct quotations from the Bible, perhaps a post-tridentine move. There is no modern edition; I read the copy at Harvard's Houghton Library.

7.   See D. P. Walker, *Spiritual and Demonic Magic from Ficino to Campanella* (University Park: Pennsylvania State Univ. Press, 2000; first pub. 1958), 8–10, although Ficino is more interested in how music travels through the inner ear into the brain. See also Gary Tomlinson, *Music in Renaissance Magic: Toward a Historiography of Others* (Chicago: University of Chicago Press, 1993), 101–44.

8.   Le Fèvre, *Meslanges*, ed. Gorris, 295, note.

9.   Guy Le Fèvre de la Boderie, *La Galliade* (1582), ed. François Roudaut (Paris: Klincksieck, 1993), with full notes, bibliography, and an outline of the contents.

Simone Maser, "Musique et harmonie des quatre mondes ou le cercle IV de *La Galliade* de G. Lefèvre de la Boderie," *Renaissance and Reformation* 6 (1982): 11–33, has helpful diagrams, explanations of how music relates to the humors, and citations of other Renaissance musical theorists with Platonic, kabbalistic, and Pythagorean tendencies. See also her *"La Galliade* ou le mariage du ciel et de la terre par Guy Le Fèvre de la Boderie," *Renaissance and Reformation* 26.2 (1990): 121–46, a handy description that notes (123) the influence of Postel and the excitement caused by the supernova of 1572. François Roudaut, *Le point centrique: Contribution à l'étude de Guy Le Fèvre de la Boderie 1541–1598* (Paris: Klincksieck, 1992), includes many citations of Ficino, Postel, and others. François Roudaut, ed., *Poésie encyclopédique et kabbale chrétienne: Onze études sur Guy Le Fèvre de La Boderie*, with a preface by Jean Céard (Paris: Champion, 1999), has several essays on *La Galliade*.

10.   "[O]bscurci de nuées néo-platoniciennes," quoted from H. Bousson's *Rationalisme* (1957) by John McClelland in a review of François Secret, *L'ésotérisme de Guy Le Fèvre de la Boderie* (Geneva: Droz, 1969), in *Modern Philology* 68 (1971): 380–82.

11.   See R. E. Asher, *National Myths in Renaissance France: Francus, Samothes and the Druids* (Edinburgh; University of Edinburgh Press, 1993); pp. 156–67 examine Le Fèvre's use of a fabricated history that by 1578 most French scholars had rejected. Asher notes that legends of royal Trojan descent in, e.g., Ronsard's *dynastic* epic *La Franciade* (or in *The Faerie Queene*) had a different tonality from—and could be hard to reconcile chronologically with—the Berosian pseudohistory that sustains Le Fèvre's *nationalism*. (Could this be another reason he denies that his poem is an epic?)

12.   For a number of such anecdotes see my " 'Formes of Joy and Art': Donne, David, and the Power of Music," *John Donne Journal* 25 (2006): 3–36.

13.   Nan Carpenter, "Spenser and Timotheus: A Musical Gloss on E. K.'s Gloss," *PMLA* 71.5 (1956): 1141–51, cites verbal overlap between E. K.'s gloss and Hoby's translation of Castiglione's *Courtier*. She dismisses Basil because (I suspect) she was unaware of the degree to which his praise of the psalms' musical effects had entered English commentary.

14.   I have no evidence that Shakespeare read Le Fèvre, but the parallel between this section of the Fourth Circle and Ulysses' speech on degree is striking. In "Good Friday 1613, Riding Westward," Donne's reference to a spherical human soul and the divine hands that "tune all spheares at once" would have pleased Le Fèvre.

15.   There is no question that Le Fèvre was attached to Anjou, but I see no allusions to him in the Calendar of State Papers, although his brother Antoine figures as ambassador to James I.

16.   Plantin's wife Magdaleine is L'ANGE PLEIN D'AIMANT (188). On the copy digitized for the Bibliothèque Nationale's Gallica website, p.189, an early modern hand has added an anagram next to Le Fèvre's own L'UN GUIDE ORFEE: "UN DIEU LE FORGÉ" (a god made him).

17.   A point made by Gorris, *Diverse Meslanges Poétiques*, 55, although such reaching out was probably less a modern toleration than a hope for reconciliation.

18.   In 1580, with effusive praise, Bellot dedicated his *Maistre d'escole Anglois* or *The English Scholemaister* (London: Purfoot), to Anjou. Sonnets to Elizabeth appeared the next year in his *Jardin de vertu et bonnes moeurs* (London: Vautrollier).

19.   Thriftily recycled from Le Fèvre's translation that same year of Ficino's *Religion chrestienne*. My thanks to Roger Kuin for a blank verse translation: "As from the

round Corona's Infinite,/Wisdom flows to th'eternal springhead green,/So its perennial stream in circling forms/Fall'n into Time, turns round within this World./ Israel in Luz drank from its fertile spring;/With it Moses watered the solemn ground/Bathed by the Nile; great agile Mercury/Drew from it; Orpheus still explores its depths:/Plato divine diverted it from Egypt/To the far town where Pallas bore her Olive;/From Athens Denis fixed it on the Seine:/And peerless Paris thus was made the store of/Minerva's city, Thrace, Egypt, and Luz:/There the worlds knowledge closed its circle full." Denis is Paris's Saint Denis and Luz the place where Jacob had his dream of the ladder connecting Heaven and Earth, later called Bethel (Gen. 28:19).

20. Carol Kaske kindly transcribed and translated for me the relevant passage in her copy (Paris, 1618) of *De numerorum mysteria* by Petrus Bungus (Pietro Bongo), first published in 1585. Writing on the number 17 (416), Bungus notes, e.g., that the letters of "XVII" reshuffled give "VIXI": I have lived (i.e., am dead). Evidence shows, furthermore, that 17 "usually portends earthquakes, conflagrations, floods, and many other disasters." True, 17 is the hypotenuse of a right triangle with 12 (a good number) on its other sides—288 for the two sides squared and summed and 289 for the hypotenuse squared (the rules allowed the square of the hypotenuse to be one unit off). See Michael J. B. Allen, *Nuptial Arithmetic: Marsilio Ficino's Commentary on the Fatal Number in Book VIII of Plato's* Republic (Berkeley: University of California Press, 1994), 56–58; a note on p. 130 notes that the sum of the first seventeen numbers is 153, number of the fish that the Apostles net after the Resurrection (John 21:11).

21. See my *French Poets and the English Renaissance* (New Haven: Yale University Press, 1978), 46–47, on Spenser's addition of a fifteenth line to a sonnet by du Bellay that he translated for Van der Noot's *Theatre* and on the symbolism of 7 and 8.

22. Mack Holt, *The Duke of Anjou and the Politique Struggle During the Wars of Religion* (Cambridge: Cambridge University Press, 1986), 96–104. Arthur Golding translated and Ponsonby printed a French description, published by Plantin, of Anjou's entry into Antwerp, complete with the giant Druon Antigonus to whose story Spenser probably alludes in the Munera and Pollente episode of Book V; see "Belge" in the *Spenser Encyclopedia*.

23. *Exposition of the Psalms 1–31*, trans. Maria Boulding (Hyde Park, NY: New City Press, 2000), 72. For other comments on Sion as *specula* or watchtower see Allan K. Jenkins, "Erasmus' Commentary on Psalm 2," *Journal of Hebrew Scriptures* 3 (2001), archived by the National Library of Canada. For Erasmus, the watchtower is the "mountain of the gospel teaching, from which we look down on whatever the world considers exalted." I thank Carol Kaske for reminding me of Jerome's definition of "Sion" as *specula*.

24. In the *Divine Comedy* Beatrice guides the pilgrim to contemplate the indescribable "love that moves the sun and the other stars" and the male Virgil can reach only the perimeter of Paradise. Spenser's reversal may be less a symptom of misogyny than a (Protestant?) refinement of Una's allegorical role. The true Church and unitary Truth can lead Redcrosse to the point where thanks to God's mercy (and to the soul's becoming merciful) he can contemplate God's City, but the vision itself is more available to the individual soul than to any earthly institution, even one that

is also Christ's bride. Or perhaps Spenser reflected that to have Truth/Unity/ Church/Bride ascend these hills, or to have Mercie ascend the second one, would entail the complexity of having them gaze at a vision of themselves. In Niels Hemmingsen's *The Faith of the Church Militant*, trans. Thomas Rogers (London, 1581), John is carried "by a prophetical spirite" into "the contemplation of the beautie of the Church of Christe" (I2v), the conventional meaning of the New Jerusalem. John Bale's *Image of Both Churches* (London, 1570) is likewise explicit: John's vision is of "the true congregation of God compact together in the unitie of one perfecte Christian faith" (Mmm2). But in Spenser's allegory the city is that of a king and Una, figure of that church, is left behind in the House of Holiness and even Mercie is apparently left downhill.

25.   Quoted (but not from the Geneva Bible) in T. W.'s *Ladder of Paradise* (London: Aggas, 1580), C2v; this little book is translated from a *Scala Paradisi*, once ascribed to Augustine but by the Carthusian Guigo II. It offers advice on interior ascent and the pleasure of contemplation but I see no Platonism. In terms of Psalm 24, St. George, with blood on his hands and work to do, is no more ready for Jerusalem than Moses was for the Promised Land. David's Orphic nature is not my subject here, but on the power of these musicians to create concord see *FQ* IV.ii.1–2. Davidic harping is cosmic as well as pious. For du Bartas, it resonated with the "cieux organisés": the psalmist's touch "right cunningly/Combined with his voice draws downe sweet harmony/From th'organized heav'ns, on Harpe that still shall sound/As long as daies great star shall ore our heads go round" ("Babilon," from the *Seconde Sepmaine*, trans. William L'isle [1595], H2), and Le Fèvre uses the same phrase ("Cieux organizez") when describing Orpheus (Circle IV.355, tying the heptachord also to the seven-flamed candelabra). For a brief mention of David and Le Fèvre, see Simone Maser, *L'Image de David dans la littérature française* (Orléans: Les Éditions David, 1996), 93–94.

26.   In his *Praelections upon the Sacred and Holy Revelation of S. John*, trans. George Gifford (1573), William Fulke comments that John is taken to a "high place" so that from this "beholding place" he "might in contemplation the whole figure of the newe Jerusalem her situation and placinge"; he adds that although the Babylon of the Antichrist had seemed glorious and Jerusalem poor, the renewed Jerusalem is "a magnificall citie to behold" (T2). For Fulke, the Antichrist is Rome. Is there any hint of this in Spenser? Certainly for most Protestants the restored Jerusalem was not only the non-Babylon but the non-(papal)Rome. Needless to say, this is not what the view from Le Fèvre's hill of contemplation reveals.

27.   Ellrodt, 35.

28.   Baldassar Castiglione, *The Courtyer*, trans. Thomas Hoby (London: Seres, 1561), Xx3v. It may have been literary tact that made Spenser limit himself to three hills.

29.   Quoted from Stephen Batman, *Batman Uppon Bartholome* [Bartholomaeus Anglicus] (London, 1582), C6v. Batman quotes the opening of the *Metamorphoses* on human posture and on the next page (D1) cites Pythagoras on the soul as "a concord of melodie."

30.   Robert Southwell, *An Epistle of Comfort* (London, ?1587), N6.

31.   *A Right Christian Treatise, Entituled S. Augustines Praiers*, trans. Thomas Rogers (London, 1581), i1v. Explicitly Platonic, Rogers's *Anatomie of the Minde* (London: Charlewood, 1576) is less syncretic than classical.

32.   Euclid, *The Elements of Geometrie*, trans. H. Billingsley with added commentary by John Dee (London, 1570), *1v, in a preface citing Pico and other Neoplatonists.

33.   Ellrodt sees in Redcrosse's descent, together with a stress on Christian love, a more Christian than Platonic tonality, but just as Socrates goes about his ordinary life at the end of the *Symposium*, so too at the end of *The Courtier* we return to an ordinary day (a rosy one, to be sure, with cool air blowing from the planet Venus). Like Plato, Walter Hilton's *Scala Perfectionis*, printed in 1494 and several times thereafter in early modern England, describes a ladder, not a hill, although in the early chapters, devoted to contemplation, a mental ascent enables the soul to see "ghostly lyghtnynges from the hevenly Iherusalem that is Jhesu" (ch. 25, heading).

34.   Was John's position on the isle of Patmos often imagined as atop a mountain? The Medieval and Renaissance illustrations of St. John that I have seen tend not to make much of verticality here below, focusing on the prophet's (usually) upward gaze, although he sometimes has a small rocky mound on which to stand or kneel.

35.   Another image Spenser might have noted with appreciation is one that the printer John Day used for his title pages. *Certain Select Prayers, Gathered out of S. Augustines Meditations . . . Also his Manuell, or booke of the Contemplation of Christ* (1577) shows Hope and Faith gazing at the Hebrew letters of God's name from the sides, while Charity and her children lie below, likewise looking up Near Charity is a town with ruins. Neither Faith nor Hope carries her traditional insignia but it is easy to think of the sisters in Spenser's House of Holinesse. An extraordinary "hill of contemplation" is in a long poem published with Sir William Denny's *Pelecanicidium, or, The Christian Adviser Against Self-Murder* (London, 1653). Denny describes an upward trek through many stanzas shaped like hillocks of verse, some of which represent the "Downs of Cogitation" (X2v).

36.   Georges Poulet, *Les Métamorphoses du cercle* (Paris: Plon, 1961), 3, 5.

37.   Seth Weiner explains the triadic and "perfect" time made by the arrangements on Book VI's Mt. Acidale in "Minims and Grace Notes: Spenser's Acidalian Vision and Sixteenth-Century Music," *Spenser Studies* V (1985): 91–112.

38.   On Spenser's numerological imitation of the sun's imperfect circuit see A. Kent Hieatt, *Short Time's Endless Monument* (New York: Columbia Press, 1960).

ANDREW ESCOBEDO

The Sincerity of Rapture

This essay explores what it means to say that Spenser adheres to a poetics of erotic rapture. As it functions in Spenser's poetry, erotic rapture seizes the will, redirecting it toward the distant prospect of union with an idealized beloved. The enraptured lover loses the capacity for free choice; his or her love continues to bear traces of the initial shock of seizure, motivating rather than liberating. This loss of liberty comes with a gain of authenticity; erotic rapture is above all, for Spenser, a marker of the lover's *sincerity*. The notion of erotic sincerity sheds light on the critical debate about Spenser's conspicuous dramatization of Scudamour's choice when he takes Amoret away from the Temple of Venus (*FQ* IV.x.53). Scudamour, this essay argues, is a lover whom love has not quite seized, so he is obliged to *decide* whether or not to pursue his courtship of Amoret. His aggression springs from under-motivation; he is oddly insincere. Spenser's model of erotic rapture has precedents in medieval love poetry and Petrarchan lyric, but his most important source is Plato. After surveying the trope of rapture in Plato and Spenser, I return to the Temple of Venus to consider the implications of this trope for Scudamour's choice. This consideration takes us in turn to Chaucer, then Cicero, and finally back to Plato.

*H*AVING WON THE SHIELD of Love and passed by Doubt, Delay, Danger, and the garden of lovers; having entered Venus's Temple, portered by Concord, Love, and Hate; and seeing the statue of the hermaphroditic Venus attended by her priestesses, Scudamour at last prepares to complete his quest for Amoret. Yet before he seizes her from among a bevy of womanly personifications, Scudamour does the most extraordinary thing: he chooses. This choice occurs when he sees Amoret,

Whom soone as I beheld, my hart gan throb,
  And wade in doubt, what best were to be donne:
  For sacrilege me seem'd the Church to rob,
  And folly seem'd to leave the thing undonne,
  Which with so strong attempt I had begonne.
  Tho shaking off all doubt and shamefast feare,
  Which Ladies love I heard had never wonne
  Mongst men of worth, I to her stepped neare,
And by the lilly hand her labour'd up to reare.   (IV.x.53)

Most scholarly studies of this episode seek to determine whether Scudamour makes a positive or negative choice here. Opinions range from interpreting the abduction as a brutal "violation" to reading it as "a vigorous and healthy invasion by the male viewer."[1] Yet my interest, at least initially, lies not in evaluating the justice of Scudamour's decision but rather in the fact that Spenser dramatizes a choice in the first place. It is nearly unique in *The Faerie Queene*. Spenser first presents the psychological experience of uncertainty ("wade in doubt"), then a process of deliberation in which Scudamour weighs options (to commit either "sacrilege" or "folly"), and finishes with the dramatic resolution of uncertainty ("shaking off all doubt") in the form a distinct choice ("I to her stepped neare"). Here we have the impression, which we rarely do in the poem, that a character's deliberate choice will change the course of the narrative.

Critics have insufficiently savored the surprise of this moment. Spenser's characters usually do not seem to make deliberate choices so much as their decisions appear to be consequences of earlier narrative events. Of course, they "make choices" in that they perform actions that are not directly compelled by external agents: in this minimal sense, all literary characters have free will, and there are no volitional distinctions to be made. But Spenser, unlike poets such as Sidney or Milton, doesn't dramatize these actions as choices, but instead makes them appear as effects of narrative momentum or moral character. Even at those moments in which the narrative explicitly offers multiple options, Spenser almost never allows his characters to deliberatively select one option over another. For example, Amoret "did cast" (III.vi.53.1) her love to Scudamour rather than to her other suitors at Faery court, but Spenser declines to make these suitors distinctive in any way: with no sense of the alternatives among which Amoret is selecting, her casting does not come across as much of a deliberate choice. As another example, consider Britomart's options at the flaming gate of Busirane's House: go forward or go back (basically the same options that Scudamour later confronts at the Temple of Venus). At first she demurs, noting that indiscreet action "[i]nglorious and beastlike is" (III.xi.23.2). But then, hearing Scudamour's despair, she resolves to "try extremities of chaunce" (24.8) rather than retire. We might, through an external process of interpretation, make sense of Britomart's sudden swing from one option to its opposite, but Britomart does not herself make this sense for us through a deliberative contemplation of the two options. She doesn't choose it in the way that Scudamour does.

This odd exception to typical Spenserian poetics demands our attention all the more because it occurs in an episode that withholds choice, when Scudamour seizes Amoret against her will, denying her "her wished freedome" (IV.x.57.5). Doubling this irony is the fact that Prince Arthur, just prior to Scudamour's account of the Temple of Venus, has insisted that it is precisely ladies like Amoret "[t]o whom the world this franchise ever yielded,/That of their loves choice they might freedom clame" (IV.ix.37.6–7). Scudamour appears to have purloined the choice that ought to belong to Amoret. Yet we should resist the common assumption that Scudamour, by denying Amoret her freedom, encroaches on what Spenser sees as the right of women (or men, for that matter) to choose whether or not they fall in love and with whom. No one, at least no virtuous lover, gets to choose this in *The Faerie Queene*. In this poem, love seizes you or not; if it does, your subsequent freedom, such as it is, lies in refusing to transfer your love to another. Part of Scudamour's problem, as this essay will suggest, is that he is a lover whom love has not quite seized, and so he is obliged to *decide* whether or not to pursue his courtship of Amoret. His aggression springs from his under-motivation; he is oddly insincere.

I have elsewhere discussed the function of "daemonic" personification to explain Spenser's disinclination to account for ethical behavior in terms of deliberate choice.[2] In this essay, which I intend as a complement to the former one, I explore what it means to say that Spenser adheres to a poetics of erotic rapture. By *rapture*, I mean something different from Gordon Teskey's account of allegorical capture (which relies on a model of repressive constraint) as well as something different from Katherine Eggert's account of poetic rapture (which relies on a model of open-endedness).[3] Yet it will be obvious that I owe much to these two views. Erotic rapture, as it functions in Spenser, to some extent combines these models: it is a seizure that overwhelms the will while simultaneously implying the future possibility of purposeful volition. Yet this subsequent sense of purpose does not yield a capacity for free choice; instead, it continues to bear the trace of the initial shock of seizure, motivating rather than liberating. The loss of liberty comes with the gain of a certain species of erotic authenticity, because rapture is above all for Spenser a marker of the lover's *sincerity*. This model of erotic rapture has precedents in medieval love poetry and Petrarchan lyric, but Spenser's most important source is Plato. After surveying the trope of rapture in Plato and Spenser I'll return to the Temple of Venus to consider the implications of this trope for Scudamour's choice. This consideration will in turn take us to Chaucer, and then Cicero, and finally back to Plato.

Plato's Divine Madness

Discussions of Platonism in Spenser's poetry often emphasize a process of abstraction in which the initial shock of love is smoothed away by a vision of the good.[4] Yet this is not the only story of the dialogues, and it is not the story that Plato's Renaissance followers cared about the most. In popular dialogues such as the *Phaedrus* and the *Symposium*, violent rapture persists as a model of virtuous action and knowledge. The modern commentator who has perhaps seen this most clearly is the German Catholic philosopher Josef Pieper, who, despite an inclination to Christianize Plato, identifies erotic madness as the foundation of Plato's sexual ethics:

> If we consider all the aspects of *mania* which Plato mentions, we shall have to say that he uses the word to mean, primarily, a being-beside-oneself, a loss of command over oneself, surrender of autarchic independence and self-control; a state in which we are not active, but passive. . . . [W]hen [*mania*] happens, it does so in such a manner that *sophrosyne* and all that goes with that is forcibly annulled, however much the dignity of the human person depends on it. Inspiration takes the form of *theia mania*, of the self's not-being-with-the-self.[5]

In this account, rapture is not merely a beginning that the Platonic scheme leaves behind, but rather it represents a self-alienation that permanently changes the moral agent. Keeping this interpretation in mind as we review relevant passages from Plato and his Renaissance redactors will prepare us to avoid certain misunderstandings about love and free choice in Spenser.[6]

Erotic rapture in Plato is sudden, compulsive, and violent. It involves a temporary and salubrious evacuation of reason brought on by an encounter with beauty. In the *Phaedrus*, Plato's Socrates explains that sages of old understood that "the greatest blessings come by way of madness [*mania*], indeed of madness that is heaven-sent" (244a).[7] Of the four primary kinds of *mania*—prophetic, mystic, poetic, and erotic—Socrates reserves his highest admiration for erotic madness. He makes it clear that the voluntary faculties of reason have nothing to do with the initial experience of beauty. The soul, having fallen from its vision of the pure being and entered a body on earth, encounters a beautiful person:

> But when one who is fresh from the mystery, and saw much of the vision, beholds a godlike face or bodily form that truly expresses beauty, first he shudders [*ephrize*] and then there overtakes [*hupēlthen*] him the awe which the vision inspired, and then reverence as at the sight of a god, and but for fear of being deemed a very madman he would offer sacrifice to his beloved, as to a holy image of deity. Next, with the passing of the shudder, a strange sweating and fever seizes [*lambanei*] him. (251a–c)[8]

The language of arrest and seizure (*phrissein, huperchomai, lambanein*) underscores that love is something that *happens to* a virtuous soul. Lovers don't deliberate about whether to have this experience or not, and there is no hint that a prior-existing temperance, such as Aristotle would later advocate, might mitigate rapture's assault.

Indeed, Plato contemptuously dismisses the possibility of free calculation in love by exposing Lysias's speech (which Phaedrus initially reads to Socrates) as a false model. In Lysias's misguided interpretation, nonlovers surpass lovers because they are "free agents under no constraint," and so can "regulate their services by the scale of their means, with an eye to their own personal interests" (*Phaedrus* 231a). The nonlover says to himself, "I am the master of myself, rather than the victim of love" (233c). Freedom is just another name for parsimony, and such ungenerous comportment provides no path to virtue, so far as Plato is concerned. The *Symposium* likewise underscores the falseness of free agency in erotic attachment. Pausanius cautions that lovers must accept servitude as the condition of erotic virtue, the lover "lawfully enslaving himself to the youth he loves, in return for his compliance, the latter lawfully devoting his services to the friend who is helping him to become wise and good" (184d–e). True lovers are just free enough to give up their freedom, entering a relationship of mutual thralldom.

Plato's preference in these passages for rapturous lovers over calculating ones recalls David M. Halperin's account of the distinction between erotic desire and irony in the Platonic dialogues: "In moments of intense, overwhelming sensation, we have little awareness of context and no attention to spare for more than one set of meanings. In such states, we become literalists: we can experience only one kind of thing."[9] Rapture collapses the gap between experience and expression upon which irony thrives and which might allow the agent a "perspective" on the situation confronting him. Part of Plato's point is that erotic desire has no perspective. Halperin does identify a deeper irony in the Platonic account of love, namely, the gap between what we think we want (a lover's body or person) and what our desire really wants (transcendent beauty or being): "Love's ironies . . . come down to a single paradox: the object of desire is not what you think it is."[10] Yet this irony provides no mastery for lovers, but rather hurls them deeper into the abyss of misrecognition. I suggest that this helplessness, which rapture both exemplifies and signifies, constitutes a Platonic version of erotic *sincerity*. It is an odd kind of sincerity, to be sure, since it consists not so much in coinciding with yourself but rather relinquishing a self that might fail to coincide. If you really are the master of yourself at the first moment of encounter, as Lysias recommends, then you are not really a lover.

This is not to deny that erotic *mania* presents a danger in Platonism: rapture is both a promise of authentic virtue and a risk of degradation, an ambiguity that emerges as the hallmark of Spenserian eroticism. Not all agents can manage their soul's response with equal success. Plato details his notion of the tripartite soul—rational (in the head), passionate (in the heart), and appetitive (in the lower abdomen)—in the *Republic* (435b–444e) and the *Timaeus* (69d–72d). In the *Phaedrus*, he famously figures this model of the soul as a chariot, with a driver in control of two horses, one noble and passionate, the other wanton and vainglorious (246a–b). This is precisely where erotic rapture can go wrong: if the rational charioteer fails to control the appetitive horse, the initial experience of rapture degenerates into mere lust (*Phaedrus* 253c–254e). If rational control wins out and the lovers resist sexual consummation, a philosophical calm does indeed soften the initial feeling of rapture: "their days on earth will be blessed with happiness and concord . . . they have won self-mastery and inward peace" (256a–b). Yet it is important not to exaggerate this calm in Plato's thought, since even sexual lovers gain bliss:

> Such a pair as this also are dear friends, but not so dear as that other pair, one to another. . . . When death comes they quit the body wingless indeed, but eager to be winged, and therefore they carry off no mean reward for their lovers madness [*mania erotikē*], for it is ordained that all such as have taken the first steps on the celestial highway shall no more return to the dark pathways beneath the earth, but shall walk together in a life of shining bliss, and be furnished in due time with like plumage the one to the other, because of their love. (256c–e)

The point to grasp here is not only the obvious idea that sexual passion, though subordinate to purely spiritual love, remains a legitimate form of affection in Plato, but that erotic *mania* persists as a model of spiritual reward. The oft-cited "ladder of love" does not *only* abstract from passionate rapture to spiritual calm, but, on the contrary, rapture reappears on the upper steps, as the prophetess Diotima teaches Socrates in the *Symposium*: "Whoever has been initiated so far in the mysteries of Love and has viewed all these aspects of the beautiful in due succession, is at last drawing near the final revelation. And now, Socrates, there suddenly bursts upon [*ezaiphnēs katopsetai*] him that wondrous vision which is the very soul of the beauty he has toiled so long for (210e211a).[11] This is the same kind of language that attended the lovers initial, rapturous vision of physical beauty. It guarantees the authenticity of the attainment of true beauty.

Later commentators did not miss this language of rapture or fail to observe its prominence as a theme in Plato's thought. The third-century philosopher Plotinus, a crucial disseminator of Platonic ideas, echoes the vocabulary of seizure in his account of beauty, insisting that spiritual loveliness ravishes souls even more violently than physical loveliness: "they must be delighted and overwhelmed [*ekplēxin labein*] and excited much more than by those beauties we spoke of before . . . [experiencing] wonder and a shock of delight [*ekplēxin hēdian*] and longing and passion.[12] In Plotinus, beauty has the force of an overwhelming blow (*ekplēxis*). Likewise, Plato's most important Renaissance editor, Marsilio Ficino, repeatedly notes in his commentaries the centrality of Platonic *mania*, which he usually translates as *furor* or *alienatio*: "Whoever experiences any kind of spiritual possession is indeed overflowing on account of the vehemence of the divine impulse and the fullness of its power: he raves, exults, and exceeds the bounds of human behavior. Not unjustly, therefore, this possession or rapture is called madness and alienation" [*Itaque occupatio hec sive raptus furor quidam et alienatio non iniuria nominatur*].[13] Ficino maintains Plato's sense of violent erotic possession (*occupatio, raptus*), and even more than Plato underscores the encounter with otherness (*alienatio*) that such possession entails. Erotic rapture temporarily sets you outside yourself, and to complain that such alienation compromises self-control or reason misses the point: "Anyone who condemns intemperate love on the grounds that it is a frenzy, that is, an alienation of the intelligence, errs. For the love that alienates a soul, which has been seized by a god and raised above man, is also a frenzy, though a frenzy we should venerate since it comes from a god."[14]

Rapture and Freedom in Spenser

Spenser finds in this Platonic tradition of erotic rapture—of *mania, ekplēxis, raptus, furor*, and *alienatio*—a model of virtuous love even more central than the commonly cited abstraction from physical to spiritual.[15] In claiming this, I have no wish to deny that other traditions, such as Petrarchan lyric and medieval romance, inform Spenser's representation of the arrest of beauty. The *coup de foudre* was a literary commonplace in Spenser's time.[16] Yet Spenser derives a combination of several elements from Platonic rapture that he would not have found elsewhere, at least not with the same set of interlocking significances. Crucially, it supplies Spenser with a means to potentially distinguish inconstant from constant love within a fictional world that works against constancy. *The Faerie Queene* functions according to a protocol of hermeneutic ambiguity, such that a hero's progress nearly always coincides with a narrative movement from simple to complex patterns of meaning that make it difficult to discern what actually counts as progress. Spenser's heroes are not deceivers, but they live in a world in which an assertion of virtue remains incomplete in itself, potentially qualified by other contexts and episodes that call it into question. In a poetic landscape such as this, rapture stands out because it is unmistakable as rapture. Certainly, its *consequences* following the moment of seizure are uncertain, but rapture itself never functions as a calculated deception or ambiguity. The false Florimell, under the mechanical guidance of a built-in sprite, perfectly replicates the behavior of a virtuous woman in love (III.viii.7–8, 10, 14), and it is precisely this *distance* between truth and expression that precludes the possibility of *mania* for her. You can fake almost anything in *The Faerie Queene*, but you can't fake rapture.

In the poem's typical scheme, the rapture of beauty temporarily dispossesses the lovers it assaults of their reason and voluntary control. In doing so, it creates the occasion for either virtuous feeling or crass sexual impulse, the former usually accompanied by a (Platonic) intuition of "beauty itself." In the case of virtuous feeling, the rapture divides the lover's life into a distinct before and after, between a prior drifting freedom and a subsequent sense of ethical purpose. This sense of purpose, although requiring the exertion of moral will, does not present itself as a set of choices to be made but rather as a series of shocks that, echoing the original experience of rapture, inspire the lovers (sometimes painfully) to pursue their moral goals. Spenser does not, of course, have his lovers follow the ladder of love up to the contemplation of pure beauty or goodness, but it is not clear how he would manage that in a heroic romance epic. Love in *The Faerie Queene* is less strictly teleological than Platonic love, yet it is nonetheless purposive, and Spenser imagines this purpose to derive from an experience of Platonic rapture.

Most often, erotic seizure represents the start of a conversion from sexual or social immaturity to a mature care for others. Arthur, Marinell, Artegall, and Britomart leave behind their youthful traits (sadism, priggishness, savagery, and naiveté, respectively) not through a process of reason or choice but through the *mania* of love. Seeing or hearing their beloveds for the first time, Arthur is "ravished with delight" (I.ix.14.6), Artegall suffers "secret fear" and "trembling horrour" (IV.vi.21.3 and 22.8), Marinell's "stubborn heart, that never felt misfare/Was touch with soft remorse and pitty rare" (IV.-xii.12.4–5), and Britomart feels "sudden joy, and secret feare withal" (IV.vi.29.3). The assault of love victimizes all of these characters, cruelly denying them their self-control for a time, but in so doing it imbues them with a sustained (if fallible) sense of virtue. Arthur shifts from riotous youth to a knight of grace, Artegall from a savage knight to a knight of justice, Marinell from proud indifference to solicitude, Britomart from girlish innocence to martial womanhood.[17] (Scudamour does not quite fit into this list, as we will discuss.) This "conversion" to ethical purposiveness does not simply leave the moment of erotic ravishment in the past. Rapture continues to seize the characters in reiterations of the original assault of beauty, as when Arthur, recounting his first vision of Gloriana to Redcross and Una, suddenly becomes pale and faint (I.ix.16), or when Britomart, watching the reunited Amoret and Scudamour embrace, is briefly overcome with passion for her own love (III.xii.46).

Of course, the lovers must rely on their moral character to modulate the initial experience of erotic rapture, and therein lies the simultaneous risk and promise of love that Spenser adapts from Plato. If critics have found it notoriously difficult to maintain a clear separation between love and lust in *The Faerie Queene*, this difficulty stems in part from the common origin both feelings have in the arrest of beauty. The sight of Gloriana leaves Arthur "ravished with delight" (I.ix.14.6), and the sight of Belphoebe likewise enraptures Braggadocchio, though he, "with her wondrous beauty ravisht quight,/Gan burne in filthy lust" (II.iii.42.4–5). Neither character chooses to feel ravishment, and neither exactly chooses to respond virtuously or basely: rapture activates what is already in them. The heroes do not deliberate and then decide how to respond to ravishment, but rather let erotic instinct guide them, as Artegall does despite his urgent passion for Britomart:

> Yet durst he not make love so suddenly,
>   Ne thinke th'affection of her hart to draw
>   From one to other so quite contrary:
>   Besides her modest countenance he saw
>   So goodly grave, and full of princely aw,
>   That it his ranging fancie did refraine,
>   And looser thoughts to lawfull bounds withdraw;
>   Whereby the passion grew more fierce and faine,
> Like to a stubborne steede whom strong hand would restraine.
>
> (IV.vi.33)

Strikingly, Artegall's effort at temperance makes his desire both more lawful and more dangerously intense. Spenser's metaphor of the "stubborne steede" may owe something to Plato's description, in the *Phaedrus* (254b–e), of the increasingly violent efforts of the soul's appetitive horse to resist the governing bridle of the rational charioteer. As Plato notes, some lovers succeed in this restraint, and some do not. Because a model of erotic seizure so fully dispossesses the lover of voluntary response, the initial modulation of desire becomes a tricky affair: in the moments following his rapture, Artegall comes perilously close to Braggadocchio. As in Plato, rapture supplies the initial, overwhelming energy that the lover's ethical character tries to channel in an appropriate direction, but the sheer risk of erotic *mania* is never far from Spenser's mind.

This model of erotic sincerity, even though it includes Britomart, is at least slightly gendered male in Spenser's mind, since he usually depicts the sincerity of his female lovers not in terms of rapture but rather in terms of suffering and enduring. As Melissa E. Sanchez has observed in a splendid discussion about friendship and political sovereignty in *The Faerie Queene*, Amoret's bondage confirms the authenticity of her love for Scudamour: "the sincerity of her choice becomes legible through Busirane's violence."[18] We could say much the same of Florimell's trials for the sake of Marinell. In Spenser, virtuous girls tend to suffer for love, whereas virtuous boys tend to be enraptured into it. My Platonic focus in this essay leads me to concentrate on the latter, but in both cases sincerity becomes manifest through a kind of constraint.

Indeed, as the foregoing discussion already suggests, Platonic rapture in Spenser acquires both its power and instability from a denial of choice, in the sense of Plato's dismissal of a lover's "free agency," or what Spenser censures as "liberty."[19] This does not amount to saying that Spenser advocates an erotics of rape, for he always disapproves of forcing someone to receive desire against his or her will, as Busyrane tries to do to Amoret or Proteus to Florimell. We can still speak of "consent" in Spenserian eroticism, but only as an acquiescence to an external pressure, not as a considered decision to love or not. Spenser thinks that his lovers ideally ought to have the freedom to do (or not do) what they want, but they cannot will what they want, to borrow Arthur Schopenhauer's formula of desire. Artegall, as we have seen, desists from leaping on Britomart, knowing that such an act would violate her will, even though she already loves him. But Spenser describes the knight's subsequent courtship as an assault in which he "did lay/Continuall siege unto her gentle hart," until "at the length unto a bay he brought her" (IV.vi.40.4 and 41.3). The language of siege and hunt is a metaphor for persuasion, of course, but Spenser's formulation of Britomart's acceptance of the knight's love reveals the limited purview of volition in desire: "she *yielded* her consent/To be his love, and take him for her Lord" (41.7, my emphasis). As a lover, Britomart is servant to her lord, just as Arthegall becomes "a Ladies thrall" (IV.vi.28.8). Pausanius's mutual thralldom (*Symposium* 184d–e) is as free as love gets in *The Faerie Queene*.

If this model strikes us as somewhat unstable, it is because rapture can always go wrong. A lover such as Artegall, newly ravished by the sight of the wicked Radigund, may consent to be "her thrall," "willfully" abandoning his moral responsibilities (V.v.17.5, 8). This kind of possibility confirms Joseph Loewenstein's claim that in Spenser's work "the *arresting* power of beauty constitutes both a narrative and poetic problem."[20] Yet Spenser offers no sense that an ethics of free will might assuage this problem of arrest, certainly not in the form of A. Kent Hieatt's suggestion that the poem promotes a "room of one's own for decisions" about love.[21] In Spenser's version of Platonic rapture, the room is not simply one's own, and one doesn't make decisions in it. Hieatt does marshal important evidence for his view, namely, those statements in the poem that echo the Chaucerian dictum (from the Merchant's tale) that mastery cannot compel love.[22] These statements are significant, and demand interpretation. Britomart censures Malecasta's knights' attempt to force Redcross to change his love by telling them, "Ne may love be compeld by maistery;/For soone as maistery comes, sweet love anone/Taketh his nimble winges, and soone away is gone" (III.i.25.7–9). Duessa, taunting Scudamour with Amoret's supposed infidelity, informs him, "For love is free, and led with selfe delight,/Ne will enforced be with maisterdome or might" (IV.i.46.8–9). Satyrane, proposing that (the false) Florimell be awarded to the knight of her choice, says in indirect discourse that "Sweete is the love that comes alone with willingness" (IV.v.25.9). And finally, as we noted earlier, Arthur chides the knights for continuing to battle over possession of Florimell since "of their loves choise [ladies] might freedom clame" (IV.ix.37.7).

What do these assertions of erotic freedom amount to? The clearly compulsive nature of love in *The Faerie Queene*, including virtuous love, signals immediately that we cannot take them as Spenser's advocacy of erotic freedom *tout court*. Local ironies undercut three of the statements: the mastery of Cupid *does* in fact compel Britomart to love, the false Florimell's choice of Braggadocchio is hardly sweet, and Arthur's claim is immediately contradicted by Scudamour's demonstration that Amoret had no choice in the Temple of Venus. Furthermore, three of the assertions speak to contexts in which knights try to determine a woman's love by battle. Spenser does indeed find this kind of mastery illegitimate, precisely because it seeks to override the imperatives of authentic rapture. Lovers surely *should* have the freedom to refuse any external compulsion to abandon the beloved whose beauty has already enthralled them. Here we can distinguish between Duessa's freedom "led with selfe delight"—a version of the "free agency" that Plato despises in the *Phaedrus*—and the more limited freedom of consent and faithfulness. Duessa's formulation in fact represents a casual indifference to any single beloved, describing the freedom of the false Florimell, who looks at every knight "[a]s though she wished to have pleasd them all" (IV.v.26.7), or the freedom of Paridell's easy welcome to the wound of love:

But nothing new to him was that same paine,
Ne paine at all; for he so oft had tryde
The powre thereof, and lov'd so oft in vaine,
That thing of course he counted, love to entertaine.

(III.ix.29.6–9)

This kind of love, to recall Halperin, is ironically detached from itself; it has escaped mastery at the cost of authentic intensity. Such lovers simply drift because love pushes them in no particular direction.[23] To some degree, then, both casual love and erotic rapture eschew external mastery, but in fundamentally different ways. No human mastery can force the casual love of the false Florimell or Paridell to commit to a single beloved, nor force the ravished Redcross or Amoret to love someone other than their beloved (although *another* ravishment can force this, as the example of Arthegall confirms).

But if consenting fidelity is the primary sense of these statements against mastery, their language of freedom and choice also speaks to the poem's anxiety about rapture. Rapture *is* different from rape for Spenser: the former violently makes you want something, the latter violently makes you engage in something you don't want.[24] Yet both phenomena override the will, temporarily denying the characters their self-control. Spenser sees no way around this risk. Unlike Milton, whose best-known moment of moral artistry demands that Adam choose virtue *despite* the promptings of love, Spenser nearly always imagines that virtue *needs* love as its prompt and fuel. His heroes gain the momentum of moral purpose through an initial seizure of their volition, a loss of autonomy violent enough to render the lover a victim. Free choice in love represents the underdetermined version of rapture, exampled by Duessa, the false Florimell, and Paridell. Yet the overdetermined version of rapture, and sometimes uncomfortably close to it, is rape, exampled by would-be violators such as Sansloy, Busirane, Proteus, and Lust. This is why the poem both praises love as a noble god of Platonic proportions and condemns it as a tyrant.

Scudamour's Choice

Loci amoeni such as the Bower of Bliss or the Garden of Adonis have intrigued and perplexed readers with their rich multiplicity: there is too much to see in one view. The Temple of Venus perplexes us, by

contrast, because something seems to be missing. The basic tonality of
the episode is unnervingly inconsistent. Is the lesson of Scudamour's
adventure that the fidelity of love more than compensates for its pain,
as he clearly tells us in stanza 2 of the temple canto, or that the pain
of love exceeds its rewards, as he clearly tells us in stanza 3? Does
Scudamour think that he is worse off than lovers who are "free from
·feare and gealosye" (28.5) or better off, since "Much dearer be the
things, which come through hard distresse" (28.9)? Spenser also
makes it difficult to determine how we ought to respond to Scudamour himself in this episode. Critics have often suggested that the
first-person perspective of the episode, the hero's biased recollection
of what happened, requires that we not take seriously his claim of
victory. But the third-person narrator has already confirmed victory,
of a sort, at the beginning of Book IV, when he tells us that Scudamour fetched Amoret "From twentie Knights, that did him all assay:/
Yet fairely well he did them all dismay:/And with great glory both
the shield of love,/And eke the Ladie selfe he brought away"
(IV.i.2.4–7). Spenser also implies real sympathy for Scudamour during
his embrace with Amoret in the 1590 conclusion of Book III
(xii.44–45). On the other hand, this is the same hero we saw child-
ishly pounding his head on the ground at Busirane's gate
(III.ix.7–13, 26–27).

Spenser likewise refuses us ready evidence to determine whether
Scudamour makes the right or wrong choice when he decides to
seize Amoret. In one sense, when he "her labour'd up to reare"
(IV.x.53.9) from the temple, the gesture recalls Amoret's deliverance
from Busirane's house when Britomart, "uprearing her from ground"
(III.xii.40.1), rescues her from torture. In another sense, the seizure
is anything but a deliverance, since it is so clearly *against* Amoret's
will (IV.x.57). As I have suggested, erotic rapture in the poem does
temporarily deny the lover voluntary control, but Scudamour does
not ravish Amoret with his beauty, as Artegall does to Britomart
(IV.vi.26): Scudamour uses force. Yet is force wrong in this episode?
Although Womanhood berates Scudamour as "over bold"
(IV.x.54.2), Scudamour is "emboldned" when he sees the statue of
Venus "with amiable grace/To laugh at me, and favour my pretense"
(56.3–4). This laughing endorsement, along with that of Concord
earlier in the narrative (36), makes it hard to see the episode offering
a straightforward condemnation of an overaggressive male. Despite
Laurel L. Hendrix's excellent research on the ambiguity of godly
laughter in *The Faerie Queene*, Spenser's Venus, who in the Garden
of Adonis did "reape sweet pleasure of the wanton boy" (III.vi.46.3),

is no stranger to the compulsive mastery of love.[25] She seems to be laughing with genuine approval.

With these perplexities before us, we would do well to heed Judith H. Anderson's advice and avoid a reading of the temple of Venus that is "closed, settled, and determinate—wholly on top of things."[26] Anderson herself carries out a superbly unsettling reading of the episode by exploring one of its primary literary sources, Chaucer's *Parliament of Fowls*, in which the narrator, a would-be student of the art of love, recounts a dream in which he was led to the temple of Venus and then to a gathering of birds preparing to select mates. Through a nuanced comparison, Anderson attributes the tonal oddness of the episode in part to a mixture of Chaucerian irony and Scudamour's self-absorbed passion. My only demur with this interpretation is that it understates the issue of choice common to both texts. Chaucer goes out of his way in *Parliament of Fowls* to note that the formel, the young beauty coveted by the male birds, possesses the prerogative to accept or decline the advances of her admirers: "But natheles, in this condicioun/Mot be the choys of everich that is heere,/That she agre to his eleccioun"; "she hireself shal han hir eleccioun/Of whom hire lest."[27] Indeed, at the end of the poem, the formel chooses to accept no suitor, opting to wait another season before selecting a mate. Anderson insists that "the relevance of the formel's freedom to Amoret's situation is moot. Amoret's lack of freedom is a consequence of Scudamour's vision, and her consent is not an option available within its terms."[28] Yet although the second half of this statement is true, the first half overlooks the possibility of an ironic relevance: Spenser bases the denial of Amoret's "wished freedome" on a Chaucerian original explicitly characterized by female prerogative.

Furthermore, Scudamour's unusually dramatic process of doubt and choice, when he sees Amoret, finds a parallel in the Chaucerian narrator's uncertainty at the entrance into the temple of Venus, when he encounters the gates of bliss and danger:

These vers of gold and blak iwriten were,
Of whiche *I gan astoned to beholde.*
For with that oon encresede ay my fere
And with the other gan my herte *bolde;*
That oon me hette, that other dide me colde;
No wit hadde I, for errour, for to *chese*
To entre or flen, or me save or lese.   (141–47, my emphases)

The narrator's astonishment and boldness anticipates the "doubt" and "emboldened" confidence (*FQ* IV.x.53 and 56) that Scudamour feels in Spenser's rendition. Spenser appropriates the speaker's choice, at the entrance of the temple of Venus, and shifts it to the climax of his version, when Scudamour seizes Amoret. The latter part of Chaucer's poem features the capacity of the female beloved's freedom; the latter part of Spenser's episode features the female beloved's lack of freedom and the male lover's effort of decision. The Chaucerian intertext surely works to thematize the issue of choice, yet Spenser has radically changed the terms. He does so to accommodate the erotic protocols of his poem, which work according to an ethic of rapture rather than the Chaucerian ethic of freedom.

What is Scudamour choosing? He is choosing between the "sacrilege" of robbing a temple and the "folly" of giving up (IV.x.53), which is to say he chooses whether to be bold or not. The language of *boldness* throughout the episode confirms this, language that links his doubt not only to *Parliament of Fowls* but also to Britomart's puzzlement over the competing messages of "be bold" and "be not too bold" in Busirane's castle.[29] Unlike Scudamour, Britomart does not *choose* between these two options—she does not even understand what they mean—but she follows her ethical and erotic instincts to go forward "with bold steps" (III.xii.50). Scudamour deliberates and decides, yet his options sound curiously extreme: if he decides to be bold and take Amoret, he commits sacrilege and becomes *too bold*; if he decides not to be too bold and leave Amoret, he commits folly and becomes *insufficiently bold*. We could interpret the lose-lose quality of these options to reflect Scudamour's limited moral character—Hieatt calls Scudamour "a very thrusting young knight," and Elizabeth Fowler complains that the knight "concludes that, rather than requiring [Amoret's] voluntary consent, his action must be based upon his own worth."[30] Yet Scudamour understands his choice not as one between the beloved's voluntary consent and the lover's self-worth, but between seizure and withdrawal. Perhaps Scudamour *should* have formulated better options, but the episode never implies that voluntary consent is a possibility in the temple. This is a place in which Cupid's "law compels all creatures to obay," even in Cupid's absence, a law that provokes lovers' laments "through loves constrayning" (IV.x.42 and 43). Spenser's translation of the Lucretian hymn to Venus, uttered just before Scudamour sees Amoret, confirms love's constraining effect, as Anthony Esolen suggests: "At virtually every opportunity Spenser overgoes Lucretius in celebrating the wildness of love's power."[31] True, in the garden outside the temple one set of lovers is "lincked in true harts consent" (26.4), yet significantly these are pairs of male friends, not heterosexual couples (27): Spenser values them, but does not offer them as a model for Scudamour and Amoret.

Scudamour's problem is not that he makes an imprudent choice or that he miscalculates his options. Rather, his problem is that he has not been enraptured by love and so has to make a choice at all. Critics routinely point out that the story of Amoret and Scuda-mour—unlike that of the other primary characters in the poem—remains unfinished in the 1596 version of the poem, leaving the two lovers on the brink of reunion without quite letting it happen.[32] Generally unnoticed, however, is the manner in which Spenser matches this imperfect conclusion with an imperfect beginning. The narrator has told us that Amoret, after her fosterage in the Garden of Adonis, came to the fairy court, where she fell in love with Scuda-mour, "To whom her loving hart she linked fast" (III.vi.53.3). But what about Scudamour: when or how did he fall in love with Amoret? I am not seeking biographical detail in the way one might of a character in a modern novel. Instead, I point to the poem's odd silence on this matter compared to the distinct moments of rapture experienced by Marinell, Arthur, Artegall, and Britomart. Scudamour certainly suffers for love, but we never *see* the moment in which he undergoes Platonic *mania*. The poem provides no division between his pre—and post-rapture character, because that distinct moment of *ekplexis* is denied him.[33] At the beginning of the account of his adventures Scudamour briefly mentions "the day that first with deadly wound/My heart was launcht, and learned to have loved" (IV.x.1.7–8). Did this day of wounding occur *before* his journey to the Temple of Venus? If so, he seems to have forgotten about it by the time he sets out:

What time the fame of this renowmed prise
   Flew first abroad, and all mens eares possest,
   I having armes then taken, gan avise
   To winne me honour by some noble gest,
   And purchase me some place amongst the best.
   I boldly thought (so young mens thoughts are bold)
   That this same brave emprize for me did rest,
   And that both shield and she whom I behold,
Might be my lucky lot; sith all by lot we hold.

(IV.x.4)

The *time* when news of the Temple's prize circulated abroad seems
curiously askew from the *day* when Scudamour received his love
wound. In the stanza above Scudamour appears motivated by a desire
for martial honor, not by love's deadly wound. Of course, in this
poem such motivations are not mutually exclusive, but in Scudamour's account of his intentions they seem unusually separate, as if
he cannot remember the one at the same time as the other.

   This is not to say that Scudamour does not love Amoret, but that
his pursuit of her is mixed with other motives. The lack of erotic
rapture by beauty, leaving open the distance between emotion and
expression, leaves him *too free*, too able to calculate his actions with
an eye to self-interest or self-protection. This distance, rather than
making him more effective, ends up producing a recurring unsteadi-
ness in his character, so that he asserts his will excessively or insufficiently, and seems to us alternately silly and dangerous. Even at the
moment of decision he abstracts from his situation to gauge ("I
heard . . . Mongst men of worth") which course of action will most
likely secure success. Nothing wrong with this as far as choices go:
rational decisions require consulting external criteria of evidence and
logic. Yet, in Spenserian love, this volitional gap between motive
and action creates a space of potential inauthenticity that makes it
hard to distinguish genuine erotic intentions from self-interested
ones. Once this gap opens in Scudamour, it likewise infects Amoret
with insincerity—or, if one prefers a psychological reading, Scudamour projects insincerity onto Amoret in his narration: "She often
prayd, and often me besought,/Sometime with tender teares to let
her goe,/Sometime with witching smyles" (IV.x.57.1–3). This does
not sound like the Amoret we have come to know in *The Faerie
Queene*: here she uses affectionate expression as a means to manipulate
others, the way a Duessa or Malecasta would. Spenser tries to stave
off, or at least mitigate, this version of love with erotic rapture.
Scudamour represents an example of the virtuous lover unmotivated
by that rapture. His *choice* to take Amoret from the Temple of Venus
signifies not his agency but rather a deficiency of inspiration, a species, in this poem, of insincerity.

   The Chaucerian intertext merits this attention to erotic choice
in the episode, as does the textual genealogy behind Chaucer. *The
Parliament of Fowls*, employing Scipio Africanus as the narrator's guide,
recalls and spoofs Cicero's *Somnium Scipionis*, transforming a dream-
vision about the sage Roman general to a dream-vision about a
grumpy love counselor. Chaucer's narrator even tells us that he was
reading the *Somnium* when he fell asleep (92–112), echoing the claim

of Cicero's narrator, Scipio the Younger, that talking about his ances-
tor before bed provoked his dream about him.[34] Cicero's text concerns itself little about choice—Scipio Africanus merely mentions
that his descendent will soon face a "viam ancipitem fatorum," or
two-fold path of destiny (IV.xii.12)—yet of more relevance to
Spenser may be the source lying behind the *Somnium*: Plato's Myth of
Er. We cannot, of course, be sure precisely which Platonic dialogues
Spenser read and which he did not, nor would the Chaucer-Cicero
connection alone automatically lead him to Plato's *Republic*: Spenser
could have read Thomas Newton's English translation of the *Somnium*, published twice, in 1569 and 1577.[35] Yet educated Elizabethans
were also likely to encounter Scipio in Macrobius's influential *Commentary on the Dream of Scipio*. The work was a touchstone for the
medieval and Renaissance understanding of dreams, and E. K. mentions Macrobius twice, in the General Argument and in the March
gloss to the *Shepheardes Calender*; E. K. also ascribes to Spenser a
poem, now lost, entitled *Dreames*.[36] If Spenser was familiar with the
Commentary, as it seems likely that he was, in the opening pages he
would have read about the "striking similarity" between Cicero's
Somnium and Plato's Myth of Er.[37] Macrobius makes clear that Cicero
deliberately imitates Plato, and for him the two texts seek the same
set of goals.

The post-death recollections of the Pamphylian warrior Er, coming at the very end of the Plato's *Republic*, cannot serve as a "source"
for the Temple of Venus in the ordinary sense, since the Er story
concerns itself with the afterlife punishments and rewards of human
beings, as well as with the process by which souls undergo reincarnation. Yet Plato's scene, like Spenser's, unfolds in a sacred space with
cosmic resonances, and furthermore the primary theme of the Er
story is in fact the issue of moral free will, an unexpected emphasis
in a dialogue that has scarcely said a word about the issue throughout.
According to Er, the souls are brought before the throne of *Anangkē*,
the principle of necessity, and one at a time obliged to choose what
kind of life they will live in their next iteration on earth:

Souls that live for a day, now is the beginning of another cycle
of mortal generation where birth is the beacon of death. No
divinity [*daimōn*] shall cast lots for you, but you shall choose
[*hairēsesthe*] your own deity [*daimōn*]. Let him to whom falls the
first lot first select a life to which he shall cleave of necessity.
But virtue has no master over her, and each shall have more or

less of her as he honors her or does her despite. The blame is
his who chooses [*helomenou*]. God is blameless.[38]

Beyond the theme of reincarnation, Spenser might have found congenial in this description the mixture of freedom and necessity with
which Plato describes moral choice. Spenser has little interest in *anangkē* as a cosmological principle: Jon Quitslund rightly notes that
Spenser nearly always prefers the term destiny over necessity.[39] Yet
in the Er story Plato is discussing the necessity of character, and so
this passage speaks to some of the fundamental ways in which Spenser
conceives that individuals achieve moral action. Importantly, although Plato argues here against a notion of fatality that would make
our choices irrelevant, he certainly makes no claim for the complete
absence of determinism. The soul freely selects a *daimōn* who then
guides that soul, of necessity, through the next life, and the Greek
term *daimōn* blends the notions of a prompting voice (a function of
character, *ethos*) and a destiny (a function of external necessity). The
first soul, for example, selects a life hastily, and then laments that this
life includes the "fate" [*heimarmenēn*] of eating his own children
(619c). Knowing about this fate does not leave the soul free to avoid
it; it's locked in as a feature of character. As Er reports, "the choice
[of the next life] was determined for the most part by the habits of
their former lives" (620a).

Spenser's Temple of Venus is not a philosophical treatise on the
interplay of freedom and necessity, and Scudamour is making a choice
about love, not reincarnation. Yet like the Myth of Er, Spenser's
episode suggests the degree to which the freedom of a choice does
not guarantee its virtue. Exertions of the will can be motivated by
necessity and still entail moral responsibility. We can profitably think
of the daimonism of the Er scenario, blending character and necessity,
as a philosophical template for the daemonic quality of Spenser's
titular heroes, who are "fated" to evolve into the virtue they represent and whose allegorical essence pushes them to behave as they do.
In such a scenario, choices are more the effects of character and
experience than the causes of these things. This determinism imbues
choices with their sincerity, whereas the absence of determinism
tends to yield flightiness rather than freedom. Indeed, in the Er story
the first *named* soul who chooses a new life, Orpheus, uses its freedom
rather thoughtlessly, electing to be a swan "because from hatred of the
tribe of women, owing to his death at their hands, it was unwilling to
be conceived and born of a woman" (620a).

This example of choice as irrational pique lays claim to relevance
for the final stanza of the temple episode, when Scudamour compares

his rescue of Amoret to the occasion when "Orpheus did recoure/ His Leman from the Stygian Princes boure" (IV.x.58.4–5). In the most common versions of this myth, Orpheus loses his beloved a second time by turning around to confirm that she is actually behind him. Beyond the possible irony of this myth of failure for Scudamour's triumph, Orpheus's *looking back* signals a lack of faith and resolve. Ovid, for example, describes the moment as a mixture of distrust and overeagerness that resonates with Scudamour's simultaneous underreaching and overreaching: "hic, ne deficeret, metuens avidusque videndi" [he, afraid that she might fail him, eager for the sight of her].[40] Plato, in the *Symposium*, anticipates this interpretation:

> Thus heaven itself has a peculiar regard for ardor and resolution in the cause of love. And yet the gods sent Orpheus away from Hades empty-handed, and showed him the mere shadow of the woman he had come to seek. Eurydice herself they would not let him take, because he seemed, like the mere minstrel that he was, to be a lukewarm lover, lacking courage to die as Alcestis dies for love, and choosing rather to scheme his way, living, into Hades. And it was for this that the gods doomed him, and doomed him justly, to meet his death at the hands of women. (179d)

Plato's Orpheus refuses to give himself over to the risk of love, scheming, and calculating how most safely to achieve his goal. He *chooses*, in the weak sense of the term, and gains only the shadow of his beloved, unlike Alcestis, who uncalculatingly surrenders herself to death with the result that she gains both life and love. If the history of Western erotic discourse since Plato has often aligned rapture and death, it has done so because both phenomena attest so persuasively to a lover's sincerity.[41]

NOTES

1.   The first view comes from Sheila T. Cavanagh, *Wanton Eyes and Chaste Desires: Female Sexuality in "The Faerie Queene"* (Bloomington: Indiana University Press, 1994), 98; and the second from Theresa Krier, *Gazing on Secret Sights: Spenser, Classical Imitation, and the Decorums of Vision* (Ithaca: Cornell University Press, 1990), 147.

2.   Escobedo, "Daemon Lovers: Will, Personification, and Character," *Spenser Studies* 22 (2007): 203–25.

3.   Teskey: "In the more powerful allegorical works this prevenient violence is unexpectedly revealed in moments that are so shocking in their honesty that they are consistently misread as departures from allegorical expression. Such moments literalize a metaphor from Neoplatonism, the moment of *raptio*, or "seizing," in which Matter, perversely resisting the desire of the male, must be ravished by form before being converted and returned to the Father" (*Allegory and Violence* [Ithaca: Cornell University Press, 1996], 18). Eggert: "As opposed to figuring poetry as genital rape, a tool for single-minded exposure, penetration, and comprehension of a feminized scene, *The Faerie Queene* also, if only intermittently, hints at poetry as a vehicle for rapture, a suffusion of delight that suspends the quest and admits a multiplicity of both erotic and epistemological pleasures" ("Spenser's Ravishment: Rape and Rapture in *The Faerie Queene*," *Representations* 70 [2000]: 1–26, at 2).

4.   For example, in his otherwise impressive essay on Platonism and the figure of Florimell, Patrick Cheney emphasizes only the process of abstraction in the Platonic scheme, ignoring the prevalence of rapture. See " 'And Doubted Her to Deeme an Earthly Wight': Male Neoplatonic 'Magic' and the Problem of Female Identity in Spenser's Allegory of the Two Florimells," *Studies in Philology* 86 (1989): 310–40.

5.   Pieper, *Enthusiasm and Divine Madness: On the Platonic Dialogue "Phaedrus"* (1962), trans. Richard and Clara Winston (South Bend, IN: St. Augustine's Press, 2000), 49, 56.

6.   In the following discussion I will make only a few distinctions between "Plato" and his various characters (Socrates, Diotima, Pausanius, etc.) because the Renaissance for the most part received the ideas they voiced as "Platonic," even though the original Greek audience would have found such distinctions important.

7.   All English passages from Plato are from *The Collected Dialogues of Plato*, eds. Edith Hamilton and Huntington Cairns (New Jersey: Princeton University Press, 1961). This collection reprints R. Hackforth's translation of the *Phaedrus* (1952) and Michael Joyce's translation of the *Symposium* (1935). References will be made parenthetically in the text. All passages and phrases from the original Greek are from *Platonis Opera*, vol. 2, ed. John Burnet (Oxford: Oxford University Press, 1901).

8.   I have made R. Hackforth's translation slightly more literal in order to avoid obscuring the verbs of rapture that I wish to highlight.

9.   Halperin, "Love's Irony: Six Remarks on Platonic Eros," in *Erotikon: Essays on Eros, Ancient and Modern*, ed. Shadi Bartsch and Thomas Bartscherer (Chicago: University of Chicago Press, 2005), 48–58, at 49.

10.   Ibid., 52.

11.   Again, I have made the translation slightly more literal in order to avoid obscuring the language of seizure.

12.   Plotinus, *Ennead* 1.6 ("On Beauty"), Loeb Classical Library (Cambridge: Harvard University Press, 1966), 244–45.

13.   Ficino, *Commentarium in Phedrum* (1496), edited, with facing-page translations, by Michael J. B. Allen in *Marsilio Ficino and the Phaedran Charioteer* (Berkeley: University of California Press, 1981), 84.

14.   Ficino, *Commentum cum summis capitulorum* (1496), in ed. Allen, 141–42.

15. The question of where Spenser got his Platonism from—Plato himself, or Plotinus, or medieval Platonism, or Renaissance Neoplatonists—has been extensively debated. Robert Ellrodt, in *Neoplatonism in the Poetry of Spenser* (Geneva: Droz, 1960), has voiced skepticism about Spenser's direct engagement with Plato; arguments for a more direct influence have come from Alastair Fowler ("Emanations of Glory: Neoplatonic Order in Spenser's *Faerie Queene*," in *A Theater for Spenserians*, ed. Judith M. Kennedy and James A. Reither (Toronto: University of Toronto Press, 1969], 53–82); Elizabeth Bieman (*Plato Baptized: Toward an Interpretation of Spenser's Mimetic Fictions* [Toronto: University of Toronto Press, 1988]); and Jon Quitslund (*Spenser's Supreme Fiction: Platonic Natural Philosophy and* The Faerie Queene [Toronto: University of Toronto Press, 2001]). I have little to add to the debate about specific sources except my conviction that Spenser absorbed the main doctrines of Platonic thought thoroughly enough that they emerge with some coherence in his poetry.

16. For touchstone studies of the Petrarchan and courtly sources of Spenser's love poetry, see C. S. Lewis, *The Allegory of Love: A Study in Medieval Tradition* (Oxford: Clarendon Press, 1936), and Thomas P. Roche, Jr., *The Kindly Flame: A Study of the Third and Fourth Books of Spenser's "Faerie Queene"* (Princeton: Princeton University Press, 1964).

17. In the case of Britomart, it is true that her mission to found a British dynasty comes from Merlin in III.iii, but Merlin merely helps determine what Britomart will do with her love; he does not help her decide whether she loves or not, a question that has already been definitively answered by the mastery of Eros in III.ii.

18. Sanchez, "Fantasies of Friendship in *The Faerie Queene*, Book IV," *ELR* 37:2 (2007): 250–73, at 259. Although Sanchez places more emphasis on Amoret's freedom in Book III than I do, I have found her insight about the link between suffering and sincerity in the poem an excellent corrective to my focus on rapture.

19. For example, when Mirabella was "Ladie of her libertie" she "Did boast her beautie had such soveraine might,/That with the onely twinckle of her eye,/She could or save, or spill, whom she would hight" (VI.vii.31.5–8). Likewise, Prince Arthur confesses that his time of "libertie" (I.ix.10.7 and 12.4) was characterized by the "looser life" (12.6) of adolescent sadism, when he "joyed to stirre up strife,/In middest of their mournfull Tragedy,/Ay wont to laugh, when them I heard to cry,/And blow the fire, which them to ashes brent" (10.3–6). Also see my comments about erotic liberty in "Daemon Lovers," 216–17.

20. Loewenstein, "Echo's Ring: Orpheus and Spenser's Career," *ELR* 16 (1986): 287–302, at 291n12, emphasis in original.

21. Hieatt, "Room of One's Own for Decisions: Chaucer and *The Faerie Queene*," in *Refiguring Chaucer in the Middle Ages*, ed. Theresa M. Krier (Gainesville: University Press of Florida, 1998), 147–64.

22. Ibid., 156–58. To avoid foisting evidence on Hieatt that he may not want, I should note that he does not mention Satyrane's statement about the freedom of love, which I discuss below.

23. Of course, Spenser *can* find humor in casual love, as the examples of the Squire of Dames or Hellenore and the Satyrs suggests. *The Faerie Queene* offers a range of sexual tonalities, not only a single note.

24. Relevant here is Katherine Eggert's distinction between rapine poetry, which depends on metaphors of penetration and violation, and rapturous poetry, which modulates and complicates the teleological thrust of the narrative ("Rape and Rapture in *The Faerie Queene*").

25. Hendrix, " 'Mother of laughter, and wellspring of blisse': Spenser's Venus and the Poetics of Mirth," *ELR* 23 (1993): 113–33.

26. Anderson, "The 'covert vele': Chaucer, Spenser, and Venus," *ELR* 24 (1994): 638–59, at 657.

27. *Parliament of Fowls*, lines 407–09 and 621–22, in *The Riverside Chaucer*, ed. Larry D. Benson (Boston: Houghton Mifflin, 1987).

28. Anderson, 658n34.

29. See A. Kent Hieatt, "Male Boldness and Female Rights: What the Isle of Venus Proposes," *Spenser Studies* 13 (1999): 269–72.

30. Hieatt, "Room of One's Own for Making Decisions," 154; Fowler, "The Failure of Moral Philosophy in the Work of Edmund Spenser," *Representations* 51 (1995): 47–76, at 57.

31. Esolen, "Spenserian Chaos: Lucretius in *The Faerie Queene*," *Spenser Studies* 11 (1990): 31–51, at 42.

32. E.g., see Hendrix, 113–14.

33. David Lee Miller has reminded me in an email correspondence that Scudamour does experience rapture in his reunion with Amoret at the end of the 1590 *Faerie Queene* (III.xii.44–46). Quite true, and indicative of the particular experience of Eros that Spenser found appropriate as an ending to his poem. Yet the cancellation of this passage in the 1596 *Faerie Queene* calls our attention all the more to the fact that the Scudamour who narrates the Temple of Venus episode has never experienced that rapturous reunion.

34. Cicero, *De Re Publica* IV.x.10, ed. Clinton Walker Keyes, Loeb Classical Library (Cambridge: Harvard University Press, 1970), 262.

35. Newton, trans., *The Booke of Marcus Tullius Cicero entituled Paradox Stoicorum . . . Wherunto is also annexed a Philosophical Treatyse of the same Authoure called Scipio his Dreame* (London, 1569); and *Fovvre Severall Treatises of M. Tullius Cicero* (London, 1577).

36. *Yale Edition of the Shorter Poems of Edmund Spenser*, ed. William A. Oram (New Haven: Yale University Press, 1989), pp. 23, 63, and 19. See also Carol Schreirer Rupprecht's entry on "Dreams" in *The Spenser Encyclopedia*, ed. A. C. Hamilton (Toronto: University of Toronto Press, 1990), 226–27.

37. Macrobius, *Commentary on the Dream of Scipio*, trans. William Harris Stahl (New York: Columbia University Press, 1952), 81.

38. Plato, *Republic* 617d–e, in Hamilton and Cairns, eds. Passages from the Greek original from *Platonis Opera*, vol. 4, ed. John Burnet (Oxford: Oxford University Press, 1902).

39. Quitslund, 145.

40. Ovid, *Metamorphoses* 10.56, ed. G. P. Goold, Loeb Classical Library (Cambridge: Harvard University Press, 1984).

41. The best modern discussion of this alignment remains Georges Bataille, *L'Erotisme* (Paris: Editions de Minuit, 1957).

KENNETH BORRIS

Platonism and Spenser's Poetic: Idealized Imitation, Merlin's Mirror, and the Florimells

To exempt his own work from the censures of poetry current in early modern cultural politics, Spenser embraces a poetic of idealized imitation that seeks to represent ideals rather than conventional reality, and thus promote pursuit of virtue and truth. Much of that program derived from favorable Platonizing theories of the verbal and visual arts. Yet serious sixteenth-century advocacy of poetry had to reckon with Plato's influential critique of poetry in the *Republic*, and Spenser does so in his allegory of poetics in Books III and IV of *The Faerie Queene*. By encountering Merlin's mirror, Britomart assimilates a mimetic image that motivates great enterprise, and that story seeks to demonstrate the inspirational power of right poetry. The poet further explores the ethical responsibilities of artistic creation through his invention of beauteous Florimell. Her contrast with the False Florimell, a spurious copy created by a witch, corresponds to the Platonic distinction between icastic (truthful) and phantastic (falsified) modes of representation in the arts. Whereas Plato's *Republic* had condemned almost all poetry for multiplying illusions doubly removed from the reality of the Ideas, and thus misleading its audience while badly inflaming their passions, Spenser's allegory indicates that is rather the effect of phantastic poetry, or the art's abuse. Through his contrary practice of icastic imitative idealism, Spenser finesses the *Republic's* critique to portray himself as a philosopher-poet correlative to that dialogue's valorized philosopher who awakens minds to reveal truth. Central to this endeavor is Spenser's correlation of eros with heroism, for which he invokes the authority of Socrates at the outset of the 1596 *Faerie Queene.*

Spenser Studies: A Renaissance Poetry Annual, Volume XXIV, Copyright © 2009 AMS Press, Inc. All rights reserved.

The mimetic art is far removed from truth.
—Plato, *Republic* 10.598b[1]

Wisdom and all her sister virtues; it is the office of every poet to beget them.
—Plato, *Symposium* 209a

S TEPHEN GOSSON'S ANTIPOETIC campaign around 1580, invoking the authority of Plato among others, instances a general European phenomenon that polylingual learned writers such as Spenser experienced fully.[2] Aside from Lodovico Castelvetro, poetry's advocates agreed that it properly instructs as well as delights, for it could hardly seem estimable otherwise.[3] Even they condemned those whom they thought violated such standards, and so Ronsard finds Ariosto's "Poësie fantastique . . . contrefaict & monstrueux," while Polyhymnia accepts only "some few" contemporary English poets in Spenser's *Teares of the Muses* (1591).[4] Although Christian ideology conditioned much of the debate, implicitly and otherwise, its central text among knowledgeable participants was Plato's *Republic*, which banishes most kinds of poets and poetry from the ideal commonwealth.[5] Yet since his *Ion*, his *Phaedrus*, and his later followers afforded means to glorify poetry, many of its advocates throughout sixteenth-century Europe sought to rebut its detractors accordingly, and so did Spenser.[6] Among his various writings, Books III to V of *The Faerie Queene* most evince this endeavor. The stories of Merlin's mirror and the doubled Florimells constitute a self-reflexive allegory of poetics engaging Platonic thought about poetry to justify Spenser's art; mock contrary literary theories, tastes, and practices; and claim the status of a philosopher-poet. Florimell's vindication against her impostor in the Legend of Justice symbolically realizes that objective.

Within *The Faerie Queene*, Spenser often examines its own and other signifying practices, as in its proems and representations of Error, Archimago, Gloriana, Acrasia's Bower, Bonfont/Malfont, and the Graces. The *Republic* is one of few texts the *Letter to Ralegh* acknowledges,[7] and Spenser would have found it significant not only because of its famous critique of poetry and its centrality, along with Aristotle's *Poetics*, for current mimetic understandings of the art, but also because the poet had strong affinities for philosophical idealism as his *Fowre Hymnes* most obviously show. Questions of appropriate poetics particularly arise at the start of Book III because Acrasia's Bower has just demonstrated the potentially ambiguous allures of art and apparent beauty. Hence poetry's opponents like Gosson alleged, as

Spenser says, that its "pleasing baite" for readers' "fancies" induces "follie" (IV.pr.1).[8] Even Sir Philip Sidney conceded that "poesy may not only be abused," but because of its "sweet charming force" can "do more hurt than any other army of words."[9] As love was often defined as the desire for beauty in Spenser's time, following Plato,[10] so the poet's central books of love and amity broach issues of esthetics, including the value of poetic beauty. For Spenser, much of poetry's power arises from its verbal and imagistic potencies in the domains of esthetics, desire, and representation. How, then, can its stimulative force be rightly used? That typical concern of early modern literary theory, practice, and reception suffuses the 1590 *Faerie Queene*, and fully surfaces in the proem for Book IV. The stories and other contents of Books III and IV are so interrelated that the latter's proem is partly retrospective.

Just as that proem invokes Socrates, Platonism is central to Spenser's stories begun in Book III, including their allegory of poetics. In these books appears the poet's character most associated with beauty, Florimell, who provides means of exploring its implications, effects, and challenges to human apprehension. Much of the reception of Books III and IV focuses on their programmatic engagements with Platonic thought about love, beauty, generation, the soul's origins, cosmology, and the creative relations of Form and matter.[11] Yet Spenser's allegorical assessment of Platonic poetics in his central books has been largely unexplored,[12] and so this study newly clarifies his own poetic, esthetics, philosophical affinities, and conceptions of poetry's value.

To appreciate this allegory of poetics we must understand its contexts in early modern thought and cultural politics, and my first and second sections outline the literary and esthetic issues at stake. I first assess Spenser's relation to former concepts of literary art as an imitative representation of some apparent or hypothetical reality. I will use the terms "mimesis," "imitation," and their cognates in that sense throughout, for I am not concerned here with emulation of prior writers and texts, nor with presentational techniques such as narration and dramatic impersonation. Spenser draws on early modern Platonizing conceptions of inspirational furor, idealized imitation, and icastic poetics to finesse Plato's critique of poetry in the *Republic* and advance his own claim to illuminate truth. Such considerations animate the poet's depiction of the effects of Merlin's mirror upon Britomart, and his portrayal of the doubled Florimells.

The representation of beauty, my second section explains, has pivotal importance for Spenser's development of his poetic and these two narratives. In the *Phaedrus* Plato argues that the manifestations

of Beauty have greater potential to awaken and enlighten minds than
those of any other Idea (250bd). Understanding beauty similarly,
Spenser thus assumes that poetry's esthetic potential is also psycha-
gogic. As the central books address the creation, evaluation, reception, and significance of beauty, so for this poet these issues entail
assessment of art's imagistic fashionings and the responsibilities of
literary creativity.

In the stories originating in Book III, the allegory of poetics has
two main components addressed in sections three to five: Britomart's
imagistic metamorphosis; and Florimell's contrast with her bad imitation. In Merlin's mirror, Britomart perceives an image of "a comely
knight" that impels her to undertake a momentous quest (III.ii.24).
This story not only demonstrates love's powers (as in standard readings), but also poetry's. Despite being dismissed in Plato's *Republic*
as apparitions that provoke passions and obscure reality, imagistic
simulacra such as we find in mimetic fictions can effect genuine good,
Spenser shows, and his endeavors to fashion readers much depend
on those means.

Yet like Sidney he allows for harmful poetry too, and sections four
and five show that the story of the Florimells juxtaposes Spenserian
imagistic imitation with its epitomized travesties. Florimell is Spenser's creation. Platonizing opponents of poetry would have demanded
how she could in some sense figure forth true beauty, conducive
to enlightenment, rather than merely adding yet another delusive
semblance to the world's manifold illusions. Spenser's response is to
contrast his Florimell with an exemplary bad imitation, False Florimell. She and her fictive creator, a witch, instantiate the poetics of
delusory enchantment opposed to his own procedures of idealized
imitation. This opposition correlates with early modern poetic usages
of Plato's distinction between phantastic art, which propagates illusions, and its icastic counterpart, which seeks mimetic authenticity.
Doublings of true and false agents and images appear throughout *The
Faerie Queene*, and the icastic/phantastic distinction already affects
Book I.[13] Yet in the Florimells' story it becomes a central theme
complementing the contrast between genuine and merely apparent
beauty. Spenser mocks phantastic poetics, those beguiled by false
beauties in life and art, and the social prevalence of such delusions.
Culminating in the impostor's exposure and Florimell's vindication,
discussed in section five, this narrative represents Spenser's poetic as
a means to dispel illusion and reveal truth.

For study of sixteenth-century writers such as Spenser, usage of
"Platonic" and its cognates should be aptly historicized. A generalized Platonic movement appeared to extend from antiquity into that

time, and so our present concern to distinguish what we would now call "Neoplatonic" adaptations would be anachronistic in most Spenserian circumstances.[14] I will use the vocabulary of "Platonism" in that expanded sense, and specify variants only if needful in particular contexts. Literary scholarship should also allow for the breadth and divergences of views comprised in former Platonic philosophies.[15] As Spenser's writings from the *October* eclogue to the *Fowre Hymnes* show, he was strongly drawn to Platonism, and his allegory of poetics responding to Plato's *Republic* is not anti-Platonic, because his advocacy appropriates much from Plato and later Platonists. When I cite other Platonic texts, my argument need not assume the poet had read them in particular, for the relevant doctrines were widely reported. But there is now plenty of evidence, including more here, to show that the poet was well versed in Platonism when writing *The Faerie Queene*.[16] The true poet was to be, as Sidney and others remarked, "the right popular philosopher," and for poetry's advocates it was not only the original source of the intellectual disciplines or "the first philosophy" but, to enhance its status further, a part or instrument of philosophy.[17] Spenser's epos reflects and fulfills that theory. Confronting Plato's expulsion of poets in the *Republic*, Sidney's *Defence* maintains that "the wiser a man is, the more just cause he shall find to have [Plato] in admiration," and concludes that this philosopher is poetry's "patron" who condemned only its "abuse"(104, 108–09). Spenser's allegory of poetics in Books III and IV indicates that Plato deeply challenged and yet energized his creativity. One of Socrates' last acts was to take up writing poetry "on imaginative themes," and in the *Republic*, he sincerely asks to be shown in prose how it can benefit the search for truth (*Phaedo*, 60c–61c; *Republic* 10.607c–8b). *The Faerie Queene* grants his wish poetically, the better to demonstrate the art's philosophical value.

1. SPENSER AND IDEALIZED IMITATION

> The work of the creator, whenever he looks to the unchangeable and fashions the form and nature of his work after an unchangeable pattern, must necessarily be made fair and perfect, but when he looks to the created only and uses a created pattern, it is not fair or perfect.
>
> —Plato, *Timaeus* 28ab

Following Plato and Aristotle, among other ancient authorities, the poetics of Spenser's time assumed that poetry is fundamentally a mimetic art that presents images of its subjects as if they are present and engages its audience accordingly. Questions of mimesis were pivotal for literary understandings and judgments, and self-reflexive explorations of the central issues are to be expected in Spenser's heroic poem. Not only was that genre to be culturally encyclopedic, but its exemplars were to manifest the height of poetic art in comparison to their precursors, and the climate of reception appeared to ensure that much of their evaluation would revolve around their mimetic qualities. But assumptions about mimesis were radically different from what we would now expect. Though Plato's and Aristotle's conceptions of it differ, the analogical and synthetic impulses of sixteenth-century thought ensured that Aristotle's was much Platonized, so that his *Poetics* appeared a different text than what we now have.[18] Especially in the latter half of that century, poetics and art theory in general thus tended to privilege "idealized imitation," whereby verbal and visual artists could endeavor to indicate intelligible universals through the sensuous particulars of their creations.[19] Renaissance theories and practices of such "high mimetic" imitation, as I will also call it, tended to involve at least some diffuse Platonism.[20] For Sidney, the poet bypasses the "brazen" world compromised by the Fall, to imitate ideals instead, and manifest a "golden" world supposed to reflect a heightened reality. Although literary theory of the time was eclectic, and both Sidney's poetic and Spenser's are hybrids, Sidney's has important Platonic affinities,[21] and Spenser's overgoes his Platonism. In *The Faerie Queene* Spenser represents his poesis as an enraptured icastic expression of formative ideals that parallels the processes of divine creation.[22]

While Platonism in one aspect fueled early modern attacks on poetry, in another it was, along with Horatian and Aristotelian approaches, a major means of positive literary thought. Promoting philosophy as the sovereign means to discern truth, Plato's *Republic* alleges that most poets and types of poetry stimulate disorders of the passions and propagate illusions by imitating the world of appearances, itself a mere reflection of the Ideas. But higher estimates of poetry and the visual arts appear in other dialogues such as the *Ion* and *Phaedrus*, and in the evolving Platonic tradition those comments came to underwrite, particularly through the contributions of Plotinus, Proclus, and Marsilio Ficino, insistence on art's value as a potentially inspired means of enlightenment.[23] The corpus of Plato's writings and their Neoplatonic elaborations ensured that certain literary principles, topics, and debates appeared distinctively Platonic: for example, how poetry as an imitative art relates to education and the pursuit of Truth (a main topic of the *Republic*). In Renaissance writings favoring poetry, doctrines and concerns indicating Platonic influence include 1) the poet's divine furor; 2) poetry's capacities for raising readers' minds toward truth through apt representation; 3) its relationship to a world composed of imitations; 4) its ethical, political, epistemological, and pedagogical value; 5) its legitimacy, expressed as defense of poetry, partly according to theological and ethical standards; 6) its proper allegorism; 7) its proportional harmonies with the cosmos, deemed God's creation.[24] Not all need be present to indicate Platonic affinity. But much of Spenser's *oeuvre* clearly addresses these principles—the seventh, for example, most of all in *The Faerie Queene*'s Acidale episode. Here I only have scope to discuss his relation to the first and, at length, the second and third.

Drawn from passages of Plato's *Phaedrus* and *Ion* that now seem somewhat ironic, the doctrine of the visionary *furor poeticus*, if accepted, determines much of the apparent nature, scope, and significance of poetic enterprise.[25] Hence Sidneians have argued that, though Sidney's *Defence* evinces much Platonism, it does not dominate his theory because he dissociates himself from the doctrine of poetic fury.[26] But Spenser did not do so. Exploring poetic inspirations, his *October* eclogue acknowledges the potentially interrelated Platonic ecstasies of eros and poetic creation, while the commentator "E. K." declares that Spenser endorses "ἐνθουσιασμὸς and celestial inspiration" in his treatise on poetics, *The English Poete* (now lost).[27] Gabriel Harvey's commendatory poem for the 1590 *Faerie Queene*, partly a means of guiding its reception, applauds Spenser's "sacred fury." In the second installment published in 1596, the "sacred" muses infuse "goodly fury" into "the mindes of mortall men" (VI.pr.1–2). Surveying the loci of revelation, Book I includes Parnassus, where "the thrise three learned Ladies play / Their *heauenly* notes," with the Mount of Contemplation, Mount Sinai, and the Mount of Olives (I.x.53–56; my emphasis). Though subordinating his own creation of Cleopolis to the New Jerusalem there, and hence his own poetry too, Spenser insists that the heightened realm of his invention is nonetheless "for earthly frame, / The fairest peece, that eye beholden can." *The Faerie Queene* not only brings readers to ascend Contemplation's Mount, but mediates that vision (I.x.58–59). Colin Clout has privileged access to correlative visionary heights upon Mount Acidale, where divinities, the Graces, attend his piping. The doctrine of poetic furor maintains that the poet's highest attainments arise from an external intervention, not from native genius or art, and Colin says of the Graces, "none can them bring in place, / But whom they of them selues list so to grace" (VI.x.19).[28]

Endorsement of poetic furor had decisive importance in poetics because literary art thus becomes a suprarational means of revelatory insight beyond the scope of narrowly Horatian and Aristotelian theories.[29] At the outset of *The Faerie Queene*, its author appears at once the "all too meane" vessel infused by "sacred" powers, yet their chosen one who blazons their visions abroad (I.pr.1). Even if all four of his *Hymnes* date from around 1595–96, as Robert Ellrodt improbably claims,[30] they would nonetheless show that the poet remained committed to this Platonic ideology of rapture.

The *Phaedrus* and *Ion* could thus be used, together with some hints in the *Republic*,[31] to argue that poetic imitation could somewhat reflect the Ideas beyond the phenomenal world's degraded reflections. Such a poet could bring some enlightenment like Plato's representative philosopher in the *Republic*, who leaves the cave and returns to inform its benighted denizens of the sun-bright realms above (7.514a–21d). Plato's banishment of poets from his model republic would then apply only to those who promoted moral and social disorders, and Platonists could legitimate "right poetry" as a socially beneficial means of piercing the world's deceptive illusions.[32] While complementing Horatian delightful teaching, Platonic literary didacticism entails a distinctive visionary idealization.

By locating *The Faerie Queene*'s action in his own invented faery realm, Spenser rejected imitation of any conventional reality. His notions of appropriate poetic imitation would have complemented Sidney's unoriginal golden model: hence Spenser's invention of his esthetically and morally heightened poetic world. Yet his enthusiasm for "enthusiasmos" implies still greater idealization. The soaring *Fowre Hymnes* further instantiate this difference of mentalities, for Sidney never wrote anything like them. As Spenser's Contemplation episode indicates, through his creation of Faery he seeks to mediate between the New Jerusalem and the mutable world, by transposing the latter into a high mimetic mode supposed to be more indicative of ideals. In that sense they are the ground and prime objective of his representation. And yet, in accord with the norms of early modern idealized imitation, Spenser's images are heuristic and provisional because, however heightened, they can only reflect and intimate the higher reality they betoken.[33] As the poet indicates in his *Hymnes*, relatively full awareness of that signified would have been assigned rather to the realms of contemplative ecstasy, afterlife, or Platonic preexistence. Though all Spenser's assertions of poetic fury claim some such vision, by definition it remains beyond words and images, so that he seeks pragmatically, by various strategies of accommodation such as allegory, to draw readers' attention beyond the phenomenal world toward an inspirational transcendent reality.[34] Not only contemplative, this process is to refashion lived realities by changing minds and hence behavior. Spenser's warrants for such philosophically oriented sociopolitical engagements would have included Plato's *Republic*, his *Laws*, and his personal ties to Dion of Syracuse.

Though the Platonizing aspects of Spenser's faery mimesis have been little explored to date,[35] the basic procedure was current enough to be summarized in Sidney's *Defence*. In surpassing the fallen productions of nature to body forth ideals, the Sidneian heroic poet presents characters who substantiate them, somewhat revealing the virtues; and through the forming power of his ideas,[36] that maker's mind creatively echoes his Maker's, even "with the force of a divine breath" (78–79, 98). Sidney and Spenser would most likely have absorbed their notions of idealized imitation from its more expansive contexts in Italian literary theory. The poet represents some Idea "absolutely eternal and durable," Bernardino Tomitano urged in 1545, whereas other things "are born perishable and mortal, . . . subject to constant mutation."[37] Around 1555 Girolamo Fracastoro declared, "the poet . . . does not wish to represent this or that particular man as he is with many defects, but . . . , having contemplated the universal and supremely beautiful idea of his [C]reator, makes things as they ought to be."[38] Torquato Tasso, one of Spenser's chief literary models, explains in his *Discorsi del poema eroico* (1594) that the poet is an imitator "of existing things," and what exists is "the intelligible" rather than "the visible" or sensible world, just as "Plato . . . put visible things in the genus of non-being and only the intelligible in the genus of being" (32).[39] Treatises on the visual arts, to which Sidneians have further linked Sidney's high mimetic doctrines, also disseminated such theories.[40]

Most directly stated in *The Faerie Queene*'s *Letter to Ralegh*, its proems, and its title pages for the successive books, the whole poem's fundamental conceit is that each book's manifold stories express a virtue so that their particulars resolve in that concept, while all those stories, books, and virtues coalesce in magnificence as it tends toward glory. Spenser entitles Book I, for example, "The Legend of the Knight *of the Red Crosse*, OR *Of Holinesse*." He thus encourages readers to interpret the poem's world in a way parallel to Platonic and Christian Platonist readings of the phenomenal world, through which it appears a sensory expression of higher concepts that render its profusions intelligible.[41] According to Plato's fable of the cave, the philosopher's central duty is to promote that kind of interpretation; Spenser's program to fashion readers "in all vertuous and gentle discipline" addresses the pedagogical criteria of Platonic and Horatian poetics in a manner informed by Christian Platonism.

The proem of each book outlines Spenser's artistic procedure in composing that book's fundamental ideal to be amplified through imitative projection: he draws the concept of each titular virtue from his sovereign's mind. Introducing the whole *Faerie Queene*, Book I's proem expresses that project most generally: the poet's "argument" is his sovereign's "true glorious type," envisioned in his thought (I.pr.4). In Book III he stretches his quill "so high" as to portray the virtue of Chastity, "shrined" in her "perfections" (III.pr.1–3). Book V's proem makes Justice ("Most sacred vertue she of all the rest,/ Resembling God in his imperiall might") virtually interchangeable with the sovereign herself ("Dread Souerayne Goddesse, that doest highest sit/In seate of iudgment, in th'Almighties place). Thus strategically blurring his categories, so that his procedures evoke the divine Idea of Justice through these doublings or approximations, the poet represents his concept of the virtue through the sovereign's "great justice" instrumentalized in Artegall (V.pr.10–11). Most clearly expressing the Platonic affinities of Spenser's poetic, Book VI's proem invokes the muses' "goodly fury" (VI.pr.2). To represent Courtesy, the poet journeys into "vertues seat . . . deepe within the mynd," correlative to a divinely originated "sacred noursery/Of vertue" sprung from "heauenly seedes of bounty soueraine," to seek an authentic "patterne" (VI.pr.2–6). He deduces it from the sovereign's "pure minde," and returns it to her through the poem (VI.pr.6–7).

As Spenser's "great workmaister" creates the universe according to a "Paterne" or "perfect mould" in the first hymn to beauty (lines 29–49), so the poet begins each book of *The Faerie Queene* by seeking a formative perfect pattern to be adumbrated in the book's creation. The procedure is fundamentally Platonic as the quest for perfection indicates.[42] The poet uses the words "perfect" and "perfections" in Book III's proem, and all the proems posit a transcendental paradigm or ideal, surpassing the capacities of ordinary human perception in its "exceeding light" (II.pr.5).[43] What the poet offers is "so diuine a read" that every proem promises its book will, if read aright, provide some insight into "perfect things" (V.pr.11, VI.pr.5). Both Spenser's hymns to beauty clearly evince the philosophically idealist capacities of his vocabulary of perfection.[44]

Like other contexts in *The Faerie Queene*, such as the Contemplation episode, Spenser's proems indicate that his representations of ideals are provisional, in the sense already explained, so that his artefact can point to but not reproduce its formative paradigm. The first proem maintains that the whole poem's foreconceit surpasses its expression: the "true glorious type," reflecting "grace and Maiestie diuine," is "The argument," but of an "afflicted stile" (I.pr.4). Addressing more than the poet's social inferiority relative to his queen, this context defines his creative procedure. The 1590 installment's final proem expands this point. As no art, whether visual or verbal, can adequately express the "perfections" of Chastity's ideal, Spenser says, still less can he himself do so. Yet since even "choicest witt" cannot "figure playne" that "glorious pourtraict," he "in coulord showes may shadow itt" (III.pr.3). The poem is the penumbra of the poet's creative ideal. Renaissance theories and practices of idealized imitation tended to mix Platonic and Aristotelian principles, and did so in varying proportions. Yet Spenser portrays his art as a means of "shadowing" a higher reality in a somewhat diminished way, so that the world here is at least notionally a Platonic one of reflections. Moreover, his insistence on the supremacy of the artist's conceptual model relative to the artefact, and hence on the latter's comparative insufficiency, is markedly Platonic.[45] For Platonists, Form is transcendent, matter recalcitrant, and the intelligible and phenomenal realms disjunct. Since materialization thus incurs degradation, high mimetic creativity cannot fully manifest its formative idea. From Platonic standpoints such art retains value insofar as its images may spark some rekindled awareness of intelligible reality. If nature is presumed to be fallen, art's function in striking such sparks is particularly privileged.[46] But its images are to enhance intellectual apprehension, not ends in themselves or, in effect, idols. Tasso's high mimetic theory of heroic poetry thus maintains that readers "try to raise their own minds" to the presented images of illustrious virtue, whereupon "their intellect itself becomes a painter who . . . paints in their souls forms of courage, temperance, prudence, . . . and every other virtue." The poet's images, like a mystical theologian's, are to "awaken the mind."[47]

While evoking the imitative idealizations of contemporary Platonized poetics, whereby poets seek to represent some Idea or the Ideas, Spenser conceitfully reinterprets the method. For Sidney, "the skill of each artificer standeth in that *idea* or fore-conceit of the work, and not in the work itself" (*Defence*, 79). From the outset Spenser defines his sovereign as "Mirrour of grace and Majestie diuine," so that his conceptual model partly reflects divine glory, or "her makers great magnificence" (I.pr.4, II.ii.41). Her light is to "raise" his thoughts to produce the mental paradigm for his "argument": her "true glorious type" (I.pr.4). Rather than professing direct access to the Ideas, then, this poet claims to derive his exalted conceptual paradigms of glory and the virtues from his sovereign's mind, and their value is implicitly authorized by the doctrines of creation in

God's image (the human mind thus somewhat reflects God) and of providential monarchy. In another proem Spenser represents that creation through a brief horticultural allegory, whereby the gods originally planted the virtues "in earth," figuratively in the substance of created humanity (VI.pr. 3, compare Genesis 1:26–27, 2:19). Yet by regarding the sovereign's mind the poet extrapolates a higher creative model, her "true glorious type," further evoked by the name Gloriana.[48] In doing so the poet becomes comparable to a Platonic lover who, as he ascends beauty's scale to seek its paradigm, refines an ideal of the beloved and other beauties in his mind to restore the "first perfection" of their transcendental origin. Spenser's *Hymnes* further evince this technique, and he applies it to the queen herself in *Colin Clouts*.[49] Exemplary womanhood, the soul, or the mind had long seemed to furnish mirrors of divinity,[50] and the sovereign's "pure mind" appears a brilliant revelatory mirror of ideal virtue in Book VI's proem (pr.6). By these means in *The Faerie Queene*, the poet circumvents the artistic hubris of less nuanced claims to imitate the Ideas.[51] He praises the queen while avoiding mere flattery (he imitates her idealized type, not her); asserts his artistic agency, which perceives and expresses her true type; focuses his whole epos on the sovereign as inspiration for its formative archetypes; and secures what would be, by Christian Platonist standards, an arguably valid basis for his mimetic project. Ideals thus form his poetic matter, he claims, so that he does not simply imitate our material world, presumed to be fallen, but creates one altogether more intelligible, anew.

Spenser's attendant imagery of solar enlightenment has apt Platonic resonances. In the *Republic* Socrates famously cautions that Truth must be apprehended indirectly and by degrees, like perceiving the sun through its reflections in water (7.515e–16c). We have seen that Spenser's tactful high mimetic procedure approaches the Ideas indirectly (hence my preference for the term "ideal" to designate the Spenserian creative paradigm, rather than "idea"). Not the sun itself but only "*Like* Phoebus lampe," the sovereign's light is to irradiate his "feeble eyne" to "raise" his "thoughtes" toward the glorious archetype (I.pr.4; my emphasis). The sovereign provides a counterpart of the sun, as it were, on which he can gaze, and his vision exceeds his readers', he implies, for he can perceive and body forth her idealized archetype. Yet he tells his sovereign, his personified sovereign ideal, or both[52] that he must use "couert vele" and "shadowes light" so that "feeble eyes your glory may behold/Which ells could not endure those beames bright/But would be dazled with exceeding light" (II.pr.5).[53] Spenser's interest in "accommodated" modes of depiction anticipates Milton's in *Paradise Lost*, although that important aspect of *The Faerie Queene* has been little explored to date.

Since Spenser seeks to illustrate his poem's animating ideals of virtue through his heroic representations, he imitates the former more than any individuals. "In the Persons of Agammemnon and Ulysses," Spenser's *Letter* observes, Homer "hath ensampled a good governour and a vertuous man," and Virgil's "like intention" appears "in the person of Aeneas," while Ariosto's and Tasso's heroes epitomize moral and political philosophy. Similarly, Spenser explains, he seeks "to pourtraict in Arthure . . . the image of a braue knight perfected in the twelue priuate morall vertues, as Aristotle hath deuised, the which is the purpose of the first twelue books." Hence the prince figures forth Spenser's consummate virtue, magnificence (715–16). Not only Aristotle's treatises on moral philosophy and their reception history are relevant, but also his *Poetics*, just as the context addresses theory of genre and literary characterization.[54]

Though the *Poetics* as it is now understood has neither Spenser's "perfected" hero nor his didactic emphasis, it had those applications in the later 1500s.[55] The poet positions his poem in relation to leading concerns and concepts of contemporary literary theory, and shows his familiarity with that discourse (primarily Italian at that time, whether vernacular or Latin).[56] Writing on romances, Giambattista Cinzio Giraldi declares "Aristotle said that the poet's aim was to induce good mores in the minds of men" (1554).[57] In Francesco Robortello's important Latin commentary on the *Poetics* (1548), Aristotelian characterization approaches Platonic Ideas, as in some later commentaries too. For a poet to portray wise Ulysses, Robortello advises, "he should not be considered as he actually was; but . . . should be transferred into the realm of the universal and depicted in the way in which the perfect 'wise' and ingenious man is ordinarily described by the philosophers."[58] Aristotle assumes that "poetry relates more of the universal, while history relates particulars," and " 'universal' means the kinds of things which it suits a certain kind of person to say or do, in terms of probability or necessity: poetry aims for this, even though attaching names to the agents."[59] But Robortello's Aristotle has become Horatian and Platonized, and sixteenth-century poetics often explained poetic universality according to the Platonic doctrine of Ideas.[60] Whereas Aristotle stresses literary plot and action, in Renaissance idealized imitation they come to serve representation of ideals. Just before Sidney cites Aristotle as his authority on mimesis, he insists on poetry's creation of a golden world, so that his Aristotle is somewhat Platonized (*Defence*, 78–80).

Likewise eclectic, Spenser's nominally Aristotelian account of Arthur's characterization involves Platonic and Horatian instructive priorities, allegorism, and the idealizing practices of both Plato's *Republic* and the *Cyropaedia* of Socrates' student Xenophon (*Letter*, 715–16).[61] Among the literary genres of the late sixteenth century, heroic poetry most of all was supposed to provide edifying conceptual models.[62]

Yet in Renaissance verbal and visual idealized imitation, pursuits of abstraction and vivacity converged. Enlivening the ideal, which required some strategic particularization, addressed interrelated criteria of credible verisimilitude, delight, *enargeia*, and moving the audience to embrace the manifested paradigm. Notwithstanding Una's allegorical role, she appears a memorably engaging personality, like Redcross and many others in *The Faerie Queene*. Yet however vivid, their representation is high mimetic, based on fundamental abstraction, and Spenser limits their particularity because, rather than being self-sufficient, it is to stimulate readers' apprehension of the signified ideal.[63] So generalized are Spenser's heroes and heroines that their personal traits remain sketchy and their facial features unknown. Aside from Redcross and Arthur's armaments, which are symbolic attributes, what do they look like? When lifted, Una's veil discloses no traits except radiant "beautie" and "glorious light" (I.vi.4, xii.23). Even the lengthy blazon of Belphoebe defies description through its mercurial diversity of comparisons, insistence on her inexpressibility and "heauenly" aspect, and central textual crux, the half-blank line (II.iii.22–26). Book VI's heroine Pastorella, who never speaks, is just "full fayre of face, / And perfectly well shapt in euery lim" (VI.ix.9). We can never approach Gloriana. The attenuated specificity of Spenser's positive characters indicates their provisional status in focusing ideals. Likewise, in presenting his settings, typically generalized except for particular symbolic features, Spenser avoids insignificant description or accidental particularities. The whole action's situation in Faery marvelously heightens the poet's images with numinous unearthliness.

High mimetic technique depended on the compilation of the abstracted model through apt selection of sensory indications, and the painter Zeuxis famously exemplified that procedure. As Cicero said, Zeuxis combined the best qualities of five beautiful girls to portray Helen's "surpassing beauty," for "in no single case has nature made anything perfect," and Tasso adopted this method to formulate his ideal of the heroic poem.[64] For Renaissance exponents of idealized imitation, Socrates' procedures for apprehending Beauty would have clarified the production of mental paradigms. Beauty, he advises, is to be apprehended in all its earthly manifestations, to enable conceptual refinement of its archetype (*Phaedrus* 249c–53c; *Symposium* 210a–12a). The high mimetic artist would develop such a pattern (not necessarily of beauty), then seek to depict it insofar as possible. Although the result was necessarily provisional in Platonic idealized imitations, as we have seen, their creators could ascribe to them a higher status than the ordinary world or any art that imitated it. Representation of the ideal was to foster its expression in minds and lives.

As Plato's theory of mimesis in the verbal and visual arts focused on their relation to the discernment of truth, so it yielded an evaluative distinction between "icastic" and inferior "phantastic" modes of imitation that informed much early modern high mimetic art theory. Whereas icastic art presents a correct likeness or copy, Plato observes, its phantastic counterpart gives an appealing but deceptive semblance through *trompe l'oeil* (*Sophist*, 235–37). By Spenser's time the scope of this distinction had encompassed broader issues of Platonic truth and value in the arts. If literary fiction could be icastic in some sense, and thus a means of authentic representation, not only could mimetic theory affirm poetry's moral instrumentality, but it could contest the common antipoetic charges that fictions are falsifications.

The major new Plato edition of the late sixteenth century, issued in three annotated folio volumes in 1578, with parallel Greek and Latin texts, makes the icastic/phantastic distinction central to Plato's poetic. Queen Elizabeth is the first volume's dedicatee, and the translator, Jean de Serres, gave complete sets both to her and to Sir Philip Sidney. De Serres provides a preface for each dialogue, and in the first volume presents the *Ion* as Plato's study of "the art of poetry in general."[65] This preface probably influenced Sidney's *Defence*, and possibly E. K.'s remarks on poetic furor in Spenser's *Calender*.[66] De Serres's mostly Latin comment uses some Greek, which I translate in square brackets. For Plato, de Serres explains, "the entire art of poetry is a certain enthusiasm . . . or ['divinely enraptured representation']." And "it is a common teaching of Plato that Poetry is [mimetic], although in what way and how far needs to be considered. In the *Sophists* [i.e., *Sophist*] he teaches that . . . the [mimesis] of poetry is various and sundry. One is [icastic], which presents true and agreeable images, while another is [phantastic], which deludes by the presentation of false images" (154). Now poetry "is designed for a certain delectation, but applied to the end of teaching and persuading," and "teaches by delighting, by imitating things that are absent and offering them . . . as though they were present" (154–55).

When we seek to distinguish between icastic and phantastic modes of imitation, de Serres advises, our test should be poetry's "primary function, to teach by delighting":

> For [the icastic mode] forms its images so that they are addressed
> suitably to the reason, and they are designed to achieve the best
> of purposes, so that they delight while teaching, and they teach
> with genuine honesty, since they are contained in a praisewor-
> thy subject matter. . . . [The phantastic mode], in contrast, pro-
> duces things in a base manner, and deals with ugly and
> despicable things. To this end, it spreads muck as it chooses,
> and by its seductions introduces many false and vicious things
> into the souls of men. The latter [i.e., the phantasic mode]
> should be rejected, but the former is not unworthy the study
> of honorable men, nor does it offend moral principles. Rather,
> it sometimes provides a great force to bolster virtue and honesty,
> and to temper men. . . . For surely good poetry is [like a psycha-
> gogue], an epithet of Hermes as leader of dead souls to the
> underworld—that is, because by this moderation it better insin-
> uates and instills pleasant thoughts in our very souls. (155)

The phantastic mode is superficially seductive yet a corrupting influence, and base or ugly and despicable in that sense. Though its domain of falsified art is analogous to Acrasia's Bower, not only sensual
temptation is at stake, but also whatever could impair the soul's
pursuit of truth and virtue. In closing his preface, de Serres exclaims,
"how I wish there were not so many examples of [phantastic] or
vicious poetry, and not so great an abuse of poetry by depraved
men" (156).[67]

In late sixteenth-century poetics, the icastic/phantastic distinction
further entered major literary debates about the legitimacy of Dante's
and Ariosto's departures from verisimilitude and historical realism.
Among the various literary genres, heroic poetry most of all was to
produce marvels, as Aristotle had indicated; but what was a poet's
appropriate latitude in creating them?[68] Just as usage of Platonic conceptions was flexible, different theorists employed the icastic/phan-
tastic distinction in different ways, and sometimes implicitly, without
using its characteristic terminology.[69] Yet the early modern tendency
to privilege truth as the ultimate touchstone of poetic value ensured
that their poetics were somehow finally icastic in principle.

Since *The Faerie Queene* and Dante's *Commedia* both present their
own invented worlds, Torquato Tasso's dispute with Dante's advocate Jacopo Mazzoni about icastic versus phantastic representation is
particularly revealing for study of Spenser, while further showing
how topical indeed these concerns were in late sixteenth-century

literary culture. Here we must distinguish between two types of truth acknowledged in former poetics: that of factual particulars, and the universalized "poetic truth" of abstract concepts.[70] Trying to uphold both to maximize adherence to truth, Tasso's *Discorsi del poema eroico* (1594) maintains that "the most perfect poetry imitates things that are, were, or may be," so that flying horses, centaurs, and the like are inappropriate, and "things that either happened or might have happened" trump more fanciful inventions (30). Yet Tasso's literary realism is philosophically idealist: he assumes that the poet should primarily imitate intelligible, not sensory things, because only the former have actual being (32).[71] Icastic imitation thus includes not only the events and possibilities of the natural world, but also, for example, angels and the evangelists' symbols in the Book of Revelation. He proposes that the mind may have not one but two faculties of imagination or fantasy, the higher being intellective, or what Dante may call *alta fantasia*, an icastic capacity of insight into intelligible being. But in any case, Tasso concludes, genuinely poetic imitation is indeed icastic. In its high disclosure of truth, the poet like "the mystical theologian" is "to lead to the contemplation of divine things and thus awaken the mind with images" (32–33).

Though Tasso contextually attacks Mazzoni for advocating phantastic imitation in the latter's *Della difesa della "Commedia" di Dante* (1587), formerly one of the most authoritative treatises on poetics, Tasso somewhat misrepresents his adversary. Mazzoni, who was to succeed Francesco Patrizi as Chair of Platonic Philosophy at the Sapienza, the University of Rome, valorizes the phantastic mode only insofar as it becomes icastic in effect. Since he seeks to allow more scope to poetic invention and production of marvels than Tasso, Mazzoni does not reject phantastic imitation outright, but classifies it into legitimate and illegitimate types. The false type presents deceptive images that disorder the intellect and will, and immoderately arouse the passions.[72] Yet, whereas icastic poetry in Mazzoni's account "takes a true subject from history," thus presenting factual truth with some inventive scope (88), the legitimate type of phantastic poetry (Dante's type), excels it by propounding "feigned things to our intellects in order to regulate the appetite," and "often it contains under the outer covering of fiction *the truth of many noble conceptions*" (83, my emphasis; see 108–09). It is validated by conceptual truth and hence, we may say, "icastic phantastic."[73] For Mazzoni the Song of Solomon, for example, is "replete with the most beautiful poetic fantasies," and "phantastic in regard to the literal sense, but icastic in regard to the allegorical sense."[74] His assumptions about reality and the objects of true imitation are philosophically idealist like Tasso's.

Hence Tasso and Mazzoni both use Platonic resources to raise poetry's potential status according to Plato's criteria. Whereas Plato had warned that poetic imitations propagate degraded reflections of the phenomenal world's already second-rate imitations of the Ideas, Tasso's icastic and Mazzoni's "icastic phantastic" modes give poets means to resolve the disorientations of that existential hall of mirrors. But in granting poets the most latitude to create their own imaginative worlds that are icastically revealing, Mazzoni's theory opens the readiest exit. Such considerations may well have been fundamental to the development of Spenser's fabulously inventive allegorical poetic. In any case, its very inventiveness indicates that his conceptions of poetic truth, hence optimal icastic representation, were more like Mazzoni's than Tasso's. Yet for both, and Spenser too as his commitment to allegory's conceptual vindications shows, the touchstone of representative validity remains in some sense icastic truth.

Plato's icastic/phantastic distinction also had much currency among Elizabethan literati. George Puttenham similarly distinguishes between the "phantastical" disordered imagination, and the "euphantastic" one proper to "all good Poets," "illuminated with the brightest irradiations of knowledge and of the veritie and due proportion of things."[75] George Chapman insists that Homer's "all-comprising Poesie" is not "phantastique, or meere fictive, but the most material and doctrinal illations of Truth." This advocate of Homeric allegory means that Homer's epics are icastic in some sense allowing for inner truth (including the marvellously inventive *Odyssey*), but assumes the term is familiar enough to remain tacit.[76] In the *Defence* Sidney warns that "man's wit may make poesy, which should be icastic (which some learned have defined: figuring forth good things), to be fantastic (which doth, contrariwise, infect the fancy with unworthy objects)," and hence "please an ill-pleased eye with wanton shows of better hidden matters" (104). The golden world of Sidneian right poetry is implicitly icastic, whereas art imitating his brazen world of fallen nature would fill readers' minds with degraded phantasms. Sidney's understanding of "icastic" imitation accords with Mazzoni's conception that I have called "icastic phantastic," because Sidney insists on "that high flying liberty of conceit proper to the poet," that creates "another nature, . . . either better . . . , or, quite anew, forms such as never were in nature," such as "Chimeras" (77–78). Tasso would not grant so much inventive scope, nor does de Serres appear to. And by stressing *"figuring forth,"* Sidney's account of the icastic mode more readily evokes the "inner truths" of allegory than de Serres's.[77] When Sidney maintains that the heroic poet "teacheth and moveth to the most high and excellent truth," he says in effect that, among the literary genres, the heroic poem can best fulfill poetry's icastic potential.

As Spenser and his closest associates linked his poesis with enraptured fury, his literary Platonism surpassed Sidney's, hence presumably also his interest in Plato's icastic/phantastic distinction. I subsequently use "icastic" as Sidney defines it: "figuring forth good things" while allowing much latitude for imaginative invention warranted by some inner or oblique truth. Despite using different categories and terms, Mazzoni similarly interprets icastic representation at best, to justify Dante; and so would that other allegorical fantasist, Spenser. Though modifying Plato's usage in the *Sophist*, this definition of "icastic" befits the commitment of Renaissance Platonic literary advocacy to poetry's moral and epistemological value, and thus has much in common with de Serres's account, among others. If the phenomenal world is delusive, icastic poesis must depart from conventional reality by presenting imagistic indicators of a higher truth.

I will also use Sidney's complementary definition whereby "phantastic" texts "infect the fancy with unworthy objects," spuriously pleasing their audiences "with wanton shows." From Platonic standpoints, such mimetic dissimulations increase attachment to the phenomenal world's appearances, and further obscure authenticity.

Heroic poetry attracted the highest literary expectations, and insofar as Spenser sought to fulfill them, he would have engaged contemporary debates about poetic mimesis. At the outset of Book II he already anticipates how some will judge his "antique history" "th'aboundance of an idle braine/ . . . and painted forgery" (pr. 1). Even to advocates of poetry such as Ronsard and Tasso, *The Faerie Queene* would have appeared too inventive to be sufficiently truthful or icastic; yet others like Mazzoni would have admired its pursuit of inner poetic truth through fictional inventions. Not only Spenser's proems reflect upon his version of idealized imitation, but also his stories about imagistic effects or productions, and doubles such as the Florimells. *The Faerie Queene*'s fanciful romantic allegorism was not "provincial and old-fashioned by contemporary Italian standards,"[78] but profoundly responsive to contemporary debates about questions of value in the arts, not just in England, but continentally too, just as Spenser had long studied current French and Italian literary culture. His approach to poetic representation reflects trends in literary thought specific to the late sixteenth century, advanced by Agnolo Segni and Paolo Beni as well as Mazzoni, and in mannerist theories of the visual arts.[79]

2. Beauty in Spenser's Faery Poetic

We must look for those [makers, i.e.,**δημιουργοὺς**][80] who by the happy gift of nature are capable of following the trail of true beauty and grace, that our young men . . . may receive benefit from all things about them, whence the influence that emanates from works of beauty may waft itself to eye or ear like a breeze that brings from wholesome places health, and . . . harmony with beautiful reason.

—Plato, *Republic* 3.401cd

Fundamental to Spenser's idealized poesis is a cult of beauty that motivates much of his writing from *The Shepheardes Calender* to his final publications while alive, such as the *Fowre Hymnes*.[81] Throughout the sixteenth century, the verbal and visual arts often engaged love's Platonic theorizations as "the desire for beauty," and so do the tales Spenser launches in *The Faerie Queene*'s central books of interpersonal love and desire. Those stories further reflect upon the esthetic and rhetorical responsibilities of poetry as it seeks to represent beauty. Many poetics of the time, including Spenser's, assumed esthetic considerations are central to poetry's beneficial potential: "The Renaissance was no less sensitive to the virtue of beauty than to the beauty of virtue."[82] Spenser's evaluation of beauty's significance, abuses, and modes of appearance in Books III and IV entails assessment of the power and value of imagistic mimesis, just as the contrast between his prime avatar of beauty and her impostor, Florimell and False Florimell, expresses that of the icastic and phantastic imitative modes.

Addressing his nurture of Pegasus in a letter dated 1637, Milton avowed his habitual search "day and night" for the "idea of the beautiful, as for a certain image of supreme beauty, through all the forms and faces of things."[83] Around a century earlier, Fracastoro had maintained that "what perfection and beauty are, only the great artists know." "The poet by nature is one who can be seized and moved by the true beauties of things, and who . . . is able to speak and write through them. Those are true poets who, contemplating the Idea of their own art, strive to omit no beauty" (69, 71). The poet, Giulio Cesare Scaligero assumed, creates images whose beauty surpasses what exists in nature.[84] Sixteenth-century interest in beauty's implications for poetics partly arose from the renewed currency of Hermogenes' stylistic treatise *Concerning Ideas*. His seven incipiently Platonic archetypes of style include Beauty, which inheres both in the general harmonious proportionality of a work, and in the style of particular contexts.[85] Such was his vogue that Spenser's friend Gabriel Harvey called himself "Pseudo-Hermogenes" in *Rhetor* (1577).[86] Aiming to define "the most perfect and most beautiful" heroic poem in *Discorsi del poema eroico*, Tasso assumes that poetry in general "seeks and yearns for beauty," and concentrates on "the idea of the beautiful more than any other" idea (6, 14, 171). Yet since "the heroic poem is the most beautiful" among "all" poetry's kinds, the delight of "wonder at the beautiful" is "its very own." Though Tasso insists that the other Hermogenic Ideas are also relevant, he somewhat follows Fracastoro in conjecturing that it may not be "too far wrong" to consider "the idea of the beautiful" the heroic poet's specific "goal."[87] Love's thematic suitability for the genre follows from beauty's importance, Tasso observes; indeed "Isocrates held that all the grace and charm of Homer's poems spring from the beauty of Helen" (46).

Renaissance theories of idealized imitation, at least somewhat indebted to Platonic thought even when invoking Aristotle, tended to base their claims that such art promotes truth and virtue upon its capacities to produce compelling representations of beauty.[88] The cultural diffusion of Platonic love theory had ensured wide familiarity with the importance of beauty in Plato's epistemology. Among all the supersensible Ideas, he maintains, only Beauty's earthly reflections have an irresistible luster. For the others, such as Justice and Temperance, "so dull are the [perceptual] organs wherewith men approach their images that hardly can a few behold that which is imaged." But "for beauty alone this has been ordained, to be most manifest to sense and most lovely of them all" (*Phaedrus* 250bd). Hence Plato assigns beauty unique potential to reawaken human minds and disclose, beyond the evanescent material realm of the senses, the splendor of the world of being (for Christian Platonists, heaven and divinity). Conceived as the desire for beauty, love rightly pursued affords a means of enlightenment, a rapture analogous to but excelling poetic furor, and "the source of the greatest goods that can befall us" (*Phaedrus* 244a–49e, 265a–66b). Poets treating love and beauty could consider themselves most inspired. Traditional Christian notions of the physical world as "the book of nature" revealing the creative Word further encouraged early modern Platonizing attributions of spiritual significance to beauty.

By rendering ideals in a sensuously beautified aspect, verbal and visual artists sought to imbue them with beauty's appeal. Alluding to the *Phaedrus* as just cited, Sidney especially so defines the heroic poet, who "teacheth and moveth to the most high and excellent truth": "if the saying of Plato and Tully be true, that who could see virtue would be wonderfully ravished with the love of her beauty—this man sets her out to make her more lovely in her holiday apparel."[89] Sidney further assumes that the right poet in general does not paint "Lucretia whom he never saw, but painteth the outward beauty of such a virtue," so as to range "into the divine consideration of what may be and should be." Relative to philosophers, such a poet seems to promise readers only delight, yet presents "the form of goodness (which seen they cannot but love)"—in other early modern words, beautifully (*Defence*, 81, 93; cp. 90). In *Discorsi del poema eroico* Tasso seeks to maximize poetry's beauty (hence its powers of pleasurable attraction) as already shown, while defining the "most excellent" poet and poetry as delightful means to instantiate and promote the good (13–14).

Beauty was fundamental for Spenser's poetic too. *The Faerie Queene*'s stories survey human responses to beauty through many amorous pursuits, and the poem's beauties of style and content are to promote its adumbrated ideals. Many in Spenser's time, including the poet, would have assumed that those beauties are not only decorative but *participate* in the good. Representations of beauty in *The Faerie Queene* tend to reflect upon the value, objectives, and mimetic procedures of art, as well as the use and abuse of its esthetic capacities, often through self-reflexive allegories. When Colin Clout turns up in this poem, he attends the goddess of beauty's holiday resort, Mount Acidale, together with the Graces themselves, who bestow "on men all gracious gifts" to "make them louely" (VI.x.23). Just as the Graces nurtured Florimell there, she epitomizes Spenserian beauty (IV.v.5).

A central thematic word in *The Faerie Queene*, "fair" is by far the most common descriptive adjective in the 1590 text (we still lack such data for its successor),[90] and Spenser's unique version of Faery is his projected realm of the esthetic. The poem involves much verbal play between "fay," "fair," and "fairy," including their cognates and variant spellings, such as the lexical group "fayre," "fayrely," "fayrer," and "fayrest." At the outset Spenser announces he sings "Of Faerie knights and *fay*rest Tanaquill," and Faery's capital Cleopolis, where the "fairest Fary Queene doth dwell," seems "The fairest city" except for the New Jerusalem, or "fairest peece, that eie beholden can" (I.pr.2, I.x.58–59; my emphasis).

Beauty's significance in Spenser's poetry is fundamentally revelatory, for he assumes "beautie . . . was made to represent/The great Creatours owne resemblance bright" (IV.viii.32).[91] From that standpoint, which combines Christian concepts of nature's book and the divine image with Platonic doctrine as in the *Phaedrus*, all manifestations of true beauty (whether humanly embodied, otherwise natural, or artificial) would have such significance.[92] Condemning the fallen world's abuses of beauty in Book IV, Spenser concludes by juxtaposing "heauens face," the sublime visage of the dawn implicitly betokening its presumed Creator, with the darkened world and dimmed vision of humankind (IV.viii.34).

Also attributing revelatory import to feminine beauty in general, Spenser addresses women as "Fayre ympes [i.e., offshoots, offspring] of beautie, whose *bright shining beames*/Adorne the world with *like to heauenly light*" (III.v.53; my emphasis). Belphoebe appears a "heuenly pourtraict of bright Angels hew" or "glorious mirrhour of celestial grace," her face ineffable (II.iii.22, 25). When Timias looks to the "skies" for help, *she* manifests instead, her "matchlesse beautie" "ful of diuinities,/And gifts of heauenly grace" (III.v.34). With her wondrous "beautie," Britomart enables "contemplation of diuinitee" (III.ix.23–24; cp. IV.vi.19–24). "Shyning with beauties light, and heauenly vertues," Amoret "plainely" appears "The heauenly pourtraict of bright Angels hew" (IV.v.13, x.52). Florimell's "blazing beauties beame" sheds "rare light" inducing an "extasye" or daze, for her "angels face" is "Adorn'd with all diuine perfection" (III.viii.22, IV.xii.34). The narrator observes, "T'adore thing so diuine as beauty, were but right" (III.vii.11). Spenser's more discursive *Hymnes* unfold the Christian Platonist doctrinal contexts of these passages.

Such devotions as Spenser recommends them in *The Faerie Queene* would not have deserved charges of idolatry,[93] for he emphasizes the body is "God's worke," or "The wondrous workmanship of Gods owne moulde,/Whose face he made" (II.x.1, I.x.42). Insofar as human beings are "images of God in earthly clay" (I.x.39), they would reflect divine perfections to a unique degree, just as Britomart resembles "The maker selfe . . . in her feature" (IV.vi.17), or Belphoebe mirrors "celestiall grace" (II.iii.21–25). The turret-head of Alma's anthropomorphic castle, which expresses the soul's rule "in all beautie excellent" (II.xi.2), is "likest . . . vnto" God's "owne blessed bowre" (II.ix.47). So while Contemplation can disclose a vision of the New Jerusalem, the later books of interpersonal love and desire assume that human beauty can be wondrously revelatory, and it already has some such significance in Book I.[94] Una is "That floure of faith *and beautie* excellent" (I.vi.15; my emphasis). Brightening into "glorious light" after the dragon's demise, her "heauenly beautie" and "sunshyny face" afford a "celestiall sight" transcending the poet's expression (I.xii.21–23; cp. I.iii.4).

Throughout *The Faerie Queene*, Spenser's descriptions of beauty, his accounts of divine revelation, and his symbols of Truth pointedly share topoi of illumination and astonishing or dazzling radiance. These associations reappear in his *Hymnes*, where beauty's light can reveal divinity.[95] In Una's case, the poet describes her emphatic beauty according to solar biblical motifs that do *not* refer to beauty (such as the Woman Clothed with the Sun; "the children of light" or "Sonnes of day"; transfigured Christ's face like the sun, Matt. 17:2). Transferred to beauty in Spenser's contexts, these descriptions further evoke its radiance in Platonic tradition, and its related epistemological value.[96] Una's sunny disposition subsumes Plato's hypothetical dazzling sun of Truth in the *Republic*, and its myriad refractions in later Platonisms, as in Ficino's *De sole*. Also dazing beholders with "sunny beames" are Fidelia's face (I.x.12); Arthur's diamond shield when unveiled, a main touchstone of Truth in *The Faerie Queene* (I.vii.35, viii.19); "th' Almighties lightning brond" (I.viii.21); and the New Jerusalem's "things diuine" (I.x.67). The poet applies motifs of revelatory illumination to various female beauties aside from Una, just as Britomart's "beautie" gives "light vnto the day" (III.i.43). The story of Florimell, the poem's central exemplar of beauty, climaxes with her vindication according to solar symbolism (V.iii.17–28). The "faire beames" of Gloriana, Spenser's "Idole of *her makers* great magnificence," dazzle with "exceeding light" (I.pr.4, II.pr.5, VI.x.4; my emphasis). For Spenser genuine earthly beauty is the wondrous and somewhat synechdochal sign of a transcendental signified. He describes his images of such beauty so as to suggest that idealized meaning.

Yet despite beauty's visionary, divinely authorized force in Spenser's view, it has only a soft power, as it were, vulnerable to abuses, misrepresentations, and misapprehensions. Plato likewise complains that some treat beauty bestially, without due reverence (*Phaedrus*, 250e). In Book IV the poet observes that, though "beautie" was "made to represent" the Creator, a primal lapse of the world rendered it "the baite of bestiall delight," and so, in appearance, "faire grew foule, and foule grew faire" (IV.viii.30–32). *The Faerie Queene* implicitly expresses that view, further articulated in the *Hymnes*, from the outset.[97] Books I and II feature myriad spurious beauties such as Archimago's fabricated false Una, who seems "of beautie soueraigne Queene"; Duessa's "forged beauty"; and Lucifera's "blazing beautie"; not to speak of Philotime's and Acrasia's (I.i.48, ii.36, iv.8). And even true beauty's revelation may be misconstrued or misappropriated, as when Sansloy and Sylvanus lust for Una's "beautie" (I.vi.4, 15). Yet Spenser nonetheless urges its inspirational, enlightening potential, like Plato, and seeks to promote its apt appreciation and pursuit through his art.

Among *The Faerie Queene*'s celebrated beauties, "*Florimell* the fayre" ("Fayrest of faire, that fairnesse doest excell," "the fairest

Dame aliue") is its prime means of exploring the reception and significance of true beauty (III.v.8, IV.ii.23, III.i.18). The bounds of
Spenser's faery representation preclude her being Beauty or its Idea.
Yet just as she embodies material beauty to an exceptional extent, so
she reflects intelligible beauty exceptionally well. Much as Plato assumes that, among all the Ideas, Beauty is most manifest to sense,
Florimell marvellously focuses beauty's ideal. Her symbolism includes
perceived beauty in general, and especially as it evokes desire while
also affording opportunities for heightening awareness of ideals and
reality beyond appearances. Hence her solar associations and numinous aspect.

The diverse kinds of admiration and pursuit that Florimell occasions instance the modes of "beauties chace" or "the chase of beauty
excellent" (III.i.18–19, iv.45, v.5). For some, like the forester and
old fisherman, she represents irresistible sex, in effect, and the latter
thus seeks to violate "beautie" (III.viii.36). Not only do many who
desire her see nothing beyond her physical beauty, misapprehending
that sign as its own signified, but they even prefer her bad imitation
(V.iii.17). Yet she also has more discerning adherents (the best are
relatively few), whom she inspires with devotion that yields more
or less chivalric actions. Romance-epic idiom thus epitomizes the
broader range of positive effects that desire for beauty can produce,
including "workes of wise sages" and the various attainments of good
lovers (IV.pr.2–3). So "all the noble knights of *Maydenhead*" adore
her, and the bravest rush "To sauegard her, ywandered all alone"
(III.viii.46–47). Satyrane glorifies her "in all / His famous conquests."
Florimell can immediately motivate him, Arthur, Guyon, Timias,
Peridure, and Calidore to extraordinary efforts, and it is the Knight
of Justice who renders the homage of returning her lost cestus in
Book V.[98] The beauty contests that unfold from Books III to
V—"The controuerse of beauties soueraine grace" or "Turneyment
for beauties prise"—reflect beauty's thematic importance in those
books and its centrality for Florimell's significance (IV.v.2, vii.3). In
doing so, these pageants provide means to assess rival claims upon
beauty, expose misperceptions, and satirize varied social abuses. Florimell's girdle is to be "The prize of her, which did in beautie most
excell," and though her bad imitation seems the winner at first,
Florimell herself turns out to be "the fayrest," winning the contest's
prize (V.iii.24–27).

To appreciate her story's sometimes misconstrued Platonic aspects
we must review some of Platonism's fundamental esthetic principles.[99] Many have assumed that Renaissance Platonists equate perceived beauty with good, since some of their statements may seem

to do so.[100] But their views on that were actually complex, and so such remarks should be more broadly contextualized. Whereas Spenser's second hymn says "all that faire is, is by nature good" when celebrating beauty, as Platonists often reverently said when praising it, his fourth pointedly shifts the emphasis: "all that's good, is beautifull" (*HB*, line 139; *HHB*, line 133). This latter aphorism expresses the fundamental Platonic criterion for evaluating beauty.[101] For Platonists, human beauty is primarily internal, its material expressions relatively accidental, even to the extent that beauty is incorporeal.[102] "The beauties of the body," their master declares, "are as nothing to the beauties of the soul."[103] Likewise in the *Amoretti* Spenser distinguishes between transitory physical beauty and "true beautie" which inheres in "gentle wit,/and vertuous mind," "diuine and borne of heauenly seed" (Sonnet 79). A beautiful soul can have an ugly body, his second hymn explains, if defects of its matter impair expression of form (hence Socrates); and the high inner potential that outer beauty signifies can be corrupted by abusive "will" (hence a handsome murderer).[104] Encountering "spiritual loveliness . . . in the husk of an unlovely body," an evolved Platonic lover "will find it beautiful enough to fall in love with and to cherish" (*Symposium* 210bc).

Spenser's esthetic representations accord with Platonism's fundamental distinction between true beauty and apparent beauty. As the poet relates the former to Truth and the Good in Una's case, so his bad characters who seem attractive, such as Duessa, Acrasia, and Florimell's impostor, are not truly beautiful. Though deceptively seeming "like beautie," Castiglione's Bembo warns, outer glamor or wanton appeal are "unworthie of so honourable and holy a name" (311). Florimell's virtue, signified by her special relationship with the Cestus that she pointedly regains, authenticates her relation to true beauty (V.iii.27–28), for feminine chastity symbolizes purity or goodness in this allegory.

Since Spenser, like Bembo, assumes beauty's earthly appearances are ambiguous, much of *The Faerie Queene* portrays confusions about beauty as well as its abuses, so as to heighten readers' capacities of evaluative discernment.[105] Platonism likewise assumes our world is one of becoming, full of manifold illusions, so that we must carefully assess appearances to glean intimations of truth and develop appropriate esthetic perceptions. For Plato, once again, among all the Ideas' reflections in our world, Beauty's most readily disclose the transcendent world of being (*Phaedrus* 250bd). While likewise assigning beauty revelatory value in *The Faerie Queene*, Spenser portrays it in such a way as to demonstrate the challenges of perceiving it aright in a world of illusions correlative to Plato's.[106] In effect, the poet explores how Plato's account of human misperceptions of reality in the *Republic* affects his doctrines of love and beauty in the *Phaedrus* and *Symposium*. Insofar as early modern literature engages Plato's theories of love and beauty, it tends to focus on the tensions, already integral to those dialogues, between human desires, bodies, and transcendental aspirations. Finally, though Florimell and Marinell are to marry, that would not have been necessarily un-Platonic as some suppose, because their marriage has symbolic roles compatible with Platonism anyway, and Christian Platonists could allow for sex and marriage.[107]

Florimell's initial manifestation as the ever-elusive object of pell-mell desire, with the lustful forester in hot pursuit, as well as the more chivalrously desirous Arthur, Guyon, and Timias, focuses much of the apparent nature, impact, and reception of beauty as Renaissance Platonists conceived it in their philosophy and art. Its power to prompt desire (imaged here as impassioned equestrian pursuit) and elude its devotees (none of Florimell's pursuers here can apprehend her) were standard topoi.[108] Contextually likened to a comet, the embodied revelation of Florimell's beauty seems a heavenly prodigy, at which "the people stand aghast" (III.i.16). In *December*, Colin Clout says that beauty transformatively appeared in his life like "A comet" heralding love's "raging fyre."[109] Though comets had long been considered sublunary atmospheric phenomena that presaged disaster, the renowned astronomer Tycho Brahe and others had redefined them as miracles that God produces among the superlunary planets and fixed stars, like wondrous fireworks signifying divine glory.[110] Both these cultural understandings befit Spenser's allegory of beauty. Just as Florimell herself is the mainly passive quarry of desire, beauty in general affects its perceiver largely in accord with what she or he brings to that vision.

The "griesly" forest setting for Florimell's spectacular advent expresses the paradoxes inherent in the appearance of such formal perfections in the sublunary realm of matter. Somehow materialized, they become apprehended through the physical media of the senses and flesh, and implicated in the passions and bodily desire. Those are instantiated here by the prowling beasts (expressing the subrational animalities of embodiment) and by the Forester himself, riding his "tyreling Iade" in an allegorized satire of lust's sexual mountings (III.i.14, 17).[111] The ensuing Malecasta episode features a progressive scale of seduction that travesties its implied antitype, the Platonic scale of ascent for apprehending idealized beauty.[112]

Spenser's central books of love and amity examine beauty's significance and the applications of esthetics to life, art, poetics, and the personal and social pursuits of truth and goodness. At issue are the nature and effects of beauty; the validity, variety, and range of its expressions; the possibilities of its apprehension and misapprehension; and the status of artistic images and imitations. Since the poet finds beauty so exalted, his creation of Florimell as its primary symbol entails dangers of falsification which he seeks to contain by presenting her antitype, the False Florimell. Thus "good by paragone / Of euill, may more notably be rad," and he finally sets both together, "Of both their beauties to make paragone" (III.ix.2, V.iii.24). This strategy of depiction seeks to expose falsities and mass delusions regarding beauty, while addressing the ethical responsibilities of art in the dissemination of influential images. Spenser's depiction of the False Florimell constitutes a stylized, phantastic imitation, as if in ironic quotation marks, that indicates the contrary icastic character of both Florimell and his other idealized images in general.

3. Britomart and Merlin's Mirror

The mimetic poet sets up in each individual soul a vicious constitution by fashioning phantoms far removed from reality and by currying favor with the [soul's] senseless element.

—Plato, *Republic*, 10.605c

Spenser introduces his third book with a proem that assesses the capacities of poets, painters, and his own *Faerie Queene* to depict "vertue" and "beauty." Though the visual and verbal arts cannot adequately reproduce these ideals, they may still, with sovereign "pardon" and Platonic resonances, produce provisional imagistic reflections through "colourd showes," "shadow," and "mirrours more then one" (III.pr.1–5). The seminal event of the ensuing Britomart plot epitomizes such esthetic concerns. An "image" she has seen in Merlin's magic mirror fills her mind with desire to seek that vision's fulfillment (III.i.8.6–9). While various interpretive approaches can be applied,[113] the Britomart fable launched together with Florimell's in Book III clearly revolves around the mediation, status, and power of mentally assimilated images. In *The Faerie Queene* these arise through stimuli, agencies, passions, and faculties including Alma's Phantastes, the Bower's bad genius, his good counterpart Agdistes, and eros. The poem's good and bad enchanters partly adumbrate the possibilities of artistic influence, and so does the narrative of Merlin's mirror.[114] Drawing on Plato's *Republic*, antipoetic discourse argued that poetic images lack truth-content, overstimulate the passions, and confuse their audiences. Through Britomart's experience and the Florimells' adventures, Spenser explores how his art can instead attain a relative esthetic authenticity that affords means of inspired vision, despite the general currency of deceptive illusions. This allegory of poetics preemptively appropriates and mocks some basic antipoetic critiques.

The initial phases of Britomart's experience with Merlin's phantasmal mirror enact some main ill effects that poetry's detractors ascribed to the art in general. By at first showing how deeply Britomart's vision in the mirror impassions, possesses, and transforms her, the poet grants that the arts of imagistic representation wield great power over minds, and acknowledges concerns about artistic influence upon the public. Yet he proceeds to demonstrate right poetry's benevolence, for though Britomart's encounter with the mirror may initially appear to subject her to a harmful illusion, that experience turns out to have revealed a truth, and thus launches a quest with momentous consequences. Neither the image Britomart perceives in the mirror nor her desire that it inspires, we find, are ever merely illusory. A self-reflexive demonstration of the icastic capacities of Spenser's poesis, the narrative of Merlin's mirror draws on antipoetic discourse, the condemnation of poetry in general rather than only its abuses, so as to mock and dismiss that critique.

"Like to the world it selfe," Merlin's surrogate mirror-world has especially clear analogies with expansive mimetic narratives such as *The Faerie Queene*:

> It vertue had, to shew in perfect sight,
>> What euer thing was in the world contaynd,
>> Betwixt the lowest earth and heuens hight,
>> So that it to the looker appertaynd. . . .

(III.ii.19)

Following ancient precedents such as Plato's *Republic* among others (10.596d–99e), Renaissance poetics commonly portrayed fictions as "mirrors" of nature; yet assumed that much of what appears in them depends on what different readers bring to their reading.[115] On Merlin's enchanted glass, Spenser remarks, "Who wonders not that *reades* so wonderous worke?" (III.ii.20; my emphasis). Merlin's "wondrous" creative powers, like those of his antitypes Archimago and Busyrane, arise from "wordes" and "writing straunge characters" (III.iii.12, 14). Elsewhere Spenser calls *The Faerie Queene* "this fayre mirrhour," and its characterizations present Elizabeth with "mirrours more than one" (II.pr.4, III.pr.5). As Merlin's mirror is "a famous Present for a Prince/And worthy worke of infinite regard," so too *The Faerie Queene*: both are *specula*, as it were, wherein much of past and future good and ill may be discerned (III.ii.18–22).

Gazing upon Merlin's fabulous orb, Britomart finds the "fayre visage" that appears to her there has somehow thus been *"written* in her heart" (III.ii.29; my emphasis). This effect figures the correlative power of poetry's imagistic representations to seize, impassion, and transform minds. That potency motivated much of Plato's critique in the *Republic* (10.602a–08b), as well as later antipoetic detraction, and yet also inspired Renaissance advocacies of the art that sought to harness its capacities for good while condemning abuses. Here the assimilated image becomes "infixed" in Britomart's "bowells," considered the seat of the passions, and forms a rankling "vlcer" growing "daily more and more" (III.ii.39). In terms unwittingly recalling standard motifs of antipoetic discourse, as I will show, Britomart laments that, having perceived a "shade and semblant" in this "wondrous" creation, she was "pleased with that seeming goodlyhed," and swallowed "Vnwares the hidden hooke with baite" (III.ii.38). After inducing disturbing "dreames, and . . . fantastick sight" (III.ii.29), it brings her to "feed on shadowes, . . . /And like a shadow wexe," or "pyned ghost" (III.ii.39, 44, 52). "I fonder loue a shade," she complains, "the body far exyld" (III.ii.44). A vocabulary of illusion implying progressive recession from reality characterizes Spenser's account of the mirror's seemingly ill effects on its apparent victim.

In these passages and those on the Florimells, the poet's imagery and diction of shadow, shade, semblances, reflections, and phantoms (also called shades in another sense) have Christian Platonist ontological implications unapparent to the characters but important for the allegory. In Plato's usage, followed by later Platonists, such terms express the diminished, illusory, reflective nature of all that we ordinarily take for reality, relative to the resplendent Ideas.[116] In Spenser's proems for Books II and III, besides the *Letter to Ralegh* on Faery's queen, "shadow" evokes that meaning along with its further senses of figuration and type, and clearly has its Platonic significance in several *Amoretti* and both hymns to beauty.[117]

From Plato's standpoint in the *Republic*, poetry's apparently pleasing representations not only overexcite the passions and impair reason but multiply its devotees' illusions by reflecting nature's reflections of the Ideas. Hence poetry's enthusiasts lead doubly apparitional lives, and that is Britomart's predicament as we have just seen her describe it. The philosopher's allegation that poetry produces "phantoms" at several "removes from reality, . . . without knowledge of the truth," follows from its contextual definition as a kind of imitative "mirror." Complaining that many credit poets with knowledge of "all the arts and all things human pertaining to virtue and vice, and all things divine," Plato likens them to "some magician" (compare Spenser's Merlin) whom people suppose "all-wise," yet who deceives his public with tricks of imitative artifice (10.596d–605c). Here Plato specifically targets Homer, epic's prototypical exponent. The supposedly universal wisdom of his epics underwrote the genre's definitive encyclopedism and much of its sixteenth-century prestige.[118] The initial effects of Merlin's mirror on Britomart reflect a range of antipoetic allegations current in Spenser's time, particularly as formulated in the *Republic*.

Having thus sampled and represented that discourse, Spenser demonstrates its deficiencies. Platonic advocates of poetry used Plato's theories of furor and icastic imitation to develop poetics of the image that claimed to promote pursuit of truth and the good. Sidney similarly advocates poetic manifestation of a golden world surpassing nature in such a way as to manifest ideals and inspire readers to pursue them; his paradigmatic heroic poet provides images of "virtue" made "more lovely in her holiday apparel," so that "the image of each action stirreth and instructeth the mind," inflaming it "with desire to be worthy"(78–79, 98). Spenser's avowed end of fashioning readers "in vertuous and gentle discipline" would in his view depend on such assimilation of images that positively move and transform the mind (*Letter*, 714). Neither would have assumed that always happens, or even to the same extent when it does, for early modern reader-response theories acknowledged that some readers are perverse or incorrigible.[119] As edification dominated former advocacy of art, so both writers remained committed to poetry's potential to fashion and inspire "right readers."

When Glauce first seeks to deal with her charge's strange possession by "The shadow of a warlike knight" (III.ii.45), her advice on how to make the best of it unwittingly accords with basic principles of Renaissance icastic and idealized imitation. Glauce advises, "No shadow, but a body hath in powre" (III.i.45), and so, rather than remaining committed to the penumbra, as it were, they seek to pursue the adumbrated reality, or refer the imagistic sign to its true signified by pursuing the actual source of the image that Britomart absorbed from Merlin's mirror. In the allegory of poetics, this correction of the heroine's initial mode of perceiving and understanding the mirror's image expresses an exemplary correction of responses to art, and especially to Spenser's. A certain kind of perceived shadow, he indicates, can inspire its beholder to pursue truth's fulfillment beyond the world of shadows. Likewise, icastic poetry's images were to be referred to the validating truths they seek to indicate, and the fictional integuments of allegory to their animating conceptions.

Hence the Britomart plot allegorically addresses the problems of poetic insufficiency mooted in Book III's proem. Though poetry that aspires to represent ideals of virtue and beauty can only "shadow" them in "coloured showes," Spenser assumes (III.pr. 2–3), his following narrative proceeds to show how these imagistic approximations of truth can nonetheless evoke positive realities with inspirational force. In this sense, Britomart's ultimate response to Artegall's image models the experience of "right readers": those whose reactions to the poem's favorable images accord with the principles of Spenserian ideal imitation.

This implicit poetic advocacy partly depends on astute appropriation of Platonic love psychology. For Platonists, and Spenser addresses this theory in his *October* eclogue, *Amoretti*, and *Hymnes*, the lover's mind or soul becomes a mirror reflecting the beloved's image, which the lover venerates, refines, and assimilates, so that both may seek to become that ideal—hence love's positively inspirational potential.[120] This is what happens to Britomart, and love transforms her so much that she changes into a knight to pursue the knightly image in her mind. Yet the crucial difference here is that she has never actually seen or met Artegall himself. Until much later, her experience of love and her desired lover remain *virtual*—gained through the marvelous mirror analogous to beneficent textual mirrors, which imprints its contents within her. Whereas poetry's detractors, including Plato, alleged it harmfully provokes readers' passions, Britomart's case indicates that art's imagistic powers, even those involving eros, can produce surrogate experiences that can have real beneficial consequences. Arthur's dream of Gloriana, which may have been reality because he finds pressed grass where she had lain in his reverie, has similar implications (I.ix.13–16).

When Glauce asks Merlin for advice about Britomart's predicament, their discussion unwittingly amplifies the allegory of poetics. This "*sad euill*, which doth her infest," Glauce complains,

> Doth course of naturall cause farre exceed,
> And housed is within her hollow brest,
> That either seems *some cursed witches deed*,
> Or *euill spright*, that in her doth such torment breed.

> (III.iii.18; my emphasis)

At this the wizard laughs. The terms of Glauce's indictment and Spenser's usage of a benevolent sorcerous persona parody conventions of antipoetic discourse. For example, Plato's *Republic* and Gosson's treatises represent poets as suspect enchanters, poetry as their spell, while Gosson adds witchcraft and deviltry.[121] Merlin's laughter here ventriloquizes the poet's at poetry's detractors. Britomart's predicament, the magician insists, is actually her "good fortune" (III.iii.19). Its effects in stimulating her heroic pursuit of an ideal parallel those that high mimetic poetry was to have upon right readers. Spenser further mocks antipoetic criticism by representing it, in effect, within ironic double quotation marks, for Glauce herself does not fully believe what she says here. Though she assumes that Britomart's condition is serious unless remedied, she is nonetheless discreetly seeking to hide much of the truth from Merlin, whom she does not actually fool at all (III.iii.15–24).

This allegory indeed anticipates the commentary on poetics in Book IV's proem. There, a "rugged forehead" condemns Spenser's "looser rimes" for their representations of love. These allegedly lead "fraile youth" astray with

> false allurement of that pleasing baite,
> That better were in vertues discipled,
> Then with vaine poemes weeds to haue their fancies fed.
>
> (IV.pr.1)

Britomart similarly complains that the "semblant of a knight" she saw in Merlin's mirror "*pleased* with . . . *seeming goodly-hed*," so that she swallowed "Vnwares the hidden hooke *with baite*" (III.ii.38; my emphasis). To Glauce she seems infested with "wicked euill" (III.ii.32; cp. iii.16, 18). While this proem's representative detractor likely portrays William Cecil, Lord Burghley, his censures typify antipoetic discourse. Among others, Plato had made similar remarks in the *Republic*, and Gosson in various treatises. The bishop of London, John King, had denounced Sidney's "Arcadia, & the Faëry Queene, and Orlando Furioso" in a sermon delivered in 1594: "it may be the sin of this lande and age of ours (perhaps the mother of our atheisme) to commit idolatry with such books."[122]

As Book IV's proem and Book III's self-reflexive allegory of Glauce's complaint and Merlin's response are homologous in thought, so Spenser's answer to that proem's representative detractor amplifies the first two stanzas of Canto iii in Book III. There, Spenser distinguishes love from lust and from "base affections" as a "sacred fyre" kindled in the heavens, "thence pourd into men." Committed to "true beautie" and "vertue," that "sweete fit" is a means of providence that inspires "all noble deedes and neuer dying fame," including "th'Heroes high intents," and further effects "destined descents" (III.iii.1–2). In Book IV's proem, love rightly understood is the "roote" of "honor and all vertue," that culminates in "glorious flowres of fame,/That *crowne* true lovers with *immortall blis*," alluding to the Christian crown of glory (IV.pr.2–3; my emphasis).[123] Contrary to the antipoetic critique summarized in this proem's first stanza, Spenser argues that his poem promotes such heavenly love. Rather than corrupting people's fancies with false allurements (as if some vile witch's work, in Glauce's terms), it can thus be profoundly enlightening.

This mimetic "(h)eroism" is central to Spenser's poesis, and so is its main statement, the proem to Book IV, in *The Faerie Queene*'s physical structure. While Socrates, "the father of Philosophie," is Spenser's human authority on love's value here, the poet conceives his inspirational sovereign or sovereign ideal in Book IV as a "sacred Saint" comparable to both Venus and Christ: "Queene of loue, and Prince of peace from heauen" (IV.pr.3–4). Heightening the contextual Christian Platonism, the poet's implicit play on "eros" and "hero" underwrites his claim that love animates the highest human achievements in thought and deed:

> all the workes of those wise sages,
> And braue exploits which great Heroes wonne,
> In loue were either ended or begunne. . . .
>
> (IV.pr.3)

When asked "what is the meaning of the word *hero* (ἥρως, in the old writing ἔρως)," Socrates says "the name . . . signifies that they were born of love," for it "is only a slight alteration of Eros, from whom the heroes sprang" (*Cratylus*, 398cd). Although "the association of 'heroes' with love" had thus become "common" as Hamilton's *Faerie Queene* notes (410n), the context here is pointedly Socratic. Plato had defined love as desire for beauty, a standard assumption in the *trattati d'amore*, and Books III and IV assess beauty's role in inspiring (h)eroism, as the local references to Venus and Platonic love philosophy indicate. Contrary to poetry's detractors, Spenser argues that his (h)eroic poem can itself be a means of grace and providential guidance.

The Britomart story demonstrates that discreetly presented thesis. After Glauce charges that his mirror has evilly bewitched Britomart, Merlin insists

It was not, *Britomart*, thy wandring eye,
   Glauncing vnwares in charmed looking glas,
   But the streight course of heuenly destiny,
   Led with eternall prouidence, that has
   Guyded thy glaunce, to bring his will to pas.
....
   Therefore submit thy wayes vnto his will,
And doe by all dew meanes thy destiny fulfill.

                                 (III.iii.24)

The ensuing narrative fulfills Merlin's claims for his mirror's potentially providential role, because Britomart's vision and resultant relationship with Artegall culminate in the Tudors. In the allegory of
poetics, the effects of Merlin's "worlde of glas" correspond to those of
right poetry when rightly read. This beneficent prophetic enchanter
propitious to love supplements Colin Clout as a Spenserian proxy;
the poet has Cuddy call Colin the oracular "Priest" of love's mysteries
in *Colin Clouts* (lines 823–34), and Spenser composed four hymns on
love and beauty. The self-reflexive allegory of the mirror's impact
on Britomart insists on the inspirational power of the poetic image
that provisionally indicates beauty and virtue. Such poetry conduces
(h)eroism, Spenser assumes, by awakening readers' desires for these
ideals. Britomart's vision and its effects reflect upon their momentous
correlate, Arthur's dreamed or real encounter with Faery's queen,
which launched his quest. The visions of Spenser's readers in the
depths of his textual mirror are to reflect those of his protagonists
in Faery.

4. THE DOUBLED FLORIMELLS

> Is it an imitation of a phantasm or of the truth?
> —Plato, *Republic*, 598b

Like Thomas Lodge, Sidney, and many other sixteenth-century advocates of poetry, Spenser considers some poetics, writers, and fictions
misleading or corrupt, and his story of Florimell's impostor satirizes
them as well as their gullible enthusiasts.[124] Until late in Book V,
Spenser rarely uses the word "idol" in *The Faerie Queene*, yet twice
applies it to the witch's creation, the False Florimell, and not only

because she is wrongly idolized (III.vii.11, IV.v.15).[125] In late six-teenth-century literary discourse "idol" was a standard and not neces-sarily pejorative term for the mimetic image that the poet fabricates, based on the Greek εἴδωλον (which yielded the further term εἰδωλοποιός, "image-maker"), from the root verb εἴδω, meaning "resemble," as Mazzoni explains.[126] In Plato's usage, εἴδωλον applies to apparitions, shadows, and likenesses in general, hence to mimetic simulacra. When Guyon describes Gloriana as "th'Idole of her makers great magnificence," referring to her reflection of divine glory, Spenser's usage of the term partly alludes to her function as an imagis-tic signifier (II.ii.41).[127] Likewise an "idol" in the former literary sense, but *in malo*, the False Florimell focuses the misrepresentations of phantastic art, in contrast to Florimell's instantiation of Spenser's idealized poetic. The "cursed witches deed" that wrought Brito-mart's imagistic enchantment in Glauce's complaint is actually en-acted here. In Gosson's view, like the divine Edward Dering's, poets give readers "cuppes of *Circes*," "bewitching" them.[128] Spenser's alle-gory of poetics appropriates the portrayal of poets as bad enchanters in antipoetic discourse, so that Merlin's antitype the witch epitomizes poets who degrade the art.

This implicit satire targets more than poetasters and audiences, whether courtly or not, who are undiscerning in their pursuits of beauty and love. While Spenser's commitment to icastic imitative idealism motivates much of the satire, his version of that theory is not austere. For example, the False Florimell's parodic blazon implies mockery of love-poets who, as Lodge and Sidney complained, stimu-late sensual appetites to induce delight without edifying value (III.-viii.6–7).[129] Yet Spenser and Sidney exploit poetry's erotic potential, and for Spenser physical beauty, though inferior to its supposed sources, is nonetheless to be celebrated. For them, what validates literary eroticism is some implied benefit to readers, society, or both, and that principle of justification drawing on early modern poetics, philosophy, and theology encompasses these writers' subject matter in general. In pursuit of beauty, truth, and the good, *The Faerie Queene* gains poetic license to survey the world, including characters as diverse as Arthur, Archimago, Una, Helenore, and Malbecco.

Since Spenser valorizes mimetic idealism and the quest for truth in his poetic and in his creation of Florimell, his account of her impostor satirizes art that disseminates illusions, and its public recep-tion. It is fundamentally art that is not in pursuit of truth, and thus merely humors and misleads its audience. Such art would be phantas-tic and nonidealized, for Spenser's mimetic idealism seeks to forsake the world's shadows or deceptive appearances, insofar as possible, the better to approach truth. Though many cannot tell the true and false Florimells apart, these apparent doubles crucially differ. Not only does the impostor befit Plato's definition of the phantastic as overdone, as I will soon show; but she is relatively deficient in existence or being, as section five explains, just as she disappears when directly compared with the true Florimell (V.iii.24).[130]

In any case, writing to Harvey around 1580, Spenser condemned literary quests for patrician favor and for applause from "pleasing the people," because such efforts court "follies" and reap "the base praise which rewards/Ignominious nonsense."[131] Whereas he treats some poets generously in *Colin Clouts* (1595), he condemns the English literary milieu, including "all" poets except a "few," in *Teares of the Muses* (1591).[132] His satire of bad poetics in the Florimells' story could include popular English drama. Though representing the muses of comedy and tragedy sympathetically, and thus approving those genres in principle, Spenser's *Teares* laments their current decline.[133] Plato's critique of dramatic poetry in the *Republic* included male theatrical transvestism,[134] and a masculine spirit animates Florimell's impostor (III.viii.8). Just as many are thus deceived, Spenser's representation of "her" satirizes the prevalence of poor esthetic judgment in general. Yet "she" could have further suggested cross-dressed English theatricality. On account of Spenser's learned polylingual comparatism, the satire of bad poetics in the Florimells' story includes ancient, Neo-Latin, and vernacular continental literatures.

When resplendent Florimell shelters by chance at the witch's hovel, the hag's lazy son, who symbolically slumbers through the brilliant day in "slothfull shade," falls in "brutish lust" with her and she flees (III.vii.12–19). The comparison of her initial impact upon him to "the bright Sunne" dazing "feeble eyne" evokes Plato's analogy of the dazzling sun of Truth in the *Republic* contrary to the shadowlands of lived illusions (III.vii.13). The witch's son's lustful response parallels Sansloy's and Sylvanus's to Una. When Florimell flees, the witch first consoles her son's dismay by sending her "hideous beast" to retrieve the beauty or consume her. This creature "likest . . . to an *Hyena*" and comparable to Maleger signifies "corrupted flesh" in a lusty aspect (III.vii.22, 30), and the witch herself somewhat suggests perverse intellect and imagination, or "wicked wit" (III.viii.5). Spenser thus satirizes lustful desires for beauty: only the beast returns, incapable of apprehending the beauty herself or, figuratively, beauty. Ficino comparably maintains that beauty can only be known through the spiritual senses (reason, sight, hearing), and eludes the physical ones (touch, taste, smell).[135] Having exchanged beauty for the beast, the son despairs and his progenitor creates the phantasmal Florimell as consolation.

In this mock-etiology of apparent but spurious beauties, they culturally originate as facile surrogates for their elusive and demanding counterpart, and render its discernment and pursuit all the more difficult. As Spenser's depiction of Acrasia's Bower anticipates, their over-elaboration most readily identifies them, for they are phantastic in Plato's sense. Rather than seeking to maintain fidelity to the original insofar as possible, the imitator attempts to enhance the semblance's appearance through interventions that deceive the beholders' senses (*Sophist* 235d–36c). Likewise, faced with the witch's phantasm, "euen Nature selfe enuide the same, / And grudg'd to see the counterfeit should shame / The thing it selfe" (III.viii.5). This semblant evinces "much more goodly glosse" than the reality (IV.v.15). Spenser terms both Merlin's created mirror and the False Florimell "wonderous worke" (III.ii.20, viii.5), and the latter travesties the former in the allegory of poetics. Whereas Merlin's mirror presents Britomart with a sign inducing pursuit of its genuine signified, the bad enchantress creates an illusion of glamour that deceives perception in order to conceal its total disjunction from what it purports to be (Florimell, cynosure of beauty). Obscuring its own status as a representation, it causes its admirers to seek fulfillment in the superficiality of its imposture and directs them to nothing whatsoever beyond itself, hence to admiration of falsity. Whereas Merlin's kind of semblant leads to a truth beyond itself, his antitype's amplifies illusions, so that "many it mistooke" (III.viii.5).

Spenser, we have seen, warns that his representations, like Merlin's here, are provisional means of referral that necessarily *fall short* of their signified ideals. His icastic poesis infused with philosophical idealism seeks to practice veracious imitation by pursuing beauty, truth, and the good, yet respecting the limits of representation. What do Spenser's genuinely beautiful characters, particularly Florimell, look like? His generalized and idealized descriptions of their features, often involving radiance, downplay material coordinates so as to gesture beyond them. Whereas Spenser's blazon of Belphoebe's beauty involves many "heauenly" elements suggesting numinous mystery (II.-iii.22–26; likewise III.v.51–54), the witch conglomerates specific inert objects, then instills a wicked male sprite to animate that "carcase dead." To define Florimell and his poetic, Spenser produces her bad imitation in the phantastic mode, as if to say *"this* image is what *mine* are *not."* Florimell herself is "no . . . fantasticke sight," and that assurance plays on the adjective's technical sense in Platonic literary discourse to epitomize the allegory of poetics (III.viii.23).

Since her phantastic semblance seems the reality, "Or fayrer . . . , if ought algate / Might fayrer be" (III.viii.9), that prototypical denizen of shade the witch's son rejoices in the apparently immediate presence of beauty. His equally shady lady "Him long . . . with shadows entertain'd, / As her Creatresse had . . . ordain'd" (III.vii.10). As the impostor's bodily substance is snow from "a shady glade" (III.viii.6), so she finally vaporizes when confronted with Florimell's beauty comparable to the sun (III.vii.13, V.iii.10, 14–28). The witch and her phantom exemplify the imagistic dissemination of baited "false allurement," of which Spenser himself stood accused, along with his correlate Merlin in Book III, as if they had done, as Glauce says, "some cursed witches deed" (IV.pr.1, III.iii.18). The bad enchantress produces an illusion unsubstantiated by Spenser's touchstones of truth, virtue, and authentic beauty on which he seeks to base his idealized imitation, to render his fictions icastic.

Yet in a world replete with illusions, empty shadow-shows most readily please, so long as they provoke and titillate desires, and many soon celebrate the witch's imposture. The False Florimell's relentless coquetry tantalizes them with illusory prospects of consummated desires for beauty, and through her covert transvestism Spenser mocks the gullibility of those who pursue spurious beauties. (We may now compare television, Hollywood, glamorized consumerism, and ideological misperceptions.) Mimetic artists whom Plato condemns produce only what "appears beautiful to the ignorant multitude" (*Republic*, 10.602b). The False Florimell's devotees are all somewhat correlative to her prototypical shadow-lover, the witch's son. From him she forcibly passes to the archetypal false knight, Braggadocio, another creature of illusions. Then to Ferraugh, next Blandamour thus "cast . . . in a foolish trance," yet rivalled in that by Paridell. At the Tournament of Beauty, where the fairest is to be awarded Florimell's stray cestus and coupled with the most valiant knight, she herself seems lost. But "all" adjudge her impostor "the Paragon . . . / Of beauties praise," and "full many," with few exceptions, desire her (IV.v.9, 16, 23). Hence "all together" become "wroth," "Each" professing "to be her paramoure," and they seek "new battle," "nigh mad," without "reasons rule" (IV.v.24, 27). Their desires, perceptions of pleasure, and aspirations have come to be focused on an unworthy object that, former moral philosophers would say, stimulates and empowers the earthbound appetitive part of their souls, undermines the rational part, obscures truth, and produces both inner and outer disorders expressed in their dissensions. Plato's *Republic* ascribes these effects also to wrongful art (10.604c–6d).

In that dialogue, Socrates likewise describes "the life of the multitude," who "vainly" strive "to satisfy with things that are not real the unreal and incontinent part of their souls." "Are not the pleasures with which they dwell inevitably commingled with pains, phantoms of true pleasure, illusions of scene painting, so colored by contrary juxtaposition as to seem intense in either kind, and to beget mad loves of themselves in senseless souls, and to be fought for, as Stesichorus says the wraith (εἴδωλον) of Helen was fought for at Troy through ignorance of the truth?" (9.586bc).[136]

That quite widely reported alternative Helen myth, whereby beauty's fabled exemplar remained chastely hidden in Egypt, while what went to Troy was a fake made from a cloud, was likely Spenser's main fictional model for Florimell's phantasmal impostor.[137] We have seen that his allegory's conceptual models include Plato's icastic/phantastic distinction and discussions of mimetic phantasms. The philosopher's formerly well-known illustrative use of the false Helen in the *Republic* links the central precedent for Spenser's fiction with his conceptual applications engaging Platonism.

Plato contextually uses the false Helen and her deluded admirers' frenzies of desire to exemplify the condition of those focused only on materialities, who thus pursue false pleasures, things relatively unreal, untrue, and unsatisfying, confined to the domain of transience (9.585b–87b):

> those who have no experience of wisdom and virtue but are ever devoted to feastings and that sort of thing are swept downward . . . and roam to and fro throughout their lives, but they have never transcended all this and turned their eyes to the true upper region . . . , nor ever been truly filled with real things, nor ever tasted stable and pure pleasure, but with eyes ever bent upon the earth and heads bowed down over their tables they feast like cattle, grazing and copulating, ever greedy for more of these delights, and in their greed kicking and butting . . . , they slay one another in sateless avidity. . . . (9.586ab)

Spenser's account of the False Florimell's Tournament of Beauty in Book IV uses many animal similes to stress the brutal, subrational impulses at play (IV.iv.47). Plato's critique is psychic as well as social, for this bestial state arising from the soul's domination by its appetitive and contentious parts entails "inner dissension." Yet those ruled by their rational, wisdom-loving part cling to "what is ever like itself and immortal and to the truth," or to what "more truly *is*." This is the way of being "more truly filled and satisfied" with "true pleasure," rather than "ignorance and folly." "If a thing has less of truth," Socrates observes, "has it not also less of real essence or existence?" (9.585be).

Whereas Plato's context focuses on attaining real pleasurable fulfillment through pursuit of truth and wisdom, Spenser's usage of the false Helen motif addresses false apprehensions of beauty and resultant distortions of desire, including those abetted by spurious artistic imitations. However, for Platonists genuine beauty, truth, and goodness are correlative. So understood, the pursuit of beauty, if aptly undertaken, becomes a potent means of enlightenment: hence its high significance in the *Phaedrus*, the *Symposium*, and the Renaissance *trattati d'amore*. Spenser's application of the false Helen motif to the evaluation of beauty thus complements its usage in the *Republic*, for the poet thereby mocks the distractions of false beauty that could impair pursuit of its genuinely illuminating counterpart.

Spenser's allegory of the Florimells further complements Neoplatonic allegoresis of beauty's role in the *Iliad*. Helen thus signifies apparent material beauty, and the passions and conflicts she inspires express the confusions and degradation it produces in minds oblivious to its insufficiencies and intelligible source. The Trojans' defeat and the Greeks' return home express mental victory over the attractions of matter, enabling pursuit of intelligible beauty.[138] In Spenser's story, the False Florimell and her many admirers instance spurious beauty and the delusions of its reception (including those of phantastic art). Florimell herself and her relatively few faithful adherents focus beauty's inspirational potential in reflecting intelligible beauty. Her alienation and persecution by various abusers, correlative to Una's in Book I, satirize true beauty's reception otherwise, "Despisd and troden downe of all that ouerran" in a lapsed world (IV.viii.32).

In any case, Spenser's enthusiasts of false beauty are like Plato's bovine multitude who stampede after illusions of apparent pleasure, deserting reality, truth, and enlightenment. To resolve their bellicose rivalry for Florimell's fake after the tournament, Satyrane has her choose whom she wishes, and she selects Braggadocio, the greatest exponent of illusory pretensions, whose disjunction from reality epitomizes that fault of her admirers. For Spenser truth and goodness are the touchstones of authenticity in judging the world's deceptive appearances. Among all the knights assembled at this Tournament of Beauty, only Britomart and Triamond can resist the False Florimell's appeal, because their full commitment to virtue enables apt evaluation. Britomart prefers Amoret's "vertuous gouernment," and Triamond maintains fidelity to Canacee (IV.v.20–21).

Throughout Spenser's story of the doubled Florimells, the poet contrasts the many deceived by spurious simulacra, and their illusory prospects of pleasurable fulfillment, with the few who seek the realities beyond appearances. When Trompart unveils Florimell's impostor at the second beauty contest, the people think her "surely *Florimell*," or if not,

> That *Florimell* her selfe she then did pas.
> So feeble skill of perfect things the vulgar has.
>
> (V.iii.17)

As so often in *The Faerie Queene*, despite the fiction's outwardly chivalric idiom, this vulgarity does not coincide with any literal social status, for those deceived have been mainly knights.[139] It is rather a learned commoner's ironic trope mocking esthetic and epistemological poverties of the mind—and not just poor skill or knowledge of the perfect things and ideals he seeks to illuminate, but the inadequacies of the mind itself, just as even Marinell "Ne wist . . . what to thinke, or to deuise" here (V.iii.18). The theme of forsaken Truth characterizes not only Book I (expressed in Una's ecclesiological wanderings, doublings, and abandonments), but also Books III to V, for the Florimell plot depicts the misadventures and misapprehensions current in the likewise potentially revelatory domain of desiring, pursuing, and representing beauty, in both life and art.

5. FLORIMELL'S SOLAR AUTHENTICATION

> What . . . would be the study that would draw the soul away from the world of becoming to the world of being?
>
> —Plato, *Republic* 7.521d

Rival claims upon beauty at last resolve in the Legend of Justice through Artegall's intervention, according to a solar symbolism that validates Florimell, the Cestus, and their proper congruence. In constructing a fable that emphasizes the elusiveness of true beauty and transcendent ideals in the world, Spenser allows for skeptical counternarratives about them, but only in the context of a conclusion that valorizes that beauty, together with virtue and truth. Florimell's vindication symbolically applies to all that she represents, to such commitments, and to her creator's poetic.

Suspecting some imposture, Artegall sets Florimell

by that snowy one,
Like the true saint beside the image set,
Of both their beauties to make paragone,
And triall, whether should the honour get.
Streight way so soone as both together met,
Th' enchanted Damzell vanisht into nought:
Her snowy substance melted as with heat,
Ne of that goodly hew remayned ought,
But th'emptie girdle. . . .

(V.iii.24)

The true beauty negates the false, revealing the latter's relative unreal-ity. The impostor's dissolution resolves the fundamental imagistic contrast between the real Florimell's solar radiance (e.g., III.vii.13, IV.xii.34), and her surrogate's assemblage from well-shaded snow and inferior lights (III.viii.6–7).

Solar imagery especially pervades the tournament and subsequent beauty contest immediately preceding Florimell's victory. The pre-liminary tournament tests the proposition that her beauty excels all others (V.iii.4, 15). Her side wins under the ensign of a shield bearing "the Sunne brode blazed in a golden field," analogous to Arthur's "sunshiny" or "sunlike" shield (I.viii.20, V.viii.41), and borne by the Knight of Justice (V.iii.10–12). When Trompart later reveals her impostor's presence, in effect

two sunnes appear in the azure skye,
Mounted in *Phoebus* charet fierie bright,
Both darting forth faire beames. . . .

(V.iii.19)

But the challenge is illusory as her competitor's immediate meltdown confirms, like a marvelous rainbow vanishing (IV.iii.25).

These two meteorological similes have pointed allegorical signifi-cance. Both the parhelion (double sun) and the rainbow were consid-ered apparitions produced by *reflection*, so that both similes complement Platonic analysis of appearances and realities here. Ac-cording to sixteenth-century meteorology, largely based on Aristot-le's *Meteorologica*, a rainbow or dual sun appears when a cloud in apt circumstances is seen to reflect the sun like a mirror.[140] Mock suns, for instance, "are nothing else but Idols, or Images of the sunne, . . . as in a glasse."[141] Neither phenomenon is objectively real: Aristotle had interpreted both rainbows and mock suns as types of optical illusion produced by refraction of the observer's vision (*Meteorologica*, 3.2–6).[142] Whereas some meteorological phenomena "have a true substance indeed, as raine and haile: others . . . have no more but a bare apparence, without any reall substance."[143] Natale Conti reviews this former science in his mythographical discussion of Iris, goddess of rainbows.[144]

Analogies of reflection are fundamental to Platonic epistemological, esthetic, metaphysical, and ontological discourse. In the *Republic*, Plato uses such phenomena to explain that we live in a world of becoming that seems real but is illusory relative to the world of being that it reflects: the Forms or Ideas. Whereas the arts in that dialogue multiply our illusions by reflecting the reflections, later theories of idealized imitation recuperated Platonic grounds of artistic authenticity.

Spenser's context distinguishes what *should* be admired from its counterfeit that generally passes current through mass delusion. This valorization of forsaken yet present truth not only applies to judgment of the nature of reality, the significance of beauty, and the pursuit of truth, but also to the arts and poetics. As well as being a preeminent exemplar of beauty, who has nonetheless been abused and deserted for a fake, Florimell is Spenser's own creation, a poetic image, presented in contrast to a bad imitation. By inducing the latter's disappearance, their direct comparison affirms the contrary substantiality of the poet's high mimetic poesis. Unlike apparitions such as mock suns and phantastic artifices, which "vanisheth away" and "into nothing goe" like rainbows, however wondrous (V.iii.25), Spenser's creation has in some sense real existence and value, he implies. Such a claim would assume that his art expresses higher reality to an extent surpassing other modes of imitation, so that it more fully partakes of being. Likewise, the celestial sun transcends phenomena of the corrupted sublunary domain such as rainbows and mock suns. From Plato and Tasso's standpoints, once again, we should put "visible things in the genus of non-being and only the intelligible in the genus of being." In that case, as Tasso says, imitation of what exists "belongs to the icastic imitator," whose practice is one of idealization.[145]

Central to the vindication of all that Florimell represents here, the solar imagery reflects Plato's epistemological analogies of the sun as in the *Republic* (6.508a–7.521c), as well as its biblical and Christian Platonist associations.[146] In Book III, Florimell's disappearance occasions Arthur's complaint about night and the obscurities of human perception. There, darkness is infernal and daylight heavenly, associated with "Truth" and "The children of day" as "the blessed seed."

Presiding over their ultimate triumph over darkness and "sinne" is the sun-giant Titan, a trope for the Son as *sol gigas* (III.iv.57–61).[147] Solar imagery at this bride and bridegroom's marriage in Book V epitomizes the heavenly ideality to which Spenser refers the manifestations of virtue and beauty (e.g., VI.pr.3–4). In her exemplary beauty, radiantly spotless Florimell is one of the poet's Women Clothed with the Sun, like Una and Gloriana. If interpreted as prodigies, the mock sun and rainbow could signify divinely authorized admonition to forsake illusion, and maintain redemptive hope.[148] But they mainly function here as analogies of reflective apparition from natural philosophy, for Spenser associates portentous interpretation of mock suns with ignorance of "natures worke" (V.iii.19.5–7).[149] His eclectic Christianity subsumes much Platonism, and he often alludes to the *Republic*'s solar analogy and attendant cave of shadows. That Platonic context treats the discernment of reality as opposed to illusion: precisely what is at stake in the final juxtaposition of Florimell and her impostor. Plato thus defines the philosopher's mission, to which that of the right poet, Spenser implies, is correlative.

In the *Republic*, Socrates declares that the sun is to the human eye, vision, and its objects as "the good is in the intelligible region to reason and the objects of reason" (6.508c). Though the Idea of the good is "the cause of knowledge and of truth," it surpasses them both, "fair as they both are," in its "inconceivable beauty" (6.508e–9a). The context addresses the quality of the soul's intellectual vision. When the soul "is firmly fixed on the [intelligible] domain where truth and reality shine resplendent it apprehends and knows them and appears to possess reason, but when it inclines to that region which is mingled with darkness, the world of becoming and passing away, it opines only and its edge is blunted, and it . . . seems as if it lacked reason" (6.508d).

Further expounding this analogy of the sun, Socrates recounts his fable of the prisoners long incarcerated in a cave (7.514a–21c). Throughout their lives, they have only seen flickering shadows projected on a wall by a fire's half-light, and so these constitute their apparent reality. Yet if one were freed, he would not only come to see the means and actual objects of projection, but upon leaving the cave, would discover the world, the heavens, and the dazzling sun (7.516bc). The condition of those prisoners is ours, Socrates argues, for our lives are bound to the world of becoming, so that we merely see reflections of the Ideas unless we forsake our illusions to enter the world of being through intellectual vision. The freed prisoner's departure from the cave and contemplation of the heavens corresponds to "the soul's ascension to the intelligible region," while the sun itself correlates with "the idea of good, . . . the cause . . . of all that is right and beautiful, giving birth in the visible world to light, and . . . in the intelligible world being the authentic source of truth and reason" (7.517bc). Hence Socrates advocates "an art of the . . . conversion" of the mind's vision, "from a day whose light is darkness to the veritable day" (7.518d, 521c). Like a prisoner freed from the cave who returns to enlighten its inmates, those with philosophically "waking minds" who "have seen the reality of the beautiful, the just, and the good" are to promote such conversions (7.520bc).

Spenser seeks to practice such a beneficial art, and so we must recur to his invocation of Socrates, "the father of Philosophie," where the poet defends his art against the "Stoicke censours" averse to his advocacy of (h)eroism. There, Socrates is a *philo*sophical educator, one who "to his Critias, *shaded oft from sunne,*/ Of loue full many lessons did apply" (IV.pr.3; my emphasis). Whereas Robert Ellrodt claims that by "Critias" Spenser meant "Phaedrus" here but blundered, thus establishing "beyond doubt" the poet's ignorance of basic Platonic texts, this is a compact allegory involving Spenserian onomastic wordplay and complex Platonic intertextualities.[150] These include not only the *Phaedrus* and *Symposium*, the chief dialogues on love and beauty; but also the *Republic*, a text fundamental for former debates about the value of poetry; and the *Apology*, where Socrates defends himself, like Spenser here, against charges of corrupting "fraile youth" (IV.pr.1). Platonic philosophy as rediscovered, reinterpreted, and popularized in the Renaissance stressed the potential of love and beauty to inspire pursuit of wisdom, truth, and virtue. In this case Critias typifies those who receive such Socratic counsel, and the context alludes to emancipation from the shadows of misperception, famously expressed by the analogy of the sun and related fable of the cave. These two lines on Critias also readily allegorize the Socratic project of enlightening the mind, for the name evokes the Greek κριτικός.[151] Referring to capacities of judgment (like many of its derivatives such as the Latin *criticus*), that word denoted in one sense "the power of discerning." The poet thus honors ancient Platonism while aligning his own poesis with that philosophy's Christian redevelopments, for its original intellectual light, he assumes, was dappled: "shaded oft from sunne" (IV.pr.3). But not *always* shaded. Wittily reinterpreting Plato's fable of the sun beyond the dark cave in the *Republic*, the poet's trope implies that Philosophy's father has his limitations: presumably most of all for Spenser because Socrates was shaded from the Son (who was often the tenor of former English solar wordplay). But that Platonic philosopher remains the major human authority whom we are to "Witnesse" on love, and the specific exemplar of "wise sages," who shed some light in his "full manie lessons" about it. Since the poet himself brings a new "lesson" of love here (a pointed correspondence of diction, and the proem's emphatically penultimate word), he represents himself as a Socratic inheritor who, as a philosopher-poet, promises a brightened vision of eros (IV.pr.5).

In this context responding to detractors, Spenser's chosen Socratic exemplar partly functions as an authorization of his own poetic, particularly for *The Faerie Queene*'s diverse representations of (h)eroism. Seeking to promote modes of love that elucidate beauty, truth, and the good, the poet finesses the *Republic*'s critique of poetry by appropriating the mission Socrates assigns to philosophers. Spenser's allusion to the Platonic tropes of the sun and privation from sunlight is particularly apt here because the fable of the cave stresses that the denizens of its shadow-world would not only misunderstand and ridicule anyone who sought to enlighten them, but would, if possible, kill him (7.517ac). So ended the Father of Philosophy, as in Plato's *Apology*; yet while noting how his own endeavor furrows influential foreheads (IV.pr.1), the poet proceeds with it nonetheless. Not merely a pragmatic local strategy, Spenser's alignment of his poetic with the Socratic project both comments on the prior volume's contents and reception, and defines the reader's approach to the second three books. For minds that can be awakened, he assumes, *The Faerie Queene*'s mode of esthetic fairness affords heightened perceptions of reality. The others will enjoy their shadows.

McGill University

NOTES

1. Plato, *Collected Dialogues*, ed. Edith Hamilton and Huntington Cairns, trans. various (Princeton: Bollingen-Princeton University Press, 1961). Used throughout; except I use Loeb for the Greek.

2. Gosson, *The Schoole of Abuse* (London: Thomas Woodcocke, 1579), STC 12097, sig. A2b–3a. His antipoetic crusade continues in *An Apologie of the Schoole of Abuse* in his *Ephemerides of Phialo* (London: Thomas Dawson, 1579), STC 12093, fols. 81a–92b; and *Playes Confuted in Five Actions* (London: Thomas Gosson, 1582), STC 12095. See Peter C. Herman, *Squitter-wits and Muse-haters: Sidney, Spenser, Milton and Renaissance Antipoetic Sentiment* (Detroit: Wayne State University Press, 1996); Concetta Carestia Greenfield, *Humanist and Scholastic Poetics, 1250–1500*

(Lewisburg: Bucknell-Associated University Presses, 1981); Bernard Weinberg, *A History of Literary Criticism in the Italian Renaissance*, 2 vols. (Chicago: University of Chicago Press, 1961), Index, s.v. "Defence of poetry."

3. Castelvetro defines poetry's end as pleasure (without invoking instruction). See his *On the Art of Poetry* (*Poetica d'Aristotele vulgarizzata et sposta*), trans. Andrew Bongiorno (Binghamton: Medieval & Renaissance Texts and Studies, 1984).

4. Ronsard, "Au lecteur" (1572 preface to his *Françiade*), in Vol. 7 of *Oeuvres complètes*, ed. Paul Laumonier, rev. ed. (Paris: Lemerre, 1914–19), 67. Spenser, *TM*, lines 580–94. For citations of Spenser's poetry aside from *The Faerie Queene* I use *The Shorter Poems*, ed. Richard A. McCabe (Harmondsworth: Penguin, 1999), and his abbreviations of Spenserian titles (504–05).

5. "All Renaissance [literary] theorists felt themselves obliged to deal with Plato's banishment of the poets. . . . The defence of poetry in the Cinquecento is largely a reply to Plato." Weinberg, *Literary Criticism*, 1:251.

6. An English example is Henry Dethick's *Oratio in laudem poëseos* published in the early 1570s, in J. W. Binns, ed., trans., *Latin Treatises on Poetry from Renaissance England* (Signal Mountain: Summertown, 1999), 39–41.

7. For discussion of Plato's role in Spenser's *Letter*, see Kenneth Borris, "Reassessing Ellrodt: Critias and the *Fowre Hymnes* in *The Faerie Queene*," this volume; and Wayne Erickson, "Spenser's Letter to Ralegh and the Literary Politics of *The Faerie Queene*'s 1590 publication," *Spenser Studies* 10 (1989): 147–51.

8. *The Faerie Queene*, ed. A. C. Hamilton, Hiroshi Yamashita, and Toshiyuki Suzuki (London: Longman, 2001). Used for that poem throughout.

9. Sidney, *Defence of Poetry*, in his *Miscellaneous Prose*, ed. Katherine Duncan-Jones and Jan van Dorsten (Oxford: Clarendon, 1973), 104. Hereafter also cited parenthetically in my text. Similarly Gosson's respondent Thomas Lodge, *"Reply to Gosson"* (actual title unknown; London, 1580?), STC 16663, sig. B2b–3a.

10. Compare, e.g., Spenser's *TM*, lines 363–64: love's fire is "with beawtie kindled." See John Charles Nelson, *Renaissance Theory of Love: The Context of Giordano Bruno's "Eroici furori"* (New York: Columbia University Press, 1958).

11. See, among others, Jon A. Quitslund, *Spenser's Supreme Fiction: Platonic Natural Philosophy and "The Faerie Queene"* (Toronto: University of Toronto Press, 2001), chs. 6–7; Sean Kane, *Spenser's Moral Allegory* (Toronto: University of Toronto Press, 1989), ch. 3; Patrick Cheney, " 'And Doubted Her to Deeme an Earthly Wight': Male Neoplatonic 'Magic' and the Problem of Female Identity in Spenser's Allegory of the Two Florimells," *Studies in Philology* 86 (1989): 310–40; David O. Frantz, "The Union of Florimell and Marinell: The Triumph of Hearing," *Spenser Studies* 6 (1986): 115–27; David W. Burchmore," Triamond, Agape and the Fates: Neoplatonic Cosmology in Spenser's Legend of Friendship," *Spenser Studies* 5 (1985): 45–64; Jerome S. Dees, "Spenser's Anti-Neoplatonism," and Elizabeth Bieman's response, "Neoplatonism: The Ghost in Spenser's Fictions," both in David A. Richardson, ed., *Spenser: Classical, Medieval, Renaissance, and Modern* (Cleveland: Cleveland State University Press, 1977), 271–305, 306–13; Dwight J. Sims, "Cosmological Structure in *The Faerie Queene*, Book III," *Huntington Library Quarterly* 40 (1977): 99–116; his "The Syncretic Myth of Venus in Spenser's Legend of Chastity," *Studies in Philology* 71 (1974): 427–50; Lila Geller, "Venus and the Three Graces: A Neoplatonic Paradigm for Book III of *The Faerie Queene*," *JEGP* 75 (1976): 56–74; James Nohrnberg,

The Analogy of "The Faerie Queene" (Princeton: Princeton University Press, 1976), ch. 4; Thomas P. Roche, Jr., *The Kindly Flame: A Study of the Third and Fourth Books of Spenser's "Faerie Queene"* (Princeton: Princeton University Press, 1964), ch. 3.

12. See Richard McCabe's complementary essay in this volume. The joint appearance of our essays is a happy coincidence because we conceived and wrote them independently. Some prior discussion of the Florimells' relation to Plato's icastic/phantastic distinction appears in Nohrnberg, *Analogy*, 143–51; and Jon A. Quitslund, "Beauty," in A. C. Hamilton, et al., eds., *The Spenser Encyclopedia* (Toronto: University of Toronto Press, 1999), 82; hereafter designated *SE*.

13. See Nohrnberg, *Analogy*, 106–17; Quitslund, "Beauty," *SE*, 82; his *Supreme Fiction*, 299–305. The polarity of the icastic/phantastic distinction, which lacks typical Platonic intermediations, complements that of biblical doublings of agents and images *in bono et in malo*. On the latter, see Carol V. Kaske, *Spenser and Biblical Poetics* (Ithaca: Cornell University Press, 1999), chs. 1–2.

14. See Jon A. Quitslund, "Platonism," *SE*, 546; his *Supreme Fiction*, 11–13; Michael J. B. Allen, "Ficino, Marsilio," *SE*, 305.

15. Plato's dialogues are dialogic explorations, not a coherent body of doctrine. Likewise Platonism had diverse relations to, e.g., Christianity, sex, marriage, and poetics. See n23, n99.

16. In *Neoplatonism in the Poetry of Spenser* (Geneva: Droz, 1960), Robert Ellrodt granted Spenser's interest in Platonism from the *Calender* onward, but claimed the poet's Renaissance Platonic learning postdates even the 1596 *Faerie Queene*. See Borris, "Reassessing Ellrodt," in this volume.

17. Sidney, *Defence*, 87. See Weinberg, *Literary Criticism*, ch. 1. Aristotle had influentially argued that poetry mediates between philosophy and history (*Poetics* 1451b). For ancient texts I use Loeb editions throughout unless otherwise stated (as for Plato, e.g., n1).

18. As Plato's and Aristotle's concepts of reality differ greatly, so do their views of poetic imitation. Aristotelian mimesis involves consideration of plot, action, and formal structure absent from Plato. See Stephen Halliwell, *Aristotle's Poetics* (London: Duckworth, 1986), ch. 4; Richard McKeon, "Literary Criticism and the Concept of Imitation in Antiquity," in R. S. Crane, ed., *Critics and Criticism: Ancient and Modern* (Chicago: University of Chicago Press, 1952), 147–75. Yet sixteenth-century reception of the *Poetics* merged it with Horatian and Platonic notions. See Baxter Hathaway, *The Age of Criticism: The Late Renaissance in Italy* (Ithaca: Cornell University Press, 1962). Also his *Marvels and Commonplaces: Renaissance Literary Criticism* (New York: Random House, 1968), 43–60; Lawrence C. Wolfley, "Sidney's Visual-Didactic Poetic: Some Complexities and Limitations," *Journal of Medieval and Renaissance Studies* 6 (1976): 220–22; Weinberg, *Literary Criticism*, 1: 57, 60–65, 304, 453; and his "Robortello on the *Poetics*," in Crane, 319–48.

19. As John M. Steadman explains, "idealized imitation" has both ethical implications (re moral absolutes and content) and aesthetic ones (re ideal beauty, structure, and form). In my usage the term's scope includes both applications, for they were intertwined in the Renaissance, as in *The Faerie Queene*. See Steadman's *The Lamb and the Elephant: Ideal Imitation and the Contexts of Renaissance Allegory* (San Marino: Huntington Library, 1974), xi n1, 172n6. On literary aspects of idealized imitation,

see also especially Baxter Hathaway, *Age of Criticism*, chs. 1–13. See further Mindele
Anne Treip, *Allegorical Poetics and the Epic: The Renaissance Tradition to "Paradise Lost"*
(Lexington: University Press of Kentucky, 1994), ch. 4, Appendix B; Annabel M.
Patterson, "Tasso and Neoplatonism: The Growth of his Epic Theory," *Studies in
the Renaissance* 18 (1971): 105–31; her *Hermogenes and the Renaissance: Seven Ideas of
Style* (Princeton: Princeton University Press, 1970), 35–43, 201–05; Walter R.
Davis, *Idea and Act in Elizabethan Prose Fiction* (Princeton: Princeton University Press,
1969), ch. 2. On the visual arts, see Erwin Panofsky, *Idea: A Concept in Art Theory*,
trans. Joseph J. S. Peake (Columbia: University of South Carolina Press, 1968). Also
E. H. Gombrich, "*Icones Symbolicae*: Philosophies of Symbolism and their Bearing
on Art," in his *Symbolic Images: Studies in the Art of the Renaissance* (Oxford: Phaidon,
1972), 123–95; Rensselaer W. Lee, *Ut Pictura Poesis: The Humanistic Theory of Painting*
(New York: Norton, 1967); Anthony Blunt, *Artistic Theory in Italy 1450–1600* (Oxford: Clarendon, 1969).
20.   A main precedent was Cicero, who himself cites Plato. See Steadman, *Lamb
and the Elephant*, 127–28, 151–52, 196–97.
21.   See Michael Raiger, "Sidney's Defense of Plato," *Religion and Literature* 30
(1998): 21–57; John C. Ulreich, Jr., " 'The Poets Only Deliver': Sidney's Conception of *Mimesis*," *Studies in the Literary Imagination* 15 (1982): 67–84; D. H. Craig,
"A Hybrid Growth: Sidney's Theory of Poetry in *An Apology for Poetry*," *English
Literary Renaissance* 10 (1980): 183–201; John P. McIntyre, "Sidney's 'Golden
World,' " *Comparative Literature* 14 (1962): 356–65. Wesley Trimpi differently claims
that Sidney rejects Neoplatonic attitudes toward poetry in "Sir Philip Sidney's *An
Apology for Poetry*," in Glyn P. Norton, ed., *The Cambridge History of Literary Criticism:
Volume 3, The Renaissance* (Cambridge: Cambridge University Press, 1999), 187–98.
However, Sidney's appropriation of Plato's icastic/phantastic distinction indicates
some Platonic affinity. In any case Sidney's text demonstrates that Platonic and
Neoplatonic views of poetry had considerable topical interest for Elizabethan literati.
22.   Sections three to five further document this thesis argued in this section.
Compare Sidney, *Defence*, 78–79, 104. Further citations on idealized and icastic
imitation follow in appropriate contexts. For the poet as creative demigod, see
Giulio Cesare Scaligero, *Poetices libri septem: Sieben Bücher über die Dichtkunst*, ed. Luc
Deitz and Gregor Vogt-Spira, 5 vols. (Stuttgart-Bad Cannstatt: Fromman-Holzboog,
1994), 1: 70–72 (1.1). Also Torquato Tasso, *Discourses on the Art of Poetry* (*Discorsi
dell'arte poetica*), trans. Laurence F. Rhu, in his *The Genesis of Tasso's Narrative Theory*
(Detroit: Wayne State University Press, 1993), 131; and Weinberg, *Literary Criticism*, 1:263.
23.   See Plotinus, *Enneads*, trans. Stephen MacKenna, 4th, rev. ed. (London: Faber,
1969), 1.6.3, 5.8.1; Proclus, "On the More Difficult Questions in the *Republic*: The
Nature of Poetic Art," trans. Thomas Taylor, rev. Kevin Kerrane, in O. B. Hardison,
Jr., et al., eds., *Medieval Literary Criticism: Translations and Interpretations* (New York:
Ungar, 1974), 50–63. Even Plato's *Republic* anticipates possibilities of idealized artistic imitation. See G. M. A. Grube, *The Greek and Roman Critics* (Toronto: University
of Toronto Press, 1965), 54–55.
24.   On point seven, see Craig: 189–90; Hathaway, *Age of Criticism*, 91, 96–97, ch.
33; Alastair Fowler, "Introduction," in Richard Wills (or Willes), *De re poetica*, ed.,

trans. Fowler (Oxford: Blackwell-Luttrell Society, 1958), 30–34. Points one to six derive from Weinberg's overview in *Literary Criticism*, chs. 7–8. On the points aside from poetic furor (obviously relevant), see, e.g., 1:261, 293–96, 301–04, 338, 345; on allegory's Platonic aspect, 1:257–58, 264–67, 278–79. Though literary allegory was favored from various standpoints, Weinberg most associates it with Platonic advocates of poetry. I agree because Platonic criteria obliged them to establish poetry's epistemological and social value, and to do so they had to promote its "inner truth." For Platonists, the world's appearances are distortions, so that poetic truth had to go much beyond them.

25.   *Phaedrus* 245a, 265b; *Ion* 533d–5a. For Marsilio Ficino's views, important for the Renaissance, see his *Commentary on Plato's "Symposium" on Love* (*De amore*), trans. Sears Jayne (Dallas: Spring, 1985), 7.13–15; Arthur Farndell, comp., trans., *Gardens of Philosophy: Ficino on Plato* (London: Shepheard-Walwyn, 2006), 53–58.

26.   Sidney, *Defence*, 109. For the argument that Sidney's literary Platonism, though substantial, does not dominate his poetic, see, e.g., Craig: 188–89. However, Sidney's position on poetic inspiration is complex; compare *Defence*, 76–79, 111, 121.

27.   *October*, lines 83–84, 88–94, 109–10 and gloss; "Argument."

28.   Spenser also asserts poetic furor in *CCH*, line 823; *HL*, line 28; *HB*, line 2; *HHB*, line 1.

29.   "The deity . . . uses [poets] as ministers, along with soothsayers and godly seers; . . . it is the god himself who speaks, and through them becomes articulate to us." *Ion*, 534cd. For some Renaissance applications, see Dethick, 39; Weinberg, *Literary Criticism*, 1:319–21.

30.   Ellrodt, *Neoplatonism*, ch. 1. See Borris, "Reassessing Ellrodt," in this volume.

31.   See Grube, *Greek and Roman Critics*, 54–55.

32.   So argue, e.g., the encyclopedist Lodovico Ricchieri and literary theorist Scipione Ammirato; see Weinberg, *Literary Criticism*, 1:257–59, 279.

33.   "Heuristic" here bears its sense "serving to find out or discover," while "provisional" means "adapted for present needs or for the time being," "accepted or used in default of something better" (*OED*, 2nd ed., "heuristic" A adj.; "provisional" adj. A 1a). Gombrich, e.g., discusses such concerns of former mimetic idealism, though without those terms, in "*Icones Symbolicae*," 151–60.

34.   In its unfolded aspect, what Christian Platonists would have called the Ideas in the mind of God; in its infolded aspect, God or the One. See Patterson, "Tasso and Neoplatonism": 108–09.

35.   By "Platonizing" here I mean a diffuse, much-filtered and redeveloped Platonism. See Steadman's astute summary in *Lamb and the Elephant*, 40–41; also David Lee Miller, *The Poem's Two Bodies: The Poetics of the 1590 "Faerie Queene"* (Princeton: Princeton University Press, 1988), 54–55, 68–82. Patterson assumes Spenser positions his faery "precisely" between "man and the angels," with "the Platonic Ideas" (*Hermogenes*, 203–04). Although Spenser's faery is a heightened world, his positive images are idealized yet provisional, not presented as Ideas, for those were presumed beyond human capacity to reproduce fully. See *Phaedrus* 247c; Torquato Tasso, *Discourses on the Heroic Poem* (*Discorsi del poema eroico*), trans. Mariella Cavalchini and Irene Samuel (Oxford: Clarendon, 1973), 171 (hereafter also cited parenthetically within my text).

36.   I say "ideas" here in lower case because, in early modern theories of idealized imitation, the artist's mind is only analogous to God's, hence possessed of "quasi-ideas" (in Panofsky's phrase, 39): inevitably provisional, however illuminating. On different possible early modern senses of "idea" in contexts addressing verbal or visual imitation, see Steadman, 172n6, and on Spenser, 40–41.

37.   Weinberg, *Literary Criticism*, 1:265; compare 1:615, on Lionardo Salviati.

38.   Fracastoro, *Naugerius*, trans. Ruth Kelso (Urbana: University of Illinois Press, 1924), 60. Hereafter also cited parenthetically within my text. Compare Weinberg, *Literary Criticism*, 2: 727–29; Hathaway, *Age of Criticism*, 139–43, 157.

39.   Tasso further outlines his Platonic views of poetics in his dialogues such as *Il Messagiero* (published 1582) and *Il Ficino, overo de l'Arte*, apparently written around 1592/3. See Patterson, "Tasso and Neoplatonism": 105–31.

40.   See, e.g., Geoffrey Shepherd and R. W. Maslen, eds., *An Apology for Poetry*, 3rd, rev. ed. (Manchester: Manchester University Press, 2002), 140–41.

41.   Christians had long interpreted the world in such a way, as in, e.g., Augustinian Platonism; idealized art theory with its recognized Platonic affinities was partly attractive for that reason. Compare 1 Cor. 13:12: "now we se through a glasse darkely: but then shal we se face to face." Also Romans 1:20: "The invisible things of him, that is, his eternal power and Godhead, are seene by the creation of the worlde, being considered in his workes." *The Geneva Bible*, introd. Lloyd E. Berry (Geneva, 1560; facsim. rpt. Madison: University of Wisconsin Press, 1969); used for biblical citations throughout.

42.   Compare Plato's demiurge, *Timaeus*, 28–29. On perfection's role in Platonic poetics, see Hathaway, *Age of Criticism*, chs. 8–9 (esp. 139).

43.   Compare I.pr.4.2, 7.

44.   Compare *HB*, lines 32, 40, 216; *HHB*, lines 46–47, 105, 295–96.

45.   Compare Plotinus, *Enneads*, 1.6.3, 5.8.1. See Panofsky, 16–32, 94–95, 120–21; Robert L. Montgomery, *The Reader's Eye: Studies in Didactic Literary Theory from Dante to Tasso* (Berkeley: University of California Press, 1979), 45, 103–05.

46.   Apart from Christian notions of fallen nature, Plotinus, e.g., had noted these implications of "mimetic idealism." As Ficino emphasized, instruction was supposed to rekindle innate impressions of the Ideas. See Panofsky, *Idea*, 25–32, 56–57; Gombrich, "*Icones Symbolicae*," 151–60.

47.   Tasso, *Discorsi del poema eroico*, 5, 32.

48. Compare 2 Cor. 3:18: "we all beholde as in a mirrour the glorie of the Lord . . . , and are changed into the same image, from glorie to glorie." On Gloriana's correlations with Sapience in *HHB*, see Jeffrey P. Fruen, "The Faery Queen Unveiled? Five Glimpses of Gloriana," *Spenser Studies* 11 (1994): 56, 82n9.

49.   Compare *HB*, lines 211–24, *CCH*, lines 608–27. Spenser further treats this Platonic doctrine in *October*, lines 91–96; various *Amoretti*; and other *Hymnes*. Compare *Phaedrus* 252d–53b; Ficino, *De amore*, 2.8, 6.6, 7.1; Castiglione, *Courtier*, 317.

50.   See Herbert Grabes, *The Mutable Glass: Mirror-imagery in Titles and Texts of the Middle Ages and English Renaissance*, trans. Gordon Collier (Cambridge: Cambridge University Press, 1982), 78–81, 88–89, 121.

51.   For Fracastoro, the poet is to imitate God's Idea (*Naugerius*, 60). Likewise Cristoforo Landino, Ficino, and Tasso, according to Patterson, "Tasso and Neoplatonism": 108–17.

52. Since the poem is called *The Faerie Queene*, its references to the queen encompass its eponymous ideal as well as Elizabeth. The *Letter to Ralegh* advertises Spenser's creation of Gloriana, archetype of glory. In the first proem, he pointedly produces the queen's "glorious type." The poet's addresses to the sovereign relate as much (and sometimes more) to his sovereign concept as to Queen Elizabeth I.

53. Compare VI.x.4, which similarly introduces Colin's art as a means of visionary insight; and, on the glorious light of God and Sapience, *HHB*, lines 114–40, 239–301.

54. Following Jerry Leath Mills, "Spenser's Letter to Raleigh and the Averroistic *Poetics*," *English Language Notes*, 14 (1976–77): 246–49.

55. Hence, *pace* Mills above, sixteenth-century discussions of Aristotle's *Poetics* account much better for Spenser's idealized and didactic interpretation than Averroes's twelfth-century account.

56. See Steadman, 138–40; Borris, *Allegory and Epic in English Renaissance Literature: Heroic Form in Sidney, Spenser, and Milton* (Cambridge: Cambridge University Press, 2000), chs. 1, 3.

57. Giraldi, *On Romances* (*Discorso intorno al comporre dei romanzi*), trans. Henry L. Snuggs (Lexington: University of Kentucky Press, 1968), 51.

58. Cit. Weinberg, "Robertello," 334.

59. *Poetics*, 9.1451b; trans. Stephen Halliwell.

60. See Hathaway, *Age of Criticism*, chs. 8–12, and *Marvels and Commonplaces*, 43–60. Steadman assesses Aristotelian and Platonic aspects of idealized imitation (127, 151–52), and concludes Spenser's practice is primarily Platonic (40–41). The Platonizing aspects of early modern high mimetic art had a partly Ciceronian basis, for Cicero says he seeks to delineate an "unsurpassable ideal" of oratory, just as sculptors and painters refer to "an intellectual ideal" in representing beauty, beyond its copies we can sense. "We can nevertheless grasp it by the mind and imagination. . . . These patterns of things are called . . . ideas by Plato," and "they exist for ever" (*Orator* ii.7–10, trans. H. M. Hubbell). Castiglione similarly describes portrayal of the perfect courtier, 13.

61. In the *Republic*, Socrates envisions an "ideal" city's "pattern . . . laid up in heaven" for those who wish contemplatively to become its citizens, 9.592ab. On Plato in Spenser's *Letter to Ralegh*, see n7.

62. Compare Tasso, *Discorsi dell' arte poetica*, 108: "Epic . . . needs the highest virtues. . . . Indeed, the sum of all these virtues appears in some of these characters" (i.e., in heroic poems).

63. Compare Hathaway: "Literary critics in all ages have assumed that poetry is some kind of reconciliation of the universal and the particular, but the important question for any given period is the extent to which the taste and metaphysics of the time move the emphasis one way or another." *Age of Criticism*, 130.

64. Cicero, *De inventione*, 2.1.3; trans H. M. Hubbell; Tasso, *Discorsi del poema eroico*, 6.

65. De Serres, Argument for the *Ion*, in Plato, *Platonis opera quae extant omnia*, 3 vols. (Geneva: Henri Estienne, 1578), 1: 528–29. S. K. Heninger, Jr. translates this preface in "Sidney and Serranus' *Plato*," *English Literary Renaissance*, 13 (1983): 146–61. I quote the preface's Latin in Heninger's translation, cited parenthetically in my text hereafter. I thank Faith Wallis for consultation on two Greek phrases.

66. Heninger, "Serranus' *Plato*": 156–59.

67. De Serres's discussions of some other Platonic dialogues further address the icastic/phantastic distinction. See M. J. Doherty, *The Mistress-Knowledge: Sir Philip Sidney's "Defence of Poesie" and Literary Architectonics in the English Renaissance* (Nashville: Vanderbilt University Press, 1991), 134, 169.

68. Aristotle, *Poetics*, 1460a (Stephen Halliwell's translation uses "awe" for the relevant effects.) See Hathaway, *Age of Criticism*, 350–53, 390–96; also his *Marvels and Commonplaces*, chs. 2–4.

69. Among the Italians: Lodovico Castelvetro, Francesco Patrizi, Lionardo Salviati, Jacopo Mazzoni, Torquato Tasso (on them, see Hathaway, *Age of Criticism*, especially 350–53, ch. 29), Tomasso Correa (see Weinberg, *Literary Criticism*, 1:321), Gregorio Comanino (in *Il Figino*, 1591), and Scaligero, *Poetices*, 5:490–99 (7.1.2). Among the English: Sidney, George Puttenham, and George Chapman (discussed subsequently), and likely Gosson, who demands that poetry present an "Image of trueth" (*Playes Confuted*, sig. D5ab). For Milton's interest, see Paul Stevens, "Milton and the Icastic Imagination," *Milton Studies* 20 (1984): 43–73.

70. Compare Hathaway, *Age of Criticism*, chs. 10–11.

71. "In all this theorizing of Tasso there is . . . a hidden Platonism" that "sees behind every poem or every part of a poem an Idea which the poet seeks to imitate." Weinberg, *Literary Criticism*, 1:341.

72. Mazzoni, *On the Defense of the Comedy of Dante: Introduction and Summary*, trans. Robert L. Montgomery (Tallahassee: Florida State University Press, 1993), 82, 97. Hereafter also cited parenthetically within my text. Mazzoni summarizes his treatise's argument in this introductory section. Only it and the first three books were published in 1587; the last four were printed in 1688. See Murray Krieger, "Jacopo Mazzoni, Repository of Diverse Critical Traditions or Source of New One?" in Rosario P. Armato and John M. Spalek, eds., *Medieval Epic to the "Epic Theater" of Brecht* (Los Angeles: University of Southern California Press, 1968), 97–107.

73. The end of Mazzoni's introduction clarifies his argument. Earlier, e.g., he says poetry is not necessarily concerned with the true, and must valorize the credible instead (78–79, 86). But for him the highest type of poetry is governed by "the civil faculty," by which he means moral philosophy, and instructively promotes truth and the good, through what we may call the "icastic phantastic" mode (98–99, 108–09). Compare Hathaway, *Age of Criticism*, 199–200.

74. Mazzoni, *Della difesa della "Comedia" di Dante* (Cesena: appresso Bartolomeo Raverio, 1587), Book III, ch. 6 (413).

75. Puttenham, *The Arte of English Poesie* (London, 1589), sig. D3b–4a. Similarly Ronsard, *Abbregé de l'Art poetique françoys*, in *Oeuvres complètes*, ed. Jean Céard et al., 2 vols. (Paris: Gallimard, 1993–94), 2: 1178.

76. Chapman, "To the Earle of Somerset" (dedicatory epistle for Chapman's *Odyssey*), in *Chapman's Homer*, ed. Allardyce Nicoll, 2 vols. (Princeton: Bollingen-Princeton University Press, 1998–2000), 2:5.

77. On Sidney's commitment to literary allegorism, see Borris, *Allegory and Epic*, ch. 4.

78. As Steadman alleges, *Lamb and the Elephant*, 117. But the *Orlando furioso* was still very widely admired, Tasso had just published the *Gerusalemme liberata*, and both were considered allegorical.

79. On these trends, see Hathaway, *Marvels*, 45; Panofsky, *Idea*, ch. 5.

80. For the translation's "craftsmen" I substitute "makers" here. The context broadly addresses, e.g., painting, weaving, poetry, architecture.

81. As yet, beauty's Spenserian significance and poetic role, though central for this poet, have been little studied. See Quitslund, "Beauty," *SE*, 81–82; Kenneth Borris, "Sub Rosa: Pastorella's Allegorical Homecoming, and Closure in the 1596 *Faerie Queene*," *Spenser Studies* 21 (2006): 143–51.

82. Quoting Steadman, *Lamb and the Elephant*, xi n1.

83. Milton, *Epistolarum familiarum*, trans. David Masson, in Volume XII of *Works*, ed. Frank Allen Patterson et al. (New York: Columbia University Press, 1936), 27.

84. Scaligero, *Poetices*, 1:70–72 (1.1).

85. Hermogenes, *On Types of Style*, trans. Cecil W. Wooten (Chapel Hill: University of North Carolina Press, 1987), 54–64. Cf. Patterson, *Hermogenes*, ch. 1, 53–56. For Tasso and Spenser, beauty has much more contextual relevance and both stylistic and thematic importance than Patterson recognizes, partly because of their Platonic affinities. See, e.g., Quitslund, "Beauty," *SE*, 81–82.

86. Patterson, *Hermogenes*, 24–25.

87. Tasso, *Discorsi del poema eroico*, 172–73; compare 13. For Fracastoro, "there is practically only one sort of subject which is absolutely beautiful, the heroic" (*Naugerius*, 64).

88. See Steadman, *Lamb and the Elephant*, xxii, 124–27, 172n6, 174n7.

89. Sidney, *Defence*, 98. Compare *Phaedrus* 250bd; Cicero, *De officiis* 1.5.14, *De finibus* 2.16.52.

90. See Hiroshi Yamashita et al., eds., *A Comprehensive Concordance to "The Faerie Queene" 1590* (Tokyo: Kenyusha, 1990), 1143. "Faire" and "fayre" jointly have 480 instances; "great," apt for heroic poetry, ranks second (399).

91. See Borris, "Sub Rosa": 143–51. In *Amoretti*, Sonnet 61, the beloved is "The glorious image of the makers beautie." Also *CCH*: "the beame of beautie" is "sparkled from aboue," and "Beautie" is "the burning lamp of heauens light" (lines 468, 873). Spenser's *Hymnes* present his notions of beauty's revelatory power at length.

92. Spenser's *Hymnes* unpack these notions. Compare *Phaedrus* 250bd (quoted earlier) and Spenser's *HL*, lines 113–16: "in this mortall frame/ . . ., nought more diuine doth seeme,/ Or that resembleth more th'immortall flame/ Of heauenly light, then Beauties glorious beame." And *HHB*, lines 104–40: divine Love's diverse creations express "his beautie" as in a "booke, To read." Also *HB*, lines 29–54. Fundamental to Spenser's thought on humanity's relation to beauty is the doctrine of the divine image. Divine Love created man "According to a heauenly patterne," "his owne like mould," to produce a "louely shape" apt for love, reflecting his own (*HHL*, lines 106–19). Likewise man's "immortall mynd" contains "sparks" of Love's creative "heauenly fire" impelling embrace of what "seemes on earth most heauenly," Beauty (*HL*, lines 97–112). The divine image is implicit, there, in "mynd" and "sparks." The basic creation myth of the *Hymnes* and *Colin Clouts* is that Love creates all according to the pattern of Beauty. In Spenser's etiology of beauty's earthly manifestations in *The Faerie Queene*'s Garden of Adonis episode, he associates the goddess Venus with the planet, its astrological functions, and apparently beauty's formative Idea: thence "all the world deriues the glorious/ Features of beautie . . . / With which high God his workmanship hath deckt" (III.vi.12).

93.   See Sean Kane, "Idols, Idolatry," *SE*, 387–88; Herman, *Squitter-wits*.

94.   Spenser further explores his conceptions of *human* beauty's revelatory potential in his *Hymnes*. Compare *HL*, lines 103–19; *HB*, lines 29–56, 85–140, 162–68, 183–89, 211–31; *HHL*, lines 106–19; *HHB*, lines 113–40.

95.   Nothing on earth "resembleth more th'immortall flame of heauenly light, then Beauties glorious beame" (*HL*, lines 113–16). Compare *HB*, lines 90–105, 120–33. *Heauenly Beautie* celebrates "that soueraine light,/From whose pure beames all per-fect beauty springs" (lines 295–96). In that hymn, "immortal light," "Truth," "vertue," and "ineffable beautie" conjoin in God's presence (lines 169–210). In effect, beauty is the esthetic effulgence of truth and good.

96.   Plato speaks of Beauty's "brightness" and "pure . . . light," *Phaedrus* 250ad. Ficino relates beauty to light in *De amore* 2.5, 5.6, 6.17. For Castiglione's Bembo, beauty is "an influence of the heauenly bountifulnesse," "holy," "an heauenly shin-ing beame" or "shining . . . light" (*Courtier*, 304, 308, 313, 319).

97.   Compare *HL*, lines 176–87; *HB*, lines 148–75; *HHL*, lines 105–26.

98.   III.i.18, iv.45–47, vii.31–6, viii.28; V.iii.27.

99.   In "Spenser's Anti-Neoplatonism," Dees assumes that certain views he ascribes to *The Faerie Queene* are "anti-Neoplatonic" (292–98, 301). Yet at least most of them are well within the ambit of Renaissance Platonisms. His respondent Bieman finds his model of Neoplatonism too narrow ("Neoplatonism," 306–13). Following Dees in "Allegory of the Two Florimells" (314n7), Cheney claims Spenser thus satirizes "Neoplatonic man" (314). Yet Neoplatonists varied, and the witch's son cannot satirize Neoplatonism *in principle*, because he lusts for beauty, perceiving only its physical aspect, whereas early modern Neoplatonists strongly advocated its spiri-tual dimension. The son's portrayal could partly satirize *corruptions* of Neoplatonism, as well as Epicurean or libertine anti-Neoplatonism such as Pietro Aretino's. Cheney astutely insists that Spenser spiritualizes physicality (338–39n). That is the basis of the poet's long-term fascination with Platonizing views of love and beauty, evident in his writing from the *October* eclogue to his *Hymnes*, and of his Christian Platonist erotic mysticism, whereby he finds virtuous feminine beauty revelatory as I have shown. See, e.g., T. Anthony Perry, *Erotic Spirituality: The Integrative Tradition from Leone Ebreo to John Donne* (University, AL: University of Alabama Press, 1980).

100.   Though Ellrodt represents Castiglione's *Courtier* as if its speaker Bembo simply asserts that "outwarde beautie [is] a true signe of the inward goodnesse" (309; *Neoplatonism*, 27), Bembo's subsequent statements strongly qualify that remark (310–11, 319–20).

101.   "When we hear that 'Beautie is alwaies good' from a Platonist, . . . he speaks of true Beauty—the Beauty that emanates from or is reflected from a higher level." Bieman, "Neoplatonism," 316.

102.   See Spenser, *HB*, lines 90–115. Also Ficino, *De amore*, 2.9, 5.3, 6.18; Castigli-one, *Courtier*, 319–20.

103.   *Symposium* 210b. Hence Socrates concludes the *Phaedrus* by praying "to be-come fair within," 279bc.

104.   *HB*, lines 141–58; with my own parenthetical examples. For Castiglione's Neoplatonist Bembo, physically beautiful females may become corrupt because of bad nurture, lovers' provocations, poverty, deceits, and other causes; for "like causes

may also beautifull men become wicked" (*Courtier*, 311). On defects of matter impairing beauty's outer expression, compare the *Courtier*, 310; Ficino, *De amore*, 6.6, 18.

105. Kaske considers Christian aspects of this Spenserian procedure in *Biblical Poetics*, chs. 1–2.

106. Compare, e.g., Castiglione's Bembo: "the beauties, which we dayly see with these our dimme eyes in bodies subiect to corruption, . . . be nothing else but dreames and most thinne shadowes of [intelligible] beautie" (319–20).

107. Such precedents include Plato's sexually active male couples who gain "shining bliss" after death (*Phaedrus* 256ce); and Plotinus's assurance that procreative love can be "on the right path" (*Enneads*, 3.5.1). Bembo allows for "worthie" sexual lovers in the *Courtier* (306–07). Renaissance Platonisms could accommodate diverse views on sex and marriage, including erotic mysticism, and uses of copulation to symbolize contemplation, as in Leone Ebreo's *Dialoghi d'amore*. See, e.g., Perry, *Erotic Spirituality*.

108. For the topos of beauty's elusiveness, see Borris, "Sub Rosa": 166.

109. *December*, lines 55–60; compare "E. K.," Argument, and gloss for "Comete," line 59.

110. See Clarisse Doris Hellman, *The Comet of 1577: Its Place in the History of Astronomy* (New York: Columbia University Press, 1944); and Paul H. Kocher, *Science and Religion in Elizabethan England* (San Marino: Huntington Library, 1953), 165–80.

111. "Jade" had the bawdy sense "over-used whore," a usage Spenser's "tyreling" reinforces. Compare Plato, *Phaedrus* 250e: he who is impure looks upon beauty irreverently, "and surrendering to pleasure he essays to go after the fashion of a four-footed beast, . . . consorting with wantonness." See Gordon Williams, *A Dictionary of Sexual Language and Imagery in Shakesperean and Stuart Literature*, 3 vols. (London: Athlone, 1994), s.v. "jade."

112. The stages of seduction had been similarly schematized in non-Platonic ways (see, e.g., Alastair Fowler, "Six Knights at Castle Joyous," *Studies in Philology*, 56 [1959]: 583–99). But Spenser's context differs, hence also the implications of his progression. Even Ellrodt would concede that Books III and IV treat love in a generally Platonized way (*Neoplatonism*, 34), and the Platonic scale of amorous ascent had been well popularized, as by Castiglione.

113. See, e.g., Linda Gregerson, *The Reformation of the Subject: Spenser, Milton, and the English Protestant Epic* (Cambridge: Cambridge University Press, 1995), ch. 1; Elizabeth J. Bellamy, *Translations of Power: Narcissism and the Unconscious in Epic History* (Ithaca: Cornell University Press, 1992), 201–11.

114. See Quitslund, *Supreme Fiction*, ch. 3, Index, s.v. "Merlin"; Genevieve Guenther, "Spenser's Magic, or Instrumental Aesthetics in the 1590 *Faerie Queene*," *ELR*, 36 (2006): 194–95. She claims the ethical function of Spenser's verse depends upon the reader's belief in devils, and conflation of poetic agency with demonic agency. Yet early modern treatises on literary theory rarely evince any concern with such matters. To what extent are *The Faerie Queene*'s devils figurative? Sixteenth-century commentaries conventionally allegorized magicians and magic in Italian romantic epics.

115. On literary mirrors, cf. Hathaway, *Age of Criticism*, Index, s.v. "Mirror theory"; M. H. Abrams, *The Mirror and the Lamp: Romantic Theory and the Critical Tradition* (New York: Oxford University Press, 1953), 30–35. On sixteenth-century reader-response theories, see Borris, "Sub Rosa": 158, 163–64. On Spenserian mirrors generally, see Herbert Grabes, "Mirrors," *SE*, 477–78.

116. Plato uses semblances, reflections, phantasms, and phantoms in this way throughout his analysis of reality in the *Republic*, including his account of the mimetic arts such as poetry and painting. For this usage of shadow, opposed to solar enlightenment, the definitive Platonic context is the *Republic*'s fable of the cave (7.515a–17e, 520cd). Compare Castiglione's Bembo: relative to heavenly or intelligible beauty, "the beauties . . . we dayly see with these dimme eyes . . . be nothing els but . . . thinne shadows" (*Courtier*, 320). Also Ficino, *De amore* 6.17. This term "shadow" had complementary Christian implications, for in one biblical sense it figured earthly life's lack of reality relative to God: "we are as strangers before thee . . . : our dayes are like the shadowe upon the earth, and there is none abiding" (1 Chr. 29:15; similarly Job 8:9, Ps. 102:11, 144:4). Compare 1 Cor. 13:12: "For now we se through a glasse darkely: but then shal we se face to face."

117. Compare *Amoretti*, Sonnets 83, 88; *HB*, lines 68, 168; *HHB*, lines 273, 291. *Letter*, 716: "in some places else, I doe otherwise shadow her."

118. On Renaissance assumptions of Homer's universal knowledge and their generic effects, see Borris, *Allegory and Epic*, ch. 1.

119. Borris, "Sub Rosa": 158, 163–64.

120. See *October*, lines 91–96; *Amoretti*, Sonnets 22, 45, 88; *HL*, lines 130–33, 190–237; *HB*, lines 179–82, 211–31. Compare Plato, *Phaedrus* 252d–53b, 255d; *Symposium* 178c, 179ab. Also Ficino, *De amore* 2.8, 6.6, 7.1; Castiglione, *Courtier*, 313, 316–17.

121. Plato, *Republic* 10.598d, 601b, 608a, 607c. Gosson, *Schoole of Abuse*, sigs. A2b, A6a, D1a; *Apologie of the Schoole of Abuse*, fols. 84a, 87b; *Playes Confuted*, sigs. D8b–E1a.

122. Later published in King, *Lectures upon Jonas* (Oxford: Joseph Barnes, 1597), STC 14976, 355. For the broader context, see note 2 above.

123. Depicted as a garland in, e.g., Geffrey Whitney, *Sic probantur*, in his *Choice of Emblemes*, introd. John Manning (Aldershot: Scolar, 1989), 224. Compare 1 Cor. 9:25, 1 Pet. 5:4, Rev. 2:10, Jas. 1:12.

124. Compare Herman, *Squitter-wits*, ch. 5.

125. Spenser uses "idol" most frequently in the Belge episode of Book V, that satirizes alleged Spanish and papal tyrannies according to Protestant exegesis of the Book of Revelation.

126. Mazzoni, *Defence*, 45–46. See Hathaway, *Age of Criticism*, ch.7; Weinberg, *Literary Criticism*, 1:62, 301, 325.

127. Compare εἴδωλον in the sense image in the mind, idea. Also, Gloriana's symbolism goes much beyond Queen Elizabeth. Even insofar as Faery's queen relates to Elizabethan England's, various theological and political doctrines authorized Elizabeth's apparent reflection of divinity.

128. Gosson, *Schoole of Abuse*, sigs. A2b, A6a, D1a. I silently correct "*Cicres.*" Also see his *Apologie of the Schoole of Abuse*, fols. 84a, 87b. For Dering, see Herman, *Squitter-wits*, 49.

129. Lodge, *"Reply to Gosson,"* sig. B2b–3a; Sidney, *Defence*, 103–04.

130. Just as even Plato approved certain kinds of art in the *Republic*, Platonic art theory, especially in its Neoplatonic elaborations, allows for modes of representation that have different proximities to reality or being. Though all mimetic art reflects the Ideas to some extent in that view, some types are deemed especially remote from that source and hence unreal, relative to others. Hence idealized, icastic art could claim to be more real than its phantastic, nonidealized counterparts. See, e.g., Tasso, *Discorsi del poema eroico*, 32.

131. "To a Man Most Eminent," trans. Rudolf Gottfried, in *Familiar Letters*, in Spenser's Variorum *Works*, ed. Edwin Greenlaw et al., 10 vols. (Baltimore: Johns Hopkins University Press, 1932–57), 10: 257 (lines 176–81).

132. E.g., *TM*, lines 547–58, 583–93.

133. By 1580 Spenser had reportedly written nine English comedies himself, apparently Ariostan *commedia erudita*, but never canonized them through publication. See Harvey, *Familiar Letters*, in Spenser, Variorum *Works*, 10:459, 471–72.

134. For Plato, theatrical impersonations further multiply illusions and debase human character, partly because males assumed female roles in ancient Greek drama (*Republic*, 3.392a–8b, 10.604d–5b).

135. Ficino, *De amore*, 5.2–3.

136. A. C. Hamilton notes this Platonic passage's relevance to the Tournament in his *Faerie Queene*'s first edition (London: Longman, 1977), 463n, though not in the second.

137. See Roche, *Kindly Flame*, 152–62; Nohrnberg, *Analogy*, 114–19, 572–74.

138. See Nohrnberg, *Analogy*, 116–19, 573–74; Robert Lamberton, *Homer the Theologian: Neoplatonist Allegorical Reading and the Growth of the Epic Tradition* (Berkeley: University of California Press, 1986), 197–201; and his "Neoplatonists and the Spiritualization of Homer," in Robert Lamberton and John J. Keaney, eds., *Homer's Ancient Readers: The Hermeneutics of Greek Epic's Earliest Exegetes* (Princeton: Princeton University Press, 1992), 131–33.

139. On Spenser's advocacy of personal merit against inherited privilege, see Borris, *Allegory and Epic*, 158–60, ch. 7.

140. For an overview, see S. K. Heninger, Jr., *A Handbook of Renaissance Meteorology* (Durham: Duke University Press, 1960), 8–15, ch. 4. Aristotle, *Meteorologica*, 3.2–6. See further Thomas Hill, *A Contemplation of Mysteries* (London: Henry Denham, 1574?), STC 13484, fols. 40a–45b; William Fulke, *A Goodly Gallerye . . . of Meteors* (1563), ed. Theodore Hornberger (Philadelphia: American Philosophical Society, 1979), 72–75, 80–81.

141. Fulke, *Meteors*, 80.

142. Or as "Plutarch" says in *De placitis philosophorum* (now attributed to Aëtius), when a rainbow appears to us, "our sight . . . is rebated and beaten backe" by aerial dew-drops, "and by that meanes there is presented unto it [i.e., our sight] a Rainbow." From Plutarch, *Morals*, trans. Philemon Holland (London: Arnold Hatfield, 1603), STC 20063, 828.

143. As "Plutarch" explains Aristotle's view in *De placitis*, 828.

144. Conti, *Mythologiae*, trans. John Mulryan and Steven Brown, 2 vols. (Tempe: ACMRS, 2006), 2:779–84. Conti presents Aristotle's view and some alternatives.

145. Tasso, *Discorsi del poema eroico*, 32. Though Spenser's understanding of icastic poesis differs from Tasso's as explained in section one, they would agree on its basis in truth.

146. On Spenser's Christian and Platonic sun symbolism, see Alastair Fowler, *Spenser and the Numbers of Time* (London: Routledge, 1964), ch. 8; Nohrnberg, *Analogy*, Index, s.v., "sun," "day."

147. See Nohrnberg, *Analogy*, 273–74. Compare Mal. 4:2 on "the Sunne of righteousness," designating Christ "because in him self he hathe al perfection, and also the justice of his father" (Geneva gloss). Also 1Thess. 5:5–6, Eph. 5:8, John 12:36.

148. See Heninger, *Handbook*, 143–44; Fulke, *Meteors*, 75; Hill, *Mysteries*, fol. 15a (commenting on a prior catalogue of meteorological prodigies).

149. Pliny scientifically dismisses portentous interpretations of rainbows. *Historia naturalis*, 2.60.

150. Ellrodt, *Neoplatonism*, 96–97. For full discussion of both Spenser's Critias references, see Borris, "Reassessing Ellrodt," in this volume.

151. An onomastic connection that Michael F. N. Dixon observes yet interprets differently in *The Polliticke Courtier: Spenser's "The Faerie Queene" as a Rhetoric of Justice* (Montreal: McGill-Queen's University Press, 1996), 55–56.

CATHERINE GIMELLI MARTIN

Spenser's Neoplatonic Geography of the Passions: Mapping Allegory in the "Legend of Temperance," *Faerie Queene*, Book II

This analysis of Book II argues that *The Faerie Queene* charts a geography of physical places connected by the Platonic and Neoplatonic hierarchy of the four physical elements (earth, water, air, and fire) and the positive and negative passions associated with them. Earth stands for the more primitive or "dark" energies of the "lower" soul, the fleshly basis of its earthly existence but also for the foundation of life. Water stands for its "vegetable" or sentient capacities, sensuality on the one hand, but also fluidity or motion on the other. Air stands for the psyche's "drier" or more mental functions as well as its potential self-absorption, to which Sir Guyon nearly succumbs in Mammon's Cave. Fire represents the alternately spiritual and self-destructive passions, zeal and wrath. Like Spenser's other knights, Guyon must successively master each of these levels of his physical, human nature, or, failing that, sink to a lower level. Combined with a zodiacal system linked to the four elements and humors, this relatively simple Neoplatonic system effectively charts Guyon's moral progress through a full "cosmic year" complete with beginning, middle, and end points. It also explains intervening episodes that no longer seem random or digressive within this framework, including the strangely deferred ending of Book II. Besides illuminating the complex geographical substrate of Spenser's allegorical artistry, this essay demonstrates his heavy reliance on Neoplatonic schemas of vice, virtue, and the passions long ago discovered by Frances Yates in the French academies of the sixteenth century and by Rosemund Tuve in Barnabe Googe's translation of *The Zodiake of Life*.

Spenser Studies: A Renaissance Poetry Annual, Volume XXIV, Copyright © 2009 AMS Press, Inc. All rights reserved.

S PENSER'S USE OF of emblematic architecture to express mental and moral states throughout *The Faerie Queene* could hardly be
more obvious, yet ironically, much recent criticism has obscured,
ignored, or simply denied the existence of geographical paths
connecting its symbolic houses and castles. Christopher Burlinson sweepingly rejects all "semiotic readings of space" in the
poem, including any that attach moral meaning to physical paths
or structures, while Jon A. Quitslund questions whether anything
like "a finished cosmos . . . is mapped for us in the poet's articulate design." Quitslund does note elements of a mannerist design
in which spatial parts relate to one another if not to a larger
whole, but for Burlinson, all "in-between spaces exist in the
poem only insofar as they are needed to describe an approach to
one of these locations. . . . This being so, any sense that the poem
consists of a single, integrated 'landscape' becomes difficult to
maintain"; Spenser "clearly declines to depict a spatial continuum." Thus while he admits that the poem creates a "mosaic-like
arrangement . . . of elements" constructed (as in Angus Fletcher's
seminal analysis of allegory) by fundamental oppositions such as
" 'saluage forests' and 'court,' " he denies that these dichotomies
graph a continuous or "coherently imagined" spatial world.[1]
Commenting specifically on Book II, Joanne Woolway Grenfall
emphatically agrees: its terrain is "uncharted and unchartable" in
terms of graphs or tables, even though contemporary Protestants
increasingly used "maps of the Holy Land as visual aids to guide"
them "through the unfamiliar lands of Old Testament narrative."
Grenfall concedes that these maps "had a theological as well as a
more national/political significance" well understood by
Spenser, but argues that his choice of a typological rather than a
fully allegorical mode prohibits their use in *The Faerie Queene*.[2]
Typology thus has the same nugatory function for Grenfall as
mosaic arrangements have for Burlinson: neither somehow permits geographical continuities, even though both types and mosaics possess spatial dimensions.[3]

These assessments are at least partially true: the geography of
The Faerie Queene includes both types, which link disjunctive
temporal events, and mosaics, which juxtapose disjunctive figures. In that respect, it obviously lacks the interlocking grids or
routes of modern city maps. Yet even today, the term "geography" need not refer to point-by-point mapping, which is not
what we actually find in Spenser's poem. *Webster's Unabridged
Encyclopedic Dictionary* defines geography more globally as the systematic "differentiation of the earth's surface, as shown in the

character, arrangement, and interrelations . . . of such elements as climate, elevation, soil, vegetation, population, land use" according to
"their relative size and position." Spenser's Proem to the final book
of *The Faerie Queene* shows that he understands his poetic topography
in a similar sense. Remarking that the variegated "waies" of his poem
have sometimes made for "tedious trauell," he still finds them "so
exceeding spacious and wyde,/And sprinckled with such sweet variety,/Of all that pleasant is to eare or eye," that his "dulled spright"
is moved to begin anew (VI.pr.1).[4] Yet as C. S. Lewis, Isabel MacCaffrey, and Wayne Erickson all agree, these "waies" are more diagram-
matic than naturalistic. Synthesizing the approaches of the former
two critics, Erickson describes the universe of *The Faerie Queene* as
including both

> a horizontal dimension of spatial and temporal geography and
> a vertical dimension of topographical and cosmological geogra-
> phy. The horizontal—the earthly setting in the fallen
> world—intersects the vertical—an ontological spectrum ex-
> tending from heaven to hell—on the plain in Faeryland where
> much of the action of the poem occurs. In general, vertical
> shifts in the setting—up a mountain, down into a valley or cave,
> up or down into a building—reflect changes in the ontological
> status of the event portrayed. At the upper limit of Faeryland
> lie what C. S. Lewis named the "allegorical cores[s]," such
> places as the Mount of Contemplation. . . . At the lower limit
> lie their demonic counterparts, such places as the dungeon of
> Orgoglio.[5]

This geography is obviously remote from modern conceptions of
space, but not from those current in Spenser's day. As late as Sir
Walter Ralegh's *History of the World,* newer and more accurate con-
figurations of the world still tended to succumb to the customary
idealization found on both biblical and pilgrimage maps. John G.
Demaray shows that this traditional idealization discouraged the realistic drawing of even familiar town streets, "let alone the town itself,
or the region, or the wider world. . . . [The] geographical world and
its places, supposedly ordered by underlying spiritual essences, were
generally conceived of and rendered" in symmetrical, iconographic
shapes rather than in empirically accurate form. He finds this older
patterning prominent in *The Faerie Queene,* where Gloriana "has her

seat in a tower of glass found to mirror the ancient stone tower on
the terraced, pyramidal hill or Tor of ancient Glassenbury,' modern
Glastonbury, the oldest pilgrimage center in England where, in the
poem, Joseph of Arimathea is said to have brought relics of the Cruci-
fixion."[6] Such symmetries also underlie the "ritual" structure and
action of allegory, yet that does not necessarily make its symbolic
places wholly space-less or disconnected. [7] These places are in fact
meant to be read much like literary emblems or the devices on early
modern frontispieces, where viewers construct meanings by linking
iconic edifices to the glades, gardens, pools, and paths that surround
them. Spenser was clearly familiar with landscapes of this kind, not
only from emblems but also from courtly quest literature and literary
commentaries on classical and modern epics. Whether in poetry or
in synthetic visual-verbal devices, word-emblems were "meant to be
visualized, and believed in as facts." Even when their details are
strangely or surreally combined, "individual object[s] in the picture
are real, concrete, visual, and believed." [8] Taking a clue from this
tradition, this essay will trace the more textually subliminal yet real
paths between the places visited by Spenser's knights, routes typically
"plotted" by their passage through the four successive elements of
the Platonic cosmos—earth, water, air, and fire (*Timaeus*, 31B–32C).

These four elements simultaneously chart the physical and spiritual
ascent of the hero and his passions, emotions traditionally connected
to the body through its four humors and four "souls," vegetable,
animal, angelic or rational, and divine. Much as Erickson suggests,
after a knight has successfully navigated one of the lower elements in
this fourfold, he vertically ascends to the next material level, but if
he becomes enmeshed in its "temptations," he falls into a more
negative psycho-material dimension. The overarching cosmic principles at work in this schema have been long recognized by critics
ranging from one of Spenser's first commentators, Sir Kenelm Digby,
to one of his most recent, Harry Berger, Jr. Berger shows that Spenser
conventionally expands upon the principle "first elaborated by Plato
in the middle and later dialogues, that the structure of the world is
isomorphic with the structure of the soul—a notion found in various
forms in the work of Aristotle, Virgil, Augustine, and in the general
assumptions of classical and Christian cosmology."[9]

As in the iconic maps studied by Demaray, the habit of projecting
the body on to its cosmic source and destiny persisted well into the
seventeenth century. Caterina Albano finds it in the maps of Gerard
Mercator, Helkiah Crooke, and many others who continued to in-
scribe their geographical projects within a theological framework.

This practice long allowed the *imago dei* or human form to retain its traditional status as " 'an epitome of the whole creation.' "[10]

In his introduction to *The Theatre of the Empire of Great Britain* (1611), John Speed further expanded the analogy between "anatomy and cartography, based on the juxtaposition of body and mind, land and state, bodily parts and geographical elements," in order to emphasize "the reciprocity between microcosm and macrocosm" that "follows from the analogous organising principles which ensure their proper functioning. . . . The analogy of body and space is thus processed through an image of natural order in which single elements are perceived both functionally and hierarchically as the individual components of an ideal harmonious unity." This analogy is naturally not limited to the four elements; it appears in a wide variety of interrelations between bodies and both natural and artificial landscapes. Because corporeality was frequently represented as an artifice reflecting the structure of the cosmos, connections between internal and external spaces were also common. In anatomical engravings of the 1550s, for instance, "the dissected body is presented as a space and framed by compass bearings more proper to maps."[11] Rosemond Tuve additionally notes the frequent use of astronomy in literary "maps" like *The Zodiake of Life,* a popular handbook and probable influence on Spenser, which Barnabe Googe translated in 1565 from the 1537 original of Marcellus Palingenius. This work uses the signs of the zodiac to depict " 'twelue seuerall labours, painting out most liuely, the whole compasses of the world, the reformation of manners, the miseries of mankinde, the pathway to vertue & vice, . . . the misteries of nature, and diuers other circumstances of great learning' ": a plan that fulfills the same " 'general end' " as *The Faerie Queene* and *Shepheardes Calender.*[12] Mixed geographies of this type ultimately take their origin from the classical birth of medicine and geography as interrelated sciences. These "new" disciplines united "the optical practices of cartography and geometry" in a "particular 'way of seeing' " which joined "the Greek *thea* ('outward appearance') and *hora* ('to look closely')" in the display and analysis of both the body and the physical world.[13]

In the microcosm of the poem, Spenser was well aware that complex comparisons between the body and the surrounding world could be "graphed" in even a single sentence. John Hoskins (1566–1638) gives an example drawn from Sir Philip Sidney's *Arcadia* which could just as easily apply to Spenser's Alma: "Philoclea was so environed with sweet rivers of virtue that she could neither be battered nor undermined."[14] Since such analogies are infinitely expandable, *The*

Faerie Queene can construct spatio-temporal routes between "pinna-
cles" like the House of Alma and the higher and lower places that
surround it simply by investing their intervening vice and virtue
figures with elemental symbolism. Thus to reach their highest heavenly or "fiery" peaks of virtue, each of Spenser's knights must first
master the trials posed by "lower" earthy or watery places of his soul,
which he typically encounters in surrounding caves, tunnels, forests,
shady pools, or stagnant lakes and their inhabitants. Once these trials
are met, the knight can enter airier or more open plains, but if he
fails, he will be confined to ever darker physical enclosures. While
hardly creating an empirical landscape, passages up and down the four
elements embedded in this geography chart relatively continuous
allegorical progresses or paths.[15] Along the way, fallen yet worthy
heroes also depend upon allies or helpers who have conquered or
resisted the same "elemental" enemies to rescue them from their
"dark places."

The work of Frances Yates and her school is relevant here, since
it shows that sixteenth-century Italian and French Neoplatonists
commonly used geography to "map" their elaborate conceptions
of faculty psychology and virtue. These Neoplatonic schemes were
imported to England along with the hermetic philosophy of Marsilio
Ficino and Giordano Bruno, who strongly influenced the Sidney
circle. Although generally building on medieval cosmogonies, these
systems were transformed by fresh understandings and translations of
Plato. With this in mind, both John Erskine Hankins and Quitslund
object to Robert Ellrodt's view of *The Faerie Queene* as indebted only
to medieval Platonism and Renaissance popularizations of Platonic
aesthetics, with no direct influence from either ancient Platonism or
learned Renaissance Platonists such as Ficino. In fact, as Quitslund
points out, Ellrodt contradicts himself since he does concede that
Spenser was "decisively influenced" by the quite learned Renaissance
Platonism of Louis Le Roy.[16] According to Yates, Spenser can additionally be linked to the attempts of Ficino and his followers to
harmonize religion, philosophy, and myth, to find a secret Platonic
harmony underlying all religions. Like Francis Bacon long after them,
they and their heirs searched for the "pia filosofia" concealed in the
elemental myths variously adumbrated by "Pythagoras, Plato, Empedocles, and Democritus," all of whom had "the Egyptians for
masters."[17] The same basic impulse lay behind the emblematic "science" of imagery, which "the rational disciplines would arrive at
separately" from the poets, who applied it in deeper, more intuitive
ways. All followed the common practice of simultaneously segregat-
ing and relating physical and moral levels of meaning. In a typical
gloss, Natale Conti explains that "the 'physical' meaning of the

Bellerophon story" relates "to the movement of the elements, whilst its 'moral' meaning is that of the conquest of the passions."[18]

Yates notes the even more familiar fact that since Neoplatonism typically sought to merge Platonic with Aristotelian ethics, its definitions of virtue commonly merged Plato's understanding of "the good" as a balance of pleasurable and painful passions with Aristotle's golden "mean between the extremes of opposite vices." In either case, reason ideally mediates between the two opposing "sides, or different levels, of man's nature," which must work with, not against his complex physical and moral passions.[19] Reaching the apex or "summit" of balanced virtue was thus regularly conceived by Neoplatonists as a literal ascent up a geographical scale or hillside surrounded by "cloudy swamps of the vices." Beyond them lay a symbolic "central mountain on the summit of which are the temples of the intellectual virtues grouped round an upward mounting flame." This fire "represents the heavenward direction of the whole personality, both intellect and will." In the characteristic conception of Bartolommeo del Bene, separate parts of the

> City of Truth, the valleys, the plain, and the mountain, correspond to the three kinds of human life: the way of the brutish and sensual life, the way of the active political life, and of the moral virtues; and the way of the contemplative life and of the intellectual virtues. From the base of the central mountain issue twenty rivers of pleasure and pain; in the valleys of the vices their waters spread unregulated, producing swamps, marshes, and clouds; beside the highways of the moral virtues they run in well-regulated canals. These rivers represent the emotions, flowing from the inmost core of the personality, and used either for good or evil.
>
> Here is presented in an easily grasped pictorial form the psychology of the Palace Academy debates, with their Aristotelian classification of the virtues into moral and intellectual, and their insistence that the emotions are not evil in themselves, but that virtue consists in the right use of their power [see Fig. 1].[20]

Spenser's version of this mapping is only a little less elaborate. Both his knights of Holinesse and Temperance, Redcrosse and Guyon, chart a synthetic Christian/Platonic conquest *and* fulfillment of the passions, but since Redcrosse aims to attain the highest fulfillment

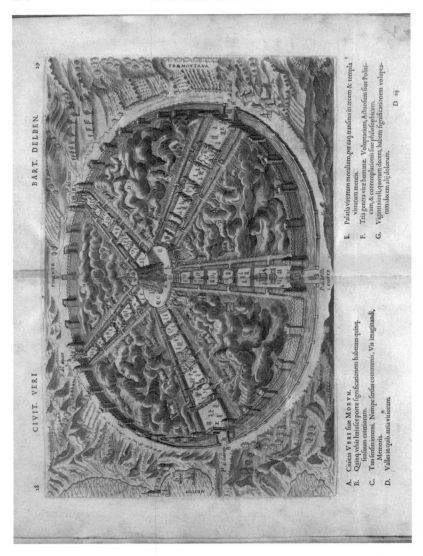

Fig. 1. The City of Truth, from Bartolommeo del Bene, *Civitas veri* (Paris: Apud Ambrosium et Hieronymum Drouart, 1609), 28–29. By permission of Houghton Library, Harvard University.

or form of love, the zeal or "fire" of God, his final victory is figured by his defeat of an irascible dragon, his own negative counterpart. In contrast to this holy quest, temperate Guyon aims to fulfill the lesser or "second table" moral commandments dealing with pure or temperate love of neighbor and material goods, which he accomplishes by perfecting his "airy" or free ability to balance competing affections and desires. In destroying Acrasia's Bower of Bliss—the lair of the "flaming" siren whose dark erotic mischief he must avenge—he therefore employs only the "cold fire" of rigorous temperance.[21] Yet both journeys also symbolize the knights' *common* attainment of the Aristotelian "mean" of virtue, the balance between opposing drives of cowardice and prideful wrath, indolence and concupiscence, which each encounters both in the form of temptresses and in fallen male alter egos along the way. Thus at the lowest point of his quest, Redcrosse is temporarily captured by the twin "idols" of worldly pride and zeal, Orgoglio, the pompous, bellowing son of Earth and Wind (I.vii.9, viii.11), and Duessa, the lustful "daughter" of fleshly religion; while at the lowest point of his saga, Guyon is temporarily captured by the "idol" of worldly concupiscence, Mammon, who offers him Philotime (false pride or honor) as his bride.

As in the reworkings of pagan myth studied by Jean Seznec, it is nevertheless impossible always to work out Spenser's schemata methodically. In either case, the " 'immense net of learning' " figured in miniature is not just encyclopedic but disproportional, not only in the individual work of art "but also from the point of view of the thought which they embody. Sometimes current decorative themes are used with no sign of any organic arrangement which indicates a carefully thought-out program. Sometimes, on the other hand, everything reveals the artist's subservience to the order imposed by the mind." In general, however, Spenser's patterns are no more arbitrary or erratic than those of other mythographers, where "learned diagrams of every sort—theological, geographical, mineralogical, medical—are combined according to the laws of numbers and the divisions of physical space."[22] George Boas adds that in innumerable schemata of this kind,

Most important because seldom rejected, was the theory of the four elements: Earth, Water, Air, and Fire. This, as everyone knows, was an all-embracing theory, for with each element were correlated not only certain perceptual characteristics, but also dynamic properties on which a physics could be erected,

and psychological traits extending throughout the animal kingdom, human beings, and even the planets. . . . Second, the main
scientific interest was astronomy and after that alchemy.

Thus "as far as intellectual simplicity and elegance go," the elemental
system "was not far from perfection," although its many Renaissance
elaborations hardly remained simple (see Fig. 2).[23]

Enjoying a "continuous and prolific tradition," the elemental tetrad was an omnipresent organizing principle in vastly disparate fields
of Renaissance knowledge. Citing Pierre de la Primaudaye's remark
that " 'All the foundation of every deepe studie and invention, must
be settled upon the number of fower, because it is the roote and
beginning of all numbers,' " S. K. Heninger notes the enormous
extent of its interrelated uses:

> In natural philosophy, the tetrad explained the arrangement of
> the four elements; in theology, it represented the symbiosis
> between Christ and the evangelists; in medicine, it balanced
> the four humours and differentiated the four ages of man; in
> psychology, it constituted the four faculties of the soul; in mete-
> orology, it presented a wind rose . . . ; in astrology, it organized
> the twelve signs of the zodiac into four seasons; and in alchemy,
> it showed how the philosophers' stone is the perfect center of
> the universe.[24]

The central role of the four literally foundational elements derives
originally from Hesiod and Pythagoras, but more proximately from
Plato and his commentators. In this Platonic lineage, Heninger finds
Macrobius at once "representative" and "remarkable" in striking a
balance between elemental stability and transmutation.[25]

Macrobius particularly set the stage for poetic adaptations of his
Timaean source by clarifying it as follows:

> We know, according to Plato (that is, according to the sanctuary
> of truth itself), that those bodies alone are closely held together
> which have a mean interposed between extremes to create a
> strong bond. When that mean is doubled the extremes are
> bound not only firmly but even indissolubly. . . . Now . . . the
> number four is the first of all numbers to have two means.

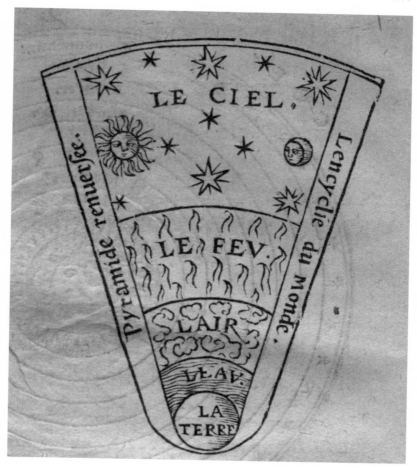

Fig. 2. The Elemental Cosmos, from Charles de Bouelles, *La geometrie pratique* (Paris: Chez Hiérosme de Marnef et Guillaume Cavellat, 1566), fol. 60b. By permission of the Thomas Fisher Rare Books Library, University of Toronto.

> Borrowing the means from this number the Creator of the
> universe bound the elements together with an unbreakable
> chain, as was affirmed in Plato's *Timaeus*: in no other way could
> the elements earth and fire, so opposed and repugnant to each
> other. . . , be mingled together by the two means of air and
> water.

As Heninger says, Macrobius then "expands upon Plato by inserting
the four basic qualities as the bonds between adjacent elements":

> Earth is dry and cold, and water cold and moist; but although
> these two elements are opposed, the dry to the wet, they have
> a common bond in their coldness. Air is moist and warm and,
> although opposed to water, the cold to the warm, nevertheless
> has the common bond of moisture. Moreover, fire, being hot
> and dry, spurns the moisture of the air, but yet adheres to it
> because of the warmth in both. And so it happens that each
> one of the elements appears to embrace the two elements bor-
> dering on each side of it by single qualities.[26]

As we have seen, these secondary qualities allowed the four elements to be associated not just with the four humors and seasons (hot
and dry for summer, cold and moist for winter, hot and moist for
spring, and cold and dry for autumn) but with every level of creation.
The human microcosm was no exception, as La Primaudaye testifies:
"It is the common use in schooles to teach, that man is a little
world, and that within him the bodie is composed of elements, the
reasonable soule is celestiall, the vegetable power common to men
and plants, the sense common to brute beasts, the reason participated
to Angels: and finally the image of God is therein seene & considered."[27] Yet given its Macrobian potential for transmutation, the
system is fundamentally unstable, often being expanded into a pentad,
as La Primaudaye seems to suggest, or contracted into a triad in which
the "brutal" or vegetable levels were fused—although these were just
as often balanced by a fourth or fully divine soul above the rational
level often identified with angels (see Fig. 3).

Spenser's clearest indication of his commitment to the most Pla-
tonically orthodox fourfold scheme appears in the concluding passages
of both *Colin Clouts Come Home Againe* and the *Hymne in Honour of
Love*. Although Ellrodt admits that the latter clearly expresses the

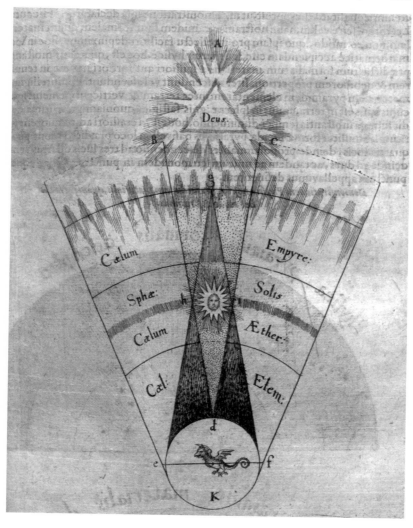

Fig. 3. The Cosmic Hierarchy, from Robert Fludd, *Utriusque cosmi majoris scilicet et minoris metaphysica, physica atque technica historia* (Oppenheim: Johann-Theodor de Bry, 1617), 165. By courtesy of the Department of Special Collections, Memorial Library, University of Madison-Wisconsin.

"Platonic idea that God joined the elements by introducing 'means'—that is water and air—between the extremes of earth and fire," which seems directly "reminiscent of *Timaeus* 32b–c," he nonetheless doubts Spenser's claim that his *Fowre Hymnes* were early compositions. Thus, as usual, he rejects Plato's relevance to the cosmology of *The Faerie Queene*.[28] Heninger disputes this claim by arguing that the tetrad at once provides "the fore-conceit" of Spenser's *Shepheardes Calender* and his allegorical epic, and Quitslund agrees: "the four elements constituting the world's body and the conditions of the soul's embodiment" underlie *The Faerie Queene*'s geography, although he does not consider their structural or mapping function.[29]

Spenser's *Hymne in Honour of Love* clarifies that function by providing a precise Platonic/Lucretian description of how Love's entry into Chaos brings forth the fourfold "essences" of creation. Much as in Luigi Berra's *L'Accademia delle Notti Vaticane,* these essences then create "the heaven, the stars, the sun, the moon" above, and below, "fire, air, water, earth, and many other beautiful things . . . filled with fervour or set on fire by Love."[30] Burlinson also notes that Spenser's *Hymne in Honour of Love* is indebted to this tradition, which Bacon later continues in his myth of "Cupid, or the Atom" in the *Sapientia Veterum.* Yet Burlinson incorrectly supposes that the *Hymne*'s "Platonic rejection of the material" world jars with the "materialized, materially replete descriptions" of places and things in *The Faerie Queene.* Both works in fact closely agree on the divine origins of matter in either Venus or her son Cupid.[31] In the *Hymne,* the "chyld" of Venus acts as "the force of this new flame" (line 8) or "kindled . . . fire" (line 28) from which all creation springs.[32] Cupid is also paradoxically "the eldest of the heavenly peares" and, as Plato's *Symposium* relates, the most lately born from "Plentie and . . . Penurie" (lines 53, 55–56). This first/last conundrum requires a full relation of Cupid's role in creating *both* mind and matter, for according to Spenser, he not only "reignest in the mynd," but also in "all the bodie" which he "doest frame" from Chaos (lines 43–44).

Since the passage in question is less familiar than it should be, it warrants citing at length:

> ere this worlds still moving mightie masse
> Out of great Chaos ugly prison crept,
> In which his goodly face long hidden was
> From heavens view, and in deepe darknesse kept,
> Love, that had now long time securely slept
> In Venus lap, unarmed then and naked,
> Gan reare his head, by Clotho being waked.

And taking to him wings of his owne heate,
Kindled at first from heavens life-giving fyre,
He gan to move out of his idle seate,
Weakely at first, but after with desyre
Lifted aloft, he gan to mount up hyre,
And like fresh eagle, make his hardie flight
Through all that great wide wast, yet wanting light.

Yet wanting light to guide his wandring way,
His owne faire mother, for all creatures sake,
Did lend him light from her owne goodly ray:
Then through the world his way he gan to take,
The world, that was not till he did it make,
Whose sundrie parts he from them selves did sever,
The which before had lyen confused ever.

The earth, the ayre, the water, and the fyre,
Then gan to raunge them selves in huge array,
And with contrary forces to conspyre
Each against other, by all meanes they may,
Threatning their owne confusion and decay:
Ayre hated earth, and water hated fyre,
Till love relented their rebellious yre.

He then them tooke, and tempering goodly well
Their contrary dislikes with loved meanes,
Did place them all in order, and compell
To keepe them selves within their sundrie raines,
Together linkt with adamantine chaines;
Yet so that in every living wight
They mixe themselves, and show their kindly might.

So ever since they firmely have remained,
And duly well observed his beheast;
Through which now all these things that are contained
Within this goodly cope, both most and least,
Their being have, and dayly are increast
Through secret sparks of his infused fyre,
Which in the barraine cold he did inspyre.

(lines 57–98)

Rising from the "cold" of earth to the pinnacle of fire, Cupid's four elements thus structure "every living wight," including "man, that breathes a more immortall mynd" (line 103), and aspires to a still higher invisible, "immortall flame." This flame's earthly form is "Beauties glorious beame" (lines 115, 116), which in its truest or "original" shape, Spenser Neoplatonically understands not just as physical beauty but also as moral perfection. Beauty's heavenly "glory" is thus naturally opposed to the delusory charms of a Duessa, Lucifera, or False Florimell, who are all soon belied by their surroundings, companions, or origins. For as Ficino remarks, "only by divine inspiration can men understand what true beauty is, what legitimate love is, and in what way one ought to love," although false love gives clear "signs" of its "earthly filth" through its addiction to Bacchus and Priapus.[33]

Spenser's view of the elements again parallels La Primaudaye's more extensive vision in *The French Academie* (first English translation, 1586), where the "whole" of the universal frame is

> compounded of vnlike elements, of earth, water, ayre, and fire, . . . preserued by Analogie and proportion, which they haue together: and as we see in a mans body . . . : in a house, . . . a politike body . . . and . . . euery body mingled with heate, colde, drie and moiste, is preserued by the same reason of analogie and proportion which they haue together: so it is in euery commonwealth, well appointed and ordered, which consisting of many and sundry subiects, is maintained by their vnitie, beeing brought to bee of one consent and will, and to communicate their workes, artes, and exercises together for common benefite and profit.[34]

Hence as in *The Faerie Queene,* here each element like each virtue simultaneously contributes to the microcosmic or individual part and also to the macrocosmic whole. And just as each Spenserian knight represents a single virtue that contributes to that whole, so his attainment of this ideal requires his individual perfection of each successive element of his whole nature, earthly, watery, airy, and fiery. Since the soul's components have the same secondary qualities as the cosmic elements—hot, cold, moist, and dry—they can be alternately represented as deserts of parching heat or beaming light or as floods of either refreshing or destructive waters. Yet in either case, the passions *inside* the human frame precisely reflect the *outside* or external landscape through which it passes.

As the foregoing implies, the secondary qualities of the elements carry a double valence of positive and negative attributes which in turn generate Spenser's forking "pathes and alleies wide/With footing worne" (I.i.7). These "forks" mark the point where the knight will either successfully pass through or become entrapped in the landscape that lies ahead. Heninger shows that wide or beaten paths mark a leftward or "evil" turn in the Pythagorean Y or crossroads; yet even after a wrong turn or detour, the elements often remain relatively ambiguous.[35] As the lowest, most inert, passive and "cold" element in this system, earth is usually linked with deficiency, vice, or filth. Errour obviously represents this aspect of earth: specifically, abiogenetic, abnormal or abortive forms of nature or nurture. Lying deep within the "durtie ground" of her den, she ceaselessly breeds and poisonously feeds an "ill fauored" and "uncouth brood" who share her hatred of light, and by extension, viable life. Her vomit reveals that her semi-digested food consists of "eyeless" creatures like frogs and toads, the source of her foul milk. When deprived of it, her vermin-like offspring ("fowle, and blacke as inke") cannibalistically feed on her equally fatal blood. In every respect, then, they occupy the most primitive and unnatural level of animate or animal life, which Spenser compares both to creatures born from the "fertile slime" of the flooding Nile and to noisome gnats. These life forms all inhabit an earthy geography of wet, cold, dark and dank "shades" lacking in life-giving light (I.i.15–16, 20–23). Yet at other times earthy, abiogenetic birth is oppositely linked to "pure" spontaneous generation and procreation, as in the Chrysogone episode of Book III (vi.8). Kenneth Borris further notes that similar binaries also operate in the quest's resting points or castles, where the lowest or most "earthy" level of both Alma's and Lucifera's houses is "built from matter like 'Aegyptian slime.' " The overriding difference is that Lucifera's dwelling is uneven, rotten, and imminently decomposing while Alma's pure "body" (much like Charissa's house in Book I) is a well-proportioned castle of health. Yet since both are "built" from earth, Borris argues that the closely intertwined rites of passage performed in Books I and II mark parallel, not disjunctive ascents from flesh to spirit by Redcrosse and Guyon.[36] In general, then, like body and soul, earth and fire may be opposites, but they are also naturally interdependent and potentially benign elements in both the macrocosm and microcosm.

Carol Kaske explains that this aspect of Spenserian aesthetics derives from the tradition of biblical "romance," which typically presents evil as a false look-alike, example, or image of good. Bad examples sometimes "masquerade" as good, but at other times they

simply counter it, so that even seemingly transparently "evil" reptil-
ian images may serve *in bono* as well as *in malo,* the two basic faces
of biblical polarity.[37] Both Plato's *Phaedrus* and *Republic* and Aristotle's
De anima and *Nicomachean Ethics* similarly distinguish between positive and negative aspects of the same passions, which all further subdi-
vide into concupiscent and irascible affections. The former are always
considered more "earthy" or lowly, and the latter more heroic or
aspiring passions. Spenser signals his conformity to this tradition by
linking concupiscence to "lowly" earth and water, and irascibility,
the pagan counterpart of Christian spirit and zeal, to air and fire.
Yet this upper level can only be attained not just by controlling but
by cooperating with the lower ones. Hence as in Alma's house (as
Borris notes), the lower appetites "are not only both domesticated
and subservient but fully humanized, becoming handmaidens who
follow her movements and directives, rather than constituting unstable, potentially restive and unruly beasts that precede and in a sense
lead the directing agency," as in the case of Plato's Phaedran charioteer.[38] Poorly managed or corrupt "lower" appetites would admit
Maleger's bestial armies within Alma's chaste walls, but in her domain
they instead serve as positive supporters of the temperate passions.

Space hardly permits a thorough exploration of the entire nexus
of elemental geography governing Book II, some of which has already
been traced by Walter R. Davis in the Medina and Braggadochio
episodes of Cantos ii and iii.[39] Since Davis further shows that the
four separate chambers of Mammon's Cave feature the same four
fatal "elemental" affections Guyon encounters before entering it in
Canto vii, the Mammon episode provides an appropriate place to
begin.[40] First, however, we must recall that Guyon had first met
Amavia and then Phedon, who jointly represent the descent of love's
higher "fire" into its earthiest or "basest part" (II.i.57). Phedon thus
becomes a murderer and Amavia a suicide whose once "alabaster
brest" stains not just a nearby fountain's "cleane waues with purple
gore," but the lap holding her unfortunate child and all the grassy
soil beneath (II.i.39–41). He next met Phaedria, whose Lake of Idleness stands for watery stagnation, and finally, Cymochles and Pyrocles, the Castor-and-Pollux-like enemy "twins" who respectively
stand for wavering and fiery instability, as the Greek meaning of their
names indicates. This elemental symbolism is evidently more Platonic
(or Timean) than del Bene's Aristotelian pictorialization of the virtues
of Temperance, Fortitude, Magnificence, Liberality, Magnanimity,
and the rest, yet Spenser's general approach to mapping paired passions and virtues is not unrelated to del Bene's geographical model
of ascent.

Drawing upon work by Tuve, Heninger, and Alastair Fowler, James R. Fisher shows that the paths, crossroads, and places visited by the knight are all similarly invested with cosmic significance. To mark the balance between extremes, he argues, Guyon's quest begins at the vernal equinox, the beginning of the year in Aries, or the "sign" of Belphoebe. Aries is of course a sun or fire sign, but as Belphoebe's name ("fair moon") indicates, she actually unites the sun and moon, the perfect Aristotelian balance of the zodiac, whose constellations require both "the sun to mark out the pathway, [and] the moon to mark the twelve divisions." Her "golden Bauldricke" (II.iii.29), Fisher further explains, evokes the symbolic "belt" of the zodiac, itself divided between earth, water, air, and fire signs. These help to mark Guyon's moral and temporal progress toward Acrasia or Capricorn, the wintry sign of the goat, so that his final purging of her Bower appropriately occurs under the sign that Macrobius considered the gateway to immortality. In terms of the zodiac, then, Belphoebe or spring and Acrasia or winter provide the antithetical poles of Guyon's quest. Belphoebe presides over the life-giving vernal equinox that sets him on his course, and Acrasia over the artificial illusion of spring, the Bower, beneath which (as beneath Duessa's sensually alluring garb) lies the sexual sterility and spiritual death associated with the winter solstice.[41]

In the middle of this quest Guyon encounters two other female antitheses, Phaedria, who reigns at the summer solstice, and Alma, who embodies the moral and physical maturity of the autumnal equinox. Fisher adds that since Alma represents not only autumnal "ripeness" but also the balance needed to attain it, her castle is placed between autumn equinox's two signs, Virgo and Libra, symbols respectively of restraint and of careful weighing or prudence. Tuve supports this general notion by noting that the quester in *The Zodiake of Life* similarly seeks Dame Virtue under the sign of Virgo, an episode additionally featuring a "dark death-like garden" very like the last place Guyon visits before escaping Mammon's Cave, the Garden of Proserpina.[42] As Acrasia's diametrical opposite, Alma has not felt "Cupid's rage" despite her comparable "ripeness" for two reasons variously noted by Fowler and Hankins: she has made her body a temple of holiness, and she unites the two opposing qualities personified by Shamefastness and Prays-desire, "the sense of shame and the desire of honour."[43] Because prudence also resides in the "library" or repository of her mind, which similarly balances memory and imagination (the latter is ruled by "Phantastes," where Cupid often "rages"), her house is balanced between the two solstices where "the

sun is at its low points," that is, where day and night are most unequal. According to Fisher, Phaedria's and Acrasia's domains are thus
situated at the opposite of either equinox, seasons "when the sun is
at its peak crossing the equator" and night and day are nearly equal.
This situation is partly relative to one's perspective, since "from
anywhere on earth, the equinoxes are those points where day and
night are of equal length, . . . [but] "the length of either day or night
at a solstice depends on which hemisphere the viewer inhabits. From
a solar perspective, however[,] . . . the sun can be said to 'fall' from
its peak at an equinox to either of its low points at a solstice." Around
these cosmic signposts he locates other "elemental characters" who
do not always appear in the exact order of the zodiac, although like
Maleger, the archer who combines the dark, wintry signs of Scorpio
and Sagittarius, they generally conform to its plan.[44]   After encountering Braggadochio and Phedon, "goaty" symbols of the destructive
male ego also associated with Mordant, the first victim of Acrasia's
lust, Guyon meets Cymochles and Pyrochles, the self-destructive
"twins" of air and fire. Then at the center of his quest he finally
meets Mammon, whose cave lies below the earthy sign of the bull in
Taurus. The Gemini should astrologically follow Taurus, yet Guyon's
second and final encounter with Cymochles and Pyrochles actually
does take place after leaving Mammon's Cave. The money-god's
female counterpart is Phaedria, the temptress jointly associated with
the watery and airy signs of Aquarius, Pisces, and Cancer (Fisher,
24), who separates the knight from his Palmer even though, unlike
Cymochles, Guyon never becomes her lover. As an airier form of
Phaedria's watery sloth, Cymochles shares her association with the
"wavy" or "wavery" path of sensual intemperance. Its attractions are
represented by the glittering, infertile lightness of airy bubbles and
empty laughter, for Spenser the most dangerous threat to the temperate soul:

A Harder lesson, to learne Continence
    In ioyous pleasure, than in grieuous paine:
    For sweetnesse doth allure the weaker sence
    So strongly, that vneathes it can refraine
    From that, which feeble nature couets faine;
    But griefe and wrath, that be her enemies,
    And foes of life, she better can abstaine;
        Yet vertue vaunts in both their victories,
And *Guyon* in them all shewes goodly maysteries.

                                                    (II.vi.1)

Yet Phaedria proves too foolishly idle actually to attract a pure "airy" soul like Guyon, who represents the positive lightness and dryness of Aquarius.[45] She nevertheless exercises some residual power over him, for his easy "escape"—much like Redcrosse's easy conquest of Errour—increases his natural sanguinity, the "humour" associated with air. This humor in turn makes him more susceptible to Mammon, Book II's "alchemical" equivalent of that primally evil magician, Archimago. Mammon is literally a miner and refiner of gold, but also figuratively a magus who uses it to transform "base metal" or people. Guyon's potential weakness to his figurative power is signaled by his faint upon leaving the Cave: after becoming inured to its metallic "fumes," he chokes on his first breath of pure air, especially as he is also faint from lack of food or sleep, forms of nurture as unnatural to Mammon as to Errour. His faint leaves him in the power of Pyrochles and Cymochles, the irascible and concupiscible twins about to despoil him when Arthur charges in with an appropriately homeopathic remedy: fire fights fire. The moral seems to be that Arthur has been strengthened by his previous encounters with their egoistic vices, which Guyon has known only abstractly from his Palmer's remarks on Phedon, Mordant, and Amavia (II.i.57–59).

These lessons are recapitulated as Phedon sorrowfully gives Guyon and his Palmer an account of his "capture" or betrayal by Philemon or "self-love," who tricked him into believing that his true love Claribell was false by asking her maid to masquerade as the mistress. After seeing him make love to this "illusion," Phedon flies into a violent rage and murders both his friend and his fiancée, thus succumbing to the same temptation Redcrosse faced when Archimago deceived him with the false Una. In response, the Palmer outlines the elemental process by which the soul decays into its vegetable and animal components once its rational light kindles into jealous fire:

> Wrath is a fire, and gealousie a weede,
> Grief is a flood, and loue a monster fell;
> The fire of sparkes, the weede of little seede,
> The flood of drops, the Monster filth did breede:
> But sparks, seed, drops, and filth do thus delay;
> The sparks soone quench, the springing seed outweed,
> The drops dry vp, and filth wipe cleane away:
> So shall wrath, gealousie, griefe, loue dye and decay.

(II.iv.35)

These comments explain that Phedon experienced no sudden "death" of love, but a gradual destabilization of each elemental link in his psyche, here clearly represented as a tetrad of earth, water, air, fire. Once the degeneration of each is complete, wrath or concupiscence (or in Phedon's case, a combination of both) extinguishes the higher light of the soul. This decline can only be prevented by restraining negatively earthy or selfish "elements" when they are but "weake and wan," for once they get the bit in their teeth, "Strong warres they make, and cruell battery bend/Gainst fort of Reason, it to ouerthrow" (II.iv.34).

Successful resistance to such attacks is later shown through Alma's response to Maleger's onslaught against her "fort" of temperate affections, but Phedon has already lost that battle at every level. The lowest level on this scale of affections is human "loue" understood as earthy sexual desire, which when intemperate or selfish, becomes "monstrous" and "filthy." It then breeds the "weed" of jealousy from the "flood" of grief caused by suspicion or lack of trust. Spenser's *Hymne in Honour of Love* contrastingly shows a very different kind of earthly love ascending the scale to holy fire by absorbing the higher and more fluid nature of pure water and air. Its pure "fluids" do not dissolve in floods of grief but, balanced by airier bliss, produce kindly drops of compassion. Ficino's *Commentary on Plato's Symposium* similarly teaches that divine or rational intuition strengthens rational love, much as an angel in the form of a "*Cupido*" later assists the rational Palmer to preserve Guyon from his faint until Arthur comes to the rescue. These scenes also foreshadow the theme of Book III, where chaste love derived "from heaven and different from the source of 'base affections' and 'filthy lust' ([III.iii]1.5–6)" empowers mortal minds to order and direct "all their actions . . . aright" (2.2–4).[46] The opposite obviously occurs when "mixed" affections like Phedon's go awry: muddy oceans of grief "water" the false imagination's "weede of little seede," inflame the "air" of the mind with jealous delusion, and finally kindle sparks of wrath that darken its mental "lamp" and usher in bloody sin. A similar degeneration has earlier doomed the faithless Mordant, the suicidal Amavia, and their blood-stained infant, Ruddymane.[47] By reversing this descent, the temperate soul attains its freedom by wiping away earth's filth, drying up unruly drops of grief, and uprooting the "seeds" planted by the airy imagination before they can be watered and "grow" into fires of deadly hate. Yet jealous rage aside, intemperate souls like Phedon also fail to free themselves because they secretly share a slothful form of selfishness or self-love not unlike that of his false friend or the indolent Phaedria.

Philemon's self-centeredness seems to consist in using others as objects of his own pleasure, including the pleasure of "infecting" them with his own vices. A similarly hidden bond between apparent contraries connects Cymochles and Pyrocles, who equally if oppositely pervert the highest Aristotelian virtue, magnanimity.

As the true opposite of them all, Guyon survives Mammon's Cave by successively resisting each of the elemental passions that would otherwise subject him to the fire of "*Plutoes* griesly rayne" (II.vii.21). Ruled by Proserpina and Mammon's daughter, Philotime, the Cave's final chamber literally leads to the mouth of hell, although like Mammon and the rest of his Cave, it molders more than burns. Combining all the worst elements of Errour's den and Lucifera's Castle, this poisonous cavern lies a little beyond Phaedria's "*Ydle lake*" in a "desert wilderness" leading to Mammon's "Gloomy glade." Here Guyon finds the "vncouth, saluage" "Money God" shut off "from heauens light" like Errour (vii.39, vii.3), but unlike her slimy den, his "shades" are blackened by a smoke that stains his face, eyes, and hands "cole-blacke" with its fiery residue, a combination of rust and dust (vii.3, 4). These corrupted, earthy elements of fire superficially support his sinister claim to be the "greatest god below the skye," one who "bounteously" channels his "mountains" of material goods "into an ample flood" flowing from the "hollow earth" where they "haue their eternall brood" (vii.8). Yet since Mammon represents an ontological reversal of the natural flow of water and light from high to low, from the true God to earth's fertile womb, his "floods" are not life- but grief-inducing. That has been the case ever since "the quiet wombe" of Guyon's "great Grandmother" earth was first "wounded" as Mammon-like metallurgy began to pollute her "veines" with "His greedy flames, and kindled life-deuouring fire." Earth's macrocosmic descent from the golden age thus follows the same pattern of corruption as the microcosmic soul. First the earth becomes polluted, then "fountaines of gold and siluer" take the place of life-giving water, and finally the air burns with a "huge desire/ and pompous pride" that can never warm like the sun's natural fire (vii.17).

Guyon personally experiences this cosmic descent as Mammon's Cave reveals the consequences of "guiltlesse blood pourd oft on ground" by greed (II.vii.13). This blood is a variant of both Orgoglio's gore-stained floors and the bestial "carkases" that litter Lucifera's dungeons (I.v.49), both of which contain more "purely" prideful victims of Mammon's "worldly muck" (II.vii.10), or ambition. His own deadly emotions are personified by the figures who line the "beaten broad high way" leading to the first of the Cave's four chambers: "Cruell Reuenge, and rancorous Despight, / Disloyall Treason, and hart-burning Hate," "gnawing Gealosy," "trembling Feare," and "Lamenting Sorrow" (vii.21, 22). Behind the first door lies an "vgly feend, more fowle then dismall day," who longs to seize Guyon with his "cruell clawes" if he succumbs to any of his lower senses, that is, "if euer couetous hand, or lustfull eye, / Or lips he layd on thing, that likte him best" (vii. 26, 27). These three temptations of sight, taste, and touch obviously exclude hearing or smell since Mammon's screaming fiends, night birds, and sulphurous fires can appeal to neither, but Spenser adds a fourth sensual temptation, sleep or "forgetting," to balance out a chamber filled with victims of the lowliest earthly desires. Their sins are further suggested by the dark figure of "*Arachne*," whose smoky web represents the most primal or subhuman desire for "prey." Within her dusty, decaying walls no light penetrates, while her floor is strewn with carcasses surrounded by ancient, double-barred treasures that can never be opened (vii.28–30). These subhuman sinners have apparently forgotten not only that their sensitive or "vegetable" needs are secondary rather than primary, but also that Mammon cannot supply either; hence they suffer the "yron whip" and "bloudy knife" of self-inflicted abjection (vii.21).

His second and higher chamber includes all the "airier" pleasures that current money can buy: all "the worldes blis, . . . / To which al men doe ayme, rich to be made." Its "couetous Spright" or presiding miser is not quite so primally repulsive as the "feend" of the first, suggesting that his pleasures occupy a higher or more "animal" level of "blis." The Spright's "airier" nature is also suggested by his longing to snatch Guyon away "More light then Culuer in the Faulcons fist," yet he is doomed to fail because Guyon knows that real bliss is not animal but rational. It lies in being "Lord of those, that riches haue, / Then them to haue my selfe, and be their seruile sclaue" (II.vii.32–34). This rebuttal forces Mammon to take his guest to the very source of money's power over men, the "liquid waues" of metal and sweat needed to refine gold from crude metal. Combining the higher powers of water and fire, the processes that create this "fountaine of the worldes good" are directed by "Deformed creatures" whose eyes sparkle "with feruent fyre," "fiers *Vulcans* rage to tame" (vii.35–38). Yet as Guyon's opening remark indicates, their gold *only* flows, never fills, especially since Mammon's slaves can never apportion wealth to the real needs of those who have "cause to vse" it (vii.38–39). Obviously, then, these three chambers do not precisely follow the natural order of the elements, yet all lead to the fourth and fieriest level of his Cave. Rather than the iron doors leading to

the others, the entrance to this level is framed by a broad gate of
beaten gold guarded by a golden man with an iron club, which
suggests that its brightness merely disguises its earthy or "Iron Age"
tools, methods, and values. *Disdayne*'s "Sterne . . . looke, . . . full of
stomake vaine" burns with a truly Luciferian or earth-despising pride
in wealth that makes "him scorne all creatures great and small / And
with his pride all others powre deface" (vii.41). Thus while his glittering "brightnesse" makes that "darknesse light," he cannot enlighten much less "enliven" anyone; like the regal counterparts of
his pride, he has too deeply perverted his natural source.
"Decked . . . / With crownes and Diademes, & titles vaine," Philotime's court represents both false glory and false beauty. Her "broad
beauties beam" may shine brilliantly in her palace's "dim shade," but
she has clearly lost both her "natiue hew" and her true honor
(vii.42–45).

"Wrought by art and counterfetted shew," Philotime nevertheless
attracts "Thereby more louers vnto her . . . call," which neatly summarizes the nature of her vain and artificial court (II.vii.45). Its true
queen Proserpina actually reigns below with Pluto (or Plutus, the
mythical money god), but her spirit remains in the Garden that Guyon views after refusing Philotime's hand. Here Mammon offers him
Proserpina's silver stool and golden apples, temptations which recall
the "stony" food, godlike honors, and ill-gotten kingdoms Satan
offered Christ in the wilderness. The consequences of accepting these
"gifts" are obviously symbolized by the garden's poisonous trees and
herbs of death, which are watered by the hellish Cocytus itself
(vii.52–56). Were Guyon seduced by any of these "attractions," his
airy soul would decline into the lowest deep represented by Pluto /
Lucifer, the false or failed Olympian light-bearer(s) whose unfounded
pride at once occupies the highest and "lowest" rung on the ladder
of concupiscence. For them as for all those who climb the golden
chain Philotime offers her "lovers," the higher they go, the lower
they fall into living rivers of death. Suffocating rather than burning,
her victims have all literally "swamped" the seeds of life-giving earth
and air with fiery floods of lust, although these vices are predictably
subdivided into two basic types, "vegetable" sins of earth and water,
and animal sins of air and fire. Tantalus symbolizes the vegetable soul
who even in hell can think only of eating and drinking, while Pilate
represents the animal ambition that would pass false judgement on
the "lord of life" himself. Imagining worldly honor and ease to be
greater than justice ultimately deludes Pilate into vainly attempting
to wash away his guilt in the muck of Cocytus. Thus like Mammon's
other victims, he is tortured by the very elements he intemperately

indulged. Just as Tantalus "steeps" in the "cold liquor" of earth and water, Pilate wallows in the "feculent" filth created by "his labour vaine and idle industry," animal "waste" that can never cleanse him (vii.58, 61; cf.10). Like Phedon, all therefore suffer from a failure to refine each of the elemental faculties they have instead corrupted.

After resisting each animal, vegetable, and mineral temptation in reverse order, Guyon not only beguiles "the Guyler of the pray" (II.vii.64) but receives the "prevenient grace" or heavenly fire consistently associated with Arthur.[48] Yet this "providence" only temporarily dispels the combined force and fraud of Pyrochles' and Cymochles' attack, since the temperate man must personally confront these twin opposites of the just and airy Alma in preparation for his final confrontation with the debased and watery Acrasia, the perfected imperfection of Phaedria and her idle lake. Both fallen females are thus associated with what Davis calls the Cymochlean or pleasure-loving elements in man, the vegetative "excess of the bodily and defect of the spiritual," whose opposite is Pyrochlean fire, the "ireful . . . excess of the spirited and defect of the bodily."[49] Together they also represent "willfully refused grace" (II.viii.52), the obvious antithesis to both Arthurian fire and to Alma's and Guyon's airy balance.

At the very bottom of the scale of intemperance we find Maleger, the lowly or unerotic earthy senses that unworthily attack Alma's House. His true female counterpart is thus not Acrasia but Errour, for while Acrasia physically perverts the erotic energies leading to holy fire, Maleger and his legions can corrupt only the "male" or non-procreative aspects of animal desire. Literally chthonic creatures, they spring "with outrageous cry/ . . . /Out of the rockes and caues" armed with primitive weapons, wild and hollowed-eyed with the "stiffe vpstanding heares" (II.ix.13) of frightened or paralyzed beasts. These descriptions culminate in their comparison to lions and tigers, but their basic character as earthy bodies without souls also associates them with the lowest moving things, including a "swarme of Gnats" (II.ix.16) that recalls both Errour's brood and Arachne's smoky web. The defense is again conducted by Arthur, and since Guyon takes no part in this battle, Davis seems correct to suppose that he is Alma's male counterpart or "animus," and vice versa.[50] As a rational "virgin bright," the temperate Alma appropriately wears a lily white robe and a crown of roses (ix.18–19), symbols of the resurrection that mark her as a bride of Christ awaiting marriage to her "spouse."[51] While her Castle is firmly grounded in earth, it thus points toward the heavens, so that in comparison with Lucifera's palace, hers is almost literally a castle in air. Although in time "it must turne to earth; no earthly thing is sure," her "circle sett in heauens place"

marks her eternal destination, as does its "goodly diapase" or harmony resembling the music of the spheres (ix.21–22).

This reading is supported by the standard Christian belief set forth
by Ficino and other commentators on the rational soul, which has
"nothing at all to do with the generation of the body or its first
formation[;] that is the task of the vegetal soul or, as Ficino says, the
non-rational life of the world." Once the rational soul "arrives, it
takes over the task of 'organizing' the body from the vegetal and
sensible souls, which become united with it and under its direction. . . . [A]t death it separates from its companion . . . souls, and
proceeds to the destination adjudged to it by God." On earth it acts
as "the very principle of form," as "Spenser writes in 'an Hymne in
Honour of Beautie', 132–33." [52] The rational soul's essence, heavenly
destination, and final reformation into an imperishable body are here
summed up in Alma's "Turret" or watchtower, one

> Like highest heauen compassed around,
> And lifted high aboue this earthly masse,
> Which it suruewd, as hils doen lower ground;
> But not on ground mote like to this be found,
> Not that, which antique *Cadmus* whylome built
> In *Thebes*, which *Alexander* did confound;
> Nor that proud towre of *Troy*, though richly guilt,
> From which young *Hectores* bloud by cruell *Greekes* was spilt.
>
> (II.ix.45)

Unlike edifices built by pagan magic or for pagan glory, Alma's Castle
is ultimately incorruptible, just as her bodily form is ultimately resur-
rectible. Its immortality is signaled both by the watchtower's light-
giving beacons and its resemblance to "that heauenly towre, / That
God hath built for his owne blessed bower" (ix.46–47), which A.
C. Hamilton glosses as the New Jerusalem.

Thus like other Neoplatonists, Spenser seems to believe that the
united mind of man reflects the "in-dwelling" of God, still another
tetrad or "golden square." For in Alma's symbolic mind or watchtower, judgment and memory are balanced by imagination, which
is subdivided into Eumnestes and Anamnestes to make a fourfold. [53]
Yates points out that her house as a whole reflects this balance: its
partly circular and triangular—or partly masculine and feminine—proportions are intersected by a "cube, or quadrate, . . . the
elemental world of the four elements: the seven is the celestial world
of the seven planets; the nine proportioned equally" (II.ix.22) "is the

supercelestial world of the nine angelic hierarchies, which form into
the Triangle of the Trinity. All three elements are present in man as
well as in the universe."[54] As this remark indicates, depending on
how one counts, Spenser uses a variety of numerical patterns. The
Alma episode additionally features all five senses along with their
enemies, the seven deadly sins, although the latter are not described,
presumably because Spenser expects the reader to recall their appearance in Lucifera's Castle. His use of vertical maps nevertheless remains
a constant, as shown by the hierarchic beast imagery used to describe
the five fallen senses. The corrupters of sight are likened to sharp-
eyed "biting" predators (owls, dogs, gryphons, and lynxes), while
corrupt hearing—the next highest faculty—is compared to stealthy
reptiles and beasts who (like human falsehood) appear or attack without warning (deer, wild boar, and snakes; II.xi.8, 10). The enemies
of smell are odiferous "devils" of various kinds (apes, hellhounds, and
fiends), while lower down the scale, perverted taste is represented by
greedy ostriches, "loathly Toades," and swine (xi.12). The final
"troupe most horrible of hew" consists of creeping and crawling
things: "ugly Vrchins," snails, and spiders (xi.13), ultra "earthy" creatures associated with "evil" touch.

Yet as soon as Alma's "Patrone" (II.xi.16), Arthur, marches out
against them, Spenser returns to his familiar elemental symbolism.
Collectively raining down from the "high mountaine" of earthy pride
and ambition, Maleger's legions threaten "to ouerflow/With suddein
fury all the fertile playne" that the "sad husbandman," the faithful
worker in the field, has carefully cultivated (II.ix.18). Arthur first
experiences these earthy forces as an elemental flood of frozen rain
or "heaped hayle," and next as airy, dry "withered leaues" blown
by "the wroth Western wind," who strips the trees of their crown
of "locks." Against these forces of dry water and air he appropriately
sets "the fierce *Spumador* borne of heauenly seed," a foaming stallion
who represents the moist spirit of water blending with air (ix.19).
His charge then calls the opposing "Capteine" of air into action,
Maleger riding like "the winde" on a swift tiger barely touching the
ground. He himself is composed of mere wind, "of such subtile
substance and vnsound,/That like a ghost he seem'd, whose graue-
clothes were vnbound" (II.xi.20, 26). As the living spirit of bodily
death, Maleger is perhaps Guyon's truest opposite, as cold and dry
as dead air, "pale and wan as ashes," "His body leane and meager as
a rake,/And skin all withered like a dryed rooke,/Thereto as cold
and drery as a Snake" (xi.22).

The chief supporters of this living death's head (he even wears one
as "an Helmet light"—some Spenserian humor here, II.xi.22) are

Impotence and Impatience, the ultimate "ends" of concupiscence and irascibility, and thus the eternal "patrons" of characters like Cymochles and Pyrochles, Tantalus and Pilate. Embodied as twin "Hags," the capital "I" sisters manage to unseat Arthur, who must be rescued by his weaker squire, again (as in Guyon's rescue) representing the power of grace (xi.30–31) overcoming ill-fortune, exhaustion, or importunity. Newly inspired by this gift of grace, Arthur's spirit is literally reignited against Maleger:

> Like as a fire, the which in hollow caue
>   Hath long bene vnderkept, and downe supprest,
>   With murmurous disdayne doth inly raue,
>   And grudge, in so streight prison to be prest,
>   At last breakes forth with furious infest,
>   And striues to mount vnto his natiue seat;
>   All that did earst it hinder and molest,
> Yt now deuoures with flames and scorching heat,
> And carries into smoake with rage and horror great.
>
> (xi.32)

With Arthur's irascible soul thus inflamed, the spiritless Maleger would soon gasp out his earthy "spright" if not for his Antaeus-like ability to regenerate it from the cold and moist earth (xi.38, 42, 43). From this power he gains his darkly "airy" ability to exist as "Flesh without bloud, a person without spright,/Wounds without hurt, a bodie without might," "most strong in most infirmitee;/Like did he did neuer heare, like did neuer see" (xi.40). The reference is ambiguous—either Arthur never saw such a "ghost" before, or it behaves like a blind and deaf "body"—but in any case, Maleger certainly represents the absolute emptiness of the body in the absence of spirit. He seems dead even while alive, an earthy "wind" hearing only sounds of "horrour and confused cr[ies]" (xi.20). Arthur finally defeats this Antaeus figure by strangling him in midair and casting him into a "standing lake" (46), the opposite of the waters of life.

At this point, Hankins finds Maleger clearly representing "spiritual death from the subjection of the soul to the passions and lusts of the body," so that his demise prefigures the final death awaiting the damned at the resurrection of all the dead.[55] He further argues that the standing lake alludes to the Book of Revelation's burning lake, since two spiritually fatal and damnable suicides immediately occur here: Impatience's death by water, and Impotence's self-impalement with a "cursed dart" of hate—uncontrolled, infertile desire smoldering with impotent fire (II.xi.47). Hence, like Maleger, both Hags

will perish eternally, while Arthur's wounds are soon healed with
the finest fruits of earth and water (wine, balm, and spices) in Alma's
house of health.

After these malign spirits of earth, water, air, and fire are defeated,
it remains only for Guyon to himself "fight fire with fire" in confronting the most difficult form of concupiscence to resist, the sexual
desire more "lightly" represented by Phaedria. The latter is linked
to the lower vegetable affections through her sleep-inducing "sermon" to Cymochles on the lilies of the field (II.vi.17–18), while
Acrasia's watery realm corrupts and infects the higher "animal spirits"
by depriving them of air. Since Guyon first learned of her fatal powers
by the side of a fountain, his final trip past Acrasia's fountain brings
him full circle.[56] Although this canto is rooted in well-known enchantress myths taken from Homer, Ariosto, and Tasso, Spenser's
version is more deeply saturated with figures of death-giving water
than any of the others. In order to complete their "goodly frame of
Temperaunce" (II.xii.1), Guyon and his Palmer first spend two days
at sea, "Ne euer land beheld, ne liuing wight," until on the symbolic
third day they pass through the "*Gulfe of Greediness* . . . /That deepe
engorgeth all this worldes pray" and vomits it up, much in the manner of Homer's Charybdis (xii.2–3). Opposite lies the Rock of Reproach, which like Homer's Scylla is shunned by all living things.
Here as in Arthur's assault on Maleger and his forces, a descending
scale of elements foreshadows what Guyon is up against. The Rock
first sends "storm" troopers down its dreadfully high, craggy, and
bleak mountain peaks, while its magnetic stone cruelly paralyzes and
wrecks all those who come too close. All fish and fowl detest it
except for hoarse "Seagulles" and "Cormoyraunts," noisily irrational
and predatory "birds of rauenous race" (xii.8). These consume the
shipwrecked victims of "lustfull luxurie and thriftlesse wast" in the
part of the Gulfe where its "streame more violent and greedy
growes," draining straight down to the "darke dreadfull hole" of
Tartarus, as always, a place of smoky air and eternal fire (xii.9, 5–6).

The temptations leading to this hell-mouth are framed by the
deceptively "faire and fruitfull" Wandering Islands "floting the floods
emong" (II.xii.10, 12). Here we again meet Phaedria and her wandering "boat withouten ore" in a watery playland haunted by mermaids
"making false melodies" to distract the unwary from the nearby quick
sands and whirlpools of thriftlessness (xii.15, 17). These liquid elements reinforce the lessons taught by the Gulfe and the Rock of
Reproach in a different key, for on their other side lies the final
"*Whirlepoole of decay*," a watery type of hell presided over by a "wrathfull *Neptune*" without a "puffe of wind" or spark of fire (xii.20, 22).

Neptune's realm at once recalls Mammon's Cave and foreshadows Acrasia's Bower, a smothering realm of illusion "disguiz'd/By that same wicked witch, to worke vs dreed" through the sensuous powers of imagination gone astray (xii.26). Like Neptune's Sea monsters, dreadful fish, and the sirens who lie ahead, this entire realm represents the pathless wandering of "Phantastes" separated from the two helpers who assist him in Alma's house, judgment and memory. Acrasia symbolically replaces them with two types of the fallen imagination, Genius with his wine bowl and Excesse with her false enchanted cup (xii.49, 56–57). Guyon casts the cup aside but proves as vulnerable to the wanton maidens who attract him by half-revealing, half-concealing their charms in Acrasia's fountain as he earlier had been to Neptune's sirens. These inhabit the outer banks of a fluid domain destined to shake the firmness of all his "elements," earthly, watery, airy, and fiery, since "nature" itself supports them:

> With that the rolling sea resounding soft,
>   In his big base them fitly answered,
>   And on the rocke the waues breaking aloft,
>   A solemne Meane vnto them measured,
>   The whiles sweet Zephirus lowd whisteled
>   His treble, a straunge kind of harmony;
>   Which *Guyons* senses softly tickeled,
>   That he the boateman bad row easily,
> And let him heare some part of their rare melody.
>
> (xii.33)

Earth and waves, wind and the heavenly "fire" of harmony all disguise the fact that the pleasant land he is about to enter is really filled by gross fogs, dull vapors, and desert "wastes" of ocean, which together hide "heuens chearefull," fiery face (xii.34).

As the sirens suggest, the intemperance of Acrasia's isle so confuses the primordial elements that they seem about to return to the symbolic Chaos from whence they issue in Spenser's first *Hymne*: "this great Vniuerse seemd one confused mas," extending from the birds of heaven to the beasts of the field. The latter "roard outrageously," no doubt stung by the lust and gluttony that Acrasia's "misrule" encourages (II.ix.34–39).[57] The fence separating their concupiscent chaos from her beautiful Bower is "but weake and thin;/Nought feard theyr force, that fortilage to win,/But wisedomes power, and temperaunces might/By which the mightiest things efforced bin" (II.xii.43). Hence Guyon and his Palmer are alone protected by the

inner "fences" that the Bower itself at once lacks and illusorily maintains by using art to disguise its nature. Acrasia's Art, "halfe in scorne/
Of niggard Nature, like a pompous bride/Did decke her, and too
lauishly adorne,/When forth from virgin bowre she comes in th'
early morne" (xii.50). The skill that should serve as nature's hand-
maiden has become her procurer, a point driven home by Acrasia's
venereal practice of what appears to be a form of temple prostitution.
Yet the watery weakness of her real allure is doubly betrayed both
by the lack of any real "fence" between her Bower and the elemental
and animal perversions just beyond and by Guyon's effortless destruction of her apparently immortal "art." Simply summoning his "rigour
pittlesse" to destroy her Bower's "goodly workmanship" in a sudden
"tempest of . . . wrathfulnesse," Guyon reveals that her attractive
"dungeon" is actually a sty—hence Grille's famous anger at losing
his "hoggish forme" (xii.83, 86). Guyon's sudden wind or "cool"
fire also helps explain why Acrasia is not destroyed like Orgoglio or
Maleger, but merely bound in "chaines of adamant" before being
deported to Gloriana's court (xii.82). A more fundamental reason
may be that soulless bodies are far more perishable than the flames
of eternal desire, which may be bound but not eradicated until the
true Bridegroom returns.

Yet where, finally, does this journey take us? If it is by now clear
that Spenser persistently graphs his moral plot on an elemental hierarchy, where does it lead? Certainly not to any final resting place,
palace, or even symbolic betrothal like the one that concludes Book
I, but only to an empty "desert" waste, "of the fayrest late, now
made the fowlest place" (II.xii.83). In part, this blankness signals the
"chastening" liberation of Acrasia's latest victim, the newly freed
Verdant, the redeemed or at least redeemable counterpart of Mordant,
the deadliest type of venereal intemperance. Verdant's release symbolically begins as soon as he and Acrasia are netted in the act of lust, a
net Spenser borrows from Vulcan's crafty exposure of the adulterous
Venus and Mars. Since the net is now wielded by Guyon *and* his
Palmer, it apparently signifies the vastly superior power not of craftsmanship but of the even more "learned" art of temperance, a rational
discipline taught by pilgrims like the Palmer to disciples who would
recuperate the "spoils" of lust, including the loss of warlike manhood
symbolized by Verdant's forsaken weapons and "sleeping praise"
(xii.80). Yet this skill stakes out no real space: Guyon and his friend
simply ready themselves to "depart, whilest wether serues and
winde," now that the seas have become temperate or serviceable
(xii.87). This mild weather certainly signals the victory of Temperance over Acrasia, but not, apparently, over any territory unless, as

Heninger suggests, it is the Platonic or Timean "place" of immortality, a perfect circle or " whole larger than the sum" of its parts," whose substance " is secondary in importance to the form itself."[58]

As for Guyon, Fowler and Fisher believe that he has completed a real path, not only between two fountains that have proved poisonous for either Mordant or Verdant, but also through a cosmic circle tracing the "descent of the soul down the Milky Way," or through all 360° of the zodiac. For Fisher, this circuit symbolizes Guyon's *imitatio Christi,* or "man's motion though all Time and all Space, the two concepts irrevocably joined in the metaphor of the Zodiac," while Fowler more simply describes it as fulfilling "a race or 'course' " analogous to "the fulfillment of an astronomical periodic cycle." If either is correct, Spenser's literary problem in drawing this "map" may be likened to Mercator's dilemma, that of making a two-dimensional map (with longitude and latitude) express the four dimensions of space/time. Mercator's solution was circular in one way—to imitate the three-dimensional globe, he placed gored global sections separated by star signs on a two-dimensional map—which according to Fisher, Spenser does in narrative time.[59] His identification of the Knight of Temperance with Christ seems much more dubious, but these conjectures at least suggest another, more satisfactory "circle" that might be drawn here. First, even if Acrasia's isle does represent a false summer—a captive and debauched "greenness," as Verdant's name suggests—marked by the winter solstice, Guyon's destruction of her Bower cannot represent a "putting off" of the flesh in preparation for the Platonic place of rebirth at the sign of Capricorn simply because he does *not* die but lives on into the next book.[60] There he is soon defeated by the more powerful Britomart, a knight whose "burning" but chaste love—a more truly Christlike virtue—surpasses his cool temperance. Meeting her after again taking leave of Alma in Book III (i.1), his circle is not actually complete until he learns the limits of his own virtue from the knight who first brings him "to grownd" through "secret powre vnseene" (III.i.7). While "death sate on the point" of Britomart's "enchaunted speare," Arthur again providentially comes to the rescue, but this time to assuage *Guyon's* "wrathfull will with reason," and to reconcile "goodly temperaunce" with "affection chaste" (III.i.9–12). If this coda for Guyon's quest indicates his true "rebirth" into higher knowledge, it would additionally indicate Spenser's final revision of Plato in representing this hero's accomplishment. As the philosopher taught, the immortal soul ascends to renewed life hereafter; yet as the Christian poet teaches, on earth its "reincarnations" into new spiritual phases or degrees demand *not* a forgetting but a remembering: in this case, a clear recollection of the spiraling stairs linking Temperance and Chaste Love on the way to their final mountain top, the heavenly ring of fire.[61]

The University of Memphis

Notes

I would like to thank Meredith Donaldson Clark for her useful bibliographical assistance, Professor Kenneth Borris for his very valuable editorial suggestions, and the late Professor Michael Fixler for numerous exchanges on the nature of the Platonic tetrad or fourfold. The anonymous readers of this essay should also be credited for their expert and meticulous objections and advice.

1. Jon A. Quitslund, *Spenser's Supreme Fiction: Platonic Natural Philosophy and "The Faerie Queene"* (Toronto: University of Toronto Press, 2001), 66, 69; Christopher Burlinson, *Allegory, Space, and the Material World in the Writings of Edmund Spenser* (Cambridge: D. S. Brewer, 2006), 41, 28, 29–30. I partially agree with Quitslund, but argue that the poem's "deep organizing structures" (66) are much more explicit than he indicates.

2. Joanne Woolway Grenfell, "Do Real Knights Need Maps? Charting Moral, Geographical, and Representational Uncertainty in Edmund Spenser's *The Faerie Queene*," in *Literature, Mapping, and the Politics of Space in Early Modern Britain,* ed. Andrew Gordon and Bernhard Klein (Cambridge: Cambridge University Press, 2001), 24–38; quoting 24, 26, 27.

3. Grenfell's argument rests on a common but mistaken belief that typology and allegory are mutually exclusive modes, a view promoted by Barbara Lewalski's *Protestant Poetics and the Seventeenth-Century Religious Lyric* (Princeton: Princeton University Press, 1979), but not supported by the majority of allegorists in theory or in practice. For a critique and revision of this view, see my study of Milton's epic, *The Ruins of Allegory:"Paradise Lost" and the Metamorphosis of Epic Convention* (Durham: Duke University Press, 1998), 18–20, 56–57. On the compatibility of the "mapping functions" of types, figures, and allegory, see Angus Fletcher, *Allegory: The Theory of a Symbolic Mode* (Ithaca: Cornell University Press, 1964), 179–80; on the concrete aspects of the mosaic or "cosmic image," see 70–146. On Spenser's "mapping" as a function of the opposition between the temple and the labyrinth, see Fletcher, *The Prophetic Moment: An Essay on Spenser* (Chicago: University of Chicago Press, 1971).

4. Spenser, *The Faerie Queene*, ed. A. C. Hamilton et al., 2nd ed. (Harlow: Longman, 2007); cited throughout.

5. Wayne Erickson, *Mapping "The Faerie Queene": Quest Structures and the World of the Poem* (New York: Garland, 1996), 5. On Erickson's use of MacCaffrey's "mapping" of a geography similarly based on horizontal or "unfolded" and vertical or "infolded" dimensions of human experience, see 62–66. Erickson also finds Northrop Frye's "outline of the [poem's] cosmic realms . . . accurate" (65), but much of his own mapping is generic rather than topographical.

6. John Demaray, *From Pilgrimage to History* (New York: AMS, 2006), 19, 33, 37–38.

7. Fletcher, *Allegory*, 87–146.

8. Peter M. Daly, *Literature in the Light of the Emblem*, 2nd ed. (Toronto: University of Toronto Press, 1998), 93. See also John Erskine Hankins, *Source and Meaning in Spenser's Allegory* (London: Oxford University Press, 1971), 24, 35–36, 55, 66–71. Along with commentaries on Virgil's *Aeneid*, Hankins cites Tasso's *Allegoria* from his *Gerusalemme Liberata* and chivalric journeys like Jean Cartigny's *Voyage of the Wandering Knight*, translated into English by William Goodyear in 1581. Dorothy Atkinson traces the extensive influence of the latter on Book I, Canto 10; see "The Wandering Knight, the Redcross Knight, and 'Miles Dei,' " *Huntington Library Quarterly* 7 (1944): 109–34.

9. Harry Berger, Jr., "The Spenserian Dynamics," in his *Revisionary Play: Studies in the Spenserian Dynamics* (Berkeley: University of California Press, 1988), 28. (This book chapter first appeared as a 1968 article.) On Digby, see Quitslund, *Supreme Fiction*, 13.

10. Caterina Albano, "Visible Bodies: Cartography and Anatomy," in *Literature, Mapping, and the Politics of Space*, 89–104, citing Crooke, *Microcomographia* (1615), 89.

11. Albano, "Visible bodies," 93, 95.

12. Rosemond Tuve, "Spenser and the *Zodiake of Life*," in her *Essays*, ed. Thomas P. Roche (Princeton: Princeton University Press, 1970), 65. Tuve cites the title page of Barnabe Googe's translation of *The Zodiake of Life* (London: Robert Robinson, 1588).

13. Derek Gregory, *Geographical Imaginations* (Oxford: Blackwell, 1994), 16.

14. John Hoskins, *Directions for Speech and Style*, ed. Hoyt H. Hudson (Princeton: Princeton University Press, 1935), 9–10.

15. Yates believed that Spenser's extremely physical interpretation of Aristotelian vice and virtue was assisted by the credence that Neoplatonists generally gave the Pseudo-Aristotelian *Problemata*, which outlines a similar ascent from "the sphere of earth through the spheres of the other three elements, thence up through the spheres of the planets to the higher divine realms." Frances Yates, *Elizabethan Neoplatonism Reconsidered: Spenser and Francesco Giorgi* (London: Warburg Institute, 1977), 12. She does not, however, cite chapter and verse, although she may be giving a very loose translation of Book XVII, "Problems Connected with Animate Objects," 1–3. See [Pseudo] Aristotle, *Problems*, trans. W. S. Hett (Cambridge, MA.: Harvard University Press, 1961), 365–67.

16. Quitslund, *Supreme Fiction*, 120–21, 240; Quitslund stresses the importance of Stephen Batman's revised encyclopedia and its Neoplatonic discussion of the four elements. See also Hankins, *Source and Meaning*, 235–39, which notes Ellrodt's useful corrections to earlier simplifications (238, 243, 263), but objects to his thesis that Spenser's Platonism is an amalgam of medieval and current popularizations, uninformed by learned Renaissance Neoplatonism until around the mid 1590s. For that thesis, see Robert Ellrodt, *Neoplatonism in the Poetry of Spenser* (Geneva: Droz, 1960).

17. Frances Yates, *The French Academies of the Sixteenth Century* (London: Warburg Institute, 1947), 3. Yates cites Pico from the first page of *Heptaplus*, his dedication to Lorenzo di Medici.

18. Yates, *French Academies,* 130.

19. Yates, *French Academies,* 110–11. Like Carol Kaske below, however, Yates finds the ultimate roots of these systems in biblical tradition, the Church Fathers, and Aquinas; see 110, 118.

20. Yates, *French Academies,* 112.

21. As Alastair Fowler similarly observes, "After his visit to Alma . . . Guyon shows little sign of any emotion that could be called irascible. . . . He resists concupiscence not by the substitution of any opposite passion, but by his integration." *Spenser and the Numbers of Time* (New York: Barnes & Noble, 1964), 107. This remark does, however, overlook Guyon's "tempest of . . . wrathfulness" in destroying the Bower (II.xii.83), although there he simply enlists irascibility to support reason against concupiscence, the essence of the Bower's attractions. This "balancing" again represents standard moral philosophical advice in the Renaissance, derived ultimately from Plato's *Republic.* There reason and thumos (the equivalent of irascibility) were supposed to combine in controlling unruly appetites. Borris suggests that the conclusion of Book II may imply Guyon finally falls short of this ideal, which would explain why Britomart easily defeats him in Book III (personal communication); but Guyon's soul also seems to have regained its internal harmony after the Bower is destroyed and he and his Palmer are about to set sail for home. In that case, his defeat would simply suggest the superiority of chaste love to temperance (see my conclusion).

22. Jean Seznec, *The Survival of the Pagan Gods: The Mythological Tradition and Its Place in Renaissance Humanism and Art,* trans. Barbara F. Sessions (New York: Pantheon, 1953), 126, 124.

23. Franz Boas, "Philosophies of Science in Florentine Platonism," in *Art, Science, and History in the Renaissance,* ed. Charles S. Singleton (Baltimore: Johns Hopkins University Press, 1967), 239–54; quoting 241.

24. S. K. Heninger, *Touches of Sweet Harmony: Pythagorean Cosmology and Renaissance Poetics* (San Marino: Huntington Library, 1974), 170. Heninger cites Pierre de la Primaudaye from *The French Academie,* trans. T. Bowes (London, 1586), 177.

25. Heninger, *Touches of Sweet Harmony,* 164.

26. Macrobius, *Commentary on the Dream of Scipio* [I.vi.23–28], trans. William H. Stahl (New York: Columbia University Press, 1952), 104–05. Cit. Heninger, *Touches of Sweet Harmony,* 164, 166.

27. Heninger, *Touches of Sweet Harmony,* 311–12, 341. La Primaudaye is cited, 343.

28. Ellrodt, *Neoplatonism,* 126. Ellrodt is somewhat inconsistent here, since he first insists that these ideas were drawn from Le Roy but then shows that both Le Roy and Natalis Comes make Plato's account of the birth of Love "relevant to ethics rather than cosmogony" (125). The problem is that, like Plato's account, Spenser's *Hymne* is actually more cosmogonic than ethical. For Ellrodt's chronological argument against Spenser's early Platonism (including the long parallel to the first *Hymne* in *Colin Clouts Come Home Againe*), see 13–24; but see note 16 above.

29. Heninger, *Touches of Sweet Harmony,* 313–16, 372; Quitslund, *Supreme Fiction,* 162. Quitslund is more concerned with the four elements as a *discordia concors* and with their contribution to constructing a natural cosmos in the poem (162–76).

30. Luigi Berra, *L'Accademia delle Notti Vaticane* (Rome, 1915), 48.

31. Burlinson, *Allegory, Space, and the Material World,* 17–18.

32. Citing Spenser's hymn from *The Complete Poetical Works of Spenser,* ed. R. E. Neil Dodge (Cambridge, MA.: Houghton Mifflin, 1908).

33. Ficino, Speech VI, *Commentary on Plato's Symposium on Love,* trans. Sears Jayne (Woodstock, CT.: Spring Publications, 1985), 107.

34. La Primaudaye, *French Academie* (1586*),* 301. Cit. Yates, *French Academies,* 126–27.

35. Heninger, *Touches of Sweet Harmony,* 356, 269. On the Pythagorean Y in both Virgil and Spenser, also see Hankins, *Source and Meaning,* 68.

36. Kenneth Borris, "Flesh, Spirit, and the Glorified Body: Spenser's Anthropomorphic Houses of Pride, Holiness, and Temperance," *Spenser Studies* 15 (2001): 17–52; quoting 23–24. See also 18–22. Hankins supports the same line of thought by noting that "The 'slimie nature' of the earth is the *limus terrae* of which God made Adam; Spenser assumes that it was also used for the other animals. His account seems to be an interpretation of Genesis in terms of Lucretius, who wrote that in their first creation animals emerged from 'wombs' in the earth, in the manner of plants." *Source and Meaning,* 285.

37. Carol Kaske, *Spenser and Biblical Poetics* (Ithaca: Cornell University Press, 1999), 37. She also discusses this technique's debt to the Church Fathers; see 35–37.

38. Borris, "Flesh, Spirit, and the Glorified Body," 38. Borris's scheme loosely parallels mine but outlines a tripartite rather than a four-fold set of oppositions and omits the four elements. Aside from the *Timaeus,* commonly recognized sources for both systems derive from *Phaedrus* 246a–48b, 253c–56e, and *Republic* 440e–44e.

39. Walter R. Davis, "The Houses of Mortality in Book II of *The Faerie Queene,*" *Spenser Studies* 2 (1981): 121–40. Davis's treatment of these episodes is highly compatible with but not identical to the patterns suggested here. Instead of a simple fourfold scheme, he uses a combination of quadratic and triadic patterns, the former based on a "landscape of action divided about equally between land and water, and the Pyrochlean and Cymochlean elements" (127), which I relate to fire and air but he does not. He does, however, similarly relate these landscape patterns to the ascending order of the vegetative, sensitive (animal or emotional) and intellectual souls (123), to which I would add the heavenly spirit of fire, which Davis instead discusses in Jungian terms (126). He is also more directly concerned with relating these patterns to the four levels of allegory, an aspect of the ascent implicit but not developed here.

40. In this insight Davis precisely anticipates me: he notes that Mammon's "four rooms are governed by the [four] elements" which he perverts but Alma refines, and that "The House of Mammon is both a summary of the world he [Guyon] has experienced in the adventures of the first six cantos and a dim type or *figura* of the world he will grasp toward the end." See "The Houses of Mortality," 134–37 (quoting 135, 136–37).

41. James R. Fisher, "Certaine Signes of the Zodiac: The Shape of Spenser's Allegory in Book II of *The Faerie Queene,*" *Constructions,* 8 (1993): 10–14, 20, 24–25; quoting 14. Fisher's system is at once an extension and a simplification of Alastair Fowler's astrological analysis of Book II in *Spenser and the Numbers of Time,* 80–121, which takes into account not just the signs of the zodiac but their houses, presiding

deities, and numerical identifications. Many of Fowler's points are valuable, but they often seem over-complicated and too unwieldy for literary allegory.

42. Fisher, "Signes of the Zodiac," 14, 18; Tuve, "Spenser and *The Zodiake of Life*," 67.

43. Hankins, *Source and Meaning*, 55–56, 11. Fowler agrees that Alma and her Castle represent Spenser's vision "of sanctified human nature"; see *Spenser and the Numbers of Time*, 87–88, quoting 88.

44. Fisher, "Signes of the Zodiac," 12, 24, 30. Fisher simply regards Maleger as a type of Sagittarius (10), but since this sign is a "positive" fire sign, his negativity fully makes sense only in combination with the "earthiness" of Scorpio. These two signs are also the binary opposites of Alma's signs, Virgo and Libra.

45. Fowler, *Spenser and the Numbers of Time*, 94–101. Aquarius is of course the "water-pourer," but Fowler shows that Ficino's *De vita coelitus comparanda*, III.v, regards it as the "airiest" of signs (96). In its driest or most malign aspect, it also the most inimical to life. This association seems somewhat problematic since for Spenser, temperance *fosters* life, but Fowler seems to think that its saturnine qualities have a homeopathic effect on intemperance (101). The point is interesting, but I believe that associating Guyon with sanguinity rather than melancholy makes more sense (see below).

46. Quitslund, *Supreme Fiction,* 151.

47. Fisher gives a similar interpretation without noting the reversal whereby Guyon must ascend, *not* descend (as he assumes) like Phedon, "through a symbolic Chain of the Elements" representing the tetrad of wrath, jealousy, grief, and love. "Certain Signes of the Zodiac," 21.

48. For the common gloss on "Arthur as the instrument of heavenly grace [come] to rescue the fallen hero," see Hamilton, ed., *Faerie Queene*, 225n (on II.viii.1). Arthur's association with fire is clearly established in Book I. His armor is compared to the "glauncing light of *Phoebus* brightest ray" (I.vii.29) and his shield to a "light . . . that heuens light did pas,/Such blazing brightnesse through the ayer threw,/That eye mote not the same endure to vew" (I.viii.19). In the next stanza, the "flashing beames of that sunshiny shield" blind Arthur's enemies like the blaze of the sun (I.viii.20). In Book II and beyond, he continues to serve as the "fire" of divine vengeance.

49. Davis, "Houses of Mortality," 134.

50. On Alma as both the perfected type of the temperate body and the "home" of Guyon's feminine *anima*, Shamefastnesse, see Davis, "Houses of Mortality," 123–25; on Guyon's need for a feminine supplement in postmodern terms, see David Lee Miller, *The Poem's Two Bodies: The Poetics of the 1590 "Faerie Queene"* (Princeton: Princeton University Press, 1988), 209–14.

51. See Borris, "Flesh, Spirit, and the Glorified Body," 34–38.

52. Hankins, *Source and Meaning*, 270, citing Ficino's *Commentarium in Philebum,* appendix xxi; and Vincent de Beauvais, *Speculum Naturale,* in *Opera* (Douai, 1624), xxiv.31 (1733A).

53. On its "golden squire" or square, see Piotr Sadowski, "Spenser's 'golden squire' and 'golden meane': Numbers and Proportions in Book II of *The Faerie Queene*," *Spenser Studies* 14 (2000): 107–31.

54. Yates, *Elizabethan Neoplatonism Reconsidered*, 7–8.

55. For an extended discussion and defense of this interpretation, see Hankins, *Source and Meaning*, 84–87, which anticipates my rejection of the common gloss on the lake as baptism. To me this seems extremely unlikely since Maleger is that part of the human "animal" that *cannot* be baptized, the earthbound "old Adam" who refuses grace.

56. See Fowler, *Spenser and the Numbers of Time*, 94–95, for a fuller exploration of this theme.

57. One meaning of her name (from the Greek *a-kratos*) is anti-rule, although in Aristotelian terms she also stands for incontinence.

58. In both Christian and Platonic thought, "The circular form . . . makes the clearest and fullest statement about the infinity and eternity" of God and his divine plan. Heninger, *Touches of Sweet Harmony*, 372.

59. Fowler, *Spenser and the Numbers of Time*, 85, 81, quoting 81; Fisher, "Certaine Signes of the Zodiac," 25–26, 17.

60. For the alternative reading, see Fisher, "Certaine Signes of the Zodiac," 31; Fowler, *Spenser and the Numbers of Time*, 99.

61. On this theme, see also John C. Bean, "Cosmic Order in *The Faerie Queene*: From Temperance to Chastity," *SEL* 17.1 (Winter, 1977): 67–79. Bean adopts a Platonic approach mainly through Ficino, but he is not concerned with Platonic circles or elements.

JON QUITSLUND

Melancholia, Mammon, and Magic

Focusing on Guyon's encounter with Mammon, this essay examines melancholia in *The Faerie Queene* in relation to Marsilio Ficino's *Three Books on Life*. Ficino recognizes melancholia as a serious malady, but he also claims that some melancholics are extraordinarily intelligent and creative. In Spenser's poem, some melancholy characters (Despair, Mammon, and Maleger, for example) are dangerous, while others (Phantastes, the youthful sage in Alma's castle, and the poem's most idealistic lovers) appear in a more positive light. Ficino traces the causes of a melancholy temperament to astrological factors. Saturn's influence predisposes an individual to inquire into the depths of experience, aspiring also to self-transcending knowledge and power. The ill effects of black bile can be tempered by habits that nourish the vital *spiritus* and connect the human microcosm with beneficial daemons and angels. Describing heavenly influences that can be captured to cure melancholia, Ficino stresses the importance of Phoebus Apollo, Venus, and Jupiter, the "Three Graces." Two engravings by Dürer, *St. Jerome in His Study* and *Melencolia I*, provide pictorial analogues to architectonically significant passages in Books I and II of *The Faerie Queene*; the pattern of textual echoes and contrasts continues in Book III. A Platonic program emerges from details in Guyon's encounter with Mammon, his sojourn in Alma's castle, and his testing in the Bower of Bliss. This sequence is capped by all that is revealed in the Garden of Adonis canto (*FQ* III.vi) under the aegis of the three Graces.

Spenser Studies: A Renaissance Poetry Annual, Volume XXIV, Copyright © 2009 AMS Press, Inc. All rights reserved.

It's always night, or we wouldn't need light.
—Thelonious Monk[1]

L IKE " 'ROUND MIDNIGHT," his best known composition,
Thelonious Monk's dictum speaks to a cross-cultural basis for
the complex emotions called melancholia and the deep involve-
ment of those emotions with creativity. With Monk's words
in mind, I will turn toward some landmarks in Renaissance
culture in which the dynamic interplay of night and light is explored.

This essay offers a wide-ranging discussion of melancholia in
The Faerie Queene. By a circuitous route, it will arrive at a
focus on Sir Guyon in his encounter with Mammon and the
narrative's descent into Mammon's underworld. My argument
proceeds first through Marsilio Ficino's *Three Books on Life,*
placing Ficino's diagnosis of the consequences of being born
under Saturn within the framework of a treatise that covers
several other topics, all of which offer ways to counter the ill
effects of severe melancholia. I will argue that Ficino's treatise
helps us to understand *The Faerie Queene,* and that his rationale
for therapeutic magic should be taken seriously by readers of
Spenser. I remain committed to the proposition, advanced tentatively in *Spenser's Supreme Fiction,* that "the poet's worldmaking and the procedures of a magician whose power comes from
the daemon Love may be much alike."[2] I will say at the outset,
however, that anyone who embraces the possibility of therapeutic magic, along with any poet who aims to move readers toward
virtuous action, must also confront the possibility of failure and
a return of the melancholy theme, "It's always night."

I

Most readers of *The Faerie Queene* are acquainted with melancholia and recognize the traits of that distemper in several of
the poem's characters, but the subject has not received a deep
treatment specific to Spenser.[3] As an obvious trait in major
and minor characters on the dark side of the poem (Night,
Aesculapius, Despair, Mammon, Huddibras, Maleger, and Malbecco), melancholia is presented to us as something to be feared,
and to be avoided if possible. The poem's melancholy lovers
(Timias, Marinell, Amoret, Florimell, and Priscilla) receive sympathy in their predicaments, but they are somewhat culpable,

never glamorous in their suffering. Redcrosse, Una, Arthur, and Britomart experience melancholy at times, but they are not overcome by it. And last but not least, since Merlin's role in the poem resembles the poet's own, when the great seer looks into the future with Britomart and Glauce his "spirite" is first enabled, then in the end overcome in a "halfe extatick stoure," by a prophetic *furor* that is akin to melancholia (III.iii.21 and 50).

The figure of Phantastes, one of the "three honorable sages" (II.ix.47) lodged in the turret of Alma's castle, is "full of melancholy," and a special case. He occupies a position of prestige, yet his appearance—"Bent hollow beetle browes, sharpe staring eyes,/That mad or foolish seemd"—is as grotesque as Mammon's, indicating that he was "borne with ill disposed skyes,/When oblique *Saturne* sate in the house of agonyes" (52). Fowler observes that while Saturn's influence is to be expected in a book dominated by Aquarius, "we are hardly prepared to find it exerted in the Castle of Alma itself" (*Numbers of Time* 101). I follow Hamilton's commentary in correlating the three sages and their rooms with the three higher faculties of the soul (fantasy or foresight, judgment or understanding, and memory), and also with the future, present, and past, all constituting an allegory of Prudence, the intellectual virtue most closely allied with the moral virtue of Temperance.[4]

What is melancholia, as manifested in a figure so "mad or foolish" as Phantastes seems to be, doing in an allegory of Prudence, and what could the wild energy in his chamber possibly contribute to the future-oriented education of Guyon and Arthur? Melancholia typically afflicts older people, and it is surprising to find it embodied in a young man with a hyperactive imagination. The unnamed figure in the central chamber tempers the younger and older sages associated with the imagined future and the past. More than the others, he stands for Spenser's model poet, the "goodly reason" who keeps "All artes, all science, all Philosophy" (53) in order, but his mediating role requires the participation of imagination and memory. No single moment and no part in Spenser's narrative universe stands alone. The rationalizing artifice that puts intellectual faculties in three distinct rooms partially obscures the fact that consciousness functions within a continuum. Guyon and Arthur both desire to be disciples of reason alone, but to do so would be to opt out of their narratives. The melancholy Phantastes possesses an undisciplined energy that stimulates rational judgment (and Guyon and Arthur), although this energy can also be bewildering and subversive.

I think that Phantastes, in his chamber filled with "idle thoughts and fantasies,/Deuices, dreames, opinions vnsound,/Shewes, visions,

sooth-sayes, and prophesies" (51), represents a part of Spenser's experience as a poet that in the context of Book II he could only represent
in caricature.[5] Isabel MacCaffrey saw in these stanzas "one of Spenser's most visible efforts to defuse the potentially diabolic energy of
poetry by advertising imagination's inherent duplicity."[6] For Spenser,
and perhaps for Sidney as well, when we consider practice along
with theory, the imagination's *eikastic* power is indistinguishable from
phantastic energies until judgment imposes its second thoughts.[7] And
judgment, like Guyon for most of his journey, is pedestrian. In Phantastes, melancholia is not morose and withdrawn, but young and full
of curiosity. Considering Phantastes and looking forward from Book
II to Books III and IV, MacCaffrey observes, "The counter-rational
power of love and the counter-factual power of imagination are
close kin."

In his thorough discussion of sadness, mourning, and melancholy
in Book I, Douglas Trevor treats sadness and melancholy as antithetical traits: sadness is characteristic of a soul properly oriented to God
and its heavenly destiny, while melancholy is a disorder originating
in the body that may fatally infect the soul.[8] While he recognizes that
due to Marsilio Ficino's influence, melancholia was regarded in some
quarters as evidence of intellectual profundity even though it was a
dangerous condition, Trevor dissociates Spenser from that way of
thinking: the poet "nowhere offers even a provisional endorsement
of genial melancholy" ("Sadness" 348, n. 24).

On the contrary, I believe that the solemn sadness attributed to
Redcrosse and to many other characters—an emotion seen also in
the poet's self-image—is closely akin to what Trevor calls "genial"
melancholy. With a careful reading of parts of Ficino's *Three Books
on Life* as my foundation, I will propose that coming to terms with
melancholia, even in its morbid form, was central to Spenser's endeavor in *The Faerie Queene*. I will examine Guyon's encounter with
Mammon and the trial of his temperament in Mammon's cave as a
test of this thesis.

II

Ficino's *Three Books on Life* (usually referred to hereafter as *De Vita*),
first published in Florence in 1489, found a large audience across
Europe during the sixteenth century.[9] The book's success was partly
due to the enterprise of printers, and to translators who produced

versions in German, French, and Italian, but most of the credit must
go to Ficino himself, even if he never imagined how many readers
he would find for his encyclopedic treatise. Addressed in its opening
pages to the hard core of the book-buying public, the growing numbers of *litterati* and *studiosi*, and somewhat glamorizing their chosen
way of life, *De Vita* spoke to the aspirations and anxieties intrinsic
to all aspects of humanism. It offered good counsel and profound
learning, tempered by serious play—less ironic than the lively wit of
Erasmus, but imaginative enough to engage its readers in speculative
consideration of human nature and the cosmos.

In chapter i of *De Vita*, the opening sentence is addressed to "anyone who enters upon that rough, arduous, and long journey which
barely, at the last, by continual hardship leads through to the high
temple of the nine Muses." Claiming to be "the first to attend as a
physician sick and invalid scholars" (109), Ficino proceeds quickly in
subsequent chapters to identify the insidious hazards faced by his
acutely self-aware readers. Tacitly, he assumes that they will be free to
pursue self-directed quests (a rosy scenario that would-be intellectuals
down through the centuries have been quite willing to accept); he
dwells instead on the factors affecting health and happiness that self-
discipline and intellectual inquiry can anticipate and attempt to control. Ficino's treatise was thus perfectly suited to a social world in
which care of the self was a central concern. In all its emphasis on
self-fashioning in accordance with the ideals of an elite culture, *De
Vita* has much in common with Spenser's *Faerie Queene*. Ficino's
voice, that of a guide who combines the qualities of a mentor and a
physician, resembles that of Guyon's guide, the Palmer.[10]

De Vita is a hybrid text containing much, especially in Book III,
that would be out of place in a standard medical treatise. Ficino's
aim seems to be to address everything under the sun, and the high
heavens too, that concerns the health, enlightenment, and long life
of his readers. In a brief chapter ii, after surveying the vital organs of
the body and emphasizing that they must be cared for, he proceeds
to scold "the priests of the Muses" for their neglect of "that instrument with which they are able in a way to measure and grasp the
whole world. This instrument," he goes on to say, "is the spirit,
which is defined by doctors as a vapor of the blood—pure, subtle,
hot, and clear. After being generated by the heat of the heart out of
the more subtle blood, it flies to the brain; and there the soul uses it
continually for the exercise of the interior as well as the exterior
senses" (111). As later chapters make clear, this *spiritus* not only connects the soul and intellect with all parts of the body, but is the
instrument through which external forces, from the physical world

and all the spheres beyond the moon, can act either beneficially or harmfully upon the microcosm of an individual human life.[11]

Chapter ii distinguishes between three types of spirit: natural (enabling the liver to produce blood), vital (generated in the heart and carried with blood through the body), and animal (the more sublime, rising to and residing in the brain). When he says that through this spirit we "are able in a way to measure and grasp the whole world," Ficino hints that human power is not limited to perception of and discourse about the cosmos (measurement), but extends to the management (Ficino's verb is *capere*, to grasp or capture) of cosmic forces through magical doctrines and practices. Books I and II will deal with conventional medical methods for care of the body and spirit, including diet and exercise; Book III, *De Vita coelitus comparanda*, will reach higher and capture more of the visible and invisible universe, "obtaining life from the heavens."

As everyone in medieval and Renaissance studies knows, health and long life depend upon maintaining a harmonious mixture of the four humors. All of us are inclined to some excesses, and it was common knowledge in early modern and earlier centuries that astrological factors and unhealthy habits predisposed individuals to specific forms of intemperance. Ficino observes that scholars are apt to neglect physical exercise and to be "busy [*negotiosus*] in the brain and the mind" (113). In their *otium* they produce an excess of phlegm, while their *negotium* creates an excess of black bile, the melancholy humor. The effects of phlegm are simple (it "dulls and suffocates the intellect"), and easily remedied by exercise, diet, and hygiene. The causes and effects of melancholy are more profound, and they require more elaborate attention.

Why are the *litterati* so prone to melancholia? The three causes of their condition—celestial, natural, and human—can be seen as a vicious circle, but once it is understood, remedies can be found. The first order of causes, celestial, will be evident in a natal horoscope and the alignment of planets day by day: influences from Mercury and Saturn favor the development of curiosity, perseverance in the investigation of doctrines, and a retentive memory, but the same influences produce a cold and dry complexion, given to melancholia (113). The cause that Ficino terms "natural" pertains to the effects upon the soul itself of "pursuit of the sciences, especially the difficult ones," and of contemplation that turns inward "to the center of individual subjects," then "carries one to the contemplation of whatever is highest" (113–15). In Ficino's description of intense study and contemplation, black bile is associated with the center of things and the depths of the earth, but also with Saturn, the most distant of planets. An excess of the melancholy humor figures as both cause and effect of the soul's activity, and it both depresses and exalts consciousness.

Ficino recognizes melancholia as a malady, a miserable state that may be dangerous and require a physician's attention, but he also claims that some melancholics are extraordinarily intelligent and creative, not in spite but because of their distempered constitution. In chapter v he discriminates between praiseworthy and deplorable forms of melancholy; his emphasis falls on the positive benefits of the disposition. Citing Aristotle (actually pseudo-Aristotle, in the misattributed *Problems*), he claims "that all those who are renowned in whatever faculty you please have been melancholics." Plato and Democritus are quoted in support of a theme developed in many of Ficino's other works: "intellectually outstanding" efforts in poetry and other endeavors involve disciplined effort but also require the *furor* that accompanies melancholia (117).

After distinguishing between "natural" melancholy and the dehumanized condition produced by "adustion" (when black bile is kindled and burned up), Ficino observes, "Only that black bile which we call natural, therefore, leads us to judgment and wisdom—but not always." The best is easily corrupted into the worst of conditions. A gift of the heavens and the result of prolonged effort can become a cursed state: "we hope for nothing, we fear everything, and 'it is weariness to look at the dome of the sky' "—quoting from Virgil's description of *infelix Dido* (*Aeneid* IV 451). Unlike the other humors, black bile is unstable, tending toward the extremes of hot and cold (119–21).

We have already seen how important the spirits are to Ficino's understanding of the human organism and its health. Adustion degrades or consumes the corporeal spirit produced by the blood, resulting in madness if not controlled. The later chapters in Book I describe habits and choices that will promote vitality, and chapter xxvi, the last, advises "lovers of truth" to nourish their "incorporeal spirit, i.e., the intellect," with philosophy which prepares the mind for the light of religious truth. Those in possession of a "serene mind," living "in the light of God, which is always and everywhere present for us," are able to rise above melancholia (161–63).

Book II, *De Vita longa*, composed after the completion of Book III, adds to the discussion of diet and daily habits in Book I and brings the entire treatise nearly into balance: Books I and II together are almost as long as Book III.[12] In the attention given to planetary influences and nurture of the medical *spiritus*, Book II provides a bridge to Ficino's more philosophical and esoteric concerns in Book

III. In chapters xiv and xv, Book II is enlivened by Ficino's summoning first Venus, then Mercury, to address his aging readers. From *alma Venus*, the goddess invoked memorably by Lucretius (and by a tormented lover in Spenser's Temple of Venus, *FQ* IV.x.44–47), we hear a *iocosum oraculum* and a recommendation to enjoy gardens and green things of all kinds, since they delight the eye and nourish vital spirits (203–09). Mercury interrupts, asking the elderly (among whom Ficino includes himself) why they should listen to Venus, *semper puella*, when what they need is a broader understanding of the role of reason, the five senses and five ages of man, and all the planetary influences that may lengthen their lives (209–15).

Venus and Saturn are antithetical influences, and both tempt us to excess. In chapter xvi, Ficino drives the point home: "from opposite sides Venus and Saturn ensnare the flight of our spirit. She through her pleasure lures to external things, while he through his, recalls us to the internal. If they move the spirit at about the same time, they distract and dissipate it" (215). "The best discipline," he says, "is to recall to the mean those declining to either side through certain pursuits and remedies of Phoebus and of Jupiter, who are the middle planets between Saturn and Venus" (217).

These rudimentary references to the zodiac's cycle of influences become an elaborate system of astrological calculation and sympathetic magic in the course of Book III. The influence of Saturn and of black bile is placed in a broad context; the benefits to be derived from Phoebus, Jupiter, and Venus (the "three Graces"), touched upon in Book II, are described at length in Book III. Rather than being regarded deterministically as a gift that is apt to turn into a curse, birth under Saturn becomes an occasion to develop mastery of occult cosmic forces, affirming the freedom of adept and prudent individuals to shape their own ends.

Readers of the *Three Books on Life* today encounter a worldview and attitudes toward a healthy quality of life that may seem familiar in some respects, although much of Ficino's deductive reasoning and Neoplatonic lore remains inert: hard to comprehend even with Carol Kaske's resourceful introduction and notes, and unbelievable even after being understood. This is especially true of Book III. If we assume that Spenser was acquainted with Ficino's *De Vita* (a hypothesis worth testing), what was he likely to have thought about Ficino's most esoteric propositions, and in general, his "magical thinking"? There is no definitive answer to this question: everything depends on how one reads Spenser's poetry and the cultural matrix in which one places it. Some aspects of Ficino's Neoplatonism appear to have been irrelevant to Spenser's interests as a poet, but I believe that several of his fundamental principles (among them, the rationale for what D. P. Walker has called "spiritual" magic) illuminate subtle and significant features of *The Faerie Queene.*

Strange as they may seem today, most of the basic ideas developed in *De Vita coelitus comparanda* were consonant with mainstream culture in Ficino's time and over the course of the sixteenth century. That the little world of human nature is hierarchically arranged and linked to the cosmos by elaborate correspondences was a truth universally acknowledged among educated people; medical opinion, ethical and political discourse, the plots and metaphors in literature, and religious devotion all worked within that framework. Ficino's logic and his appeals to venerable authorities only pushed the cultural envelope, becoming over-ingeniouss at times and on rare occasions flirting with heterodoxy.

"Since the heavens have been constructed according to a harmonic plan and move harmonically and bring everything about by harmonic sounds and motions, it is logical that through harmony alone not only human beings but all things below are prepared to receive, according to their abilities, celestial things." This sentence opens chapter xxii, one in a series that explains in detail how *coelestia* are "captured" by things below (362–63). Similar statements appear at several points in Book III. In the universe as Ficino describes it, the heavens are spacious, yet not vast. The principles of analogy and mediation provide for continuity from top to bottom,[13] and everything is in motion, giving and taking vitality from one level to another. Mobility is the very essence of life throughout the cosmos. At the end of *De Vita*, in a letter to three friends, "most beloved brothers in the hunt for truth," Ficino observes poignantly, "Nothing is more expansive [*amplius*] than the heavens, nothing more vital. Conversely, the earth is very small and it has the least life of anything in the cosmos. Finally, since we live by heaven and in time, the more widely we absorb these, the more and the longer do we live" (405).

How is the capture and absorption of celestial vitality made possible? The potential for this resides in the nature of things; that potentiality is carried through pregnancy and labor by art. Nature herself is an *artifex* and a sorceress, using the attraction of masculine to feminine to bind everything together (385–87). In all the arts, from farming to medicine to magic, their human practitioners are imitators of nature. Within the human microcosm and the cosmos surrounding and informing it, the basis for communication and mobility is the *spiritus*, intermediary between physical bodies and their souls. The magical operations from which, according to Ficino, we can derive both physical and spiritual benefits are only the most disciplined and specialized activities involving this intermediary agent. As Gary Tomlinson has shown, "the spirit was the nexus of perception. On it the stimuli of the external senses were impressed as images or phantasms. There they were regarded and judged by the soul in the act of sensation. Moreover, in response to them the soul conceived its own purer images or phantasms; this was the function of the imagination or phantasy."[14]

Magic, then, belongs in a continuum with aesthetic experience, whether in response to natural beauty or to art. "While experiencing, therefore, the motion of shining water, of clear air, of a fire that is not too close, and of the sky, you will receive the motion of the life of the world, if you yourself also move lightly, and in almost the same way—executing as many gyrations as you can without dizziness, traversing the celestial bodies with your eyes, and revolving them in your mind" (291). Those celestial bodies promote the natural, vital, and animal spirits' healthy functions in us, since planetary influences were active in our formation: Jupiter and the sun beginning in the first phase of fetal development, Venus in sexuality, and Mercury (with Apollo, the sun) "insofar as it [i.e., the animal spirit] ministers sense and imagination to the mind" (293). Saturn, of course, is a special case: "Through the influence of Saturn alone, the substance of spirit is properly neither created nor recreated at any time, but it is always recalled by him from the outer to the innermost faculties and subjects and often from the lowest to the highest. For this reason he helps one contemplate the more secret and the higher subjects" (295).

The mixed blessings of Saturn and melancholy had been the focus of anxious attention in Book I of *De Vita*; in Book III, Ficino contemplates "the more secret and the higher subjects" in order to obtain powerful remedies for his own and other scholars' constitutional vulnerability. His efforts to explain how images benefit those who contemplate them, and how words and songs elevate the spirits of those who hear them, take us to the heart of Book III and may shed some light on Spenser's practices as a poet.

The images whose reputed power Ficino analyzes in chapter xx are of two kinds: votive statues representing specific celestial influences and inscribed gems worn as talismans. Ficino admits to some uncertainty about their effectiveness and says, "I prefer medicines to images by far," but he adds, "Yet the Arabs and the Egyptians ascribe so much power to statues and images fashioned by astronomical and magical art that they believe the spirits of the stars are enclosed in them" (351). Here and at other points in Book III, Ficino is a sympathetic interpreter of esoteric doctrines that he *wants* to believe are true, or at least not in conflict with the truth. "The Arabs say that when we fashion images rightly, our spirit, if it has been intent upon the work and upon the stars through imagination and emotion, is joined together with the very spirit of the world and with the rays of the stars through which the world-spirit acts" (350–53).

If it is important that the fashioner of an image has been "intent [*attentissimus*]," so must its user believe fervently in its power: "it is my opinion that the intention of the imagination [*imaginationis intentionem*] does not have its power so much in fashioning images or medicines as it does in applying or swallowing them" (353). Like the light bulb in a therapist's hands, the spirit must *want* to change. Kaske's note on the term *intentio* (452–53, n. 7) is helpful here: I take it that, stimulated by the well-fashioned image, an attentive imagination is activated to transmit, via the animal spirit, an emotion-laden image to the mind's higher faculties. Love, faith, and hope are all involved in assimilating benefits derived by art from the world-spirit: the individual is by no means a passive recipient of the stars' (or the magician's) designs.

Chapter xxi adds to what has been said about images an account of "the power of words and song for capturing celestial benefits." Ficino gives words, song, and instrumental music a privileged and pivotal place in the ascending order of seven human activities that connect our lives with heavenly benefits: they are "rightly dedicated to Apollo whose greatest invention is music." Conveniently, the sun occupies the middle position in the seven planetary spheres. The materials of lesser types of medicine, such as stones, plants, and ointments, are assigned to the moon, Mercury, and Venus. Music and poetry are followed in the hierarchy by "the strong concepts of the imagination—forms, motions, passions—which suggest the force of Mars," then by deliberations of human reason (aligned with Jupiter), and finally, in Saturn's sphere, we come to "the more remote and simple operations of the understanding" (357). Ficino's aim here, and again in chapter xxii (363–65), is to connect human consciousness with a universe perceived as harmonious and open to upward movement.

The arts sacred to Apollo rely on imitation. Ficino reinterprets this truism quite radically; for him the musician and the poet, like participants in a ceremony or ritual, are imitating the orderly life to be found in the world-spirit or (if the focus of an invocation is more specific) in the daemon associated with a specific planet. "We strive to adapt ourselves to this multifarious and occult influence by the same studied methods we use every day to make ourselves fit to receive in a healthy manner the perceivable light and heat of the

Sun" (357). And one imitative act produces another: Ficino expects the singer's example to prompt his audience to imitate his intention and be similarly inspired. The mysterious effects of music, and especially of song, are evidence of "something approaching a life of its own" within the artistic performance (Tomlinson 111).[15] It consists of "air, hot or warm, still breathing and somehow living; like an animal, it is composed of certain parts and limbs of its own and not only possesses motion and displays passion but even carries meaning like a mind, so that it can be said to be a kind of airy and rational animal" (359). This "animal" is endowed by its creator with the capacity to serve as an intermediary, between heaven and earth and from person to person. It may be relevant here that in schematic representations of the four elements and four humors, air is aligned with the sanguine humor, opposite earth and black bile.

When Ficino reintroduces Saturn as a participant in the world-system interacting with human lives, he denies that songs can be used to capture that planet's benign influence and avoid its adverse effects. The moon, Mars, and Saturn "have voices but not songs"; Saturnian voices "are slow, deep, harsh, and plaintive" (361). We can seek health and support from Jupiter, who "tempers" Saturn (365–67), but as Ficino says in the next chapter, "let us first of all search out the inclination [*instinctum*] of our nature and of our daemon" (375). Saturn is one of several determinants of that inclination. Chapter xxiii introduces two guardian figures, the *genius* that represents, in the form of an external spirit, an individual's innate qualities (the *ingenium* that may either prosper or encounter adversity in later life), and the "daemon," another spirit, representing qualities appropriate to the profession or way of life that the individual has chosen.[16] Ficino uses the distinction between genius and daemon to counsel against pursuing a career that leads to conflicts between these two guardians (371–75).

With a subtle message to convey, Ficino follows a circuitous path, often reiterating a theme in order to enlarge its range of reference. Chapter xxiv, while it is not the last in the book, includes a valedictory message to his fellow "*litterati, Musarum cultores.*" He puts their Saturnian inclination in context: they are "primarily [*imprimis*, which can mean "in the first place"] Mercurial, and Solar besides." Those who excel in "eloquence, in amiability, in dignity, in charm" owe those qualities to both Venus and Apollo. "A person who is more inclined to laws or natural and public philosophy, should be aware that he has Jupiter for a patron." Saturn's influence has dwindled, it seems, to that of an *éminence grise*. In a celebratory mood, Ficino invokes Apollo and Bacchus, jointly the creators of wine. The spiritual body, he says, should be "nourished with its own four subtler elements": wine in place of earth, odor of wine rather than water, song and sound for air, sunlight for fire. In keeping with their allegiance to Apollo, he urges his brothers to "live in the light," and "waking or sleeping, always breathe living air, air living with light" (377–79).

De Vita begins in gloom, stressing the isolation and the risks to health involved in an introspective life; it ends in sunlight and camaraderie. Ficino goes to great lengths to overcome the earthbound inertia that can result from Saturn's influence, and to enliven the aspirations and intellectual zeal that also characterize melancholia. Through his doctrine of intermediary spirits, generated within the human body and capable of communicating with analogous spirits in the heavens, Ficino provides a foundation—not in demonstrable facts but in respectable authorities and rational argument—for enthusiastic belief in human agency and creative potential. As represented in *De Vita*, especially in Book III, human beings (those best equipped by nature and nurture, at least) are free agents; their knowledge is power, and the world in which they find themselves will be generous in response to their actions. Human nature is porous, open to influence and dependent on tenuous connections. Those influences are not all beneficial, and success in life depends upon courting the benefits while tempering the adverse effects as much as possible. Ficino implies that all experience has a spiritual dimension; experience is also culturally mediated, based in nature and the conditions of embodiment but shaped by various arts. Imagination is a weathervane: it can be set spinning by turbulent humors, but it also issues directives to discursive reason. Reason in turn can act in ways that discipline the imagination and connect it with external spiritual presences.

Ficino had prepared for the sun-filled conclusion of *De Vita coelitus comparanda* near its beginning. In chapter iv he emphasizes that "all the celestial goods" can be drawn into the spirit by relaxing in the sun—"with this caution, however, that you should carefully avoid drying yourself out under the summer's heat" (259–61). Chapters iv through vii (259–77) explain how Jupiter, Phoebus Apollo, and Venus, with the moon in a favorable aspect, provide the most balanced and beneficial influences on our natural, vital, and animal spirits: the triad of Jupiter, the sun, and Venus are, in Ficino's astrological frame of reference, the three Graces. I think that these heavenly influences enliven the dancing figures on Spenser's Mount Acidale, summoned by Colin's bagpipe and encountered by a suspicious Calidore. The three planets' cornucopia of "all the gifts of grace and

chastitee" (III.vi.2) is more explicitly identified in the natal horoscope provided for Belphoebe and Amoret (discussed below, page
349). Both the Garden of Adonis canto and the episode on Mount
Acidale take us to the source of Spenser's poetic inspiration, associated with Venus and her benevolent daemonic allies.

I will argue that Ficino's astrologically based therapeutic magic
belongs in the ideological matrix supporting our poet's creative process. I am not asserting that any episode in *The Faerie Queene* offers
to its readers the kind of musical magic that Ficino recommends in
Book III of *De Vita*. Spenser had reason to doubt his readers' openmindedness, so he is not an explicit advocate of magical practices. I
do think, however, that *The Faerie Queene* is a world in which magic
is sometimes possible—and not only the wicked magic of Archimago,
Duessa, Acrasia, and the witch who devises the false Florimell. If
Calidore's behavior on Mt. Acidale typifies a good part of Spenser's
readership, we could say that they were tone deaf and didn't believe
their eyes. In the end, however, Calidore listened eagerly to the
poet's explication of his ecstasy, and I see Spenser offering his readers
a mediated account of magic and its limited efficacy. On Mount
Acidale, after the charmed culture-bringers have been dispersed
(along with the shepherd's own *amoretta*) and Colin has broken his
pipe, he speaks at length (VI.x.21–30) about the meaning that survives
his experience of loss. Colin descends, then, to a discourse somewhat
like Ficino's in *De Vita*, more explanatory than incantatory. Perhaps
the strongest motive at work in Spenser's poetry was an effort to
achieve the re-enchantment of a fallen world, but especially in the
parts of his "vnperfit" poem published after 1590, his achievement
took the form of negotiations between what might be and what
will be.

III

Interpreting the esoteric thought and practices of a Renaissance magus today is an uncertain undertaking; scholarly specialists, enthusiasts, and serious amateurs such as myself work from different vantage
points within an *epistème* removed from the culture we seek to understand. And trying to imagine what Spenser, for example, made of
Ficino's ideas is even trickier: it is impossible to avoid guesswork and
wishful thinking. Reading Ficino is a challenge that many patient
and resourceful readers of Spenser have been reluctant to accept, or

have undertaken with a jaundiced view of Florentine Neoplatonism. Ficino is not for everyone; but isn't the same thing true, *mutatis mutandis*, of Spenser?

There is, or has been historically, an odd division within Spenser studies where the poet's work in relation to Ficino and similar writers is concerned. On the one hand, Spenser is seen to have held some very idealistic opinions (about love and beauty, for example, and the demi-divine character of his queen), and these opinions are sometimes explained as consequences of his dalliance with Neoplatonic ideas and sentiments. In some accounts a vaguely defined Neoplatonism is mixed up with "courtly love" and Petrarchism. This is an old-fashioned attitude that has enjoyed a long half-life. The more modern approach to Spenser's poetry, coming out of the old New Criticism and flourishing anew in the context of several theory-based critical methods, regards Spenser not as a naïve child of the *Zeitgeist*, but as nobody's fool, and among the shrewdest of poets. According to this way of reading Spenser, he only *seems*, at times, to be offering allegiance to clichés, and he was certainly too smart to be taken in by the esoteric lore and speculative systems to which Ficino was so devoted. From this perspective, Spenser's actual beliefs must be *sui generis*, not aligned with any ideological position.

I firmly believe that Spenser was very intelligent, and not a follower of fashions. I'm not certain, however, that I understand what being intelligent entailed in his culture. Intelligence in our culture, I submit, involves something more than a skeptical attitude toward authority figures and received opinions. It includes an awareness of marginal phenomena that is equal to or greater than one's attention to things that are central, familiar, and useful. I suppose I am biased to believe that something similar was expected of intelligent people in Ficino's time, and in Spenser's a century later. Esoteric thought, along with terms of art and guild secrets, had a marginal but important place in the literary culture of earlier centuries, and this tradition can be traced as far down as early twentieth-century Modernism, if not beyond. Therefore, although it's not for everyone, esoteric thought should be taken seriously by cultural historians.

One way to level the field for interpreting poets such as Spenser, in the company of esoterically oriented philosophers such as Ficino and Pico della Mirandola, is to consider them all as imaginative writers, involved in doing similar kinds of cultural work within an intellectual movement committed to inquiry, synthesis of fresh perspectives, and reform. Harry Berger points in this direction when he observes, "The central image which emerges from Pico's *opera*—with the possible exception of the *In astrologiam*—is not the world view which Pico sets forth but rather Pico setting forth his world view."[17] Like Pico's *Oration on the Dignity of Man*, Ficino's *De Vita* is a kind of performance. Its rhetoric isn't self-centered, but one gathers that the treatise emerged from a physician's efforts to heal himself.

In the first and last chapters of *Music in Renaissance Magic* (1–43, 247–52), Gary Tomlinson has reflected upon the hermeneutic challenges presented by "the great distance of magic from our own historical and cultural perceptions and presumptions" (2). He cautions against the "hegemonic" thinking that still infects many enterprises in the human sciences: in this way of thinking, "otherness" is not rejected as erroneous or unintelligible, but the superiority of our own purchase on reality is taken for granted, and we are especially pleased to encounter thinkers in past ages who, on occasion, appear to think like us. I can't say that I have entirely avoided this tendency, but I agree with Tomlinson that it should be resisted. He quotes with approval Gadamer's statement that "the true home of hermeneutics [is a] place between strangeness and familiarity."[18] In my experience, a certain amount of distance and strangeness invites patient attempts at understanding and encourages bold interpretation; one wants to be, like Britomart, bold yet not too bold. As Tomlinson describes it, Gadamer's "true home" is a place where dialogue is possible, although foreignness and uncertainty limit both the possibility of critical consensus and access to "Aha!" moments.

In his brief concluding chapter, Tomlinson ponders a question that Foucault raised when he confronted discontinuities in history: "What does it mean, no longer being able to think a certain thought?"[19] Tomlinson is led to imagine a place beyond the middle ground. "On that other side there is a place where magic works. This I think we must accept almost as a matter of faith, faith in anthropological difference and in people's abilities to construct through language and deed their own worlds, unfettered by the world rules others have made." I am reluctant to imitate Tomlinson's leap of faith. He affirms that somehow, Ficino's musical magic (and his magical amulets and animated statues too, I suppose) must have been effective in accordance with his rationales for them. Tomlinson loses me when he goes beyond imagining the ability to think a certain thought—a thought that we can no longer replicate with any confidence—to imagining the successful performance of actions that are no longer possible. I agree that we have no basis for saying that Ficino's magic was impossible or fraudulent, but I would prefer to say only that within the world he experienced and imagined, it was plausible to *believe* in magic. And even though much that Ficino says makes sense to a patient reader today, we can't know exactly what it meant, in his culture or in Spenser's, to believe in "obtaining life from the heavens." What Ficino describes bears some comparison to meditation and liturgical devotion, yet it is not the same; it looks more mysterious, and in the Protestant world of Elizabethan England, it must have felt somewhat dangerous. (Ficino himself met with accusations of heterodoxy, and some editions of *De Vita* omit Book III entirely.[20])

It is clear that the astrology and pneumatology found in *De Vita coelitus comparanda* responded to a felt need for relief from the complications of a melancholy temperament, and to a correlative readiness to believe in magical practices. The book's currency in learned circles across Europe, even in Protestant lands, testifies to cultural conditions not peculiar to the elite of Florence. The experience of melancholia that Ficino described was symptomatic, or so it seems to us now, of bewildering forces at work in Early Modern culture. Since the emphasis in medicine of the Renaissance was on the maintenance of health rather than the elimination of specific diseases, and since the temperament responsible for melancholia was something one lived with for better and for worse, we shouldn't expect the recommendations found in *De Vita* to result in a cure. Like the genetic vulnerabilities and chronic conditions we experience today, melancholia could only be palliated.

If we're going to approach melancholia in terms appropriate to fifteenth- and sixteenth-century cultures, it must be seen in the context of the four humors and their different mixtures of hot or cold and dry or moist qualities. Melancholia presented a baffling array of behaviors tending to extremes. It was in some sense a consequence or symptom of the dichotomizing habits and balancing acts deeply rooted in western traditions, and pandemic within the new learning of the Renaissance. Melancholia occupies one quadrant of a circle, opposite the sanguine temperament, and Saturn's influence is strongest in Aquarius, one of the lunar signs according to Ptolemy's *Tetrabiblos*. On the zodiacal circle, Aquarius is directly opposite Leo, in which the sun is dominant.[21] In this light, we can understand Ficino's emphasis on the efficacy of Phoebus Apollo, Jupiter, and Venus in counteracting the negative effects of Saturn's influence.

We have seen how Ficino created a context in which melancholia could be understood and overcome. Kaske has commented on his preference for "more-and-less over either/or thinking" (Introduction 44); I would add that he also likes to set up both/and relationships. The same is true of Spenser, not because he learned these habits of mind from Ficino, but because they pervaded Renaissance culture.

As an instance of this, and a preface to consideration of Guyon's encounter with Mammon, I will digress to comment on two of Albrecht Dürer's engravings, *St. Jerome in His Study* and *Melencolia I*. Although it is possible that Spenser was acquainted with these engravings, I am not arguing for any sort of "influence." I think, however, that Dürer and Spenser made similar uses of ideas and astrological motifs derived ultimately from Ficino and the intellectual traditions brought together in his work.

Both of the engravings date from 1514; with a third, *The Knight, Death and Devil*, from 1513, they are known as Dürer's *Meisterstiche*.[22] In his classic study of Dürer, Erwin Panofsky denies that the three images are "companion pieces," but "they form a spiritual unity in that they symbolize three ways of life which correspond, as Friedrich Lippmann pointed out, to the scholastic classification of the virtues as moral, theological and intellectual."[23] The relationship of the two engravings from 1514 is especially interesting: "That Dürer conceived of these two prints as spiritual 'counterparts' within the triad of the 'Meisterstiche' can be concluded from the fact that he was in the habit of giving them away together and that collectors looked at and discussed them side by side. No less than six copies were disposed of as pairs while only one copy of the *Melencolia I* was given away singly and no impression of the *Knight, Death and Devil* changed hands together with either of the two other prints" (156).[24]

Panofsky's comments on the three *Meisterstiche* set the two engravings from 1514 off against the *Knight*, from 1513: he represents the *vita activa*, while St. Jerome and the personification of melancholia stand for two different choices, separated from the world and from heroic effort. Each is an intense and austere commitment; the voluptuary's unexamined life is not even considered. St. Jerome has chosen the *vita contemplativa*; his bishop's hat hangs on the wall behind him, next to an hourglass, and the crucifix on the corner of his desk, combined with the skull on the sill of his window embrasure, provide focal points for devotion. At his uncluttered desk, St. Jerome is writing. Since no books are near at hand, we can conclude that he is neither translating the Bible nor involved in controversy. I suppose he is writing a letter; Jerome's correspondence was much admired in the Renaissance and Reformation, and Erasmus was at work on his monumental edition of the *Epistolae* at the same time Dürer executed this print.[25] (The saint's concentration on his writing bears comparison to the artist's concentration on his engraving.) The act of writing, rather than reading or prayer, connects the solitary saint with the world from which he has withdrawn, and potentially with posterity.

Connections with the external world are evident in Dürer's definition of the picture space. We don't see St. Jerome in a monastic
cell, but in part of a generously proportioned alcove, at least as wide
as it is deep, adjacent to the larger room in which the viewer stands.
We consider the picture through a kind of proscenium frame. A halo
envelops the saint's bowed head, and sunlight, streaming through
windows in a thick wall, fills the room with delicate shadows and
strong light. A small dog and a lion are sleeping in the foreground.
The tame lion figures in St. Jerome's legend and thus in pictures of
him; it also stands for Leo in the zodiac, and places the scene in July,
when the sun has reached its zenith. As portrayed in this engraving,
St. Jerome is blessed by the most beneficial of astrological circumstances. All that Ficino has to say about Phoebus Apollo and the
Graces in De Vita coelitus comparanda has a bearing on this image: it
is antithetical to Saturn's sphere of influence. But the closest correlative to St. Jerome in His Study within Ficino's De Vita will be found
in the lyrical last chapter of Book I, which addresses "lovers of truth
[homines veritatis cupidi]" and urges them to cultivate "the incorporeal
spirit, i.e., the intellect," with more zeal than they devote to "the
corporeal spirit." In St. Jerome at his writing desk, Dürer embodies
"a serene mind," prepared to venerate "divine truth." Of this truth,
known by Socrates and fully revealed by Christ, Ficino says, "The
mind was created for seeking and receiving it no less than the eye
was created for beholding the light of the Sun" (161).

In its pictorial design and its burden of meaning, Melencolia I offers
innumerable contrasts to St. Jerome. At a glance, the two pictures can
be read in terms of a simple in bono/in malo opposition, but Melencolia
I rewards any amount of patient attention; what it portrays is simply
"other," beyond moral categories. Seen in relation to the other two
Meisterstiche, which are idealized representations of the active and
contemplative ways of life, this third alternative is obscure, even
tragic. In Saturn and Melancholy, Dürer's portrayal of melancholia is
related to the emergence, during the Renaissance, of "homo literatus,
dedicated neither to an active life nor to religious contemplation,
but to the 'vita speculativa.' "[26]

There is nothing attractive about the stolid, brooding, earthbound
angel personifying melancholia. The area in which she sits, exposed
to moonlight and the night air, is cluttered like a workspace, but
nothing encloses it. Everything about Melencolia I is disorienting, yet
heavy with significance. It is hard to stop pondering the picture,
shifting one's focus between superficial generalizations and the undis-
closed depths of individual emblems. Panofsky offers a useful summary: "The ground is littered with tools and objects mostly

pertaining to the crafts of architecture and carpentry," and he observes that the two most obtrusive objects, "a turned sphere of wood
and a truncated rhombo-hedron of stone, . . . bear witness to the fact
that the terrestrial craftsman, like the 'Architect of the Universe,'
applies in his work the rules of mathematics, that is, in the language of
Plato and the *Book of Wisdom*, of 'measure, number, and weight.' "[27]
Turned inward, lost in deep thought, the angel sits among reminders
of the hierarchical order of things toward which the leaning workman's ladder points, but she is alienated from her surroundings. In
the distance we see a placid body of water and points of land, suggestive of a flood. This background indicates a season under the sign of
Aquarius, which is opposite Leo in the zodiac and at the height of
Saturn's influence.

The only activity in the picture invites a comparison with St.
Jerome at his desk. Centrally placed, perched on a grinding wheel,
a figure that Panofsky describes as "a morose little *putto*" is writing
something on his slate. Should we call the slate a *tabula rasa* and
identify this infant with the faculty of imagination in its first phase
of development? Panofsky lends some credence to the idea that while
St. Jerome in His Study depicts a mind that has gained serenity, in the
other we see the lowest level of consciousness, an imagination that is
rudimentary in the child and decadent in the adult figure. Panofsky's
commentary ends with an explanation of the Roman numeral I in
the engraving's title. He notes that in the first version (completed in
1509/10) of Heinrich Cornelius Agrippa's *De Occulta Philosophia*, the
effects of Saturn's influence and the *furor melancholicus* fall into three
categories, depending on which of the brain's faculties (imagination,
reason, and mind) is dominant in an individual and his chosen profession. (Agrippa's book borrowed much of its substance from Book III
of Ficino's *De Vita*, but departed from Ficino in this respect.) In a
person whose imagination is the strongest faculty (a craftsman or
an architect, an artist or, perhaps, a poet), melancholia can inspire
extraordinary creativity within the imagination's domain, which is
the physical rather than the metaphysical world. Panofsky concludes
that *Melencolia I* specifically designates the "artist's melancholy," belonging "to those who 'cannot extend their thought beyond [location
and] space.' "[28]

Examination of Dürer's engravings has provided an instance of
Ficino's influence on the arts; it has also taken us out of Italy, into
the northern Renaissance and the turbulent early years of the Reformation. Marsilio Ficino and Agrippa of Nettesheim didn't breathe
the same air. Although Agrippa—a kind of intellectual magpie, even a
charlatan—helped to disseminate some of Ficino's ideas, they became

objects of curiosity in his hands, controversial and even dangerous in the eyes of some, and appealing to others who were attracted to controversy.[29] In my view, Spenser participated in the northern Renaissance but also responded deeply to the sunnier Mediterranean outlook of Ficino, just as he did to the lively heroic poems of Boiardo, Ariosto, and Tasso.

I V

Turning now from Ficino, Dürer, and Agrippa toward Spenser and preparing to examine Guyon's encounter with Mammon, my first point of reference will be Alastair Fowler's *Spenser and the Numbers of Time*, for its account of Book I in *The Faerie Queene* as the Book of the Sun and Book II as the Book of the Moon.[30] Fowler explains how significant the parallels and differences between episodes in the two Books are, and how Saturn and the sign of Aquarius figure in Book II. "The sequence followed by Spenser in moving from Leo (Book I) to Aquarius (Book II) is a natural one, responsive to the complementary or reflective relationship of the two books" (98). He draws extensively on Ficino's *De Vita* to explain "how the lunar and other planetary influences in Book II are related. Luna stands as a mean between Mars and Saturn, on the one hand, and Venus, on the other." He goes on to say that "Guyon's task is to communicate the mediating influence of Luna," but his "temperamental inclination towards the rigour of Mars and the self-denial of Saturn" make his commitment to temperance a struggle (112–13).

When Guyon tells Arthur of his devotion to Gloriana, and of the "infinite desire" that an awareness of "the beauty of her mind" inspires, he must be aware that among her suitors, in relation to "her bounty, and imperiall power," he will never be more than an also-ran (II.ix.3). Arthur and Guyon both pursue their quests—one for love, the other for revenge and the distant prospect of renown—in a secular world. It is open to heavenly grace on rare occasions (more on this when we come to Guyon's guardian angel), but when Arthur complains that "Heauen doth to me enuy" an opportunity to meet Gloriana, Guyon can only offer cold comfort: "Fortune, the foe of famous cheuisaunce/Seldom . . . yields to vertue aide,/But in her way throwes mischiefe and mischaunce" (ix.7–8). At this point, we are meant to recall the passage at the beginning of Canto ix in Book I where Arthur is prompted by Una to reveal "what secret wound/

Could euer find, to grieue the gentlest hart on ground" (I.ix.7).
These are the neatest moments of symmetry in the Books I and
II; they accompany Arthur's rescues of Redcrosse and Guyon, each
accomplished in the eighth cantos of their respective books. Other
variations on the themes of Book I are more playful, adding ornaments to an elaborate structure.

The complementary narratives that will include Guyon's encounter with Mammon begin around the midpoint of Book I. Having
run away from the House of Pride, Redcrosse is pursued by Duessa,
who finds him resting "foreby a fountaine side,/Disarmed all of yron-
coted Plate," enjoying "the cooling shade" (vii.2–3). Soon the knight
is enthralled by Duessa once again, and he has drunk of the fountain,
participating in the disgrace of a nymph who had "Satt downe to
rest in middest of the race" (5). "Pourd out in loosnesse on the grassy
grownd" (7), Redcrosse is too phlegmatic and vulnerable to avoid
capture by Orgoglio.

At the corresponding point in Book II, Guyon has left Phaedria
and the lake of Idleness, unmoved by her offers of giddy pleasure.
He is still separated from his guide, the Palmer; he takes comfort
only in "his owne virtues, and praise-worthie deedes," making his
way "through wide wastfull ground,/That nought but desert wild-
ernesse shewed all around" (II.vii.2). Guyon seems stronger and safer
than Redcrosse had been, but unlike Redcrosse, he will never receive
even a glimpse of a transcendental destiny. In this Protestant epic,
his satisfaction with his own virtues is not praiseworthy. Coming
through the waste land, Guyon finds relief at last in "a gloomy glade"
(4), reminiscent of the "gloomy glade" where Redcrosse had relaxed
with Duessa (I.vii.4): perhaps he's not so safe after all. In the grove's
"secret shade," Guyon meets Mammon, whose grandiose sense of
himself is reminiscent of Orgoglio.

Mammon also resembles Despair, "that cursed man" whom Redcrosse, not yet fully recovered from his near-death confinement in
Orgoglio's dungeon, encountered in his "darkesome cave" (I.ix.35)
before his regeneration in the House of Holinesse. Just as Redcrosse
had been naïve and eager to debate with Despair—"Certes (sayd he)
hence shall I neuer rest,/Till I that treachours art haue heard and
tryde" (32)—Guyon argues with Mammon (II.vii.8–20). Where Redcrosse almost gives in to despair, Guyon gives in to curiosity about
the "secret place" where Mammon "can safely hold/So huge a masse,
and hide from heauens eie" (20).

Who, or what, is Mammon? Guyon is unsure: "What art thou
man, (if man at all thou art)?" (7). A. C. Hamilton calls him "an

infernal creature"; Anne Lake Prescott describes him as "a personification of wealth, as were Plutus, Pluto, and Dis according to the mythographers."[31] Originating in the Aramaic word for "riches," *mamona* began as a collective noun and became a personification before being recruited into the ranks of demons, whence he was interpreted as an instigator of mortal sin. A kind of paranoia is at work in this development: inequity becomes iniquity. In Agrippa's enumeration of demons in his *Three Books of Occult Philosophy*, "the Tempters and Ensnarers have the last place, one of which is present with every man, which we therefore call the evill *Genius*, and their Prince is *Mammon*, which is interpreted covetousness."[32] It would be fitting if Spenser's Mammon were such a demon, since the episode in Canto vii is followed by the appearance of Guyon's guardian angel (II.viii.5–8), whom Agrippa would call his good Genius.

For a long time I entertained the notion that Mammon is not in fact a demon, but a man so far gone in melancholia that he *thinks* he is a demon, or perhaps something grander:

> God of the world and worldlings I me call,
>   Great *Mammon*, greatest god below the skye,
>   That of my plenty poure out vnto all,
>   And vnto none my graces do enuye:
>   Riches, renowme, and principality,
>   Honour, estate, and all this worldes good,
>   For which men swinck and sweat incessantly,
>   Fro me do flow into an ample flood,
> And in the hollow earth haue their eternall brood.
>
> (II.vii.8)

The self-absorption evident in "I me call" could indicate an all too human delusional state, but in literature, demonic tempters also exhibit such traits, and they often appear in human form endowed with special powers, including the power to impose their schemes and lies on people who should know better. Some of Spenser's other denizens of the underworld are melancholy, and his narrative asks us to believe that Mammon's "secret place" (20) in the hollow earth is more real than a madman's fantasy.

Guyon's descent into Mammon's underworld is educative, like Virgil's descent with the Sibyl in Book VI of the *Aeneid*, but it is framed as a temptation. As in Redcrosse's encounter with Despair, some culpability and a risk of failure is involved in the testing of Guyon's virtue. Mammon is not an inner voice like Despair, but an alien adversary. He is even alien to the world as Guyon sees it—but Guyon's understanding of himself and his place in the world may be based on illusions. It seems that without promptings from his adversary, Guyon can't enter fully into the ideal life he imagines for himself. Using Anthony Wilden's Lacanian terminology, Sean Kane has commented brilliantly on the "mirror game" that Mammon and Guyon play: an "imaginary self" is asserted "through competition with a negated 'imaginary other.' " Structuring the encounter in these terms, Kane observes that "it is in a divided state that Guyon seeks some meaning from Mammon, the one among the tempters of Book Two whom the knight resembles in his melancholy isolation."[33]

By the middle of stanza 20, at the end of his heated debate with Mammon, Guyon's view of the world has begun to change. Now he needs to know "What secret place . . . can safely hold/So huge a masse, and hide from heauens eie" (20). Mammon had presented himself as a man of unlimited generosity, and Guyon disdained his offers, but he is fascinated by secrets that Mammon has not yet revealed. Secrets in Spenser are always ethically ambiguous: they promise intimate or esoteric knowledge, and knowledge may also be power, but some form of transgression is always involved in getting it.

Guyon reacts with awe and perhaps with envy to the idea that Mammon's wealth is entirely secure. Was it ill gotten, yet effectively hidden from "heauens eie"? And where can such wealth be preserved "from wrong and robbery"? Guyon has been living by Christ's injunction in his sermon on the mount: "Lay not up for yourselves treasures upon earth, where moth and rust doth corrupt, and thieves break through and steal" (Matt. 6.19). Idealism has not provided him with security; it has prompted vague aspirations. Making the first move in the debate that leads to his underworld, Mammon shows that he understands the darkness in Guyon's heart: "Or if to thy great mind, *or greedy vew*/All these [i.e., the "mountains" of wealth above ground] may not suffise . . . " (9, emphasis added). Guyon's response is condescending and sarcastic: "Regard of worldly mucke doth fowly blend,/And low abase the high heroicke spright." When he adds, "Faire shields, gay steedes, bright armes be my delight,/Those be the riches fit for an aduent'rous knight" (10), he finesses the price that someday must be paid for such equipment. Mammon replies in a single stanza, calling his adversary "Vaine glorious" and claiming that "money can thy wantes at will supply" (11). Guyon fills the next six stanzas with a fervent sermon, concluding with a nostalgic portrayal of "The antique world, in his first flowering youth" (16), and a denunciation of mining as rape and "Sacriledge" (17).

Guyon shows himself to be heavily invested in values that Spenser defends with his authorial voice throughout *The Faerie Queene*. His is the dominant voice in this debate, but Mammon has the last word, renewing his generous offer:

Thou that doest liue in later times, must wage
Thy workes for wealth, and life for gold engage.
If then thee list my offred grace to vse,
Take what thou please of all this surplusage.

(18)

Guyon is free to refuse, and he quibbles: does some "bloodguiltinesse or guile" attach to "these goods"? Hamilton's notes show how Mammon's responses to his scruples parody several passages in the New Testament. These are fingerposts to the reader, but the narrative is still over-determined in favor of Guyon's going along with Mammon. His willingness to be led "by and by/Through that thick couert" (20) is open to several interpretations. Some *curiositas* is at work in his "great mind, or greedy vew,"[34] and he is also honor bound to prove himself as "an aduent'rous knight," ready for any test of his virtue.

V

Before going further in an examination of Guyon's experience, I want to consider the author's perspective on his character. I am far from the first to find Guyon a somewhat unsympathetic figure,[35] set up by Spenser to explore the limitations as well as the fundamental strengths of the virtues on which Book II focuses: temperance, of course, but also continence and the intellectual virtue of prudence, as codified by "Aristotle and the rest." Guyon is admirable, and of all the poem's characters he is the closest to being a humanist's Everyman, but something is lacking in him even when he does the right thing. Redcrosse is often described as "sad," and Guyon is not, but he strikes me as the loneliest of Spenser's heroes. The difference between Redcrosse and Guyon is indicated in Book II's opening stanzas, when Archimago, seeking "that godly knight" (2), happens instead upon Guyon, "A goodly knight" (5). At this point, Guyon's goodliness is apparent only in his "harnesse meete,/That from his head no place appeared to his feete." How good is the man hidden within this suit of armor?

If we consider Mammon's canto in relation to other cantos of instruction, our interpretation will respond to the poem's structure, and will be more author-centered than character-centered. Canto vii of Book II is one of several passages that evoke some part of Book VI in Virgil's *Aeneid*. The descent to Mammon's domain echoes Aeneas's descent with the Sybil to Pluto's realm and the darker part of his journey through the underworld (*Aen.* VI 262–636). In the different environment of Book III, we come to the antithesis of Mammon's underworld in Canto vi, when Spenser describes the somewhat unearthly paradise of the Garden of Adonis, which alludes to Virgil's Elysium and Anchises' philosophical discourse (*Aen.* VI 637–751). The last part of *Aeneid* VI, 752–886, where Anchises names the heroes who will descend from Aeneas and Lavinia, is imitated in Merlin's prophetic encouragement of Britomart (III.iii.21–50). This prophecy is ironically relevant to Guyon's circumstances, since he resembles *pius* Aeneas but is given no place in any line of succession.

The patterns of likeness and difference that link Books I and II, then, are developed further in Book III. Planetary deities and astrological influences continue to figure in the structures of meaning; Venus emerges in Book III as a dominant and benevolent presence, in contrast to the women who are represented as predatory in Books I and II. Attention has already been given to Ficino's emphasis on the benefits to be derived from the three Graces (Jupiter, Apollo, and Venus), and there will be more to say (see below, page 349) about their presence in Book III. Comparing Mammon's domain to that of Venus in the Garden of Adonis will conclude this essay, after we have considered Guyon and Mammon more closely.

The poet's attitude toward money and Mammon is complex and somewhat conflicted. Ill fortune and a lack of worldly success figure prominently in Spenser's legend. Some twenty years after his death in London in 1599, Ben Jonson commented to William Drummond that, burnt out of his home in Ireland, Spenser "died for lake of bread in King Street." Jonson also said that he had "refused 20 pieces sent to him by my Lord of Essex, and said he was sorry he had no time to spend them."[36] Ruth Mohl considers these anecdotes factually false, but it is true that Spenser endured great hardships in Ireland, and the high-mindedness in his reputed response to Essex was a real trait of his character, seen within *The Faerie Queene* in his objections to Lord Burghley's lack of respect for him.

Although Spenser would have been no more likely than Guyon to join in the crowd around Mammon's daughter Philotime, striving to catch a link in the golden chain that she holds (II.vii.46), it is clear from all of his poetry that he harbored worldly ambitions, and early in his career, when he may have been developing plans for Book II, he wasn't at all indifferent to wealth. In 1580, collaborating with his close friend Gabriel Harvey, he published *Three proper, and wittie, familiar Letters*, and his principal contribution to the collection was a letter in Latin verse. Showing off his familiarity with the Roman poets and moralists, he advises Harvey to "chart a mid-course"; he should avoid appearing either too foolish or too wise. "Nor, if you are prudent, should you over zealously condemn luxuriant pleasures, nor a mistress finally won in marriage, nor the offer of gold."[37]

After the lines just quoted, Spenser goes out of his way to insert a parenthetical allusion to two old soldiers from the early history of Rome, exemplars of incorruptible virtue but *viris miseris* ("poor chaps") in the ambitious young poet's eyes. One of them, M. Curius Dentatus, was remembered by Roman moralists and Renaissance humanists for his indifference to wealth. In Sir Thomas Elyot's version of the story, he rejected a bribe, saying that he "had leuer haue dominion ouer them that be riche than he himselfe to haue richesse."[38] It seems that in 1580, Spenser regarded such old-fashioned virtue as unworthy of emulation. As a young man on the verge of marriage, he must have been eager for a generous patron's support and reluctant to voice any criticism of the wealthy and powerful. Ten years on, however, when Guyon is shown a roomful of "richesse," identified by Mammon as "the worldes blis, . . . the end,/To which al men doe ayme, rich to be made" (32), he refuses this "grace," declaring a preference "to be Lord of those, that riches haue,/Then them to haue my selfe, and be their seruile sclaue" (33). These lines deserve emphasis, coming as they do at the midpoint of the canto's 66 stanzas. The position Guyon takes remains problematic, however, since so far as we know he has no prospects of being "Lord" over anyone, rich or poor. The will to power that he expresses in stanza 33–power not in Mammon's gift, but power nonetheless—is at odds with his later boast, "All that I need I haue" (39).

It is as an exemplar of power (and pretensions to power) in the secular world that Mammon is a complex and interesting figure. His place within the total economy of *The Faerie Queene* exceeds his significance as Guyon's tempter. Mammon has something in common with Archimago, and more with Acrasia and Busirane: all practice a demonic sort of magic. Mammon presents himself as the overlord of an underworld that reveals the real forces at work in the world above. He promises control over those forces, and bliss as the end result. Of course, like the poem's other wicked magicians, Mammon is an illusionist; his success depends on a kink in his victim's imagination that is congruent with a demon's will to power.

Spenser's attitudes toward the many forms that power took in his culture were nuanced and ambivalent. He is widely criticized for complicity with the Elizabethan state, and in specific instances that criticism is valid. A position aloof from the public world wasn't attractive to him, however. I think that Spenser was acutely sensitive to the ways in which his authority as a poet was entangled with the authority and legitimacy of his nation's central institutions, and with the person, both symbolic and all too human, of his Queen. Like the Fox in *Mother Hubberds Tale*, whose argument for amoral freedom mocked "the golden age of *Saturne* old" and claimed that "this might better be the world of gold:/For without golde now nothing wilbe got" (*MHT* 151–53), Mammon poses a threat to Elizabethan ideals. His daughter Philotime, on her "stately siege of soueraine maiestye" (44), parodies both Gloriana and Elizabeth. And Spenser presides, in his author function, within a world where parody has its place along with fervent devotion and extravagant praise.

Many Spenserians will recall along with me Humphrey Tonkin's characterization of Spenser as "a man who kept everything." An urge to encompass the world in his book is evident in his portrayal of the three sages in the turret of Alma's castle (II.ix.45–58); each fills his room with "all" that pertains to his faculty. This urge is demonically parodied in Mammon's avarice and his claim to be "God of the world." Avarice, the self-consuming hoarding of money, is one of the traits emblematic of melancholia,[39] and when we consider that money, as a medium of exchange, is a signifying system, it becomes clear that Mammon should be included among the poem's characters who, in their wicked negativity, adumbrate the poet's positive powers.

Among the scene-setting stanzas at the beginning of Canto vii is this description of Mammon's treasure:

> And round about him lay on euery side
> > Great heapes of gold, *that neuer could be spent*:
> > Of which some were rude owre, not purified
> > Of *Mulcibers* deuouring element;
> > Some other were new driuen, and distent
> > Into great Ingowes, and to wedges square;
> > Some in round plates withouten moniment:
> > But most were stampt, and in their metal bare
> The antique shapes of kings and kesars straung and rare.
>
> > > > > > > > (5, emphasis added)

Mammon's "huge threasury" of gold is in many forms, from "rude owre" to coins stamped with "antique" rulers' heads, but it seems that none of it could pass as current. Its value belongs to the distant past or the future. This is telling: it is a symptom of Mammon's melancholia, which can be understood as an inability to live in the present. Guyon objects to Mammon's hiding his wealth "apart/From the worldes eye, and from her right vsaunce" (7), and he returns to the same theme after being shown the subterranean storehouse of Mammon's wealth and the furnaces from which it comes: "what needeth mee/To couet more, then I haue cause to vse?" (39). His response to "greedy *Tantalus*" is of a piece with this practicality: "vnto all that liue in high degree,/Ensample be of mind more temperate,/To teach them how to vse their present state" (60). Mammon's attempts to distract and demoralize Guyon only prompt him to base himself more firmly in a real and practical world.

Guyon's focus on the "right vsaunce" of money, not on gold as something to covet and hoard, suggests that he has been well schooled in Aristotle's *Ethics* and in the tradition of commentary that developed around that book. Book V of the *Ethics*, concerning justice and equity, includes three chapters (iii to v) devoted to fairness and equality in transactions between dissimilar individuals; chapter v, the most important for our purposes, deals with reciprocity in economic life, explaining why communities need money and how "it measures all things."[40] Communities consist of "people who are different and unequal" (a physician and a farmer, for example), and "they must be equalized." Money accomplishes this by introducing a "middle term," a common denominator (1133a15–20; Ostwald 125). In the Aristotelian tradition of ethical and economic thought, money did not represent "richesse," as it does for Mammon and his followers, but "need, which holds everything together" (1133a27–29; Ostwald 126). Money is also the means by which ordinary human needs can be satisfied. In a stable social order, assuming that prices are constant and money has a reliable value (Aristotle recognized that this wasn't always the case), money provides for exchanges in the future that aren't necessary in the present (1133b12–18; Ostwald 127).

There is a close connection between justice in a community and its monetary system; an unjust social structure is apt to be reflected in a flawed system of exchange, and vice versa. Guyon's encounter with Mammon doesn't provide a straightforward diagnosis of the economic problems that troubled Tudor England, but the canto does offer, between the lines, a description of alarming symptoms. Mammon and Guyon talk at cross purposes, and between their extreme positions, the middle ground of a pragmatic monetary policy goes un-articulated.

Guyon's encounter with Mammon reveals how uneasy Spenser was with the centralizing and commodifying of power and favor, grossly during the reign of Henry VIII but also under Elizabeth. Behind Mammon's demonic claims to godhead lurks an inconvenient truth that Elizabeth was obliged to confront early in her reign: that royal power and the nation's health depended upon the integrity of England's coinage, which had been badly debased during her father's reign. Advised by Sir Thomas Smith and Sir Thomas Gresham, Elizabeth took steps to call in and remint coins, but supplying a sound currency proved very difficult, and she was never able to bring inflation under control.[41] Mammon is a spectral image of real economic anxiety.

It is my sense that Spenser regarded all the forms of centralized authority with a mixture of awe and jealousy. (Consider how Gloriana and Cleopolis figure in the poem: summoned into consciousness as a ghostly paradigm of things political, but ontologically untethered, and kept on the poem's distant margin.) As the author of *The Faerie Queene*, he enjoyed a kind of sovereignty but often adopted a rustic mask, modest and self-effacing. In turn, within the poem Queen Elizabeth was both his sovereign and his subject, as Louis Montrose has shown.[42] Spenser was a defender of Elizabethan ideals and a subtle critic who occasionally bent his romance in the direction of satire. Mammon's underworld, therefore, and Philotime's court within it, can be viewed as an exposé of deep-rooted economic problems, persisting within the workings of Elizabeth's own court.

VI

My argument has strayed from its beginnings with the subject of melancholia. Ficino's views will help me bring this essay to a close. I will summon his spirit; let's imagine how he might respond to Guyon's experience.

*   *   *

The character calling himself Mammon is familiar to me from the underworld of moneylenders and the writings of moralists describing the seven deadly sins. Avarice is not prominent among the traits of studiosi like myself, but of course we depend upon friends and patrons with money, so the temptations presented by Mammon are real enough. Some readers of this poem may be enticed or overpowered by his promises. He offers a frightful example of the physical and spiritual effects of Saturn's influence: black bile predominates in him, and its adustion has led to madness. He is first seen "sunning his threasure hore," *and it seems that he is lost in a foolish superstition. If this wretched creature were a man, I would urge him to leave this* "gloomy glade" *and make his way to a verdant garden, to bask in Phoebus Apollo's benevolent rays, enjoying sweet music and overflowing glasses of golden wine. His dismal* "yron cote all ouergrowne with rust" *shows that Mars has intensified the ill effects of Saturn. But perhaps I am dwelling too much on the poem's surface: we should understand Mammon not only in terms of the effects of melancholia, but as a demon capable of imposing those effects on anyone susceptible to his influence.*

We learn at the end of this canto that, having descended underground, Guyon was obliged to spend "three dayes of men" *there, lacking both food and sleep. One is reminded of our Lord's three days of temptation in the desert, but the plain sense of this narrative should be noted as well. Guyon may not be innately predisposed to melancholy, but he is bound to experience it, exposing himself to such risks when his body, spirit, and mind together need fresh air, daylight, good food and drink, and regular hours of rest. These things having been said, I must admire Guyon for patterning his behavior not only on that of our Savior at the beginning of His ministry, but also on the descent of Aeneas to the underworld before he proceeds to embrace his fate in Latium.*

The author of this poem loves subtleties and puzzles—as much, perhaps, as our Dante does. Spenser must wish to be numbered among the studi-osi—*even the* studiosissimi. *He reserves the deepest meaning and the highest pleasures in his poem for readers who are similarly studious. Notice how he begins the canto:* "As Pilot well expert in perilous waue,/That to a stedfast starre his course hath bent,/ . . . So Guyon." *This is a glancing allusion to Palinurus, the pilot of Aeneas's ship: his abrupt fall into the sea makes the arrival of the Trojans' ships on the coast of Italy into an occasion for grief rather than celebration. My friend Cristoforo Landino, a poet and a scholar, says in his commentary on Virgil that Palinurus stands for* "appetite resisting reason"; *in his opinion, Palinurus must be left behind so that Aeneas, the intellect, can take control and lead his people* "into a tranquil port."[43] *That may be so, but I mourn the fall of Palinurus and his death at the hands of savages; I see a cruel fate at work in these events, and in the other losses and sacrifices that Aeneas is compelled to accept. My melancholy nature shows in this, I suppose. I see myself in this poet's* "Pilot well expert," *whose* "stedfast starre" *is obscured by foul weather; he must rely* "Vpon his card and compas," *just as Guyon, all alone, must rely upon* "his owne virtues, and praise-worthie deedes."

In my treatise De Vita, *I urged young men such as Guyon to remember what* Plato *taught in his* Phaedo *and* Republic, "that every person has at birth one certain daemon, the guardian of his life, assigned by his own personal star, which helps him to that very task to which the celestials summoned him when he was born."[44] *I also advised them to look within themselves, to know and nurture their* ingenium, *their individual talent. I believe that those who choose their path in life unwisely will* "labor in vain, and their supernal patrons [will] desert them." *It is not immediately clear that Guyon knows well enough what is best for him; my friend Cristoforo would find fault with his appetite for dangerous knowledge. He debates well with Mammon, but what drives him to engage in this debate? Does he show strength in stanza 20 when he expresses interest in the* "secret place" *where the mass of Mammon's wealth is hidden, or is his curiosity a weakness, as it is in melancholics? These questions can only be pondered after further inquiry. So Guyon enters the underworld, like Aeneas and Dante before him, by* "A darksome way, which no man could descry,/That deep descended through the hollow growid,/And was with dread and horror compassed arownd." *This poet draws his readers into* curiositas *even as he counsels them against it!*

At the end of my Books on Life, *in a letter to three good friends,* "most beloved brothers in the hunt for truth," *I urged them to seek freedom from care and tranquility of mind, and to live* amplissima—*expansively. I cited the advice of Pythagoras:* "beware lest you ever chance to be narrowly confined" (403–05). *Guyon goes against this advice, allowing curiosity to overrule prudence. The series of spaces that he travels through or looks into are oppressive, but the spaces themselves are for the most part described as* "ample," "Lyke an huge caue," "large and wyde." *Guyon risks everything for the sake of fully understanding himself and his place in the world; he avoids confinement by remaining modest and steadfastly refusing Mammon's offers. I observed that* "a person who is stimulated into scrutinizing curiously the depths of secret things, should know himself to be not only Mercurial but Saturnine. Under Saturn's leadership too are all those who delve as far as possible into any pursuit, especially those who neglect other affairs" (*De Vita* III xxiv 377).

Mammon urges Guyon not only to neglect his proper duties, but even to renounce them. In a scene that parodies the splendor of a royal presence chamber (and also parodies Homer's golden chain, the guarantee of cosmic order, inverting it to mean "Ambition, rash desire to sty"), *we are introduced along with Guyon to Mammon's daughter,* "fayre Philotime." *The father offers—*"if that thou lust"—*his daughter's hand in marriage: a most disgusting invitation. Confronted with this demonic distortion of the courtly world he aspires to inhabit, Guyon remains temperate: he knows himself to be* "fraile flesh and earthly wight,/Vnworthy match for such immortall mate," *and he adds,* "yet is my trouth yplight,/And loue auowd to other Lady late." *Guyon's vow of love, not lust, and his commitment to the truth of his fealty to the Faerie Queen offer proof of his sincerity. He has withdrawn into himself, rejecting worldly definitions of success and happiness. Mammon responds, still trying to prove his claim to be* "God of the world and worldlings." *Still hoping to overpower Guyon's self-restraint, he descends further into the infernal depths. But I must refresh myself.*

✶ ✶ ✶

Much has been written about the last and darkest phase of Guyon's ordeal, his introduction to the Garden of Proserpina (51–64); I can't add much that is original to the existing scholarship.[45] The garden named for Proserpina (although she is absent from it), stocked with poisonous herbs and mysterious symbols, is literally central to the first three books of *The Faerie Queene.*[46] Accompanying the "siluer seat" (53), where Guyon is urged "To rest thy weary person, in the shadow coole" (63), is "a goodly tree" bearing golden apples, "the source of all the fateful fruit of mythology," as Geoffrey G. Hiller observes in *The Spenser Encyclopedia* (s. v. "apples"). Hiller also notes that it parodies the Tree of Life in *FQ* I.xi.46–48, by which Redcrosse is revived to triumph on the morning of his third day of battle. Guyon "much wondred at this tree" (56), which shades the entire garden, with branches that reach beyond its bounds and droop into the river Cocytus, flowing around the garden's perimeter and filled with the bodies of the damned. His susceptibility to melancholia is being sorely tested.

Guyon's attention is focused on Tantalus and Pilate, the one complaining bitterly against the gods' injustice and the other confessing his own injustice: both are cautionary examples of hubris, at the extremes of the "forward" and "froward" behavior that Spenser examines throughout Book II.[47] And melancholia, as Ficino would remind us, drives its sufferers to both extremes. The symbolic golden apples and silver seat epitomize the same bipolar pattern: they invite and resist interpretation, and both require renunciation. Mammon's efforts to initiate Guyon into a demon-driven worldliness contain, at the canto's end, an initiatory ordeal of a different kind. I find merit in the suggestion by John Upton, Spenser's first scholarly editor, that Guyon's ordeal bears comparison to the Eleusinian mysteries. While taking us to the depths of human degradation and damnation, Spenser also refers us, through the admonitory figures of Tantalus and Pilate, to the divine and cosmic order that they violated. And as Douglas Brooks-Davies has pointed out, invoking Proserpina and her mythic context shifts the focus from Mammon's sterile accumulation of riches to the seasonally renewed stuff of daily life.[48]

Our discussion of the Mammon episode began with consideration of the echoes and parallels that link Book II to Book I. Now it is possible to add more details to that account and to prepare for broadening the scope of this discussion by a brief consideration of the ways that Book III builds upon the pattern developed in Book II. Brooks-Davies notes that Proserpina is present by name in Book I as well as in her hellish garden in Book II: Archimago invokes her when he calls up the spirit that becomes the false Una (I.i.37), and she figures in the House of Pride when we are told that Lucifera, superficially as bright as the sun, is in fact the daughter "Of grisly *Pluto* . . . / And sad *Proserpina* the Queene of hell" (I.v.11). Lucifera, like Philotime, presents a parodic image of Queen Elizabeth's power and glory[49]—the dark side of the moon, as it were—and it is to Guyon's credit that he confronts that face of power at its source, rather than sneaking away as Redcrosse does, only to fall prey to Duessa soon afterward.

Redcrosse is defeated by Orgoglio in Canto vii of Book I; his "slombred sencelesse corse" is thrown in the castle's dungeon before "he could out of his swowne awake" (15). The analogous moment in Canto vii of Book II occurs in the last stanza, when Mammon returns Guyon to "liuing light":

> all so soon as his enfeebled spright,
> Gan sucke this vitall ayre into his brest,
> As ouercome with too exceeding might,
> The life did flit away out of her nest,
> And all his sences were with deadly fit opprest.
>
> (66)

One is tempted, in the interests of parallelism, to regard Guyon's faint and his subsequent vulnerability as indicators of his error and weakness, but in my opinion this gives too little credit to Guyon and misinterprets what has happened to him.

★   ★   ★

Let me summon Ficino to offer his interpretation of stanza 66: *I am fond of such expressions as* "liuing light" *and* "vitall ayre," *and I welcome Guyon's return from his exhausting ordeal. He is a young man dedicated to learning, and I have advised all such people,* "Whether waking or sleeping, always breathe living air, air living with light" (*De Vita* III xxiv 379).

Guyon's condition at this point, and indeed all of his lonely experience since parting from his companion and mentor, brings to mind my description, near the beginning of De Vita, *of the cumulative effects of melancholia and the behavior prompted in us by black bile. I have observed that to pursue knowledge, especially the sort that is difficult to make one's own,* "the soul must draw in upon itself from external things to internal as from the circumference to the center." We must be "fixed in the center," *and this* "is above all the property of the Earth itself, to which black bile is analogous." *It is in this light that I understand Guyon's fascination with Mammon and his willingness to follow him into the underworld. His persistence in withdrawal and introspection is understandable too, but it takes its toll, even though Guyon achieves a philosopher's detachment from everything that Mammon reveals to him. Some have said that the mind is its own place, but it can become a prison before we know it. As I have said,* "frequent agitation of the mind greatly dries up the brain," *and* "with too little physical exercise, superfluities are not carried off and the thick, dense, clinging, dusky vapors do not exhale." And finally, "sometimes in its too vehement agitation, [the soul] either in a way flies out of [the body] or sometimes seems as if to disintegrate it" (De Vita I iv 113–15). *In the stanza I have commented upon, the poet seems to be describing such a collapse, caused by physical debility and imprudent, but almost heroic, agitation of the soul.*

*   *   *

The opening stanzas of Canto viii transport us from hell to heaven. In Canto vii, Mammon's attitude toward Guyon had combined a phony show of generosity with "inward wrath" (51) and the open contempt of his last address, "Thou fearefull foole/Why takest not . . . /Ne sittest downe . . . " (63). When Guyon finally asks to be returned to the surface, Mammon is "constraynd t'obay" (66): he has power only over "worldlings." In the lyrical pair of stanzas that open Canto viii, beginning, "And is there care in heauen?" an anxious concern for Guyon's welfare is answered by assurances of "th'exceeding grace/Of highest God," flowing from a heaven of "blessed Angels" in "siluer bowers." Over against Mammon's descent from one gloomy and secret place to another, we are asked to imagine the bright and urgent flights of angels: "How oft do they with golden pineons, cleaue/The flitting skyes, like flying Pursuiuant,/Against fowle feendes to ayd vs militant?/ . . . And all for loue, and nothing for reward." The narrative then resumes with the Palmer, who has made his way back to Guyon. He is caught up in the urgent movement: a voice calls "lowd and cleare,/Come hether, come hether,

O come hastily" (3), and he finds Guyon "slumbring fast/In senceles dreame" (4).

In stanza 3, the narrator had called Guyon's state a "traunce," and the same word is used again in stanza 53, where he finally awakes. Commentators on this episode have agreed that in his trance (termed a "swowne" in the canto's quatrain argument), Guyon remains ignorant of all the forces that come to his rescue. The word "traunce" has roots in French (*transe* and *transir*, both referring to a chilled, numb, fearful state) and Latin (*transire*, to cross over). If Guyon undergoes any sort of initiation in Mammon's underworld, it is a parody of illumination; escaping from the underworld, he enters a cold and dark liminal state, reviving only after Pyrochles and Cymochles have been dispatched by Arthur.

Beginning in stanza 3 with the cherub's call for help, the narrative in Canto viii focuses for several stanzas on the Palmer's subjective state: what he hears, sees, and feels, first in response to Guyon and then to the "faire young man,/Of wondrous beauty, and of freshest yeares," with a face like Apollo's, "adornd with sunny rayes" (5). Stanzas 3 through 9 expose the limits of the Palmer's understanding, and of our own. Stanza 5 registers the Palmer's rapt attention to the cherub's beauty; the language carries an erotic charge. In stanza 6 the narrator steps in with a comparison of Guyon's angel to "*Cupido* on *Idaean* hill," without his "cruell bow . . . /And mortall arrows," sporting with Venus and "his goodly sisters, *Graces* three." This perspective is for the reader's benefit, supplementing what is apparent to the Palmer.[50] His attraction to the fair youth lapses into a confusion of "fear and wonder"; rendered speechless, he hears "the childe" address him with respect, assure him that Guyon will recover and will be cared for "vnto the end." And then, warning that "euill is at hand him to offend" and reminding Guyon's mentor to watch over his "pupil," the angel vanishes. With "his slow eies beguiled of their sight," the embodiment of practical reason stands for a while, "sore affraid," before kneeling to feel for Guyon's pulse (7–9). At the end of this episode, after Guyon has returned to consciousness, Spenser leaves us to guess at the impact on the Palmer of his brush with supernatural love and beauty. He seems eager to forget all about it. The guardian angel's presence and disappearance go unmentioned when he explains to Guyon "the whole debate,/Which that straunge knight [i.e., Arthur] for him sustained had" (54). The narrative of Book II gets back on track with Arthur as the angel's surrogate.

When Ficino commented (above, pages 338–41) on the risks that Guyon took in debating with Mammon and yielding to curiosity about his wealth and power, he mentioned Plato's teaching that each

individual "has at birth one certain daemon, the guardian of his life."
He recommended choosing a path in life consistent with one's *genius*
and *ingenium*. To quote *De Vita*: "The misfits, while they do things
unsuited to their celestial patrons, labor in vain, and their supernal
patrons desert them" (III xxiii 371). These "supernal patrons" are
"stars and daemons (or guiding angels divinely stationed on guard)"
(375). Clearly, Guyon has not alienated his patrons, yet he must do
without assurances that they will protect him. Living on an earthly
plane more limited in its vertical dimension than the poem he inhabits, Guyon finds his pleasure in being reunited with the Palmer ("I
ioy thy face to vew," 53), and he bows in reverence to Prince Arthur,
"As to the Patrone of his life" (55).[51] Firsthand knowledge of "the
mighty Queene of *Faery*" and "the beauty of her mind" (ix.3–4)
seems to be the extent of his acquaintance with anything ineffable.

VII

Structural patterns and verbal echoes within episodes in *The Faerie
Queene* provide an unfolding context for each character's limited
perspective, and readers who are moved to emulate Guyon's example
can, if they enter fully into the fiction, take comfort in knowledge
not available to their hero. Guyon's angel enters the poem in league
with benign astrological influences, sharply contrasted with the Saturnian forces at work in Mammon's canto. As a messenger, the angel
resembles Mercury in the *Aeneid*, but Spenser doesn't reinforce that
parallel; instead, he describes the angel with references to "*Phoebus*
face" and a harmless, playful Cupid in the company of Venus and
the Graces. I read stanzas 5 and 6, along with similar evocations of
the unarmed Cupid in the Proem to Book I (3–4), in the parlor of
Alma's castle (II.ix.34), and in the Garden of Adonis (III.vi.49–50),
as programmatic references to the supernal goodness that, according
to Ficino, can be derived from the heavens as antidotes and tempering
agents, counteracting adverse effects of the melancholy humor.

Guyon's encounter with Mammon and his several engagements
with Pyrochles and Cymochles stand in obvious contrast to the temptations of the Bower of Bliss—in contrast, and yet there is continuity
as well, as Spenser anatomizes the entropic tendencies of both irascible
and concupiscent passions. It is also customary to compare the Bower
of Bliss to the Garden of Adonis, centrally placed in Book III and
an *omphalos* for the entire poem: Acrasia's artifice, sex, and sorcery
stand in contrast to the nurturing life force of Venus and Adonis.

These familiar contrasts have drawn attention away from significant thematic differences between the central locales in Books II and III, Mammon's underworld and the "ioyous Paradize" dedicated by Venus to Adonis, "Wher most she wonnes, when she on earth does dwell" (29). The echoes of Virgil in Mammon's underworld and Venus's paradise have already been noted (above, page 334). Tartarus and Elysium are juxtaposed in Book VI of the *Aeneid*, and within the more elaborate pattern of episodes in Spenser's poem, Virgil's twofold account of the other world provides a fundamental structure. In its celebration of procreative love and cyclical vitality within the natural order of things, the Garden of Adonis canto offers correctives to the values promoted by both Mammon and Acrasia.

Melancholia is present in each of these episodes, manifested in different ways: in the character of Mammon and within Guyon himself, as a motive driving the imagination of a *locus amoenus*, and as an undercurrent in the reflections that Spenser's fiction prompts. In Mammon's case, melancholia is the stimulus for avaricious hoarding and for a resentful, delusional preoccupation with earthly power. In Acrasia's sunlit realm, melancholia is an attitude to be attenuated in luxurious leisure, cultivating the suspended animation of art while acutely aware of human mortality. "Gather the Rose of loue, whilest yet is time,/Whilest louing thou mayst loued be with equall crime" (II.xii.75): these lyric lines describe the need to believe in Acrasia's sorcery and the erotic stimulation that it calls into fictive existence. In the Garden of Adonis, mortality is inescapable, but neither that fact nor the emotions it arouses distract the poet from affirmation of all that is natural.

"All things decay in time, and to their end do draw": Venus herself—"great mother *Venus*"—must accept this harsh truth as she witnesses the destruction wrought by "wicked *Tyme*" and mourns "The losse of her deare brood, her deare delight" (III.vi.39–40).[52] These lines, near the middle of Spenser's description of Venus's earthly paradise, remind us that we are in neither Plato's timeless realm of Ideas nor an innocent Eden. The Garden's pleasures are compensatory; it is a memorial to Venus's lost lover, "subiect to mortalitie,/ . . . And by succession made perpetuall,/Transformed oft, and chaunged diuerslie" (47). Promoted to being the perpetual partner of Venus, Adonis enjoys a unique status in Spenser's fertility myth, but other mortal lovers are mentioned (45), having been given perennial lives as flowers and in poetry.

The Bower of Bliss and the Garden of Adonis can be regarded as false and true versions of a reiterated dream, imagining a mythic place where sexuality triumphs over time. It would be more accurate, I believe, to say that the two episodes together point to a conclusion that neither narrative, with its burden of ideals and fantasies, is entirely true in isolation from the other—the truth being that sexuality is both prolific and devouring.

The male players in these two scenarios, Verdant and Adonis, are alike but their destinies differ radically. Having yielded to Acrasia's "sorceree/And witchcraft" (II.xii.72), Verdant remains a beautiful young man but he no longer cares for "warlike Armes, the idle instruments/Of sleeping praise" (79–80). Dallying with Verdant as he slips in and out of consciousness, Acrasia "through his humid eyes did sucke his spright,/Quite molten into lust and pleasure lewd" (73). "Strongly bound" but "soone vntyde" and provided with "counsel sage" by the Palmer, Verdant returns to his senses "both sorrowfull and sad" (82, 84): after his temporary escape from the human condition, he feels a melancholy sense of loss. Adonis's story ends differently; it is a myth rather than a moral exemplum. In the version received from Ovid, Adonis rejected Venus's persuasions to love and was killed by the boar that he had hunted in spite of her warnings. In Spenser's version of the myth, Venus mourns his death and revives his spirit, "Lapped in flowers and pretious spycery,/By her hid from the world." Although Venus, "when euer that she will,/Possesseth him, and of his sweetnesse takes her fill" (III.vi.46), her power is such that in losing his mortal identity, Adonis is not depleted, but becomes "the Father of all formes," enjoying "eternall blis" (47–48).

Both Acrasia and Venus employ magical arts to prolong the pleasure that they find in beauty. In the terms used by D. P. Walker in his classic study of Renaissance magic, Acrasia's art is demonic and at odds with nature, while that flowing from Venus is spiritual and life-affirming. Mammon's demonic magic can be considered in the same light; no less than Acrasia and in contrast to Venus in her garden, Mammon offers an escape from time and loss, but finds value only in lifeless things.

Spenser clearly intended for comparisons to be made between the Garden of Proserpina and the "stately Mount," the allegorical *mons Veneris*, "in the middest" of the broader "first seminary/Of all things, that are borne to liue and dye" (43, 30). On the top of Venus's mountain "A gloomy groue of mirtle trees did rise,"

And in the thickest couert of that shade,
   There was a pleasant Arber, not by art,
   But of the trees owne inclination made.

                             (43–44)

In contrast to the myrtle trees associated with Venus and sexuality, the garden frequented by Proserpina during her season in the under-world is dominated by "mournfull *Cypresse*," and "goodly garnished/ With hearbs and fruits, . . . /Fitt to adorne the dead and deck the drery toombe" (II.vii.51–52). The antithesis is further elaborated:

> And in the midst thereof a siluer seat,
> With a thick Arber goodly ouerdight,
> In which she often vsd from open heat
> Her selfe to shroud, and pleasures to entreat.

                                                                    (53)

This is Spenser at his most sardonic, saying that Proserpina used to "shroud" herself from the infernal heat during her wintry season in hell. And the "pleasures" that she called for were unlike those avail-able to Venus "when euer that she will" with Adonis in her "pleasant Arber." Presumably, "that same fruite of gold" and "that same siluer stoole" of Guyon's final temptation (63) are reminders of the trans-gression—tasting forbidden fruit—that first doomed Proserpina to spend the barren part of every year with Pluto.

The contrast between Mammon's domain and that of Venus with Adonis is not the same as that linking the two versions of paradise. As befits their association with astrological and temperamental oppo-sites, the worlds of Mammon and Venus have almost nothing in common. There is one passage in the description of the Garden where Spenser, zealous to account for everything in "the chaungefull world" (33), alludes to a place reminiscent of Mammon's cave. Hav-ing said that Adonis no longer needs to fear "that foe of his,/ . . . that wilde Bore," he has to explain its whereabouts. In the Adonis myth as it came down to Spenser, the boar is associated with winter and death; in the poem, it stands for "malice" and lawless cru-elty—energies opposed to nurturing love and joy. All that the boar stands for can't be eliminated from the world, but only "emprisoned for ay." The place Venus finds for this purpose is "a strong rocky Caue, which is they say,/ Hewen vnderneath that Mount, that none him losen may" (48): the boar can't be turned loose, nor can he be forgotten.

I have argued elsewhere that this cave beneath the mount of Venus is not, as some say, a frightening aspect of the goddess's powerful sexuality, but is instead a cloacal space.[53] As such, it is aligned, even identified, with Mammon's "excremental netherworld,"[54] a sunless place where gloom is unrelieved by diurnal or seasonal change, where work is endless and effort unrewarded. What kind of magic emerges from this anal/infernal region? Mammon is a charlatan, a confidence man, something like an alchemist. He doesn't bargain with Guyon as Mephostopheles did with Faust, but Guyon's adventure can be seen as a well-tempered variation on the themes of Faust's tragedy.

Throughout this essay I have been working toward a claim that in the Garden of Adonis canto, Spenser invokes images and concepts consistent with Ficino's rationale for therapeutic magic in Book III of *De Vita*. Many details indicate that the canto was conceived with Mammon's canto in mind. The name of Chrysogone is best construed as "gold-producing," and when Spenser describes her marvelous conception of Belphoebe and Amoret (III.vi.2–9), blessed by "*Titan faire*" and other celestial influences, he creates an elaborate antithesis to the miserable sight of Mammon in his "delue,/sunning his threasure hore" (II.vii.Arg.). The twins' natal horoscope could not provide more generous blessings. "*Ioue* laught on *Venus* from his souerayne see,/And *Phoebus* with faire beames did her adorne,/And all the *Graces* rockt her cradle being borne" (2), and when he explains what "reason teacheth" about this "straunge ensample of conception," Spenser adds the moon's benign effect: Apollo's "faire sister for creation/Ministreth matter fit" (8–9). As noted earlier, Ficino regarded the triad of Jupiter, Phoebus Apollo, and Venus (his three Graces), with the moon allied with Venus, as sources of the celestial *spiritus*, and antidotes to Saturn's malignant effects.[55]

In the two halves of Book III, Canto vi, Spenser shows us therapeutic magic at its source, "obtaining life from the heavens." A magician's agency, elsewhere embodied in Merlin, is an aspect of Spenser's author function here. The narrative in Canto vi describes rare accidents and discloses esoteric information with quiet authority—a far cry from the intensity characteristic of Phantastes, and yet there is a connection between the multicolored depiction of "Infinite shapes of thinges dispersed thin" on the walls of Phantastes' chamber (II.ix.50) and the "Infinite shapes of creatures . . . bred" in the Garden's "sundry bed[s]" and "endlesseranckes" (35). An individual imaginative faculty may be as frantic and disordered as "many swarmes of Bees" after their hives are full of honey (II.ix.51), but in the hierarchically ordered cosmos of causes and effects as Spenser envisioned it, a place exists, accessible to the poet's "erected wit," that is as orderly as a honeycomb, full of the preexistent forms that are the source of multitudinous life in the physical world, in individual minds, and in the incantatory language of a poem.

In stanzas 30 to 42 of the Garden of Adonis canto, describing "the first seminary/Of all things" and the triumph over "wicked *Tyme*" of "continuall Spring, and haruest there/Continuall," Phantastes is at work in concert with the other faculties of a consciousness that embraces past, present, and future as a continuum. Ficino would, I believe, see in these stanzas an instance of communication between the internal vital spirits that make individual life and consciousness possible, and the all-encompassing *spiritus mundi* that supports both life and meaning. In stanzas 43 to 51, describing the "stately Mount" of Venus, the apotheosis of Adonis, the reconciliation of Psyche and Cupid with Venus, and the fostering of Amoret, we can all respond with wonder at Spenser's bold reorientation of love's mythology. These stanzas don't offer the last word, of course; this is only the beginning of Amoret's story, and her "sore,/Sore trouble" is anticipated before the canto ends. But the heights reached here are not, like the depths plumbed in Mammon's underworld, laid before us to be rejected.

The George Washington University

Notes

1.   The epigraph's proximate source is Thomas Pynchon's novel *Against the Day* (New York: Viking Penguin, 2006), where it also appears as an epigraph. Previously, the words were quoted in the liner notes for *That's the Way I Feel Now*, an album of tributes to Monk produced by Hal Willner (A & M Records SP-6600, 1984).

2.   *Spenser's Supreme Fiction; Platonic Natural Philosophy and* The Faerie Queene (Toronto: University of Toronto Press, 2001), 266.

3.   Bridget Gellert Lyons's entry, "melancholy," in *The Spenser Encyclopedia* provides an overview, noting that the term "could refer to a pathological state or simply to a temperamental disposition," and surveying the contexts and characters in which melancholia is displayed within *The Faerie Queene*. Alastair Fowler's discussion in *Spenser and the Numbers of Time* (London: Routledge & Kegan Paul, 1964), 101–12, has not been superseded. In *Spenser's Supreme Fiction*, I dealt in passing with mourning and melancholia, primarily with reference to the Garden of Adonis (219–26).

4.   Lynette C. Black, "Prudence in Book II of *The Faerie Queene*," *Spenser Studies* 13 (1999): 65–88; Helen Cooney, "Guyon and his Palmer: Spenser's Emblem of Temperance," *Review of English Studies* 15 (2000): 169–92. Grant Williams, "Phantastes's Flies: The Trauma of Amnesic Enjoyment in Spenser's Memory Palace," *Spenser Studies* 18 (2003): 231–52, comments on the significance of Phantastes in the contest between memory and forgetting that is fundamental to subjectivity in Book II.

5.   Michel de Montaigne, a self-described melancholic, provides in his essay "On Idleness" an interesting point of comparison to Spenser's portrayal of Phantastes. He

offers a string of similitudes for his mind's undisciplined energy in solitude: first it is fallow land producing "hundreds and thousands of different kinds of useless weeds," then a woman without a man to impregnate her properly. "I find," he says in conclusion, "it gives birth to so many chimeras and fantastic monstrosities, one after another, without order or fitness, that, so as to contemplate at my ease their oddness and their strangeness, I began to keep a record of them, hoping in time to make my mind ashamed of itself" (*The Essays: A Selection*, trans. M. A. Screech [London: Penguin Books, 1993], 9–10).

6.   Isabel G. MacCaffrey, *Spenser's Allegory; the Anatomy of Imagination* (Princeton: Princeton University Press, 1976), 241–42.

7.   On this point, see *Spenser's Supreme Fiction*, 53–54.

8.   "Sadness in *The Faerie Queene*," in *Reading the Early Modern Passions; Essays in the Cultural History of Emotion*, ed. Gail Kern Paster, Katherine Rowe, and Mary Floyd-Wilson (Philadelphia: University of Pennsylvania Press, 2004), 240–52, at 245.

9.   Throughout, I will cite Marsilio Ficino, *Three Books on Life*, Medieval and Renaissance Texts and Studies, vol. 57 (1989), ed. and trans. Carol V. Kaske and John R. Clark (Tempe, AZ: Arizona Center for Medieval & Renaissance Studies, 2002). On the book's popularity, see Kaske's introduction, 3.

10.   The Palmer's deliberate pace and his staff are mentioned when he is first introduced (II.i.7); not until xii.41 are we told that it is made "of that same wood" as Mercury's caduceus. The caduceus was also an attribute of Aesculapius, and through him it became a physician's emblem. (See *The Spenser Encyclopedia*, s. vv. "Aesculapius" and "Mercury.")

11.   See Kaske's note 1 on this chapter (412), and her introduction, 42–44.

12.   An imbalance in the substance of the two halves remains (not that there's anything wrong with that): Kaske's expert commentary on Book III requires more than twice the pages devoted to Books I and II.

13.   See Kaske's introduction, 40.

14.   *Music in Renaissance Magic* (Chicago: University of Chicago Press, 1993), 121. Tomlinson's discussion of Ficino's *spiritus* doctrine and its sources is extensive: see 105–34. Kaske's introduction, 40–53, also discusses the places that *spiritus* occupies in Ficino's cosmology and his conception of human nature, together with its importance in the rationales for astrology and magic. I have discussed Spenser's uses of the terms "spright" and "spirit" in *Spenser's Supreme Fiction*, 176–81; see also 105–07, 122–23, 263–66.

15.   Adding something to D. P. Walker's interpretation of this passage, Michael J. B. Allen suggests that the song is, in effect, a daemon: *The Platonism of Marsilio Ficino* (Berkeley: University of California Press, 1984), 25–27.

16.   Regarding Ficino's views on an individual's *ingenium*, *genius*, and personal daemon, see Allen's *Platonism of Marsilio Ficino*, 7–22, and also his *Nuptial Arithmetic; Marsilio Ficino's Commentary on the Fatal Number in Book VIII of Plato's* Republic (Berkeley: University of California Press, 1994), 88–89.

17.   Harry Berger, Jr., *Second World and Green World: Studies in Renaissance Fiction-Making* (Berkeley: University of California Press, 1988), 227. I have developed a related train of thought in *Spenser's Supreme Fiction*, 85–87.

18.   *Music in Renaissance Magic*, 21; see 23–27. Tomlinson quotes from *Truth and Method*, 262–63.

19.   *Music in Renaissance Magic*, 247; the quotation is from *The Order of Things*, 50.

20.   See Kaske's introduction, 8–12 and 55–70.

21.   See fig. 2 in Fowler, *Numbers of Time*, 97.

22.   The engravings are not reproduced here, but are readily available in print and as downloads from internet sources.

23.   *The Life and Art of Albrecht Dürer*, 4th ed. (Princeton: Princeton University Press, 1955), 151.

24.   Patrick Doorly, "Dürer's *Melencolia I*: Plato's Abandoned Search for the Beautiful," *Art Bulletin* 86 (2004): 255–76, rejects much of Panofsky's interpretation; on the strength of a 1986 article by Robert Grigg, he says that this claim that the two *Meisterstiche* were conceived as a pair has been "discredited" (276n125).

25.   Erasmus's edition, prefaced by his exemplary *Vita Hieronymi*, was published by Johannes Frobenius in 1516. On the importance of Jerome for Erasmus and other humanists, see Lisa Jardine, *Erasmus, Man of Letters* (Princeton: Princeton University Press, 1993), 55–82; also Peter W. Parshall, "Albrecht Dürer's St. Jerome in His Study: A Philological Reference," *Art Bulletin* 53 (1971): 303–05.

26.   See Raymond Klibansky, Erwin Panofsky, and Fritz Saxl, *Saturn and Melancholy: Studies in the History of Natural Philosophy, Religion, and Art* (New York: Basic Books, 1964), 241–47.

27.   *Life and Art of Dürer*, 156–57; cf. 160–68. Doorly (269–70) rightly identifies Panofsky's "rhombo-hedron" as a failed attempt at fashioning a dodecahedron. The significance of that regular solid derives from Plato's *Timaeus*, 55c: see Francis M. Cornford, *Plato's Cosmology: The* Timaeus *of Plato* (Indianapolis: Bobbs-Merrill, n.d.), 218–20, where Plutarch is cited, interpreting the dodecahedron as symbolic of heaven, light, aether, or the fifth substance (i.e., the quintessence).

28.   *Life and Art of Dürer*, 169–70; cf. 168. On p. 170, the quotation cited by Panofsky is "cannot extend their thought beyond *the limits of* space" (emphasis added). He is quoting for a second time a statement by Henry of Ghent, whom he introduced on p. 168: according to this scholastic philosopher, there are melancholics "in whom the imaginative power predominates over the cognitive one," and such men "become excellent mathematicians but very bad metaphysicians, for they cannot extend their thought beyond location and space which are the foundations of mathematics." I would note that in late classical and medieval Latin the term "mathematici" sometimes refers to astrologers.

29.   Discussion of Agrippa is beyond my scope here; see *Spenser's Supreme Fiction*, 43–45, 121–24, and *The Spenser Encyclopedia*, s. v. "Agrippa." English readers in Spenser's generation were familiar with both the skeptic and the esoteric sides of Agrippa's paradoxical personality. His treatise *Of the Vanitie and Vncertaintie of the Artes and Sciences*, first published in Latin in 1530 and often reprinted, appeared in English in 1569 and was reprinted in 1575. Harvey cites Agrippa in his exchange of letters with Spenser; Sidney's *Defence* owes a debt to him. Portions of Agrippa's *De Occulta Philosophia*, including passages taken verbatim from *De Vita coelitus comparanda*, appear in the vernacular encyclopedia, *Batman vppon Bartholome* (1582).

30.   *Numbers of Time*, 63–121; on Aquarius and Saturn in Book II, see 94–106. It should be noted that Fowler was the first scholar writing on Spenser to see the relevance of Ficino's *De Vita*.

31. See Hamilton's edition at II.vii.7.5, and Prescott, s. v. "Mammon," in *The Spenser Encyclopedia*.

32. *Three Books of Occult Philosophy*, III.xviii, quoted in James Nohrnberg, *The Analogy of* The Faerie Queene (Princeton: Princeton University Press, 1976, 1980), 331.

33. See *Spenser's Moral Allegory* (Toronto: University of Toronto Press, 1989), 58–59, 64–67.

34. Harry Berger, Jr., was the first to describe Guyon's vulnerability as *curiositas*: see *The Allegorical Temper: Vision and Reality in Book II of Spenser's 'Faerie Queene'* (New Haven: Yale University Press, 1957), 22–27.

35. For two recent opinions, see Grant Williams, "Phantastes's Flies" (cited above, n. 4); and Paul Suttie, "Moral Ambivalence in the Legend of Temperance," *Spenser Studies* 19 (2004): 125–33.

36. Quoted and interpreted by Ruth Mohl in her biographical entry in *The Spenser Encyclopedia*, 671.

37. Quoting from Richard A. McCabe's prose translation of ll. 66–77 in "Ad Ornatissimum virum": Edmund Spenser, *The Shorter Poems* (London: Penguin Books, 1999), 160–61 and 578.

38. See Hamilton's note on the source of Guyon's response to Mammon's temptation, II.vii.33.

39. In *Melencolia I*, this trait is played down, but Panofsky documents it in several other images: see *Life and Art of Dürer*, 162–63 and figs. 210–14.

40. I will cite the *Nichomachean Ethics*, trans. Martin Ostwald (Indianapolis and New York: Bobbs-Merrill, 1962); V iii comprises 1132b21–34a15 in Bekker's numbers. I will refer to the translation as "Ostwald," followed by a page reference.

41. On Henry VIII's debasement of the currency and Elizabeth's response, see Nicholas Mayhew, *Sterling, the History of a Currency* (New York: John Wiley, 2000), 42–47, 56–61, and C. E. Challis, *The Tudor Coinage* (Manchester: Manchester University Press, 1978), 118–29. Sir Thomas Smith's *Discourse of the Commonweal of This Realm of England* (composed in 1549, revised in 1576, published anonymously in 1581) offered a clear-eyed account of the English economy and its problems; for an account of Smith's career and thought, see Neal Wood, *Foundations of Political Economy; Some Early Tudor Views on State and Society* (Berkeley and Los Angeles: University of California Press, 1994), 191–235. It is likely that Spenser was familiar with Smith's *Discourse of the Commonweal*, since Gabriel Harvey revered him as a mentor and patron.

42. Louis Adrian Montrose, "The Elizabethan Subject and the Spenserian Text," in *Literary Theory / Renaissance Texts*, ed. Patricia Parker and David Quint (Baltimore: Johns Hopkins University Press, 1986), 303–40; and "Spenser's Domestic Domain: Poetry, Property, and the Early Modern Subject," in *Subject and Object in Renaissance Culture*, ed. Margreta de Grazia, Maureen Quilligan, and Peter Stallybrass (Cambridge: Cambridge University Press, 1996), 83–130.

43. *Virgilius cum commentariis quinque* (Lyons: Jacques Sachon, 1499), fol. 215v, quoted in *Spenser's Supreme Fiction*, 109–10. See *Aeneid* V 835–63, and VI 337–83 for Aeneas's encounter with Palinurus's troubled spirit in the underworld.

44. *De Vita* III xxiii 371. Kaske's note supplies references to *Phaedo* 107d–08b and *Rep.* 10.617d–e, 620d–e, with further loci in Latin literature for the doctrine of individual *genii*.

45.   Scholarly interest in this part of the episode with Mammon began with the first annotated edition of *The Faerie Queene*, John Upton's (1758): he proposed that some aspects of Guyon's ordeal resembled initiation into the Eleusinian mysteries. Frank Kermode developed the idea in a seminal essay, "The Cave of Mammon," first published in 1960. Along similar lines, Alastair Fowler says, "indeed Guyon himself re-enacts the myth of Proserpina" (*Numbers of Time* 82–83). Douglas Brooks-Davies broadens the argument for the relevance of ancient mysteries and fertility cults considerably: see his article, "mysteries," in *The Spenser Encyclopedia*, which summarizes evidence and opinions developed in other publications. In the *Encyclopedia*, see also "Tantalus, Pilate" by Anne Lake Prescott.

46.   Hamilton's note on stanzas 53–55 reminds us that this is one of the places where the pregnant phrase "in the midst" appears: these stanzas occupy the "numerical midpoint of the *1590* edition."

47.   William Nelson, *The Poetry of Edmund Spenser* (New York: Columbia University Press, 1963), 182–84.

48.   *The Spenser Encyclopedia*, 486b. As I have observed elsewhere (*Spenser's Supreme Fiction* 38), Spenser's fascination with the figures of Ceres and Proserpina can be traced to his assimilation of themes in Ovid and Ariosto, evident as early as 1580 in his verse letter to Gabriel Harvey.

49.   See Paul Suttie, "Edmund Spenser's Political Pragmatism," *Studies in Philology* 95 (1998): 56–76, at 64–65.

50.   For comments on Spenser's comparison of the angel to Cupid, see R. M. Cummings, "An Iconographical Puzzle: Spenser's Cupid at *Faerie Queene*, II, viii," *Journal of the Warburg and Courtauld Institutes* 33 (1970): 317–21.

51.   Cf. Theresa M. Krier, *Gazing on Secret Sights; Spenser, Classical Imitation, and the Decorums of Vision* (Ithaca, NY: Cornell University Press, 1990), 94–99, where Guyon's predicament is compared to that of Aeneas.

52.   I have discussed this aspect of the Garden in *Spenser's Supreme Fiction*, in a segment titled "The Work of Mourning" (219–26).

53.   See *Spenser's Supreme Fiction*, 215–18.

54.   The phrase comes from Grant Williams; he points out that the entrance to Alma's castle resembles a mouth, while when Guyon follows Mammon, he enters "from the anal not the oral side." See "Phantastes's Flies" (reference in n. 4 above), 242.

55.   See *De Vita* III iv–vii (259–77), discussed above, page 334. Nohrnberg, *The Analogy of* The Faerie Queene 461–70, explicates Ficino's various comments on the Graces with reference to Belphoebe, Amoret, and Florimell; Hamilton's note on III.vi.2 provides references to other scholarship on the horoscope.

KENNETH GROSS

Green Thoughts in a Green Shade

Spenser's Garden of Adonis, while clearly a cosmological fiction and a picture of the hidden processes of nature, is also a garden of mind, a garden of thought. It is an image of the life and motions of human thought, thought's modes of continuity, change, and survival. It reflects the poet's sense of the ontology of mental phenomena like memories, dreams, and phantasms; it shows us the human mind in its generativity, its pleasure, as well as its violence, its way of inhabiting loss. In broad terms, Spenser's vision of this place (or collection of places) reflects profound shifts in Renaissance ideas about the mind, about the space of thinking, specifically in its freedom of play and its intensely secular, time-bound character; for all that it speaks of hidden, even quasi-divine energies, it presents a moving order that remains cut off from any clear transcendental grounds of meaning. In its ambiguity as well as its radical opacity, the Garden also offers a fiction of mind that anticipates more modern pictures of mental process.

Il faut cultiver notre jardin.

—Voltaire, *Candide*

E DMUND SPENSER'S GARDEN of Adonis, which holds the center of *FQ* III, the book of chastity, is most obviously a cosmological fiction, a picture of cosmic fact, an account of how the order of forms in the world both exists and comes into being. Spenser seems to want it to provide us with an image of all of the creative processes that are required for life. The episode lets us see the created world itself as a complex, moving, sexualized landscape, as both *natura naturata* and *natura naturans*, as act and potency at once. This world contains within itself a principle of ordered change. He also shows us the Garden as something both present and hidden, fallen and unfallen,

Spenser Studies: A Renaissance Poetry Annual, Volume XXIV, Copyright © 2009 AMS Press, Inc. All rights reserved.

both inside and outside the visible, phenomenal world. It is indeed less a place than a process, a form of motion and transformation, one hard to measure according to any fixed or singular myth of transcendental order. It is a garden of ongoing temporality as much as a garden of pristine origins or final reckonings—if this episode shows Spenser composing an apocalypse, as one scholar has suggested, it is an apocalypse of the middle.[1] An image of the care and support of natural being, it is as much a salvage-yard as a nursery or lying-in hospital, as James Nohrnberg comments—it is a place haunted by a sense of things dying and embalmed as well as restored and reborn.[2] Its generative power is close to that of the frightful but prolific Chaos that lies within or below the garden.[3] In creating this imaginary place—or rather this collection of places (the four-line argument to the canto, indeed, refers to "The Gardins of Adonis")—Spenser gives us at once a landscape and a map of that landscape. Or, perhaps you could say, he shows us a map whose signs and symbols have begun to take on a life of their own (under the generative force of a love that the poet represents most clearly in the coupling of Venus and Adonis, even as it is diffused more widely through the Garden as a whole). Most significant is what the episode says about the life of forms in time, including the various forms of time itself, the various images of change, preservation, and contingency that our tradition offers. Spenser's great conceptual risk is to place time at once at the center of the Garden, to make time its constitutive element, and yet to make time the Garden's enemy, its "troubler." At the center of the Garden is something that wrecks all centers.

I want to add to this broad description a further intuition or speculation. My thought is that this metaphysical garden is also a garden of mind, a garden of thought; this garden is an image of the motion of thought, of its mode of life, its survival and force of continuity as well as its mode of dying. In dwelling so much on the work of time in the Garden of Adonis, Spenser is writing about the temporality of thought, its mutability, something that speaks to his understanding of both thought's violence and its mournfulness. Like other iconographies of thinking, as Angus Fletcher describes them, Spenser's garden also gives us an image of the opacity of thought, an image of how thought recedes from representation into "uncouth forms," even as the poet intimates something about our strange attachment to such opacity.[4] The ontology of the Garden, that is to say, reflects the ontology of thought as well as the ontology of the natural world or of being in general; it reflects the ontology of mental phenomena like memories, dreams, and phantasms, productions of a mind that to Spenser seems as dangerously generative as the sun-warmed mud of the Nile River.[5] The way things move and change within the Garden reflects the movement of thought; it gives us an image of how thought comes to us, its ambition and size, its environment, what thought bears of the ideal and of the material. From one perspective, Spenser's image of thought in the Garden reflects deep shifts in Renaissance ideas about the mind, about the space and domain of thinking, in particular its increasing secularity, its worldliness and isolation from any clear transcendental origin. From another, it speaks to the conditions that will make possible the poetry of Romanticism.

Samuel Taylor Coleridge spoke about Spenser's Faerie, with its unfixed boundaries and shifting thresholds, as essentially a domain of mental space.[6] And yet the idea of a thought-ful Garden of Adonis is not an obvious one. For one thing, Spenser is rarely so bluntly hermetic in his allegory; his secrets are open secrets. He ordinarily gives readers clearer clues about his subject, as in the case of the allegory of mental faculties in the Castle of Alma, Book II, canto x, even if he also typically departs from and complicates those clues, opens his emblematic images up to larger relations, lets them slip the mooring of their original frame of reference. (This complicating drift of reference is indeed central to Spenser's mode of poetic thinking.) When he wants to show us some agent or piece of landscape as a projection of a character's mental state he usually signals us more clearly, as in Book I, at those moments when Redcrosse encounters enemies who are the externalized images of his own error, faithlessness, and despair. In contrast to these cases, the possibility of reading an allegory of mind within the Garden of Adonis—so much more obviously an image of cosmic and natural process—depends on a more blank or arbitrary sort of allegoresis than is characteristic of the poet. It may indeed feel rather like the imposed allegory of Philo or Fulgentius. As a thought experiment about an allegory of thought, such a reading indeed threatens to become tautological.

The title of this paper brings in the supporting analogy of Andrew Marvell's "The Garden," a poem that makes quite explicit the image of the garden as a place of thought and reflection, that indeed frames the garden as itself a model or diagram of the mind, a picture of the mind's way of measuring and containing the world, even as it sets the world at a distance. Marvell's garden offers a picture of the mind's way of reflecting both upon the world and upon itself—the idea of the speaker's withdrawing *into* his garden yielding up an image of a garden created *within* the mind, "Annihilating all that's made / To a green thought in a green shade."[7] "The Garden," like Milton's "Il Penseroso" (one of Marvell's source texts), draws on older poetic traditions (especially pastoral) that identify garden spaces as sites of reflection, places of mental work and mental play, as if a representation of thought were peculiarly fitted to a domain where natural forces are subjected to and reshaped by human artifice. The example of Marvell may indeed suggest how a later poet might have read Spenser's fiction in the Garden of Adonis. There are strong limits to the analogy, though, however heuristically useful it is. Not only is Marvell analytic where Spenser is synthetic, Spenser shows us no obvious thinking subject in his Garden, no explicit image of a mind or of thinking either containing or contained by the Garden (just as he shows us no gardener, though he does give us a gatekeeper, an entity named, appropriately enough, Genius). Yet this lack, I will argue, is exactly part of its strength as an image of thinking—that the process of thinking is there so diffused, so weirdly impersonal (for all that the poet says he knows the pleasures of the Garden personally, "by trial"). We feel the element of thought not in the representation of a thinking subject—as we might find it in Shakespeare or Milton—but in the movement from detail to detail of the description, in the invitation to make sense of the gaps and hidden connections which that movement suggests.

Neoplatonic cosmogonies from Plotinus to Bernardus Sylvestris and Marsilio Ficino tend to posit a primal, transcendental mind as a controlling agent within cosmological action. This primal, mental unity not only reflects on itself but, as it were, thinks by overflow and emanation the hierarchical world of Ideas from which the lower human and natural world takes its orders. Plotinus, for example—in a model followed by Renaissance Neoplatonists such as Ficino—describes eternal Nous or Mind creating the material world as a moving, temporalized image of the intelligible one, a world that in turn ideally longs for and even progresses back toward its fixed, eternal origins. The pattern mirrors the Biblical image of a God at once making a world and "seeing" that its forms and orders are "good." The following lines from Plotinus show us the cosmos seen under the aspect of thought, as a product of the procreative power of Mind; they offer at the same time an image of the fecundity of human contemplation:

> Begetting originates in contemplation and ends in the production of a form, that is, a new object of contemplation. In general, all things as they are images of their generating principles produce forms and objects of contemplation. . . . Moreover, animals generate due to the activity within them of seminal reasons. Generation is a contemplation. It results from the longing of pregnancy to produce a multiplicity of forms and objects

of contemplation, to fill everything with reason, and never to cease from contemplation. . . . All the faults met with in begotten things or in actions are due to the fact that one did stray from the object of one's contemplation. The poor workman resembles the producer of bad forms.

(*Enneads* III.viii.7)[8]

Such a picture underlies that important strain in Renaissance thought that links the work of the human maker or thinker to the work of a creating God, a thinker of the first idea, as Wallace Stevens puts it. It is a model that allows human art to discover and possess within itself something of the original, hidden orders of nature, and to create thereby a consonance or marriage of spiritual and material realms—even though Plotinus reminds us as well of those distracted workers in the factory of mind who produce illusions and violent fantasies that separate us from the real.

This tradition, in which an idealized image of human thought is projected onto the workings of the cosmos, is a central part of Spenser's inheritance in the Garden of Adonis episode—crucially mediated by an idea "developed by the Stoics . . . taken up by Plotinus and elaborated by Augustine," in which the created world, bound to time, is envisioned as a divinely adorned or inseminated garden, nature and temporal existence being driven by what are called "seminal reasons" or *logoi spermatikoi*, planted in matter and shaping its development.[9] We can find versions of this picture of creation as ideation in Renaissance authors from Leon Battista Alberti to George Puttenham. The lines from Plotinus just quoted suggest that this is an analogy that keeps the activity of mind in touch with the material and sexual orders of creation, even as it is touched by the possibility of error and failure. Yet even if we see here the general background of Spenser's invention, this model of two mirroring or interinvolved minds—cosmic and human—is too idealizing to catch at the more elusive, suspended quality of Spenser's picture of mind in the Garden, an image that so starkly cuts the powers of the Garden off from any articulated, transcendental measures or hierarchies, steeping it inescapably in the soil—at once volatile and "fruitful"—of temporal process. Spenser explores more radically what is at stake in imagining the products of mind at work in the world, what the wishes and costs are of that projection. In the process, Spenser's text also reminds us implicitly that any such cosmic garden as we find in Plotinus or Ficino should be seen not just as the metaphysical ground but also as the created product of allegorical thinking.

One other analogy for an allegory of mind in Spenser's Garden can be found in a passage from Nicholas of Cusa's *De Mente Idiota*. To convey his sense of the mind as a living substance that is, at once, a human possession and yet similar to the absolute substance of God, Cusanus describes it as a kind of fantastically generative seed planted within human beings. "Because the mind is a 'divine seed' that conceptually enfolds within its own power the exemplars of all things, it is at once placed by God (from whom it has that power, by virtue of having received it from God) in a suitable earthen body, where it can bear fruit and can unfold from itself, conceptually, an all encompassing unity of things."[10] The mind's power displays itself especially in a quasi-divine capacity to supply paradoxical, always shifting and conjectural pictures of both its own work and the truth of God, even as the mind remains essentially cut off from final access to either—something that Cusanus is at pains to make clear. (It is at moments like this that Cusanus often feels like a Renaissance precursor of Immanuel Kant.) For Cusanus, the mind's own contradictions wall it off from any such absolute knowledge, much as the human soul is cut off from free access to original innocence as a result of the Fall. Here, as Ronald Levao puts it, the constructive aspect of human vision dovetails with the destructive or skeptical side, making terminal points into liminal ones (impossible probabilities).[11] For Cusanus, while he links the work of mind to an image of natural generation, will not link that mind genealogically or metaphysically to any higher, cosmic process of thinking; such a link is itself, indeed, only one more speculative analogy. In this Cusanus is close to Sir Philip Sidney in his *Defence of Poesie*. For while Sidney does at times suggest that the poet's words reflect his understanding, however uncertain, of the eternal archetypes, he also stresses the strange autonomy of the poet as maker of literary *kosmoi*, his way of becoming "in effect another nature" that brings forth things in a space that has no certain ground within higher or hidden orders of creation.

And yet, it seems to me, even to link Spenser's allegory of mind to those of Cusanus or Sidney is to speak in a very rough, imperfect fashion. It may clarify the possible connection for Renaissance writers between minds and gardens, but it doesn't really get at the conceptual complexity of Spenser's design, nor adequately account for the troubling fact (troubling, that is, if one accepts my reading as a useful possibility) that Spenser never makes the link with thinking explicit, nor places a thinker within the Garden.

To get at what I am after, it is better to start with a more general sort of conceptual analysis, the working out of a poetic conceit. In Canto vi of Book III, let us say that we get a picture of mind not as a cave, archive, treasure house, foundry, court, labyrinth, theater of memory, or house of phantasms, but rather as an ancient and generative soil, a nursery or storehouse of "germens." We see in the Garden an image of the mind's generosity and its receptiveness, its fecundity and its powers of delight. We see the mind as a place in which thoughts circulate without clear origin, a site in which they are clothed in form and sent into the world, and a place to which thoughts can return from the world, where they are sorted, replanted, and reformed. We also see in this garden an image of how thoughts are stored, treasured, and preserved for future use. At the same time, we see thoughts as things that may be buried, frozen, trapped, and mourned over. The Garden shows us the mind as something that is both inside and outside the world, a microcosm that contains, or tries to contain, "all things," "all creatures," all forms (as well as "all plenty" and "all pleasure"). It is figured as a place of refuge from the world, a place to withdraw into, a place to keep secrets safe from the prying eyes and envious desires of others. Yet it is not a pristine or timeless safe house, rather it is a ground soaked in and watered by time and change, threatened by violences from both within and without that are yet involved deeply with its fecundity. In this garden we see an image of the mind as something that is able to terrorize itself, even to keep secrets from itself, a domain whose most mysterious and productive centers hover over a buried chaos and a buried monster. (Here he suggests how allegory tends to become a mode of terror.)

This analogizing, however suggestive it may be, is yet too static. If one feels the Garden as itself a mode of mental space this is also because, in reading the text, one is so aware of the speed and complexity of the poet's own mind as he works to invent this place on the page, always turning and reshaping the terms of his description. One struggles as one reads to grasp the unstable temporal and metaphysical dimensions of what is described, the very excess of specification about boundaries and thresholds contributing to this feeling. In the moving map that constitutes the Garden of Adonis, one senses the poet responding to his own figures as he writes, answering the questions, fears, and hopes that his description opens up with fresh images and speculations. It is as if in the stanzas that unfold the Garden or Gardens of Adonis the poet overheard himself thinking. This process, this speed of change, lends an unpredictable, groundless feel to his account of this ground of thought. Spenser's shifting, even frenzied cosmogonizing indeed reminds me less of Neoplatonic or hexameral allegory than of the freer, more self-consciously dramatic projections of cosmic analogy in Shakespeare. I am thinking, for example, of Lear's speeches during the storm scene, where he becomes a kind of mad magus, generating so many conflicting, transparently willful or defensive *kosmoi* of justice and revenge, each linked to and yet undoing the others—one of his visions projecting, indeed, the apocalyptic wish to "spill" in one moment "all germens . . . that make ingrateful man" (3.2.8–9),[12] imagining a cosmic seedbed only to call for its destruction. The volatility of Spenser's imaginative work is especially clear when we come to the vexed matter of time in the Garden.

At the risk of flattening out the episode, it will be useful to trace a rough summary of the canto's central movement. We begin by reading of a place that seems, as I said, set apart from the burdens of death and dissolution. From what we are first told, the "state of life"—that also includes the realm of earthly death—is a domain that is invaded *from* the Garden, as if the Garden were outside or beyond earthly life. The Garden is a refuge from life, the poet insists, a protected paradise. Despite this insistence, this momentary wish, however, the Garden's place within the cycle of death and life becomes more and more emphatic as the canto progresses. As one reads, as the voice of the narrator explores the Garden, the idea of time looms up more and more as both a part of the system and as a threat to the Garden's processes. Time sticks to its forms; its work makes those processes indeed seem self-destructive. As if to show us concretely, by an exemplary anecdote, how imperfect substances "catch" form and feature in the Garden, a personification of Time itself suddenly looms up as a "great enimy" to all things that live in the place (stanza 39). While this version of Time does mow things down with his scythe, as does that image of Time derived from the Greek god Kronos, he also—in a more powerful revision of the tradition—beats down the Garden's plants with his "flaggy wings," Time's violence being embodied in the tools of his progress or flight. Time thus converts this eternal pleasure garden into a fallen place, through which the goddess Venus walks mourning, like Yahweh walking through Eden after the fall in Genesis (stanza 40). Yet no sooner does the poet's mind bring into view so dangerous an enemy than he tries to undo that enemy—not so much denying Time's presence as dissolving its destructive agency into a larger movement or principle. If Spenser cannot sustain his first lie against time—the idea that his Garden is untouched by death—he tries in compensation to frame a second, more dialectical time-fiction. The image of winged Time, perhaps because it is a cliché as much as a veritable psychic menace, turns in the lines that follow from a promise of discontinuity into one of continuity. Time, that is, suddenly turns from being a breach of order into being a part of a more paradoxical order, an order in which time exists as a gift, a form of grace or blessing. ("But were it not, that *Time* their troubler is" [stanza 41].) This turn is most striking in that stanza where, against the image of Time as entropic destroyer, we suddenly get the great, redemptive enjambment of "There is continuall spring and harvest there / Continuall, both meeting at one time" (stanza 42). It's an attempt to hold together beginning and ending, spring and fall, within a subtler dialectic. Time is now represented as a relation, a precarious relational unity, rather than as a creature or personification in its own right.[13] This more mobile, labile form of time, the expression of both the pleasure principle and the reality principle, undoes that work of mind by which time is the reified object of fear, an idol or a demon more than a proper god.

As if reassured by this new imagining, the poet moves forward to reveal more hidden things within his Garden. In particular, he shows us the "gloomy grove" concealed at its center, formed of myrtle trees, safe from the malice of the Stygian gods (stanzas 43–44). It's a place where loss and restoration, pain and pleasure, mingle all the more complexly. Significantly, it is not just a place of earthly origination but a place of memory, a place that holds the memorial emblems ("every sort of flowre") into which dead poets, workers in the domain of memory, have been transformed by the work of other poets (stanza 45). As is the case with other Ovidian transformations, these flowers represent both forms of survival and forms of ruin. We see in them redemptive figurations of poetic work and fame (fame as the enemy of time), but also an array of clichéd relics or commonplaces (verbal time-servers, you might say).[14] The plenty of this grove is a little like the plenty of the rhetorical *copia* which Renaissance rhetoricians expected to furnish the mind of the writer—supply and waste both meeting at one time. One may recall here the passage in Plato's *Phaedrus* where Socrates invites Phaedrus to think about "gardens of Adonis," those small clay forcing pots filled with fast-growing and fast-dying plants that were used as part of an annual ritual celebration in honor of the death and rebirth of the lover of Venus. (Spenser might have known from Pliny that this ritual was celebrated especially by prostitutes.)[15] These miniature "gardens" were, in ancient Greece, a proverbial image for all sterile, rootless, and quickly withering things. Such pots offered derisory reflections of true life, their rapid powers of growth constituting, paradoxically, a violence against nature, "a greenness that conceals death," as Theophrastus wrote in his treatise on plants, as opposed to the sturdier life of plants sown in the ground and tended by a proper gardener. Such gardens, Plato's

Socrates argues, provide a precise metaphor for the mutability and
mortality, even bastard-like status, of thoughts that are committed to
the illusory fixity of the written word—something that nourishes
only oblivion, as opposed to the means by which thoughts are sustained and opened up to response by the vivifying powers of dialectic.
I suspect that it would be less jarring to some readers if I called the
Garden of Adonis a garden of textuality rather than a garden of mind
or a garden of thinking, an image of what Terence Cave has called
"the cornucopian text."[16] But even if this is partly true, even if Spenser's exploded image of those imploded pots constitutes a wild rejoinder to Plato's slander of the written word, a mythic defense of
writing's preservative powers, that image yet calls out to a different
order of things, something that takes us beyond the world of the text.

To continue the analysis: Pushed by his own fiction to show us
something more extreme, more paradoxical, Spenser discovers
among these flowers at the Garden's center the figure of Adonis.
This wounded figure appears, as one reads, as if from nowhere; he
is no longer lost, we are suddenly told, but instead preserved within
the Garden, where Venus always meets him and takes her solace from
him. He lies in the center "lapped in flowres and pretious spycery"
(stanza 46), an image that suggests at once seduction and mourning,
not to mention sacrifice. Crucial as it is to his picture, Spenser lends
the idea of Adonis's survival a distinctly speculative cast. He is, as it
were, a hearsay survivor, as the poet writes in the line immediately
preceding that quoted above: "There yet, some say, in secret he does
ly." Spenser conjures up Adonis here to give a more local habitation
and name to the idea that dying things might not only be preserved
in the Garden but become the sources of the world's ongoing life.
This rumored lover of Venus, vulnerable, embalmed, is indeed
quickly converted by Spenser's lines into the "Father of all formes,"
one who lives "eterne in mutabilitie" (stanza 47). Whatever we make
of this resonant paradox, the meaning of the dying and reborn Adonis
cannot be contained by seeing in him simply a myth of natural generation and regeneration. Spenser's image of Adonis, boy and man,
child and father at once, is closer to those vexed figures of poetic
perpetuation framed in Shakespeare's sonnets. The embalmed and
eroticized Adonis composes (as certain recurrent tropes in Shakespeare's sonnets do) a figure of wish and will, a figure of desire that
is joined to a stark sort of disenchantment. If the Garden of Adonis
presents us with an image of nature, it is nature as the source and
habitation of that which is unnatural. In this context, Spenser reaches
beyond the resilient voicing of universal lament such as we hear in
his "Ruines of Time" or in the closing stanzas of the Mutablitie

Cantos. In the Garden, the image of time as ruinous and destructive is transformed into, or accommodated to, a vision of time as charity, gift, time as a sustainer of growth—a figure that echoes conventional images of Time as father of truth or unfolder of providential order, but one that is more troubling insofar as Spenser's argument keeps the Garden's orders of recuperation so strongly within the secular world, within the cycle of earthly life and death. Furthermore, Spenser's Adonis is no happy thinker of green thoughts within a green shade; he is rather strangely passive, unthinking, unresponsive, unconscious; no author, no executor, no magus. Therein lies something of both his power and his erotic charm (the erotic charm of thought as well as of the sexual body). One might ask, indeed, whether the recumbent Adonis is not in fact the hidden dreamer of the garden world that contains him, as Lewis Carroll's Red King in *Alice in Wonderland* is said to be dreaming the world in which he sleeps, and so can be awakened only at the peril of the world's collapsing.[17] We may have a hard time thinking him because he is thinking us.

Harry Berger, Jr. notes that the description of Adonis is linked by verbal echoes to Spenser's picture of the horrible womb of Chaos lying below the Garden. This linkage in part supports the allegorical reading of Adonis, proposed by some scholars, as an image of matter, the never-dying stuff of creation, always changing its shape, always buried and unburied. Adonis here is the "Father of all formes" in his endless potency for receiving form. Such a reading is suggested by the text itself, but it hardly does justice to this figure's association with the realm of Chaos. The life-giving Adonis is also linked to that deathly boar, his own murderer, locked below the bower on top of the Garden's central hill. As Berger also suggests, Spenser's ambiguous use of pronouns in fact places the boar, just for a moment, as the possible referent of a line that more properly describes Adonis himself as living "in eternall blis." Spenser's wording even associates this buried enemy with Venus herself. Such connections help support Berger's argument that, in such a scene, Spenser is not just framing an image of cosmic or natural generation, but an image of the mind, especially of the creative consciousness that must work in the world, in time. The presence of the boar, he argues, suggests traces of a consciousness of death, and of poetry's complicity with death, that is at the center of this garden of human thought. They show us the thought of death, "the pull of death beneath the dream of perpetual regeneration."[18] The complexly infolded image suggests, indeed, that this form of death is bound up strangely with eros; it is the reality principle and the pleasure principle both meeting at one time. Again, the poem speaks not just of inhuman or material activities of decay, ruin, or entropy; it speaks of a death or murderousness that haunts the human mind and human desire. For one thing, Spenser here touches on the mind's violent will to mastery and on its tendency to fixate itself, as if the mind in its very copiousness were also bound up with a deathly compulsion to repeat, or to wound itself by giving form to its fears in the guise of terrifying clichés. Shakespeare's "Venus and Adonis," itself a stark, de-allegorizing response to and revision of Spenser's mythopoetic fiction, is more direct about this link between eros and death. Shakespeare's vocal Venus makes her dead lover not so much the father of all forms as the father of all of love's paradoxes and contradictions, even identifying Adonis with death itself, which takes concrete shape in that poem not as a "wide womb" but rather as a "wide wound."[19] But the lesson is not solely a skeptical or bitter one for Berger. He suggests, indeed, that the closeness of Adonis to the destructive boar—a double of winged Time—suggests a desire to transform eros from an impersonal, unconscious energy, or the conscious will for an escape from pain into momentary pleasure; rather, it can become a conscious, human, shaping force that understands its own relation to time, history, and loss, that must work *through* "death, suffering, and tension toward the development and fulfillment of a single human soul, toward the knowledge of true love whereby each soul recognizes the value of the other. It is because this must be understood that the boar is neither killed nor exiled but kept fast in the cave of consciousness as it is already in the cage of the body."[20]

Berger's reading of the iconography of thought in this episode has its limitations; for one thing, it does not meet the fact that this image of something "kept fast in the caves of consciousness" is so caught by a feeling of things *un*conscious, buried, unknown, unreadable. (Though perhaps some acknowledgement of this is implicit in Berger's idea of "*caves* of consciousness"—caves within gardens.) Nonetheless, his account is just and useful in keeping faith with a sense that Spenser here shows us something within us as well as outside us, a form of thought, a form of knowing. Northrop Frye famously called this central tableau of the Garden, and of Book III of *The Faerie Queene* as a whole, an "erotic Pietà."[21] It is a metaphor that at least begins to catch the complexity, the strangeness of the way that Spenser here marries a scene of pleasure and generation to a scene of loss and mourning, showing us that passive love-object, corpse, child, father, lying in the arms of that hungry, joyous, mournful lover, goddess, mother, both placed above their enjailed or enshrined destroyer. It is one of the most complex forms the poet gives to his dream of things that are "eterne in mutabilitie." It is the place where his dream of a redemptive, if still vulnerable, shape of time or temporal existence becomes densest, most articulate in its poetic particularity and yet also most opaque and mysterious; the image of existence hovers over and roots itself within the unsayable. In this it also gives us a crucial image of the motion and power of the mind, of human thought, thought steeped in the element of time, thought that must also include its own abysmal, perhaps defensive, but still generative opacity; it is the image of a knowing that itself resists being known.

In a response to the talk from which this essay emerged, James Nohrnberg suggested that the sort of mentalistic interpretation of a basically physical allegory I've attempted here opens up the door to reading any thought-provoking or thought-ridden site in Spenser as an allegory of mind. Hence, he proposed, Proteus's realm could be read an image of the mind's copiousness and prolific fancy, Mount Acidale as an allegory of the mind's capacity for reverie, the Bower of Bliss as a picture of the hungover or strung-out mind, Phaedria's isle as the bored or daydreaming mind sinking into inanition, Despair's cave as an image of the mind desolated, and Busirane's house as an image of a mind traumatized or fixated or morbidly preoccupied by sex. Or we might measure the Garden, seen as a place of mind, against the house or cave of Mammon. The cave could be seen—here still I am following Nohrnberg's improvised readings—as an image of how human thoughts are buried, smelted, forged and re-forged, stamped with meaning but hoarded uselessly, adored for purely external reasons, driving worldly appetite for fame. The cave is an image of the mind filled with hoarded words, stuffed with unproductive opinions or *doxa*, with thoughts that have become blank coins or counters rather than generative seeds. (This would make Mammon's cave a parodic translation of Eumnestes' chamber in the house of Alma—or perhaps a strange jamming together of the chambers of all three of Alma's counselors, Eumnestes, Phantastes, and the nameless middle counselor, images of the activities of memory, imagination, and reason.) I acknowledge the force of this warning (which itself illustrates the poem's latent power of self-reflection).[22] Still, there is something peculiar in the way that an allegory of mind is made possible in the Garden of Adonis. Perhaps that is because the Garden is at once so unlike any other place in *The Faerie Queene* and yet the most typically Spenserian thing; it is an image of the thing—place and process—that drives Spenser's poem, its nuclear reactor, its hidden springs of energy and delight, in particular the source of the poem's capacity for conceptual metamorphosis and the endless generation of possibility. The power of this analogy has something to do with the way that Spenser's Garden explodes into a cosmic dimension and gives a quasi-eternal life to those small, imploded forcing pots that are elsewhere images for the empty, trashy, unnatural productions of human thought. Spenser is not someone who considers mind and nature as essentially one and the same, even if he sees why human beings might wish them to be. If the account of the Garden of Adonis is driven in part by such a conceptual fantasy, it also shows us its limits, where it falls apart or reveals its costs, the darker appetites it fulfills. It is an image of the mind making itself up even as it seems to make up nature, an activity supported by and pitched against the mind's and nature's capacities for change.[23]

NOTES

1. Angus Fletcher describes the Garden of Adonis episode as a peculiarly radical moment in Spenser's poem, an instance of writing in which fundamental ambivalences about the relation of such polarities as life and death are not displaced, as they often are in Spenserian allegorical narratives. In this rare instance of a passage from allegory into something like true myth, true anagogy, the poet rather "maintains an equality between the polar opposites of the ambivalent attitudes and almost insists they must be joined, the apocalypse being thus gained in a moment of total consciousness." See *Allegory: The Theory of a Symbolic Mode* (Ithaca: Cornell University Press, 1964), 321.

The current essay was first delivered in oral form at the International Spenser Conference, Cambridge University, 8 July 2001, as part of a session on "Thinking in *The Faerie Queene*."

2. James Nohrnberg, *The Analogy of* The Faerie Queene (Princeton: Princeton University Press, 1976), 530–31. Cf. also pp. 554–55: "No garden is complete without a compost heap, and Spenser's is no exception:

> For in the wide wombe of the world there lyes,
> In hatefull darkenesse and in deepe horrore,
> An huge eternall *Chaos* which supplyes
> The substances of natures fruitfull progenyes.

(III.vi.36)

The horror of the scrap pile and the loss of being is here, and yet matter without form is merely the reverse of form without matter, and both are a kind of limbo."

3. Nohrnberg, *Analogy of* The Faerie Queene, 532, speaks of this Chaos as the "double" of the Garden. Jon Quitslund also reflects well on the analogy in *Spenser's Supreme Fiction: Platonic Natural Philosophy and* The Faerie Queene (Toronto: University of Toronto Press, 2001), 204–06.

4. On "iconographies of thought," see Angus Fletcher, *Colors of the Mind: Conjectures on Thinking in Literature* (Cambridge, MA: Harvard University Press, 1991),

especially 15–34 and 166–88. The current essay, I should say here, has more in common with Fletcher's pragmatic manner of exploring metaphors and iconographies of thinking in literature—an approach much indebted to Ludwig Wittgenstein's *Philosophical Investigations*—than with Gordon Teskey's probing but more insistently Heideggerian reflections on Spenser and thinking. See for instance his recent and moving essay, "Thinking Moments in *The Faerie Queene*," in *Spenser Studies* 22 (2007): 103–25. See also the comments later in this essay on Harry Berger, Jr.'s reading of the Garden of Adonis as an allegory of poetic making. Among other things, I share Berger's sense that Spenser's description of the Garden contains a number of different gardens, and further that as we read we have the strange sense of seeing the poet's mind moving, even escaping, from one imaginary garden to another.

5.   Reflecting on the life of the Garden as it unfolds "in the *longue durée* of millennia past and yet to be," Quitslund adds that "it also suggests comparison to the human imagination, famous for its capacity to bring to virtual life things never seen on sea or land. (To the 'infinite shapes' here, compare the 'infinite shapes of things dispersed thin' in writing on the walls of Phantastes' chamber in II ix 50)" (*Spenser's Supreme Fiction*, 203).

6.   See *Coleridge's Miscellaneous Criticism*, ed. Thomas Middleton Raysor (Cambridge, MA: Harvard University Press, 1936), 36.

7.   "The Garden," lines 43–44, quoted from Andrew Marvell, *The Complete Poems*, ed. Elizabeth Story Donno (Harmondsworth: Penguin Books, 1972), 101.

8.   See *The Philosophy of Plotinus*, trans. Joseph Katz (New York: Appleton-Century-Crofts, 1950), 50. Nohrnberg, *Analogy of* The Faerie Queene, 658, cites this passage to illustrate his reflections on Spenser's Mount Acidale as a source and refuge of poetic thought, linking the purpose of this place to the recuperation of self and being that goes on as well in the Garden of Adonis. It is in links such as these that one feels that Wallace Stevens has Spenser (and especially the Garden) in mind when he speaks of ways in which the act of poetic making "refreshes life so that we share,/ For a moment, the first idea," an idea that joins our wishes for an immaculate beginning and for an immaculate end, even as a place like the Garden speaks to a greenness, a form of origin, a "muddy centre" that preexists (and stands apart from) human thought. See Wallace Stevens, *Collected Poetry and Prose* (New York: Library of America, 1997), 330–31.

9.   The words in quotes are from Quitslund, *Spenser's Supreme Fiction*, 228. The most extensive discussions of the idea of "seminal reasons" in relation to the Garden of Adonis can be found in Robert Ellrodt, *Neoplatonism in the Poetry of Edmund Spenser, Travaux d'Humanisme et Renaissance* XXXV (Geneva: E. Droz, 1960), 70–90; John E. Hankins, *Source and Meaning in Spenser's Allegory: A Study of* The Faerie Queene (Oxford: Oxford University Press, 1971), 241–72; and James Nohrnberg, *The Analogy of* The Faerie Queene, 534–68. This "time fiction" and its relevance to the Garden is also the subject of a subtle analysis in Frank Kermode's *The Sense of an Ending: Studies in the Theory of Fictions* (New York: Oxford University Press, 1967), 74–81. Quitslund's discussion of this tradition as it shapes the Garden of Adonis, especially in his chapter on "The Platonic Program of the Garden Canto" (*Spenser's Supreme Fiction*, 227–66), helps save the idea from becoming a mere truism,

suggesting among other things its relevance to the complex theme of erotic education in this episode.

10.   *De Mente Idiota*, Chapter 5, in *Nicholas of Cusa on Wisdom and Knowledge*, ed.
and trans. Jasper Hopkins (Minneapolis: Arthur J. Banning Press, 1996), 547. Ronald
Levao, *Renaissance Minds and their Fictions: Cusanus, Sidney, Shakespeare* (Berkeley:
University of California Press, 1985), 73, also cites a passage in Cusanus's *De quae-
rendo Deum* (1445) that dialectically relates human understanding to a seed that
contains within itself innumerable worlds, none of which could in itself contain the
power of the seed. "Cusanus considers the power of the human understanding,
which, through its geometrical progressions, not only takes the measure of the seed,
but reveals to itself a range beyond this world or an infinity of worlds." The seed
metaphor is elsewhere used forcefully in Cusanus's account of human consciousness,
as in the *De Visione Dei*, where he exemplifies the mind's power to know God's
power of origination and sustenance by describing how a visible tree provokes the
mind's eye to imagine or conjecture its hidden origins: "Then with the mind's eye
I see that this tree existed in its seed not in the manner in which I here behold it
but potentially. I consider attentively this seed's admirable power, wherein were
present the whole of this tree, all its nuts, the entire seminal power of the nuts, and
in the seminal power of the nuts, all tress. And I discern that this power is never at
any time fully unfoldable by the motion of the heaven." It is a process of knowing
in which eventually, he acknowledges, he "must pass beyond all seminal power that
can be known and conceived and must pass into that ignorance wherein remains no
seminal power or force at all" (*De Visione Dei*, chapter 7, in Hopkins, *Nicholas of
Cusa on Wisdom and Knowledge*, 690–91).

11.   See Levao, *Renaissance Minds and their Fictions,* especially 67–98.

12.   I quote the text of *King Lear* from Shakespeare, *The Complete Works*, ed. Stanley
Wells and Gary Taylor (Oxford: Oxford University Press, 1988), 925.

13.   In an earlier essay, "Shapes of Time: Spenser's Stanza," *Spenser Studies* 17
(2004): 56–69, I discuss this stanza (III.vi.42) as an example of how Spenser's language and prosody implicitly mirror his ideas about temporal change and continuity
in the Garden of Adonis, and in *The Faerie Queene* more generally.

14.   Harry Berger, Jr. speaks of the memorial flowers of the grove as images of
poetic *topoi*, fragile creations of verbal memory, that may by dint of the individual
poet's attention, labor, and art become something closer to archetypes of cultural
and mental history. See his essay, "Spenser's Gardens of Adonis: Force and Form in
the Renaissance Imagination," in *Revisionary Play: Studies in the Spenserian Dynamics*
(Berkeley: University of California Press, 1988), 146–47.

15.   Quitslund, *Spenser's Supreme Fiction*, 221–23, argues that Spenser may have
been aware of the ancient cult of Adonis, and that in this episode he is contributing
to the almost cultic veneration of Philip Sidney, sponsored by his sister, the Countess
of Pembroke, after his untimely death—Sidney would then not only be the dead
Amintas referred to in stanza 45, but Adonis himself. (Spenser directly compares the
dead Sidney to Adonis in "Astrophel," line 152, one should recall.)

16.   See Terence Cave, *The Cornucopian Text: Problems of Writing in the French
Renaissance* (Oxford: Oxford University Press, 1979).

17.   I borrow this analogy from Nohrnberg, *Analogy*, 43–44, who evokes it very
elegantly in trying to describe the paradoxical relation of Prince Arthur to Gloriana

in Spenser's poem. Arthur is contained in Faerie, the dream kingdom of Gloriana, even though she is also glimpsed within his own dream vision. This seems to control the circumstance of their never at all meeting in the course of the poem. "Alice is told that if she were to awaken the Red King she would disappear, for she is what the Red King is dreaming. One supposes that a premature recognition of Arthur by Gloriana would have had a similar annihilating effect on *The Faerie Queene*" (44).

18. Berger, *Revisionary Play*, 144.

19. "Venus and Adonis," line 1052, in Shakespeare, *The Complete Works*, 234.

20. Berger, *Revisionary Play*, 150. Berger's desire to find an image of "consciousness" in the situation of the apparently unconscious Adonis I find particularly suggestive here—it tries to catch the sense that, though asleep, dead, or embalmed, Adonis is the site of a relentless activity of making and remaking, and not just a passive object of Venus's hungry desire.

21. See Northrop Frye, "The Structure of Imagery in *The Faerie Queene*," in *Fables of Identity: Studies in Poetic Mythology* (New York: Harcourt, Brace, & World, 1963), 82.

22. In his preface to *The Analogy of* The Faerie Queene, Nohrnberg writes that "Everyone will be able to supply examples of 'the poem about the poem within the poem,' but an insistent reading of the text in this way will also yield a more general perception: the equation of the poem's more prominent internal agents with the various mental operators implied by the mere existence of the text. . . . The poem regularly comments on its own mode of being" (xiii).

23. I should say that Donald Cheney's reflections on the Garden as, most fundamentally, an image of nature and natural process, including the processes of a generative and wounding love, continue to be important for my understanding of Spenser's fiction, here and throughout this essay. See *Spenser's Image of Nature: Wild Man and Shepherd in The Faerie Queene* (New Haven: Yale University Press, 1966), 117–41. At closing I would also mention Rosalie Colie's brilliant and often forgotten discussion of what she calls Spenser's "anamorphic" Garden in her *Paradoxia Epidemica: The Renaissance Tradition of Paradox* (Princeton: Princeton University Press, 1966), 329–52. Especially useful is her account of some of the contradictory descriptions of temporal process in the Garden, and her sense of how Spenser makes matter and form both seem, from different points of view, at once inside and outside the Garden; both matter and form are seen as at once eternal and subject to change. In more general terms, it is Colie's sense of the fierce, paradoxical activity of thought displayed in the Garden that has stayed in my memory.

AYESHA RAMACHANDRAN

Edmund Spenser, Lucretian Neoplatonist: Cosmology in the *Fowre Hymnes*

This essay reconsiders the relationship between Spenser's earthly and divine hymns in terms of the dialogic possibilities of the palinode, suggesting that the apparent "recantation" of the first two hymns is a poetic device used for philosophic effect. I argue that Spenser uses the poetic movement of action and retraction, turn and counterturn, to embody a philosophical oscillation and synthesis between a newly rediscovered Lucretian materialism and the Christian Neoplatonism, traditionally ascribed to the sequence. The stimulus for this seemingly unusual juxtaposition of two fundamentally different philosophies is the subject of the *Fowre Hymnes*: the poems are not only an expression of personal emotion and faith, but seek to make a significant intervention in the late sixteenth-century revival of cosmology and natural philosophy. Therefore, the essay takes seriously the hymns' generic claim towards the grand style of philosophic abstraction, showing how Spenser explores the dialectic between matter and form, chaos and creation, mutability and eternity, through his repeated emphasis on the creation. Each hymn contains a distinct creation account; together they contrast a vision of a dynamic, de-centered, material cosmos (identified textually with the cosmos of Lucretius's *De rerum natura*) with the formal symmetry and stable order of the Christian-Platonic universe. In this syncretic relationship between Lucretius and Plato, Spenser may have seen a powerful model for harmonizing the traditionally opposed motivations of poetry and philosophy, and for reconciling, albeit very uneasily, a concern with the flux of worldly experience and a desire to comprehend cosmic stability and formal order.

Spenser Studies: A Renaissance Poetry Annual, Volume XXIV, Copyright © 2009 AMS Press, Inc. All rights reserved.

*I*N THE DEDICATION to the *Fowre Hymnes,* Spenser offers one of the few explicit autobiographical narratives to be found among his printed poems:

> Having in the greener times of my youth composed these former two Hymnes in the praise of Love and Beautie, and finding that the same too much pleased those of like age and disposition, which being too vehemently caried with that kind of affection, do rather sucke out poyson to their strong passion, then hony to their honest delight, I was moved by the one of you two most excellent Ladies, to call in the same.[1]

This story, with its tale of attempted retraction, has presented Spenser scholars with a puzzle: are the *Hymnes* a hybrid work comprised of two youthful Petrarchan poems and two later religious corrections to the poet's *giovenile errore*? Why did Spenser feel moved to publish a hymnic palinode in 1596, the same year he published the six-book *Faerie Queene*? Perhaps more importantly, does the mystery of chronology and autobiography help illuminate the subject of the *Hymnes* themselves? The propositions of Robert Ellrodt, in his 1960 study, have done little to settle these questions of motive and content. Despite claiming that the poems could not have been composed before 1595 through a discussion of the "Neoplatonism" of Spenser's poetry, Ellrodt only threw into sharper relief Spenser's story of retraction and the possibility that it may be a fiction.[2] Why did the poet insist on this fiction? And what exactly was Spenser recanting in his own work?[3]

Long considered the apotheosis of sixteenth-century English Neoplatonism, particularly in the form of Petrarchan poetry, the *Hymnes* are perhaps the least studied poems of the Spenserian corpus. While there is critical consensus about their importance, we have yet to grasp firmly their relationship to the poet's other works or to the sociopolitical matrix into which Spenser has so successfully been reinserted in the last twenty years of scholarship. In fact, the determined absence of topical detail in the *Hymnes,* as well as their sheen of formal symmetry, have made them somewhat impenetrable to critical approaches based on historicist methods and political interests; the handful of essays on the poems treat either their philosophical sources or their formal structure.[4] Thus, we might note that the *Hymnes* have seemed paradoxically both too easy and too difficult to approach. Their juxtaposition of earthly love and beauty with heavenly love and beauty seems to argue for the dynamic of conversion, a turn away from erotic error towards penitential faith characteristic of Petrarchan poetry and even of many figures in the *Faerie Queene*. However, their earnest tone and obvious claim to a philosophic grand style seem to demand mastery of the highly syncretic and often abstruse philosophies of the Renaissance for successful understanding.

Yet Spenser's palinodic frame for the *Fowre Hymnes* in the dedication's story of origin provides us with a powerful key to understanding the poems. Indeed, it is worth noting that not only the dedication, but also *An Hymne of Heavenly Love,* contain palinodic gestures, as though Spenser meant to thematize the movement of action and retraction, turn and counterturn within the work as a whole. The palinode or recantation was of course a much-used lyric trope in the Renaissance.[5] Its classical source is Stesichorus's ode recantation of the *Helen,* famously imitated and discussed by Socrates in the *Phaedrus* (243a), while its best known Renaissance imitator might be Petrarch, whose *Rime sparse* is framed as a palinode, an Augustinian recantation of juvenile erotic experience.[6] This turn away from either erotic *nugae* or *errori* to grand devotional themes, whether in Socrates' repudiation of erotic *furor* or in Petrarch's turn towards the "Vergine bella," was simultaneously a sign of humility and ambition, a double-edged gesture that suggested genuine conversion as well as ironic self-consciousness. Moreover, Plato's anecdote about the trope's origin reveals how it became implicated in the vexed relations between poetry and philosophy: he tells of how Stesichorus, blinded because of his disparagement of Helen, was miraculously restored to sight when he penned the Palinode—a tale that Spenser significantly repeats in one of E. K.'s notes to the "Aprill" eclogue of *The Shepheardes Calender*.[7] The palinode thus signals philosophic enlightenment, and by the late sixteenth century, it contained the promise of deliverance from the blindness of erotic seductions both literal and poetic.

Not surprisingly, as the Platonic example suggests, the palinodic gesture was not limited to poets alone. One philosophic case from the Quattrocento in particular stands out. Later in life, Marsilio Ficino, often considered the most significant source of Spenser's Neoplatonic interests, discussed Socrates' palinodic performance in the *Phaedrus* and repented some of the opinions he had held in his early "Lucretian" phase as a youthful error. In a well-known letter to Martin Preninger, he claimed to have burned works composed when he was younger, most notably what may have been a commentary on Lucretius's Epicurean epic, *De rerum natura*.[8] While Ficino's repudiation was not entirely fictional, the vehemence of his assertion belies the continuing impact of the Roman poet on his work: the early *De quattuor sectis philosophorum* (1457), which considers the central tenets of the Old Academy of Plato, the Peripatetics, the Stoics, and the Epicureans, cites Lucretius with approval, while the influence is evident in such texts as his widely read commentary on Plato's *Symposium (Commentarium in Convivium Platonis De Amore), De voluptate,* his comprehensive discourse on erotic pleasure, and even the vast *Theologia platonica*.[9]

The history of turning away from youthful error to philosophic maturity is, however, not quite the straightforward intellectual and spiritual ascent that it appears to be in these Spenserian and Ficinian instances. Ironically, the very doubleness of the palinode alerts us to the continuing significance of what has been recanted. As Patricia Phillipy notes suggestively, the palinode contains dialogic possibilities, indicating a constant motion between multiple positions, so that the position of the initial ode is never quite abandoned for the palinode. Thus, Ficino's strategy of philosophic distancing through the trope of retraction, provides a suggestive parallel to Spenser's dedicatory gesture, not least because Spenser uses a poetic topos derived from Lucretius—the counterpoint of "poyson" and "hony" in the dedication echoes the famous simile of honey and wormwood in *De rerum natura*.[10] More importantly, however, to notice the palinodic nature of Ficino's repudiation of his youthful Lucretianism is to become aware of Epicurean traces in his work and thus to destabilize the seemingly monolithic edifice of Renaissance "Neoplatonism" for which his name is often a placeholder.[11] Such awareness opens up the traditional critical framework of Neoplatonism to embrace not only theories of love and transcendence, but also the dilemmas of matter and form, the relations between the natural world and the divine.[12] And consequently, it suggests that Spenser's own dedicatory recantation to his overtly Neoplatonic *Hymnes* may also be haunted by a prior, Lucretian strain.

Turning towards this shadowy, palinodic aspect of Ficinian Neoplatonism and Spenser's own possible engagement with it enables us to take a fresh look at the *Fowre Hymnes*. My goal here is not so much to assert new sources for the *Hymnes,* that most dense of Spenserian texts, but to show how the synthesis of radically different philosophic traditions in the work may signal Spenser's participation in the late sixteenth-century revival of cosmology and natural philosophy. Despite the prevailing Platonic consensus in interpretations of the

Hymnes, scholars have also pointed uneasily to their infamous philo-sophic inconsistencies, excusing Spenser on the grounds of syncretism or poetic license. But the task of rescuing the poet from such charges of philosophic inadequacy, particularly in the complex realm of Neo-platonic thought, has made it difficult to focus on other, non-Neopla-tonic, aspects of the *Hymnes.* The dedication, however, provides a way out: Spenser significantly counterpoints "earthy or naturall" love and beauty to "heavenly and celestiall" ones, designations that indi-cate a concern not only with theology and the erotic psychologies of Neoplatonism, but also with the discourses of early modern natural philosophy.[13] In fact, the *Fowre Hymnes* can be seen as Spenser's explo-ration of the dialectic between matter and form, chaos and creation, mutability and eternity—all important themes for the late poems. In the syncretic relationship between Lucretius and Plato advanced by so many Renaissance writers, Spenser may have seen a powerful philosophic model for reconciling, albeit very uneasily, a concern with the flux of worldly experience and a desire to comprehend cosmic stability and formal order.

Such a description alerts us to the wider philosophical scope of the *Hymnes,* which includes the creation and ordering of the universe (described in each of the hymns) as well as the problem of matter and its appropriate relationship to the soul or divine spirit. For Re-naissance Neoplatonism itself was not only concerned with love, though it has often been limited to commentaries on the *Symposium* and the *Phaedrus.* The renovation of a medieval Platonism founded on the *Timaeus* gave early modern natural philosophers a powerful alternative to the Christian-Aristotelian science prevalent throughout the period.[14] Moreover, the inflections of Lucretian Epicurean-ism—already present within the currents of Ficinian Neoplatonism, as I will demonstrate—only became stronger as the sixteenth century progressed, ultimately culminating in the matter theories of Gassendi, Descartes, and Newton. Recent work on the involvement of six-teenth-century writers such as Pontus de Tyard, Louis le Roy, and Giordano Bruno in the diffusion of new natural philosophies suggests that we need to rethink Spenser's place within the currents of con-temporary philosophical discourse.[15]

To focus on the cosmology of the *Hymnes* in this manner is there-fore to move away from a psychological approach to the poems as an expression of personal emotion and faith and to take seriously their generic claim towards the grand style of philosophic abstraction. Spenser himself designates the first two hymns and their preoccupa-tions as the products of "greener times"—a metaphor that recalls the many seminal gardens of material origin in his poetry—and thereby urges us to consider the relationship between the *Hymnes* and works such as the *Faerie Queene* and *Colin Clouts Come Home Againe* with their corresponding cosmogonic accounts. I therefore extend philosophic questions to ask what generic and literary historical relationship the *Hymnes* may have to the project of epic in the sixteenth century and how they may help us to understand the arc of Spenser's poetic career.

I

The problem with Neoplatonism, notes Robert Ellrodt, is that we seldom know what exactly it refers to.[16] A similar sentiment could describe the protean genre of the Renaissance hymn. Despite the identification of classical precedents in the Homeric, Callimachan, and Orphic hymns, despite a fairly clear sense of the poem's structural features, the term remains notoriously slippery and, in the sixteenth century alone, describes such varied works as Marullus's *Hymni naturales,* Ronsard's *Hymne de France,* and Spenser's *An Hymne of Heavenly Beautie.*[17] In formal terms, Renaissance writers found it difficult to distinguish between the ode and the hymn—Ronsard rearranged poems between his books of *Odes* and *Les Hynnes,* while Milton in 1645 published a hymnic poem as the *Ode on the Morning of Christ's Nativity.* Moreover, in terms of function, the appreciation of the hymn as an invocation to classical deities for religious worship overlapped with Christian liturgical practices and hymnic forms in the Bible (such as the Song of Songs and the Psalms).[18]

It was clear that the hymn was to be considered a poem of power, one that invoked divine or natural pantheistic energies, whose incantatory powers were enchanting and transformative.[19] This quasi-magical aspect of the hymn made it the form of choice for philosophers and theologians, practitioners of the *prisca theologia* as well as reformers on both sides of the religious divide. Marullus's *Hymni* were, for instance, probably influenced by both Ficino and Pico, while Marot's *Psaumes* were among the works that Ronsard may have sought to surpass with his *Les Hynnes* of 1555. To write a hymn in the sixteenth century was thus to stake a philosophic claim, to assert the status of poet as *vates*. It was a poetic gesture in the grand style, comparable to the epic, perhaps even one that transcended the worldly, imperial epic by its vaster, cosmic and spiritual ambitions. Thus, Francis Cairns observes that the classical hymn was not a fixed genre like the *komos* of Greek tragedy:

Nor is it a genre in the other sense of the word, in which it is used to refer to kinds of literature like epic, elegy or lyric; for these kinds of literature are each characterized by metre and length, and more important, they are mutually exclusive. "Hymn" is not characterized by metre or by length, and hymns can be found in epic, elegy, lyric etc.[20]

The flexibility of the form and its ability to combine secular and religious, personal and public themes made the hymn a potent, respectable mode for an ambitious Renaissance poet. If extended theoretical treatment is a mark of cultural importance, it is significant that Scaliger's mammoth *Poetices libri septem* devotes an extensive section to describing and classifying the hymn, followed by commentary on the contemporary hymns of Marullus and Vida.[21]

In generic terms, then, the hymn may have offered an alternative to the *rota Virgilii* with its culmination in the national epic.[22] Homer, after all, had written not only the *Iliad* and the *Odyssey,* but also the "Homeric" hymns, a work that Renaissance philologists such as Jean Dorat considered a late composition.[23] To write successful hymns, the poet had to transcend worldly success and become a scholar-initiate, a philosopher always seeking the truth of the nature of things. When Ronsard published his hymns, for instance, Dorat wrote with pleasure, "Naturae rerum cantica docta sonas" ["You sing learned songs about the things of nature"].[24] In this model, the writing of hymns could perhaps come to seem more significant than the completion of an epic.

Spenser's decision to write a set of hymns in the complex rhyme royal stanza reminiscent of the Italian *canzone* must be seen in this context of generic interplay. And here the example of Ronsard may in fact, as Anne Prescott has pointed out, shed light on the shape of Spenser's literary career.[25] By the mid-1590s, Spenser, like Ronsard before him, was a would-be epic poet with an incomplete *magnum opus* and waning support at court. The other poems of this period—the *Complaints,* the *Amoretti* and *Epithalamion,* and *Colin Clouts Come Home Againe*—all register strong dissatisfaction with court politics and seem to withdraw into the private sphere. The 1596 *Faerie Queene* itself reflects a breakdown of the triumphal martial epic promised by the 1590 installment: the erotic meanderings of Book IV, the violent justice and frustrated political ambitions of Book V, and the destructive intrigues of Book VI are modulated by an increasing turn away from the dirty business of governance towards cosmic allegories and philosophical speculation. In fact, the second half of the epic seems to pick up where the Gardens of Adonis left off, as the elemental river marriage of Book IV, the astrological proem of Book V, the vision on Mount Acidale all seem to lead towards the *Cantos of Mutabilitie.*

Also in 1596, in contrast to the ragged edges of his unfinished epic, Spenser presented the perfectly polished symmetries of the *Fowre Hymnes.* Where the epic is plagued by doubt, a nagging lack of closure and the subversion of a so-called "Vergilian" national project, the *Hymnes* are accomplished poems whose entwining rhymes and cyclical stanzaic structure imitate the philosophic stability which they seek to find and express. Here, Spenser comes close to representing in formal terms the paradoxes of eternity and mutability that fill the later poetry, from the *Epithalamion's* stance as being for "short time an endless moniment" to Nature's verdict about steadfastness and change in the *Cantos* ("all things stedfastnes doe hate/And changed be: yet being rightly wayd/They are not changed from their first estate"). In this, the *Hymnes* may be seen as the culmination of a "cosmological turn" in Spenser's poetry, already apparent in Book III of the *Faerie Queene.*

When read alongside *The Faerie Queene,* the hymns reveal preoccupations that are not evident at first glance: their meditations on love and beauty, the beloved theme of Neoplatonizing Petrarchan poets, now become a frame for investigations of cosmic order. *An Hymne in Honour of Beautie (HB),* for instance, begins with an apparently commonplace invocation to Venus, but it contains an unexpected allusion that would perhaps only be intelligible to readers of the *Faerie Queene:*

> Therto do thou great Goddesse, queene of Beauty,
> Mother of Love, and of all worlds delight,
> Without whose soverayne grace and kindly dewty,
> Nothing on earth seemes fayre to fleshly sight,
> Doe thou vouchsafe with thy love-kindling light,
> T'illuminate my dim and dulled eyne,
> And beautifie this sacred hymne of thyne.
>
> *(An Hymne in Honour of Beautie,* lines 15–21)

The invocation of this hymn echoes Spenser's striking translation, in the epic's fourth book, of Lucretius's invocation to Venus (itself often described as a hymn) that opens *De rerum natura:*

Great *Venus*, Queene of beautie and of grace,
The ioy of Gods and men, that vnder skie
Doest fayrest shine, and most adorne thy place,
That with thy smyling looke doest pacifie
The raging seas, and makst the stormes to flie;
Thee goddesse, thee the winds, the clouds doe feare,
And when thou spredst thy mantle forth on hie,
The waters play and pleasant lands appeare,
And heauens laugh, & al the world shews ioyous cheare.

                                                    (IV.x.44)[26]

Aeneadum genetrix, hominum divomque voluptas,
alma Venus

. . . . .

quae quoniam rerum naturam sola gubernas
nec sine te quicquam dias in luminis oras
exoritur neque fit laetum neque amabile quicquam,
te sociam studeo scribendis versibus esse,
quos ego de rerum natura pangere conor

. . . . .

quo magis aeternum da dictis, diva, leporem.

[Mother of Aeneas and his race, darling of men and gods, nurturing Venus . . . since without you nothing comes forth into
the shining borders of light, nothing joyous and lovely is made,
you I crave as partner in writing these verses . . . grant to my
speech, goddess, an ever-living charm.]

                        (*De rerum natura* I, lines 1–2, 21–28)[27]

Venus here is "hominum divomque voluptas," which Spenser renders closely as "all worlds delight" (*HB*) and "joy of Gods and men"
(*Faerie Queene*) while the key Lucretian dictum that Venus "rerum
naturam sola gubernas" provides a textual precedent for Spenser's
insistence on the goddess's complete control of the world.[28] Significantly, the language of light, so often attributed to Ficinian Neoplatonism, is here associated with the coming-to-life of generation
("dias in luminis oras") rather than the transcendental purity of the
divine—a feature that Spenser retains in his evocation of the "love-
kindling light" that physically brightens the obscurity of his vision.

In the space of seven lines, the dense rime-royal stanza of the *Hymne* condenses the main tropes of Lucretius's verse.

Spenser's fluid assimilation of this Venerean energy into the images of astral influence (lines 43–44), generative power (lines 50–55), and seductive aesthetic deceptions (lines 64–91) in *An Hymne in Honour of Beautie* completes a shift of emphasis already begun in the epic: over the course of the middle books of the *Faerie Queene,* the figure of Venus becomes disentangled from Petrarchan or Ovidian love (as in the tapestries of Malecasta's castle) and associated with cosmological generation (as in the Gardens of Adonis, the Temple, Isis Church). In the *Faerie Queene,* Spenser's translation of Lucretius acts as the lament of a lover at the Temple of Venus; significantly, however, instead of being a mere erotic complaint, the lament/hymn of Book IV celebrates the cosmic and cosmogonic power of Venus, looking back to the Gardens of Adonis in Book III even as it points ahead to the elemental river marriage that concludes the fourth book.[29] This figure is not merely the mythic goddess of love meddling in erotic disputes, the Ovidian mischief-maker who came to symbolize the unruly erotic instinct for the Renaissance. The Lucretian Venus is a natural philosophical principle, a muse-goddess who can inspire a poem on the nature of things because, as the life-force itself, she *is* the nature of things.[30]

Venus Genetrix, the origin of all things and the erotic energy that fuels the generative process, emblematizes Lucretius's epic treatment of the origin of the universe and its workings. She also signals Spenser's attempt to fuse Neoplatonic thought and Lucretian cosmology. As a figurative node in both philosophical traditions, Venus symbolized the transformative power of erotic love and the dynamism of matter itself. She could evoke mystical rapture as well as sexual fervor, transcendence as well as a Grylle-like entrapment in the flesh. To recognize the double face of Spenser's Venus is thus to revisit the philosophic underpinnings of the *Hymnes.*

My argument for the influence of Lucretius on Spenser's poetry is not new. Spenserians may well remember how, in the 1920s, a furious battle broke out in the pages of *Studies in Philology* when Edwin Greenlaw suggested that in addition to the obvious Platonic impact on Spenser's poetry, there was another discernable influence—that of Lucretius and the Epicurean philosophy which he celebrates in *De rerum natura.*[31] Greenlaw was attacked by several noted critics for suggesting that Spenser might be guilty of precisely what we have seen Ficino, one of his key sources, wrestling with: a peculiar reconciliation of Platonism and Lucretian Epicureanism. How could

Spenser, a staunchly militant Protestant, possibly espouse the materialist philosophy of an atheist? How could this be consistent with the dualist ontology of Christian Neoplatonism? But if the tricky question of just how an ardent Neoplatonic poet could draw on Lucretius remains to be addressed fully for Spenser's obvious borrowings in the *Faerie Queene,* it has yet to be posed for the *Fowre Hymnes,* where it is less overt but perhaps even more significant. [32]

Since Ellrodt's seminal work, scholars have attributed Spenser's philosophical hybridity in the *Hymnes* to such Christian Neoplatonists as Louis le Roy, Leone Ebreo and Guy le Fèvre de la Boderie.[33] However, recent explorations of these figures (particularly Le Roy) have revealed a complex contemporary engagement with Epicureanism and other alternate cosmologies.[34] Le Roy's insistence on mutability in *De la vicissitude ou variete des choses en l'univers* (1575), for instance, speaks to a persistent concern with the relation between matter and form, particularly with the troubling persistence of matter through an ever-changing array of forms (a theme that will be the basis of Mutability's argument in Spenser's *Cantos*). As Michel Jeanneret concedes, such an emphasis on matter and flux is "too variegated to classify or even encompass in a coherent survey"; nevertheless, the threads he carefully extracts from the "tangled network of sources" are tellingly *not* Platonic: the pre-Socratics, Lucretius, Pythagoras.[35]

II

Plato and Lucretius are strange bedfellows, even in the syncretic, not always consistent world of Renaissance philosophy. And yet, there is an identifiable tradition of linked commentaries on the Greek philosopher and Roman poet dating from at least the mid-Quattrocento.[36] Poggio Bracciolini's discovery of the manuscript of *De rerum natura* in 1417 was an important event in Florentine humanist circles. Leonardo Bruni translated the invocation to Venus into Italian in the form of the *Canzone a Venere* ("O Venere formosa"); Leon Battista Alberti translated a part of the third book into hendecasyllabic lines and inserted them into his *Theogenius;* Lucretius's influence is marked on Angelo Poliziano's *Rusticus* and *Stanze per la giostra,* a text that is closely imitated by Tasso in his depiction of Armida's island, and which Spenser, in turn, echoes carefully in the Bower of Bliss.[37] But most importantly, from the perspective of the history of ideas, *De rerum natura* exercised a powerful fascination on Marsilio Ficino, prompting the palinodic gesture that we have already seen. Hiro Hirai, perhaps the latest scholar to note the influence of Lucretius on Ficino, observes that the Florentine philosopher cites the poet in his commentary on the *Philebus,* clearly incorporating the Lucretian concept of the *semina rerum* into his version of Platonic philosophy.[38] James Hankins and Michael Allen both point to the extensive sections on Lucretius in the *Theologia Platonica,* but there is as yet no substantive study on the relationship between the two figures, despite suggestive clues within both the Ficinian corpus and that of his circle. In fact, Alison Brown argues provocatively for a "Lucretian counterculture" in Florence of the early sixteenth century, under the Soderini regime, identifying Niccolò Machiavelli as a prominent Epicurean.[39] One product of the Florentine school, for instance, was the *Hymni naturales* of Michael Marullus, a set of natural philosophical hymns that exhibit a peculiar synthesis of Lucretian and Platonic thought.[40] Marullus had probably already encountered Lucretius through his association with Giovanni Pontano, whose circle in Naples would produce some of the most interesting and influential commentaries on *De rerum natura,* and whose own astronomical poem, *Urania,* would be enthusiastically championed by Gabriel Harvey, among others, in England.[41]

If Ficino, the single most important translator and commentator on Plato in the Renaissance, wrestles so explicitly with the Lucretian legacy, it was perhaps inevitable that the critical fortunes of Plato and Lucretius would be linked within the Florentine circle and by their descendents and imitators. Among the Cinquecento writers who invoke Lucretius repeatedly alongside other Platonizing gestures, the most prominent are Torquato Tasso and Giordano Bruno, both important influences on Spenser's poetry. Palingenius, an important Neo-Latin poet and author of the *Zodiacus vitae,* an often-proposed source for the *Fowre Hymnes,* writes his "Neoplatonic" astrological poem in Lucretian verse and offers his own version of materialism.[42] Similar entwining is also evident among French humanists of the sixteenth century and it is most likely through this French channel that Spenser may have been exposed to *De rerum natura.* Lambin's important edition of Lucretius (1564), prepared with the assistance of Jean Dorat, attracted a new audience and led to a new spate of commentaries. Louis le Roy refers to the poem in his Platonic commentaries; its influence marks the poetry of the Pléiade, particularly Pontus de Tyard and Jean-Antoine de Baïf. Most intriguingly, a synthesis of Neoplatonism and Lucretian Epicureanism may also be discerned in the hymns of Ronsard, one of Spenser's evident models.[43]

Situated amid this roster of famous names, Spenser's combination of Neoplatonic and Lucretian elements appears to participate in a well-established tradition. Moreover, as Greenlaw observed trenchantly almost a century ago, Spenser's interest in cosmology and the philosophy of Nature would suggest an affinity with the Roman poet who attempted to explain, quite literally, "the nature of things" in hexameter. But there is more. The existence of a tradition linking Plato and Lucretius, by both poets and philosophers of the fifteenth and sixteenth centuries, suggests that Spenser is engaging with a specific set of cultural and generic markers that align his poetic *oeuvre* not only with the imperial and nationalistic ambitions of Vergilian epic, but also with a parallel tradition of the philosophic, cosmological epic epitomized by Lucretius and Ovid.[44]

While the *Faerie Queene* repeatedly announces its desire to be considered a rich foundational poem of fictionalized national history, the poem often veers away from these professed goals into the famous set-pieces of cosmological mythmaking, a trope that continues in the so-called minor poems, particularly *Colin Clouts Come Home Againe,* with its river marriage and cosmogony, and the *Fowre Hymnes,* each of which contains a creation account. There is, however, a crucial irony that informs these overtly philosophical musings in Spenser's poetry, for, as Socrates says in the *Republic,* there is an ancient quarrel between poetry and philosophy. Plato's famous condemnation of the poets, and the long Middle and Neoplatonic traditions advocating the *separation* of poetry and philosophy, culminates in Ficino's own denunciation of poetry as a mode of philosophizing and suggests that poets like Spenser should not contaminate or dilute the pure intellection of philosophy with the ornate aesthetic pleasures of poetry. While Ficinian Neoplatonism offered a bridge between metaphysical transcendence (that is, the attainment of the Good) and aesthetic temptation (the pleasures of the Beautiful), it too systematically separated poetry, with its fictional excesses, from the serious business of a rationally grounded philosophy—especially if that philosophy were to include cosmological speculation.[45] Towards whom then could poets with philosophizing ambitions, like Spenser, look for a model?

"The poems of sublime Lucretius," as Ovid describes the *De rerum natura,*[46] exemplified the powerful potential of synthesizing poetry and philosophy: indeed, Lucretius's famous image of honey and wormwood used to describe the *dulce utile* of poetry when conjoined to philosophy has a long and distinguished inheritance ranging from Virgil, Ovid, and Horace to their post-classical and Renaissance imitators.[47] Ironically enough, for poets with philosophical longings and

Neoplatonic sympathies—such as Scève, Peletier du Mans, Tasso, Bruno, and Spenser—Lucretius suggested a way out of the Platonic bind, since he, opposing Epicurus's dislike of the poets, composed a poem that celebrated and disseminated his teachings. In the invocation to Book IV of *De rerum natura,* Lucretius foregrounds this unprecedented fusion:

> iuvat integros accedere fontis
> atque haurire, iuvatque novos decerpere flores
> insignemque meo capiti petere inde coronam,
> unde prius nulli velarint tempora musae;
> primum quod magnis doceo de rebus et artis
> religionum animum nodis exsolvere pergo,
> deinde quod obscura de re tam lucida pango
> carmina musaeo contingens cuncta lepore.
> id quoque enim non ab nulla ratione videtur;

> [I love to approach undefiled fountains, and there to drink deeply; I love to pluck fresh flowers, and to seek a distinguished garland for my head from a source where, before this time, the Muses have adorned no brow; first, because I teach of great things and proceed to free the soul from the knots of superstition; next because I compose an illuminating poem on a dark subject, touching every part with the Muses' charm. This use of poetry does not seem to be without reason.]

> (IV, lines 2–10)

By invoking the *topoi* of poetic facility (the Muses' spring, the flowers of eloquence), Lucretius calls upon the power of poetic utterance to ease the expression of complex philosophic subjects though the clear light of his verse ("lucida carmina"). This expressive movement of dispelling philosophic obscurity through poetic light mimics the poem's stated purpose of liberating the mind from the bonds of superstition. No less important is his assertion of originality: not only will he rejuvenate philosophy with the potent infusion of poetry, he will also be the first poet to bring philosophy into the domain of poetry. *Both* disciplines will be enriched by their union.

Spenser must have found Lucretius's aspirations both visionary and seductive. The illuminating power of Lucretian poetry offered a striking alternative to the dark conceit of allegory that sought to hide philosophical truth from the uninitiated. Such a conception of poetry as an epistemological tool is of course central to Spenserian poetics, and serves to explain a peculiar image in the final stanza of the Proem to Book II of the *Faerie Queene*:

> The which O pardon me thus to enfold
>   In couert vele and wrap in shadows light,
>   That feeble eyes your glory may behold
>   Which ells could not endure those beames bright
>   But would bee dazled with exceeding light.
>
> (II.Proem.5)

The emphasis on enlightenment and revelation *through* poetic veiling seems logically unintelligible, and in fact, in his notes to the Longman edition, A. C. Hamilton flags this as an inversion of a traditional topos, that of poetic fictions covering up truth. However, when placed alongside the Lucretian invocation, Spenser's emphasis on light and brightness seems to evoke the idea of the *lucida carmina*, the illuminating poem that reveals rather than hides. More interestingly, this passage provides yet another instance of Spenser's attempt to juxtapose Plato and Lucretius. The "couert vele"—a phrase which translates the Macrobian *integumentum* well known from medieval Neoplatonic commentaries—is at first glance a Platonic image for poetic fictions; however, Spenser yokes on to the same concept a Lucretian understanding of poetry as revelatory rather than obscuring in function.

Against this background, which I have sketched all too briefly, the "Neoplatonism" of the *Fowre Hymnes* begins to look somewhat different. The Lucretian influence identified by Greenlaw almost a century ago no longer seems a heretical incompatibility, but rather a powerful inflection within an acknowledged Neoplatonic tradition. While it is impossible to pin down with precision, I emphasize this natural philosophical, Lucretian strain in Spenser's verse to highlight a particular aspect in his poetic practice, one which reveals rather different preoccupations than the traditional focus on the poet of romance-epic or love lyric. Unlike Castiglione or the *petrarchisti* whose lyric emphasis was primarily on the psychology of love as a civilizing force, Spenserian poetry—like the metamorphic figure of Venus to which Spenser was so attached—stretched beyond the confines of specific genres to embrace a vaster philosophical subject. In this, he may, like so many of his contemporaries, have been inspired by the cosmological speculations of *De rerum natura*.

In fact, Lucretius's emphasis on Venus as the source of the natural, material world helps us to revisit one of the most important structural features of Spenser's *Hymnes*: each hymn contains a distinct creation account based on an identifiable philosophic system. Near the beginning of each poem, the narrator's perspective widens dramatically from his own plight as languishing lover or penitential devotee to take in the sweep of the entire universe, from its moment of nascence to its perfect aesthetic fulfillment as a *kosmos,* a beautiful, ordered system. But the contrasts between each of the creation accounts and cosmic systems—loosely Empedoclean in *An Hymne in Honour of Love,* Platonic (from the *Timaeus*) in *An Hymne in Honour of Beautie,* based on Genesis in *An Hymne of Heavenly Love,* and loosely Aristotelian (with its *scala naturae*) in *An Hymne of Heavenly Beautie*[48]—each variously persuasive in its own right, foreground a crucial epistemological problem that may be seen as the subject of the *Hymnes* as a whole: what is the first cause of all things? What does the foundation of the universe rest upon? What animates this world?

While such questions of origin and etiology were not uniquely Lucretian by any means, it is nonetheless striking how often, during the course of the sixteenth century, they were associated with an interest in the Roman poet. By the 1580s, a number of poetic works, many exhibiting Lucretian influence, were articulating similar dilemmas—Pontus de Tyard's *L'Univers* (1557; 1587), Du Bartas's *La sepmaine* (1578), and Bruno's *Degli eroici furori* (1585) are among the best known examples. A debate on cosmic order even appears as a set-piece in Sidney's *New Arcadia* as Pamela and Cecropia argue whether the universe is ruled by chance or providence. For Spenser, as for Sidney and others, speculations about cosmic order may have been a corollary to speculations about the right foundation of political order, a connection he makes explicit in the proem to Book V:

> For that which all men then did vertue call,
>> Is now cald vice; and that which vice was hight,
>> Is now hight vertue, and so vs'd of all:
>> Right now is wrong, and wrong that was is right,
>> As all things else in time are chaunged quight.
>> Ne wonder; for the heauens reuolution
>> Is wandred farre from, where it first was pight,
>> And so doe make contrarie constitution
> Of all this lower world, toward his dissolution.

> For who so list into the heauens looke,
>> And search the courses of the rowling spheares,
>> Shall find that from the point, where they first tooke

Their setting forth, in these few thousand yeares
They all are wandred much.

(The Faerie Queene, V.Proem.4–5.5)

Here, Spenser posits a causal relationship between moral, political degeneration and cosmic decay. The destabilization of an original cosmic order symbolized by the straying zodiac, a trope used both by Palingenius and Bruno, echoes a sense of widespread philosophic turmoil and implicitly suggests that rectifying the political order necessitates a rethinking of the cosmic whole. Significantly, Lucretius's invocation to Venus in *De rerum natura* is also framed as a response to corruption and violence, caused, in that case, by the Roman civil wars; for writers in Italy, France and later England, the Latin epic's confrontation of political upheaval through a meditation on cosmic order may have seemed very compelling.[49]

Spenser's turn to cosmogonies in the *Fowre Hymnes* thus begins to look like the responses to questions of origin and order that surface repeatedly in late sixteenth-century texts. Each hymn posits a source for the beginning of the world and the resulting narratives contain crucial differences: Amor as the ordering energy of the world (*HL*) contrasts sharply with the Platonic demiurge (*HB*), who in turn seems quite different from the "trinall triplicities" (*HHL,* line 64) or the figure of Wisdom, who is invoked as the source of creation in *An Hymne of Heavenly Beautie* and derives from Proverbs 8 and the apocryphal Wisdom of Solomon. While Neoplatonic texts typically did tend to conflate such varied accounts (as we have seen with the uneasy but frequent synthesis of Lucretius and Plato), they could not entirely eliminate the dissonances. Spenser's separation of these creation narratives into discrete units invites an investigation of their differences, and opens several avenues for study: what is the relationship between "love" (the force of desire) and "beautie" (the material of attraction) as foundational *cosmic* elements, and how do they reflect the traditional dualism of matter and form? Spenser had already explored an answer to this question in the Gardens of Adonis, but do the *Hymnes* diverge from or reinforce that mythic system? How is "heavenly love" (the "pittie" of an incarnate, material God) related to "heavenly beautie" (formal, abstract sapience, the Wisdom of the Old Testament)?

At the heart of these questions is the fundamental problem of understanding how the torment of the material world, filled with pangs of desire, mutability, duplicity, and violence, relates to the Ideal, transcendent order of an (imagined) world of theistic or philosophical perfection. This dilemma is already evident in the proem to

the fifth book of *The Faerie Queene,* where Spenser mourns the gap
between the ideal and the actual, highlighting relentlessly the distance
between his ideal of Justice and its pragmatic manifestation in figures
such as Talus. Thus the lovers' agony in *An Hymne in Honour of Love*
parallels the anguish of Christ in *An Hymne of Heavenly Love* not only
because the love of Christ for humanity supersedes by its magnanimity the solipsistic passions of the poet-lover, but because *both* confront
the pain that comes with having a material body, both seek transcendence and fulfillment in a greater whole. Similarly, the idealizations
in *An Hymne in Honour of Beautie* and *An Hymne of Heavenly Beautie*
focus on the epistemological problem of separating false appearances
from true knowledge, of discerning correctly the "Paterne" of the
universe. In an important sense, then, the *Fowre Hymnes,* like the
Cantos of Mutabilitie, confronts the perception of worldly contingency
and yearns for the stability of philosophic, divine order. Its characteristic flights of imagination and poetry, its contemplative ascents and
material descents into the desiring body, are assays that seek to bring
these two opposed poles into clearer relation. And it is in this oscillation between matter and form, mutability and eternity that we might
discern the legacies of Lucretius and Plato within Spenser's thought.

III

Questions of cosmic origin permeate Spenser's work as early as the
1590 *Faerie Queene* with its mythic gardens. Spenserian gardens offer
moments of pause within the narrative from which matters of creation—both aesthetic and cosmogonic (and indeed, these are often
linked)—may be posed and examined: the Faery garden where Elf
and Fay meet and procreate in the *Antiquitee of Faerie Lond* of Book
II; the Bower of Bliss with its excesses of sterile aesthetic creativity;
the Gardens of Adonis which suggest the birth of the world. While
the Faery Garden with its Ovidian cosmogony lightly masks an account of creation very similar to Genesis, the Bower and the Gardens
have been linked to Epicurean pleasure and Lucretian materialism
respectively.[50] These allegorical gardens of the 1590 *Faerie Queene*
reappear in other poems: in the pastoral *Colin Clouts Come Home
Againe,* where Colin teaches Cuddie about the nature of love in a
garden-like setting, evoking the cosmic Venus-Cupid (also in a garden); and in the pastoral Mount Acidale episode of the sixth book
of the *Faerie Queene*; in the "silver bowers" (*HL,* line 23) "blossomes

of the field" (*HB,* line 78) and "Paradizes" that conclude each of the *Fowre Hymnes.*[51] In each of these cases, the pleasure gardens of epic become the spaces in which, appropriately enough, Spenser investigates the nature of eros. What is puzzling, however, is that in almost every instance (and with increasing frequency in the later poems), Spenser associates the investigation of desire in gardens with cosmological speculation—we might count five different cosmogonic narratives in the works I have outlined above—an association that reaches its culmination in the *Fowre Hymnes.*

The prevalence of this pattern across Spenser's poems suggests that questions of love and cosmology are closely interlinked in Spenser's later poetry, and that we ought not to separate them. The significance of the garden setting itself gives us a clue. Not only was Spenser drawing on the *locus amoenus* tradition of classical epic and Italian romance, and not only did the garden recall the original Edenic paradise, but to those with more than a passing interest in philosophy, the garden evoked the private, pastoral school of Epicurus, known as "the Garden," a famous spatial counterpoint to the public nature of Plato's Academy, the Lyceum where Isocrates and Aristotle taught, and even the Stoa Poikile where Zeno is said to have met his students. Tales of the Epicurean Garden, an enclosed space conducive to both *ataraxia* (detachment, tranquility) and hedonism, were readily available in accounts by Cicero and Diogenes, and it seems likely that Spenser's allegorical gardens with their distinctly materialist elements, their investigation of pleasure and cosmology, recall the philosophical significance of this model.[52] Of course, gardens as locations for philosophic myth appear in key Platonic texts as well: in the *Republic's* myth of Er (613e-621), in the *Phaedrus* (which takes place in a grove), and in the *Symposium* (203b-c)—another point of contact between Platonic and Epicurean systems.

The continuity between these philosophical gardens and the *Fowre Hymnes* is evident in Spenser's repetition of the cosmogony in *Colin Clouts* as the creation account in *An Hymne in Honour of Love*. Both poems refer to the paradox of Cupid's birth and both offer a vision of the earth formed by the conjoining of antagonistic elements, characteristic of Epicurean physics:

> For by his [Love's] powre the world was made of yore,
> And all that therein wondrous doth appeare.
> For how should else things so far from attone
> And so great enemies as of them bee,
> Be ever drawne together into one,

And taught in such accordance to agree?
Through him the cold began to covet heat,
And water fire; the light to mount on hie,
And th'heavie down to pieze; the hungry t'eat
And voydness to seek full satietie.
So being former foes, they wexed friends,
And gan by little learne to love each other:
So being knit, they brought forth other kynds
Out of the fruitfull wombe of their great mother.
Then first gan heaven out of darknesse dread
For to appeare, and brought forth chearfull day:
Next gan the earth to shew her naked head,
Out of deep waters which her drownd alway.
And shortly after everie living wight,
Crept forth like wormes out of her slimie nature,
Soone as on them the Suns life giving light,
Had powred kindly heat and formall feature . . .

                    (*Colin Clouts Come Home Againe,* lines 841–62)

For ere this worlds still moving mightie masse,
Out of great Chaos ugly prison crept,
In which his [Love's] goodly face long hidden was
From heavens view, and in deepe darknesse kept,
Love that had now long time securely slept
In *Venus* lap, unarmed then and naked,
Gan reare his head, by Clotho being waked.
    . . . . .
Then through the world his way he gan to take,
The world that was not till he did it make;
Whose sundrie parts he from them selves did sever,
The which before had lyen confused ever.

The earth, the ayre, the water and the fyre,
Then gan to raunge them selves in huge array,
And with contrary forces to conspyre
Each against other, by all meanes they may,
Threatening their owne confusion and decay:
Ayre hated earth, and water hated fyre,
Till Love relented their rebellious yre.

He then them tooke, and tempering goodly well
Their contrary dislikes and loved meanes,
Did place them all in order, and compell
To keepe them selves within their sundrie raines,
Together linked with Adamantine chaines;
Yet so, as that in every living wight
They mixe themselves, and shew their kindly might.

(*HL,* lines 57–91)

These two passages have typically been discussed in relation to each other since both identify Love as the creative source of the universe. Neither, however, is uniquely Platonic. Instead, both substitute a theory of spontaneous generation through the ordering principles of attraction and repulsion (personified in classical philosophy as Empedocles' Love and Strife or Lucretius's Venus and Mars) for the more orthodox architectural metaphors of the Platonic demiurge who is always an *artifex,* a maker.[53] In *Colin Clouts,* Love separates an apparently preexisting chaos of confused elements, while *An Hymne in Honour of Love* makes this chronology somewhat clearer by suggesting that Love is born at the very moment when "this worlds still moving mightie masse,/Out of great Chaos ugly prison crept."

It is crucial to observe here that Spenser implicitly denies the theory of creation *ex nihilo* in favor of the materialists' view of preexisting cosmic matter—a topic that Du Bartas and Tasso both vigorously argue against in their hexamera, and which is still a vexed issue for readers of Milton's *Paradise Lost.*[54] In fact, the loosely Empedoclean account of creation outlined in these poems seems to be another Spenserian variation on a set of famous passages in *De rerum natura*:

Denique tantopere inter se cum maxima mundi
pugnent membra, pio nequaquam concita bello,
nonne vides aliquam longi certaminis ollis
posse dari finem?

. . . . .

Sed nova tempestas quaedam molesque coorta
omnigenis e principiis, discordia quorum
intervalla vias conexus pondera plagas
concursus motus turbabat proelia miscens . . .

. . . . .

diffugere inde loci partes coepere, paresque

cum paribus iungi res, et discludere mundum
membraque dividere et magnas disponere partes . . .

. . . . .

Sic igitur terrae concreto corpore pondus
constitit, atque omnis mundi quasi limus in imum
confluxit.

[Since the greatest members of the world fight so hard together,
stirred by most unrighteous war, do you not see that some end
may be given to their long strife? . . . . But a sort of strange
storm, all kinds of beginnings gathered together into a mass,
while their discord, exciting war amongst them, made a confusion. . . . In the next place parts began to separate, like things
to join with like, and to divide the world and put its members
in place and to arrange its great parts. . . . In this way, therefore,
the heavy earth became solid with compact body, and all the
mud of creation, flowed together.]

(*De rerum Natura* 5, lines 380–83, 436–45, 449–54, 495–97)

Lucretian language ("pugnent membra, pio nequaquam concita bello . . . ," "Discordia . . . turbabat proelia") quite specifically underlies
Spenser's vision of elemental conflict ("For how should else things
so far from attone / And so great enemies as of them bee," "The earth,
the ayre, the water and the fyre, / Then gan to raunge themselves in
huge array, / And with contrary forces to conspire. . . . "). And this
is hardly surprising since the Roman poet's description of the world
emerging from chaos was one of the most influential set-pieces of
classical poetry for Renaissance writers. Both Du Bartas and Milton
draw on it for their accounts of Genesis, Bruno returns to it in several
treatises, and Spenser had already alluded to it in his Gardens of
Adonis (*Faerie Queene* III.vi.36).

The similarities between the Spenserian and Lucretian passages
cited here are nevertheless striking, not least because Spenser appears
to have followed quite carefully the progression of events in the
Roman epic's cosmogony. The narrator imagines a dynamic, fertile
chaos of unformed material elements, described with metaphors of
war, which gives way to the separation and recombination of the
elements into a cosmic whole.[55] Indeed, in *Colin Clouts,* Spenser offers
a number of specific textual clues that point us towards *De rerum
natura.* The invocation of the void as a spatial concept ("And voydness
to seek full satietie") was a well-known Lucretian tag, and perhaps

the earliest use of the word in this cosmological sense in English.[56] The emergence of Spenser's earth from the waters of the ocean as an enormous womb bringing forth life spontaneously depends on another Lucretian echo ("slimie wormes" imitates "omnis mundi . . . limus in imum/confluxit") and clearly identifies the "fruitfull wombe of their great mother" in Colin's narrative as the earth itself rather than chaos. And perhaps most tellingly, the emphasis on an animate, generative *matter* that makes no mention of a metaphysically distinct form, spirit, or soul is distinctly Lucretian.

However, Spenser's Lucretianism in *Colin Clouts* is contained within an Empedoclean frame, which mitigates somewhat the atheistic anti-teleological thrust of the Epicurean cosmogony.[57] Ellrodt has shown how Empedoclean thought could be neatly assimilated into Neoplatonic philosophies because of its rhetoric of love and strife.[58] And yet, the important nexus between Empedocles and Epicurus is one that Spenser would have been well aware of: Empedocles is the only philosopher (apart from Epicurus) whom Lucretius discusses with approval, and the Lucretian dichotomy of Venus/Mars is itself derived from the Empedoclean cycles of Love and Strife.[59] Moreover, Estienne's *Fragments* of the pre-Socratic philosophers, published in 1573, and Diogenes Laertius's well-known *Vitae,* would have enabled Spenser to distinguish the so-called naturalistic philosophers (Heraclitus, Democritus, Empedocles, and Epicurus) from the Neoplatonists, while recognizing the ways in which they had been assimilated by the Platonic tradition. Given these crosscurrents of Renaissance philosophy, Empedocles may have helped Spenser mediate between the atheistic materialism of Lucretian Epicureanism and the mystical devotions of the Neoplatonic writers.

It is no accident then that the stridently materialist cosmogony of *Colin Clouts* is softened in *An Hymne in Honour of Love,* even though the basic elements remain the same: Spenser removes the more extensive Lucretian allusions (the emergence of the earth-mother, the generation of animals), and focuses instead on Love's active subjection of antagonistic elements and enforcement of order. But even as Spenser shifts from a Lucretian vision of animate matter in motion to a more Empedoclean account of Love as a creative agent (who seems here to resemble an allegorized demiurge), he retains key phrases from *De rerum natura*: "confused" and "confusion" along with the "great Chaos" allude not only to the condition of elemental disorder (*discordia . . . turbabat . . . miscens*) but to the intermingling of the elements so necessary for *kosmos*. Moreover, Spenser's image of "the worlds still moving mightie masse" may translate Lucretius's vision of the "moles et machina mundi" (*DRN* 5.97), following

Marullus's hymn to Amor, which seems to have served as the model for *An Hymne in Honour of Love*.[60] In this poem, Marullus presents a cosmogony with Love as the creative agent in terms that are almost identical to Spenser's account:[61]

> Quid, quod et novas Chaos in figuras
> Digeris primus docilemque rerum
> Mutuis nectis seriem catenis
>   Pace rebelli?
>
> Quid, quod, antique superata Anance
> Suscipis mundum placidum regendum?

[And again, you organize Chaos into new forms, you are the first, and you enchain the docile line of things with mutual bonds in a rebellious peace. And again, triumphing over Ananke, you undertake to govern the calmed world.][62]

Marullus's vision of Amor's triumph over Ananke finds a counterpart in a peculiar detail of Spenser's hymn—in the English version, Love awakens to create because of Clotho, the youngest of the Moirai, identified in Plato's *Symposium* as the daughters of Ananke (necessity). The chains used to bind the elements in the *Hymne* echo the "mutuis catenis" of Marullus, while Spenser's entire stanza is, in effect, an elaboration of the elemental "pace rebelli." The structural and thematic similarities between the *Hymni naturales* and Spenser's *Hymnes* are yet to be studied in detail, but they merit attention particularly because Marullus's poems epitomize the unlikely synthesis between Lucretian and Neoplatonic philosophies that I have been tracing in Spenser's poetry.[63] It has long been observed, for instance, that Marullus's hymn to Amor in Book I of the *Hymni* modifies Lucretius's invocation to Venus in *De rerum natura*, transferring the creative energy from the goddess to Cupid/Love.[64] Spenser makes a similar substitution in *An Hymne in Honour of Love*, only to quote his Lucretian source, appropriately enough, in the invocation to Venus that begins the *Hymne in Honoure of Beautie* (lines 15–21).

This peculiar juxtaposition of a Lucretian philosophy of matter and erotic energy (*voluptas*) against the visionary transcendence promised by Christian Neoplatonism occurs in a precise pattern in the first two hymns. In *An Hymne in Honour of Love*, a Lucretian-Empedoclean creation account is framed by Petrarchan-Neoplatonic love discourse, while the pattern is reversed in the companion *Hymne in Honour of Beautie,* where the invocation to a Lucretian Venus frames a Platonic account of creation and a Neoplatonic meditation on the problem of beauty-as-form. If the torments of desire in the first hymn are experienced as physical and material, in the second, we are presented with the epistemological dilemma of distinguishing between "goodly beautie" and the "outward shew of things." As the cosmic creationism of Love glides into a reflection on beauty, so the celebration of the beautiful "Paterne" leads to an exhortation to love ("Therefore to make your beautie more appeare,/It you behoves to love . . . ," *HB,* lines 183–84). Significantly, as several critics have argued, there is no steady ascent along a Neoplatonic ladder of love because the two hymns are perfect thematic and rhetorical mirrors for each other; they emphatically do not follow a (perhaps expected) logic by which the second thematically erases and substitutes the first in a hierarchy of philosophic ascent.

IV

This extended discussion of Lucretian imagery in the first hymn raises at least two substantive questions for the interpretation of the work as a whole. First, why might cosmology, and specifically cosmogony, be central to Spenser's poetry? In a now classic article, Harry Berger discusses the cosmogonies in *Colin Clouts* and *An Hymne in Honoure of Love* only to argue that Spenser is not particularly interested in cosmology but in ethics, psychology and politics, so that the cosmic awakening of Love corresponds to a "coming to consciousness" of the self.[65] A similar emphasis on poetic subjectivity at the expense of the cosmic thought-experiment is at the center of Ellrodt's influential analysis. While these theoretical approaches have yielded rich treatments of Spenser's narrative technique, sociopolitical context and biographical motivations, what might be gained from investigating the cosmological turn in the later poems, particularly in the light of recent studies on the scientific contexts of the late sixteenth century?[66]

The second question I want to raise harkens back to Greenlaw's pioneering analysis of Spenser's Lucretianism: why indeed would a devout Protestant engage so closely with the atheistic materialism of Lucretius? Specifically, how does an appreciation of the Lucretianism in the first two hymns affect an understanding of the work as a whole, particularly given the theological emphasis of the second pair? The

issue is central to Spenser's presentation of the *Fowre Hymnes'* structure as palinodic and forces us to consider whether the hymns of
Heavenly Love and *Heavenly Beautie* simply supersede those to *Love*
and *Beautie,* recanting the youthful error of "greener times" in favor
of religious conversion.

As critics of Greenlaw's thesis argued almost a century ago, Spenser
was clearly no thoroughgoing materialist (as for instance, the monist
Milton would be).[67] His poems, especially the *Hymnes,* are suffused
with the language of light, fire, air, and desire, rejecting the grossness
of earthly matter as might be expected of a good Protestant. And
indeed, when Spenser's materialism does find expression, it is a peculiar mixture of Platonic and Lucretian elements, as for instance, in
this passage from *An Hymne in Honour of Beautie*:

> Thereof as every earthly thing partakes,
> Or more or lesse by influence divine,
> So it more faire accordingly it makes,
> And the grosse matter of this earthly myne,
> Which clotheth it, thereafter doth refyne,
> Doing away the drosse which dims the light
> Of that faire beame, which therein is empight.
>
> For through infusion of celestiall powre,
> The duller earth it quickneth with delight,
> And life-full spirits privily doth powre
> Through all the parts, that to the lookers sight
> They seeme to please. That is thy soveraine might,
> O *Cyprian* Queene, which flowing from the beame
> Of thy bright starre, thou into them doest streame.
>
> (*HB,* lines 43–56)

These stanzas oscillate between the dualism of Platonic ontology (the
Idea of beauty is infused into inert matter) and an evidently vitalist
materialism (this "influence" and "infusion" suggest the physical fluidity of the "life-full spirits"). Spenser's verses linguistically enact the
steady movement from "grosse matter" to animate spirit, as the
rhymes shift subtly from *refine/myne* to the ethereality of *light/em-
pight/ delight* before turning back to the physical realm through the
same rhyme (*sight/might*). Never quite committing to an unambigu-
ous Platonic hierarchy of form over matter, the words themselves
dance around the impregnation ("quickneth with delight") of matter

by animate spirits. While such a vision of matter taking on life could potentially be assimilated into a Plotinian vision of emanations, Spenser's insistent identification of the life-force with Venus suggests otherwise.[68] We might, moreover, also recall the central stanzas of the Gardens of Adonis episode in the *Faerie Queene* where the inter-mingling of Venus and Adonis, matter and form is inextricable, as are the elements of Platonism and materialism; here, Spenser's use of the archaic verb "empight" evokes the same botanical metaphor of planting.[69]

More importantly, perhaps, both these stanzas provide an account of the origin of life, but also struggle with the epistemological conse-quences of dualism: positing a dichotomy of body and soul, matter and spirit creates the dilemma of distinguishing appearance from essence—a question that the hymn relates back to the Phaedria's song and the Bower of Bliss:[70]

> Why doe not then the blossomes of the field,
> Which are arayd with much more orient hew,
> And to the sense most daintie odours yield,
> Worke like impression in the lookers vew?
> Or why doe not faire pictures like powre shew,
> In which oftimes, we Nature see of Art
> Exceld, in perfect limming every part.
>
> (*HB,* lines 78–84)

As the submerged allusion to Matthew 6:28–29 suggests, this passage of the *Hymne* confronts the dilemma of materiality itself—faced with the inevitable corruption of the flesh how do we transcend corporeal-ity?[71] Competing philosophies provided different answers, and the jarring incompatibility between Spenser's address to Venus and his allusion to Matthew suggests an ongoing struggle between the imper-atives of the sensual world and the desire for eternal perfection. In Book II of *The Faerie Queene,* the didactic impetus of the epic estab-lishes a clear moral distinction between the overwrought world of the senses (epitomized by the hedonistic Bower of Bliss) and the need for restraint as a form of order; but in the *Hymnes,* the moral inflections of this dichotomy are less clear as Spenser struggles to separate matter (superficial physical attractiveness) from form (inter-nal, soulful beauty).

The problem is only more acute in the second pair of overtly religious hymns, where the experience of matter leads to a rapturous contemplation of pure form. Indeed, the fine balance in the first pair of hymns between the physical focus of Lucretian materialism and the meditative magic of Neoplatonism's dualist ontology may be responsible for what David Miller insightfully describes as the "metaleptic relation between the heavenly hymns and the earthly model they purport to imitate, correct, and supplant in a single gesture."[72] Thus, *An Hymne of Heavenly Love* is almost obsessed with images of the suffering body of Christ: "that most blessed bodie . . . /He freely gave to be both rent and torne" (lines 148–50); "loves deepe wounde, that pierst the piteous hart. . . ./And sharply launching every inner part,/Dolours of death into his soule did dart" lines 156–59); "What hart can feele. . . ./Or thought can think the depth of so deare wound? Whose bleeding sourse their stremes yet never staunch" (lines 62–65). Meditation on the materiality of the Incarnation leads to an exhortation to love selflessly like the Son, but ends with an apostrophe to the earth, which is, significantly, also a synecdoche for the poet himself, man in all his material substance: "Then rouze thy selfe, O earth, out of thy soyle . . ." (line 218). The model for transcendence here is not enraptured contemplation of cosmic order itself (as it will be in *An Hymne of Heavenly Beautie*) but the mortification of the individual's flesh—literal in the case of Christ, but metaphorically imitated by his followers who will finally approach the purity of heavenly love only through the sentient body:

> Then let thy flinty heart that feeles no paine,
> Empierced be with pitiful remorse,
> And let thy bowels bleede in every vaine,
>
> . . . . .
> And let thy soule whose sins his sorrows wrought,
> Melt into tears, and grone in grieved thought.
>
> (*HHL,* lines 246–52)

The corporeality of Spenser's language in these passages contrasts strikingly with the ethereality of his images elsewhere in the hymns, and it is arguably the physical concreteness of the poem, its emphasis on the visceral, that has led to its frequent praise as the most powerful of the four.

In contrast, *An Hymne of Heavenly Beautie* turns away from the individual material body to a vision of the entire created cosmos strongly reminiscent of Du Bartas's *La sepmaine* (1578). Significantly, the poet now turns away from the sacrifice of the Son celebrated in the hymn of *Heavenly Love* and introduces the apocryphal Old Testament figure of Wisdom as the culminating figure of the *Fowre*

Hymnes.[73] Spenser seems to distinguish Sapience from the Trinity and draws on Proverbs and the Wisdom of Solomon, where Wisdom is closely associated with the creation; in fact, most of the final hymn delights in the creation before even introducing Sapience as the source of heavenly beauty.[74] This turn away from the Trinity (even though Spenser does praise "God" before the enthroned "sovereign dearling of the *Deity*") demands more attention for its unexpected shift of theological focus. It is a move similar to the final stanzas of the *Cantos of Mutabilitie* where "Dame Nature" seems to replace the traditional Christian deity that we might expect.[75]

The figure of Wisdom in the Hebrew Bible is a mysterious figure. A personification who may be based on Near Eastern goddess cults and who is depicted as the child of God (Proverbs 8:22–30), she stands for the order embedded in the universe, the "Paterne" or trace of divine agency in the world. As John Collins argues persuasively, Wisdom embodies a kind of natural theology, forming "a bridge between creation and created," providing a rather different model for understanding the relations of God and the universe.[76] Human beings might understand the presence of the divine through Wisdom, that is, the understanding of order in the visible world. From this perspective, Wisdom, the abstraction of form and order in the cosmos, becomes the counterpart to the incarnate Christ who ennobles matter itself.

In an important sense then, the second pair of hymns replicates the interlocking pattern of matter and form found in the first two hymns. An emphasis on bodily experience in both the hymns on love balances the contemplative mode of the hymns on beauty, which present the concept of "Beautie" as the order in the cosmos. This structure is also evident in the cosmogonic accounts of the hymns: creation in the hymns on love is presented as a process, an elemental coming together, while in the hymns on beauty, it is an accomplished, constructed product.[77] It is in this context that the Lucretian-Platonic dialectic that I have been describing becomes most interesting. For Spenser appears to have treated the problem of cosmic order, of matter and form, through two carefully separated perspectives, one in the light of classical philosophy without the benefit of Christian revelation, and one in the light of Revelation.[78] This distinction between classical and Christian would seem typical, even too typical, for a sixteenth-century poet—until we note that there is no clear subordination of classical to Christian, no syncretic "Christianizing" of classical materials. Significantly, the conceptual patterns that emerge between the first and second pair are strikingly similar and even complement each other, suggesting that the *Hymnes* do not advance a narrative of ascent and religious conversion or transcendence. The elaborate palinode of the dedication seems to have been pointing to this juxtaposition all along—an apparent recantation that is not quite a recantation at all.

Stony Brook University

NOTES

1. All citations to the *Fowre Hymnes* are from William A. Oram, ed., *The Yale Edition of the Shorter Poems of Edmund Spenser* (New Haven: Yale University Press, 1989).

2. See Robert Ellrodt, *Neoplatonism in the Poetry of Spenser* (Geneva: Droz, 1960), 13–24.

3. The question of Spenser's recantation of the first two hymns has been discussed by several critics—see for instance, Enid Welsford, *Fowre Hymnes and Epithalamion: A Study of Edmund Spenser's Doctrine of Love* (New York: Barnes & Noble, 1967) and Mary Oates, "Fowre Hymnes: Spenser's Retractions of Paradise," *Spenser Studies* 4 (1983): 143–69. See also the brief but suggestive comments in David Lee Miller, "Spenser's Poetics: The Poem's Two Bodies," *PMLA* 101, no. 2 (1986): 173.

4. The literature on the *Hymnes* is surprisingly slim. The most exhaustive treatment remains that of Ellrodt; some other analyses that discuss the hymns at some length include: Welsford; Einar Bjorvand, "Spenser's Defence of Poetry: Some Structural Aspects of the *Fowre Hymnes*," in *Fair Forms: Essays in English Literature from Spenser to Jane Austen*, ed. Maren-Sofie Rostvig (Totowa: Rowman & Littlefield, 1975), 13–46; Philip Rollinson, "A Generic View of Spenser's Four Hymns," *Studies in Philology* 68 (1971): 292–304; Leigh DeNeef, *Spenser and the Motives of Metaphor* (Durham: Duke University Press, 1982), 77–88; William Nelson, *The Poetry of Edmund Spenser: A Study* (New York: Columbia University Press, 1963), 97–115; Maren-Sofie Rostvig, "Images of Perfection," in *Seventeenth Century Imagery: Essays on the Use of Figurative Language from Donne to Farquhar*, ed. Earl Miner (Berkeley: University of California Press, 1971); Terry Comito, "A Dialectic of Images in Spenser's *Fowre Hymnes*," *Studies in Philology* 74 (1977): 301–21; Jerome Dees, "Spenser's Anti-Neoplatonism," in *Spenser, Classical, Medieval, Renaissance, and Modern: Proceedings from a Special Session at the Twelfth Conference on Medieval Studies in Kalamazoo, Michigan, 5–8 May, 1977*, ed. David A. Richardson (Cleveland: Cleveland State University Press, 1977), 271–305; Oates; Stella P. Revard, *Pindar and the Renaissance Hymn-ode, 1450–1700* (Tempe, AZ: Medieval & Renaissance Texts & Studies, 2001); William A. Oram, *Edmund Spenser* (New York: Twayne Publishers, 1997), 263–80; Elizabeth Bieman, *Plato Baptized: Towards the Interpretation of Spenser's Mimetic Fictions* (Toronto: University of Toronto Press, 1988), 152–62; and Patrick Cheney, *Spenser's Famous Flight: A Renaissance Idea of a Literary Career* (Toronto: University of Toronto Press, 1993). Other studies will be cited only as necessary.

5.   For an illuminating study of the form, see Patricia Berrahou Phillippy, *Love's Remedies: Recantation and Renaissance Lyric Poetry* (Lewisburg, PA: Bucknell University Press, 1995). On its origins see Leonard Woodbury, "Helen and the Palinode," *Phoenix* 21, no. 3 (Autumn 1967): 157–76.

6.   Of course, Stesichorus's recantation to the *Helen* is not actually concerned with repudiating juvenile erotic experience in favor of later, more mature, spiritual experience. The ode recantation to the *Helen* is an apology for depicting a flawed Helen in the epic, and an attempt to reinstate a pristine version of the heroine. However, Stesichorus's poem remains the first instance of this poetic mode, one which was adapted by later writers for the opportunities that it offered for portraying a flexible, changing poetic self.

7.   Phillippy, 261.

8.   The nature of the "commentary" is not fully known; in his letter to Martin Preninger (in *Op.*, 1: 933), Ficino refers to "commentariolis in Lucretium meis." See Marsilio Ficino, *Supplementum Ficinianum. Marsilii Ficini Florentini Philosophi Platonici Opuscula Inedita et Dispersa. Primvm, Collegit et Ex Fontibus Plerumque Manuscriptis*, ed. Paul Oskar Kristeller (Florence: L.S. Olschki, 1937), vol. II, 81–87; Paul Oskar Kristeller, *Studies in Renaissance Thought and Letters* (Rome: Edizioni di storia e letteratura, 1956), 191–211; Raymond Marcel, *Marsile Ficin, 1433–1499* (Paris: Société d'édition les Belles Lettres, 1958), 354–55; James Hankins, *Plato in the Italian Renaissance* (Leiden: E.J. Brill, 1994), vol. 2, 454–59; Michael J. B. Allen, *Synoptic Art: Marsilio Ficino on the History of Platonic Interpretation* (Florence: L. S. Olschki, 1998), 114; Christopher S. Celenza, "Pythagoras in the Renaissance: The Case of Marsilio Ficino," *Renaissance Quarterly* 52, no. 3 (1999): 690; and Alessandro Polcri, "Una sconosciuta corrispondenza tra Marsilio Ficino e Girolamo Pasqualini e il volgarizzamento del *De Magnificentia* e del *De Quatuor Sectis Philosophorum* dedicato ad Antonio di Tuccio Manetti," *Interpres* 19 (2000): 45–83.

9.   For instance, in Speech VII of his commentary on the *Symposium*, chapters v, vi and xi, Ficino cites Book IV of *De rerum natura* at length for examples of the pains of erotic desire.

10.   See *De rerum natura* I.936–43, repeated almost verbatim at IV.11–18. The trope is discussed extensively in Valentina Prosperi, *Di soavi licor gli orli del vaso: la fortuna di Lucrezio dall'Umanesimo alla Controriforma* (Torino: Aragno, 2004).

11.   The question of defining "Neoplatonism" is, of course, a vexed one, since the term encompasses a wide range of philosophical positions including syncretic compilations of works not only by Plato, Plotinus, and the Alexandrian Platonists, but also such figures as Zoroaster, Pythagoras, Hermes Trismagistus, the Kabbala, and even Aristotle.

12.   Literary scholars of the sixteenth century have typically focused on Neoplatonism as it relates to the erotic discourse of the period, a connection made explicit not only in Ficino's commentaries on the *Symposium* and the *Phaedrus*, but on Neoplatonizing interpretations of Petrarchan poetry (for instance, in Pico's famous commentary on Benivieni's *Canzone*). Perhaps the most influential instance of this relationship is the fourth book of Castiglione's *Il libro del cortegiano*; this background, as it is relevant for Spenser, is surveyed concisely in Welsford, 3–36. However, as an entire system of thought, Neoplatonism was concerned not only with the problem of

desire, but also with metaphysics, epistemology and natural philosophy; in this, the ongoing importance of the *Timaeus* cannot be ignored. Other important philosophic *loci* within the Platonic corpus for early modern philosophers include the *Laws* and the *Parmenides;* a useful approach to this aspect of Neoplatonic philosophy is provided by Michael F. Wagner ed., *Neoplatonism and Nature: Studies in Plotinus' Enneads* (Albany: State University of New York Press, 2002). For a discussion of Platonic natural philosophy with specific regard to Spenser, see Jon Quitslund, *Spenser's Supreme Fiction: Platonic Natural Philosophy and the Faerie Queene* (Toronto: University of Toronto Press, 2001).

13.   The strangeness (and thus, importance) of Spenser's use of the word "naturall" is noted in passing by Rollinson, "A Generic View," 294. It is through this emphasis on "natural" hymns that Rollinson connects the *Fowre Hymnes* to the *Hymni naturales* of Marullus. A case for Spenser's interest in natural philosophy is made in two classic articles by Edwin Greenlaw; see "Spenser and Lucretius," *Studies in Philology* 17 (1920): 455–84; and "Spenser's Mutabilitie," *PMLA* 45, no. 3 (September 1930): 684–703.

14.   One of Ellrodt's most important contributions for studies of Spenser and Neoplatonism was his focus on the importance of the *Timaeus* and Middle Platonism more generally; see especially 96–97. However, Ellrodt's focus on medieval interpretations and assimilations of the *Timaeus* ignores the role that it played in the development of new directions in sixteenth-century natural philosophy—see for instance Gretchen Reydams-Schils, *Plato's* Timaeus *as Cultural Icon* (Notre Dame: University of Notre Dame Press, 2003); Thomas Leinkauf, ed., *Plato's* Timaeus *and the Foundations of Cosmology in Late Antiquity, the Middle Ages and Renaissance* (Leuven: Leuven University Press, 2005); Thomas Johansen, *Plato's Natural Philosophy: A Study of the* Timaeus-Critias (Cambridge: Cambridge University Press, 2004); and M. R. Wright, ed., *Reason and Necessity: Essays on Plato's* Timaeus (London: Duckworth, 2000).

15.   See for instance Hilary Gatti, *Giordano Bruno and Renaissance Science* (Ithaca: Cornell University Press, 1999) and "The Natural Philosophy of Giordano Bruno," *Midwest Studies in Philosophy* 26, no. 1 (2002); Michel Jeanneret, *Perpetual Motion: Transforming Shapes in the Renaissance from Da Vinci to Montaigne*, trans. Nidra Poller (Baltimore: Johns Hopkins University Press, 2001); and William Eamon, *Science and the Secrets of Nature: Books of Secrets in Medieval and Early Modern Culture* (Princeton: Princeton University Press, 1994).

16.   Ellrodt, 9.

17.   Significantly, there is no substantive critical work devoted entirely to the Renaissance hymn. Useful individual studies that discuss the matter of genre include: Revard; Philip Ford, *Ronsard's Hymnes: A Literary and Iconographical Study* (Tempe, AZ: Medieval & Renaissance Texts & Studies, 1997), 107–18; P. L. Ciceri, "Michele Marullo e i suoi *Hymni Naturales*," *Giornale storico della letteratura italiana* 64 (1914): 289–357; the introductory essay to Marullus, *Hymnes naturales*, ed. and trans. Jacques Chomorat (Geneva: Droz, 1995), 7–17; Michel Dassonville, "Eléments pour une définition de l'hymne ronsardien," in *Autour des "Hymnes" de Ronsard*, ed. Madeleine Lazard (Geneva: Editions Slatkine, 1984), 1–32; Philip Rollinson, "The Renaissance of the Literary Hymn," *Renaissance Papers* (1968): 11–20 and "A Generic View," 292–304.

18. On the Christian tradition of the hymn, see the useful summary of Henry Spitzmuller, *Poésie latine chrétienne du Moyen âge, IIe-XVe siècle* (Paris: Desclée de Brouwer, 1971).

19. On this function of lyric poetry, see Thomas M. Greene, "Poetry as Invocation," *New Literary History* 24, no. 3 (1993): 495–517.

20. Francis Cairns, *Generic Composition in Greek and Roman Poetry* (Edinburgh: Edinburgh University Press, 1972), 92.

21. Scaliger's comments on the hymn appear in sections 1.45 and 3.92–95 of the *Poetices*, and are largely based on Menander's *On the Hymns to the Gods*. See Giulio Cesare Scaligero, *Poetices Libri Septem. Sieben Bücher Über Die Dichtkunst*, trans. Gregor Vogt-Spira, Luc Deitz, and Manfred Fuhrmann (Stuttgart-Bad Cannstatt: Frommann-Holzboog, 1994) and Menander, *Menander Rhetor: Edited with Translation and Commentary*, trans. D. A Russell and Nigel Guy Wilson (Oxford: Clarendon Press, 1981).

22. Patrick Cheney has argued for a reconsideration of Spenser's poetic career, claiming that he "reinvents the Virgilian Wheel" (62) by creating a four-stage model from pastoral to epic to love-lyric to hymn, where the turn from love-lyric to hymn involves an Augustinian moment of conversion, a "salvific telos." My argument seeks to extend Cheney's insightful exploration in its emphasis on Spenser's self-conscious turn from epic to hymn, but I am less persuaded by the Petrarchan-Augustinian recantation for which he argues. I see Spenser's turn away from the immediate subject of history and politics, not as a movement towards heaven and salvation, but towards cosmology (an important focus of both the *Hymns* and the *Mutabilitie Cantos*), which seems to be an extension of similar philosophic concerns with just order into a wider sphere.

23. For a useful discussion of Dorat's lectures on Homer, see Ford, *Ronsard's Hymnes*, 111–13.

24. Dorat's comment is cited in Pierre de Ronsard, *Oeuvres complètes*, ed. Paul Laumonier (Paris: Hachette, 1914), 8:4–5. We might hear perhaps in Dorat's phrase, "Naturae rerum" an echo of Lucretius's *De rerum natura*, which Dorat was helping Lambinus to edit.

25. Anne Prescott suggests that the classical Vergilian model of a poetic career may not have been the only one available to Spenser. She points usefully to the case of Ronsard, who never managed to complete an epic, and who chose increasingly to be identified as a love poet, arguing that studies of poetic careers may be served by deploying an "inter-careerist model." See Anne Lake Prescott, "The Laurel and the Myrtle: Spenser and Ronsard," in *Worldmaking Spenser: Explorations in the Early Modern Age*, eds. Patrick Cheney and Lauren Silberman (Lexington: University of Kentucky Press, 2000), 63–78. Such an analysis may well help us understand the importance of the hymns within Spenser's *oeuvre* as a whole. On the relationship between Spenser's poetry and Ronsard's, see Alfred W. Satterthwaite, *Spenser, Ronsard, and Du Bellay: A Renaissance Comparison* (Princeton: Princeton University Press, 1960). The importance of French writers more generally for Spenser (particularly, Du Bellay, Ronsard, and Du Bartas) cannot be underestimated; the classic work remains Anne Lake Prescott, *French Poets and the English Renaissance: Studies in Fame and Transformation* (New Haven: Yale University Press, 1978).

26.   All citations of *The Faerie Queene* are from Edmund Spenser, *The Faerie Queene*, eds. A. C. Hamilton, H. Yamashita, and T. Suzuki (New York: Longman, 2001).

27.   All citations of *De rerum natura* are from Titus Carus Lucretius, *On the Nature of Things*, trans. W. H. D. Rouse (Cambridge: Harvard University Press, 1975).

28.   Anthony Esolen notes that the doctrine of nature being the only controlling power in the world was theologically problematic from a Christian point of view. He points to Lucretius's identifications of "natura creatrix" and "fortuna gubernans" as the ruling forces of the universe; see Anthony Esolen, "Spenserian Chaos: Lucretius in *The Faerie Queene*," *Spenser Studies* 11 (1994): 32. The problem of whether the world was governed by chance or nature—or the providential wisdom of a deity—was at the center of natural philosophic debates in the late sixteenth and seventeenth centuries, with implications that extended beyond physics into ethics and politics. A related problem was the proper relationship of a creative nature to the supreme creative deity. Spenser avoids an overt confrontation of these questions in the *Hymnes*; however, by balancing the first two hymns, with their invocations of Love/Venus as unpredictable rulers of the universe, against the second pair, with their insistence on a Christian teleology, he implicitly raises the issue.

29.   On the Lucretian elements in Book IV of *Faerie Queene*, see Theresa M. Krier, *Birth Passages: Maternity and Nostalgia, Antiquity to Shakespeare* (Ithaca: Cornell University Press, 2001), 202–33.

30.   It is worth noting that this Lucretian figure differs in significant ways from the iconography of the Platonic Venus (though the Neoplatonic tradition often distinguished between two versions of Venus—Venus Urania and Venus Pandemos). A useful parallel example of the difficulty of mediating between Neoplatonic and Lucretian versions of Venus can be observed in the debate over the right interpretation of Botticelli's *Primavera*: Charles Dempsey, for instance, challenges the influential Neoplatonic analyses of the painting by Panofsky and Gombrich, pointing to the Lucretian intertext (among other classical poems) on which it is based; see Charles Dempsey, *The Portrayal of Love: Botticelli's Primavera and Humanist Culture at the Time of Lorenzo the Magnificent* (Princeton: Princeton University Press, 1992). For the Neoplatonic studies see Erwin Panofsky, *Renaissance and Renascences in Western Art* (New York: Harper & Row, 1969); Ernst Gombrich, "Botticelli's Mythologies: A Study in the Neoplatonic Symbolism of His Circle," *Journal of the Warburg and Courtauld Institutes* 8 (1945): 7–60.

31.   Greenlaw, "Spenser and Lucretius"; see also "Spenser's Mutabilitie."

32.   Until a tentative recent revival of the issue, the question of Spenser and Lucretius has been limited to the pages of the Variorum edition of the *Faerie Queene* and the footnote identifying the intertext for exuberant song of the lover in Book IV. Recently, the publication of several articles on Spenser's interest in Lucretius or Epicureanism suggests a revival of the topic: see Anthony Esolen, "Spenser's 'Alma Venus': Energy and Economics in The Bower of Bliss," *English Literary Renaissance* 23 (1993): 267–86, and "Spenserian Chaos"; Wendy Hyman, "Seizing Flowers in Spenser's Bower and Garden," *English Literary Renaissance* 37 (2007): 193–214. For a more thorough treatment of the subject see Stephen Buhler, "Spenser and the Epicurean Traditions" (Unpublished dissertation, UCLA, 1989).

33.   See for instance, Ellrodt, 100–105, 114–20, 183–93; Bieman; and Quitslund, *Spenser's Supreme Fiction*. For a concise discussion of specific points of Neoplatonism

in the *Hymnes* and *The Faerie Queene*, see also Carol Kaske, "Neoplatonism in Spenser Once More," *Religion and Literature* 32, no. 2 (2002): 157–69.

34.   Jeanneret, 29–49; Luzius Keller, *Palingène, Ronsard, Du Bartas: trois études sur la poésie cosmologique de la Renaissance* (Berne: Francke, 1974); Werner L. Gundersheimer, *The Life and Works of Louis Le Roy* (Geneva: Droz, 1966), 104; Albert-Marie Schmidt, *La poésie scientifique en France au seizième siècle* (Paris: Albin Michel, 1938). Ellrodt notes that Le Roy cites Lucretius several times (101). Guy le Fèvre de la Boderie is a particularly interesting and understudied figure in this regard (though he is soundly dismissed by Schmidt as a hazy Neoplatonist and second-rate successor to Scève and Pontus de Tyard): *La Galliade*, a seemingly mystical, "Neoplatonic" work, seems to bear the mark of an Epicurean physics on closer reading, which is hardly surprising given that de la Boderie was the first translator of Cicero's *De natura deorum* into French. Even though Cicero's work is an anti-Epicurean polemic, it became one of the important sources for Epicurean philosophy in the Renaissance because of its thorough description of the main tenets.

35.   Jeanneret, 29.

36.   Extensive studies of the reception of Lucretius in the Renaissance are few, though the subject is currently enjoying something of a revival. I have drawn on the following works for the discussion that follows. On the Italian humanists' reception of Lucretius see: Eugenio Garin, "Ricerche sull'epicureismo del Quattrocento," in *La cultura filosofica del Rinascimento italiano: Ricerche e documenti* (Milan: Bompiani, 1994), 72–87; Maria R. Pagnoni, "Prime note sulla tradizione medievale e umanistica di Epicuro," *Annali della scuola normale superiore di Pisa, Classe di lettere e filosofia* ser. 3, vol. 4 (1974): 1443–77; Michael Reeve, "The Italian Tradition of Lucretius," *Italia medioevale e umanistica* 23 (1980): 7–48; Susanna Gambino Longo, *Savoir de la nature et poésie des choses: Lucrèce et Epicure à la Renaissance italienne* (Paris: Champion, 2004); and Prosperi. On the reception of Lucretius outside Italy see: George Depue Hadzsits, *Lucretius and His Influence* (New York: Longmans, Green and Co, 1935); Reid Barbour, *English Epicures and Stoics: Ancient Legacies in Early Stuart Culture* (Amherst: University of Massachusetts Press, 1998); W. B. Fleischmann, *Lucretius and English Literature, 1680–1740* (Paris: A. G. Nizet, 1964); Simone Fraisse, *L'influence de Lucrèce en France au seizième siècle: une conquête du rationalisme* (Paris: A.G. Nizet, 1962); Charles Harrison, "The Ancient Atomists and English Literature of the Seventeenth Century," *Harvard Studies in Classical Philology* 45 (1934):1–79. A more philosophical treatment of the subject is offered in Hans Blumenberg, *The Legitimacy of the Modern Age* (Cambridge: MIT Press, 1983).

37.   On Bruni's poetry, see E. Santini, "Le produzione volgare di Leonardo Bruni Aretino e il suo culto per le tre corone fiorentine," *Giornale storico della letteratura italiana* 60 (1912): 289–337. On Tasso's use of Lucretius see Prosperi. On Spenser's imitation of Tasso see David Quint, "Tasso," *The Spenser Encyclopedia*, ed. A. C. Hamilton at al. (Toronto: University of Toronto Press, 1990).

38.   Hiro Hirai, *Le concept de semence dans les théories de la matière à la renaissance de Marsile Ficin à Pierre Gassendi* (Turnhout: Brepols, 2005), 55–56.

39.   Alison M. Brown, "Lucretius and the Epicureans in the Social Context of Renaissance Florence," *I Tatti Studies* 9 (2001).

40.   See Cesare Federico Goffis, "Il sincretismo lucreziano-platonico negli *Hymni Naturales* del Marullo," *Belfagor* 24 (1969): 386–417.

41.   On Pontano's interest and use of *De rerum natura* see Charlotte Goddard, "Pontano's Use of the Didactic Genre: Rhetoric, Irony and the Manipulation of Lucretius in *Urania*," *Renaissance Studies* 5 (1991): 250–62; Stephen J. Campbell, "Giorgione's 'Tempest,' 'Studiolo' Culture, and the Renaissance Lucretius," *Renaissance Quarterly* 56, no. 2 (2003): 299–332. For a discussion of Harvey's citation of Pontano among other favorite authors on astronomical subjects, see Mary Parmenter, "Spenser's 'Twelve Aeglogves Proportionable to the Twelve Monethes,'" *ELH* 3, no. 3 (1936): 196.

42.   Ellrodt argues for Palingenius as an important source for the *Hymnes* (98). Recent work on Palingenius has, interestingly, pointed to his philosophical heterodoxy, particularly his interest in Lucretius—see Foster Watson, *The Zodiacus Vitae of Marcellus Palingenius Stellatus: An Old School-book* (London: P. Wellby, 1908), 69; Keller, 9–60; Yasmin Haskell, "Renaissance Didactic Latin Poetry on the Stars: Wonder, Myth and Science," *Renaissance Studies* 12, no. 4 (1998): 495–522, and "Between Fact and Fiction: The Renaissance Didactic Poetry of Fracastoro, Palingenio and Valvasone," in *Poets and Teachers: Latin Didactic Poetry and the Didactic Authority of the Latin Poet from the Renaissance to the Present*, eds. Yasmin Haskell and Philip Hardie (Bari: Levante, 1999), 77–103.

43.   See Malcolm Quainton, *Ronsard's Ordered Chaos: Visions of Flux and Stability in the Poetry of Pierre de Ronsard* (Manchester: Manchester University Press, 1980) and Isidore Silver, "Ronsard's Reflections on Cosmogony and Nature," *PMLA* 79, no. 3 (1964): 219–33.

44.   On Lucretius as an epic poet see most recently Monica Gale, *Lucretius and the Didactic Epic* (Bristol: Bristol Classical Press, 2001) and *Myth and Poetry in Lucretius* (Cambridge: Cambridge University Press, 1994); as well as David West, "Lucretius and Epic" in *Oxford Readings in Lucretius*, ed. Monica Gale (Oxford: Oxford University Press, 2007), 289–99.

45.   See Allen.

46.   Ovid, *Amores* I.XV.23–24: "carmina sublimis tunc sunt peritura Lucreti, / exitio terras cum dabit una dies . . . " ["The poems of sublime Lucretius will perish / only when, one day, the earth itself is ruined."]

47.   See Prosperi.

48.   It is worth noting that all of these accounts can be (and have been) subsumed under the umbrella of "Neoplatonism," in part because of the ways in which the Neoplatonic tradition absorbed other philosophic positions. A useful account of this process, particularly with regard to Aristotle, is George Karamanolis, *Plato and Aristotle in Agreement? Platonists on Aristotle from Antiochus to Porphyry* (Oxford: Clarendon Press, 2006).

49.   For an interesting discussion of Italian writers' imitation of Lucretius's connection between political and cosmic turmoil, see Campbell, "Giorgione's 'Tempest,' " 322–23. The link is particularly evident in the partial English translations of Lucretius by John Evelyn and Lucy Hutchinson, both written during the English Civil Wars.

50.   On the Epicureanism and materialism of Spenser's allegorical gardens see: D. C. Allen, "The Rehabilitation of Epicurus and His Theory of Pleasure in the Early Renaissance," *Studies in Philology* 41, no. 1 (1944): 1–15; Hyman; Greenlaw, "Spenser and Lucretius"; Esolen, "Spenser's 'Alma Venus' "; and Buhler.

51.   We might recall that "paradise," a word Spenser uses repeatedly, derives from the Greek for a (Persian) enclosed park, orchard, or pleasure ground, and was used to describe the Garden of Eden in the Septuagint (OED).

52.   See Cicero, *De finibus* 5.1.3; Diogenes Laertius, *Vitae*, 10.10 and 10.17. An inscription on the gate to the Garden is recorded by Seneca in his Epistle XXI.10: "Cum adieris eius hortulos et inscriptum hortulis 'Hospes hic bene manebis, hic summum bonum voluptas est.' " [Go to his Garden and read the motto carved there: "Stranger, here you will do well to tarry; here our highest good is pleasure." On the Garden, see R. E. Wycherley, "The Garden of Epicurus," *Phoenix* 13, no. 2 (1959): 73–77; Alastair Small and Carola Small, "John Evelyn and the Garden of Epicurus," *Journal of the Warburg and Courtauld Institutes* 60 (1997): 194–214. Moreover, as Hiro Hirai has recently shown, the language of "semence" (seeds, sowing, botanical growth), used to describe problems of origin, is a powerful metaphor that pervades early modern thought, and derives from a heady mixture of Stoic *logoi spermatikoi*, Lucretian *seminae rerum*, and Platonism.

53.   The Yale edition of Spenser's shorter poems glosses these passages as Neoplatonic, given the identification of Love as the first cause of the universe. However, the actual nature of cosmic coalescence described in these passages is quite different from the Platonist and Neoplatonist emphasis on creation as making, fashioning, shaping where architectural metaphors predominate. While such vitalistic theories were certainly made to fit under the umbrella of "Neoplatonism" in the fifteenth century, they are ontologically distinct and were increasingly seen to be such by the late sixteenth century. The contrast as well as the uneasy fusion of spontaneous generation and demiurgic creation is evident, for instance, in Du Bartas's *La sepmaine*, which Spenser may well have drawn on, particularly for the vision of the cosmos in *An Hymne of Heavenly Beautie*. For a thorough and useful discussion of vitalism/ spontaneous generation versus Platonic metaphysics, see Matthew R. Goodrum, "Atomism, Atheism and the Spontaneous Generation of Human Beings: The Debate over a Natural Origin of the First Humans in Seventeenth-Century Britain," *Journal of the History of Ideas* 63, no. 2 (2002): 207–24; Henry Harris, *Things Come to Life: Spontaneous Generation Revisited* (Oxford: Oxford University Press, 2002); and Hirai.

54.   The problem of chaos in *Paradise Lost* as well as its Lucretian antecedents is very suggestive for analyses of Spenser; see especially John Leonard, "Milton, Lucretius, and 'the Void Profound of Unessential Night,' " in *Living Texts: Interpreting Milton*, eds. Kristin A. Pruitt and Charles W. Durham (Selinsgrove: Susquehanna University Press, 2000),198–217, and David Quint, "Fear of Falling: Icarus, Phaethon, and Lucretius in *Paradise Lost*," *Renaissance Quarterly* 57, no. 3 (2004): 847–81.

55.   I use "cosmic" here in its etymological senses of order and beautiful form as well as the entire universe (from the Greek *kosmos*)—a semantic node that clarifies why the creation narrative in *An Hymne in Honour of Love* ends with a seemingly abrupt shift to the subject of beauty: "Therefore in choice of love, he doth desyre/ That seemes on earth most heavenly, to embrace/ The same in Beauty, born of heavenly race." If Love brings about the cosmos, it both effects and is drawn towards beauty (that is, *kosmos*); the Neoplatonic paradigm for the interactions of love and the Beautiful is here given a cosmological twist.

56.   On the semantic history of the "void" see Leonard, "Milton, Lucretius, and 'the Void Profound of Unessential Night,' " 203, who points out that the OED lists

Milton's use of "void" as the first instance of the word in English to mean the vastness of empty space. Spenser's "voydness" may however trump Milton's primacy in this regard.

57. Empedoclean cosmology is slippery on the issue of teleology, which is one of the key points of contention between Lucretian Epicureanism (firmly antiteleological) and Neoplatonism (firmly teleological); this slipperiness (which is more strongly evident to modern scholars because only fragments of Empedocles' work remain) was probably clearer in classical antiquity. On the trickiness of this question, see Gordon Campbell, "David Sedley, Lucretius and the Transformation of Greek Wisdom," *Bryn Mawr Classical Review* (October 29, 1999), http://ccat.sas.upenn.edu/bmcr/1999/1999–10–29.html; the notes to Campbell's edition of Book 5 of *De rerum natura* are also helpful; see Gordon Campbell, *Lucretius on Creation and Evolution: A Commentary on De Rerum Natura 5.772–1104* (Oxford: Oxford University Press, 2003).

58. Ellrodt, 101, notes that Le Roy enlists Empedocles to elucidate Plato; he also notes Ebreo's use of Empedocles in a Platonizing context (192). Before Estienne's publication of the *Fragments*, Empedocles was known mostly through treatises by the Neoplatonists (for instance, Ficino's commentary on the *Symposium* and in Leone Ebreo's *Dialoghi*), who in turn derived their knowledge from Plotinus (*Enneads* IV), among others; for a useful summary see Sacvan Bercovitch, "Empedocles in the English Renaissance," *Studies in Philology* 65 (1968): 67–80. For a discussion of the Empedoclean Love-Strife motif in *The Faerie Queene* see Jessica Wolfe, "Spenser, Homer, and the Mythography of Strife," *Renaissance Quarterly* 58, no. 4 (2005): 1263–65.

59. Lucretius, of course, drew extensively on Empedocles for his own poem, not least because Empedocles' *On Nature* expounds a philosophic system in poetic form. On the relationship between Lucretian Epicureanism and Empedocles, see David Sedley, *Lucretius and the Transformation of Greek Wisdom* (Cambridge: Cambridge University Press, 1998) and David Furley, "Variations on Themes from Empedocles in Lucretius' Poem," *Bulletin of the Institute of Classical Studies* 17 (1970): 55–64.

60. Marullus describes the universe as "Machina"—a clear reference to Lucretius in a context that is very similar to Spenser's use of the phrase: "Hic ubi missa superos sagitta/ Flectis et ipsum/ Arbitrum rerum dominumque patrem,/ Cuius auditum procul omnis horret/ Coelitum pubes, procul omnis horret/ Machina nomen./ Quid, quod et novas Chaos in figuras . . . " (*Hymni naturales* I. Amor, lines 15–21).

61. The parallels were first noted by Rollinson; see "A Generic View."

62. All citations of the *Hymni* are from Marullus, *Hymnes naturales* ed. and trans. Jacques Chomorat.

63. See Goffis; and Hirai, 59–61.

64. Marullus, *Hymnes naturales*, 48, note to lines 21–24.

65. Harry Berger, "The Spenserian Dynamics," *Studies in English Literature, 1500–1900* 8, no. 1 (1968): 8–9.

66. See works cited at note 13 above.

67. On Milton's materialism and its consequences for his cosmology and theology see Stephen M. Fallon, *Milton Among the Philosophers: Poetry and Materialism in Seventeenth-Century England* (Ithaca: Cornell University Press, 1991) and John Rogers,

The Matter of Revolution: Science, Poetry, and Politics in the Age of Milton (Ithaca: Cornell University Press, 1996).

68.   For a useful study of the natural philosophical aspects of Neoplatonism see the essays in Wagner ed., *Neoplatonism and Nature*.

69.   Compare *The Faerie Queene*, III.vi.46–47.

70.   Compare *The Faerie Queene* II.vi.15.

71.   Matthew 6:28–29: "See how the lilies of the field grow. They do not labor or spin. Yet I tell you that not even Solomon in all his splendor was dressed like one of these."

72.   Miller, "Spenser's Poetics," 173.

73.   For the female figure of Wisdom in the Bible, see Proverbs 1:22ff, 8; Sirach 24; Wisdom of Solomon 1:5, 7:22–8:1. The identification of Sapience as the Biblical figure of Wisdom is disputed. In contrast to a generation of Neoplatonist interpretations of Sapience as the Uranian Venus, or theological interpretations of Sapience as either the Holy Spirit or the Virgin Enthroned, Charles Osgood first pointed out the detailed parallels between *HHB* and the Wisdom of Proverbs and the Wisdom of Solomon—see C. G. Osgood, "Spenser's Sapience," *Studies in Philology* 14 (1917): 167–77. I find Osgood's argument persuasive and the connections he makes deserve further study, particularly in light on recent work on the Jewish Wisdom literature.

74.   For sources of the figure of Sapience see Jon Quitslund, "Spenser's Image of Sapience," *Studies in the Renaissance* 16 (1969): 181–213.

75.   The relationship between Nature and the Christian God in the *Cantos* is a matter of considerable critical debate, particularly given the last two problematic stanzas of the work. It is worth considering Spenser's movement away from a clearly identified Trinity in *HHL* to the "Deity" of *HHB* as a similar move, particularly given his focus on Wisdom, another female figure (like Dame Nature), associated with the order of the material world.

76.   The point is briefly made in John J. Collins, *Introduction to the Hebrew Bible* (Minneapolis: Fortress Press, 2004), 501. It is elaborated in John J. Collins, *Jewish Wisdom in the Hellenistic Age* (Louisville: Westminister John Knox Press, 1997), which contains an important discussion of Wisdom literature as presenting a kind of natural theology; Collins also discusses the possible influence of middle Platonism on Wisdom of Solomon. On the relationship between Wisdom literature and creation theology, see Leo G. Perdue, *Wisdom and Creation: The Theology of Wisdom Literature* (Nashville: Abingdon Press, 1994).

77.   The point is made by the editors of the Yale edition of the poem.

78.   Such a distinction might sound like a return to the conventional opposition of classical and Christian culture in the Renaissance, but what is striking is Spenser's deliberate *lack* of a hierarchical relationship between the two. Rather than simply "correcting" the first two hymns, the second pair return to similar philosophical and cosmological ruminations that suggest continuity rather than conversion.

PAUL SUTTIE

The Lost Cause of Platonism in *The Faerie Queene*

My question in this paper is whether even a cautious return to a broadly Platonic Spenser is sustainable, or whether there are reasons for regarding that vision of *The Faerie Queene* as a lost cause. Not that I doubt that the Platonic tradition, in the broadest sense, is a great influence on Spenser's poetry, but that it is one thing to draw deeply on a tradition, another to produce a work whose worldview is *of* that tradition. Thus, while *The Faerie Queene* does propose essentially Platonic accounts of its overall narrative and allegorical structures, and of certain episodes (notably the Garden of Adonis and *Mutability Cantos*), all those accounts are called radically in doubt within the poem, in most cases by being shown to be rhetorically generated in the service of specific personal or political interests. Moreover, the possibility of an alternative, non-Platonic and anti-metaphysical worldview is repeatedly glimpsed behind those interests and the metaphysical claims they generate—one whose dynamics are most strikingly encountered in the difficulties of interpreting the Garden of Adonis, but whose broader implications are seen in the wider narrative and above all in the careers of Arthur and Britomart. Chief among those implications is that the valid constitution of moral and political authority must be treated as a more urgent and intractable problem than would be so if a secure metaphysical context for moral interpretation were presupposed. Spenser's grappling with that problem's intractability culminates in the *Mutability Cantos*, where nostalgia for medieval Christian-Platonic metaphysical certainty is coupled with recognition that such certainty has been rendered unavailable by the Renaissance state's appropriation of Christian-Platonic metaphysical claims to a partisan art of power.

A S WE ARE REMINDED in Jon Quitslund's recent book *Spenser's Supreme Fiction*, the notion that Spenser is in some sense a "disciple

Spenser Studies: A Renaissance Poetry Annual, Volume XXIV, Copyright © 2009 AMS Press, Inc. All rights reserved.

of *Platoes* School" is as old as Digby's *Observations* of 1628, which is to say, pretty much as old as Spenser criticism itself.[1] But of course to say that *The Faerie Queene* is "Platonic" might mean, and has meant, very different things, some more plausible than others. For Quitslund, while Spenser is not "doctrinaire"—is not a Platonist *as opposed*, say, to an Aristotelian, and certainly not as opposed to a Christian—he does partake deeply both of what C. S. Lewis calls "The diffused and Christianized Platonism which descends to the Middle Ages through St Augustine, Boethius, Macrobius, Chalcidius, Pseudo-Dionysius, and many others," and of the programmatic Neo-platonism revived by the Florentine academy, which itself reached the Elizabethans to a large degree by indirect routes.[2] In this, Quits-lund is close to the late writings of Lewis himself, those that have one eye on the weighty polemics of Robert Ellrodt's *Neoplatonism in the Poetry of Spenser*.[3] In *The Faerie Queene*, says Quitslund, "It is useful to distinguish between the programmatic Platonic design evident in certain places and the diffuse Platonism that is present in the broad and deep discursive structures of Spenser's poetry. While the deep structures are sourceless, transmitted through Western culture like inherited traits from the gene pool, programmatic Platonism can sometimes be traced to specific sources"—above all, he argues, di-rectly or indirectly to certain of Ficino's works.[4]

My question here is whether even such a cautious return to a broadly Platonic Spenser, who integrates features of Renaissance Neoplatonism into an essentially conservative (or revivalist) medi-eval-Platonic worldview, is sustainable, or whether, as my title sug-gests, there are reasons for regarding that vision of *The Faerie Queene* as something of a lost cause. Not that I doubt that the Platonic tradi-tion, taken at its broadest, is a great influence on Spenser's poetry; but that there is a difference between drawing deeply on a tradition, and writing a work whose worldview is essentially *of* that tradition.

To take first the Platonism said to be "present in the broad and deep discursive structures of Spenser's poetry": two of the broadest ways in which we are used to thinking of *The Faerie Queene* as Pla-tonic in structure consist firstly in its regular indications that truth, while certain and unchanging, is veiled, and accessible only by way of derivative copies, secondly in the broad narrative shape proposed by the *Letter to Ralegh*, and partly realized in the poem, whereby the various knights' quests seem to emanate from and return to the still point of glory that is the Fairy Queen's court.[5] The two meet in Arthur's search for Gloriana, which as the returning vector of that cyclical narrative shape, and a quest that strives by ethical means to rise from images towards their originals, has seemed to many critics to represent the eminently Platonic "quest of eros for the heavenly beauty."[6] Notoriously, a true ladder of love is hard to find in Spenser,

even in the apparently Platonic *Hymnes* to love and beauty; and if
we are to find its like anywhere, I think it is in Arthur, who on
seeing the Queen's image on Guyon's shield aspires to its original,
thence from the beauty of her face to that of her mind (II.ix.2–3),
and potentially, as Guyon suggests elsewhere, even from her beauty
to that of the God of which she herself is but an image (II.ii.41).[7]
Arthur's love, even if an isolated case, may be an extremely important
one, firstly because his is the frame narrative and the principal ethical
example of the whole poem, and secondly because the poem (pre-
dominantly through its proems) recurrently places its reader in a
position similar to Arthur's, with a rhetorically sublimated Elizabeth
in Gloriana's place, and the poem itself, with its "colour'd showes"
(III.Pr.3), in the place of Guyon's painted shield. By such means the
poem proposes an immensely influential account of how its allegory
works, a fundamentally Platonic account according to which the literal narrative is an icon of higher meaning, inviting an anagogic
ascent from its imagery towards a still point of luminous truth somewhere above and behind its fictive multiplicity.[8]

But that the poem encourages us to believe that its allegory works
in that way does not, of course, necessarily entail its actually working
in that way: its invitingly graspable self-description may bear no
nearer relation to how the poem is actually structured than does the
equally neat scheme of the *Letter to Ralegh*, which likewise offers us
a good firm grip on all the discourse, but at the expense of misrepre-
senting that discourse in some basic respects.[9] In both cases, politics
comes into play: both the letter, and the proems which represent the
poem's allegory as a mirror of Elizabethan glory, harness invocation
of the Platonic structures I have mentioned to praise of a particular
regime. That is obvious, but also important in at least two ways.
Firstly, it suggests that we ought at least to suspend judgment as to
whether such manifestly politic accounts of how the poem works
will necessarily reflect, even in outline, how it works in fact, or rather
might simply be effects of the poem's elaborate compliment to the
regime.[10] Secondly, it raises the question whether a Platonic cosmic
order rhetorically harnessed to the praise of a particular regime can
still be a Platonic cosmic order, or whether that act of harnessing
implies another worldview essentially irreconcilable to the scheme
whose materials it assimilates. The latter is a point I shall return to.

First, though, against the idea that the poem really can be assimilated, even broadly, to the metaphysical system to which, in such
moments of self-description, it invites us to assimilate it, we may
note that even Arthur's quest for Gloriana in time becomes intermed-
dled among the poem's accidents in a way that seems to threaten the
integrity of his intendments. Critics have of course apologized in

Neoplatonic terms for Arthur's erotically motivated pursuit of Florimell, on the grounds either that she represents true, intelligible Beauty
and hence is a suitable love object for the virtuous lover, or that his
error, if it is one, "hardly seems ignoble" if Florimell is regarded as
a Platonic likeness of Gloriana, a rung in love's ladder but one step
removed from his proper goal.[11] But both readings assume secure, a
priori knowledge of what Florimell's whole story calls into question:
namely, whether there is a real or only a rhetorical difference between
the kinds of desire that her various pursuers feel for her, given that
even her would-be rescuers are all so intent on winning her for
themselves as increasingly to obscure the distinction between them
and her persecutors.[12] More widely, her story disrupts the pattern of
former books (in which Arthur was also instrumental), whereby the
narrative moved through a vertically imagined cyclical shape, down-
ward to a crisis before returning upwards in Canto viii by virtue of
a providential rescue towards its happy conclusion. Here the corresponding eighth-canto moment, in which Proteus is said by the narrator to have been sent by God to rescue Florimell in her moment
of greatest danger (III.viii.29), only confirms the different pattern
operating here, one in which we see, instead of a decisive reversal
of fortunes that enfolds the whole narrative within a single circular
movement, only a perpetuation of the oscillating pattern that Florimell has already been experiencing, a pattern of near disaster followed
by provisional escape tending towards new disaster, which drives her
story not decisively upwards towards a resolution but only ever forward in time. Such a picture of Providence can leave an ambivalent
moral impression on the reader, particularly if we observe that her
string of misadventures is not only *spun out* by such indecisive divine
interventions, but also apparently *initiated* by heavenly fiat, since it
was "the vnknowen purpose of eternall fate" that Proteus's prophecy
should be misconstrued and Marinell's and Florimell's woes begun
(III.iv.28). Hence the moral ambivalence that she sees in all her would-
be rescuers may seem also, or even primarily, to belong to the "high
God" who, like all those who act ostensibly to give her "succor"
(III.viii.29), appears to be her persecutor as much as her deliverer.

Here we touch on a larger theme; for in Book III generally, divine
purpose in human history is expressed as the promise neither of
individual perfection, nor of an apocalyptic victory of the good, but
of the perpetuation of a bloodline, whose fortunes seem interminably
to oscillate between the brink of extermination and the moments of
transient glory achieved in Troy, Rome, and "*Troynouant*"
(III.ix.44–45). Like Florimell, the sons of Troy are driven ever onwards, over land and sea, by the "fatall course" (III.ix.49) of an

equivocal destiny seemingly as intent on continually renewing their trials as on sparing them from extinction. That is the context in which the consequences of Britomart's love for Artegall—itself brought about by "the streight course of heauenly destiny / Led with eternall providence" (III.iii.24)—refuse, in spite of Merlin's assurances, to seem wholly desirable. Divine intervention in her life, as in her legend at large, is to lead not to one decisive outcome but to a continuing history of consequences, which will include not only her fertile marriage but her husband's premature death, and for their offspring not only a period of imperial rule but ages of oppressive foreign domination—and "yet the end is not" (III.iii.50). Such a genealogical rather than salvific model of providential history is neither Neoplatonic nor Christian but essentially epic in provenance.[13] Nor is it turned allegorically, as Virgil's epic had been turned, into a figure for the virtuous soul's search for the *mansuram urbem*, the city that will endure: on the contrary, the eros that drives this action, whatever its pretensions to be the upward-tending Platonic kind, in practice drives events laterally, along the repetitious, ambivalent ground of secular history, as well as itself partaking of the morally ambiguous nature of worldly events, motivating the "beauties chace" (III.i.19) in which the desire for rescue and for capture are troublingly conflated.[14] Rather than endorsing a Platonic allegorization of epic eros, the poem lets us see, and suspect, the motives of that morally clarifying reading. To return to Arthur, it is not only the morality of his desire for Florimell but the whole transcendentally anchored cyclical scheme of being on which the distinction between kinds of love depends, that has been called into question—not only the object of his quest that Arthur has lost sight of, but the order of the universe. All this turns out, startlingly enough, to be cognate with Spenser's characteristic reorientation of the received love tradition towards marriage and procreation (III.iii.1–3), which we see here not only (as we know) giving potent imaginative vitalization to the Protestant matrimonial ideal, but also implying, as its shadow, the possible inescapability of our historical condition.

Here I come to the Garden of Adonis, where again we meet the prospect, again uncertain, of elevating a fugitive beauty into an enduring principle able to extract life from the ravages of time. In so doing I pass from the Platonism said to be "present in the broad and deep discursive structures of Spenser's poetry" to one of the scenes to which "programmatic Platonism" and "specific sources" have most often been attributed.[15] Now, it *is* tempting to see the Garden—whatever it may mean in its difficult details—as broadly figuring forth the process that occurs at one of the lower levels in a graded Neoplatonic cosmos owing something to Ficino.[16] That the cyclical nature of that process, emanating from the garden and reverting to it, may remind us of the cyclical action of the Neoplatonic cosmos at large would then be an instance of the way each level in that cosmos, as an image of the highest, imitates as best it can the cyclical generative activity of the highest.[17] To that notion of the Garden as ontologically speaking a derivative image of the highest reality, we might, with Quitslund, join the Neoplatonic notion of myths, as themselves potentially images of, and fictive pointers to, a higher truth.[18] But I think that the Garden's description, in its details, not only resists but threatens to invert any such assimilation to Neoplatonic metaphysics and poetics.

That the Garden *resists* such a reading, I would express in terms of its curious and persistent unclearness not simply about what it all might mean allegorically, but even about where the boundary lies between what it means allegorically and what it means literally—between the interpretation we are trying to make, and the picture to which we are to fasten that interpretation. We are told of babes, plants, forms, lives, deaths—but they resiliently refuse to be sorted into a signifying scene on the one hand and something signified on the other. In that way the myth defies the Platonic ideal of allegorical translation, whereby we would pass from what is seen to what is meant, image to idea, in a neat anagogic movement that leaves behind all literal residue[19]—much as in Book III more widely, key images (the wounds of Timias and Marinell, Belphoebe's rose, the pursuit of Florimell) both demand and defy a decisive translation, leaving us, like the characters, entangled in a world of insistent materiality which nonetheless insists on its pregnancy with meaning, a world irreducibly "double" (III.iv.28).

I do not mean to say that Spenser's description of the Garden, attended to in sufficient detail, simply dissolves into confusion: that would be far too passive an account of the confusion that close attention to it causes. On the contrary, its brilliance is that, in spite of its multifariously self-contradictory character, it continually gives the impression that another rereading from any point x will possibly produce an interpretation consistent with x. That effect of interpretability, which never resolves itself into a satisfactory interpretation, is what has made the passage a locus of such illimitable commentary, almost all of it manifestly more interesting to the commentator who is playing the game than to those who sit down to the task of reading the resulting commentary.[20] And the reason why the game is interesting (apart from its intrinsic challenge) is that it continually throws up new uncertainties in the interpreter's mind: not only, for example, "Do I *know* that form is masculine and matter feminine, and might I make more consistent sense of all this if I tried it the other way around?" but even, "Do I know that the 'fleshly weeds' " (III.vi.32) in which a living thing is clothed are its material part, or since they give visible shape to a previously invisible entity, might they just possibly be regarded as its form? And do I then know at all how to apply those basic philosophical terms, 'form' and 'matter'?" The effect, that is, of really working at the passage is ever to encounter new doubts not only as to what you know about *it*, but as to what you really know about the metaphysical questions it purports to answer, even (or especially) certain quite consequential ones, like, "Can I tell what actually distinguishes life from death? Can I tell truth from consolatory fiction?"[21] The Garden of Adonis is a forcing bed of philosophical thought.[22]

Inherent in the foregoing account is the reason I say the Garden not only resists being assimilated to any given metaphysical framework, but threatens to assimilate the metaphysical thought that tries to assimilate it. For the experience of reading, here, is that of forming a succession of tentative metaphysical propositions at various points *x* in the text, which one then tries to expand like fields of force in order to make sense of surrounding passages apparently inconsistent with *x*. What is generated in that way is not a stable structure that can then be assumed to underlie the text as something logically and creatively prior to it, but a series of ephemeral blooms of thought, fragile notions that grow for a certain time before exhausting their soil or meeting insuperable opposition, then are duly scythed and their components taken up in a different form by the next wave of growth. We glimpse here a possibility radically non-Platonic, a world in which the phenomena come first, and are not only themselves all subject to time and change, but are the ground from which even metaphysical structures are sprouted, as fading forms thrown up, then mulched, by the wheel of time.[23] And not only metaphysical structures, but (if we expand our field of vision again to the poem more widely) the moral and political forms, too, that cling like ivy to such metaphysical trunks—be it an ethical discipline based in erotic desire, or the fragile political order of a Troy or a Troynovant. Not that I assume, a priori, that a vision according to which all order—even intelligible order—is but the ephemeral offspring of a "huge eternal *Chaos*" (III.vi.36), has imaginative precedence in *The Faerie Queene* over the intimations we also at times are given of a Platonic cosmos. But just as Platonic interpretation makes a bid to assimilate the Garden, and the poem at large, to its hierarchic structure, so in turn the Garden threatens to assimilate the poem, and Platonism, to its temporality. The two are like great rivals each laying claim to the other's territory; and which, if either, ultimately has the truer claim, is a running question as we read.

It is in that context that I would approach Carol Kaske's recent article, "Neoplatonism in Spenser Once More," which revisits by a more pinpoint approach some of the same areas as Quitslund's book.[24] Says Kaske, when Britomart fashions Artegall "in her mind,/And in her feigning fancie did pourtray/Him such, as fittest she for loue could find" (III.iv.5), her act of idealization is saved "from the charge of solipsism," and given a moral force, by the Neoplatonic doctrines "that what is loved is the idea of the beloved . . . an idea which . . . also exists in the mind of God," and "that a lover teaches the beloved to live up to this ideal image."[25] To that we may add Quitslund's suggestion, that in Britomart we see enacted the Platonic notion that the lover learns to behold in the beloved, as in a mirror, his or her own ideal self as an object of moral aspiration.[26] But the role Platonism plays in such a reading, as something which potentially "answers the charge" that the heroine acts merely from more fallible and all-too-human motives,[27] highlights the salient point that Platonic metaphysics might be no more by this point in the poem than a cobbled-together means of rationalizing ambivalent experience. In other words, while the story may in these respects invite a Platonic reading, may even depend on such a reading in order to make sense of the action as the unfolding of a benign destiny contriving to bring about the happiness and moral fulfillment of its protagonist (so much is suggested by III.iii.1–3), what remains stubbornly unclear is that Britomart's fate *is* so benign.

Certainly Britomart herself does not begin by believing so (III.ii.44), and Merlin does considerably less than she might hope in the way of clearing up her doubts. Like Arthur in the House of Alma, she would need a leap of faith to derive any comfort from the radically ambivalent history laid before her, or morally to anchor her own sense of calling in its shifting sands. But for her the advisability of such a leap of faith looks newly doubtful, for at least two reasons. Firstly, with the future as well as the past now in view, Book II's optimistic, architectural notion of the state, as something that can progressively be built up by the united efforts of succeeding generations, till it reaches "heauens hight" (II.x.2), starts to look decidedly shaky: the "sacred Peace" of a united nation (III.iii.49) may still be in prospect, but less in the form of the monumental stability of the Fairy realm, than as a brief and fragile flower, blooming intermittently in an often hostile environment, and forever subject to being blasted by the next storm that "th'heauens haue decreed" (III.iii.41). Secondly, where in Book II the politically unified nation was treated as a body whose health belongs collectively to all its members, here the question arises which that loosely Platonic metaphor had occluded—the question of how, in whose interests, and at whose expense, power is exercised *within* society (III.ii.2)—and Britomart, in particular, is given much reason to doubt whether her own interests are represented by the forces pressing for her submission, or whether committing herself morally to the path seemingly dictated to her by eros would merely be to capitulate to a tyrannical and alien will. In principle, being told that the "Imperious Loue" that "tyrannizeth" in her heart (III.ii.23) serves a higher purpose should be reassuring; but in practice, it only musters before her, under the sweeping rubric of "his will" (III.iii.24), a daunting array of masculine forces—destiny, Artegall, Merlin himself—as mysteriously motivated and potentially as tyrannical as love itself. Hence Britomart is left still looking for assurances, even after her quest has begun, of the desirability for her of reaching its goal (III.ii.8–17).

In the meantime, moreover, an apparent alternative has appeared. Ostensibly Glauce's scheme to "disguize" Britomart "in feigned armes" is merely instrumental, a "deuise" to enable her ward to pursue her desire for Artegall (III.iii.52–53). But in practice it proves to be something more. For the stirring "ensample" she sets before Britomart of the female warrior Angela at once sinks, like Cupid's arrow before it, "deepe into the mynd/Of the young Damzell," kindling in her a second "great desire" alongside the first: not connubial eros this time, but the fire of heroic emulation (III.iii.55–57). So from the start Britomart has two parallel motivations for being abroad in arms, and knighthood is for her much more than a costume, more even than a practical means of self-defense: it is an inspiring ethical discipline in its own right, which soon transforms her from a tender maid prone to "often steepe/Her daintie couch with teares" (III.ii.28) to a stern warrior whose "great courage would not let her weepe," even privately (III.iv.11), and which tempers as in a furnace her moral attitude to the world, as is felt most vividly by Marinell (III.iv.12–18). How this stern, self-assertive, androgynous, martial ethic (III.iii.56) relates to the dutiful, feminine, marital ethos urged by Merlin (III.iii.24), is another of the poem's running questions. As Spenser well knew, heroic emulation was itself open to being construed in Platonic terms[28]—yet rather than pursuing that line of thought in harmony with a Platonic reading of Britomart's love for Artegall, he sets the heroine's two sources of inspiration in tension, treating Angela's example as a basis whereon Britomart is able to seize for herself the interpretative initiative that Merlin arrogates to destiny and to himself as its spokesman. Laying hold of an alternative view of history that highlights the disputability of Merlin's version by focusing on the English nation rather than the British, and on a confirmed virgin rather than a willing wife, as the sources of ethical inspiration,[29] Britomart in practice lays open to suspicion the metaphysical underpinnings the narrator attributes to Merlin's moralizing discourse, so setting before us again (and not for the last time) the question whether a Platonic cosmic order rhetorically harnessed to the praise of a particular regime can still rightly be regarded as a Platonic cosmic order.

Not that the poem puts Britomart's alternative grounds for action above similar suspicions. On the contrary, her seizing of the interpretative initiative, by which she lays claim in her own right to chivalric moral agency, involves her in a notable readiness to be free with the facts. It is not only that she allows others to assume that a knight in shining armor must be male, but that when the assumption proves wrong she is ready to replace it with a false account of a martial upbringing (III.ii.6) and of her motives for being abroad (III.ii.7–8) which make her seem a more independent, Angela-like figure than her true history would suggest (see especially III.iii.53). Yet the effect is not to make her seem a Braggadocio; for not only in words but in deeds she carries off with emphatic success the impression she aims to create as an Amazonian "mayd Martiall" (III.iii.53). Hence her accounts of her character and aims, however false as history, regularly acquire a certain truth *en route*. When she finally appoints herself, in a crowning act of self-interpretative boldness, at once as a more competent agent for performing her virtue's defining quest than the hero assigned by Gloriana, and to the role of providential rescuer played by Arthur in previous books (III.xi.14), she steps into a breach to which the story insistently calls attention, not only by Scudamour's evident need of some such relief, but more broadly by the poem's move away from the decisive providentialism of former books to a kind so wavering and uncertain that even Proteus can briefly dress himself in its mantle.

It is in relation to this brief flowering of a career as a moral agent in her own right, and above all in her self-appointed role as Amoret's rescuer and guardian, that Britomart's encroaching matrimonial destiny seems not so much to gather her upwards to a higher purpose, as to mow her down like Time's scythe, cancelling the terms on which she has existed as an ethical character at the moment of her exit from the poem (V.vii.42–44). Not that her prior career as a "self-made man" is morally less ambiguous than the destiny that finally comes to claim her. From her remorseless felling of Marinell to her extraordinary threatening of Amoret with pretended lust (IV.i.7), she is always a morally dubious force in the story. Even in what seems her finest hour at the end of Book III, she can lay claim to the role of heaven-sent rescuer only on her own bold say-so (III.xi.14); and subsequently she will turn out to be no more immune than Arthur or any other from the charge of laying claim, herself, to the prize she at first proposes disinterestedly to rescue from danger. Hence her susceptibility in Books IV and V to the slander that assaults her on one side (e.g., IV.i.4) even as her destiny asserts itself on the other. But in this moral ambivalence she is not atypical. The whole world through which she moves is a scene of morally ambiguous action, which elicits from *all* would-be virtuous characters an attempt to take control of the ethical terms on which they mean to act; and in that forcing bed of self-interpretation, Britomart's extraordinary moral self-assertion seems less an expression of, or even a willful deviation from, some metaphysically defined ethical scheme laid out for her, than a notably vigorous growth within a garden or forest of ethical possibilities—one to be overwhelmed, indeed, only by the still more morally assertive force of her destiny. In such a context, the eros that both fires her will and closes in on her against her will, seems less the elevating Platonic force than the eminently equivocal power which both motivates and hounds Florimell, and which for one character after another imponderably blurs the distinction between rescue and capture.

I do not mean to suggest that Spenser by temperament rejects all moral forms grounded in cosmic hierarchy, and is instead a kind of secret cosmic democrat: rather, that the constitution of moral authority is treated in *The Faerie Queene* as a more serious and urgent problem than is gathered if we presuppose that the poem assumes throughout a metaphysically grounded interpretative context. Even in Book I, where a cosmic vision is most clearly ventured that enfolds the chosen earthly city and the authority of its queen within a graded hierarchy of being emanating from and tending back to God (I.x.59), the poem needs to invoke the charlatan "mayden Queene" (I.iv.8) Lucifera as a scapegoat for the occluded possibility that Elizabeth too might be a charlatan, or indeed, as Machiavelli had notoriously hinted, that the metaphysical trappings of *all* regimes might equally be politically generated, self-serving fictions (I.iv.11–12).[30] And while the first book concentrates its rhetorical energy into making Gloriana's regime, and by extension Elizabeth's, seem a safe exception to that prospect, that is a temporary expedient.

If Book I solicits from readers a leap of faith in the transcendentally grounded legitimacy of Elizabeth's regime, already Book II proceeds more empirically, attempting to define true virtue, and the true monarch who is its patron, not by means of a putative revelation from above, but from the ground up; it asks whether we can justify, in earthly terms, the faith required to ascribe moral legitimacy to a claimant of our political duty. It is not, of course, directly asserted that any such act of faith is required to accept the legitimacy of Elizabeth's claim to the throne. But the effect of reading the chronicle brought to bear as evidence of that claim (II.x.1–4) is to suggest that one is eminently necessary: for with its long list of usurpations, contested claims, and outright failures of the royal bloodline, it virtually demands the question how any clear right to rule this nation, let alone Elizabeth's specifically, could ever be derived from such an ambivalent history of seizing and clinging to power. Yet by various means, not least the exemplum of the Fairy realm (II.x.70–76), which in its perpetual peace and monumental durability so manifestly embodies a good as compared with the perennially divided human nation, the book suggests that the worthy end of social cohesion might morally justify a leap of faith in the powers that be, and hence in one's own ethical agency as a dutiful subject. Such an enquiry takes us beyond the prior question of how to tell the true from a false political and moral order, to ask on what basis we might not merely recognize but create a valid system of individual and collective moral interpretation, from amid a chaos of separately plausible but mutually competing claims. That, I think, is the open question which subsequent books inherit, and which determines the trajectory of Britomart's career.

In the 1590 version of Book III, the bold fashioning of one's own moral destiny, whether as a person or as a nation, looks like a tantalizingly real possibility: the former in the person of Britomart, the latter in the poem's use of her story audaciously to trump cynicism regarding the fictitiousness of the Tudor regime's received foundation myth, by remaking, and paradoxically reinvigorating, that myth on a patently fictional basis (that is, by poetically transmitting the bloodline of Brutus to Elizabeth not through some character derived from already suspect chronicles, but through one who is manifestly the poet's own invention).[31] But a problem is stored up for the second edition in the form of tension between the respective self-interpretative claims of the person and the nation, specifically between their irreconcilable aspirations to supreme moral-interpretative authority in the life of the individual. The poem's subsequent complicity in rewriting Britomart's character on terms she cannot control is bound up with a tough new vision which emerges in the 1596 installment, according to which the realm of moral meaning is seen as ungovernable except by force and fraud.

Hereafter, a running question is how the violence needed to establish a given interpretative dispensation might itself be morally justified; in particular, whether an *appeal to nature* might provide a deeper basis for interpretative authority. Thus in Book V the authority of moral interpretation seems to depend at once on appeal to an original natural order (a normative though counterfactual condition that justice supposedly would restore), and on the material force needed to impose that condition and subdue rival interpretative regimes; but the appeal to nature that in principle justifies political force is treated with the same skepticism that in earlier books put in doubt the truth of political foundation myths. We are made to see that the normative ideas of a "natural" law and an "original" dispensation exist in rival versions—reside as much in the hero's enemies' hands as in his own (see especially V.ii.30–33)—and accordingly that the self-interpreta-tive authority backing political force must always be subject to moral doubt, short of the complete silencing of opposition voices. Nor can that moral doubt be readily translated into a political alternative to force, for in shirking the disquieting business of violently silencing a rival moral order, one stands merely to be silenced by it: "all is the conquerer's,"[32] even morally, for the winners both write the laws, and install their readings in the very landscape by fashioning allegorical monuments from the remains of the defeated.

Much as Book V regularly claims a natural basis for justice while at the same time making clear the disputability of such claims, so in Book VI courtesy is described as the inborn virtue of a noble caste even while attention is drawn to the potential constructedness of courteous natures and above all of their effect of naturalness; hence just where virtue seems most deeply rooted in nature there is most reason to suspect duplicity and fear harm.[33] Calidore successfully emu-lates pastoral lowliness (and so wins the aggressive contest to possess the object of eros) not by dropping but by intensifying his reliance on the artful "courteous guize" that Pastorella rejects when it is seen openly (VI.ix.35), using his courtly sophistication to mask itself as the humble plain naturalness that pastoral valorizes. His behavior re-minds us of the similar artificiality of the whole pastoral literary con-vention, and of the plain style of rhetoric with which it is closely associated, even in the places where we are not granted such a candid look behind its exquisitely cultivated guise of naturalness. We are reminded, not least, that even where what we seem to see is the poet himself, humbly exhibiting inside his heroic poem his own homely concerns where "all them plaine may see" (VI.x.24), what we are really seeing is precisely his pastoral persona, a painstakingly crafted poetic mask. Book VI thus places before us the question whether Colin Clout's fragile and ephemeral vision should be taken to repre-sent a glimpse into a supernatural order of grace behind Calidore's world of instrumental and often suspiciously self-serving gracious be-havior, or only another, albeit still more exquisite, bloom of the same courteous art, made to order so as to grace with winningly elegant mythological and metaphysical resonances the poet's own eros-quest. Yet despite the book's persistent opening of avenues into such skepticism, the cultivation, in some form, of gracious na-tures—the planting, in some form, of a pale of civility—whether by political or poetic agency, remains the book's sole bulwark against the moral and political brutality of graceless lords and savage tribes, even while itself standing revealed as a dangerously duplicitous and potentially disruptive force.

On reaching the *Mutability Cantos*, the final great locus in the poem of Platonic interpretation, we would seem to have come full circle to return to the Book I's concern with grounding moral and political self-interpretation in a metaphysical order.[34] But in fact what our journey through subsequent books has gradually cast in doubt is the viability of setting even the divine nature above interpretative contestation. Here even "heauens eternall towers" (VII.vi.20) are seen as the rhetorical construct of a usurping regime trying after the fact to secure its own myth of aboriginal legitimacy (VII.vi.26–27); and though behind the dubious basis of Jove's jurisdiction deeper grounds of judgment are asserted, the powerful skepticism directed at Jove's authority finally cascades onto them as well, much as the skepticism first directed at Cynthia's authority soon cascades onto Jove's (VII.vi.12, 18).[35] For much as Book III does not simply participate in the tradition of giving the epic plot a Platonic allegorical interpretation, but puts the process of reading allegorically on view within the narrative, where its validity and motives can be suspected, so here the interpretation of the universe that confirms Jove in his imperial see (VII.vii.58–59), by not merely taking as read, but in effect reenacting in the story, the Platonic allegorization of Homeric myth that had elevated the Olympian gods from conquerors and de facto rulers into eternal hypostases in a metaphysical order, makes the Platonic version of the facts seem partial in every sense. Not that Spenser sides with Mutability, any more than with sin or the wild Irish. But he acknowledges that Nature's judgment, and the seasonal pageant which seems to substantiate it, resolve only in imaginary terms the problem Mutability represents—that in beautifully assimilating human life and labor to the orderly and deathless round of the heavens, and so reducing Death itself to a kind of Parmenidean nothing, "vnheard, vnseene" amid the plenitude of life (VII.vii.46), they occlude precisely the hard fact for which the cantos were supposed to be giving an etiological explanation, namely that Nature, at least as we know her, is "accurst" with irrecoverable loss, "By which, we all are subiect to that curse,/And death in stead of life haue sucked from our Nurse" (VII.vi.5–6). That is the stinging point to which the narrator returns our attention at the start of canto eight, when he weighs Nature's judgment and finds it wanting in any adequate consolation for such sublunary beings as ourselves, "Whose flowring pride, so fading and so fickle, /Short *Time* shall soon cut down with his consuming sickle" (VII.viii.1).

In spite of such a trenchant note of skepticism about metaphysical justifications and comforts, and about the "euerlasting glory" unfailingly attributed to the powers that be in "goodly story" (VII.vi.8), there remains in the *Mutability Cantos* a sense that political assertion is urgently necessary: Arlo, synecdoche for Ireland, is ruined by the *withdrawing* Cynthia (VII.vi.55). But the failure to find convincing moral grounds for such assertion leaves a bad taste in the mouth and a radical doubt in the mind.[36]

The terms in which Mutability is silenced, while they may owe some debt to Renaissance Neoplatonism, more overtly draw on medieval Platonic thought, a fact that Robert Ellrodt and C. S. Lewis both took as evidence of the persistence in Spenser of a medieval mindset, and that Jon Quitslund interprets as a more deliberate medieval revivalism.[37] I think it is closer to the truth, given what I have said already, to maintain with Harry Berger that the pointedly medieval character of the apparatus works "to distance [its] vision in terms of cultural time" and "to emphasize its artistic and artificial quality."[38] The distancing effect cuts two ways. On the one hand, as Berger suggests, it invites nostalgia for a consolatory fiction no longer believed in.[39] On the other hand, it suggests what has happened to despoil it of consolatory power: the medieval metaphysical vision has been appropriated as a rhetoric of power by the work of art that is the Renaissance state, its universalism debased into a pretension to universality common to every pretender to imperial authority.[40] That, it seems to me, is the sense in which *The Faerie Queene* itself ultimately treats its Platonic heritage as a lost cause—letting go, at the last, of an attractive but irretrievable Christian-Platonic vision of being, in favor of a more apocalyptic Christianity which treats the fallen world or the fallen mind as having come wholly unstuck from God's plan till all is made anew; or, from another perspective, wishing the inescapable violence of imposing moral order on the world away from God's presumptive agents into God's own presumably safer hands.

NOTES

1. Jon Quitslund, *Spenser's Supreme Fiction: Platonic Natural Philosophy and* The Faerie Queene (Toronto: University of Toronto Press, 2001), 13, quoting Sir Kenelm Digby, "Observations on the 22. Stanza in the 9th Canto of the 2d. Book of Spencers Faery Queene," in R. M. Cummings, *Edmund Spenser: The Critical Heritage* (New York: Barnes and Noble, 1971), 157.

2. C. S. Lewis, "Neoplatonism in the Poetry of Spenser" (review of Robert Ellrodt's book of that title), in *Studies in Medieval and Renaissance Literature* (Cambridge: Cambridge University Press, 1966), 149.

3. Robert Ellrodt, *Neoplatonism in the Poetry of Spenser* (Geneva: Droz, 1960); see especially Lewis's review of Ellrodt, 162–63, and C. S. Lewis, *Spenser's Images of Life*, ed. Alastair Fowler (Cambridge: Cambridge University Press, 1967), passim.

4. Quitslund 13. The works of Ficino principally cited are the *Symposium* commentary and "Five Questions concerning the Mind," and among the possible intermediaries Cristoforo Landino's *Aeneid* commentary and Heinrich Cornelius Agrippa by way of *Batman vppon Bartholome.* Quitslund substantiates, by citing contemporary examples, the *prima facie* plausibility of an Elizabeth writer's integrating medieval and Florentine Platonic thought in the way that he takes Spenser to be doing: see especially his section on *Batman vppon Bartholome,* 121–24.

5. Regarding the former, see especially Lewis, *Spenser's Images of Life,* 79–82; Alastair Fowler, "Emanations of Glory: Neoplatonic Order in Spenser's *Faerie Queen,*" in *A Theatre for Spenserians,* ed. Judith M. Kennedy and James A. Reither (Manchester: Manchester University Press, 1973), 68–72; and Quitslund, passim. Regarding the latter, see especially Fowler, 75.

6. Quoting Fowler, 72. Cf. Lewis, *Spenser's Images of Life,* 133.

7. For all references to, and quotations from, *The Faerie Queene,* see A. C. Hamilton, Hiroshi Yamashita, and Toshiyuki Suzuki, eds., *The Faerie Queene,* by Edmund Spenser, 2nd ed. (Harlow, etc.: Longman, 2001). For a succinct statement of the non-ladder-like nature of love in Spenser, see Lewis, "Neoplatonism," 151.

8. Quitslund's main emphasis in his book is a version of this. See also Thomas P. Roche, Jr., *The Kindly Flame: A Study of the Third and Fourth Books of Spenser's* Faerie Queene (Princeton: Princeton University Press, 1964), 7; Isabel G. MacCaffrey, *Spenser's Allegory: The Anatomy of Imagination* (Princeton: Princeton University Press, 1976), 24; and (from a deconstructive perspective) Gordon Teskey, "Allegory" in *The Spenser Encyclopedia,* ed. A. C. Hamilton et al. (Toronto: University of Toronto Press, 1990), 16.

9. For a critical history and interpretation of these difficulties, see Wayne Erickson, "Spenser's Letter to Ralegh and the Literary Politics of *The Faerie Queene*'s 1590 Publication," *Spenser Studies* 10 (1989): 139–74.

10. Echoing Lewis's language in *Spenser's Images of Life,* 47. The compliment, of course, even if not believed to be literally true, need not be cynical flattery, as is sometimes supposed in more recent criticism: one may also call upon the devices of panegyrical rhetoric in adornment of a cause that one genuinely supposes to be a good one. See Paul Suttie, "Edmund Spenser's Political Pragmatism," *Studies in Philology* 95 (1998): 56–76.

11. For the first, see Charles G. Smith, "The Ethical Allegory of the Two Florimells," *Studies in Philology* 31 (1934): 140–51; for the second, Fowler, 73 (to whom Arthur's pursuit of Florimell "corresponds on a loftier plane to the pursuit of False Florimell by baser characters: as the false Florimell is to the true, so is the true to Gloriana"); for a combination of the two, C. S. Lewis, *English Literature in the Sixteenth Century Excluding Drama* (Oxford: Clarendon, 1954), 382–83. For more on the critical history of this episode, see Paul Suttie, "Exemplary Behaviour in *The Faerie Queene,*" *Journal of English and Germanic Philology* 99 (2000): 313–33.

12. One of the editors of the volume presses this point, asking me, "Is there no difference between the forester and the knights? To put it starkly: are they really the same?" To which I answer, those are indeed the questions I think the poem forces on us—and (to anticipate my argument a little) on Arthur himself. I do not say that it gives us, or him, a clear answer. Or rather, the clear answer it *seems* to give—its tidy assertions of a fundamental difference between the effects of eros in a "braue sprite" and in a "baser wit" (III.v.1–2)—are left looking highly doubtful in

relation to the insistent untidiness of the action, as is any eagerness on the knights' part, or on ours, to grasp at such neat moral reassurances as satisfactory answers to such a tangled problem.

13. I do not wish to suggest that there is anything irreconcilable with Platonism in a love leading to earthly progeny, in a lover's early death, or indeed in the ups and downs of history generally. My point is rather that a love which is *justified* in historical (or more specifically in genealogical) terms is to that extent not Platonic; and moreover, that such *historical* validation of moral endeavor *is* open to looking compromised and ambivalent to the extent that time's ravages as well as its rewards are brought into view—whether at a personal level, as in the early loss of the person for whose sake the quest was undertaken, or at a national level, as in the apostasy, misery, and massacre of almost whole generations of one's descendants.

14. On the Platonizing of Virgil, see Quitslund, 108–20, on Cristoforo Landino; also Lewis, *English Literature in the Sixteenth Century*, 383.

15. Again quoting Quitslund, 13, who is the latest to do so in a list including, inter alia, Josephine Waters Bennett, "Spenser's Garden of Adonis," *PMLA* 47 (1932): 46–80, and "Spenser's Garden of Adonis Revisited," *Journal of English and Germanic Philology* 41 (1942): 53–78; William Nelson, *The Poetry of Edmund Spenser: A Study*, (New York: Columbia University Press, 1963); Roche, *The Kindly Flame*; and John Erskine Hankins, *Source and Meaning in Spenser's Allegory: A Study of* The Faerie Queene (Oxford: Clarendon, 1971).

16. See Nelson, Roche, Hankins, Quitslund. The most persuasive link to Ficino is an apparent reflection, in the poem's distinction between Venus's "heauenly hous" (III.vi.12) and the Garden as her earthly dwelling (III.vi.29), of Ficino's elaboration of the Platonic distinction between heavenly and earthly Venus. It is harder to say whether Spenser's exposure to Ficino was direct or indirect.

17. Thus, *e.g.*, for Proclus, in "greater circuits and lesser," "all things proceed in a circuit, from their causes to their causes again." *Elements of Theology*, trans. E. R. Dodds, 2nd ed. (Oxford: Clarendon, 1963), 37; cf. 30–31.

18. Quitslund, 72 and passim; there is a hint of this in Lewis, *Spenser's Images of Life*, 59.

19. We may think for example of Plato's pains in the *Republic* (see especially 529 a–c) clearly to differentiate the intelligible significance of the cave story from its sensory vehicle—*The Collected Dialogues of Plato*, ed. Edith Hamilton and Huntington Cairns (Princeton: Princeton University Press, 1961).

20. It has been widely noted how ambiguous the Garden is and how much commentary it elicits. See especially Harry Berger's speaking of the Garden's creating, through its momentous indecipherability, "the effect of allegory"—"Actaeon at the Hinder Gate: The Stag Party in Spenser's Gardens of Adonis," in *Desire in the Renaissance: Psychoanalysis and Literature*, ed. Valeria Finucci and Regina Schwartz (Princeton: Princeton University Press, 1994), 102.

21. Cf. Quitslund, 78–79, on the use of the macrocosm as a mirror for the microcosm, in order to enable a process of moral reflection.

22. For the associations of the Garden of Adonis with an ephemeral kind of philosophizing based in the instability of the written word, see Plato, *Phaedrus* 276b, in *The Collected Dialogues*, ed. Hamilton and Cairns. (Cf. Richard T. Neuse, "Adonis, gardens of," in *The Spenser Encyclopedia*, 8.)

23. Cf. Sean Kane, *Spenser's Moral Allegory* (Toronto: University of Toronto Press, 1989), 84: "With its revolving and dissolving motion, the legend is haunted by the

fear that forms may not be eternal, but are merely casual properties of some 'huge eternall *Chaos*.' "

24. Carol V. Kaske, "Neoplatonism in Spenser Once More," *Religion and Literature* 32 (2000): 157–69.

25. Kaske, 166, citing Ficino's *Commentary on the Symposium*, VI.xi.

26. Quitslund, 260, also citing Ficino.

27. Kaske, 166.

28. Probably most pertinent is the argument in Philip Sidney's *Defence of Poesy* (an acknowledged influence on the *Letter to Ralegh*) that what inspires us in characters worthy of emulation is the beautiful Idea of virtue beheld in them.

29. In case the point needs underlining, it ought to be borne in mind that one could hardly find a deeper challenge to Merlin's authorized version of history than the eponymous original of the English (III.iii.56), whose descendants are destined to dominate those of the Trojan Brutus in the future history of the land, and whose name will vie with his in its very landscape.

30 See Niccolò Machiavelli, *Discourses on Livy*, trans. Julia Conaway Bondanella and Peter Bondanella (Oxford: Oxford University Press, 1997), I.xi–xv.

31. The extreme doubtfulness of the legendary history of early Britain, and in particular of those two kings to conjure with, Brutus and Arthur, was much noted among Elizabethan historians (see, e.g., "Preface to the Reader," in *Holinshed's Chronicles of England, Scotland, and Ireland*, 6 vols., ed. Vernon F. Snow [1807; rprt. New York: AMS Press, 1965], vol. 2, A3v), and is frankly acknowledged by Spenser himself in one manuscript of *A View of the Present State of Ireland*, where he declares it "as impossible to proue that there euer was anie suche Brutus of Albanye," as to corroborate the equivalent French claims to Trojan ancestry, or Irish claims to descent from "Gathelus of Spaine"—Spenser, *A View of the Present State of Ireland*, ed. W. L. Renwick (Oxford: Clarendon, 1970), 197.

32. " . . . as Tully to Brutus saith."— *A View of the Present State of Ireland*, 9.

33. See Jacqueline T. Miller, "The Courtly Figure: Spenser's Anatomy of Allegory," *Studies in English Literature, 1500–1900*, 31 (1991): 51–68.

34. A recent example of a critic's ascribing a systematic Neoplatonic intention to the *Mutability Cantos* is Thomas Bulger's "Platonism in Spenser's *Mutability Cantos*," in *Platonism and the English Imagination*, ed. Anna Baldwin and Sarah Hutton (Cambridge: Cambridge University Press, 1994), 126–38.

35. Cf. Jacqueline T. Miller, *Poetic License: Authority and Authorship in Medieval and Renaissance Contexts* (Oxford: Oxford University Press, 1986), 102–09.

36. On the topical relevance of the figure of Cynthia in the *Mutability Cantos*, see Gordon Teskey, *Allegory and Violence* (Ithaca and London: Cornell University Press, 1996), 179. The whole of Teskey's chapter on the *Cantos* is relevant to my argument here; see especially 175, where he speaks of Spenser's having become by this point in the poem "a quiet apostate" from metaphysical thought.

37. Ellrodt 70–71; Lewis, "Neoplatonism," 151–52, and passim; Quitslund, 121.

38. Berger, "The *Mutabilitie Cantos*: Archaism and Evolution in Retrospect," in *Revisionary Play: Studies in the Spenserian Dynamics* (Berkeley: University of California Press, 1988), 268.

39. Berger, "The *Mutabilitie Cantos*," 272.

40. A recent discussion of the revolution in perspective alluded to here is Teskey, *Allegory and Violence*, chapter 4.

FORUM

The Relation of the
Fowre Hymnes to *The Faerie Queene*

RICHARD McCABE

Spenser, Plato, and the Poetics of State

Focusing on Spenser's response to Plato's controversial expulsion of the poets from his Republic, this essay analyzes the many contradictions arising from the poet's simultaneous call for political censorship of the Irish Bards and vigorous defense of his own work against the apparent opposition of Lord Burghley, Elizabeth's chief officer of state. The disquieting similarity between the accusations allegedly leveled against Spenser by Burghley, and those that Spenser in turn levels against the Bards, is used to illustrate the complexity of the debate on artistic liberty and political control that Plato initiated in the *Republic*. The essay argues that all of the publications and compositions of 1596–the second installment of *The Faerie Queene*, the *Fowre Hymnes*, *Prothalamion*, and the manuscript of *A View of the Present State of Ireland*—engage in a concerted act of authorial self-assessment and self-exculpation designed to reclaim the "laureate" status that Spenser was seen by some to have forfeited through the calling in of his *Complaints* in 1591. In particular, the *Fowre Hymnes* and *Prothalamion* (being designed as examples of the two genres of poetry allowed by Plato) are interpreted as mounting a defense not merely of the moral and political value of Spenser's own verse but of the poetic art generally.

THE CENTRAL ARGUMENT of this essay is that the publication of Spenser's *Fowre Hymnes*, in 1596 in such close conjunction with that of the second installment of *The Faerie Queene*, constitutes a deliberate act of authorial self-representation, not to say self-defense, conducted via and versus Plato in terms of the conflicting but simultaneous demands of artistic liberty and colonial censorship. Despite obvious differences of style and genre, *The Faerie Queene* and *Fowre Hymnes* are, in fact, intimately connected—as the marked correspondences between the controversial proem to Book IV and the dedicatory epistle to the countesses of Cumberland and Warwick seem to

Spenser Studies: A Renaissance Poetry Annual, Volume XXIV, Copyright © 2009 AMS Press, Inc. All rights reserved.

be designed to indicate. When approached in the context of the two other works that Spenser published or prepared for publication in 1596, the *Prothalamion* and *A View of the Present State of Ireland*, they may be seen to contribute to an ongoing debate on the ethics of "authority," both political and literary, that Spenser conducted with himself and his readership at this crucial juncture in his career.[1]

The charge against which Spenser undertakes to defend himself in the proem to *The Legend of Friendship* is grave indeed:

> The rugged forhead that with grave foresight
> Welds kingdomes causes, and affaires of state,
> My looser rimes (I wote) doth sharply wite,
> For praising love, as I have done of late,
> And magnifying lovers deare debate;
> By which fraile youth is oft to follie led,
> Through false allurement of that pleasing baite,
> That better were in vertues discipled,
> Then with vaine poemes weeds to have their fancies fed.
>
> (IV Proem 1)[2]

Spenser's very public history of opposition to Lord Burghley, and the censorship that followed it, would leave few readers in any doubt as to the identity of his critic. Their relationship was already a matter of much public comment, and the renewed attack on Burghley (who had been one of the original dedicatees of *The Faerie Queene*) might well be regarded as a response to the notorious calling in of the *Complaints* in 1591.[3] But the language of the proem indicates that although the politics of faction undoubtedly played its part, the issue with which Spenser engages is as ancient and general as it is topical and particular. The statesman accuses the poet of no less than the corruption of the young, perhaps the single most damning accusation that Socrates hurls at the poet in Plato's *Republic* in a particularly trenchant contribution to what he describes as the "old quarrel" between "philosophy and poetry" (607b).[4]

The context of Socrates' onslaught on poetry in the second and third books of the *Republic* is the education of the young and, in particular, those who are destined (as future Guardians) for public life. Allowance is made in these early books for a heavily censored species of poetics designed to inculcate moral and civic virtue but book 10 seems far less open to compromise in its denigration of poetry per se as a trivial act of imitation at two removes from truth or reality ("a form of play, not to be taken seriously," 602b), and in

its call for the banishment of poets from the ideal state which is
envisioned in books 8 and 9.[5] Unlike the earlier books it challenges
the poet's claim to contribute to civic development at the most basic
level: Socrates inquires of Homer, "tell us what city was better governed owing to you," and "What city credits you with having been
a good legislator and having benefited them?" (599d–e). As it was
commonly agreed in the Early Modern period that Socrates func-
tioned as Plato's spokesman, the philosopher's attitude posed a major
problem for those involved in the "defence" of poetry against its
many perceived enemies.[6]

In the same year in which Spenser dedicated *The Shepheardes Calender* to Philip Sidney, Stephen Gosson similarly dedicated his *Schoole
of Abuse* arguing that Plato had "banished" amorous poets from his
"common wealth" as "effeminate writers, unprofitable members, and
utter enemies to virtue" (sig 2v). Their poems, he claimed, were to
be compared to "the Cuppes of Circes [sic], that turne reasonable
Creatures into brute Beastes."[7] Four years later in *Playes Confuted in
Five Actions* (1583), he drew heavily on Plato's *Republic* to argue for
the corruptive effects of mimetic art.[8] We know from the Spenser-
Harvey *Letters* (1580) that Sidney rejected the *Schoole of Abuse*, and
in his own *Apology for Poetry*—written partially at least in response
to Gosson—he took refuge in the belief that Plato, being himself the
"most poeticall" of all Philosophers, could not have intended to suggest that the practice of poetry was inconsistent with sound education
or good governance. Appealing from the *Republic* to the *Ion*, which,
as he read it, "giveth high and rightly divine commendation to Poetrie," he argues that it was only the "abuse" of poetry that Plato
banished from the state, "not the thing." "He attributeth unto Poesie," he concludes, "more then my selfe doe, namely, to be a very
inspiring of a divine force, farre above mans wit."[9] Although Sidney
seems content to take Plato's comments at face value, modern commentators are more disposed to find in Plato's account of inspiration
by divine possession a very backhanded compliment at best. Platonic
inspiration robs poetry of all claim to what the *Republic* terms
"techne," the rational principle of understanding that for Plato forms
the very basis of morality and statecraft. When read in context, it
firmly subordinates the poet to the philosopher. Even in the *Phaedrus*,
which was often argued to give a more sympathetic view of poetry,
the poet still ranks sixth in order of descent behind the philosopher
(248e).

The accusation that his poetry corrupts the young would be particularly grievous to a poet such as Spenser who had set out, as the
Letter to Ralegh explains, "to fashion a gentleman or noble person

in vertuous and gentle discipline"—according to Gosson the "olde
discipline of Englande" was precisely what was lost through poetry.[10]
Spenser's poem is intended to be educative, and its concern with
matters of state is signaled by its carefully calculated identification of
the queen as its principal reader, a reader who is invited to see "thine
owne realmes in lond of Faery" (2 Proem 4). In fact, the *Letter to
Ralegh* seems to be designed to preempt the sort of attack that Burghley had launched. Plato's Socrates condemns poetry for its dangerous "ambiguity" (*Protagoras* 339a–47a) and the letter is written
"knowing how doubtfully all Allegories may be construed." By insisting that the poem be read as a "a continued Allegory, or darke
conceit," and by supplying a rudimentary key to that conceit, it
implies an ability on the poet's part to transcend the sort of facile
imitation deplored by Socrates and deal instead with universal or
"generall" truths, a notion originally developed in the school of Plotinus and popularized anew by Renaissance Neoplatonists.[11] The problem was that Plato's Socrates had foreseen, and dismissed, such a
defense on the grounds that "the young are not able to distinguish
what is and what is not allegory" (378d). Furthermore, because poets
appeal to the "inferior part of the soul," the passionate part that resists
reason and discipline, young people are at particular risk from the
"enchantment" ["kalesis"] of the poet's rhetorical skill. The more
aesthetically pleasurable the poetry, the more morally dangerous it
was to be regarded.[12] Viewed in this light *The Faerie Queene* would
itself constitute a sort of corruptive Bowre of Blisse into which its
young readers are led like so many unsuspecting Verdants, and Gosson's comparison of amorous verse to "the Cuppes of Circe" would
be confirmed. Spenser's poetics would then seem indistinguishable
in their effects from those of Acrasia's "song of the Rose," and just
as that song is a conscious parody of a famous passage in Tasso's
Gerusalemme Liberata (16. 14–15), the entire *Faerie Queene* might well
be dismissed as a decadent parody of "moral" epic. The vice of
"akrasia," or intemperate lack of self-command, one remembers, is
singled out in the *Republic* as one of the principal dangers to the well-
governed state.[13] The mimetic poet, according to Socrates' view,
"sets up in each individual soul a vicious constitution ["kaken po-
liteian"] by fashioning phantoms far removed from reality" in a manner directly analogous to someone who places "bad men in power
and turns the city over to them and ruins the better sort" (605b).

Spenser's response to this challenge was rendered particularly complex—and a good deal more so than Sidney's—primarily because
his activities as a colonist in Ireland served to recommend the very
arguments that, as a poet, he might otherwise have been expected to

dismiss. When confronted with what he took to be the deleterious influence of the Gaelic Bards, Spenser himself assumed the role of the "rugged forhead" whose concern for "kingdomes causes, & affaires of state" necessitated the suppression of a poetry that corrupted the young. "It is moste trewe," Irenius asserts in *A View of the Present State of Ireland,*

> that suche poetes as in theire wrightinges doe labour to better the manners of men and thoroughe the swete bayte of theire numbers to steale into the yonge spirites a desire of honour and vertue are worthie to be had in greate respecte, But these Irishe Bardes are for the moste parte of another minde and so farre from instructinge yonge men in morrall discipline that they themselves doe more deserve to be sharpelye discipled for they seldome use to Chose out themselves the doinges of good men for the argumentes of theire poems but whom soever they finde to be moste Licentious of life moste bolde and lawles in his doinges moste daungerous and desperate in all partes of disobedience and rebellious disposicion him they set up and glorifye in theire Rymes him the[y] praise to the people and to yonge men make an example to followe . . . [these] evill thinges beinge decte and suborned with the gaye attire of goodlye wordes maye easelye deceave and Carrye awaie the affeccion of a yonge minde that is not well stayed but desirous by some bolde adventure to make profe of himselfe.

>   (125)

The verbal echoes between this passage and the proem to Book IV are very unsettling. Whereas Burghley is represented as accusing Spenser of corrupting "fraile youth . . . That better were in vertues discipled," Irenius contends that the Bards are "so farre from instructinge yonge men in morrall discipline that they themselves doe more deserve to be sharpelye discipled" (125). And both passages inevitably recall *The Faerie Queene*'s own avowed intention of fashioning virtuous gentlemen. Both Burghley's critique of Spenser and Spenser's critique of the Bards are heavily reliant on the *Republic*'s insistence upon the emotive power of poetry. Herein lay the crux of the matter, for both the defenders and the detractors of poetry were fully agreed on its efficacy, moral or immoral as the case might be. Sidney's argument for the superiority of poetry to philosophy resides precisely in its power to "move," its "praxis," but it is that very power that supplies its opponents with their strongest argument (I. 171). Plato's Socrates credits poetry with the seduction of the young, an emphasis perfectly captured in Burghley's alleged dismissal of Spenser's verse as "looser rimes" that led young readers to "follie" through "false allurement" of its "pleasing baite." "Irenius" consequently displays as much concern to defend the "swete bayte" of Spenser's verse as to denigrate the Bards by comparison.

The tone of the passage from the *View* makes it clear why Spenser felt the need to respond to Burghley's criticism. As an aspirant to laureate status he cannot allow his work to be read as a mere amorous romance devoid of public concern or serious moral purpose, as the moral equivalent of that of the Bards. That would be to concede Socrates's categorization of poetry as a trivial game intended to appeal to the tastes of the ignorant multitude, like the work of the Sophists whom he equally despised. The logic of Socrates' argument is that poetry's popularity serves as an index of its depravity. One might expect Spenser to demur, yet in confronting the influence of his Gaelic rivals he utilizes essentially the same argument. The Bards, Irenius tells us,

> are hadd in soe high regard and estimation amongest them [the Irish] that none dare displease them for feare to runne into reproch throughe theire offence, and to be made infamous in the mouthes of all men/ffor the verses are taken upp with a generall applause and usuall songe att all feastes and meetinges by certeine other persons whose proper function that is which also receive for the same great Rewardes and reputation besides.
>
> (124)

The Bards play to the gallery and the resulting popularity lends them power. But the argument once again raises disquieting questions. Spenser too was enormously popular, constantly cited and praised by his contemporaries, and the "rugged forhead" has now implied that this popularity is equally indebted to the indulgence of the masses, to the favor of the ill-tutored young. It is therefore all the less surprising that Spenser opts to take the battle to the enemy camp, constructing his defense against "Platonic" condemnation from the pages of Plato himself:

Which who so list looke backe to former ages,
   And call to count the things that then were donne,
   Shall find, that all the workes of those wise sages,
   And brave exploits which great Heroes wonne,
   In love were either ended or begunne:
   Witnesse the father of Philosophie,
   Which to his *Critias*, shaded oft from sunne,
   Of love full manie lessons did apply,
The which these Stoicke censours cannot well deny.

(IV Proem 3)

The stanza provides one of the best examples in Spenser of the inextricable link between heroic poetry and love, and the choice of Socrates is particularly apt because "the father of Philosophie" had also been falsely accused of corrupting the young. But the passage introduces a notorious crux. Socrates' death at the hands of "unjust Athenians" is lamented in the Cave of Mammon episode (2. 7. 52) where his "belamy" is similarly identified as "fayre Critias" (which may, in the immediate context, be a mistake for Crito). It was with Phaedrus, however, that Plato's Socrates famously sat under a "tall, spreading plane tree" to discuss the nature of love (230b), and it is in the *Phaedrus* that Socrates recants for having represented love as evil (242c–57b) and proceeds to distinguish between "right-handed" and "left-handed" love, or ennobling and corrupting love (266a). The intrusion of Critias, who appears in several other Platonic dialogues, including the fragmentary one that bears his name, remains unexplained. As errors go it is a suggestive one, however. In the *Charmides*, Critias is one of the principal speakers who attempt to define "sophrosune," something approximating self-government or self-restraint, while in the minor "prose epic" of the *Critias* he describes the rise and fall of Atlantis. As the Platonic persona perhaps most closely associated with analysis of government through the medium of pseudo-history or myth, he is well cited in a defense of epic verse.

Yet there remains little doubt that the principal dialogue to which Spenser refers is the *Phaedrus*, a dialogue which Early Modern commentators often regarded as rehabilitating poetry as well as love, or rather of rehabilitating poetry through love.[14] According to Marsilio Ficino, the single most influential of Renaissance commentators, "since Socrates here plays not a philosophical so much as a poetical role ["non tam philosophicam quam poeticam agit personam"], he adds that he has been seized by a demon because he has disparaged

Love, the name of a god; he does this so that, in the process of dividing love, he may divide poetically rather than dialectically."[15] By linking desire to the cognitive, rather than the merely appetitive, powers of the soul, the *Phaedrus* appeared to promote a similar elevation of poetry. The fact that Socrates' second speech on love—his "palinode" or recantation—is wholly structured around the famous image of the charioteer, an image that Spenser's contemporaries regarded very much as a "continued allegory or darke conceit," merely served to confirm the widespread notion that the *Phaedrus* was far more sympathetic to poetry than the *Republic.* There is therefore every point to Spenser's invocation of the *Phaedrus* in the context of Book IV and, given the labored link between poetry and love, to the manner in which he turns from Burghley to Queen Elizabeth,

> In whose chast breast all bountie naturall,
>> And treasures of true love enlocked beene,
>> To her I sing of love that loveth best,
>> And best is lov'd of all alive I weene:
>> To her this song most fitly is addrest,
>> The Queene of love, and Prince of peace from heaven blest.
>>   (IV Proem 4)

Burghley was Elizabeth's Lord Treasurer but only she affords the "treasures of true love," and only she, it is implied, shows "bountie" to true poets. According to *Colin Clouts Come Home Againe,* published the previous year, "*Cynthia,* doth in sciences abound,/And gives to their professors stipends large" (lines 745–46). She had, in fact, granted Spenser a pension in 1591 and was hailed in *The Teares of the Muses* (line 577) as a "peereles Poetresse"—"peerelesse" being the adjective that Sidney ascribes to the archetypal poet in his *Apology* (I. 164). It would therefore seem that the *Republic's* celebrated call for a philosopher-king will be answered in a philosopher-queen—had she not recently translated Boethius's *Consolation of Philosophy* into English?—who wrote poetry herself and cultivated rather than banished poets.[16] By contrast, in a final return to the topos of true and false "treasure," the sour conclusion to Book VI implies that the "mighty Pere" whose "displeasure" Spenser suffers will be appeased only when the poet's "rimes" "seeke to please, that now is counted wisemens threasure" (VI.xii.41). The contrast between "true" and "false" treasure thus frames the second installment of *The Faerie Queene* and the insult couched in the concluding lines is pointed: since the *Phaedrus* asserts that only the "wise" are to be regarded as truly rich, those who value the Sophistic art of flattery may be "counted" neither (279c).

According to Plato's *Laws* it is primarily because we come to re-semble what we enjoy that the lawgiver should legislate for the poet (655a–59e), but Spenser contrives to reverse this situation. The sec-ond installment of *The Faerie Queene* begins with a highly placed courtier's attack on poetry, but ends with the poet's attack on the court. The reversal is all the more effective, and apparently earned, in that the second installment sees Spenser tackle what the *Republic* consistently identifies as the supreme virtue incorporating all of the others, that of Justice: "Most sacred vertue she of all the rest, / Resem-bling God in his imperiall might" (V Proem 10). In Plato, the law-giver must legislate for the poet, but in Book V the poet legislates for the lawgiver—the lawgiver in general, that is, but perhaps also one in particular. Lord Burghley's own most famous publication was entitled *The Execution of Justice in England* (1583). Like Book V it mounts a spirited defense of Lord Grey's government in Ireland, but unlike Book V it does not blame the court for the Lord Deputy's premature recall that left the Irish state "unreformed":

> But ere he could reforme it thoroughly,
>   He through occasion called was away,
>   To Faerie Court, that of necessity
>   His course of Iustice he was forst to stay,
>   And *Talus* to revoke from the right way,
>   In which he was that Realme for to redresse.
>
> (V.xii.27)

The poet here gives the lawgiver an object lesson in true justice. And as the proem to Book IV had turned from the Lord Treasurer to his queen, Book V sets Elizabeth firmly in the seat of Justice as Mercilla. At the entrance to her court in Canto ix, Arthur and Artegall witness the punishment of the Poet-formerly-known-as-Bonfont but now termed Malfont "eyther for th'evill, which he did therein, / Or that he likened was to a welhed / Of evill words" (V.ix.26). On one level the nailing of his tongue to a post is a fitting, if terrible, punish-ment for the "lewd poems" and "rayling rymes" he is credited with composing (25), but on another it returns our attention to the more general subjects of poetic reputation, artistic integrity, censorship, and the role of the poet in the *respublica*, with which the second installment of *The Faerie Queene* began. Spenser's own satires had been called in owing to their attacks on one of the highest officers of state and he too had risked categorization as "Malfont." One contemporary observer suggests that his reputation was very badly damaged by the affair: "Yt is nott yett a yeare sence he writt his booke in the prayse of the Quene," observed Sir Thomas Tresham, "which was so well liked, that her maiestie gave him ane hundred marks pencion forthe of the Exchequer: and so clerklie was yt penned, that he beareth the name of a Poett Laurell. But nowe in medlinge with his apes tayle he is gott into Ireland; also in hazard to loose his forsayd annuall reward: and fynallie hereby proove himselfe a Poett Lorrell."[17] But if Spenser was no more than a subversively political poet skulking in Ireland what was the difference between him and the bards he despised? Why should he not be subject to the same form of censorship that he advocated for them?

From "poet Laurel" to "poet Lorrell," from "Bonfont" to "Malfont," such was the apparent trajectory of Spenser's career in 1591, and it is just such an anxiety, I would argue, that lies behind the vigorous *apologia pro arte sua* presented in the proem to Book IV. It can hardly be coincidence that the book it serves to introduce, *The Legend of Friendship*, announces itself as the completion of a work by "that renowmed Poet . . . Dan *Chaucer*, well of English undefiled." If the Malfonts of the literary world are "welheds of evill words," Chaucer is the pure "well," or Bonfont, of the English tradition, and specifically of the English heroic tradition for *The Squire's Tale* was written "with warlike numbers and Heroicke sound" (IV.ii.32). By investing himself in the mantle of the supreme Bonfont, Spenser appropriates the sort of Chaucerian "authority" to which he first laid premature claim in the prefatory epistle to *The Shepheardes Calender*. "Ne dare I like," he now tells us,

> but through infusion sweete
> Of thine owne spirit, which doth in me survive,
> I follow here the footing of thy feete,
> That with thy meaning so I may the rather meete.

(IV.ii.34)

This newly inspired Chaucerian Spenser, or Spenserian Chaucer, is clearly a public laureate "on Fames eternall beadroll worthie to be fyled" (IV.ii.32). To rise from pastoral to epic poetry was the goal of the *Calender*'s Cuddy (alias Colin Clout, for "some doubt, that the persons be different," as E. K. tells us). But Cuddy is forced to admit that although "Princes palace" constitutes "the most fitt" home for epic verse (*October*, lines 80–81) it seems to be peculiarly unwelcome there—and this despite the eclogue's adoption of the very Platonic notion (taking the *Ion* at face value) of inspiration, or *enthusiasmos*, as "a divine gift and heavenly instinct not to bee gotten by labour and learning, but adorned with both." "O pierlesse Poesye," he asks in despair, "where is then thy place?" (*October*, line 79). "Colin" had returned to the controversy in *Colin Clouts Come Home Againe* (1595), supplying a horrifying vision of a largely Philistine court enamored of fake values and false verse, but his reappearance in the sixth book of *The Faerie Queene*, against all generic expectations, constitutes Spenser's strongest statement on the relationship between the arts and the state. The vision of the Graces conjured up on Mt. Acidale simultaneously encapsulates both the wonder and the vulnerability of aesthetic invention. The passage has received extensive attention, but I wish to approach it from a slightly different angle to throw some further light on the significance of the sudden disappearance of Colin's vision and the subsequent destruction of the pastoral community of which he is a member.[18] Within the Neoplatonic tradition the Graces, as figures of reciprocal beneficence, were used to symbolize not just the writer's creative energies but the patronal values that nourished them. In dedicating the third and fourth books of his *Letters* to King Matthias of Hungary, for example, Marsilio Ficino notes that their acceptance by the king marks an answer to a prayer: "our Plato, the father of philosophers," he writes,

> often used to remind his chosen disciples . . . to sacrifice attentively to the Graces so that they should become more gracious and agreeable. . . . Wherefore, in the Platonic tradition, I now command these books not only to sacrifice to the Graces, but also to dedicate themselves wholeheartedly to them. . . . Suddenly they have been seized and carried off . . . towards your lofty palace, as if it were the very temple of the Graces. . . . For thus they will owe their existence only to me, but their beauty wholly to your royal majesty. And I shall be seen to have satisfied my master Plato who commanded that only that prince be venerated in whom surpassing wisdom be joined with highest power.[19]

Spenser's problem, of course, is that Colin is not in a royal "palace" and his Graces have no "temple." Exposed on Mt. Acidale in a territory surrounded by marauding brigands, he has no patron equivalent to Ficino's Matthias. Despite all of the hopes expressed in the proem to Book IV, the figure most conspicuous by her absence from the scene is the philosopher-queen, Gloriana. "Colin" appears to be denied the gracious reciprocation of laureate status even within his own epic. The first victim of the Blattant Beast is Artegall/Lord Grey, Spenser's former patron, but its final victim is the "gentle poet" himself or rather, and more tellingly, "the gentle Poets rime" (VI.xii.40). The wider context of Ficino's address to Matthias would have seemed particularly relevant to Spenser as tensions rose in the Ireland of the 1590s: the dedicatory letter is entitled "an exhortation to war against the barbarians." The state may not have banished Spenser in the technical sense envisioned in the *Republic* but, adopting an increasingly Ovidian tone, he represents himself as alienated from the court nonetheless, geographically and temperamentally. Before the situation could change he needed to provide a clear rationale for entitlement.

Towards the close of his assault on the poets in the tenth book of the *Republic*, Socrates unexpectedly announces an exception to his rule: "we can admit no poetry into our city," he tells us, "save only hymns to the gods and the praises of good men" (607a). He has good reason for such an association because, generically speaking, the hymn and the panegyric are closely associated in Classical literature—a hymn may take the form of a panegyric to a god, and a panegyric, as we shall see, may ascribe godlike qualities to a hero. Although these are the only exceptions that Socrates is prepared to make, he throws the matter open for further debate: "nevertheless, let it be declared that, if the mimetic and dulcet poetry can show any reason for her existence in a well-governed state, we would gladly admit her, since we ourselves are very conscious of her spell" (607c). I have been arguing thus far that Spenser rises to this challenge in the defense of epic and amatory verse (and indeed of amatory epic) mounted in the second installment of *The Faerie Queene*, but I now wish to suggest that this defense was fortified by the publication of the *Fowre Hymnes* that same year.[20] Spenser, it would appear, is meeting Plato's challenge directly by defending epic and amatory verse through the very genre of "hymn" that Plato permits in the well-governed state. The dedicatory letter that prefaces the *Fowre Hymnes* is particularly interesting in this regard in its attempt to conceptualize the different strata of Spenser's poetic and personal development through the Augustinian technique of "retractation."

It is essential to realize that "retractation" is not synonymous with mere retraction in this context. St. Augustine used the term to designate a mature rehandling of subjects he had dealt with earlier in his life, just as Spenser seeks to recontextualize the first two hymns, allegedly written in youth, within a new four-part structure. When we look at the accusations allegedly made against the two early hymns we find a remarkable similarity to the accusations rebutted in the proem to Book IV. Spenser enforces the similarity by alleging that one of his two dedicatees has asked him to "call in" the hymns he had written in "the greener times of my youth" on the grounds that they "too much pleased those of like age and disposition, which being too vehemently caried with that kind of affection, do rather sucke out poyson to their strong passion, then hony to their honest delight." This is the very effect that Plato's Socrates would have predicted. His argument is that such poetry—whether narrative, lyric or dramatic—unbalanced the reason (or logistikon) by cultivating dangerous emotions rather than, as Aristotle claimed in relation to tragedy, producing some form of emotional catharsis or purgation. It might therefore seem ironic that Spenser should respond to a call for the suppression of wanton poems circulating in manuscript by publishing them to a wider audience through the medium of print. But this is precisely what the business of "retractation" involves: finding himself unable to suppress the offending pieces "by reason that manie copies thereof were formerly scattered abroad," Spenser tells us, "I resolved at least to amend, and by way of retractation to reforme them, making in stead of those two Hymnes of earthly or naturall love and beautie, two others of heavenly and celestiall." The words "in stead" should give us pause: the most literal interpretation would be that the two later hymns have displaced the early ones, yet the collection is structured in such a way as to make that reading untenable.[21] Its very title, *Fowre Hymnes*, suggests inclusiveness not exclusion.

The authorial proem to *An Hymne of Heavenly Love* dismisses as mere "follies" the "lewd layes . . . In praise of that mad fit, which fooles call love" written "in th'heat of youth," but the description is singularly inapplicable to the texts that precede it, *An Hymne in Honour of Love* and *An Hymne in Honour of Beautie*. In fact, the entire sequence is arranged in such a way as to suggest that we reach the "heavenly" through the "earthly." It is less a matter of displacement than of sublimation. The same is true of Socrates' famous recantation in the *Phaedrus*: his speech in praise of love incorporates, but subtly recontextualizes, elements of the former speech against it. In responding to Plato, and the ammunition that he gave to the enemies of poetry, it is therefore essential that the *Hymnes* should concern the nature of love and its association with heroism and self-government. Popular verse, Plato's Socrates argues, is destructive of discipline since the very purpose of education is to teach us to love beauty, rightly conceived. Poetry impedes this process, he contends, because poets deal only with phantasms or images of beauty rather than the real thing. Only the philosopher touches true reality in his attention to the realm of Ideas. The *Fowre Hymnes* are structured to mount a powerful counter-argument to that viewpoint. While Socrates had maintained that "the end and consummation of culture is the love of the beautiful" (*Republic*, 403c), it is the poet, not the philosopher, who leads us to the summit of spiritual vision in *An Hymne of Heavenly Beautie*. Accordingly, all of the imagery of fledging and flight that pervades Socrates' account of the Phaedrean charioteer is transferred to the development of poetic vision. And because the proper meaning of philosophy is "love of wisdom" (philo-sophia) Spenser conducts us toward nothing less than a vision of Sapience herself, conceived as an attribute of God:

> There in his bosome *Sapience* doth sit,
> The soveraine dearling of the *Deity*,
> Clad like a Queene in royall robes, most fit
> For so great power and peerelesse maiesty.
>
> (*HHB*, lines 183–86)

This is presented as the true source of "powre imperiall" (196), and it is from this "secret threasury"—in a significant return to the subject of "wise mens treasure"—that true riches are fetched. It is the supreme vision of spiritual reality mediated by the Christian poet in comparison to which "all other sights but fayned shadowes be" (273), a severe rebuke, this, to Plato's dismissal of poets as purveyors of phantasms. Now they are conduits of vision. In fact, the poet has attained the sort of vatic status adumbrated in Plotinus's account of "intelligible beauty" (*Enneads* V. viii. 1), and directly claimed for poetry by Sir Philip Sidney (I. 154). Spenser had previously created a number of vatic figures within *The Faerie Queene*, but this is the first time that vatic status is expressly attributed to his own authorial persona, and the endeavor is undertaken in direct relation to the much-disputed subject of "love." It is the narrator's "huge love" that enables his vision of Sapience or Sophia (l. 237). The poet is the true "lover of beauty" and, therefore, the true "philosopher."

Yet Spenser remains cautious of claiming too much. The ultimate limitations of art in the face of the ineffable are acknowledged but principally through a clever *recusatio* that draws upon Platonic arguments only to subvert them. At the outset of the tenth book of the *Republic* Socrates seeks to discredit poetry by analogy with painting in that painters produce lifelike images that lead the young and the foolish to mistake them for real people. Accordingly, in approaching his vision of Sapience, Spenser tells us that not even Apelles, famed for his depiction of Aphrodite rising from the sea, could have "purtrayd" her aright. Even had the goddess been "as faire, as fabling wits do fayne," she could not compete with Sapience (*HHB*, lines 211–17). And ancient poetry fares little better: Anacreon who "did spend/His plenteous vaine in setting forth her prayse" would have dismissed Aphrodite by comparison with Sapience as an "Idole" born of his own "fayning thought" (*HHB*, lines 219–24). How could Spenser avoid the dual pitfalls of incompetence or unwitting idolatry?

> How then dare I, the novice of this Art,
> Presume to picture so divine a wight,
> Or hope t'expresse her least perfections part,
> Whose beautie filles the heavens with her light,
> And darkes the earth with shadow of her sight?
> Ah gentle Muse thou art too weake and faint,
> The pourtraict of so heavenly hew to paint.
>
> (*HHB*, lines 225–31)

But a potent answer readily suggests itself. The Christian poet has two signal advantages over his Classical counterpart: a true God and an operative "grace." Spenser writes in an age of revelation when those—and particularly, one presumes, those *vates*—"whom God so much doth grace" (240) enjoy the vision of Sapience, a vision to which even the "father of Philosophie" could not attain. He may have been Erasmus's "St. Socrates" but he was not Spenser's. Implicit in the structure of the *Fowre Hymnes* is a subordination of the Classical to the Christian. The structure of Spenser's quartet is carefully designed to respond to a contemporary critical debate about the propriety of using the originally pagan form of the classical hymn to praise the Christian deity, a controversy analogous to the debate about whether it was possible to produce a genuinely Christian epic.[22] Spenser's first two hymns center on Cupid and Venus, his last two on Christ and Sapience. Yet the earlier hymns are not dismissed. Rather they are found, in a manner of interpretation highly popular with contemporary Neoplatonists, to adumbrate through their use of Classical mythology the more profound truths of Christianity.[23] It is not Platonic philosophy but the poet's vatic "extasy" (*HHB*, lines 261) that reveals "false beauties flattring bait" to be no more than

"vaine deceiptfull shadowes" (*HHB*, lines 291–92). Ultimately for
Spenser, as later for Milton, God is the supreme patron who transforms mere images into visions through the gift of grace. The line
of visionary ascent described in the fourth hymn incorporates "those
Idees on hie which *Plato* so admyred" (*HHB*, lines 82–83), but pointedly transcends them. In governmental terms, the terms that so preoccupied Plato's Socrates, the Platonic conception of the realm of ideas
stops far short of the "fairer" heaven,

> in which doe raine
> The soveraine *Powres* and mightie *Potentates*,
> Which in their high protections doe containe
> All mortall Princes, and imperiall States;
> And fayrer yet, whereas the royall Seates
> And heavenly *Dominations* are set,
> From whom all earthly governance is fet.
>
> (*HHB*, lines 85–91)

So much for Burghley's concerns for "kingdoms causes, and affaires
of state"! It is the Neoplatonic poet who enjoys a vision of true
"governance," not the "Stoick" statesman appropriating "Platonic"
arguments for censorship.[24] Yet censorship is by no means rejected
outright. Spenser's strategy is far more subtle. In the *Fowre Hymnes*
the moral function of the patron is ostensibly upheld through a deft
negotiation between youth and age, Classical and Christian, Eros and
Heros. Spenser is hereby enabled to represent himself as responding in
a mature and responsible fashion to a call for censorship by republish-
ing the very poems that gave offence.

Yet for all the brilliance of this device, the underlying problem
raised in Book IV persists. In practical terms the conflict between
poetic and political authority could no more be resolved in the realm
of grace than in that of ideas. A more worldly modus vivendi was
still required. As we have seen, Plato will allow no poetry in his
reformed state "save only hymns to the gods and the praises of good
men." Spenser managed to produce both in 1596 by the clever expedient of transforming his *Prothalamion* into a panegyric on the Earl of
Essex, who is compared to the demigod Hercules on whose labors
so many episodes of *The Faerie Queene* are based.[25] While the ending
of the sixth book of *The Faerie Queene* laments "a mighty Peres
displeasure" (VI.xii.41), the *Prothalamion* introduces an alluring alternative to Spenser's critic in the dazzling person of the Earl of Essex,
"a noble Peer,/Great Englands glory and the Worlds wide wonder"

(145–46). By the end of the poem the narrator sets all of his "expectation" on the possibility of patronal "espousal" at Essex House, the possibility that as the swans turn into brides, the speaker may, like Horace under the patronage of Maecenas, turn into an immortal swan by completing his epic "song" (*Odes*, 2. 20). The realms of poetics and politics would then cohere: the patron would make "great Elisas" name "glorious" through military deeds, the poet through heroic verse. At exactly the same time, of course, Spenser was also suggesting in the *View* that Essex should be made Lord Lieutenant of Ireland, that his ideal patron would also be the ideal censor of the Bards.[26]

It is particularly ironic that the "Prince of Poets in his time" should long be remembered in Ireland as the enemy of poetry. The attitudes towards Bardic poetry expressed in the *View* serve to expose not only the contradictions in Spenser's own poetic self-defense—that he should demand as poet what he withheld as colonist—but more generally in the conflicting ideals of artistic liberty and state censorship. The disquieting similarity between the accusations leveled against Spenser by the great statesman and those that he levels against the Bards illustrates the complexity of the debate that Plato initiated in the *Republic*. The claim that art influences the way in which people behave is familiar to all of us from contemporary calls for the censorship of the cinema, the television, the press, and most recently, the internet. And Plato's special concern for the effects of the arts on the young expresses itself today in the elaborate system of classification that we apply to the cinema and in the creation of a so-called "water-shed" in TV scheduling. The Elizabethans were no less aware of the matter at issue. In creating his image of the Bowre of Blisse, Spenser illustrates how all of the arts—painting, music, sculpture, and poetry—may combine to lead young Verdants into a fool's Paradise of moral decadence. The effect of the Bowre is identified as one of "enchantment" (II.xii.85), the same effect that Plato's Socrates ascribes to poetry in his use of the Greek term "kalesis." The marginal annotations appended to the *Republic* in the famous "Stephanus" edition of Plato's *Works* (1578) directly associate Socrates' concerns to the fear of "intemperance."[27] Spenser's central image of a young man in the arms of a morally debilitating woman is also remarkably similar to Plato's: Socrates professes to renounce poetry "even as men who have fallen in love, if they think that the love is not good for them, hard though it be, nevertheless refrain" (607e). Yet, Spenser's own most notorious representation of moral censorship, Sir Guyon's destruction of that selfsame Bowre of Blisse, has proved to be one of the most contentious issues in Spenser criticism. Generations of readers have decried it as, at best, a comment on the limitations of the hero's "temperance" or, at worst, a crass sop to the "Puritanism" of the age. Was Spenser making a moral point through his poetry or at its expense? The controversy illustrates how aesthetic liberty may run into conflict not merely with the dictates of state censorship but even with the ideology of moral didacticism which evolved in response to Plato's attack on literature. The *Republic* laid its trap with great precision. By insisting that true poetry necessitates "madness" while the ideal state necessitates reason, it ensures that all morally based strategies of self-defense entail a measure of aesthetic self-betrayal. Could poetry really "censor" its own content without depleting its creative energy? Without enchantment Acrasia has no power. Without Acrasia Guyon has no quest. Without both—we might as well be reading philosophy.

NOTES

1.   The manuscript of the *View* entered for publication in the *Stationers Register* on 14 April 1598 (Bodleian MS Rawl. B. 478) is dated 1596.

2.   All quotations are from *The Faerie Queene*, ed. A. C. Hamilton, rvd. ed. (London, 2001); all quotations from the shorter poems are from *Edmund Spenser: The Shorter Poems*, ed. R. A. McCabe (Harmondsworth: Penguin 1999). Quotations from *A View of the Present State of Ireland* are from vol. 9 of *The Works of Edmund Spenser*, edited by Edwin Greenlaw et al., Variorum Edition, 11 vols. (Baltimore: Johns Hopkins University Press, 1932–58).

3.   See Richard S. Peterson, "Laurel Crown and Ape's Tail: New Light on Spenser's Career from Sir Thomas Tresham," *Spenser Studies* 12 (1998): 1–35; Andrew Hadfield, "Robert Parsons/Richard Verstegan and the Calling in of *Mother Hubberds Tale*," *Spenser Studies* 17 (2003): 297–300.

4.   *The Collected Dialogues of Plato, including the Letters*, eds. Edith Hamilton and Huntington Cairns, Bollingen Series 71 (Princeton: Princeton University Press, 1961). All quotations are from this edition.

5.   For this distinction see Ramona A. Naddoff, *Exiling the Poets: The Production of Censorship in Plato's Republic* (Chicago: University of Chicago Press, 2002), 67–69.

6.   See Russell Fraser, *The War Against Poetry* (Princeton: Princeton University Press, 1970); Peter C. Herman, *Squitter-wits and Muse-haters: Sidney, Spenser, Milton and Anti-poetic Sentiment* (Detroit: Wayne University Press, 1996).

7.   *The Schoole of Abuse, Conteining a pleasaunt invective against Poets, Pipers, Plaiers, Iesters, and such like Caterpillers of the Commonwelth* (1579), sigs. 2v–3r.

8.   See Arthur F. Kinney, *Markets of Bawdrie: The Dramatic Criticism of Stephen Gosson* (Salzburg: Institut für Englische Sprache und Literatur, Universität Salzburg, 1974), 29–37.

9.   G. Gregory Smith, ed., *Elizabethan Critical Essays*, 2 vols. (Oxford: Clarendon Press, 1904), I:192. All quotations are from this edition by volume and page.

10.   Gosson, sig. 16r.

11.   See Erwin Panofsky, *Idea: a Concept in Art Theory*, translated by Joseph J. S. Peake (London: Harper and Row, 1968; first pub., 1924), 63–68.

12.   See Christopher Janaway, *Images of Excellence: Plato's Critique of the Arts* (Oxford: Clarendon Press, 1995), 140–46.

13.   For the Platonic concept of *akrasia* see C. D. C. Reeve, *Philosopher-Kings: The Argument of Plato's "Republic"* (1988; Indianapolis: Hackett Publishing Company, 2006), 131–35.

14.   Modern commentators are in dispute on the matter. For the view that Plato's attitude to poetry does not significantly alter see Christopher Janaway, "Plato and the Arts," in Hugh H. Benson, ed., *A Companion to Plato* (Oxford: Blackwell, 2006), 388–400. For the view that a reassessment of poetry is implicit in the rehabilitation of eros see Martha Craven Nussbaum, " 'This Story Isn't True': Poetry, Goodness, and Understanding in Plato's *Phaedrus,*" in Julius Moravcsik and Philip Temko, eds., *Plato on Beauty, Wisdom, and the Arts* (Totowa, NJ: Rowman & Allanheld, 1982), 102–04.

15.   *Marsilio Ficino and the Phaedran Charioteer*, ed. and trans. Michael J. B. Allen (Berkeley: University of California Press, 1981), 74.

16.   For the text of Elizabeth's translation see *Queen Elizabeth's Englishings*, ed. Caroline Pemberton, EETS, orig. ser. 113 (London: Kegan Paul, Trench, Trübner, 1890), 1–120.

17.   Peterson, 8.

18.   See especially Humphrey Tonkin, *Spenser's Courteous Pastoral: Book Six of the Faerie Queene* (Oxford: Clarendon Press, 1972), 126–42, 248–63; James Nohrnberg, *The Analogy of "The Faerie Queene"* (Princeton: Princeton University Press, 1976), 461–70.

19.   *The Letters of Marsilio Ficino*, trans. Members of the Language Department of the School of Economic Science, London, 7 vols. (London: Shepheard-Walwyn, 1975–2003), II, 1–2.

20.   For the "Platonism" of the *Hymnes* see Enid Welsford, *Spenser: Fowre Hymnes, Epithalamion* (Oxford: Basil Blackwell, 1967); Elizabeth Bieman, *Plato Baptized: Towards the Interpretation of Spenser's Mimetic Fictions* (Toronto: University of Toronto Press, 1988), 152–62.

21.   See David Lee Miller, *The Poem's Two Bodies: The Poetics of 1590 "Faerie Queene"* (Princeton: Princeton University Press, 1988), 9–14.

22.   See Phillip B. Rollinson, "A Generic View of Spenser's Four Hymns," *Studies in Philology* 68 (1971): 292–304.

23.   See Edgar Wind, *Pagan Mysteries in the Renaissance*, 2nd ed. (London: Faber and Faber: 1968).

24.   Spenser appears to subscribe here to a common stereotype of the "Stoic." Gosson predicted that he would be branded a "Stoike" because of his opposition to literature; see Gosson, sig. 27v.

25.   For the association between epithalamion (of which the *Prothalamion* is a variant) and epideictic poetry, see William E. Rogers, "The *Carmina* of Horace in the *Prothalamion,*" *American Notes & Queries* 15 (1977): 148.

26.   For Essex as a potential patron of Spenser, see Richard A. McCabe, *Spenser's Monstrous Regiment: Elizabethan Ireland and the Poetics of Difference*, 2nd ed. (Oxford: Oxford University Press, 2005), 211–12.

27.   "Poetam nullum habere cum ratione commercium, sed nutriculam esse intem-
perantium et dissolutarum cupiditatum." See *Platonis Opera quae extant omnia* (Paris,
1578), ed. and trans. Jean de Serres, 3 vols. (Paris, 1578), II. 602. The first volume
of the edition is dedicated to Elizabeth I (vol. 1). For an account of the Serranus
edition, see S. K. Heninger, "Sidney and Serranus' Plato," *English Literary Renaissance*
13 (1983): 146–61.

KENNETH BORRIS

Reassessing Ellrodt: Critias and the *Fowre Hymnes* in *The Faerie Queene*

Among Spenser's varied poems, the *Fowre Hymnes* have unique interest for readers of his allegorical romance-epic because they most openly express his interests in theology and Platonism. They may thus illuminate some of the "dark conceits" of his Faery, yet have had little such consideration to date. Contrary to Robert Ellrodt's view that all four hymns in their present form as well as their Platonic learning postdate *The Faerie Queene*, the origins of at least the first pair and their erudition should be dated considerably earlier than 1595/96. The so-called Critias crux of *The Faerie Queene* does not, as Ellrodt supposed, show that the clearly learned Platonism of Spenser's *Hymnes* postdated his heroic poem, but rather shows the reverse, by evincing much Platonic knowledge and acuity. The Platonic contents of his hymnic and heroic poems overlap in various ways. A range of examples demonstrates the heuristic value of the *Hymnes* for exploring the prospects of Spenser's faery allegorism: particularly its representations of eros, beauty, the soul, the Ideas, and Gloriana.

*A*MONG SPENSER'S SURVIVING writings, the *Fowre Hymnes* are his most discursive philosophical and theological reflections. Hence their position in his canon is analogous to *De Doctrina Christiana*'s in Milton's, and yet they may well have more broad interpretive value for Spenserians than that treatise does for Miltonists. Since *Paradise Lost* is an explicitly biblical narrative about the Fall, the topics of its allegories are relatively clear. But in Spenser's romantic epic, even basic access to its allegorism is much more encoded. There, a knight's encounter with an infant whose hands are stained and whose mother

Spenser Studies: A Renaissance Poetry Annual, Volume XXIV, Copyright © 2009 AMS Press, Inc. All rights reserved.

has just committed suicide expresses theological implications of concupiscence, and so subtly that the first recorded notices of this allegory, though now widely accepted, date from around 1960.[1] Likewise
the Belge episode's allegorical engagements with Protestant apocalyptic historiography began to receive comment only around 1991.[2]
Spenser's relatively explicit writings have great interest for the hermeneutics of his Faery, and the publication of the *Hymnes* in 1596
closely attended that of *The Faerie Queene*'s expansion, as if both may
have some correlative significance. Yet the relationship of his hymnic
and heroic texts remains relatively unexplored.

The energetic debates in Milton studies about *De Doctrina* and
its relation to Milton's major poems indicate the magnitude of this
Spenserian lacuna, for relatively few studies of *The Faerie Queene*
mention the *Hymnes*, and fewer still explore their possibilities of
interpretive comparison.[3] Yet the *Hymnes* could help clarify Spenser's
faery allegorism by indicating potential philosophical and theological
subjects and illuminating doctrinal resonances of his diction, tropes,
and imagery. They have particular value for study of Spenser's conceptions of love and beauty, Platonism, and poetic theology.

The chief deterrent to such investigation has been Robert Ellrodt's
Neoplatonism in the Poetry of Spenser, for its general argument dissociates Spenser's *Hymnes* from *The Faerie Queene* to advance an interdependent enterprise of "belittling . . . Platonic influence" on all
Spenser's poetry published before his hymnic tetralogy.[4] I am not
concerned here with Ellrodt's account of the former relations between Christianity and Platonism, nor with his categories for assessing them, nor with his reading of the hymns themselves—all of
which others have contested.[5] Nor do I address his recent essay involving Spenser's Platonism (2005), for it does not change his book's
positions at issue here.[6]

Whereas Spenser attributes the first two hymns to "the greener
times of my youth" in his dedicatory epistle,[7] Ellrodt's *Neoplatonism*
claims the poet wrote all four "in their present shape . . . some time
after the publication of *Colin Clout* in 1595, and, in all likelihood,
after *The Faerie Queene* I–VI had been entered in the Stationer's
Register in 1596": hence after 20 January that year.[8] "Spenser's most
distinctly Platonic poems," as Ellrodt considers the *Hymnes*, thus all
"belong to the later years of his life" (23). Though conceding that
the initial pair evince direct knowledge of learned Renaissance Platonists such as Marsilio Ficino (e.g., 23, 118), Ellrodt assumes that is a
new acquisition for Spenser, largely gained *after* completing his heroic
poem's second installment.[9] Until then, in that critic's view, the poet's notions of Platonism were basically medieval, with vague infu-
sions of Renaissance Platonic esthetics derived from such so-called

popularizers as Castiglione, Pietro Bembo, Louis Le Roy, and Pierre de la Primaudaye.[10] This theory requires Spenser to have shunned almost all Plato's dialogues, because nearly any direct knowledge of them beyond the first third of the *Timaeus* counts as learned Renaissance Platonism.[11] Accordingly, Ellrodt doubts "whether [Spenser] had *any* first hand acquaintance" with them, even in Latin translation (115; my emphasis).[12] From his standpoint, the *Hymnes'* interpretive relevance to Spenser's previously published poems can only be dubious at best, and so is that of virtually all Plato's dialogues, all ancient Neoplatonic texts, and all their learned Renaissance elaborations. Yet by the early sixteenth century Plato's writings, for example, had become readily accessible to anyone who, like Spenser, knew Latin.

In subsequent studies of Spenser's poems published before the *Hymnes*, especially *The Faerie Queene*, many Spenserians have nonetheless credited the poet with much more Platonic learning than Ellrodt allows him at that time.[13] Although their reservations about Ellrodt's general argument have remained largely implicit, they nonetheless challenge it by citing primary texts that he would discount or avoid for Spenser prior to 1595/96 (e.g., Ellrodt 90). Those include most of Plato's own dialogues except for the *Timaeus* (see notes 11, 12), and all of Plotinus, Ficino, and Pico della Mirandola, among others.[14] Yet since Ellrodt's book is still influential, both the present volume's topic and the forum's occasion this reassessment.

Though published in 1960, *Neoplatonism*'s original manuscript dates from 1949, and when Ellrodt came to "recast" it for publication in 1958, he did not modify "any" of his former conclusions (5). Certainly the book retains value, but we must reevaluate its evidence, arguments, and methodology in light of later scholarship. For example, Ellrodt assumes *The Faerie Queene* has only "three pieces of cosmological allegory" that could potentially involve "Neoplatonic influences": the Garden of Adonis, the Temple of Venus, and the *Mutabilitie Cantos* (61–63). But we must now at least add the Triamond narrative, the Graces episode, and the idealizing proems.[15] He further assumes that recoverable authorial intention governs the poet's writings, and claims to have reconstituted "Spenser's own mind" to "find out the true perspective."[16] "Pre-eminently conservative," "traditional," and "mainly medieval,"[17] Ellrodt's Spenserian mind maintains Christian orthodoxy, for which Platonism amounts to atmospheric decoration (e.g., 34, 58, 97, 211–16). Although the *Letter to Ralegh* insists *The Faerie Queene* is a "continued Allegory, or darke conceit,"[18] Ellrodt believes that this poet's "meaning" is "plain" (6). Any hidden meanings must be political and not metaphysical, he supposes, for Spenser would not "conceal *the true meaning* of a poem unless it were for political safety" (59; my emphasis).[19] Whereas Spenser, "as he is most commonly celebrated by contemporary criticism, has a voracious, synthesizing intelligence," Ellrodt assumes that he is Donne's intellectual inferior (18), and whereas John Milton called Spenser "sage and serious" sincerely, Ellrodt does so sarcastically (127).[20] These assumptions, procedures, and the general argument affect the local readings.

The general argument of Ellrodt's *Neoplatonism* rests on two fundamental assumptions: (1) the learned Renaissance Platonic content of the first two hymns postdates the 1596 *Faerie Queene*; (2) the poet "badly blundered" in that poem's references to Plato's dialogues (227; cf. 96–97). We must grant *both* claims in order to accept his broad conjecture that Spenser's Renaissance Platonic learning developed very late, after completing *The Faerie Queene*'s first six books (23–24, 118–19). The second one is Ellrodt's "evidence" that the poet lacked "first hand" acquaintance "with the Platonic philosophy" when composing *The Faerie Queene* (96–97; see my note 12).

Since Ellrodt concedes that the first two hymns evince substantial Platonic erudition characteristic of the Renaissance, particularly Ficinian learning, an astute reviewer remarked that, if their Platonic content significantly predates 1596, *Neoplatonism*'s general argument "falls like a house of cards."[21] That would result either if the first two hymns were written early as Spenser says, or if they have substantial content derived from earlier versions or writings. As another reviewer, C. S. Lewis, perceived, the poet's whole relationship to Platonism would thus change.[22] Anticipating such critiques, Ellrodt claims that Spenser would thus have turned against learned Platonism after a short-lived early enthusiasm (23). But that would affect *Neoplatonism*'s fundamental model of the poet's mind and intentions, and its governing assumptions about the Platonic interpretive potential of *The Faerie Queene* in relation to those hymns and otherwise. Spenser's "continued Allegory" of Faery expresses ideas through complex symbolic imagery (*Letter to Ralegh*, 714), and we should allow for current conceptions of poetic intertextuality, intentionality, counternarratives, and so forth.

There are two basic alternatives for dating the first pair of Spenser's *Hymnes*. Either he wrote them or their correlative hymnic precursors well before 1596, and his dedication's comment on that is broadly true; or they originated much closer to that date, and his dedication is deliberately misleading. No extant evidence in this case approaches the dedication's specificity. Though any argument for redating must rest on the stylistic similarity of all four, stylometric comparative dating still lacks validity, and especially when the texts are short like these.[23] Comparison with Spenser's prior poetry is problematic because their unique genre—the Renaissance classicizing hymn—strongly conditioned their style (hence, for example, the absence of archaisms, deemed apt for pastoral and epic due to Theocritan and Homeric precedents).[24] In any case, stylistic similarity cannot clarify the first pair's *date of origin* nor that of their content because, if Spenser had written those two earlier, as he says, he would reasonably have revised them somewhat, particularly in style, when he wrote the second pair, in order to produce the tetralogy for publication.[25] Ellrodt's claims for the late development of Spenser's Renaissance Platonic learning have a speculative basis disproportionate to their major interpretive consequences for the poet's canon.

Those claims also require relatively drastic redating of the first two hymns. For other proponents of redating, the extent to which the published texts subsume earlier Spenserian material has far less significance; for their purposes, it need just be substantially redeveloped at their chosen time in the 1590s, mainly in style.[26] But since Ellrodt harnesses redating those hymns to minimizing Spenser's learned Platonic content in prior publications, including the whole *Faerie Queene*, he has to maintain the hymns' chronological separation from the latter, *both* in their substantial composition *and* in their Renaissance Platonic learning. Though Ellrodt often writes as if, for his purposes, the initial hymns need merely have been based on some earlier material and *rewritten* late (e.g., 114, 211), the extent to which they subsume prior Spenserian thought and writing has *crucial* importance for his general argument. And if the first pair were substantially rewritten for publication around the mid 1590s, according to the dedication they had quite comparable precursors. It says the poet "composed" the "former two Hymnes in the praise of Loue and beautie" in his "youth" (452). Those ur-hymns, even if revised later, would thus still have been (1) formally "two Hymnes" of the same classicized Renaissance type, likewise focusing on Eros and Venus; (2) praises "of Loue and beautie"; and (3) treatments of those subjects probably involving much Platonism, as was common in the sixteenth century, since Platonic content is fundamental to the published versions.[27]

There are reasonable grounds to conclude that Spenser partly devised the dedication to reduce this book's potential to cause public controversy, and that the reservations the poet voices there about the first two hymns' amorous content are in that way somewhat disingenuous.[28] But no evidence invalidates the dedication's account of the first two hymns' origins and prior reception, and so the further we depart from it on those points the more we start freewheeling.

To date, advocates of redating those hymns have overlooked that volume's feature central for assessing the credibility of the poet's claimed chronology: the dedication is worded in such a way that, in effect, not just Spenser but one of the exalted dedicatees also attests to the first pair's earlier origin, manuscript circulation, and reception history. The poet's account entails many eyewitnesses: "many copies thereof were formerly scattered abroad" (690). And they include at least one of Spenser's two dedicatees: the sibling countesses of War-wick and Cumberland, Anne Dudley (1548/9–1604) and Margaret Clifford (1560–1616), both daughters of Francis Russell, the second earl of Bedford. Spenser declares, "I was moved [i.e., asked] by the one of you two most excellent Ladies, to call in the same" (i.e., his hymns to love and beauty circulating in manuscript). But since the dissemination of the poems precluded that, he adds, he has instead conjoined two more hymns, on heavenly love and beauty, "by way of retractation to reforme them." He dedicates all four "joyntly" to the two countesses, requesting their "patronage" for the whole cycle (690).

These were extraordinarily well-connected women of substance, and it was Margaret, "an exceedingly pious lady, a zealous puritan," who most likely intervened.[29] In *Colin Clouts Come Home Againe* (1595), Spenser says of Anne, stepsister to Lord Grey's wife,

> great *Cynthia* [i.e., the queen] her *in chiefest grace*
> Doth hold, and *next vnto her selfe aduance*,
> Well worthie of so honorable place
> For her great worth and noble governance.

Turning to Margaret, he declares "Ne less praise worthie is her sister deare" (lines 500–504, my emphasis). Their brother Sir William Rus-sell (c.1553–1613), whom Spenser likely knew, was lord deputy of Ireland from 1594 until the year after the *Hymnes* were published.

As the dedication circulated publicly in the book, so the poet had to be sure that his desired patrons would find whatever he said there unexceptionable. If he invented anything about their own involve-ment in his project, it had to have their prior approval and assurance of continuing support. Unless we assume a conspiracy between the poet and one or more countesses to launch a public hoax, versions of the "former two Hymnes in the praise of Loue and beautie" (452), whether composed in youth or not, must have been circulating in manuscript well in advance of their publication (at least by the early 1590s), and provoked one of these countesses to intervene.

Comparison to the *Letter to Ralegh* further clarifies this case. That former epistle says "many other aduentures are intermedled, but rather as Accidents, then intendments" (718). Spenser's ensuing list of such adventures includes definitely allegorical episodes, and so we have clear evidence of that statement's disingenuousness: presumably a device to deflect responsibility for unwelcome interpretations. But he avoids directly implicating anyone else in this self-exculpatory invention: it remains simply *personal.*

To massage public reception of the *Hymnes* in 1596, Spenser would not likely depart from that astutely discreet procedure of 1590. If, as Ellrodt assumes, the first two hymns substantially originated around 1596, and the poet wanted to backdate them in the dedication (23–24, 118–20), he could just have said this:

> Having in the greener times of my youth, composed these former two Hymnes in the praise of Love and Beautie, and finding that the same too much pleased those of like age and disposition, which being too vehemently caried with that kind of affection, do rather sucke out poyson to their strong passion, then hony to their honest delight, I resolved to amend, and by way of retractation to reforme them, making in stead of those two Hymnes of earthly or naturall love and beautie, two others of heauenly and celestiall. The which I do dedicate joyntly unto you two honorable sisters.

Spenser's comments on previous manuscript circulation and especially the countess's intervention, which I have deleted, make the alleged hoax more vulnerable to contradiction and difficult to execute. Since that material requires at least one countess to participate in the hypothetical deception, Spenser would have needed her prior permission and become hostage to her continuing discretion. Probably the approval of both would have been needful, for they were joint dedicatees, siblings, and both implicated here by serving as patrons. Would one have consented to endorse a hoax involving both, if the other were not to be advised? Confronted with the dedication, the other could ask questions about the texts' prior circulation and her sister's intervention.

Then there is the matter of the "many" dispersed manuscripts. Questions could be asked in Elizabethan literary circles, and manuscripts sought. Although no manuscript copies of the hymns independent from their published text are currently known,[30] we have lost vast quantities of such ephemera. Only a few fragments of Ralegh's *Cynthia* survive, and none of Gabriel Harvey's Latin epic *Anticosmopolita*.[31] Attrition would have been greatest for manuscripts whose content had entered print. Although Sir Philip Sidney's *Defence of Poetry* was not published until 1595, Sir John Harington's "Apologie of Poetrie" published in 1591 assumes his readers can consult it, and yet only two sixteenth-century manuscripts of Sidney's text are now known to exist.[32] Extracts of the 1590 *Faerie Queene* circulated before publication, yet none of those survive, despite that poem's and Spenser's literary celebrity; none of his published poems nor any portion thereof survives in autograph manuscript.[33] We have even lost many poems Spenser reportedly wrote but never published. Though the extant Elizabethan comments on them mention no hymns on love and beauty prior to the *Hymnes'* publication, the two ur-hymns could have been overlooked due to their brevity or controversial content, for example, and those writers say Spenser's unpublished works include diverse other poems beyond those they name.[34]

Since the dedication of the *Hymnes* states that the first two originated early, and adduces a countess who had intervened in their manuscript circulation, the burden of proof is on anyone who would reassign their origin or that of their main substance to the mid 1590s. In Ellrodt's view, his own inability to find learned Renaissance Platonism in *The Faerie Queene* confirms his very late dating of the first two hymns, since they do contain such content (23). But to accept this argument we have to assume that he fully apprehended the Platonic capacities of Spenser's 36,000-line allegory in 1949/58, and overlook some procedural circularity.[35] He also adduces stylistic data comparing enjambment ratios (219–23). Yet even if we were to agree that the style of all four hymns is thus correlative, and indicates much development in that form around the same date, that cannot show that the first two *originated* at that time, nor that their *content* or *Platonic learning and attitudes* did so. Yet those are the points at issue for his general argument. Further tabulating the correspondences between each hymn and each book of *The Faerie Queene*, he perceives 24 parallels between the first pair and the romantic epic, yet only 9 between it and the second pair (217–18). Moreover, 19 of the 24 pertain to the 1590 installment, and only 5 to its 1596 successor, while "the largest number of parallels to the first two hymns—and the clearest ones—occur in Books II and III" (19). These findings counter his conjecture that all the hymns originated, in their present form and substance, around 1596 (23–24). If the first pair or their precursors were composed much earlier than the last pair, the former would have the most correspondences with *The Faerie Queene*, and most of all with the 1590 text, because its time of composition, and hence the poet's concerns, would be closest to that primary hymnic material. Finally, as Phillip Rollinson observes, the first and second pairs follow disparate hymnic models: the first Michele Marullo's pseudo-pagan type, and the second Marco Girolamo Vida and Giulio Cesare Scaligero's Christian type. Hence "it is unlikely that both pairs . . . were composed at the same time in Spenser's poetic development."[36]

We may now assess *Neoplatonism*'s second foundational assumption: Spenser "badly blundered" when referring to Plato in both installments of *The Faerie Queene*, and so we should "doubt . . . any first hand" knowledge of the dialogues, even in Latin (227, 115). Here Ellrodt depends on A. E. Taylor's short note of 1924.[37] However, the poet's interests in Platonic thought about poetics, love, and beauty clearly date from at least the October eclogue in *The Shepheardes Calender* (1579), and polylingual Spenser pursued learning avidly. Along with Aristotle, Plato was one of the major authorities of Renaissance humanist thought, whom it thus behooved a poet with learned aspirations to know, and the *Letter to Ralegh* pointedly names both. Whereas I know of no clear references to Aristotle himself within Spenser's poetry, I find four to Plato or his mentor and dialogic protagonist Socrates (II.vii.52, ix.48; IV.pr.3; *HHB*, line 83). Those contexts of *The Faerie Queene*, a poem which rarely drops names, are all strategic: the *Letter*; the meditation on mortality in Mammon's cave; the representation of the mind itself at Alma's turret; the first proem for the 1596 installment. The Platonic dialogues and their representation of Socrates were not insignificant to Spenser.

Readers need only think the poet blundered if they accept Taylor and Ellrodt's interpretation of two passages referring to Critias, which can readily be interpreted otherwise. When Spenser refers to Socrates in Mammon's cave and the proem for Book IV, we encounter a name—"Critias"—other than what we might expect, for Critias's role in the Platonic dialogues is not obviously relevant to those contexts. Whereas Ellrodt's general argument needs Spenser's "Critias" references to be "grievous blunders" (96), the name has complex allusive potential. Plato's *Critias*, *Timaeus*, *Charmides*, *Protagoras*, and Seventh Letter as well as the pseudonymous *Eryxias* all involve persons so named (the Letter tacitly). Moreover, *allegoria*, which could be extensive or encompass only a few lines, was a standard rhetorical device,[38] and Spenser is an allegorical fantasist who thinks in tropes, lively images, and interpretive puzzles often involving allusive onomastic wordplay. Yet in print, allegorical consideration of the two Socrates/Critias passages dates only from Michael F. N. Dixon's notice of the second one's astute Platonism in 1996.[39] I offer a different reading.

In Mammon's underworld, we enter Proserpina's "black" garden, "Fit to adorne the dead and deck the drery tombe," including "*Cicuta* bad," or hemlock:

> With which th'vniust *Atheniens* made to dy
> Wise *Socrates*, who thereof quaffing glad
> Pourd out his life, and last Philosophy
> To the fayre *Critias* his dearest Belamy.

> The *Gardin of Proserpina* this hight.

(II.vii.51–53)

The garden itself exfoliates "Proserpina" as *prosero poena*, "I sow pain." Whereas the general context evokes horror of mortality, Socrates appears the "Wise" exemplar who, at the hour of his death, was "glad" to die, because he serenely anticipated a better afterlife and even, according to Plato's *Phaedo*, elaborated his theory of the soul's immortality. Thus he poured out his life and "last Philosophy" (or "love of knowledge") in assessing last things. Whereas Crito was a main attendant in Plato's account, here the allegorist substitutes "fayre *Critias* his dearest Belamy." What Socrates held most dear was the life of the mind, or the dialectical pursuit of truth, and Critias allusively evokes the Greek κριτικός, which refers to capacities of judgment or discernment.[40] For Socrates, those functions characterize the best part of the soul, and it is that part which he seeks most to embrace (*Republic*,10.602d–3b, 4.439d–44e). Contextually alluding to Platonic dialogues at least including the *Apology* and *Phaedo*, Spenser adduces Socrates partly as an example for Christians fearful of death. Even by cultivating natural reason, this pagan met death hopefully; Socrates himself is not in Proserpina's underworld, only the hemlock.

No Spenserian context has more strategic importance than that of the poet's second Socrates/Critias passage, for here he both introduces *The Faerie Queene*'s second installment and rebukes detractors to advocate the poem's representations of love and exalt his poetic. He chooses to do so specifically according to the Socratic model.

Works of "wise sages" and great heroes' "braue exploits" were all "either ended or begunne" in love:

> Witnesse the father of Philosophie,
> Which to his *Critias*, shaded oft from sunne,
> Of loue full manie lessons did apply,
> The which these Stoicke censours cannot well deny.

The poet further avows that his text gives the queen his own such "lesson" (IV.pr.3, 5). Taylor and Ellrodt assume that Spenser refers specifically to the *Phaedrus* here, but bungled by naming Critias, for Socrates had that conversation with Phaedrus under a plane tree. So at the outset of the *Faerie Queene*'s second three books, when Spenser sought to justify his art before the realm and his queen, and for posterity, he ineptly faked familiarity with Platonic dialogues that he had never read to adduce a Socratic role model about which he was ignorant.[41] "Was the 'poet's poet,'" Taylor asks, "a bit of a humbug?" (210).

Spenser's *Teares of the Muses* (1591) condemns unlearned poetry, and while the *Phaedrus* is allusively in play here, the stanza broadly addresses Socratic-Platonic love doctrine, and hence also the various other dialogues commenting on love, especially the *Symposium* and *Cratylus* (via the hero/eros allusion, lines 3–5; *Cratylus* 398cd).[42] There is no evidence that the particular line about Critias *must specifically* refer to the *Phaedrus* and that dialogue *alone*, hence none to warrant claims that by "Critias" Spenser really meant "Phaedrus." Reporting a conversation *on one occasion*, like Plato's other dialogues, that dialogue is *one* lesson; but Spenser writes of "full manie" here, that are also shaded "oft," and so he posits an *ongoing* Socratic pedagogy of love. To denominate a participant in continuing Socratic discourses, "Critias" was a knowledgeable Spenserian choice, for that was the name of one of Socrates' long-term philosophical associates (e.g., *Charmides*, 156a, 161c). Moreover, "shaded oft from sun" does not necessarily refer to the *Phaedrus* or any tree or trees, for shade has diverse possible sources. And could shade and sun be figurative here? In the *Republic*, the sun famously figures the light of true knowledge, broadly speaking, while shadow and darkness signify its privation (6.508a–7.518e). Spenser himself had already used such Platonic symbolism often in *The Faerie Queene*, mixed with complementary Christian conventions.[43] Critias may typify those whom Socrates instructed, or the name involves wordplay as in Book II. Hence Philosophy's father would afford many lessons on love to minds and rational judgment, both his own and others, though "shaded oft from sun," or the full light of truth. His intermittent intellectual light should presumably be brightened by the Son (formerly standard wordplay), whom the following stanza's Christian diction evokes ("sacred Saint," "Prince of peace from heauen"). Among the Platonic dialogues not only the *Republic* and those treating love or including Critias are intertextually involved, but also the *Apology*, for in the latter that social critic Socrates was accused, just like the poet here, of corrupting "fraile youth" (IV.pr.1; 23c–28b). As Plato's Critias tells of the gods' punishment of a great island realm due to its residents' bad behavior (*Critias*, 121bc), so the 1596 *Faerie Queene*'s introductory proem may well anticipate the forthcoming books' social satire and apocalypticism aimed finally at the poet's detractors (VI.xii.38–41).[44]

To this resourceful passage Spenser appends a stinger: "The which these Stoicke censours cannot well deny." By thus expropriating his detractors' assent, the poet challenges them to determine what he is saying. To do so they have to know at least the Platonic dialogues involving Critias as well as those on love, and ponder allegory's possibilities of producing imaginative truth through fictional invention. Assuming that is beyond them, and for other reasons too, he then remarks, "To such therefore I do not sing at all" (IV.pr.4.1). The poem is not for them, he declares, and he has come to speak over their heads. Such learned literary elitism was typical of the time, and heroic poetry was to be particularly enigmatic.[45]

Here and throughout, Ellrodt sets the bar for evidence of Spenser's knowledge of Plato far higher than he does for Aristotle and Calvin. Although Aristotle and Plato could formerly be conflated to varying extents, *Neoplatonism* promotes Aristotelian interpretation of *The Faerie Queene* (52–58), but overlooks the apparent difficulties in the poet's references to Plato's student. The most obvious are the *Letter*'s attribution of "twelue priuate morall vertues," or "the image of a braue knight" who is "perfected' in them, to "Aristotle"; and its designation of "magnificence" as the other virtues' "perfection," "according to Aristotle" (716). To make sense, these much–debated remarks require historicized interpretive explanation.[46] So do the Critias references, and yet Ellrodt denies them that attention, even though they appear *within* an inventive allegorical poem, not a prosaic letter. He could use the same procedure to minimize Spenser's Aristotelianism just like the poet's Platonism. This inconsistency repeats in Calvin's case, for without discussing evidence, Ellrodt assumes "Spenser certainly knew the *Institutes*" (180). But the poet never mentions Calvin, nor any of his writings, but repeatedly does so for

Plato or Socrates as we have seen. Ellrodt derives another procedure
for minimizing Spenser's Platonic knowledge from Taylor's note of
1924: we should discount the poet's specific reference to the *Republic*,
for example, because he *could* have known of that text from reading
Cicero (53–54). Likewise the *Calender*'s references to poetic furor,
Ellrodt argues, *could* have come from Minturno's *De poeta* rather than
the *Ion* or *Phaedrus* (31). Yet the latter texts are both relatively short,
and were available in the same language. Both Calvin and Aristotle
had been amply recycled too, and so Ellrodt makes assumptions in
their cases that he declines in Plato's.

The relative roles of the *Hymnes*' dedication and the *Letter to Ralegh*
in *Neoplatonism* are also revealing. Since the *Letter* "does not disclose
any metaphysical intention" in Ellrodt's view, for him it shows that
Spenser's faery allegorism excludes learned Platonic metaphysics (59;
cf. 61). We are told that while the *Hymnes*' dedicatory epistle *should
not* be taken at face value, the *Letter to Ralegh should* be (59–60).
Hence, this critic concludes, "a Neoplatonic interpretation of *The
Faerie Queene* has not 'the authors' [sic] consent" (60).[47] Like Lewis
in his review, we should query Ellrodt's notions of authorial intentionality and recall that the *Letter* is quite cagey, sometimes contradicts the poem, and describes *The Faerie Queene* as a "darke conceit,"
"clowdily enwrapped in Allegorical deuises" (714–16).[48] Although
Ellrodt insists that " 'the continued Allegorye . . . ' of the story itself
is purely ethical, historical or political" (59), Spenser situates those
concerns metaphysically (i.e., in relation to the nature of being) insofar as his poem is *also* theological, philosophical, and cosmological.
Moreover, the *Letter* announces a "generall intention" of "glory"
that could readily involve Christian Platonism, and hence also some
version of its diverse metaphysics (716).[49] Ellrodt concedes that
"metaphysical overtones . . . are not wanting in the epic," and that
"overtones in the poem itself suggest that the object of Arthur's quest
is more than the fame 'that grows on mortal soil' (to echo *Lycidas*)"
(52, 58).

Although the few authorities named in Spenser's *Letter* include
Plato, Ellrodt says the poet is thus "far from claiming the patronage
of Plato," and instead "admits he 'laboured' to satisfy the 'commune
sense' of those by whom 'is Xenophon preferred before Plato' " (59).
Both had been students of Socrates. Spenser praises "the exquisite
depth" of Plato's "iudgement," not Xenophon's, and declares his
poem follows the latter's *method* of "doctrine by ensample," rather
than by "rule" (716). That is not a depreciation of Plato's doctrines
themselves, and if it were it would apply equally to all philosophers,
including Aristotle. Moreover, the tone is regretful and somewhat

satiric. The preceding sentence mocks "the vse of these dayes, seeing all things accounted by their showes, and nothing esteemed of, that is not delightful and pleasing to commune sence. *For this reason* is Xenophon preferred before Plato . . . " (716; my emphasis). By using the passive voice, Spenser avoids endorsing that preference, and he deplores the social conditions responsible. In effect, he avows that, given his society's unfortunate state, he can best intervene for its benefit in a way accommodating its manifest lack of discernment. This context at once apologizes for his poem, asserts its social value, and insists that he himself possesses a higher vision than his community, which his poem seeks to mediate. Plato's "Commune welth" or *Republic* that Spenser adduces here complements that vision, for it condemns predominant social esteem for mere shows and things "pleasing to commune sence" (e.g., 7.514a–21c, 9.585b–87b).[50] As we have seen, Spenser proceeds to invoke Socrates directly within the poem itself, even aligning his own role with the latter's when introducing the second installment (IV.pr.1–5).

What would account for the programmatic underestimation of Spenser's Renaissance Platonic learning in Ellrodt's *Neoplatonism*? Its author has since denied suggestions of bias toward ensuring the poet's Christian orthodoxy.[51] In any case, some early modern literary contexts vital for his inquiry were relatively inaccessible in 1949/58. Ellrodt accepts that the *Calender* and *Faerie Queene* clearly involve Renaissance "esthetic Platonism" as he calls it: Platonizing doctrines of love, beauty, and poetry (9). However, in comparison to the content of the first two hymns, the expression of those ideas in Spenser's eclogues and romantic epic seems so vague or "nontechnical" in Ellrodt's view that he assumes the poet must have acquired such expertise (as opposed to looser popularized notions) very late. That assumption drives Ellrodt's interpretation of everything, including the dating of the first pair of hymns (e.g., 37–39, 99, 118–19, 211). But as Valery Rees argues in this volume, we should take into account former literary norms for assimilation of influences.[52] Already in Spenser's *Calender*, as E. K. indicates in his introductory Epistle, anyone who would "trace" its intertexts must be "well sented" indeed (29). To assess how this poet's expressions of ideas modulate from poem to poem, we must further consider his allegorism, his relation to early modern generic norms and poetics, and his early reception.

Though allegory is formalized in Spenser's *Faerie Queene*, Ellrodt assumes that only its *literal* references to Platonism can show Platonic expertise.[53] Yet in reviewing *Neoplatonism*, Lewis warns that, since the poet's faery allegory is richly polysemous, "to show that many passages do not . . . demand a Neoplatonic interpretation is not the same as showing that they do not admit it," nor does it establish that they "never suggested this to Spenser."[54] Moreover, by overemphasizing the literal aspect of Spenser's poems in his evaluation of their Platonic content, Ellrodt ends up treating them as if they are prosaic expository treatises (the poet's "meaning" is "plain," 5). If we were thus to evaluate the poet's knowledge of theology, ethics, and politics, we would be left with little beyond the introductory stanzas of cantos and find him naive on those subjects too; but we know much more goes on in that poem than is literally said there. A literalist approach is doubly inappropriate in the case of Platonism, whose progenitor, like his Renaissance inheritors, used much fabulation and symbolic imagery to express ideas. An adequate methodology for assessing Spenser's poetic treatments of philosophy and theology in *The Faerie Queene* must seriously reckon with the figurative dimension of its diction and imagery.

Sixteenth-century generic norms further clarify Spenser's diverse strategies of Platonic reference. The *Hymnes'* unique style and poetic diction accord with those for learned classicizing hymns, and that Renaissance genre had particular affinities with philosophical discourse and terminology.[55] But though Ellrodt makes much of the contrary vagueness of the October eclogue's Platonism (31–33, 39), pastoral decorum precluded attribution of learned acuity to shepherds. Spenser's intellectual resources in 1579 comprised more than what he thought apt for shepherds to say explicitly in eclogues: a medium of artful, faux-naïf obliquities where more is meant than meets the ear.

Though heroic poetry was to be encyclopedic and deeply learned, even it was to epitomize that knowledge in its lively images, as Sidney indicates.[56] Often considered a heroic poem in the sixteenth century, Dante's *Commedia* was attacked for including too much technical language, rather than following the subtler practices of Homer's presumed allegorism.[57] Spenser wrote *The Faerie Queene* in accord with that view. He eschews the technical terminology of the learned disciplines, and instead appropriates their repertoires of metaphors and figurative topoi to express their insights allegorically, such as the sun/shade topos of the *Republic*, already mentioned.[58] (Of course his usages should be assessed according to context, just as shade had various possible early modern symbolic and other connotations.) Hence the relative absence of obvious Platonic diction and philosophizing in Spenser's bucolic and heroic poems, compared with his *Fowre Hymnes*, does not in itself show that his knowledge of learned Renaissance Platonism postdated those former texts. The matter should be considered much more broadly, according to various relevant factors.

Since no one has depreciated Spenser's knowledge of Protestantism, a theological example is helpful. Concupiscence was a basic concept in Protestant definition of the effects of the Fall. Those are central to Book I and underlie much subsequent representation of the virtues and vices. But nowhere in this 36,000-line poem does Spenser use the word "concupiscence." Applying Ellrodt's methods, we would conclude Spenser was ignorant of basic Protestant theology at that time. Though Spenserians widely accept that the whole Ruddymane episode allegorizes the relation of concupiscence to Temperance,[59] they are wrong, then, for the word never appears there, and so the episode's vagueness or imprecision in expressing ideas establishes Spenser's naiveté about such matters. We could proceed through the whole poem likewise, on any subject. But rather than using such obviously technical terms, Spenser devises imagistic correlates for conceptual material in *The Faerie Queene*, and that produces much of the poem's wit, power, and wonder.

Just as Plato's authority in early modern culture encompassed poetics, assessment of Spenser's Platonic learning and affinities further requires evaluation of his responses to Plato's esthetics and their Neoplatonic developments. Ellrodt only allows for the doctrine of poetic furor (9, 31–32, 106). In order to deny the relevance of Platonic interpretation to the contrast between Florimell and False Florimell, he asserts that it does *not* relate to that between "ideal and phenomenal beauty" (a Platonic distinction), but instead opposes "Nature and false art" (47). Yet, building on the *Republic* and *Sophist*, Platonism had much to say about art's potential falsities and relations with nature.[60] As Sidney's *Defence* summarily shows, Platonizing art theory in the Renaissance had far more resources than furor, and that short treatise refers to the *Apology, Ion, Phaedrus, Republic, Phaedo, Sophist,* and *Symposium*, among others.[61] In Spenser's case, his many favorable references to poetic furor, dating from the *Calender* onward, demonstrate his continuing interest in Platonic literary perspectives. He cites the *Republic* in his *Letter to Ralegh*; and the *Ion, Phaedrus,* and *Sophist*—Plato's other dialogues central for early Renaissance poetics—are accessibly brief. Various eminent literary theorists further cited ancient Neoplatonists such as Maximus of Tyre, Proclus, Porphyry, and Plotinus, both to canvass the range of relevant authorities, and to advocate Platonizing practices of ideal and icastic imitation that, if followed by poets, exempt their work from Plato's criticisms in the *Republic*. The humanist milieu would have encouraged a somewhat enterprising enthusiast of poetry and poetics to pursue such citations of ancient Neoplatonic authorities, and he could do so in Latin if not in Greek.

To clarify the Platonic capacities of Spenser's scholarship, we may turn to early modern literary precedents, Spenser's biography, and his early reception.[62] We know the Pléiade was a major early Spenserian influence, and those poets highly valorized learning. Torquato Tasso was one of Spenser's chief models, and his voluminous prose, some of which the English poet probably read, reveals the breadth of Tasso's reading. If interpreted at face value, his *Gerusalemme liberata* could lead some to conclude he was not much interested in philosophy—quite as Ellrodt estimates ancient and Renaissance Platonism in *The Faerie Queene*. But Tasso's prose confirms his extensive reading of philosophers, including Platonists from their master through Proclus and Plotinus to Ficino and Jacopo Mazzoni.[63] There is no reason to think that Spenser was any less intellectually energetic than Tasso, and *The Faerie Queene* evinces much more interest in philosophizing than Tasso's romantic epics.

Spenser entered Pembroke College at Cambridge as an impecunious young sizar or servant-student in 1569, and "among the entertainments for Queen Elizabeth at Cambridge in 1564" had been "a 'war' between Aristotle and Plato."[64] A long-term friendship somehow developed with the older Gabriel Harvey, who became a fellow of Pembroke (1570), Greek lecturer (1573), and University Praelector of Rhetoric (1574). Spenser's languages included Latin, Italian, French, and, as his friend Lodowick Bryskett attests and the Harvey connection indicates, Greek. In an epistle to "the Gentlemen of both Universities" (1589), Thomas Nashe maintains that, "should the challenge of deepe conceit, be intruded by any forreiner, to bring our english wits, to the tutchstone of Arte, I would preferre, diuine *Master Spenser*, the miracle of wit to bandie line for line for my life, in the honor of *England*, against *Spaine*, *France*, *Italie*, and all the world." For Nashe in 1596, Spenser remains "the *sum' tot* of whatsoever can be said of sharpe inuention and schollership." Many others called this poet "learned," including Harvey, who collected and annotated an extraordinarily large multilingual library.[65] Harvey's extant marginalia, the bulk of which has been lost, cite Ficino's *Letters* once and Plato quite often.[66] Sir Walter Ralegh's library included various works of Platonic and occult philosophy, such as a two-volume Ficino.[67] Bryskett found Spenser "very well read in Philosophie"; likewise Sir Kenelm Digby, "especially the PLATONIKE"—even "a constant disciple of *Platoes* School."[68] Like formidably erudite Milton, who considered Spenser his "original,"[69] the creator of *The Faerie Queene* aspired to compose a heroic poem that could stand comparison to all its illustrious precursors, and such a text was profoundly to epitomize its culture through encyclopedic learning. Even aside from considerations of genre, in Spenser's literary milieu poets to be taken seriously were not just "superficial humanists," as Harvey observes, but "exquisite artists, & curious vniuersal schollers."[70]

Assessments of Spenser's Platonic interests should allow for at least seven engines of impetus. Aside from infusing the poet's cult of love and beauty as Ellrodt acknowledges,[71] and offering diverse resources for literary thought, such as the poetic furor that Spenser found congenial, Platonism authorized his Socratic role of persecuted truth-teller (e.g., IV.pr.1–3). Fourth, Socrates had great prestige among humanists as a prototype of wisdom and Christ.[72] Fifth, Plato was central for early modern inquiries into human reason's potential to corroborate faith. Any pagan philosophical precedents for Christianity's chief doctrines, such as the soul's immortality, appeared to provide rational supports for religious belief. Elizabethan expressions of that syncretic vogue include *The Faerie Queene*'s recourse to Socrates in treating mortality (II.vii.51–57); the translation of "Plato's" *Axiochus* attributed to Spenser (1592); and that of Philippe de Mornay's *De la verité de la religion chrestienne* (1581), undertaken by Sidney and Arthur Golding (1587).[73] Sixth, in Spenser's time poetry by definition overlapped with philosophy, as this present volume's Introduction explains, and allegorical heroic poetry did so extensively. Seventh, from Platonism's ancient origins through its diverse Christian redevelopments from late antiquity onward, it offered abundant resources for exploring the nature of being (metaphysics). As Spenser's Garden of Adonis episode, his *Fowre Hymnes*, and his *Cantos of Mutabilitie* most obviously show, yet also many other passages such as his idealizing proems or his representation of the Graces upon Mount Acidale, reflection upon metaphysical mystery was central to his poetic.[74] Though the strength, development, and effects of these seven Spenserian motives are debatable, for him they would reasonably have impelled study of at least Plato's *Symposium*, *Phaedrus*, *Republic*, *Ion*, *Sophist*, *Apology*, *Phaedo*, and *Timaeus*, with learned forays into various ancient, medieval, and Renaissance Platonisms, including Platonizing treatises on poetics, beginning in the late 1570s if not earlier. Spenser was an eclectic writer with strong Platonic and Aristotelian interests, among others,[75] that bear different weights in different contexts. While somewhat synthesizing Platonism and Christianity he tends to privilege the latter, as my reading of Book IV's proem indicates, yet not without frictions between them.

Since the origins and learned Renaissance Platonic content of the first two hymns do not likely postdate *The Faerie Queene*, those poems can illuminate its treatments of love, beauty, Platonism, poetic theology, and the soul. Even Ellrodt says "the *Fowre Hymnes* . . . turn out

to be in essential agreement with the poet's other pronouncements
on love" (23). As the doctrinal contents of those hymns and their
usages of metaphoric and other terminologies are relatively explicit,
so they provide Spenserian means to investigate the devices of his
faery allegory, document potentially relevant concepts, and support
interpretive hypotheses. For instance, the conclusive canto of the
1596 *Faerie Queene* restores Book VI's heroine to Belgard, and the
second hymn's Platonic contextualization of "belgard," an apparent
Spenserism, may clarify that word's symbolic implications in the romantic epic (II.iii.25; III.ix.52, *in malo*; VI.xi.3: *HB*, line 256).[76] Carol
Kaske's "Neoplatonism in Spenser Once More" observes that the
first two hymns expound Neoplatonic preexistence of the soul, and
it seems integral to Spenser's representations of love in *The Faerie
Queene* (162–67). The heroic poem further evokes that concept, I
would add, through its speculative topos in which a woman appears
"As if some miracle of heauenly hew/Were downe . . . descended
in . . . earthly vew" (VI.ix.8).[77] Moreover, the development of the
ideas presented in the last two hymns would reasonably have overlapped somewhat with at least some later drafts of Books IV to VI.
Spenser's apparently major revision of Book V's conclusion even
while it was in press indicates that he was prone to rethinking his
text.[78] The thought of all four hymns overlaps to some extent with
that of *The Faerie Queene*.

In Book II, for example, an epic simile about unarmed "*Cupido*
on *Idaean* hill" (literally, Mount Ida) describes the angel who descends
to help unconscious Guyon (II.viii.6), and this image of divine love
and beauty may allusively associate them with the elevated Ideas. As
in Spenser's own *Amoretti*, "idea" was commonly also spelled "idaea"
("beholding th'Idaea playne,/Through contemplation of my purest
part," 87).[79] Hence, as Philemon Holland translates Plutarch in 1603,
"Socrates and Plato suppose, that these Ideae bee substances separate
and distinct from Matter, howbeit, subsisting in the thoughts and
imaginations of God."[80] In that sense, "Idaean" means "of or pertaining to the Ideas." Now the *Hymnes* involve various ascents to
apprehend ideals of love and beauty, and the last one situates the
"*Idees* on high" adjacent to the angels' domain amidst the highest
love and beauty (*HHB*, lines 78–112). Spenser's interconnection of
these topics there assists interpretation of this simile about Cupid,
and perhaps some other contexts involving Mount Ida, which this
poet makes a preferred resort of his allegorical gods (II.xii.52). Ficino's
De amore associates the realm of the Ideas with the pagan gods insofar
as they denominated general principles or powers (such as Venus or

Cupid as Love), and with God's angelic messengers.[81] Further contexts where Spenser evinces interest in the Ideas include *The Faerie Queene*'s proems, which synthesize two Platonizing theories: artistic idealized imitation; and the refinement of a mental ideal through amorous admiration.[82]

Like Milton, Spenser was convinced of his manifest literary destiny, and sought to manage his publications and their posterity from the *Calender* onward. It is significant that he published the *Fowre Hymnes* directly after the expanded *Faerie Queene* in the same year. He had issued the 1590 *Faerie Queene* with a partial commentary, the *Letter to Ralegh*, to guide reception. To what extent was the full hymnic cycle conceived and published to adjust the reception of his previous publications;[83] provide a skeleton key to some prior allegorism; or to promote certain kinds of reflection about it? His celebratory "maiden queen" imagery used from the February eclogue onward, including his *Epithalamion*, implicitly culminates in his vision of Sapience. The *Hymnes* present a series of exalted queens each reflecting her higher and more general counterparts: from the poet's own beloved as "great Goddesse" through the soul as "virgin Queene," Pleasure as "Goddesse . . . and Queene," and Venus as "great Goddesse, queene of Beauty"or "great Soueraine." Last and highest appears Sapience, the "soueraine dearling of the *Deity*," crowned and "Clad like a Queene," with "chastest bowre" and great "dowre."[84] Structuring the chain of being in such a reflective way is fundamentally Platonic. Clearly analogous to Spenser's queen of Faery, these hymnic figures culminating in Sapience recontextualize and reconfigure that former regal symbolism. Whether that amounts to an ex post facto redefinition or an indirect elaboration of some mostly tacit aspects of Gloriana's complex meaning, it is important for understanding Spenser's poetic development, yet has had little attention.[85] The poet's faery extrapolation of his sovereign ideal or "true glorious type" from Elizabeth involves a Platonizing contemplative ascent to "raise" his "thoughts" through the inspiring effects of her "faire beames" (I.pr.2).[86] Gloriana's definitions include "mirror of grace and majesty diuine" and "the Idole of her makers great magnificence": Spenser's Sapience in brief (I.pr.4; II.ii.41).[87] Does Gloriana's symbolism telescope some correlative metaphysical hierarchy, as the structure of the *Hymnes* suggests? Of one point we can be certain: the poet's complex notions and imagery of Sapience and her glory—biblical, patristic, medieval, humanist, kabbalist, and Platonic[88]—did not all suddenly spring upon him in 1596.

McGill University

NOTES

1. See Carol Kaske, "Amavia, Mordant, Ruddymane," in A. C. Hamilton et al., eds., *The Spenser Encyclopedia* (Toronto: University of Toronto Press, 1990), 25–27. Hereafter designated *SE*.

2. See Kenneth Borris, *Spenser's Poetics of Prophecy in "The Faerie Queene" V* (Victoria: University of Victoria Press, 1991).

3. Surveying fifteen Spenser monographs published no earlier than 1981 but otherwise chosen at random, I found that eleven had indexes with no entries for the *Hymnes*, one referred to one page, and only three to multiple pages. For comparative study of Spenser's *Hymnes*, *Faerie Queene*, and minor poetry, see, among others, Carol V. Kaske, "Neoplatonism in Spenser Once More," *Religion & Literature* 32 (2000): 157–69; Patrick Cheney, *Spenser's Famous Flight: A Renaissance Idea of a Literary Career* (Toronto: University of Toronto Press, 1993), ch. 5; William C. Johnson, "Spenser's 'Greener' *Hymnes* and *Amoretti*: 'Retractation' and 'Reform,' " *English Studies* 5 (1992): 431–43.

4. Ellrodt, *Neoplatonism in the Poetry of Spenser* (Geneva: Droz, 1960), 47. Hereafter also cited parenthetically in my text. All Ellrodt references without specification of title refer to this book.

5. William Nelson's review found Ellrodt "persists . . . in using a razor to divide the stew." *Renaissance News* 14 (1961): 277–79. See further Elizabeth Bieman, *Plato Baptized: Towards the Interpretation of Spenser's Mimetic Fictions* (Toronto: University of Toronto Press, 1988), 136; Maren-Sofie Røstvig, "Images of Perfection," in Earl Miner, ed., *Seventeenth-Century Imagery* (Berkeley: University of California Press, 1971), 124; Jon A. Quitslund, *Spenser's Supreme Fiction: Platonic Natural Philosophy and "The Faerie Queene"* (Toronto: University of Toronto Press, 2001), index, s.v. "Ellrodt"; and his "Spenser's Image of Sapience," *Studies in the Renaissance* 16 (1969): 181–213.

6. In Ellrodt's recent essay, apropos of Spenser's "all-embracing" philosophical vision in *The Faerie Queene*, he says the poet's "mind welcomed the Neoplatonism *of Ficino* and Castiglione" (emphasis mine). But that sentence's note just refers us to Ellrodt's *Neoplatonism*, so that he tacitly repeats its claim that Ficino's influence upon *The Faerie Queene* was wholly *indirect*, through Castiglione and others. Ellrodt, "Fundamental Modes of Thought, Imagination, and Sensibility in the Poetry of Edmund Spenser," *Spenser Studies* 20 (2005): 1–21 (quoting 4).

7. Spenser, the *Fowre Hymnes*, in his *Shorter Poems*, ed. Richard McCabe (Harmondsworth: Penguin, 1999), 452. Cited throughout for all the minor poetry. *HL*, *HB*, *HHL*, *HHB* denote the hymns' titles.

8. In Sonnet 80 of the *Amoretti* the poet speaks of resting after his six-book race through faery, and its date of entry in the Stationer's Register is 19 November 1594. However, he would have continued to revise Books IV to VI in style and content, for he was still significantly doing so even when they were in press in 1596. See Frank B. Evans, "The Printing of Spenser's *Faerie Queene* in 1596," *Studies in Bibliography* 18 (1965): 49–67.

9. Ellrodt grants that Colin's second speech on love in *Colin Clouts* (lines 835–94) and some concluding sonnets of the *Amoretti* evince what he would call learned

Renaissance Platonism, but dates the former to "1594 or 1595," and the latter to "1593–94" (14, 40–45, 92–93). His Spenser started dabbling in that around the mid 1590s, and became most knowledgeable around 1596. But, e.g., the increasing Platonism of the *Amoretti* may well be a means of creating narrative development that was envisaged from the sequence's inception, and not any late discovery. See further Jon A. Quitslund, "Spenser's *Amoretti VIII* and Platonic Commentaries on Petrarch," *Journal of the Warburg and Courtauld Institutes* 36 (1973): 256–76.

10.   Since Le Roy was a learned Platonic commentator who cites Ficino and Pico della Mirandola, and Ellrodt thinks he influenced *The Faerie Queene*, *Neoplatonism*'s argument is somewhat self-contradictory, as Catherine Martin pointed out to me. Carol Kaske's essay in this volume similarly questions Ellrodt's "popular" classification of Castiglione. See also Quitslund, *Supreme Fiction*, 239–40.

11.   The medieval West knew Plato himself primarily through the first third of the *Timaeus* as mediated by Chalcidius and, except for the *Meno*, *Phaedo*, and part of the *Parmenides* in difficult *ad verbum* translations, lacked the other dialogues. Their recovery and dissemination in the later fifteenth century is partly what created the distinctive cultural shift we call the Renaissance.

12.   There Ellrodt is dealing with the *Hymnes*, and hence (from his viewpoint) with Spenser's state of Platonic knowledge in 1596 (23). "The not impossible influence of the *Timaeus* is not sufficiently established" (55). Spenser "*may* [sic] have known the *Republic*," but whether he "ever read" it "is doubtful" (54, 159). Also doubtful are the *Timaeus*, *Ion*, and *Symposium*; the *Phaedrus* and *Phaedo* must be "ruled out" (96–97). Ellrodt allows some possible influence of the *Timaeus* (presumably indirect) on *The Faerie Queene* (91–92), and the *Symposium* (directly or indirectly) on *Colin Clouts*, but not earlier than 1594/5 (93). Though he vacillates somewhat on Spenser's knowledge of Plato's dialogues (e.g., 227), his general argument is untenable unless Spenser had no direct knowledge of them aside from the *Timaeus* and little else, until at least 1596, when *The Faerie Queene* was published. Those that were inaccessible in the medieval Latin West (see note 11) all count as learned Renaissance Platonism.

13.   Valery Rees lists some relevant scholars at the outset of her "Ficinian Ideas in the Poetry of Edmund Spenser," in this volume.

14.   Ellrodt rejects C. S. Lewis's application of Proclus, Orpheus, and Ficino to Book IV (90). Having objected to Ellrodt's procedures in his review of *Neoplatonism* (cited note 5), William Nelson, e.g., leaves those differences implicit in *The Poetry of Edmund Spenser* (New York, Columbia University Press, 1963), but still expresses them through much citation of learned Platonic texts that Ellrodt discounts. See Nelson's index, s.v. Ficino, Pico, Plato, Plotinus.

15.   See, e.g., Patrick Cheney, "Triamond," *SE*, 698–99. For bibliography on Neoplatonism and Spenser's Graces, see Kenneth Borris, "Sub Rosa: Pastorella's Allegorical Homecoming, and Closure in the 1596 *Faerie Queene*," *Spenser Studies* 21 (2006): 143, 146–47. On the idealizing proems, which are in that sense metaphysically interpretive, see Kenneth Borris, "Platonism and Spenser's Poetic," first section, in this volume.

16.   *Neoplatonism*, 112. Thus "we [i.e., Ellrodt] . . . discovered the bent of the poet's mind," and the *Hymnes* must be read according to "their context in the poet's mind" (112, 113). "I will not attempt to read parallels into the poem before the poet's own

intention has been ascertained" (130). *Neoplatonism* is to be read accordingly (e.g., 12, 59–60,169).

17.   However, Spenser was a great innovator *au courant* with the latest cultural trends. See Quitslund, *Supreme Fiction*, 3–16, 120–30; Kenneth Borris, "Allegory, Symbol, Emblem," forthcoming in *The Oxford Handbook to Edmund Spenser*, ed. Richard McCabe.

18.   Spenser, *The Faerie Queene*, ed. A. C. Hamilton et al., rev. 2nd ed. (London: Longman, 2007), 714. Cited for the *Letter* and *Faerie Queene* throughout.

19.   But unorthodox philosophical, theological, and metaphysical doctrines have political implications. Even the Platonic Ideas themselves could be controversial, just as George Puttenham attacks understandings of divine creation that, as in Spenser's *Hymnes*, posit a formative Platonic "paterne" (*The Arte of English Poesie*, ed. Gladys Doidge Willcock and Alice Walker [Cambridge, 1936; rprt. Folcroft, PA: Folcroft, 1969], 3). Second, Spenser's allegory is complex and exploratory (see Borris, "Allegory, Symbol, Emblem"). Third, sixteenth-century poetics assumed allegories in heroic poetry would involve diverse intellectual disciplines, not just current affairs. See, e.g., Sir John Harington, "Apologie of Poetrie," in Ariosto, *Orlando Furioso*, ed. Robert McNulty, trans. Harington (Oxford: Clarendon Press, 1972), 3–7.

20.   Quoting Bart van Es, "Introduction," in *A Critical Companion to Spenser Studies*, ed. van Es (Houndmills: Palgrave-Macmillan, 2006), 5. For Milton, see R. M. Cummings, ed., *Edmund Spenser: The Critical Heritage* (London: Routledge, 1971, 163–64. In Ellrodt's context that I cite, he mocks *HB*, lines 36–40, where the "wondrous Paterne" of "perfect Beautie" is elusive, "Whether in earth layd vp in secret store,/Or else in heauen." Countering Ellrodt somewhat, Enid Welsford observes that Spenser's contemporaries likewise debated whether the Ideas are immanent in creation or remain transcendent; but she still balks at "*in earth* layd vp in secret store." However, this riddling Spenserian paradox invites us to consider how that might be so, and an effective answer is anamnesis: the Platonic theory that the embodied soul inwardly retains its preexistent apprehension of the Ideas. In this sense the Ideas exist not only on earth but *in* it, since earth was thought the body's substance and constitutes, as such, a Spenserian metaphoric topos (e.g., I.vii.9, II.ix.21). For Platonists, apprehensions of beauty reflect innate knowledge of Beauty, and so the incarnate mind is that Pattern's earthly "secret store." See Plato's *Meno*, 80e–86c; *Phaedo*, 72e–77a; *Phaedrus*, 249bc. Welsford, ed., *Fowre Hymnes, Epithalamion* (Oxford: Blackwell, 1967), 154.

21.   James A. Notopoulos, *Modern Language Review* 57 (1962): 85–86. Though Ellrodt assures us an earlier dating does not jeopardize his main conclusions or procedures, that is not so. Cf. *Neoplatonism*, 23; also Ellrodt's reply to Notopoulos above, in *Modern Language Review* 58 (1963): 459. There and in the review, "1595" should be 1596 (compare *Neoplatonism*, 23).

22.   "The lack of demonstrably [i.e., certainly] Neoplatonic echoes in the rest of [Spenser's] work would then represent, *not (as in Dr. Ellrodt's picture)*, a period when he was still ignorant of their system, but a period in which he learned to sit to it more and more loosely." Spenser's Platonic erudition would thus much predate the mid 1590s. Lewis, "Neoplatonism in Spenser's Poetry," *Studies in Medieval and Renaissance Literature* (Cambridge: Cambridge University Press, 1966), 150 (emphasis

mine). Having assumed Spenser's Platonic erudition in *The Faerie Queene* previously (see Ellrodt, 90), Lewis continued to do so in lectures published as *Spenser's Images of Life*, ed. Alastair Fowler (Cambridge: Cambridge University Press, 1967), where his citations include the *Phaedrus*, Pico, Plotinus, and Ficino.

23. "I don't have any confidence in stylometric dating of ANY text, nor do the American courts." Donald Foster, Vassar College, personal communication.

24. See, e.g., Phillip B. Rollinson, "A Generic View of Spenser's *Four Hymns*," *Studies in Philology* 68 (1971): 292–304.

25. On the hymns' intricate interrelations, see William Elford Rogers, *The Three Genres and the Interpretation of Lyric* (Princeton: Princeton University Press, 1966), 572–94.

26. First to advocate redating the first pair of hymns was Percy W. Long, who claims they were written in 1590 ("The Date of Spenser's Earlier Hymns," *Englische studien* 47 [1913–14]: 197–208). Then in the 1930s Josephine Waters Bennett appropriated Long's redating to advocate the whole hymnic cycle's "organic unity": all four can thus originate within the 1590s ("The Theme of Spenser's *Fowre Hymnes*," *Studies in Philology* 28 [1931]: 49–57 [52 on Long]). She nonetheless assumes Spenser used some older material in the first hymn (54–55), and that the current first pair's "parallel structure . . . may go back to their first composition" (55), and so she still allows for two Spenserian ur-hymns on love and beauty. See also her "Spenser's *Fowre Hymnes*: Addenda," *Studies in Philology* 32 (1935): 152–57. Mary I. Oates supposes all four in their present form date from "ca. 1590–95," but says "there is no reason to deny that the first two might have been written . . . in the poet's youth," then stylistically "revised" in the 1590s ("*Fowre Hymnes*: Spenser's Retractations of Paradise" in *Spenser Studies* 4 [1983]: 143–69).

27. Ellrodt nonetheless claims the first two hymns and the fourth were based on portions of *Colin Clouts* and the *Epithalamion*, as if "whether the poet drew for subject-matter [in those hymns] on unpublished hymns, or simply on his earlier published love-poems, is of little consequence" (21). But educated Renaissance poets knew and respected their genres, and Spenser says the first hymns were, as such, written and circulated well before their publication. Also, the influence could run the other way: from two early hymns to *Colin Clouts* and *Epithalamion*. Cf. Ellrodt, 21–23, 124–29.

28. Spenser remained somehow committed to the content of the first two hymns because he published them and in that way privileged their canonicity. He had become sensitive to public reactions to his poetic representations of love (e.g., IV.pr.1–4, VI.xii.41), and the *Hymnes*'s dedication seeks to manage those issues.

29. Richard T. Spence, "Clifford, Margaret," in H. C. G. Matthew and Brian Harrison, eds., *Oxford Dictionary of National Biography* (Oxford: Oxford University Press, 2004): 12:104; *ODNB* henceforth. Cf. Simon Adams, "Dudley, Anne," *ODNB*, 17: 63–65; Jon A. Quitslund, "Spenser and the Patronesses of the *Fowre Hymnes*: 'Ornaments of All True Love and Beauty,' " in Margaret Patterson Hannay, ed., *Silent But for the Word: Tudor Women as Patrons, Translators, and Writers of Religious Works* (Kent: Kent State University Press, 1985), 184–202, 281–83; Rosemond Tuve, "Spenserus," in Thomas P. Roche, Jr., ed., *Essays by Rosemond Tuve: Spenser, Herbert, Milton* (Princeton: Princeton University Press, 1970), 139–63.

30. See Ernest A. Strathmann, "A Manuscript Copy of Spenser's Hymns," *Modern Language Notes* 48 (1933): 217–21.

31. On Ralegh, see Peter Beal, Volume I of *Index of English Literary Manuscripts*, Part Two (London: Mansell-Bowker, 1980), 365.

32. "For all, or the most part of such questions I will refer you to Sir *Philip Sidneys* Apologie, who doth handle them right learnedly." Harington, "Apologie of Poetrie," 2. See Beal, *Index*, 484–85.

33. Extant ms. extracts of *The Faerie Queene* all postdate 1600. Yet, e.g., Marlowe and Abraham Fraunce both had some in 1587/8. See Roma Gill, "Marlowe, Christopher," *SE*, 453; Walter R. Davis, "Fraunce, Abraham," *SE*, 319. Beal inventories surviving mss. of Spenser's poems, *Index*, 523–31.

34. E. K.'s Epistle to Harvey for the *Calendar* (1579) speaks of "sondry others" (30). William Ponsonby's prefatory epistle for the *Complaints* (1591) says he has thus gathered only some "fewe parcels" of Spenser's "smale Poemes." There are "sundrie others" and "Pamphlets looslie scattered abroad," some named, others unspecified ("*& c.*"; 165). William Webbe's *A Discourse of English Poetrie* (1586) says Spenser has "plenty" of unpublished poems, some named, but also "with other." Volume I of *Elizabethan Critical Essays*, ed. G. Gregory Smith (London: Oxford University Press, 1904), 246.

35. Though Ellrodt denies any circularity (23), in this regard he basically argues that (1) learned Renaissance Platonism is not to be found in *The Faerie Queene* because the first two hymns, which certainly evince such content, postdate it, despite their dedication; (2) they postdate it, despite their dedication, because that content is not to be found in *The Faerie Queene*.

36. Rollinson, "Generic View": 297. Spenser's other poems in rhyme royal, Long observes, date from around 1590/91 (200).

37. Taylor, "Spenser's Knowledge of Plato," *Modern Language Review* 19 (1924): 208–10. Hereafter cited parenthetically in my text.

38. Cf., e.g., Puttenham, *Arte of English Poesie*, 186–88.

39. Dixon, *The Polliticke Courtier: Spenser's "The Faerie Queene" as a Rhetoric of Justice* (Montreal and Kingston: McGill-Queen's University Press, 1996), 55–56. For a survey of earlier comments, see Raymond B. Waddington, "Socrates," *SE*, 661.

40. Dixon's reading of Book IV's proem interprets "Critias" according to the same Greek word, 55.

41. Ellrodt doubts Spenser had read "any" of Plato's dialogues even by 1596 (115), and absolutely "ruled out" the *Phaedrus* and *Phaedo* (97).

42. Plato, *Collected Dialogues*, ed. Edith Hamilton and Huntington Cairns, trans. various (Princeton: Bollingen-Princeton University Press, 1961). Cited for Plato throughout.

43. See James Nohrnberg, *The Analogy of "The Faerie Queene"* (Princeton: Princeton University Press, 1976), index, s.v. "sun," "day"; Alastair Fowler, *Spenser and the Numbers of Time* (London: Routledge, 1964), ch. 8.

44. On the 1596 *Faerie Queene*'s apocalypticism, see Borris, *Poetics of Prophecy* (Book V), and "Pastorella's Allegorical Homecoming": 160–63 (Book VI).

45. See Chapman, "Preface to the Reader," in Homer, *The Iliad*, ed. Allardyce Nicoll, trans. Chapman, 2nd ed. (Princeton: Princeton University Press, 1998), 15;

Harington, "Apologie," 3–7. See further Kenneth Borris, *Allegory and Epic in English Renaissance Literature: Heroic Form in Sidney, Spenser, and Milton* (Cambridge: Cambridge University Press, 2000), chs. 1, 3.

46.   In my view, the *Letter*'s representation of Aristotle accords with late sixteenth-century understandings of that philosopher. For various explanations, see Borris, "Platonism and Spenser's Poetic," section one, in this volume; Hamilton's notes for the *Letter*, 715n, 716n; Ronald A. Horton, "Aristotle and His Commentators," *SE*, 57–60.

47.   Ellrodt puts "the authors" in quotation marks here (60) because he is quoting the *Letter*'s original title ("*Letter of the Authors*," 59) in order to insist on its privileged definition of the poet's intention, and hence of the poem's "true meaning" (59). See note 16.

48.   See Lewis, "Neoplatonism," 158–61.

49.   See Jeffrey P. Fruen, "The Faery Queen Unveiled? Five Glimpses of Gloriana," *Spenser Studies* 11 (1994): 53–88; Alastair Fowler, "Emanations of Glory: Neoplatonic Order in *The Faerie Queene*," in *A Theatre for Spenserians*, ed. Judith M. Kennedy and James A. Reither (Toronto: University of Toronto Press, 1973), 53–82; Lewis, "Neoplatonism," 157–61.

50.   On Plato and Xenophon in Spenser's *Letter*, see further Wayne Erickson, "Spenser's Letter to Ralegh and the Literary Politics of *The Faerie Queene*'s 1590 Publication," *Spenser Studies* 10 (1989): 147–51.

51.   Ellrodt, "Fundamental Modes," 16n21, rejecting Bieman's notice of *Neoplatonism*'s apparent bias (136). Yet in *Neoplatonism* Ellrodt adduces "further proof of the poet's perfect orthodoxy" (73), and says, e.g., Spenser "could declare [love] heavenly in his profane poetry, but he could not consider it as a step towards heavenly love in his religious poetry. No clear-sighted and healthy-minded man could treat it so" (149).

52.   See also Thomas M. Greene, *The Light in Troy: Imitation and Discovery in Renaissance Poetry* (New Haven: Yale University Press, 1982).

53.   "In my survey of Platonism in the *Faerie Queene*, I have thought it wise to restrict myself to an examination of Spenser's direct *statements* on love and beauty" (47).

54.   Lewis, "Neoplatonism," 160–61.

55.   See Stella P. Revard, *Pindar and the Renaissance Hymn-Ode: 1450–1700* (Tempe: CMRS, 2001), chs. 3–5; Rollinson, "A Generic View": 292–304; his "The Renaissance of the Literary Hymn," *Renaissance Papers* 1968: 11–20; James Hutton, "Spenser's 'Adamantine Chains': A Cosmological Metaphor," in Luitpold Wallach, ed., *The Classical Tradition: Literary and Historical Studies in Honor of Harry Caplan* (Ithaca: Cornell University Press, 1966), 572–94.

56.   Sidney, *Defence of Poetry*, in his *Miscellaneous Prose*, ed. Katherine Duncan-Jones and Jan van Dorsten (Oxford: Clarendon Press, 1973), 98.

57.   See, e.g., Michael Caesar, *Dante: The Critical Heritage, 1314(?)–1870* (London: Routledge, 1989), 292–93; Bernard Weinberg, *A History of Literary Criticism in the Italian Renaissance*, 2 vols. (Chicago: Unversity of Chicago Press, 1961), 2:819–911, 1106–12.

58.   See Borris, *Allegory and Epic*, 101–06.

59. See Kaske, "Amavia, Mordant, Ruddymane," 25–27.

60. The account of Florimell and her fake learnedly draws on Platonism to assess beauty and its appearances in both life and art. See Borris, "Platonism and Spenser's Poetic," this volume, sections two, three, five; and Alastair Fowler, *Spenser and the Numbers of Time* (London: Routledge, 1964), 21n2.

61. See Sidney, *Miscellaneous Prose*, index, s.v. "Plato."

62. See also Valery Rees's appendix on the Tudor currency of Platonic texts, this volume.

63. See Tasso's *Discorsi del poema eroico*, *Il Messaggiero*, *Il Ficino*, and *Il Minturno*, among others.

64. John Erskine Hankins, *Source and Meaning in Spenser's Allegory: A Study of "The Faerie Queene"* (Oxford: Clarendon Press, 1971), 236.

65. See Virginia F. Stern, *Gabriel Harvey: His Life, Marginalia and Library* (Oxford: Clarendon Press, 1979), 249–53.

66. Harvey, *Marginalia*, ed. G. C. Moore-Smith (Stratford: Shakespeare Head, 1913), index, s.v. "Ficinus," "Plato." Also "Mirandula."

67. See Walter Oakeshott, "Sir Walter Ralegh's Library," *The Library*, 5th ser., 23 (1968): 285–327. Ficino, No. 364; Pico, No. 265; Apuleius, No. 143; George of Trebizond's (?) comparison of Aristotle and Plato, No. 485. Also Hermes Trismegistus (?), No. 90; Reuchlin, No. 99; Cardano, No. 160abc; Trithemius, No. 452ab; Porta, No. 95; and various predictive physiognomers.

68. For Harvey, Nashe, et al., see Cummings, 52, 60–62, 119, 150.

69. "*Milton* has acknowledg'd to me, that *Spencer* [sic] was his Original." John Dryden, "Preface" for *Fables*, in Vol. 7 of his *Works*, ed. Vinton A. Dearing (Berkeley and Los Angeles: University of California Press, 2000), 25.

70. Harvey, *Marginalia*, 160–61.

71. Ellrodt concedes that the October eclogue's ideas "are unmistakably of Platonic descent" (31), and that Spenser's "conception of love and beauty as expressed in *The Faerie Queene*" has "a general Platonic character" (34). Also, the influence of learned Renaissance Platonists such as Ficino, "direct or indirect, may . . . be surmised whenever beauty is described in Renaissance literature as an effulgence and effluence of the Divine" (35). That is a fundamental Spenserian theme.

72. E.g., Lynda Gregorian Christian, "The Figure of Socrates in Erasmus' Works," *Sixteenth Century Journal* 3.2 (1972): 1–10.

73. The *Axiochus* was long thought Plato's, as by Ficino; see Harold L. Weatherby, "Axiochus," *SE*, 77. On Spenser's syncretism, see Quitslund, *Supreme Fiction*, 8–16.

74. See Quitslund, *Supreme Fiction*; Borris, "Platonism and Spenser's Poetic," this volume.

75. On Spenser's Aristotelian aspects, see Ronald A. Horton, "Aristotle and His Commentators," *SE*, 57–60.

76. See Borris, "Pastorella's Allegorical Homecoming": 148–51.

77. Compare I.iii.8, vi.16; II.iii.21; III.v.52, vi.1–3, vii.11; IV.v.13, vi.22, 24, xii.34.

78. Evans, "*Faerie Queene* in 1596": 49–67.

79. *OED*, 2nd ed., s.v. "idea," sb., with various examples, including Spenser's friend Bryskett.

80.   Plutarch, *The Philosophie, Commonlie Called, the Morals*, trans. Philemon Holland (London: Arnold Hatfield, 1603), 813, STC 20063. Cit. *OED*.

81.   Ficino, *Commentary on Plato's Symposium on Love (De amore)*, trans. Sears Jayne (Dallas: Spring, 1985), 6.3–7. Michael J. B. Allen informs me that Ficino's discussion there is "a preliminary foray into territory he was to explore throughout his life" (personal communication). The *locus classicus* for interpretation of the ancient pantheon in relation to Plato's Ideas is the procession of the gods through the heavens in the *Phaedrus*. See Michael J. B. Allen, *The Platonism of Marsilio Ficino: A Study of His "Phaedrus" Commentary, Its Sources and Genesis* (Berkeley: University of California Press, 1984), ch. 5, esp. 121–23; also Valery Rees, "Ficinian Ideas," in this volume, her note 29.

82.   See Borris, "Platonism and Spenser's Poetic," section one, this volume.

83.   For discussion of some retrospective "careeric" aspects of the *Hymnes*, see Cheney, *Famous Flight*, ch. 5.

84.   *HL*, lines 287–92; *HB*, lines 15, 126, 267, 274, 282; *HHB*, lines 184–85, 249.

85.   In Jeffrey P. Fruen's account of 1994, e.g., the prior such inquiries predate 1950. "The Faery Queen Unveiled?": 56, 82n9.

86.   See Borris, "Platonism and Spenser's Poetic," section one, in this volume; David Lee Miller, *The Poem's Two Bodies: The Poetics of the 1590 "Faerie Queene"* (Princeton: Princeton University Press, 1988), 70–80; Fowler, "Emanations of Glory," 67–77.

87.   Compare Spenser's address to Elizabeth in Book V's proem as "Souerayne Goddesse, that doest highest sit/ . . . in th' Almighties place,/ . . . with magnificke might and wondrous wit." In this "diuine" discourse, the English queen passes into or yields to her idealized archetype Gloriana, expressed through the forthcomimg narrative of Faery. The "most sacred vertue" of Justice resembles "God in his imperiall might" (V.pr.10–11).

88.   See Quitslund, "Sapience," 181–213.

GORDON TESKEY

A Retrograde Reading of Spenser's *Fowre Hymnes*

The *Fowre Hymnes* are presented in the epistle as a continuous series extending by Neoplatonic analogy upwards from earthly love and beauty to heavenly love and beauty. This plan gives the victory to a chilly Neoplatonism that loathes the world and is incompatible with the warmth of Christian charity. But when read backwards the hymns unexpectedly recover much of the warmth and wisdom they ineffectually claim for themselves when read forwards. In the *Hymne in Honour of Love*, instead of the continuity of the series of the hymns, we find an interesting continuity from the force that created the world to the erotic desire that rouses all living creatures to reproduce. Human beings are conscious of this desire as a higher power, Beauty, which leaves them unsatisfied in eroticism unless it has a religious and collective aspect. An orgiastic erotic heaven is therefore imagined at the conclusion of the poem—*orgiastic* in the strict sense of involving secret rites—in which lovers are lodged in ivory beds placed beside one another and stretching to infinity. At first the image seems to teach that what we experience as most private, erotic love, is also most general, distinguishing us from animals and making us human. But the image of the beds hard by one another never reconciles the discontinuity of the individual couples with the continuity of the whole. In the end, the effort to see eroticism reconciled to itself is a failure, though one that is more interesting than the failure that comes from reading the hymns in the prescribed order.

T HE FIRST CRITIC of any of Spenser's *Fowre Hymnes* was probably Margaret Clifford, Countess of Cumberland, one of the "two noble

Spenser Studies: A Renaissance Poetry Annual, Volume XXIV, Copyright © 2009 AMS Press, Inc. All rights reserved.

481

and virtuous ladies" to whom, in the epistle of 1 September 1596, the *Fowre Hymnes* were dedicated. The poet says the lady asked him to "call in" his hymns in honor of Love and of Beauty, because they endanger the morals of the young, who "do rather suck out poison to their strong passion, than honey to their honest delight." But because too many copies of those two hymns have been spread abroad for it to be possible to call them in—this being one of the commoner excuses of Renaissance epistles—the poet has resolved to "amend" and "reform" them, "by way of retractation," or rewriting, and to add two further hymns by way of correction, hymns of *heavenly* love and of *celestial* beauty.[1]

The erring hymns are addressed to Cupid and Venus, respectively, the corrective ones to Jesus and Sapience, respectively. According to the epistle, we are meant to take the second pair as a rejection of the first. But we are then meant to understand the second pair as a transumptive analogy of the first: as Cupid to Venus, so Jesus to Sapience. The analogy is transumptive because the first pair is taken up and completed in the second. The analogy is also foolish, at least when it is set forth baldly like this, without protection. The point, after all, is *not* to put the analogy baldly, thus allowing us, as we read through the poems, to enjoy the feeling of ascending through ever-higher levels of experience and wisdom. Should we happen to reflect that Cupid has little to do with Christ and Venus still less to do with Sapience, we can fall back from the implicit relation of progression to the explicit relation of rejection (*of course* they don't!), without worrying that these relations are incompatible. The continuity will return and reassert itself because the discontinuity of Cupid with Jesus and of Venus with Sapience is in the subordinate role of taking pressure off the relation of progression at moments of crisis. Whatever we make of the dialectical fiction of Spenser's *Fowre Hymnes*, it is apparent that they are cast in a series in which each must appear to ascend to a higher plane than the last. Like the heavens in *An Hymne of Heavenly Beautie*, the four hymns are to "rise more more faire, till they at last arrive / To the most faire, whereto they all do strive" (*HHB*, lines 76–77).

That image of poetry as taking flight, which like so much else in these poems would be important to Milton, is underlined at the outset of *An Hymne of Heavenly Beautie*, when the poet compares himself to the soaring falcon, mounting aloft "to contemplation of th'immortal sky" (line 25). Certainly in this final poem, which is the most Neoplatonic of the four, and the least Christian of the four, there is a strong retrospective effort by the poet to impose a simpler plan on the series than it actually has. As in Donne's "Of the Progress of the Soul," that is, the Second Anniversary, in which the liberated soul is compared to a bullet fired from a gun, we are taken up swiftly through the visible heavens of the created world, then through the invisible heavens to the Mercy Seat and throne of God, then to the idol of Sapience, lodged in God's breast, and at last out of the world altogether. We leave the world because of a subjective motivation within us, our love of God, "which loathing brings/Of this vile world, and these gay seeming things" (lines 298–99). *Loathing*?

This is the language of the penultimate stanza of the *Mutabilitie Cantos*, but with an important difference. There, what provokes Spenser to "loathe this state of life so tickle" is not the love of God but rather "that speech whyleare/Of *Mutability*."[2] Contemplating the decay of all beauty can indeed make you loathe the world; it shouldn't, though it can. But should contemplating the love of God make you loathe the world? It should not. Loathing the world is unethical on any ethical plan, and certainly on the Christian one, where such loathing would be the destruction of all charity. The early Christian Church fought a hard fight against contempt of the world, which was expressed in extreme cases by suicide, and opposed to such contempt was "charity" or Christian love, *agape*. Spenser's episode of loathing in the *Mutabilitie Cantos* is wiser than that of *An Hymne of Heavenly Beautie* because it is a passing mood and is not the final word. But to arrive at the wisdom of the *Mutabilitie Cantos* demands a more dialectically active plan of ascent than the simple steps taken—or imagined to be taken—in the *Fowre Hymnes*. The Christian has to find a way out of the world to God without ceasing to love the world, since God himself loved the world, and still does. The muddled thinking of the *Hymne of Heavenly Beautie* suggests to me that something has gone off the rails in Spenser's scheme.

Here is the hypothesis I advance: that it is possible to read the *Fowre Hymnes* against and indeed opposite to their author's declared scheme. In short, it is possible and not only possible but preferable to read them backwards. In doing so, we can recover the feeling of ascending to something better in each, even if we have to build the stairs ourselves. In the order Spenser gives the hymns, claims to philosophical and religious wisdom increase as poetic wisdom declines. I am trying to avoid saying that their poetic quality declines, although each hymn is more discursive than the last. Discursive poetry has its place, after all, and, anyway, who could fail to admire the splendid lines in the *Hymne to Heavenly Beautie* describing Sapience, "Whose beautie filles the heavens with her light/And darkes the earth with shadow of her sight" (lines 228–29). Nor are these lines the only splendid ones.

They appear in a passage where Spenser returns to *The Faerie Queene*, in particular to the language of the proem to Book III, reflecting on the incapacity of the arts—the visual as well as the poetical arts—fully to embrace what they alone allow us to see: "How then dare I, the novice of his [the *Teian* poet's] Art,/Presume to picture so divine a wight?" (*HHB*, lines 225–26); "How then shall I, Apprentice of the skill,/That whylome in divinest wits did rayne,/Presume so high to stretch mine humble quill?" (*The Faerie Queene*, 3.pr.3). But this comparison, like the comparison with the *loathing* in *The Mutabilitie Cantos*, is likewise to the disadvantage of the hymn. Not only is the verse better in the proem to Book III, the thought is better, too. There, Spenser is describing a queen, allegorically. Here, Spenser is describing an abstraction, Sapience. Sapience is a traditional figure in allegory, going back to the *Psychomachia*, but the great power of the allegory of *The Faerie Queene* is that in it abstractions are used to probe real problems in the real world. In *The Faerie Queene* as a whole, we feel the weight and the complexity of the world. In the passage at hand, Queen Elizabeth is always more real than the "colour showes" (3.pr.3) the poet weaves about her. But he tells us so, and he is pointed in the right direction: towards the world. In contrast with this, we do not believe the thought of those verses in which Sapience's beauty "fills the heavens with her light/And darkes the earth with shadow of her sight" (*HHB*, line 229). By moving away from the world into nothing, they exemplify much of what we find in the *Hymne of Heavenly Beautie*: brilliant writing to little purpose.

What is more surprising still—if one finds this surprising, as I do: indeed, I find it startling—is that the muddled effort to reconcile, in the *Hymne of Heavenly Beautie*, chilly Neoplatonism with warm Christian charity, to the total loss of Christian charity and the victory of what Neoplatonism must come to in the end, *loathing*, is corrected in the hymn that precedes it. *An Hymne of Heavenly Love* is a masterly summary of Christian doctrine and ethics that is so complete—in under three hundred lines—that Milton could have depended on it alone.

It certainly appears to be a poem Milton studied with care from an early age, so that it sank deep into his mind and influenced him unconsciously for the rest of his life. One clue to this is the seventeen-year-old Milton's appropriation of a distinctive locution from *An Hymn of Heavenly Love* in "On the Death of a Fair Infant Dying of a Cough." Milton asks if the soul of the infant was a star that fell from Heaven and which "carefull Jove . . . in fit place did *reinstall*."[3] The same word is in Spenser's hymn. After a splendidly Miltonic account of the war in Heaven and the fall of the angels into Hell, Spenser says that God saw in Heaven "a waste and emptie place" where the fallen angels once were, and resolved to fill it with a new kind of creature, raised from earth:

> Now seeing left a waste and emptie place
> In his wyde Pallace, through those Angels fall,
> [God] Cast to supply the same, and to *enstall*
> A new unknowen Colony therein,
> Whose root from earths base groundworke shold begin.
>
> (*HHL*, lines 100–104; italics added)

These lines describe the idea at the heart of Milton's conception of *Paradise Lost*, and Spenser's *Hymne of Heavenly Love*, taken entire, gave Milton the Christian-Biblical vision of history that would be the structural frame of his epic. Of course, Milton had pieces of the vision from elsewhere, too, belonging as it does to the Christian tradition. But nowhere else are the elements of that vision drawn together in such a concentrated, poetic form, and one so congenial to Milton's mind and art.

Spenser's *Hymn of Heavenly Love* does do something less congenial to Milton's mind and art, however, which is to make Christianity emotionally appealing by focusing on God's love, instead of God's power, and to exhort us to the love of God and of one another, instead of to simple obedience to God: "Him first to love, great right and reason is,/Who first to us our life and being gave," "Then next to love our brethren, that were made/Of that selfe mould, and that selfe makers hand" (*HHL*, lines190–91, 197–98). In *Paradise Lost* obedience and gratitude—"the debt immense of endless gratitude," as Satan calls it—are owed to God because he made us.[4] Abdiel asks Satan, "shalt thou dispute/With Him the points of liberty who made/Thee what thou art?" (5.822–24). Abdiel never says Satan should *love* God for making him, but rather that Satan should *obey*.

It is interesting that Milton as a poet was largely unmoved by the two definitive images of Christian worship: the baby in its mother's arms and the man on the cross. Both images are calculated to arouse the emotions of love and of pity. Spenser gives us a child "encradled . . . In simple cratch, wrapt in a wad of hay,/Between the toyle-full Oxe and humble Asse" (*HHL*, lines 225–27), animal reflections of human labor; and Spenser gives us a Christ who is "nayled on a gallow tree" (line 153). Milton was unmoved by the baby in its mother's arms and by the man on the cross because they are images of helplessness, not of power, and their appeal is to the emotions, rather than to the instincts for order and for command.

The strength of the *Hymne of Heavenly Love* is in the objectivity of its Christian vision. The poem begins to lose energy three stanzas from its end, however, beginning with the line, "Then shalt thou feele thy spirit so possest" (line 267). At this moment the objectivity is lost and our attention is turned to how we will feel, that is, to a spiritualized sensationalism. It is also from this moment that this hymn modulates towards the theme of the next, *An Hymne of Heavenly Beautie*. The decisive element in this modulation is the loss of concentration on the objective phenomenon of Christian love and an increasing effort to make the worshipping subject real, as rapturous sensation. We go from the language of the Book of Common Prayer, exhorting one to love God "With all thy hart, with all thy soule and mind" (*HHL*, line 260), to a simple, consequentialist assertion: "Then shalt thou feele thy spirit so possest,/And ravisht with devouring great desire/Of his deare selfe, . . . /That in no earthly thing thou shalt delight" (lines 267–72). Note how the auto-erotic language of such worship—"ravisht with devouring great desire"—is accompanied by dislike of all things on earth, a dislike tending, of course, to loathing.

The subjective sensuality here figured by ravishment and devouring desire is not what Christianity looks for as a consequence of loving God. Loving God is supposed to prompt us to love one another: "love is the lesson which the Lord us taught."[5] Christianity looks for humility and the loss of the subject as a center of value so that Christian love and charity—*agape*, or in Latin, *caritas*—can enter us, turning our attention back towards the world, or rather to others in the world. There is no reason in the logic of the *Hymne of Heavenly Love* for this modulation away from the object (Christian love and charity) into the sensuality of the worshipping subject. The "Then" is a purely temporal *then*, which we are invited to take for a logical *then*. The final stanza, with its "ravisht soule inspired" gazing with "bright radiant eyes" on "Th'Idee of his pure glorie," and enjoying from that sight the "sweete enragement of celestiall love," is like the *Hymne of Heavenly Beautie* that follows it: gorgeous writing to little purpose. For its contemplated object, the idea of divine glory, is not an object at all but an auto-erotic hallucination in the subject. It rises up in the mind to serve one purpose only, that of giving the weight of probability to what is happening in the subject: "sweete enragement," an ecstasy belonging to the first, not the third, of Spenser's four hymns.

An Hymne in Honour of Beautie is the most interesting, that is, the most intellectually engaging of the four hymns, as the *Hymne in Honour of Love* is the most beautiful, for the *Hymne in Honour of Love* has the jeweled particularity and daintiness of quattrocento painting, being a Petrarchan Triumph of Cupid, such as was often represented on the panels of marriage chests, *cassone*. The *Hymne in Honour of Beautie* is addressed to Venus, Cupid's "Mother deare" (line 9), because the sight of beauty arouses erotic desire. We recall that the first of Malecasta's six knights, representing the six stages of seduction, is *Gardante*, Mr. Male Gaze (*Faerie Queene* 3.1.45). The opening of the *Hymne in Honour of Beautie* is wonderful, and again reminiscent of the language of *The Faerie Queene*: "Ah whither, Love, wilt thou now carrie mee?/What wontlesse fury dost thou now inspire/Into my feeble breast?" (*HB*, lines 1–3). Love carries the poet up to the thought of what inspires love, prompting his invocation of Venus, the "queene of Beauty": "Doe thou vouchsafe with thy love-kindling light,/T'illuminate my dim and dulled eyne,/And beautifie this sacred hymne of thine" (lines 19–21). We notice that he is not concentrating eudaemonically on his own ravishing experience but on the capacity in himself to come to the sight and understanding of powers outside the self, in the objective world. The hymn is not his: it is hers, "this sacred hymne of thyne."

This orientation is touchingly stressed in the fourth stanza, when Spenser dedicates the hymn to his own lady love—presumably Elizabeth Boyle, the same who appears in the great, Mount Acidale vision of Book VI of *The Faerie Queene*—so that she will at last take pity on him and, he hopes, "streame/Some deaw of grace into my withered hart,/After long sorrow and consuming smart" (*HB*, lines 23–28).

This is followed, to keep symmetry with the Creation passage in the *Hymne in Honour of Love*, by an account of the Creation of the world from a "goodly Paterne" (*HB*, line 32), which in Milton will become the Son's "great idea" (*Paradise Lost*, 7.557). Still more important for Milton is that much longer Creation passage in the *Hymne in Honour of Love* (lines 57–98) to which this alludes, describing when "this worlds still moving mightie masse,/Out of great *Chaos* ugly prison crept" (lines 57–58). Love himself seems to move upon the face of the waters before separating the elements and linking them with "Adamantine chaines" (line 89), chains Milton will borrow to bind Satan with in Hell: "there to dwell/In adamantine chains and penal fire" (*Paradise Lost*, 1.47–48).

In the *Hymne in Honour of Beautie* the poet speculates on the origin of beauty—an "infusion of celestiall powre" (line 50) from the planet

Venus—and on the difference within beauty, erotically and aesthetically perceived. Spenser brings up reductive arguments about the purpose and nature of beauty which are not unfamiliar today, for example, that beauty gives differential reproductive advantage and is not heavenly in origin but merely "comely composition/Of parts well measurd" and "mixture made/Of colours faire" (lines 69–70 and 65–66). Our appreciation of flowers and other natural beauties may be different in degree when we love a human figure and face, but not different in kind.

The argument against this is truly interesting, and has to do with the madness of love, as we should expect from a poet steeped in the wisdom of the classics: "can proportion of the outward part/Move such affection in the inward mynd,/That it can rob both sense and reason blynd?" (*HB*, lines 75–77). Conversely, why do we not feel "like impression" (line 81), that is, raging erotic desire, for "blossomes of the field" (line 78)? And why does human beauty as we see it represented in pictures, when such beauty may be augmented by the power of art, fail to rob sense and reason blind?

> Why doe not then the blossomes of the field,
> Which are arayd with much more orient hew,
> And to the sense most daintie odours yield,
> Worke like impression in the lookers vew?
> Or why doe not faire pictures like power shew,
> In which oftimes, we Nature see of Art
> Exceld, in perfect limming every part[?]
>
> (*HB*, lines 78–84)

The poet's answer to these questions is that the aesthetic beauty which we find in the world and human beauty tending to erotic love are different in kind, not degree. Human beauty fades and decays, like flowers, but unlike these, the beauty of the beloved, even as it ages, is always dear.

Spenser comes close to making this point, but being taken up with his intellectual problem he seems to slide off it. He affirms the point when he says "That Beautie is not, as fond men misdeeme,/An outward shew of things, that onely seeme" (*HB*, lines 90–91), lines immediately followed by a stanza describing the decay of beauty in the beloved. We expect this dismaying account to be followed by an assurance that what we are witnessing in the stanza is only an outward show, and that the inner beauty is preserved and sublated:

For that same goodly hew of white and red,
With which the cheekes are sprinckled, shal decay,
And those sweete rosy leaves so fairely spred
Upon the lips, shall fade and fall away
To that they were, even to corrupted clay.
That golden wyre, those sparckling stars so bright
Shall turne to dust, and loose their goodly light.

(*HB*, lines 92–98)

The assurance seems to come in the stanza following, when the poet says that the "faire lampe" (*HB*, line 99), the light from which the inner beauty shone forth to glorify the body, "Shall never be extinguisht nor decay,/But when the vitall spirits doe expyre" (lines 101–02). The reader naturally takes this to mean that in the beloved the lamp of beauty will shine until the end of life. But at this moment Spenser ungrammatically introduces a second principal clause sharing "that faire lampe" for its subject: "shall never be extinguisht" must give way to "shall retyre" (lines 101, 103). This phrase "shall retyre" describes the return of the light of that lamp, the lady's beauty, to the planet Venus. The ungrammaticality of the stanza is not a result of carelessness but of two thoughts occupying a single verbal space, pulling the syntax in different directions:

But that faire lampe, from whose celestiall ray
That light proceedes, which kindleth lovers fire,
Shall never he extinguisht nor decay,
But when the vitall spirits doe expyre,
Unto her native planet shall retyre,
For it is heavenly borne and can not die,
Being a parcel of the purest skie.

(*HB*, lines 99–105)

One thought, the touching one, is concerned with the survival of love for the person who once was beautiful: the fair lamp of beauty shall never be extinguished in the lover's eyes, until the lady dies. The other thought is concerned only with the metaphysical substance of beauty and with where it escaped to upon the death of its container, since *it*, the metaphysical substance, cannot die, "Being a parcel of the purest skie." This is chilly Neoplatonism of the purest water. No human soul is here returning home: a metaphysical substance is returning to its purest sky, having briefly used and discarded a human body, because, after all, a body can die. For Neoplatonism, as opposed to Christian charity, the body must finally be an object of loathing and contempt.

Further interesting reflections follow in *An Hymne in Honour of Beautie*, especially on that favorite Renaissance theme, whether souls that partake more of heavenly light, which shines in their goodness and virtue, capture greater physical beauty, the soul actually shaping its body into a more pleasing form: "these faire soules . . . / Frame to themselves most beautifull and brave / Their fleshly bowre" (lines 120–24). The point is summarized in the stanza following, which concludes with the best-known couplet in the *Fowre Hymnes*:

> So every spirit, as it is most pure,
> And hath in it the more of heavenly light,
> So it the fairer bodie doth procure
> To habit in, and it more fairely dight
> With chearefull grace and amiable sight.
> For of the soule the bodie forme doth take:
> For soule is forme, and doth the bodie make.
>
> (*HB*, lines 127–33)

The strength of the *Hymne in Honour of Beautie*, what makes it so superior to *An Hymne of Heavenly Beautie*, is its concentration on the world around the speaker, rather than on the speaker himself. Or rather, the speaker sees himself dialectically—"the mirrour of his owne thought doth admire" (*HB*, line 224)—in his concentration on others: "For lovers eyes more sharply sighted bee / Then other mens" (lines 232–33). The power of that sight occasions perhaps the best stanza in the poem, in which this subjective power of a lover's eyes, when turned on the face of the beloved, transforms the objective world:

> Sometimes upon her forhead they behold
> A thousand Graces masking in delight,
> Sometimes within her eye-lids they unfold
> Ten thousand sweet belgards, which to their sight
> Doe seeme like twinckling starres in frostie night:
> But on her lips, like rosy buds in May,
> So many millions of chaste pleasures play.
>
> (*HB*, lines 253–59)

We find ourselves unexpectedly again in the neighborhood of the vision on Mount Acidale: much of the language and imagery recalls it. The extreme subjectivity with which the objective beloved is briefly captured is celebrated in a paean to Venus: "Then *Iö tryumph*, O great beauties Queene" (line 267). The entire world joins in, as a chorus "singing this Hymne in honour of thy name, / Compyld by me, which thy poore liegeman am" (lines 272–73).

That last line is awkward, but what it says is important. Everywhere he appears in *An Hymne in Honour of Beautie*, in contrast with *An Hymne of Heavenly Beautie*, the poet is particularized as an artist and as a lover. The exchange between the subject and the object becomes climactically intense in the final two stanzas of this poem, which describe the poet losing his life to his lady and recovering it from her again. Here are the final couplets of each of these stanzas: "And this same life, which first fro me she reaved, / May owe to her, of whom I it received"; "And shew what wondrous powre your beauty hath, / That can restore a damned wight from death" (*HB*, lines 279–80, 286–87).

We have observed how the *Hymne in Honour of Beautie* moves into this dialectical region from a detached, positivistic reflection on the nature of beauty and on the qualitative difference between aesthetic beauty and the beauty that arouses the madness of erotic desire. When the hymn concludes by turning back to the poet, this poet is no longer—recall that we are reading the series backwards—the pure subject of the *Hymne of Heavenly Beautie* but a real subject mediated through negotiation with the objective world; with Venus, or the problem of erotic beauty in the world; and with the focus of that problem in the poet's experience, confronting "she whose conquering beautie doth captive / My trembling hart" (*HB*, lines 275–76). Perhaps this is why, in the final stanza, which is addressed to that same *she*, his lady, "faire *Venus* dearling, my deare dread" (line 281), we find him addressing her as if she were in fact the goddess Venus—"great Goddesse of my life" (line 282)—because the lady *is* Venus dialectically, that is, so far as the poet is concerned:

And you faire *Venus* dearling, my deare dread,
Fresh flower of grace, great Goddesse of my life,
When your faire eyes these fearefull lines shal read,
Deigne to let fall one drop of dew reliefe,
That may recure my harts long pyning griefe,
And shew what wondrous power your beauty hath,
That can restore a damned wight from death.

(*HB*, lines 281–87)

The lady is the instantiation of Venus in the poet's life, and the instantiation is as goddess-like for him as is the goddess herself. He hopes she may let fall, as if from heaven, "one drop of dew reliefe," a paronomasia on *dew* and *due*, something owed him, due to him. The stanza brings together and resolves the separate persons of Venus and the lady, who at the poem's outset, in the third and fourth stanzas of the invocation, are more clearly distinct, Venus being asked to provide the *radiance* of beauty—to "beautifie this sacred hymne of thyne" (*HB*, line 21)—and the lady being implored, as if she were herself a planet raining influence, to "streame/Some deaw of grace" to soothe the scorching that this radiance has given him:

> That both to thee [Venus], to whom I meane it most,
> And eke to her [the lady], whose faire immortall beame,
> Hath darted fyre into my feeble ghost,
> That now it wasted is with woes extreame,
> It so may please that she at length will streame
> Some deaw of grace, into my withered hart,
> After long sorrow and consuming smart.
>
> (*HB*, lines 22–28)

There is no talk here of "perfect beauty" (*HHB*, line 296) in the skies, above this loathed world. I said that the verb *streame*, although it is meant of the lady, suggests the action of a planet, like Venus, raining influence. But in fact the *she* who is the subject of the verb *streame* is not specified and could be Venus or the lady. The uncertainty is momentary but deliberate, forcing us to blend Venus and the lady together, in anticipation of the conclusion, in which the two are one. Who restores this "damned wight from death," Venus or the lady? The lady, of course.

I have been reading the *Fowre Hymnes* backwards and have come to the last, which shall be first, *An Hymne in Honour of Love*, which I confess I love best, though it lacks the dialectical energies of the other hymns. It is instead almost what in the final verse its singer says it is: a "simple song" (*HL*, line 307). Yet its structure is not simple. It begins with a six-stanza invocation, in which the poet says he will compose a hymn to Love, who tyrannizes over him, in the hope that this service will persuade the god to ease the ravages of unrequited passion, restoring his "enfeebled" faculties enough for it to be possible for the poet to make the song. Hence the god of Love must be the inspirer of the hymn addressed to him as well as the cure of the enfeeblement that prevents the hymn from being made:

Come then, O come, thou mightie God of love,
Out of thy silver bowres and secret blisse,
Where thou doest sit in *Venus* lap above,
Bathing thy wings in her ambrosiall kisse,
That sweeter farre then any Nectar is;
Come softly, and my feeble breast inspire
With gentle furie, kindled of thy fire.

(*HL*, lines 22–28)

The Muses, the nymphs, and human youths are called to march in a triumph to the god in which this very hymn will be sung. The song begins, in terms Milton could not have failed to be impressed by, with the god of Love bringing world's mighty mass out of chaos; soaring like an eagle through "that great wide vast, yet wanting light" (line 70); separating the four elements which formerly were peacefully confused and are now at war with one another to their own "confusion and decay" (line 82); binding the elements in adamantine chains so that they will coexist harmoniously in creatures, "in every living wight" (line 90); infusing those living wights "with secret sparks of his infused fyre" (line 97) so that they burn with appetency and seek "To quench the flame" (line 102) by copulation; and infusing this flame into the race of mankind, "that breathes a more immortal mynd": "Not for lusts sake, but for eternitie,/Seek[ing] to enlarge his lasting progenie" (lines 103–05). With remarkable authority, Spenser delineates a continuity extending from the first warmth of affinity in the elements as the universe was created by Eros to the sting of lust in animals and the fires of erotic passion in humans.

There follows a description of the painful effects of love in men—Spenser surely means men, not women—who "make ful piteous mone/Unto the author of their baleful bane" (*HL*, lines 127–28), the *author* being the desired women, not the god. The god laughs them all to scorn, including the "mangled" poet, who asks why the god of Love, the parent and preserver of the world (line 156), is so cruel to such a faithful servant as the poet is, and why Love is generally most cruel to those who serve him best. The answer lies somewhere in the region of the assertion that love lifts the nobler mind "On golden plumes up to the purest skie" (line 178) to the contemplation of ideal beauty. Possession of this beauty is won, however, only in "the mirrour of so heavenly light" (line 196), which is the beloved: "His harts enshrined saint, his heavens queene" (line 215).

Once ideal beauty has become fixed in the poet's mind, he "casts in his unquiet thought" (*HL*, line 218) to win her favor by "brave exploit," by "conquest" and by "adventurous paine" (lines 220 and 221), driving his will, with "resistlesse hand," "Through seas, through flames, through thousand swords and speares" (lines 228 and 230). After a description of jealousy, the lover's hell, which seems an inevitable consequence of such passion, the poet describes an erotic heaven into which all these faithful lovers will at length come: "So thou thy folke, through paines of Purgatorie,/Dost beare unto thy blisse, and heavens glorie" (lines 278–79).

The final vision of the lovers in erotic paradise, like the triumph of Cupid earlier, is the reason I compared this poem to quattrocento painting, with its enameled meads and its concentration on the minute particulars of the objective world in its moments of joy. At the end of all their trials, the lovers are placed in a paradise of

> joyous happie rest,
> Where they doe feede on Nectar heavenly wize,
> With *Hercules* and *Hebe* and the rest
> Of *Venus* dearlings.
>
> (HL, lines 281–84)

After this intense but vague picture, we draw back to see the lovers from a distance in their paradise, where they "lie like Gods in yvorie beds arayd,/With rose and lillies over them displayd" (*HL*, lines 285–86). A wonderful word, *displayed*, which is so often employed in *The Faerie Queene*, as here, in its etymological sense as an unfolding, the opening-outwards of folds, of *plis*, as in Old French *despleier* and Late Latin *displicare*. The word is also used in *The Faerie Queene* for analytic discourse, discourse of the kind that opens out and explains (cf. Italian *spiegare* "to unfold," "to expound," "to interpret").[6] To the absurd spectacle of these numerous pairs of lovers embedded in such close proximity to one another, like lovemaking couples on a long suburban street where the houses have abruptly disappeared, there is a discursive element, demanding thought and interpretation.

What is being opened up for interpretation is the phenomenon of *eros* itself, which, we discover to our surprise, is a collective, not a private phenomenon. We think of eros as private and more than private. We think of eros as excluding all other events and, indeed, as excluding the rest of the world, a psychological fact symbolized by the representation of the god Eros in Spenser's cosmogonic myth, in which Eros passes through "the world that was not till he did it make" (*HL*, line 75). There is a powerful psychological sense to Donne's frequent claim that the joined lovers constitute a world entire. As he says in "The Sun Rising," "Nothing else is." It is therefore curious to see all these lovers in this hospital-ward-like scene, tucked into their ivory beds by the tens of thousands, the Kafkaesque line of them stretching out of sight. Eros is a general experience that seems singular and private and is graspable in this generality only through the private moment, the discontinuity of each bed in the series. The generality of eros can therefore be represented only by the absurd spectacle of many beds together, by the iteration of the particular moments, each ivory bed hard by its neighbor, until we break through to what the discourse of this iteration says. Perhaps this poem, or at least this culminating vision, is more dialectical than I suspected. Eros is at once particular and general. That at any rate is how true knowledge in Spenser is usually arrived at: not by drawing closer to the object and disappearing into it, as at the end of *An Hymn of Heavenly Beautie*, but by moving back, so as to take in a more comprehensive view, to see the truth *displayed*.

The lovers get out of their ivory beds from time to time, after their "hurtlesse sports" (*HL*, line 288) with *Pleasure*, Venus's daughter, to crown *Pleasure* with flowers and also to deck Venus's altar with flowers:

> There with thy daughter *Pleasure* they doe play
> Their hurtlesse sports, without rebuke or blame,
> And in her snowy bosome boldly lay
> Their quiet heads, devoid of guilty shame,
> After full joyance of their gentle game,
> Then her they crowne their Goddesse and their Queene,
> And decke with floures thy altars well beseene.
>
> (*HL*, lines 287–93)

It is a vision of what we think we hope for from eros, where eroticism is reconciled to itself and complete in itself. Certainly the poet hopes to attain that state:

> Ay me, deare Lord, that ever I might hope,
> For all the paines and woes that I endure,
> To come at length unto the wished scope
> Of my desire, or might my selfe assure,
> That happie port for ever to recure.
>
> (*HL*, lines 294–98)

More interestingly, the spectacle of the lovers at their "gentle game" (*HL*, line 291) is also an image of whatever it is we feel eludes us in eros, even at the happiest moments, which is why the lovers have to get out of those beds and engage in a collective act of worship, an orgiastic mystery, an opening-outwards to something beyond, to the elusive divinity of which their lovemaking is the sacrament, a sacrament which, like any sacrament, points beyond itself.[7] As we see in this vision of the lovers crowning *Pleasure* as their queen, completed eros would be a kind of religion, as it is so often portrayed in Italian painting after Petrarch's *Trionfi*, a regular, even dutiful celebration of erotic pleasure, which is what eroticism is in Christian marriage: a duty. The vision of the *Hymn in Honour of Love* is not at all in competition with the Christian religion, with a Christian heaven, with Christian duty, or with Christian morals, because it is a "simple song" about one thing, eros, and not another—not, that is, some *analogy* of eros.

At least it seems so to me when I delight in this poem for its naïve insistence on remaining what it is, despite the poet's *retractation*. One stanza does however seem different from the rest and recalls us to a different lesson, the one we know so well from *The Faerie Queene*: that love exists to nourish something higher than itself, *heros* being an anagram of *eros*. We saw that erotic love is at first experienced as if it is fulfilled in itself and refers to nothing outside itself, until it becomes a mystery. But in truth, at least in Spenserian truth—the truth as it is held in a noble mind—eros is the spur to something beyond it that is not religious but moral:

> Such is the powre of that sweet passion
> That it all sordid basenesse doth expell,
> And the refyned mynd doth newly fashion
> Unto a fairer forme, which now doth dwell
> In his high thought, that would it selfe excel.
>
> (*HL*, lines 190–94)

When speaking of jealousy, Spenser has the lapidary line "For love cannot endure a Paragone" (*HL*, line 251). We might choose to understand this simple statement in a higher sense, too, that would itself excel. It may be true that love cannot endure a paragon. But it has one, anyway: honor.

Harvard University

NOTES

1. Dedicatory Epistle to the *Fowre Hymns*, in *Edmund Spenser, The Shorter Poems*, ed. Richard A. McCabe (London: Penguin, 1999). References to the hymns hereafter are from this edition and are given in parentheses, abbreviated in sequence, *HL, HB, HHL* and *HHB*. My thanks to Kenneth Borris for valuable observations on this paper, among which the suggestion that the sister most likely to have made such a request is Lady Margaret. According to Richard T. Spence, in the *Dictionary of National Biography*, Lady Margaret was "an exceedingly pious lady, a zealous puritan." *Oxford DNB,* online edition, 2004–08. I am also grateful to Jon Quitslund for the observation that the critical challenge posed by the hymns is to distinguish between genuine, "speculative idealizing" and "make-believe." There is an amply supply of each, although the proportions tilt towards the latter as the hymns go on.

In the preface to his notes on the hymns, McCabe points out that by *retractation* Spenser does not mean "retraction" but "a process of rehandling," of re-treatment (706). It seems to me Spenser means both: Spenser *retracts* the earlier versions of the first two hymns; and Spenser *reworks* them so that they may be issued again, but with their new, corresponding heavenly hymns.

2. *The Faerie Queene*, ed. A. C. Hamilton, Hiroshi Yamashita, and Toshiyuki Suzuki, 2nd, rev. ed. (Harlow, UK: Pearson-Longman, 2007), 7.8.1. Subsequent references are to this edition.

3. "On the Death of a Fair Infant Dying of a Cough," in *Complete Shorter Poems*, ed. John Carey, 2nd, rev. ed. (Harlow, UK: Pearson, 2007), lines 45–46.

4. *Paradise Lost*, ed. Gordon Teskey (New York: W. W. Norton, 2005), 4.52.

5. *Amoretti* 68.14, *Shorter Poems*, 421.

6. See, e.g., *Faerie Queene* 1.7.38, when Prince Arthur addresses Una: "Faire feeling words he wisely gan *display*"; Arthur entreats Una "to *unfold* the anguish of your hart" (1.7.40); and Una replies that grief "does greater grow displaid, / If then it find not helpe" (1.7.41).

7. For a study of eroticism in its connections with religious sacraments and orgiastic rites, see Georges Bataille, *L'Erotisme* (Paris: Minuit, 1957).

JON QUITSLUND

Thinking about Thinking in the *Fowre Hymnes*

The *Fowre Hymnes* contain Spenser's most discursive poetry, and in them his handling of philosophical and theological matters is more doctrinaire than in other poems. Most scholarship on the *Hymnes* has concentrated on tracing Spenser's thought to learned sources and deciding, on that evidence, how to label his mixture of courtly, Christian, and Platonic or Neoplatonic themes. While it considers one instance of Spenser's borrowings from Ficino's commentary on Plato's *Symposium*, this essay is more concerned to relate the content of the *Hymnes* to "thinking moments" in other parts of his poetic *oeuvre*. Ideas about the heavenly source of physical beauty and its power to inspire a refined, intellectual love, explained at length in the first pair of hymns, can be found more succinctly expressed in Spenser's earlier poetry, dating back in at least one instance to the brief period, circa 1580, when he was associated with Philip Sidney. The second pair of hymns echoes the religiosity of Book I in *The Faerie Queene*; the fourth hymn, especially in its vision of "*Sapience* . . . / The soueraine dearling of the *Deity*" and its world-renouncing conclusion, also invites comparison to Spenser's posthumous *Cantos of Mutabilitie*.

*T*HINKING SERIOUSLY ABOUT Spenser's *Fowre Hymnes* after many years away from them involves me inevitably in retrospection. When I was in graduate school, casting about recklessly for a dissertation topic, I proposed undertaking a study of philosophical poems in English from the sixteenth and early seventeenth centuries. I thought I would devote a chapter each to Spenser's *Hymnes*, Chapman's *Shadow of Night*, Donne's *Anniversaries*, Greville's "treatie" poems, and Shakespeare's "Phoenix and Turtle." Tom Roche advised me to be less ambitious; he recommended that I focus on an edition of the *Fowre Hymnes*, arguing that such a project would be both challenging and limited, and would be presentable for publication soon after I completed it. I set that idea aside when I found Enid Welsford's edition of the *Hymnes* and *Epithalamion* listed as "forthcoming" in a catalogue from Blackwell's. It didn't appear until 1967, by which time I had completed a different sort of dissertation, "Studies in Spenser and the Platonic Tradition," with two chapters devoted to aspects of the *Fowre Hymnes*. Those chapters formed the basis for two essays, published in 1969 and 1985.[1]

Both in teaching and in writing for publication, I have paid much more attention to *The Faerie Queene* than to the *Fowre Hymnes*. (I suppose that Spenserians generally are most alive inside *The Faerie Queene*, and find the *Hymnes* easy to set aside, if in fact they ever read them carefully.) We see in the *Hymnes* a falling off from the fictive and multitudinous mode of Spenser's heroic poem, and, compared to his other poems published in 1595 and 1596, they are less appealing and accessible. But these comparisons are shallow criticism; they fail to consider the *Hymnes* either on their own terms or with reference to characteristics that they have in common with other poems. The *Fowre Hymnes* are as representative of Spenser's generically adventurous genius as anything else he wrote.

I won't say that I outgrew my early interest in the *Hymnes*, but while studying the matrix of influences and agendas in which *The Faerie Queene* took shape, I chose not to base my interpretation of Spenser's heroic poem on clues that might be found in them. It was convenient to accept Robert Ellrodt's argument that all of the *Hymnes*, as published in 1596, postdate Spenser's work on *The Faerie Queene*. (I have not, however, followed Ellrodt in believing that the poet did not possess an adept awareness of the Neoplatonism of Ficino and his followers when he conceived *The Faerie Queene*.) I can now acknowledge that omitting the *Hymnes* from my book–length consideration of Spenser's Platonism was only a strategic decision, limiting an already unmanageable scope of work. I am pleased to have this opportunity to make amends.

The *Hymnes* are somewhat anomalous in the context of Spenser's career, but in their structure and themes they can be linked with his other poetry, both early and late. From its roots and its first flowering in *The Shepheardes Calender* to the posthumous *Cantos of Mutabilitie*, Spenser's was consistently a totalizing vision, seeking the integration of individual consciousness with a world in which flux and cosmic order coexist, more or less in balance, competing as figure and ground for the poet's and his readers' attention. Even when his subject is frustration or fragmentation, Spenser's poetry is structurally sound and coherent. In the *Hymnes*, if not in all of his works, one gathers that an intuitive sense of the whole preceded his articulation of its parts; all of the pieces take their places within a solid framework, a *kosmos*. Any objectionable "looser rimes," such as are mentioned in the opening lines of the Proem to Book IV of *The Faerie Queene*, must have been taken out of context and misunderstood.

Even if there was some factual basis for the poet's saying that the first two hymns contain indiscreet verses from his "greener times," he was also capable of devising the tetradic structure of the *Fowre Hymnes* long before 1596. As we have them, the two pairs of hymns are linked together as firmly as Triamond and Canacee, Cambel and Cambina, the married couples who, in the first quarter of Book IV, display schematically the strife and love with which the Legend of Friendship will be concerned.[2] And tetradic patterning was not an innovation in Book IV. An interest in poetic forms and structures related to the four elements and other tetrads can be traced through *The Faerie Queene* and back to the "square" poem appended to *The Shepheardes Calender*. "Loe I haue made a Calender for euery yeare" consists of twelve twelve-syllable lines, a form that Puttenham called "the figure of most solliditie and stedfastnesse," which he associated with Aristotle's "constant minded man, . . . *hominem quadratum*."[3] What is distinctive about the use of a tetradic frame in the *Fowre Hymnes* is the poet's emphasis, within a balanced sequence of reiterated and analogical upward movements, on self-transcending desire that seeks and celebrates union with its idealized object.

I want to examine the kinds of *thinking* that Spenser engages in over the course of his two pairs of hymns. They are epideictic poems—poems of praise—but they are not celebratory in the manner of the *Epithalamion* and *Prothalamion*. Their lyric character is often overlooked, and it should not be, but it is not grounded, as in the marriage and betrothal poems, in the colorful specificity of ceremonial occasions. The subjectivity we associate with lyric forms is not pronounced in these hymns, except in a few purple passages. They comprise an intricately ordered testament of faith, and an explicit display of the kind of expert knowledge that, in his supple heroic poem, Spenser had been careful to encode in myths and imagery.

The *Hymnes* are discursive; we might as well call them didactic, although they aim to instruct and move readers by delighting them, in accordance with Sidney's formula for poetry worthy of the name. We see the poet sometimes in the act of reasoning, sometimes relating a myth or expounding an abstruse doctrine, and sometimes rationalizing, as if to justify a foregone conclusion. He constructs a network of relationships between love and beauty, and between the different kinds of love and of beauty. (Rightly understood, they are more alike than different.) He is engaged throughout in something like Psyche's labor, distinguishing truths from inferior integuments and imitations.

The *Fowre Hymnes* are presented to us with their own textual integument: we come to the first pair, in honor of the classical personifications of love and beauty, by way of a dedicatory epistle that honors two noble sisters, the countesses of Cumberland and Warwick. This epistle invites careful parsing, which it has received from almost everyone who has written on the *Hymnes*. Spenser offers an explanation of the relationship between the two pairs of hymns, but his references to poems composed in "the greener times of [his] youth" and his resolution to "amend, and . . . reforme them" with a second pair have been regarded as at best obfuscatory. This explanation provides something like the occasion that, in an earlier paragraph, I had said was conspicuously lacking in the *Hymnes* themselves.

The dedicatory epistle offers more than a defense of Spenser's seriousness as a laureate public poet. Some clarity about the compatibility of the two kinds of love and beauty, "earthly or naturall" and "heauenly and celestiall," is provided in his compliment to the two sisters, "the most excellent and rare ornaments of all true loue and beautie, both in the one and the other kind." In its superlatives and its both/and construction, this statement is entirely characteristic of Spenser, whose idea of reformation was not corrective but additive: his second thoughts don't reject the first, but dilate upon them,[4] developing a four-part suite of dances around the perennially fascinating subject of true love and beauty. The four hymns can be read and reread in any order, but no less than Eliot's *Four Quartets*, they call for interpretation in their entirety. Einar Bjorvand has shown how each of the hymns is organized around its central stanza or stanzas, where contrasts between the first and third and second and fourth are brought into focus.[5]

In Spenser's poetry, as in the culture he inhabited, thinking was never entirely separate from attitudes and acts of faith. Thinking in the *Fowre Hymnes* harks back to themes in Book I of *The Faerie Queene*, where he shows us that faith and thought are often in error, attached to false assumptions or proven wrong by unintended consequences, and that doubt, similarly, can lead to error. His approach to truth in its various forms is that of faith seeking understanding. But what is the character of the poet's faith, as we find it in Book I and in the *Hymnes*? Coleridge's concept of "poetic faith" (i.e., "a willing suspension of disbelief for the moment") is relevant to all portions of Spenser's romance narrative, even in Book I with its life-or-death theological issues. Saints' lives often resembled chivalric romances in their medieval heyday. In Spenser's Reformation-era context a suspension of disbelief in any sort of fiction was that much more essential, at the same time that the narrative inculcates an earnest Christian faith and a commitment to truth as "troth" or fidelity, a way of life rather than a body of knowledge. The first pair of hymns, which have much in common with the more secular and playful aspect of *The Faerie Queene* (especially in Books III and IV), also invoke poetic faith. That sort of imaginative attention to a body of beliefs about Eros, Venus, and love understood as "a celestiall harmonie,/Of likely harts composd of starres concent" (*HB*, lines 197–98), seems essential if readers are to "sucke out . . . hony to their honest delight" (Ded. Epistle, lines 5–6).

The second pair of hymns makes claims of a different sort on a reader's faith. Their frame of reference is more devotional than mythological and philosophical: reading them in concert with the author's intention requires a commitment to something beyond suspension of disbelief. "An Hymne of Heavenly Love" is a meditation on the grand Christian narrative of creation, fall, incarnation, sacrifice, and redemption. It calls for more than an aesthetically appreciative or historicist "as if" response. A sincere, devout response came naturally to such readers as the two countesses, but it is difficult for me, and I suppose for many other Spenserians today—even those who were raised, as I was, in the context of churchgoing.

The fourth hymn makes similar claims on a reader's assent to its truth, and its claims may be more problematic, since the Christian devotion it expresses is given an explicitly Neoplatonic cast. "An Hymne of Heavenly Beavtie" continues on the high plane reached at the end of the third hymn, without the stanzas of invocation that open the other hymns. The poet who had promised, "Then shall thy rauisht soule inspired bee/With heauenly thoughts, farre aboue humane skil" (*HHL*, lines 281–82) begins the ascent to his final vision "Rapt with the rage of mine own rauisht thought" (*HHB*, line 1). Spenser's language here verges upon baroque theatricality; many features of the fourth hymn anticipate, and probably informed, Donne's *Anniversaries*, as Gordon Teskey has pointed out.

As others have noted, such language isn't unique to the second pair of hymns: that Spenser subscribed to something like Ficino's belief in the poet's inspiration by a *furor*, as Plato had said, is evident as early as *The Shepheardes Calender*, and his true lovers' experience of "ravishment" or rapture appears throughout *The Faerie Queene*, as

Andrew Escobedo has shown elsewhere in this collection. In the hymns, as with the figure of Colin in *Colin Clouts Come Home Againe* (lines 823–26) and in *The Faerie Queene* (with Calidore in VI.x), the poet's and a devout lover's rapture are one and the same. Were these beliefs deeply held by Spenser, or are they merely conventional, chosen to accompany his costume as Colin Clout? I am still seeking an answer to this question, but unsure of its legitimacy. To the extent that Spenser's subtle mind resembled Montaigne's, a sharp distinction between personal beliefs and conventional attitudes would be inappropriate. I am confident, however, that the difference between truth and falsehood mattered to Spenser, and that he didn't accept received opinions passively.

What sort of thinking is "rauisht"? Spenser's thought seems diametrically opposed to what Heidegger, in his pivotal and influential late work, called thinking. For Heidegger, man thinks "because what must be thought about turns away from him." He goes on: "The event of withdrawal could be what is most present in all our present, and so infinitely exceed the actuality of everything actual."[6] At crucial moments in *The Faerie Queene*, evanescence and a sense of loss are constitutive of thought and action: think of Arthur's awakening from his dream of Gloriana, and think of what happens on Mt. Acidale after Calidore's appearance disrupts the Graces' dance. But in the *Fowre Hymnes*, being inspired and carried beyond oneself is what gives thought its wings, and the direction it takes is provided, through vision or in the mind's eye, by a beauty suited to one's soul.

We will better understand what is at stake in the fourth hymn's aspirations and declarations if we go back to the beginning, to examine the kind of thinking found in "An Hymne in Honovr of Love." Asking to be inspired "With gentle furie" (*HL*, line 28), the poet gives Love the central role in a creation myth, moving through "The world that was not till he did it make" (*HL*, line 75). Love moves upward, "Lifting himselfe out of the lowly dust, / On golden plumes vp to the purest skie" (*HL*, lines 177–78). While Love brings order to the cosmos, the poet distinguishes between "stedfast" and "baseborne mynds" (*HL*, lines 71–73), explaining that in steadfast minds,

Such is the power of that sweet passion,
That it all sordid basenesse doth expel,
And the refined mynd doth newly fashion
Vnto a fairer forme, which now doth dwell
In his high thought, that would it selfe excel.

(*HL*, lines 190–94)

As described in the first pair of hymns, love provides access to a beauty inherent in the soul that survives its descent "from the top of purest heauens hight" (*HB*, line 109). Spenser explains at some length (*HB*, lines 110–40) how the soul, "According as the heauens haue her graced" (116), "doth the bodie make" (133)—making it as beautiful as the substance of its "tabernacle" of flesh permits (lines 141–47). In the first hymn, love is an ordeal that is eventually justified by its reward, which is arrival "in a Paradize/Of all delight, and ioyous happie rest" (*HL*, lines 280–81). The second hymn ends similarly, in a pretty Parnassian scene where Venus, "great beauties Queene," reigns as a conqueror (*HB*, lines 260–80). Earlier, however, Spenser describes in fine detail the intellectual activity involved in mutual love between "those whom heauen did at first ordaine,/And made out of one mould the more t'agree" (*HB*, lines 206–07). Their love works upon sense impressions to create "A more refined forme, which they present/Vnto their mind" (lines 214–15). This refined love is intellectual, involving aesthetic pleasure uncoupled from desire. Shifting from "they" and "their mind" to "he" and "his thought," Spenser describes the fashioning of "An heauenly beautie" that becomes "The mirrour of his owne thought" (lines 221–24). Love of another's inner beauty becomes the means to fuller awareness of one's own identity and imaginative capacity.

The inwardness described in these stanzas is both self-absorbed and aware of a tendency to excess, "Counting it [i.e., the idealized form] fairer, then it is indeede,/And yet indeede her fairenes doth exceede" (lines 230–31). The imaginative process described here becomes more interesting if we recognize that, in describing what true lovers do (or more accurately, what love does in them), Spenser is also describing his own creative process, not only in his *Amoretti and Epithalamion* but also in *The Faerie Queene*, when he imagines allegorical characters and incidents that show us virtue in action.

The way of thinking I have been examining in the second hymn can be traced to sources of two kinds. The first and most significant sources will be found in Spenser's earlier poetry, in habits of mind, convictions, and convenient tropes developed over several decades (more on this shortly). The second will be found in books, such as Castiglione's *Courtier* and Ficino's commentary on Plato's *Symposium*, *De Amore*. There are enough echoes of Bembo's speech on beauty and the "ladder of love" in the *Fowre Hymnes* to suggest that Spenser had recently read (and surely he was *re*reading a book he had digested years before) a speech that many of his readers already knew well. With Ficino's *De Amore* the case is somewhat different. I am convinced that by 1596, Spenser had been familiar with several of Ficino's translations, commentaries, and treatises for many years, but in poems published prior to the *Hymnes*, the depth of affinities between the poet and the philosopher isn't evident in verbal echoes. Editors of the *Hymnes* have documented numerous borrowings, and close examination shows that the ideas Spenser used were carefully selected.

Chapter 6 in the sixth Speech of Ficino's *De Amore* has been cited, aptly, as a source of many details in the second hymn, beginning around line 99 and extending for more than a hundred lines.[7] The title of this chapter is "How we are caught [*capiamur*] by love,"[8] and its themes develop out of the previous chapter's description of Venerean daemons, who take advantage of astrologically determined humoral characteristics, making a person conceived "under the domination of Jupiter," for example, fall in love with another Jovian. Spenser takes seriously what Ficino says about the stars' role in love (see *HB*, lines 106–19, 190–210), but he both simplifies and adds to what Ficino had said. Spenser says nothing about Venerean daemons here, although I am confident that he followed Socrates (*Symposium* 202d–e) in viewing Venus's son, Eros—the real cosmic entity, not Cupid, the cultural icon of a decadent culture—as a daemon.[9]

In his advice to lovers, both men and women, Spenser's emphasis is on choice, not chance or the stars' compulsion:

> But in your choice of Loues, this well aduise,
> That likest to your selues ye them select,
> The which your forms first sourse may sympathize,
> And with like beauties parts be inly deckt.
>
> (*HB*, lines 190–93)

These lines gain some poignancy from the fact, well known in court circles, that Margaret Russell Clifford, one of the dedicatees of the *Fowre Hymnes*, was unhappily married to an unfaithful husband, George Clifford.[10] Ficino says nothing about such errors, or the importance of choosing wisely: that two people born under the same star will recognize their likeness and be powerfully attracted to one another is a given, even when one is outwardly less beautiful than the other. "The soul thus stricken [*pulsatus*] recognizes the image [*simulacrum*] before it as something which is its own." Ficino happily describes the position of the one whose body was less responsive to his soul's form, and Spenser follows closely his account of what happens. The inferior lover, stimulated by a physical beauty greater than his own, takes in the image of that beauty and sets it beside his own interior image of a perfection that has remained unrealized. Within the inferior lover's soul, the beauty of the beloved is idealized, and "the soul loves that reformed image as its own work." Eventually, a lover sees his beloved not as he (or she) really is, "but in the likeness of [the soul's] own innate idea, an image which is more beautiful than the body itself" (*De Amore*, trans. Jayne, 114). Three stanzas in Spenser's second hymn (*HB*, lines 211–31) make Ficino's meaning in this passage somewhat clearer than it is in my summary.[11]

I turn now to examples of Spenser's consistency, in the *Hymnes*, with his own earlier poetry. The distinction made in the first hymn between steadfast and baseborn minds is emphasized frequently in *The Faerie Queene*, and in the 1590 and 1596 segments of his heroic poem we also find Spenser describing true love as a thought process that edifies the lover, refining his mind and filling his imagination with an idealized object that disciplines desire. For example, a few stanzas after describing the effect on Artegall when he sees Britomart's face for the first time (IV.vi.19–22), the narrator explains Artegall's reluctance to "make loue" to his sworn adversary too suddenly:

Besides her modest countenance he saw
So goodly graue, and full of princely aw,
That it his ranging fancie did refraine,
And looser thoughts to lawfull bounds withdraw.

(IV.vi.33)[12]

The prime example of this trope—the civilizing effect of extraordinary beauty on a lover suited to receive its impact—appears in the *blazon* accompanying Belphoebe's first appearance, when she accidentally encounters Trompart and Braggadocchio in Book II. The poet begins with her face, focusing in the second stanza on the effect of her eyes:

In her faire eyes two liuing lamps did flame,
    Kindled aboue at th'heuenly makers light,
    And darted fyrie beames out of the same,
    So passing persant, and so wondrous bright,
    That quite bereau'd the rash beholders sight:
    In them the blinded god his lustfull fyre
    To kindle oft assayd, but had no might;
    For with dredd Maiestie, and awfull yre,
She broke his wanton darts, and quenched bace desire.

(II.iii.23)

Each of the passages quoted qualifies as a "thinking moment" of the kind singled out by Gordon Teskey in a recent article.[13] I will dilate briefly on the example involving Belphoebe, which is acutely à propos of Teskey's observation that, as distinct from the focus of traditional philosophy on questions and answers that define some entity, "Spenser's poetic thinking does not strive to make the questions disappear into answers telling us what these things are. Instead, it strives to make those questions even more strange than we had ever supposed" (116). I can't pursue all the questions that the *blazon* raises. The question that most interests me is this: What accounts for Spenser's conception of Belphoebe in these terms? Contextually, she is linked to Venus, mother of Aeneas, as Virgil conceived of her (see II.iii.33, with Hamilton's note)—a benevolent, sovereign figure, but also an austere and elusive one. In her return to the poem in Book III, however, she is associated with Diana as well as Venus. She is also identified there as the twin sister of Amoret, which further complicates matters. Is she intelligible in terms of the Neoplatonic understanding of love and beauty that we find in the *Fowre Hymnes*? I think so, but with the possible exception of Sapience, Belphoebe is a more complex figure than anything in the *Hymnes*, and the questions that spring up around her are best considered within the contexts of Books III and IV and topical allusions to court politics.

To recapitulate briefly before striking off in another direction, pertinent to the attributes of Belphoebe: we began by examining passages in the first pair of hymns that derive earthly beauty from a heavenly source and describe how love, in the steadfast minds of praiseworthy lovers, disciplines desire and leads to a more refined self-awareness, focused on the beloved's idealized beauty. While I wouldn't say that there is nothing new in the first pair of hymns, I have been interested in showing how consistent their messages, derived in part from Ficino's account of love and beauty in his commentary on Plato's *Symposium*, are with Spenser's earlier poetry. Now I want to look more closely at the stanza devoted to Belphoebe's "faire eyes . . . /Kindled aboue at th'heuenly makers light."

It has not been widely recognized how closely this stanza from Belphoebe's *blazon* resembles one of Spenser's sonnets. As published in 1595, Sonnet VIII in the *Amoretti* sequence begins, "More then most faire, full of the liuing fire,/Kindled aboue vnto the maker neere." Belphoebe's eyes dart "fyrie beames" that dazzle "the rash beholders sight," and "In them the blinded god his lustfull fyre/To kindle oft assayd, but had no might." Similarly, we read in the sonnet,

Thrugh your bright beams doth not the blinded guest
   shoot out his darts to base affections wound:
   but Angels come to lead fraile mindes to rest
   in chast desires on heauenly beauty bound.

In the sonnet's third quatrain, just as if he has been reading Spenser's hymnbook, the lover says,

You frame my thoughts and fashion me within,
   you stop my toung, and teach my hart to speake,
   you calme the storme that passion did begin,
   strong thrugh your cause, but by your vertue weak.

Considering these similarities, one might suppose that Spenser, when he composed his sonnet sequence in 1594–95, borrowed from his praise of Belphoebe and added the idea, perhaps taken directly from Ficino, that an ideal object of love has the power to reform the lover's mind. In fact, the trope I have been examining, starting from the second hymn and looking back through some of its appearances in *The Faerie Queene* and the *Amoretti*, has a longer and more remarkable history than has been indicated so far.

There is good evidence that the first fruits of Spenser's thoughts about the power residing in beautiful eyes predate the publication of the 1590 *Faerie Queene* by a decade. Although other sonnets in the *Amoretti* focus on the lady's eyes (see VII, IX, XII, XVI–VII, and XXI), Sonnet VIII may be the only one composed (with the "English" rhyme scheme used in his *Complaints*) long before the sequence devoted to Spenser's courtship of Elizabeth Boyle took shape. *Amoretti* VIII is also the only sonnet by Spenser that appears in manuscript miscellanies, among other poems composed circa 1580.[14] Ironically, this very proper love poem may be the only surviving instance of a "looser" rhyme from the "greener times" of Spenser's youth. He had reason to be proud of it, and I consider it likely that, as early as 1580, in his sonnet as well as in his *blazon* of Belphoebe, he was already thinking through the poetic strategies he would use for praising Queen Elizabeth. The sonnet's similarities to poems by Greville (*Caelica* III) and Sidney (*Astrophil and Stella* 42) suggest that the "vse of familiarity" that Spenser enjoyed briefly within Sidney's circle was not entirely devoted to reforming versification on the classical model of quantitative syllables.[15]

Spenser's sonnet closely imitates a sonnet by Petrarch, as Richard McCabe has noted.[16] Petrarch devoted many poems in the *Rime* to

praises of Laura's eyes and exposition of their effect on him. Petrarch's trope, already conventional before his time, was the subject
of scholarly attention in commentaries and lectures on the *Rime*.
Giovanni Andrea Gesualdo's edition of them, first published in 1533,
was informed by a Platonizing bias: together with other interpreters
such as Lodovico Dolce, Gesualdo interpreted Petrarch as if the four-
teenth-century poet had had access to the same ideas about love and
beauty, ultimately derived from Plato, that were current in courtly
circles during the high Renaissance. In an article published in 1973, I
undertook to show that in his imitation of Petrarch, Spenser followed
Gesualdo's commentary more closely than he did the poet's language—apparently on the assumption that Gesualdo had brought out
meaning latent in Petrarch's words.[17] It seems that in Spenser's thinking about poetry, the aim of reading—and of emulating one's predecessors—resembles the aim of true love: to penetrate superficial
beauties and bring to full consciousness the more valuable soul or
spirit hidden within poetic language.

Returning to Spenser's elaborate account in the second hymn of
the thought process involved in true love, I must confess to some
ambivalence about the poetry's literal sense.

> But they which loue indeede, looke otherwise,
> With pure regard and spotlesse true intent,
> Drawing out of the obiect of their eyes,
> A more refined forme, which they present
> Vnto their mind, voide of all blemishment;
> Which it reducing to her first perfection,
> Beholdeth free from fleshes frayle infection.

(*HB*, lines 211–17)

The next two stanzas go on in a similar vein. It all seems very
methodical, like the manufacture of a fine perfume. This dutiful
account of Ficino's rationale for a refined intellectual love makes it
clear that fear of physical passion is deeply implicated in Spenser's
preoccupation with an idealized love and beauty. And "auto-eroti-
cism" (of a spiritual sort, mind you) is not too strong a term for the
inner-directedness of this love. One is reminded of D. H. Lawrence's
scorn for what he called "sex in the head."

At its most technical, Spenser's Platonism can be exasperating.
Careful attention to the sources and the matrix of assumptions informing the *Hymnes* would be worth little if it didn't lead to a better
understanding of such poems as *Amoretti* XLV ("Leaue lady in your

glasse of christall clene"). In this tender and subtle poem, which happens to be centrally placed in the eighty-nine sonnets of the *Amoretti*, the poet seeks to draw his beloved away from her mirror to look on him, "and in my selfe, my inward selfe I meane, / most liuely lyke behold your semblant trew." He proceeds: "Within my hart, . . . / the fayre Idea of your celestiall hew, / and euery part remaines immortally." We can understand the poet's claim and feel its sincerity without reference to Ficino or the *Fowre Hymnes*, but I think something is added to the poem when we have an intellectual context for it.

Spenser's commitment to a mixture of refined sentiments (Gesualdo had called them "sentimenti Platonici") and rigorous intellectual activity represents a civilized alternative to the dominant patriarchal culture of masculine rivalry and sexual conquest, where women figured as trophy objects at best, and often as lesser objects to be chased after, used, and discarded. What we see in Spenser's love poetry, I think, is a positive adaptation to a hierarchical, status-conscious social system, in which acceptance of a subordinate position was essential to advancement, and learning of the kind that Spenser displays was a way of evening the scales, or even turning the tables. Beginning auspiciously in *The Shepheardes Calender* (although Colin Clout is represented there as unsuccessful), worshipful love is represented as a modest but ambitious person's proper attitude. In Spenser's semiotic system, following conventions already established in courtly culture, beauty stands in for other determinants of higher station, virtue, prestige, and power. By the time of Spenser's emergence as England's "new poet," the legacy of Ficino's thinking about love and beauty had been modified by a host of writers, including Leone Ebreo, Baldesar Castiglione, and Louis Le Roy, from a rationale for exquisite friendships between men into an elaborate foundation for romance and courtship, leading, in the best of all possible worlds, to companionate marriage such as Spenser envisions in his *Amoretti and Epithalamion.*

I will turn now from the implications of Platonism in Spenser's representation of intimate relationships to Platonism (or Neoplatonism, if you will) as a worldview, a cosmology that closely connects heaven and earth. Macrocosmic order, originating in love's unlimited desire for a beauty that is above its own station, forms the framework for the *Fowre Hymnes* in their entirety, which is no surprise to readers of Spenser's other poetry. Parts of three hymns describe a world-making process (*HL*, lines 57–105; *HB*, lines 29–56; *HHL*, lines 22–119) and the fourth hymn surveys God's creation in its entirety, "Beginning then below, with th'easie view / Of this base world"

(*HHB*, lines 22–23), and after "gathering plumes of perfect speculation" (line 134), reaching the throne of God in the central stanza
(lines 148–54). The dithyrambic climax that concludes the *Fowre
Hymnes* is an extended vision of Sapience, "The soueraine dearling
of the *Deity*" (lines 183–252, quoting line 184). The poet attributes
"powre imperiall" to her, saying that "Both heauen and earth obey
vnto her will,/And all the creatures which they both containe"
(lines 196–98).

The sources of Spenser's poetic thinking in his description of Sapience do not lie solely within the Neoplatonic tradition (or traditions,
if one distinguishes between pagan and Christian lines of transmis-
sion), but any response to the fourth hymn and to Sapience is apt to
be influenced by preconceptions about Spenser's allegiances in the
domain of Neoplatonic metaphysics. Having considered the provenance and precise significance of Sapience many years ago (see note
1), I am not very interested in remnants of the old controversies. I
want to consider a question: What did Spenser achieve by representing Wisdom as feminine, distinct from the Judaeo-Christian godhead, but God's "soueraine dearling"? Abstract nouns are typically
feminine in Latin, so there is a certain inevitability to the gender
of Sapientia, but Spenser treats her as a quasi-divine person, not a
personification. She is implicated in a family romance, somewhat
similar to what we find in the *Cantos of Mutabilitie*, accounting for
beautiful order rather than disorder. Again, we are presented with a
"thinking moment."

The first thing Spenser wanted to do, I suppose, was to accentuate
wisdom among the attributes of God (separate from "The instruments
of his auenging yre" mentioned in line 182), and then to claim that
all together, the creatures in heaven and earth are beautiful because
"They all partake" of the "fulnesse" of Sapience (lines 197–200). He
could have identified the personification familiar from Old Testament
and apocryphal wisdom literature with the Second Person of the
Trinity, the Logos: that would have been readily understood by his
readers, and it would have strengthened connections between the
third and fourth hymns. Alternatively, he might have presented Sapience as female and a thoroughly Neoplatonic entity. This would
have strengthened connections between the two hymns to Beauty,
the one "earthly or naturall" and the other "heauenly and celestiall"
(Ded. Epistle, lines 10–11). But this would have baffled or shocked
many of his readers, and would have been uncharacteristic of him.[18]
Instead, Spenser developed a poetic image that is intelligible in terms
of the common threads in several traditions, including the Jewish

mystical tradition of Kabbalah that had attracted adherents among esoterically oriented Christian scholars—some of them in England.

As a sovereign, even "imperiall" figure, "Clad like a Queene in royall robes" (lines 196, 185), Sapience is the most sublime of the several female authority figures in Spenser's poetry, ranging from Elisa in "Aprill" of *The Shepheardes Calender* to Nature in the *Cantos of Mutabilitie*. It appears that, to be both beloved and powerful in Spenser's poetic world, a ruler must be female. The *Fowre Hymnes* seem innocent of any political design but it turns out, in their climax, that there is a political dimension to them after all, at least from the highest vantage point. We are accustomed to thinking that after publishing six Books of *The Faerie Queene*, Spenser turned inward and, while not resting on his laurels, chose not to concern himself with large public themes. What happens in the last hymn, however, is that his grandest secular themes—national sovereignty, an organic social order, and everything evoked by the word "glory" in its worldly sense—shrink to insignificance, while the language and trappings of power are transferred to the highest heavens. Compared to Sapience, who is Gloriana, and where is Cleopolis? Gloriana herself has been interpreted as a manifestation of Wisdom,[19] and Sapience may reveal the ultimate source of Gloriana's charisma while drawing all devotion toward herself. (Spenser claims that for those who have seen Sapience, "All other sights but fayned shadowes bee," line 273.) Considering the extent of the "powre imperiall" wielded by Sapience in an intimate alliance with "God on hy" (line 193), Queen Elizabeth's domain is a mote in the distance, and her claim to sovereignty depends upon her being an earthly reflection of Sapience.

Another perspective on individual identity and the world of experience in which it is ordinarily defined opens up in the hymn's final movement, beginning around line 239 when the poet confronts his own and any man's utter dependence on divine grace for access to Sapience's "secret threasury,/ . . . Euen heauenly riches, which there hidden ly/Within the closet of her chastest bowre" (lines 246–50). The hymn conveys some feeling for the value of the self-transcending "extasy" available to those admitted by Sapience to her presence (see lines 253–66), but the poet is powerless to convey that experience itself. His choice of an expository rather than a first-person voice for these stanzas leaves it unclear whether he speaks from his own ecstatic experience, or from an unfulfilled desire for all that "they," the "worthy," are granted. In the hymn's last two stanzas, addressed to his own "hungry soule," he instructs it to "looke at last vp to that soueraine light,/From whose pure beames al perfect beauty springs," where his "straying thoughts" can "for euer rest" (lines 288–301).

Having worked backward from the first pair of hymns to see how their central theme had been developed in Spenser's earlier poetry, I will close by looking, very briefly, beyond the fourth hymn to Spenser's handling of similar subject matter in his posthumous *Cantos of Mutabilitie*. In the *Cantos* his varied repertoire of narrative materials, all handled with apparent ease and delight in his craft, gives the poet more and better opportunities for development of his ideas than he found in the *Fowre Hymnes*. In the *Cantos* he writes freely, working from long familiarity with what he knows and what he knows how to invent, whereas in the *Hymnes* it is my sense that he had something to prove. (In the *Cantos*, of course, it is Mutabilitie who has something to prove, and the poet bears no responsibility for flaws in her character or her argument.)

In the *Fowre Hymnes*, until the last two stanzas the integrity of the physical universe is not called into question, and perhaps it should have been, since both the poet's "hungry soule" and his devout readers are instructed to overcome their delight in it. At its best, Spenser's thinking involves either delight in complexity or a struggle arising from ambivalence, and ambivalence is devalued in the *Hymnes*. (In the *Cantos* it may be carried too far.) In this connection, comparison of the two presiding quasi-divine figures, Sapience and Nature, will be instructive.

As we have seen, the "fulnesse" of Sapience flows from on high into the creation and sustaining of the universe below her, while on a different level, "Plentie of riches . . . / Euen heauenly riches" are available, "out of her secret threasury," but only "to all those which thereof worthy bee" (*HHB*, lines 246–52). The fourth hymn makes a sharp distinction between knowledge of being and becoming in the physical world, which is open to all, and a mysterious kind of wealth that is available to a few: this would be knowledge, within one's own lifetime, of the super-celestial heavens. (Would only a cynical modern reader see a confidence scheme being played out here?) In the *Cantos of Mutabilitie*, the challenge posed by Mutabilitie extends only to the limits of the physical world, over which Jove presides in accordance with classical literary conventions. Nature plays a role somewhat analogous to that of Sapience in the fourth hymn. She is the authority figure, but she is wise, not Wisdom. The power that Nature exercises is enigmatic, not imperial: she is not a ruler but a judge, explaining a natural law that operates (in tandem with Mutabilitie's unruly desire) from the inside out, rather than from the top down. Nature's relationship to the transcendent God of Sabbaoth is mysterious; what is clear is that no super-celestial heavens and no angels are required to guarantee the world's order.

The *Cantos* and the *Fowre Hymnes* are nowhere more alike than in their concluding stanzas—a balanced pair in each instance. In both places, the poet renounces the vanity of his love for worldly pleasures and expresses loathing of that world. In almost the last lines of the fourth hymn, it is "the loue of God, which loathing brings/Of this vile world, and these gay seeming things" (*HHB*, lines 298–99). In the "vnperfite" ending of the *Cantos*, it is all the evidence of Mutabilitie's "sway" that "makes me loath this state of life so tickle,/And loue of things so vaine to cast away." In both poems, loathing of the world and love of God are dialectically related. The metaphysical differences between the two endings are subtle but profound. Both conclude with the prospect of blessed relief from restless change. In the last two lines of his final hymn, Spenser urges his soul, "being so possest" with pleasures derived from "that soueraine light," to "henceforth for euer rest" (*HHB*, lines 295–301). In the last lines of the *Cantos*, adding something to Nature's description of the Change that dilates being, "turning [all things] to themselues at length againe" (VII.vii.58), the poet says, "But thence-forth all shall rest eternally/With Him that is the God of Sabbaoth hight:/O that great Sabbaoth God, graunt me that Sabaoths sight" (viii.2). The last line's turn to prayer is dramatic and urgent, but it arises from confidence in the nature of being and becoming. Having turned away from "this state of life so tickle," on second thought the poet imagines "stedfast rest of all things firmely stayd/Vpon the pillours of Eternity." It is a more generous vision of the end of days than the focus on Sapience and "the closet of her chastest bowre" (*HHB*, line 249) that is set before his "hungry soule."

The George Washington University

NOTES

1. "Spenser's Image of Sapience," *Studies in the Renaissance* 16 (1969): 181–213; "Spenser and the Patronesses of the *Fowre Hymnes*: 'Ornaments of All True Love and Beautie,' " in *Silent But for the Word; Tudor Women as Patrons, Translators, and Writers of Religious Works*, ed. Margaret P. Hannay (Kent, OH: Kent State University Press, 1985), 184–202.

2. See A. Kent Hieatt's entry, "tetrads," in *The Spenser Encyclopedia*.

3. See Richard A. McCabe's note in his edition of *The Shorter Poems* (London: Penguin Books, 1999), 574, and cf. *The Yale Edition of the Shorter Poems*, ed. William A. Oram et al. (New Haven: Yale University Press, 1989), 213. Throughout, for quotations from and references to Spenser's *Fowre Hymnes* and other shorter poems, I cite McCabe's edition.

4.   Near the end of the *Cantos*, Nature says of "all things" that "being rightly wayd/They are not changed from their first estate;/But by their change their being doe dilate." Patricia A. Parker unfolds the implications of this idea in her *Inescapable Romance: Studies in the Poetics of a Mode* (Princeton: Princeton University Press, 1979), 54–64.

5.   See "Spenser's Defence of Poetry: Some Structural Aspects of the *Fowre Hymnes*," in *Fair Forms: Essays in English Literature from Spenser to Jane Austen*, ed. Maren-Sofie Rostvig (Cambridge: D. S. Brewer, 1975), 13–35, and notes in *The Yale Edition of the Shorter Poems*. The central stanzas of the first hymn (*HL*, lines 148–61) question Love's justice as "the soveraine Lord of all," since he seems to "tyrannize" his loyal subjects, while the central stanza of the third hymn (*HHL*, lines 141–47) concerns Christ's incarnation, to "make amends to God for mans misguyde." The central stanza of the second hymn (*HB*, lines 141–47) observes that "oft it falles, that many a gentle mynd/Dwels in deformed tabernacle drownd," while in the corresponding stanza of the fourth hymn (*HHB*, lines 148–54), the devout Christian approaches God's throne, "Close couered with the Lambes integrity."

6.   "What Calls for Thinking?" trans. Fred D. Wieck and J. Glenn Gray, an excerpt from *Was heisst Denken?* (1954) in Martin Heidegger, *Basic Writings*, ed. David Farrell Krell (New York: Harper & Row, 1977), 350.

7.   Hugh Maclean's notes in the first edition of his Norton Critical Edition, *Edmund Spenser's Poetry* (New York: W. W. Norton, 1968), are the most detailed and discriminating in their attention to Ficino's *De Amore*: see the notes keyed to *HB*, lines 103, 147, 198, 216, 224, and 230. See also the discussion by Robert Ellrodt, *Neoplatonism in the Poetry of Spenser* (Geneva: E. Droz, 1960), 131–37.

8.   I will cite the translation by Sears Jayne, *Commentary on Plato's* Symposium *on Love* (Dallas: Spring Publications, 1985), referring also to the edition of Ficino's Latin text, with a French translation, by Raymond Marcel, *Commentaire sur le Banquet de Platon* (Paris: "Les Belles Lettres," 1956).

9.   On Spenser's representation of Eros within the "daimonic" order of creatures, see "Platonism" in *The Spenser Encyclopedia*, 547c, and my *Spenser's Supreme Fiction* (Toronto: University of Toronto Press, 2001), 95–97, 150, 235–36, 243–44.

10.   See "Spenser and the Patronesses" (reference in n. 1), 187–92.

11.   To this discussion, which emphasizes Spenser's selective adaptation of ideas from Ficino, compare Carol Kaske's elsewhere in this collection, under the hallmark of "Preexistence": she rightly identifies Plato's *Phaedrus* as Spenser's (and Ficino's) ultimate source.

12.   For all quotations from *The Faerie Queene* I cite the edition of A. C. Hamilton et al. (Harlow and London: Longman, 2001).

13.   "Thinking Moments in *The Faerie Queene*," *Spenser Studies* 22 (2007): 103–25.

14.   See L. Cummings, "Spenser's *Amoretti VIII*: New Manuscript Versions," *SEL* 4 (1964): 125–35.

15.   In the *Letters* that he exchanged with Gabriel Harvey, published in 1580, Spenser mentions "the twoo worthy Gentlemen, Master *Sidney*, and Master *Dyer*," saying that "they haue me, I thanke them, in some vse of familiarity." See *The Poetical Works of Edmund Spenser*, ed. J. C. Smith and E. De Selincourt (London: Oxford University Press, 1912, reprinted 1948), 635b.

16.   His note in *The Shorter Poems* cites Petrarch's *Rime* 151 and 154. My own tracing of Spenser's imitations of Petrarch is indebted to W. L. Renwick's edition of the *Amoretti* in *Daphnaïda and Other Poems* (London: Scholartis Press, 1929).

17.   "Spenser's *Amoretti VIII* and Platonic Commentaries on Petrarch," *Journal of the Warburg and Courtauld Institutes* 36 (1973): 256–76.

18.   While I am confident that Spenser was familiar with the distinction made by Pausanias in Plato's *Symposium* (180d–e) between Venus Pandemos and Venus Urania, I don't find him making that distinction anywhere in his poems as Ficino and Pico della Mirandola do, locating one in the *anima mundi* and the other in the *mens angelica*.

19.   See Jeffrey P. Fruen, "The Faery Queen Unveiled? Five Glimpses of Gloriana," *Spenser Studies* 11 (1994, for 1990): 53–88.

INDEX